The
Palestinians

The Palestinians

In Search of a Just Peace

Cheryl A. Rubenberg

LYNNE
RIENNER
PUBLISHERS

BOULDER
LONDON

Published in the United States of America in 2003 by
Lynne Rienner Publishers, Inc.
1800 30th Street, Boulder, Colorado 80301
www.rienner.com

and in the United Kingdom by
Lynne Rienner Publishers, Inc.
3 Henrietta Street, Covent Garden, London WC2E 8LU

Library of Congress Cataloging-in-Publication Data
Rubenberg, Cheryl.
    The Palestinians : in search of a just peace / Cheryl A. Rubenberg.
        p. cm.
    Includes bibliographical references (p.) and index.
    ISBN 1-58826-200-6 (alk. paper)
    ISBN 1-58826-225-1 (pbk. : alk. paper)
    1. Arab-Israeli conflict—1993—Peace.   2. Israel—Politics and government—1993–
3. Palestinian Arabs—Politics and government—1993–   4. Al-Aqsa Intifada, 2000–
I. Title.
    DS119.76.R794   2003
    956.05'3—dc21

                                                                    2003041422

British Cataloguing in Publication Data
A Cataloguing in Publication record for this book
is available from the British Library.

Printed and bound in the United States of America

The paper used in this publication meets the requirements
of the American National Standard for Permanence of
Paper for Printed Library Materials Z39.48-1992.

5   4   3   2   1

An injustice anywhere is an injustice everywhere.
—*Samuel Johnson*

The sentiment of justice is so natural, and so
universally acquired by all mankind, that it seems
to be independent of all law, all party, all religion.
—*Voltaire*

Justice cannot be for one side alone, but must be for both.
—*Eleanor Roosevelt*

Justice denied anywhere diminishes justice everywhere.
—*Martin Luther King Jr.*

Reconciliation should be accompanied by justice, otherwise it
will not last. While we all hope for peace it shouldn't be
a peace at any cost but peace based on principle, on justice.
—*Corazon Aquino*

———

*This book is dedicated to
all individuals across the globe who care about peace with justice*

Contents

Illustrations

Maps

Tables

Figure

Preface

> Most American Jews know little about the realities of the Middle East except as communicated by Jewish leadership and media stereotypes. . . . Palestinians were the victims of this European syllogism, a defenseless people who became refugees in the formation of Israel. A triumph for Jews. A disaster for Palestinians. . . . Meanwhile, the Palestinian catastrophe has deepened with the loss of land and swelling refugee populations.
>
> —Marc H. Ellis[1]

With these words, Marc Ellis touches the core of the problem for most people in understanding the Palestinian-Israeli conflict. As Westerners, we tend to identify with Israel, and, for the most part, we are unable to see, much less to comprehend or empathize with, the plight of the Palestinians. Our perceptions of the Palestinian-Israeli conflict are so deeply imbued with biases and stereotypes—typically unrecognized as such—that we often do not grasp the fundamental issues.

Government officials, policy specialists, and media commentators constantly repeat such refrains as "there is no solution to this conflict" or "until the parties decide to make peace with each other there is nothing we can do to force it on them." To which I would reply, in an admittedly somewhat oversimplified manner: the solution is for Israel to end the occupation of the territories it conquered in 1967 and to allow the Palestinians to establish a viable, independent state alongside Israel. This book explicates this observation in detail and in relevant historical contexts.

My central focus is the Oslo peace process that began with the famous handshake between Yasser Arafat and Yitzhak Rabin in September 1993. Many people—Palestinians, Israelis, Americans, Arabs, and Europeans—believed at the time that the Oslo Accords were the first step of the Palestinians' journey to statehood. It is my thesis, however, that Israel never intended to withdraw from the Occupied Territories based on United Nations Security Council Resolution 242 or to permit the emergence of a territorially contiguous, genuinely independent Palestinian state. Moreover, I contend that the eruption of the Al-Aqsa intifada in September 2000 (the second Palestinian uprising) was a direct result of the failure of the Oslo peace process.

It is one of the ironies of this conflict that the Palestinians and Israel are typically presented as being equal parties. Yet, Israel is one of the strongest states in the global system and enjoys the unqualified backing of the world's sole superpower, the United States. The Palestinians are a dispersed, dispossessed, and disorganized nation of people—a party so pathetically weak in the power dynamics of this conflict that to equate it with Israel is absurd. Throughout this book, I highlight these power disparities and demonstrate the multiplicity of ways in which Israeli power represses and threatens the security of Palestinians.

In analyzing the failure of the Oslo process and its culmination in the Al-Aqsa intifada, I situate the peace process in the hundred-plus years of the Palestinian-Israeli conflict. In my judgment (though history should never be deterministic), it is impossible to comprehend the present without some understanding of how it is informed by the past. For that reason, Chapter 1 is devoted to a reconstruction of the origins and development of the conflict from the late nineteenth century through the early 1990s. Given limited space, I touch on the past issues that are most relevant today (e.g., land, refugees and the right of return, the meaning of Jerusalem, the rise of Palestinian resistance, the transformations in Palestinian tactics and objectives, and the role of world powers). But it is the very continuity of these issues that is essential to a comprehension of the conflict today. The notes to Chapter 1 are extensive and provide the reader with a wealth of source material for further reading. (In other chapters, as well, many of the endnotes serve as bibliographic essays.) Readers should note that in the endnotes where reference is made to a website, the full website address is included in "Websites for Online Research" following the bibliography. Additionally, the appendix, "Measurement and Monetary Equivalents," should be helpful when encountering foreign measurements in the book, such as dunums, hectares, and square meters.

Chapter 2 analyzes the agreements signed by Israel and the Palestinians (and the political context in which they were concluded), which constitute the contractual framework of the peace process. I begin with the 1993 Declaration of Principles and end with the July

2000 Camp David Summit and the January 2001 Taba meeting (both of which terminated without an agreement). I argue here that the Oslo process was doomed to fail from the outset because of the two-stage structure of the process, the fact that Israel's interests were specifically protected while the rights of the Palestinians were either left open to interpretation or omitted, and the absence of an impartial ombudsman. Moreover, the Oslo Accords were based on conflicting and mutually exclusive objectives. The Palestinians believed that the peace process would culminate in a sovereign Palestinian state in the West Bank, the Gaza Strip, and East Jerusalem. The Israelis believed that the *process* could serve to terminate the conflict with the Palestinians while still maintaining Tel Aviv's basic aims—including retention of the settlements in the West Bank and Gaza, preventing the return of refugees, preserving Israeli sovereignty over East Jerusalem, and continuing control over water, external borders, economic issues, security, and so on. Chapter 2 also examines in detail the issue of refugees and the right of return as a substantive illustration of the fatal flaws in the Oslo Accords.

Chapter 3 is an overview of the economic and social deterioration experienced by Palestinians living in the Occupied Territories during the years of the peace process. Here I examine the impact of closures, permits, land confiscations, new settlements, house demolitions, water restrictions, harassment at checkpoints and roadblocks, travel restrictions, and other Israeli policies. These practices, in my judgment, say more about Israel's real intentions regarding the peace process than all the various agreements.

Chapter 4 uses the city of Hebron as a case study of the foregoing, with special emphasis on settler violence and official Israeli collaboration with that violence. It also illustrates the ongoing policies of expulsion. Chapter 5 focuses on Jerusalem, illuminating Israel's efforts to de-Arabize the city so as to ensure its permanent character and status as a sovereign Jewish entity. I also look at Jerusalem from a geopolitical perspective—as the fulcrum from which roads and infrastructures have been created to bind together settlement blocs in the northern, central, and southern West Bank, ensuring a permanent Israeli presence and carving up into isolated cantons the geographic area that would be Palestine.

In Chapter 6, I analyze the Palestinian Authority (PA) in the context of the worsening life situation of the Palestinians. Through corruption, repression, destruction of the judiciary, and the like, the PA contributed significantly to the deterioration of Palestinian society and polity. In addition, its security cooperation with Israel contributed to its loss of legitimacy and to the widespread despair that overtook the populace.

Chapter 7 considers the U.S. role in the Oslo process and contextualizes it in the history of U.S. policy toward the Palestinian-Israeli conflict. U.S. support for Israel, at least since 1967, has been constant, steadfast, and unwavering. Many U.S. policymakers believe that Israel serves as a valuable strategic asset to U.S. interests in the Middle East; the U.S.-Israeli partnership is also the result of the widespread perception among U.S. citizens that Israel and the United States share common values and democratic institutions. Thus, acceding to Israel's wishes, U.S. policy has been consistent in its rejection of basic Palestinian rights and aspirations. The responsibility of the United States for the failure of Oslo is major and must be recognized.

Chapter 8 contemplates the Al-Aqsa intifada as an expression of the despair and impoverishment of the Palestinians after years of unfulfilled promises and dramatically worsening life situations. I also consider Israel's political and military responses to the Palestinian uprising and the cycle of violence that has ensued.

By way of conclusion, in Chapter 9 I consider the current Palestinian condition, looking at the complete Israeli reoccupation of the West Bank and its partial reoccupation of the Gaza Strip. It is a situation of humanitarian disaster, widespread collective punishment, fears of mass expulsion, the total absence of a peace process, and unmitigated despair and hopelessness. I conclude on a hopeful note with a discussion of the multiple grassroots movements from around the globe, including Israel, that are working on behalf of the Palestinians. Their collective energy, courage, and commitment may well prove to be a countervailing force to the traditional dictum that "might makes right."

*   *   *

I have numerous debts of gratitude, none more profound than to my editor, Bridget Julian. She enthusiastically endorsed the project from the outset, offered invaluable critical suggestions, tried to teach me nuance, and painstakingly edited nearly every chapter. Bridget has since left publishing to return to graduate school, but she remains, for me, an inspiration, a friend, and a simply beautiful human being.

I am deeply grateful to Lynne Rienner for her willingness to publish this book—for her principled commitment to scholarship outside the boundaries of conventional wisdom. I dearly hope that she will not have cause to regret her decision.

Many individuals read chapters of the manuscript as I was writing and provided invaluable critiques, suggestions, and support. In this regard I want to thank Bahjat Itayem, Samih Farsoun, Naseer Aruri, Ghada Karmi, and Kate Rouhana. I also want to express my appreciation to the anonymous reviewers who so carefully read the text and made so many extremely useful suggestions that vastly improved the final work.

As always, my deepest appreciation and ardent thanks go to my husband, Marty. He is my best friend, my companion in all things, and has supported my every endeavor during the past thirty years—even when he thought they were ill-considered. For this book, he spent untold hours working on the maps and tables, reading my endless drafts, and carefully proofing the copyedited manuscript with eyes far sharper than my own.

Note

1. Marc H. Ellis, "Caught in a Moral Dilemma," *Ha'aretz* (Jerusalem, daily, English), June 26, 2001. Ellis is a Jewish American theologian who is university professor and director of the Center for American and Jewish Studies at Baylor University in Waco, Texas.

The
Palestinians

1

The Past as Prologue

The point is that most Israelis have yet to internalize their share of the responsibility for the creation of the Palestinian tragedy and until they do so, there's no chance for peace.

—Tom Segev[1]

What is truth here? That Palestinians do exist, that their expulsion from their homeland was real, and that their national claims are just and legitimate, and have not been achieved.

—Souad Dajani[2]

This chapter presents a historical overview of the Palestinian-Israeli conflict from the perspective of Palestinians. It is not intended to be a comprehensive history but rather to provide insight into Palestinian positions in the peace process and to clarify why Palestinians insist on achieving a viable independent state in the remaining 22 percent of Mandatory Palestine (e.g., the West Bank and Gaza).

Events Prior to 1948

Palestinian Social History

Palestinians trace their historic roots in Palestine from the time of ancient Canan.[3] Whether Muslim or Christian, they share a collective memory of, and pride in, the glories of the Arab-Islamic Empire from 732 C.E. through 1258 C.E. It was the most powerful and advanced empire of its time, renowned for military conquests and brilliant intellectual achievements in medicine, philosophy, astronomy, mathematics, optics, physics, chemistry, the arts, architecture, and other fields.[4] The

Mongols destroyed Arab civilization, then exercised a brutal and tyrannical rule for nearly 260 years. In 1517, Palestine came under the domination of the Turkish Ottoman Empire; in 1917 the British took control.

Palestinians are also linked by a common language—Arabic—as well as by shared mores and folkways. These include similar forms of dress, eating habits, gender dynamics, family structures and relations, work habits, and lifestyles.[5] The basis of Palestinian social life was and continues to be the *hamayel* (patrilineal clan or lineage).[6] The centrality of land and village is the crux of their social organization, their discourse of honor, and their national narrative.[7] Christians as well as Muslims have deep religious ties to Palestine—it was the birthplace of Christianity and the site of the prophet Muhammad's nighttime ride to Paradise. It is the third holiest site in Islam and is commemorated in Jerusalem by the Dome of the Rock and the Al-Aqsa mosque—both situated on the Harem al-Sharif.[8] For Christian Palestinians, Jerusalem is equally sacred, containing the Church of the Holy Sepulcher, the Via Dolorosa, and many other hallowed places; Bethlehem, Nazareth, Galilee, and other sites throughout the country are also venerated.

Nineteenth-Century Transformations

During the first half of the nineteenth century, major economic, social, and political changes—especially transformations in class and land tenure relations—buffeted Palestinian and other Arab Ottoman subjects.[9] Palestine was an impoverished province of the declining empire, poorly administered, lacking basic infrastructure and services, and heavily taxed. The Ottoman Land Law of 1858 and the Land Registration Law of 1861 served to worsen the situation, having particularly pernicious consequences for the *fallahin* (peasants). These codes provided for the registration and issuance of deeds of title to all property; however, the *fallahin* feared that the new registers would lead to increased tax collection, extortion, and military conscription. Thus, they evaded, en masse, the registration of their lands. Conversely, the urban elite, inspired by the growing value of cash crops and by the new land laws, took advantage of peasants' vulnerability. Merchants and absentee landlords, often from Beirut, Damascus, and other far-flung cities, who were frequently also tax farmers and moneylenders, registered villages and vast landholdings in *their* names. Moreover, because the Ottoman laws made no provision for mediating relationships between landlords and tenants, most peasants, from the 1870s onward, were deprived of even the most minimal rights of land tenure. As a result, the *fallahin* were transformed into sharecroppers, tenant farmers, and rural wage-laborers and came increasingly under the control of the landowners.[10] Some found comfort in family and clan ties that were rooted in village and land—connections that engendered knowledge of who they were and their purpose in life.[11] Yet the very nature of the new land tenure system, together with the overwhelmingly agrarian character of Palestine, facilitated the influx of Zionist settlers and set the stage for the ensuing conflict. In the twentieth century, absentee landlords sold Palestinian lands to the Zionists, and the peasants represented the majority of refugees in 1947–1948. Moreover, Israel used these same Ottoman laws within the so-called Green Line (the putative borders of the Jewish state) after 1948 to expropriate land from its Palestinian citizens and, after its 1967 occupation of the West Bank, to confiscate huge tracts of land from the Palestinians therein.

Paradoxically, however, the dynamics that originated in the late nineteenth century also gave rise to the reemergence and consolidation of an Arab consciousness, accompanied by the emergence of a Palestinian consciousness. Thereafter, these twin identities—Arab and Palestinian—were mutually reinforcing, and they ultimately formed the basis of strong Palestinian opposition to the Zionist enterprise.[12]

Birth of the Zionist Movement

By the 1870s, immigrant Europeans began to sporadically construct exclusively Jewish colonies in Palestine. The first settlements were financed by a French Jewish banker-baron, Edmund de Rothschild, who purchased land from absentee landlords for seven agricultural colonies.[13] Palestinian resistance, also intermittent at first, followed quickly. In March 1886, the first clash occurred between Palestinians and Jewish immigrants. In 1893, Tahir al-Hussayni, mufti of Jerusalem and a respected Palestinian leader, began to publicly express concerns about the threat embedded in Zionist efforts to buy land and enlarge the Jewish population through mass immigration.[14]

By the turn of the century, Zionist colonization efforts became systematic, methodical, and internationally organized. In 1897, the first Zionist Congress was held in Basel, Switzerland, with the stated objective of "creat[ing] for the Jewish people a home in Palestine" by means of prodigious Jewish immigration, land purchase, settlement construction, and institution-building.[15] The congress established a group of core structures to realize this objective, including the Zionist Organization and the annual Zionist Congresses whose goal was to create a consensus among world Jewry over the nature and purpose of Zionism's political objectives. The Jewish National Fund was to raise money

worldwide for the enterprise while the Palestine Land Development
Company would purchase land, foster Jewish emigration, and organize
new settlements. The Keren Hayesod, an international umbrella organization, was to ensure that land, moneys, and other properties would be
held in permanent Jewish trust.[16] These institutions quickly birthed the
Yishuv, the prestate organizational infrastructure of the Jewish community in Palestine. The Yishuv, in turn, gave rise in 1948 to the State of
Israel, which resulted in the Palestinian al-Nakbah (catastrophe).[17]

Land and Demography in the Palestine Conflict

Ottoman census records circa 1860 illustrate the demographic composi-
tion of Palestine prior to organized European Jewish colonization. Out
of a total population of 600,000, 96 percent of the inhabitants were
Arab, including 80 percent Muslim, 10 percent Christian, and 6 percent
Jewish. Armenians, European expatriates, and others accounted for the
remaining 4 percent. Palestine was a primarily agrarian society with
510,000 peasants and only 90,000 urban dwellers. The major urban
areas were Haifa, Jaffa, `Akka, and Jerusalem, with less important cities
such as Nablus, Al-Khalil (Hebron), and Gaza. Though city-dwellers
represented but a fraction of the population, they included the vast
majority of indigenous Palestinian Jews.[18] By March 1947, owing to the
Zionist immigration efforts, the Jewish (now separated from Arab) com-
position of the total population had risen from 6 percent to 31 percent,
or 589,341 out of a total of 1,908,775.[19]

The transformations in Palestinian landownership are equally striking, though they evidence far less success in original Zionist objectives
(i.e., purchasing land) than do the demographic changes. Prior to 1880,
Jewish holdings were infinitesimal because of the community's intrinsi-
cally urban character.[20] By 1947, after fifty years of land purchase and
settlement efforts, Zionists owned only 7 percent, or 180,000 hectares,
of the total land area of Mandatory Palestine.[21] Nevertheless, the 1947
United Nations (UN) partition resolution gave the Jewish state approximately 5,500 square miles compared to a 4,500-square-mile allotment
made to the Palestinians.[22]

The Role of the Great Powers in the Palestine Conflict

The conquest of Palestine was not, however, solely a function of Zionist
efforts. Great Powers (primarily Great Britain) and, after 1947, the
United States and the Soviet Union, as well as the United Nations, con-

tributed mightily. During World War I, Great Britain played a duplicitous diplomatic game in trying to defeat its Ottoman enemies and ensure the continuation of its regional interests. It entered into three contradictory agreements involving the Arab nationalist movement (represented by Sharif Husayn, guardian of the holy sites in Mecca); the Zionist movement (in the person of Lord Rothschild, head of the Jewish community in Britain); and the French government (embodied in Charles Georges-Picot, formerly the French consul-general in Beirut).

The first agreement, known as the Husayn-McMahon Correspondence, was concluded with the Arab nationalists in a series of eight letters exchanged during 1914–1915. It involved explicit commitments by each side. The Arabs pledged to assist the British war effort by revolting against the Ottoman Turks. In exchange, the British promised to facilitate, at the war's termination, the Arab nationalist goals of independence and unity in a contiguous territorial entity that specifically included Palestine. In 1916, Britain and France secretly signed the Sykes-Picot Accord in which they agreed to divide most of the Arab world into spheres of influence, in much of which they would "establish such direct or indirect administration or control as they desire and as they may think fit to arrange."[23] France was to have authority in Syria, from which it carved out Lebanon, whereas Britain was to have control of Iraq, Transjordan, and Palestine. In 1917, Britain issued the Balfour Declaration, pledging support for Zionist objectives in Palestine. At the San Remo conference in 1920, Britain and France were given mandates for these territories (subsequently approved by the League of Nations), confirming the imperialist designs set forth in Sykes-Picot. Moreover, the mandate for Palestine contained the Balfour Declaration plus additional provisions that reinforced Zionist objectives in Palestine.[24]

Britain formally assumed the Palestine mandate in 1920 and maintained its control until May 1948.[25] Throughout this period, London presided over the growth and development of the Yishuv as well as over virtually continuous intercommunal conflict. The Palestinians resisted Zionist encroachment, whereas the Zionists, backed by the British, crushed the rebellions.[26] There were relatively minor Palestinian uprisings in 1920, 1921, 1929, and 1933, culminating in a major revolt that lasted from 1936 through 1939 (the latter is known as the Arab Revolt). It began with a labor strike, evolved into mass civil disobedience, then into armed insurrection. British suppression of the uprising was brutal and oppressive. It included the imposition of harsh emergency regulations and practices, including closure of newspapers, search-and-seizure operations without warrants, mass arrests and incarceration, deportation of political, trade union, and resistance leaders, widespread curfews, and other forms of collective punishment.[27]

1947–1948: The Fateful Years

In 1947, prior to its withdrawal from Palestine in the face of the irreconcilable conflict (although not before ensuring the viability of the Jewish prestate institutional infrastructure), Britain handed its "Palestine problem" to the United Nations for disposition.[28] A UN-appointed committee investigated the conflict and forwarded a recommendation to the UN General Assembly. The committee was split, but a slight majority favored partition. On November 29, 1947, contrary to the wishes of the indigenous population, the UN General Assembly, under strong U.S. pressure,[29] approved UN Resolution 181. It called for the division of Palestine into a Jewish state and a Palestinian state and stipulated that Jerusalem was to be a *corpus separatum*—a united city under permanent UN trusteeship. As noted, the Palestinian state was to be smaller (45 percent of the territory) than the Jewish state (55 percent), which also contained the most fertile agricultural lands. This division was made despite an incongruous population ratio (approximately 31 percent Jewish to 69 percent Palestinian). The Jewish state was to include a sizable Palestinian minority—about 45 percent of the total population; the Palestinian state would have a negligible Jewish minority. The Zionists accepted the plan (with reservations, as it fell far short of their territorial objectives), whereas the Palestinians rejected it.

An intercommunal war immediately erupted. The Zionists were organized, highly trained, and equipped with heavy weapons, whereas the Palestinians were exhausted and disorganized from three decades of resistance, leaderless (attributable to British imprisonment and expulsion of their leaders from prior insurrections), and equipped with only light arms. In short, the Palestinians were outnumbered, militarily disadvantaged, and politically unprepared to defend their homeland. Even after May 14, 1948, when Israel declared its independence and neighboring Arab brigades provided the Palestinians some assistance, they were unable to match the numerical, technological, and organizational superiority of the Israeli Defense Forces (IDF).[30] Indeed, as Israeli historian Avi Shlaim notes, the Zionists had 96,441 men under arms, whereas the combined Arab and Palestinian forces never exceeded 40,000: "at each stage of the war, the IDF significantly outnumbered all the Arab forces arrayed against it, and by the final stage of the war its superiority ratio was nearly two to one." Thus, "the inability of the

Arabs to coordinate their diplomatic and military plans was in no small measure responsible for the disaster that overwhelmed them."[31]

After 1948

The First Israeli Expansion and the Palestine Refugee Issue

By December 1948, Israel had conquered one-fourth more territory than it was allotted in the partition plan from areas that the United Nations had assigned to the Palestinian state (see Map 1.1). Israeli scholar Ilan Pappe argues that David Ben-Gurion, leader of the Yishuv and later the first prime minister of Israel, was determined "to enlarge the Jewish State at any cost and for that purpose to carry the war forth into the areas designated by the UN as the Arab State."[32] Moreover, in accordance with a prior secret agreement between the Zionists and the British-installed King Abdullah, east-central Palestine came under Transjordanian control and was later illegally annexed as the West Bank of the expanded Kingdom of Jordan.[33] Israel and Jordan divided Jerusalem, also illegally, under their respective sovereignties, and the Gaza Strip came under Egyptian military occupation.[34] Palestine ceased to exist—except in the memories of its dispossessed inhabitants.

Indeed, the success of the Zionist project in establishing a sovereign Jewish nation-state on 78 percent of historic Palestine rendered the Palestinians—Muslim and Christian—dispersed, dispossessed, and stateless. Some 770,000, more than half the total, became destitute refugees, residing in squalid camps in nearby countries, left with nothing save their longing to return to their homes and lands.[35] Moreover, Israel razed 418 Palestinian towns and villages (more than 50 percent of the total Arab property in Palestine), burned vast amounts of agricultural land, and confiscated both movable and fixed (e.g., houses and factories) property.[36]

Debates continue today as to who was responsible for the dispossession of the Palestinians. For years, it was an article of faith—especially in the United States—that the leaders of the Arab states and other Arab elements were the cause of this tragedy. Israel claimed that it was entirely blameless, and its assertion became historical "fact." Israeli historians have now turned this dogma on its head. The research of scholars such as Avi Shlaim and Ilan Pappe, as well as Benny Morris, Simha Flapan, Tom Segev, and others, has provided an entirely revised picture

Map 1.1 UN Resolution 181 Partition Map (1947) and the Rhodes Armistice Lines (1949) Showing Territory Conquered by Israel Beyond Resolution 181 Allocations

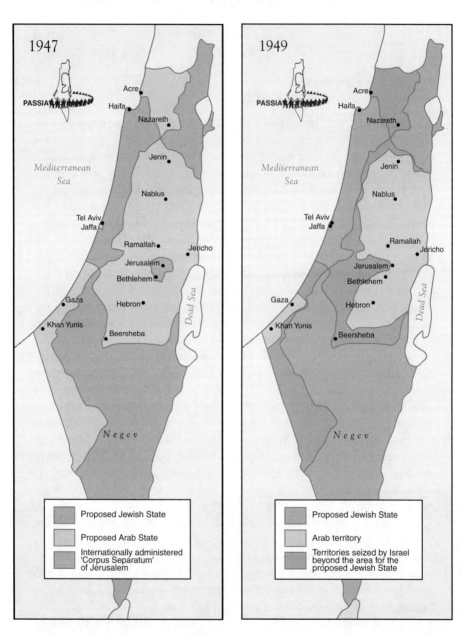

Source: Palestinian Academic Society for the Study of International Affairs (PASSIA), Jerusalem, http://www.passia.org/palestine_facts/MAPS/1947-un-partition-plan-reso.html. Accessed January 2003. Reprinted with permission of PASSIA.

of the refugee issue. Palestinian researchers such as Nur Masalha and Walid Khalidi, and Michael Palumbo likewise have broadened our understanding of the refugee question.[37]

Zionism and the Inevitability of Transfer

Prior to 1947, there was a half-century of plans, policies, preparations, and actions to empty Palestine of Palestinians.[38] Moreover, the concept and practice of transfer (read: expulsion of the Palestinians from Israel) is grounded in the very basis of Zionism—a *Jewish* state, a *state of the Jewish people* (as compared to a state wherein national citizenship inheres from birthright). The fundamental function of the Jewish state is to serve as a place for the in-gathering of world Jewry (codified in the Law of Return). Zionist leaders were virtually unanimous in believing that Zionism, if the indigenous inhabitants were allowed to remain, could not succeed in establishing a homogeneous Jewish state and fulfill its imperative of absorbing the expected influx of Jewish immigrants.[39] According to the partition plan, approximately 45 percent of the total population of the Jewish state would be Palestinian. Added to this was the Palestinian population in the territory Israel had seized from the area of the designated Palestinian state. This meant, in effect, that the state would have been binational, not Jewish, and would have negated the whole purpose of the Zionist project.

Theodor Herzl, the founder of political Zionism, had ignored the existence of indigenous Palestinians in his early writings, although in later pieces he asserted that Zionism would bring progress and prosperity to the Palestinians. Yet in private, Herzl spoke about the necessity of displacement and transfer from what would become the Jewish state. "We shall try to spirit the penniless population across the border by procuring for it employment in the transit countries [he did not say how]. . . . Both the process of expropriation [of land] and the removal of the poor must be carried out discreetly and circumspectly."[40]

Israeli historian Zeev Sternhell writes: "The building of the Yishuv was accompanied by a constant struggle with a stubborn Arab opposition. . . . Both sides understood each other well and knew that the implementation of Zionism could be only at the expense of the Palestinian Arabs. The leadership of the Yishuv did not conceal its intentions."[41] Similarly, Israeli historian Benny Morris writes: "In the months before the [1942 Biltmore] conference both [Chaim] Weizmann and [David] Ben-Gurion had expressed support for the transfer of the Arabs . . . by compulsion if necessary."[42]

The importance of David Ben-Gurion as a Zionist theoretician and statesman requires further examination of his views.[43] It was Ben-Gurion's praxis that implemented Zionism's fundamental objectives: to conquer as much land as possible, to bring as many Jewish immigrants to the state as was feasible, and to expel as many Palestinians as was achievable. He believed, above all, in the necessity to employ force and power—political, economic, organizational, and especially military—to realize these goals.[44] The fact that he was committed to, and oversaw, the expulsion of the Palestinians is reflected in this series of quotes from 1938 to 1947:

> "We must expel Arabs and take their places . . . and if we have to use force . . . to guarantee our own rights to settle in those places—then we have force at our disposal" (1937).
> "I support compulsory transfer. I do not see in it anything immoral" (1938).
> "Complete transfer without compulsion—and ruthless compulsion at that—is hardly imaginable. . . . The majority of Arabs could hardly be expected to leave voluntarily within the short period of time which can materially affect our problem" (1941).
> "[The Haganah, or prestate Zionist military force, must] adopt the system of aggressive defense; during the assault we must respond with a decisive blow: the destruction of the [Arab] place" (1947).[45]

Shabtai Teveth, David Ben-Gurion's biographer, relates Ben-Gurion's belief that only by expelling the Palestinians could the Zionists fulfill their dream of a Jewish state:

> The *compulsory* transfer of the Arabs from the valleys of the proposed Jewish state . . . could give us something which we never had, even when we stood on our own during the days of the First and Second Temples . . . a real Jewish state—a contiguous, thickly populated, agricultural bloc. . . . This is national consolidation in a free homeland.[46]

Implementation of Transfer

Between September 1947 and January 1948, approximately 70,000 Palestinians, mainly from the upper classes who sensed the coming war, left the country, the majority voluntarily. Yet they departed without their possessions and did not sell their properties, indicating their expectations to return.[47] Israeli forces, however, mostly drove out the remainder. Some fled in psychological terror upon hearing of rumors of brutal massacres in other villages, some because of the destruction of their villages (286 by August 1948), and some because they were simply caught up in the chaos and uncertainty of war and fled to safer ground.

Focused efforts to depopulate Palestine did not begin until March 1948 and took on greater intensity after April. Israeli historian Ilan Pappe records that in March Israel's forces were instructed to begin occupying areas that lay *outside* the designated Jewish state. As the Yishuv acquired more and more territory, it acquired more Palestinians, and the need to solve this predicament became increasingly acute. Thus, beginning in March and April 1948, peaking in August, and through December, the vast majority of Palestinians fled or were driven from their homes.

The existence and implementation of a program, a military strategem, devised by the Zionist high command of the Haganah, clearly attests to the significance of expulsion in the refugee flight. The program for the transfer of the Palestinians was known as Plan Dalet, or Plan D. Shlaim provides insight:

> The aim of Plan D was to secure all the areas allotted to the Jewish state under the UN partition resolution as well as Jewish settlements outside these areas and corridors leading to them, so as to provide a solid and continuous basis for Jewish sovereignty. The novelty and audacity of the plan lay in the orders to capture Arab villages and cities. . . . [Plan D's] objective was to clear the interior of the country of hostile and potentially hostile Arab elements, and in this sense it provided a warrant for expelling civilians. By implementing Plan D in April and May [1948], the Haganah thus directly and decisively contributed to the birth of the Palestinian refugee problem.[48]

Though Plan D was devised by the military, it had the support of the highest political echelons. Israeli scholar Tom Segev, considering a statement made by Ben-Gurion in March 1949, adds: "Ben-Gurion tended to ignore the human tragedy of the Palestinian Arabs. . . . 'Land with Arabs on it and Land without Arabs on it are two very different types of land,' he told his party's central committee."[49] Regarding the issue of expulsion, Pappe writes: "Plan D can be regarded in many respects as a master plan for [their] expulsion. Moreover, the Plan legitimized, *a priori*, some of the more horrendous atrocities committed by Jewish soldiers."[50] And:

> Plan D, with its specific orders of destruction and eviction [resulted in] the lower strata of the Palestinian society [being] driven out through [its] . . . implementation. . . . The massacre in Deir Yassin [also] played an important role in driving these groups out of Palestine in April and May 1948 . . . [It] had a psychological effect on the Arab community and acted as a catalyst to the exodus.[51]

Plan D was the most important blueprint for the expulsion of the

Palestinians; however, it was not the only strategy. Other methods (here summarized by Palestinian historian Nur Masalha) require mention:

> At least 122 Arab localities were expelled at gunpoint by Jewish forces. . . . 270 localities were evacuated under assault by Jewish troops: the tactic of attacking a locality from two directions, but leaving "escape routes" was particularly perfected by Yigal Allon as a deliberate method to ensure Arab evacuation. . . . 38 localities were evacuated out of fear of attack or being caught in the crossfire. . . . 49 localities were vacated under the influence of the fall of a neighbouring town. . . . 12 were evacuated as a result of psychological warfare methods, spreading rumours and whispering campaigns.[52]

Pappe writes:

> From October 1948 on the Israelis did their utmost to create a fait accompli that would render repatriation impossible. The prime objective was to demolish what was left of the abandoned Palestinian villages, almost 350 in all, so that the term itself would become meaningless. Moreover, Israel's policy-makers required the land and property for the absorption of the waves of new Jewish immigrants. . . . Even before the war it was clear to many Jewish leaders that the Arabs who left would not be allowed to return. In June 1948, Yosef Weitz wrote in a memorandum that there was a consensus among those responsible for the "Arab problem" that the best way to deal with abandoned Arab villages was by "destruction, renovation, and settlement by Jews." In August 1948, the Israeli government decided to implement Weitz's ideas to the letter.[53]

After the war, Israel took every possible step to prevent the refugees' return, including razing 418 Palestinian villages and towns and constructing kibbutzim (communal farms or settlements), moshavim (cooperative farms), and Jewish towns over the ruins. It seized all the property Palestinians left behind, and deterred by force Palestinians who attempted to infiltrate the new borders to reclaim their property or harvest their crops.[54] Yet as sociologist Samih Farsoun writes: "Even as they took flight, however, there was never a question of return: It was always a matter of when and how, not whether they would return."[55]

The Refugees from 1948

The Palestinians dispossessed in 1947–1948 represent the refugee issue we know today. According to UN figures, the refugees were dispersed as follows: 280,000 to the Gaza Strip; 190,000 to the West Bank; and 256,000 to Jordan (East Bank), Syria, and Lebanon—reaching a total, by September 1949, of 770,000. By May 1950, that aggregate had risen to 957,000.[56] In 1999, according to the United Nations Relief and Works Agency (UNRWA), the number of registered refugees and their descendants was approximately 3,677,882. Of these, 1,194,512 are living in sixty-one camps in the West Bank, Gaza, Lebanon, Syria, and Jordan.[57] UNRWA's requirements for registering refugees are stringent; thus, the actual number of Palestinian refugees is considerably higher.[58]

On December 8, 1949, the UN General Assembly established the UNRWA for Palestine refugees; it was charged with providing assistance to the refugees in the fields of food, shelter, education, and health services. It differed from the United Nations High Commission for Refugees in that it was *not* authorized to seek either the local integration or the resettlement of refugees in another country. Prior to the General Assembly's UNRWA resolution, on December 11, 1948, that body passed UN Resolution 194, which called for either the repatriation of the Palestinians to their homes or compensation paid to those who chose not to return. Since then, most of the original refugees have remained stateless (except in Jordan), destitute, and confined to the same squalid, overcrowded UNRWA camps. Resolution 194 remains the fundamental, although not the only, legal basis for the refugees' right of return.

Palestinians were thus transformed from proud *fallahin* to a disarticulated proletariat and lumpenproletariat. Arab governments neither welcomed nor embraced the refugees. In Lebanon, they have experienced continuous and extreme discrimination, oppression, and violence as well as numerous massacres.[59] In 1970, King Hussein of Jordan carried out the Black September massacre that killed some 20,000 and expelled an additional portion of the community. In Kuwait, Palestinians were afforded wide-ranging and lucrative economic opportunities but were denied citizenship, landownership, and political rights. In 1991, the Palestinian community in Kuwait—some 450,000—was expelled.[60]

About 150,000 to 180,000 Palestinians remained in their homes and on their lands in what became Israel in 1948. Many of these, however, became internal refugees subjected to compulsory migration from one place to another: from 1950 until 1966, Israel ruled its Arab citizens under a systematic military government.[61] Between 1948 and 1956, the state expropriated half of all the land owned by Palestinians remaining in Israel (i.e., those within the Green Line) for Jewish settlement.[62] To this day, Arabs in Israel (who now number approximately 900,000, or some 18 percent of Israel's total population) continue to live as second-class citizens that face exclusion, discrimination, and suspicion.[63]

All the Palestinians who left Israel, no matter what the circumstances, left behind property in the form of land, crops, orchards, industrial plants, quarries, heavy equipment, trucks, banks, bank accounts, houses, furniture, rugs, household effects, stores and warehouses full of goods, livestock (including goats, sheep, hens, and cattle), cash, jewelry, and more.[64] The value of Palestinian property lost in 1947–1948 is estimated at U.S.$57.8 billion (in 1998 dollars).[65] In 1948, Israel appointed a custodian of abandoned property to take control of everything left by Palestinians. In 1950, the Knesset (the Israeli legislature) enacted the Basic Law of Absentee Property that provided, retroactively and prospectively, for the State of Israel to confiscate all properties from anyone defined as an absentee. Essentially this meant that all the property left behind by Palestinians in 1947–1948 would be appropriated by Israel and turned over to the Jewish National Fund for administration and disbursement to Jewish immigrants.[66] To date, Israel has not paid any financial reparations to the Palestinians.[67]

Refugees, Infiltrations, and the Arab-Israeli Conflict

After the al-Nakbah and dispersion en masse, Palestinians were preoccupied with the essentials of survival and were politically quiescent for nearly fifteen years. Moreover, following the creation of the Israeli state, the issues surrounding the question of Palestine became obscured in the Arab-Israeli conflict. This all played out in a series of wars and strife that included the 1948 War of Independence, the 1956 Sinai War, the 1967 Six Day War, the July 1967–August 1970 War of Attrition, the 1973 Yom Kippur War, and the 1978 and 1982 invasions of Lebanon. Not until 1969, when Yasser Arafat and his Fateh resistance organization assumed control of the Palestine Liberation Organization (PLO), did Palestine and the Palestinians reemerge as the center of the conflict. Nevertheless, the Palestinians remained at the heart of the Arab-Israeli conflict.

After the 1948 war ended, many Palestinian refugees tried to return to their original homes and villages to retrieve movable property or find lost relatives. These efforts involved crossing Israel's borders and were considered by Israel to be infiltrations. Because this involved the Arab states as well, the issue of Palestinian infiltrations and Israeli reprisals laid the foundation for the Arab-Israeli conflict. Israeli historian Avi Shlaim writes that:

> Infiltration was a direct consequence of the displacement and dispossession of [the Palestinians]. . . . The motives behind it were largely social and economic. . . . The infiltrators were [mostly] Palestinian refugees whose reasons for crossing the border included looking for

relatives, returning to their homes, recovering material possessions, tending their fields, harvesting. . . . During the 1949–56 period as a whole, 90 percent or more of all infiltrations were motivated by social and economic concerns. . . . [As a result of] the "free-fire" policy adopted by the Israeli army, border guards, and police [in this same period] . . . between 2,700 and 5,000 infiltrators were killed . . . the great majority of them unarmed.[68]

But Israel was not content with stopping infiltrations through killing individual infiltrators. It developed a policy of massive retaliation that involved striking at the villages and areas from which Israel claimed the infiltrators had come—places that lay inside the boundaries of neighboring states. It was a policy that "greatly inflamed Arab hatred of Israel and met with mounting criticism from the international community."[69] The raids were conducted at night, were aimed at civilian targets, and violated the sovereignty of Arab states. What made matters worse from the perspective of the Arab governments was that "they were opposed to infiltration and tried to curb it."[70]

Nevertheless, Israel created a special unit within its military—Unit 101—to carry out the raids and placed Ariel Sharon in charge. Sharon initiated dozens of retaliations; an especially notable one was on the village of Qibya, within the Jordanian annexed West Bank. On the night of October 14–15, 1953, Sharon reduced the village to rubble: "forty-five houses had been blown up and sixty-nine civilians, two-thirds of them women and children, had been killed."[71] The reprisals continued through February 1955 with the Gaza raid that set off a chain reaction leading to Israel's October 1956 invasion of Egypt.[72] (Another cycle of infiltrations and massive reprisals contributed to the June 1967 war.)

The Resurgence of Palestinian Nationalism

Palestinian quiescence came to an end on January 1, 1965, when the first fedayeen (self-sacrificers) group, Fateh (meaning "conquest" or "opening," a reverse acronym for the Palestine National Liberation Movement), led by Yasser Arafat, carried out its first guerrilla operation against Israel. Soon thereafter, the Popular Front for the Liberation of Palestine (PFLP), led by George Habash, emerged and began carrying out raids against Israel. Then, Nayif Hawatmeh, one of the founders of the PFLP, split with the organization and formed his own resistance group—the Democratic Front for the Liberation of Palestine (DFLP). Numerous smaller groups arose in various places to which Palestinians had been exiled and undertook a variety of activities to "liberate Palestine."[73] Leaders and cadres of all the organizations were deeply influenced by the revolutions in Algeria and Cuba, the Vietnamese resistance to the United States, and Arab nationalism. Thus, they espoused objectives similar to those of other twentieth-century anticolonialist liberation movements, proclaiming their intention to free their homeland from foreign oppression and colonialism and to use armed struggle as the means to that end.[74]

Arab leaders understood the threat that such a revolutionary movement could pose to their interests and the status quo. Indeed, after fifteen years of Israeli reprisal raids, plus Israel's 1956 invasion of Egypt, Arab leaders wanted to avoid further conflict with Israel and thereby to absolve themselves of the Palestinian albatross. Thus, they created an organization that would give the Palestinians the illusion of determining their own destiny while simultaneously ensuring Arab state control over it. In 1964, at the first Arab summit in Cairo, Egyptian president Gamal Abdul Nasser proposed the PLO as an "independent" institution through which Palestinians could struggle on their own for their rights.[75]

In May 1964, the PLO was formally founded in Jerusalem at an assembly of 422 Palestinians from ten Arab countries. There they established the institutional structures of the organization, drafted the Palestinian National Covenant (known as the charter), as well as a declaration of independence, and wrote the General Principles of a Fundamental Law, a constitution of sorts.[76] At this juncture, however, the PLO was neither independent nor capable of struggle—not even political endeavor. It was created by Egypt, controlled by Egypt, and functioned mainly as an instrument of Egyptian diplomacy in Arab politics.[77]

By contrast, Fateh, the PFLP, the DFLP, and other groups operated independently and subscribed to different ideologies, and collectively they constituted the Palestine Nationalist Movement. They were underground, secretive, populist, activist, and radical, in contrast to the PLO, which was above ground, elitist, willing to toe the Arab states' line, and legitimized by the status-quo Arab League.[78]

In 1969, the fedayeen took control of the PLO, transformed it into an autonomous organization, and subsumed eight distinct resistance groups under its unifying umbrella.[79] The original political institutions remained intact thereafter. Because Fateh was the strongest and most populous group, its leader, Yasser Arafat, became chairman of the executive committee and leader of the PLO. Both Fateh and Arafat remained dominant from then on. Throughout Palestinian communities, the PLO became the symbol of Palestinian nationalism and the embodiment of Palestinian hope. Yet for the next twenty years, until the aftermath of the 1987 intifada, Israel, backed by the United States, vilified the Palestinians as terrorists and successfully kept a discussion of the Palestine question off the agendas for peace in the region.

The June 1967 War: A New Nakbah

In the June 1967 war, euphemistically labeled as a preemptive attack, Israel conquered in six days Egypt's Sinai Peninsula, including the occupied Gaza Strip, Syria's Golan Heights, and the West Bank, including East Jerusalem, which had been occupied by Jordan since 1948.[80] Israel immediately instituted a coercive military occupation throughout the West Bank and Gaza and began to incorporate Jerusalem under Israeli sovereignty (see Map 1.2).

The 1967 Refugees

In the context of the 1967 Six Day War and Israel's conquest of the West Bank, Gaza, and East Jerusalem, some 250,000–300,000 Palestinians fled or were driven from the West Bank and Gaza.[81] Most analysts put the figure at 300,000.[82] Immediately after the war, "thousands of Arabs were taken by bus from East Jerusalem to the Allenby Bridge" and deposited on Jordanian soil.[83] Many of the 300,000 were refugees from 1948; most went to Jordan, some to Egypt and other parts of the Arab world. On July 2, 1967, under pressure from the international community, Israel announced that it would permit the return of refugees if they applied no later than August 10 (subsequently extended to September 13). How many refugees were aware of Israel's announcement is unclear, but given the turbulence of their lives in the months after the war, it is safe to assume that the number was limited. Nevertheless, 120,000 persons applied to return; of these, Israel permitted only 14,000 to actually do so. The refugees from 1967 are officially termed "displaced persons" and they, together with their descendants, are thought to number some 1.1 million today.[84]

UN Resolution 242

On November 22, 1967, the UN Security Council, in a rare unanimous vote, passed UN Security Council Resolution 242, thought to contain the elements for a just and lasting peace in the region. It emphasized the "inadmissibility of the acquisition of territory by war" and called for Israel's withdrawal "from the territories occupied in the conflict"

Map 1.2   Israel and the
Territories It Occupied After the 1967 War

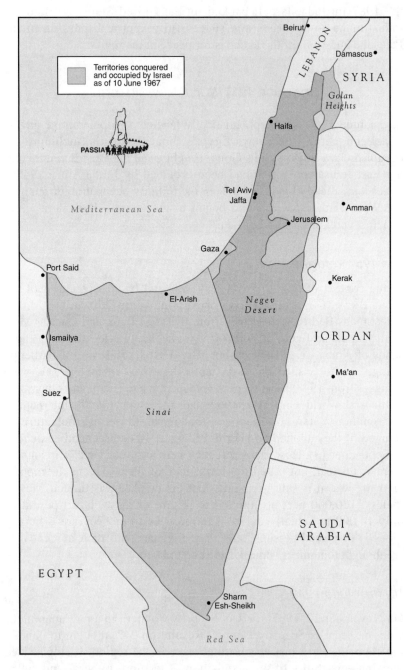

Source: Palestinian Academic Society for the Study of International Affairs (PASSIA), Jerusalem, http://www.passia.org/palestine_facts/MAPS/pdf/1967-post-june-war-israel.pdf. Accessed January 2003. Reprinted with permission of PASSIA.

in exchange for peace between Israel and its neighboring states. It specified an international conference as the means to achieve peace. (After the October 1973 war, the Security Council passed Resolution 338, which was virtually identical to Resolution 242.) The Palestinians were not specifically mentioned; rather, there was merely a reference to "achieving a just settlement of the refugee problem."[85] because of this characterization, the PLO did not accept the resolution until 1988.

The June 1967 Six Day War was another catastrophe for the Palestinians. Relatively benign Arab control over Gaza, the West Bank, and East Jerusalem was exchanged for a hostile Israeli military occupation bent on territorial expansion. Foreshadowing events to come, Israeli troops, within days of capturing the Old City, gave the 650 Palestinian residents of the Mughrabi Quarter several hours to leave and then dynamited their houses—allegedly to provide additional space for Jews to pray at the Western Wall. Within two days, the quarter was demolished. On June 28, 1967, Israel's interior minister signed a decree extending Israeli law to East Jerusalem and enlarged the municipal boundaries by twenty-eight square miles at the expense of Palestinian lands in the West Bank. Shortly thereafter, the Knesset passed legislation unilaterally enacting the "reunification" of Jerusalem, effecting its de facto annexation.[86] Palestinian residents of the city were issued residency cards, giving them a different status than their brethren in the West Bank and Gaza as well as from Israeli Jews (see Map 1.3).

In addition, within weeks of the war's end, Israeli authorities destroyed the Palestinian villages of Imwas, Beit Nuba, and Yalu in the Latrun area and expelled their inhabitants while partially destroying several neighboring villages. In September 1967, construction of the first Jewish settlements in the West Bank was begun.

Israel's Occupation of the West Bank, Gaza Strip, and East Jerusalem After 1967

The most fundamental fact, central to an understanding and analysis of Israel and the Palestinians from 1967 through the present, is that the West Bank, Gaza, and East Jerusalem remain under Israeli occupation (see Map 1.4). Since 1967, these places collectively have been known as the Occupied Territories.

The Israeli occupation has had catastrophic effects on Palestinian society, economy, cultural expression, and political rights. Israeli historian Benny Morris characterized it accurately:

Map 1.3 The Expanded
Boundaries of Jerusalem, 1967–1969

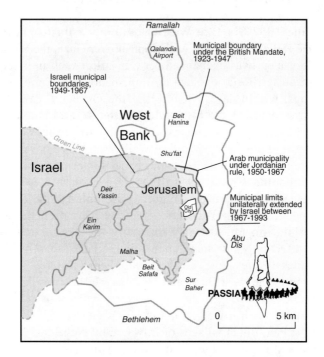

Source: Palestinian Academic Society for the Study of International Affairs (PASSIA), Jerusalem, http://www.passia. org/palestine_facts/MAPS/images/jer_maps/Jlem1947-2000.html. Accessed January 2003. Reprinted with permission of PASSIA.

Map 1.4　The West Bank (by Israeli Defined Districts) and the Gaza Strip, 1967

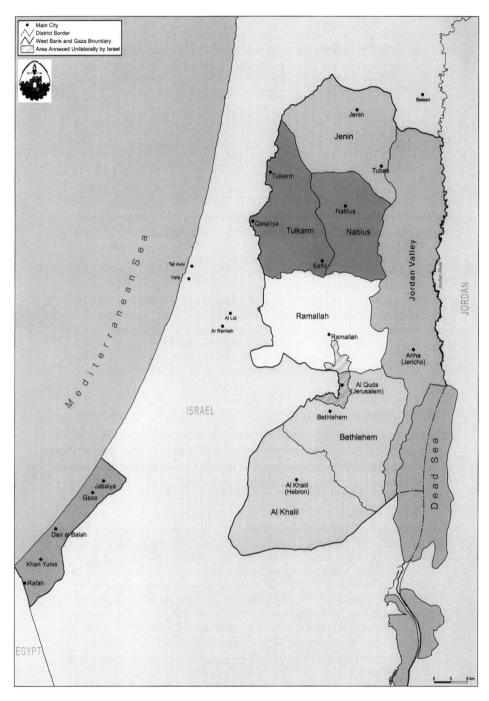

Source: Jad Isaac, et. al., "West Bank and Gaza Strip Districts According to Israeli Administration After 1967," in *Applied Research Institute, An Atlas of Palestine (The West Bank and Gaza)* (Jerusalem: Applied Research Institute—ARIJ, January 2000), p. 22. Reprinted with permission of ARIJ.

Israelis liked to believe, and tell the world, that they were running an "enlightened" or "benign" occupation qualitatively different from other military occupations the world has seen. The truth was radically different. Like all occupations, Israel's was founded on brute force, repression and fear, collaboration and treachery, beatings and torture chambers, and daily intimidation, humiliation and manipulation.[87]

Abba Eban, a former Israeli foreign minister and member of the Knesset, described the political situation of Palestinians in the Occupied Territories on the eve of the 1987 intifada (the first uprising):

> In the areas of Judea, Samaria [Israel's appellations for the West Bank] and Gaza today there are 1,300,000 Arabs and less than 50,000 Israeli settlers. The Arabs cannot vote or be elected at any level, have no degree of juridical control over the government that determines the conditions of their existence, have no rights of appeal against the judgments of the military courts, are not free to leave their land with assurance of a right to return, are not immune from judgments of expulsion from their birthplace and homeland, have no flag to revere, do not possess the same economic and social conditions as their Jewish neighbors, nor the same status for their newspapers and universities. The 50,000 Jews and those who might come in their wake have a totally different set of rights and immunities. . . . There is a society in the West Bank and Gaza in which a man's rights are defined not by his conduct or by any egalitarian principle, but by his ethnic identity.[88]

In 1986, Meron Benvenisti, an Israeli Jew who is a well-known writer and commentator, a former deputy mayor of Jerusalem, and former founder and director of the Ford- and Rockefeller-funded West Bank Data Base Project, succinctly described Israel's overall economic objectives in regard to the Occupied Territories:

> Israel's economic policy appears on the surface to be clear, consistent and deliberate. It can be summarized in a few sentences: freezing the economic development of the Palestinian sector along with encouragement of improvements in the standard of living, based on income from work in Israel; economic prosperity for individual residents alongside economic stagnation at the communal level; discouraging independent economic development that would enter into competition with the Israeli economy, and prevention of independent economic development that could enable Palestinian political forces to establish power bases, and eventually a Palestinian state. A relatively high standard of living, achieved by employment in Israel, is to create greater dependence on Israel and distract public opinion from politics; economic dependence is also achieved by the integration of infrastructure systems (roads, electricity, water); economic rewards and punishments

form part of the political and security control system of the territories. This policy appears to have been executed with great success.[89]

The extreme hardships experienced by the Palestinians under occupation led, after twenty years, to the 1987 uprising. The intifada reflected the primary dynamic in the Israeli-Palestinian relationship: ongoing Palestinian resistance to the occupation, and relentless Israeli efforts to maintain, deepen, and extend the occupation in an effort to bring the territories under Israeli sovereignty with a Jewish demographic majority. The ever-expanding settlement movement lies at the core of this effort.

The Reemergence of Palestinian Nationalism in the Occupied Territories and the War in Lebanon

By the early 1970s, the cumulative effect of two co-terminus trends gave rise to a reemergence of Palestinian nationalism within the Occupied Territories. The first involved Israel's extensive political repression, its settlement drive, and its successful effort to "de-develop" the Palestinian economy and then tie it to Israel in a structural relationship of dependency.[90] The second was related to the PLO's growing international stature after 1969 and its effective articulation of nationalist sentiments. However, the ascendance of Palestinian nationalism in East Jerusalem, the West Bank, and the Gaza Strip was of grave concern to Israel because it was an obstacle to the realization of Tel Aviv's objective of extending its sovereignty there.

Israeli leaders, in particular Defense Minister Ariel Sharon, calculated that if the PLO could be destroyed in Lebanon (Beirut was the headquarters of the PLO), and if the physical institutions—political, medical, educational, research, economic, and others—that constituted the symbolic manifestation of Palestinian nationalism could be eliminated, then nationalist sentiments in the Occupied Territories would be crushed and Israel could implement its goals over a quiescent population. Thus, Israel's 1982 invasion of Lebanon was aimed at liquidating the PLO as an organization and as the embodiment of Palestinian nationalism so that Israel could better control the Palestinians in the territories. The war had secondary objectives as well, but eliminating the PLO was paramount.[91]

Israel defeated the PLO, destroyed all its social institutions, and expelled it from Lebanon. In the process, it bombed into ashes the refugee camps in southern Lebanon, presided over massacres at Sabra and Shatilla, and killed some 20,000 Palestinian and Lebanese civilians.

The PLO elite regrouped in Tunis while the masses were dispersed to Yemen, Iraq, Somalia, and other distant destinations. Yet despite the magnitude of this devastation, among Palestinians in the Occupied Territories (and elsewhere), the strength of resurgent nationalism, as well as the PLO's influence, remained undiminished.

The Historic Compromise

PLO tactics, under the leadership of Arafat, underwent major transformation—from an almost total reliance on armed struggle to a combination of guerrilla activity and diplomacy to the use of diplomacy almost to the exclusion of other means. Guerrilla incursions within Israel peaked in 1970, then steadily declined until ceasing altogether in the early 1980s. The major terrorist operations occurred during the period 1970–1974 and for the most part were carried out by leftist groups, especially the PFLP. Later, on several occasions, some elements of Fateh engaged in terrorist activities.[92]

More significant, the PLO—again under Arafat's leadership—transformed its objectives from liberating Palestine, to establishing a democratic secular state of Palestine, and then, by 1988, to the acceptance of a Palestinian state alongside Israel on 22 percent of Mandatory Palestine. For Palestinians that meant accepting a state in the West Bank and Gaza with East Jerusalem as its capital. This historic compromise, made by the PLO at a time of internal unity and universal (excepting the United States and Israel) external legitimacy is of signal importance in understanding the PLO's expectations of the peace process that was initiated in Oslo, Norway.[93] It also underlies comprehension of the failure of that process as a result of Israel's unwillingness to relinquish control over these territories and permit the establishment of a viable, contiguous, independent, and sovereign state.[94]

The PLO had informally approved the two-state approach by 1975, and at the 1977 meeting of the Palestine National Council (PNC) the concept was further clarified, accepted, and tied to a commitment to diplomacy and negotiations. However, at the November 1988 PNC, the PLO went even further. It recognized UN Security Council Resolutions 242 and 338,[95] and it proclaimed the State of Palestine within the Occupied Territories. In so doing, the PLO explicitly abandoned earlier policies for liberation and secular democracy. The PNC also categorically rejected "terrorism in all its forms," gave express backing to the need "for security and peace in the region," and authorized the PLO's executive committee and its chairman, Yasser Arafat, to pursue these objectives solely through diplomatic means.[96] The first diplomatic step followed on December 7, when, in a joint declaration with a delegation of Jewish American leaders in Stockholm, Arafat explained that the PNC resolutions "accepted the existence of Israel as a state in the region."[97]

On December 13, 1988, the UN General Assembly convened in a special session in Geneva specifically to hear an address by Chairman Arafat after the U.S. government denied him permission to come to New York. In his speech, Arafat unequivocally reaffirmed the PLO's commitment to diplomacy and a two-state solution.[98] The following day, he gave a press conference in which he spoke of peace as salvation for both Israelis and Palestinians, "renounce[d] all forms of terrorism," called for an international peace conference, reiterated the PLO's commitment to UN Resolutions 242 and 338, and recognized Israel's *right* to exist.[99] This, then, constitutes the Palestinians' "historic compromise" with which the PLO entered the Oslo process.

The 1987 Intifada

In December 1987, the intifada—the Palestinian uprising against Israeli occupation—exploded in the Occupied Territories. It was a spontaneous, nonviolent, grassroots movement against the occupation and its attendant deprivations. It was built on a series of emerging institutions of civil society that represented every social sector, as well as on the willingness of a new generation to stand up to Israel and demand an end to the occupation.[100] The intifada crossed local political affiliations and coalesced in the Unified National Leadership of the Uprising (UNLU), which worked underground to coordinate and organize the uprising. Virtually all Palestinians participated in intifada-related activities— mass demonstrations, labor and merchant strikes, civil disobedience (e.g., refusal to pay taxes), confrontations with the military authorities, blocking roads with burning tires, and—in what became the symbol of the uprising—throwing stones at armed soldiers. The uprising was an extraordinary display of an unarmed society, reclaiming its humanity and dignity, in a struggle to throw off the yoke of twenty years of military repression.

Israel, under the direction of Defense Minister Yitzhak Rabin, responded with the Iron Fist policy of might, force, and beatings; mass arrests and detentions without charges (some 10,000 total); brutal incarcerations in hastily built camps for those charged with an offense; lengthy curfews; live fire against unarmed civilians; and other ruthless measures. Palestinians accepted this suffering and persevered because they believed that the intifada would produce a political solution—a negotiated settlement with Israel—to end the occupation and establish a Palestinian state. The original momentum of the uprising was sustained for two years despite Israel's intransigence toward any political settlement. Thereafter, the intifada, though not totally crushed by Israel, followed a series of stages that coincided with pivotal regional events.[101] First, toward the end of 1989, the center of political gravity in the Middle East shifted away from Palestine to the Iraq-Kuwait conflict. Of note, too, is the fact that while the intifada successfully brought international attention to Israel's occupation of the West Bank, Gaza, and East Jerusalem, it also had the effect of diverting attention from the Palestinian refugees in the diaspora and the question of the right of return.

The Intifada, the 1991 Gulf War, and the 1993 Oslo Accords

The Gulf War: Disastrous Decisions and Precipitous Decline

The year 1988 marked a high point for the PLO, with strong international support for the intifada, the PNC's bold historic compromise, and chairman Arafat's successful diplomacy at the United Nations and throughout Europe. However, by 1990–1991, the organization was at a nadir. The intifada was losing much of its original momentum. Israeli repression left Palestinians in the West Bank and Gaza debilitated, depressed, economically enfeebled, and without any political gains to show for their years of struggle. Additionally, Israel initiated a new, more intense settlement drive in the Occupied Territories, and inside the Green Line it expanded its population with several million Jewish immigrants from the Soviet Union. The collapse of the Soviet Union and the end of the Cold War left the PLO without the diplomatic support of a superpower, although European backing remained firm. In the Arab world, the PLO was estranged from Syria owing to a long-standing feud between Hafez Asad and Yasser Arafat; its relations with Jordan and Egypt were correct but cool; and its friends in Saudi Arabia and the Persian Gulf had begun to cut back their traditional economic aid. Only Iraq appeared to be a genuine ally, but Baghdad's support proved to be the PLO's undoing.

First, Iraq's August 2, 1990, invasion of Kuwait shifted world attention to the oil-rich Persian Gulf, leaving Palestinians in the Occupied Territories even more isolated and vulnerable to Israeli repression.

When the allied Coalition, led by the United States, began to prepare an attack to drive Iraq from its occupation of Kuwait, the Palestinian masses in the Occupied Territories and throughout the diaspora reacted with scorn and outrage at the hypocrisy. As time went on, that sentiment was transformed into overt support for Iraq. Yet the initial outpouring of mass emotion became far more nuanced, complex, and diverse. Still, the damage to the Palestinians' image in regional and world public opinion was severe. Arafat could have ameliorated the harm created in the public perception, but unfortunately he made the situation worse. His pronouncements were vague, ambiguous, and contradictory. He avoided a forthright condemnation of Iraq's actions and refrained from a candid call for Iraq to unconditionally withdraw from Kuwait.[102] As a result, the PLO's fortunes plummeted.[103]

The U.S.-led assault began on January 13, 1991, and lasted less than six weeks; Iraq surrendered on February 26. The damage to Iraq was immense, but the losses to the PLO and the Palestinians were large as well. The PLO was politically discredited owing to its failure to condemn Iraq, and European support withered precipitously.[104] The PLO was completely isolated by the Arab states—which were more united behind the United States than ever. No Arab government was willing to challenge the United States on issues relating to the Palestinians—even had one been inclined to do so. Moreover, the U.S.-Israeli alliance was firmer than ever. The PLO also experienced financial disaster as its traditional Arab donors cut off aid entirely while remittances from Palestinian labor in the Gulf ceased because the workers were expelled. Indeed, Kuwait expelled virtually its entire Palestinian population, which totaled some 450,000.[105] The new world order was a unipolar configuration, with U.S. power becoming absolute while the emasculated Soviet Union was unable to play any independent role and the PLO became isolated and discredited.[106]

The Madrid Conference

Even though Arab leaders had capitulated to U.S. pressure to join the war on Iraq, there was widespread anger against Washington among the Arab masses, which deeply resented the brutality against the Iraqi people. The Arab "street" was full of condemnations of Washington's hypocritical double standard in subjecting Iraq to the full force of U.S. military might for invading and occupying Kuwait while continually supporting Israel despite its occupation of Palestinian territory. In the war's aftermath, the United States, fearing that mass Arab outrage might threaten Arab governments that were loyal U.S. allies, and seeing the "message" of the intifada, decided to embark on a Middle East peace process.[107]

During the spring and summer of 1991, Washington initiated such a process and in mid-July presented terms for what would become the Madrid conference. The plan was the antithesis of UN Resolutions 242 and 338. According to the U.S. plan, there would be no international conference; rather, it would be a U.S.-orchestrated program. The United Nations would act merely as an observer without playing any substantive part, and Europe would also be a token spectator. Washington would chair the conference along with a nearly impotent Soviet Union. Relevant UN resolutions would serve merely as a basis for talks rather than being binding (i.e., land for peace was no longer to be the foundation for agreements). The conference itself would be essentially symbolic, setting the stage for separate bilateral talks between Israel and individual Arab states—traditional divide-and-rule tactics.

In addition, the PLO was prohibited from participating. Israel insisted that Palestinian involvement could only be as a junior member of a joint Jordanian-Palestinian team; Palestinian delegates could come from the West Bank and Gaza but not from East Jerusalem or from outside the Occupied Territories, and they could have no obvious affiliation with the PLO. Moreover, Israel demanded a veto over each individual who would take part. Additionally, the Palestinians were required to negotiate in two separate stages: the first to reach an interim self-government arrangement in the West Bank and Gaza; the second to reach a final settlement that would begin only in the third year of the interim period. There were no references to Palestinian self-determination or statehood.

These were highly unfavorable terms for the Palestinians; indeed, they were, in every respect, at odds with the PLO's fundamental policies and objectives. Yet in its weakened condition, the PLO could do little to influence or alter the U.S. proposal. The issue for the PLO basically came down to one of two choices: (1) permit Israeli-approved Palestinians from the Occupied Territories to participate, accept the terms as stipulated, and hope that the conference would constitute a first step toward more favorable conditions; or (2) boycott the conference entirely. The gut feeling of most PLO officials and Palestinians in general was to boycott. Yet the very precariousness of the organization's situation made that a risky strategy, for it might have placed the PLO on the sidelines of any talks for the long term.

The PNC convened in Algiers in September 1991, supposedly to debate and decide the issue. Arafat, however, had already decided to participate, and he used this meeting to suppress dissent and to intensely pressure PNC members to vote with him. In the end, a slim majority was persuaded to support Arafat.[108] Nevertheless, majority was not consensus. As one Palestinian American professor who had served on the PNC since 1977 wrote:

> I resigned. . . . I felt that the terms we accepted for going to Madrid were disastrous. I had voted for the two-state solution at our 1988 Algiers meeting. I could see in 1991, however, that not only were the gains of the intifada about to be squandered, but that Yasir Arafat and a few of his closest advisors had already decided on their own to accept anything that the US and Israel might throw their way, just in order to survive . . . the PLO leadership . . . concede[d] every single national aim and legal principle.[109]

Arafat's disastrous diplomatic decisions during the Gulf War were thus followed by high-handed manipulation of the PNC to sanction Palestinian participation in the Madrid conference. At Algiers, Arafat negated the principles of unity and consensus by which the PLO had successfully functioned since 1969. It proved to be a harbinger of his role in the Oslo Accords—and of the dictatorial means by which he would govern after returning to the Occupied Territories in 1994.

On October 30, 1991, President George H.W. Bush opened the first session of the Madrid conference.[110] Yet despite nearly two years of dialogue, the Palestinians made no progress on any of their objectives.[111] In the meantime, beginning with a clandestine encounter in London in December 1992, and proceeding through thirteen highly secret meetings between January and August 1993, a small group of PLO officials and Israelis met in Oslo under the auspices of the Norwegian government, with Foreign Minister Johan Joergen Holst taking the lead.[112] When in late August, Israel and the PLO announced their agreement on a set of principles to resolve the 100-year conflict, the Palestinian delegation at Madrid was stunned, as were Palestinians throughout the diaspora. Considering the lack of headway on any issue under the Madrid formula, news of the Olso Accords became disbelieving shock. Nevertheless, on September 13, 1993, Chairman Arafat and Prime Minister Rabin formally signed the Declaration of Principles on Interim Self-Government Arrangements (i.e., the Oslo Accords) in Washington, D.C.[113]

When the PLO initialed the Oslo Accords and embarked on the road to peace, the majority of Palestinians expected that the occupation—and the policies Israel used to sustain it—would end. They also assumed that the culmination of the process would be a genuinely independent Palestinian state in the West Bank and Gaza with East Jerusalem as its capital. The accords, however, were fashioned precisely to avoid these outcomes. Israel did terminate some of the occupation policies (e.g., displaying the Palestinian flag was no longer illegal, and Israel ceased interfering in the educational system). However, Israel retained the majority of its practices, and, in fact, many of the most egregious policies were implemented with greater intensity after Oslo (e.g., land confiscation, settlement construction, house demolitions, etc.) even as new methods of repression were introduced. Moreover, Israel failed to honor the accords it signed with the Palestinian Authority (PA)—the Palestinian administrative body in the Occupied Territories after 1994—and undermined the fundamental principle of the two-state peace agreement. The combination of these factors led to a second uprising, the September 2000 Al-Aqsa intifada, seven years after the Oslo process was initiated.

Israel and the Palestinians on the Road to Peace

Before examining the Oslo peace process in more detail, several issues need emphasis. The enormity of the PLO's historic compromise cannot be overstated. Under the leadership of Yasser Arafat, the PLO abandoned the idea of liberating Palestine and first proposed a democratic secular state wherein Jews and Arabs could live together as citizens of one country. When Israel rejected that, Arafat led the Palestinians to agree to a state alongside Israel in 22 percent of Mandatory Palestine. In the process, the PLO accepted UN Resolution 242 even though it was silent on the political or national rights of Palestinians. Arafat renounced terrorism despite Israel's persistent state terrorism against Palestinians in the Occupied Territories and against Palestinian communities in the diaspora (e.g., Lebanon). Perhaps most extraordinary of all, the PLO recognized Israel's *right* to exist—in effect giving Palestinian legitimacy to the Zionist usurpation of Palestine and the dispossession of its people. In its effort to establish diplomatic relations with the Jewish state, the PLO could have simply "recognized" Israel, a normal practice among states in the international system. Yet it went far beyond that requirement in a remarkable gesture toward Israel—granting it what it always stated it sought, that is, legitimacy of its right to exist.

Arafat's years of continuous efforts—speeches, letters, public forums, and so on—attempted to convince Israelis of Palestinians' sincerity in desiring to coexist in peace and normalcy. Moreover, the PLO compromises and peace initiatives were made during periods when it enjoyed internal strength and unity and international legitimacy and respect (unfortunately squandered during the Gulf War). Thus, when Arafat and the PLO agreed to the Oslo Accords in 1993, there were no further concessions the Palestinians could have been expected to make short of self-extinction as a nation of people with national, political, and human rights.

However, Israel, for its part, had rejected every Palestinian peace initiative and had not put forward one of its own. The failure of bilateral and multilateral talks under the Madrid framework suggests that Israel was not interested in a political settlement that involved recognizing Palestinians' right to self-determination in an independent state. Israel seemed to value the expansion of settlements in the Occupied Territories over an equitable solution of the Palestine conflict.

Conclusion

This chapter provided a brief overview of the Palestinian-Israeli conflict from its inception. Because this book is an account of Palestinian history and politics, and owing to space limitations, other narratives were not included. From this chapter emerges the major themes and goals that animate the Palestinian national movement through this day: injustice, statelessness, dispossession, the plight of refugees, the sacredness of Jerusalem, occupation, resistance, steadfastness, fear of transfer or expulsion, the significance of land, and the duplicity of international diplomacy. Each of these issues played out in the Oslo process.

For Palestinians, the creation of Israel, and their own concomitant dispossession and statelessness, meant that injustice remained as real as in 1948. Even among Palestinians who are not refugees, the experience of statelessness has been traumatic. Though since 1988 Palestinians have pragmatically accepted Israel on 78 percent of their former homeland, and are prepared to coexist in peace and normalcy, they strongly desire from Israel an admission of the wrong that was done to them. Moreover, the creation of a Palestinian state in that portion of Mandatory Palestine occupied by Israel in 1967, although it is considerably less than what UN Resolution 181 originally granted them, constitutes *the* fundamental Palestinian national and political objective. Even for the many Palestinians who would not go there to live today, an independent, sovereign Palestinian state is of enormous symbolic and emotional importance. For Palestinians living under Israeli occupation in the West Bank, Gaza, and East Jerusalem, such a state is a matter of survival both individually and as a social collective. All Palestinians believe that those living under occupation have the right—and duty—to resist.

The plight of the refugees—those who were forced from their

homes and lands and have spent a half-century in refugee camps—is also an issue of enormous emotional and practical significance. Palestinians hold on to UN Security Council Resolution 194 with all their might. Some Palestinians—in particular some of the PLO/PA leaders—have conceded that all the refugees cannot return to Israel, but even they demand that Israel admit responsibility for their circumstance, allow a reasonable number to return, and pay reparations to the remainder. Others—the majority—believe the right of return is sacred and inviolable. Similarly, Palestinians—Christian and Muslim—do not accept that Israel has a stronger claim to Jerusalem. They do not accept that the Jewish holy sites are more sacred than their holy sites, and they reject Jewish dominance of a unified Jewish Jerusalem.

The remaining chapters focus on seven basic interrelated issues that the peace process was supposed to resolve.

1. The political/national right of Palestinians to form an independent sovereign state on the remaining 22 percent of Mandatory Palestine.
2. Refugees and the right of return.
3. Land, especially Israel's confiscation of Palestinian land to accelerate the construction of Jewish settlements.
4. Expulsion, or Israel's ongoing effort to minimize the number of Palestinians in order to create an ethnically homogenous Jewish state or "State of the Jewish People."
5. The post–June 1967 Israeli occupation and the Palestinian right to resist it.
6. The status of Jerusalem.
7. The role of the United States in supporting Israeli policies vis-à-vis the Palestinians as well as Washington's disregard for the rights, needs, and concerns of Palestinians.

The power disparity between Israel and the Palestinians is a leitmotif because Israel has enjoyed exclusive possession of the resources of power. The imbalance has been reflected at all levels—alliance patterns and support, social and political organization and cohesiveness, military strength, economic resources, even information. Palestinians have not been able to confront Israel from anything but a position of weakness, and nowhere has this been more apparent than in the agreements that constitute the Oslo process.

In Chapter 2, I analyze and contextualize the agreements signed by the PLO/PA and Israel from the 1993 Declaration of Principles at Oslo and beyond, including Camp David and Taba (from which no accords emerged). In the agreements, Israel's power compared to Palestinian weakness permitted the former to fashion the accords to preserve its interests; Palestinians could do little more than assent if they wanted the process to proceed at all. On no issue is this more apparent than that of the refugees and their right of return; in Chapter 2 I examine this in detail.

Notes

1. Tom Segev, "A History Lesson," *Ha'aretz* (Jerusalem, daily, English), June 29, 2001.

2. Souad Dajani, "A Vision for the Palestinian Future," in Daniel McGowan and Marc H. Ellis, eds., *Remembering Deir Yassin: The Future of Israel and Palestine* (New York: Olive Branch Press, 1998), p. 123.

3. See, for example, Keith W. Whitelam, *The Invention of Ancient Israel: The Silencing of Palestinian History* (London: Routledge, 1996); G. W. Bowersock, *Roman Arabia* (New York: Columbia University Press, 1988); Amin Maalouf, *The Crusades Through Arab Eyes* (New York: Schocken, 1985); Philip Hitti, *An Arab-Syrian Gentleman and Warrior in the Period of the Crusades* (Princeton: Princeton University Press, 1987); Kamil al'Asali, ed., *Jerusalem in History*, 2nd ed. (London: Kegan Paul, 1996).

4. For a wide-ranging account of the intellectual contributions of Arab-Islamic civilization, see Seyyed Hossein Nasr, *Science and Civilization in Islam* (Cambridge, MA: Harvard University Press, 1968); see also John S. Badeau et al., *The Genius of Arab Civilization: Source of Renaissance*, 2nd ed. (Cambridge, MA: MIT Press, 1983).

5. For an account from a nineteenth-century witness, see Mary Eliza Rogers, *Domestic Life in Palestine* (London: Kegan Paul International, 1862). See also Rashid Khalidi, *Palestinian Identity: The Construction of Modern National Consciousness* (New York: Columbia University Press, 1997), pp. 35–62; and Beshara Doumani, *Rediscovering Palestine: Merchants and Peasants in Jabal Nablus, 1700–1900* (Berkeley: University of California Press, 1995).

6. Samih K. Farsoun with Christina E. Zacharia, *Palestine and the Palestinians* (Boulder: Westview, 1997), pp. 22–27.

7. For a discussion of the *masha'a* system and the relationship between the Palestinian *fallahin* and the land, see John Ruedy, "Dynamics of Land Alienation," in Ibrahim Abu Lughod, ed., *The Transformation of Palestine: Essays on the Origin and Development of the Arab-Israeli Conflict* (Evanston, IL: Northwestern University Press, 1971), pp. 122–123.

8. For a good understanding of Christian and Islamic—as well as Jewish—attachment to the Holy Land, see Karen Armstrong, *A History of God: The 4,000-Year-Old Quest of Judaism, Christianity, and Islam* (New York: Ballantine Books, 1993), and Karen Armstrong, *Jerusalem: One City, Three Faiths* (New York: Ballantine Books, 1996).

9. See Beshara B. Doumani, "Rediscovering Ottoman Palestine: Writing Palestinians into History," *Journal of Palestine Studies* 21, no. 2 (winter 1992):

5–28; 'Adel Manna, "Eighteenth and Nineteenth-Century Rebellions in Palestine," *Journal of Palestine Studies* 24, no. 1 (autumn 1994): 51–66; Alexander Scholoch (translated by William C. Young and Michael C. Gerrity), *Palestine in Transformation, 1856–1882: Studies in Social, Economic, and Political Development* (Washington, DC: Institute for Palestine Studies, 1993).

10. Ruedy, "Dynamics of Land Alienation," pp. 123–124. Also see Farsoun with Zacharia, *Palestine and the Palestinians*, pp. 38–40.

11. For an excellent analysis of the economic, social, and political transformations that swept Palestine (and surrounding areas) in the nineteenth century, see Scholoch, *Palestine in Transformation, 1856–1882;* Roger Owen, *The Middle East in the World Economy, 1800–1914* (London: Methuen, 1981). See also Roger Owen, ed., *Studies in the Economic History of Palestine in the Nineteenth and Twentieth Centuries* (Carbondale: Southern Illinois University Press, 1982). Additionally, see Moshe Ma'oz, ed., *Studies on Palestine During the Ottoman Period* (Jerusalem: Magnes, 1975).

12. Farsoun with Zacharia, *Palestine and the Palestinians*, pp. 54–55 and 21–65. On the nineteenth-century development of Palestinian consciousness, see also Khalidi, *Palestinian Identity*, and Muhammad Y. Muslih, *The Origins of Palestinian Nationalism* (New York: Columbia University Press, 1988).

13. Nahum Sokolow, *History of Zionism*, vol. 2 (London: Longman, 1919), pp. 329–331; Ilan Pappe, *The Making of the Arab-Israeli Conflict: 1947–1951* (London: I. B. Tauris, 1994), pp. 1–3, gives a slightly different account, though the substance is the same.

14. Pappe, *The Making of the Arab-Israeli Conflict*, pp. 1–3.

15. Several good, sympathetic studies of Jewish history and the Zionism movement include: Shlomo Avineri, *The Making of Modern Zionism: The Intellectual Origins of the Jewish State* (New York: Basic Books, 1981); Solomon Grayzel, *A History of the Jews* (New York: New American Library, 1968); Arthur Hertzberg, *The Zionist Idea* (New York: Herzl Press, 1960); Howard M. Sachar, *The Course of Modern Jewish History* (New York: Dell, 1977), and Sachar, *A History of Israel: From the Rise of Zionism to Our Time* (New York: Knopf, 1979); and David Vital, *The Origins of Zionism* (Oxford: Oxford University Press, 1975), and Vital, *Zionism: The Formative Years* (Oxford: Oxford University Press, 1982).

16. Mark Tessler, *A History of the Israeli-Palestinian Conflict* (Bloomington: Indiana University Press, 1994), pp. 191–192.

17. For a good discussion of the Zionist prestate institutions in the Yishuv that excluded Palestinian Arabs, see Bernard Avishai, *The Tragedy of Zionism: Revolution and Democracy in the Land of Israel* (New York: Farrar Straus Giroux, 1985), pp. 99–171.

18. Janet Abu-Lughod, "The Demographic Transformation of Palestine," in Abu Lughod, ed., *The Transformation of Palestine*, p. 140. Also see Stanford Shaw, "The Ottoman Census System and Population, 1831–1914," *International Journal of Middle Eastern Studies* 9 (August 1978): 325–338; Alexander Scholoch, "The Demographic Development of Palestine, 1850–1882," *International Journal of Middle Eastern Studies* 17 (November 1985): 485–505.

19. *General Monthly Bulletin* (London) 12 (December 1947): 686 (table 1), cited in Janet Abu-Lughod, "The Demographic Transformation of Palestine," p. 155.

20. Ruedy, "Dynamics of Land Alienation," pp. 124–125.

21. Ibid., 134–135; see Appendix: Measurement Equivalents in this book.

22. Fred J. Khouri, *The Arab-Israeli Dilemma*, 2nd ed. (Syracuse: Syracuse University Press, 1976), pp. 53–54.

23. For the letters and maps of the Husayn-McMahon correspondence, see George Antonius, *The Arab Awakening* (New York: G. P. Putnam and Son, 1946), pp. 413–427.

24. All of these documents (and other important ones through 1972) may be found in John Norton Moore, ed., *The Arab-Israeli Conflict III, Documents* (American Society of International Law) (Princeton: Princeton University Press, 1974), Sykes-Picot at pp. 24–28, Balfour Declaration at pp. 31–32, and report of the UN Special Committee at pp. 259–312.

25. A good recent account by an Israeli scholar is Tom Segev, *One Palestine, Complete: Jews and Arabs Under the British Mandate* (New York: Metropolitan Books/Henry Holt, 1999).

26. For an excellent analysis of Palestinian nationalism and resistance to Zionism before the 1948 creation of Israel, see Ann Mosely Lesch, *Arab Politics in Palestine 1917–1939: The Frustration of a Nationalist Movement* (Ithaca: Cornell University Press, 1979). Also see Yehoshua Porath, *The Emergence of the Palestinian Arab National Movement, 1918–1929* (London: Frank Cass, 1974); and Yehoshua Porath, *The Palestinian Arab National Movement from Riots to Rebellion, 1929–1939* (London: Frank Cass, 1977).

27. Farsoun with Zacharia, *Palestine and the Palestinians*, pp. 104–108.

28. For good analyses of the many issues involved in Britain's withdrawal, see William Roger Louis and Robert W. Stookey, eds., *The End of the Palestine Mandate* (London: I. B. Tauris, 1986), and Michael J. Cohen, *Palestine and the Great Powers, 1945–1948* (Princeton: Princeton University Press, 1982).

29. There are many good accounts of U.S. manipulations, pressure, and the like behind the scenes to facilitate passage of the partition resolution. Still, without the support of the Soviet Union, it is unlikely that it would have passed, U.S. efforts notwithstanding. See Harry S. Truman, *1945–1952, Years of Trial and Hope: Memoirs,* vol. 2 (New York: American Library, 1956). Also important are: John Snetsinger, *Truman, the Jewish Vote, and the Creation of Israel* (Stanford: Hoover Institution Press, 1974), and Robert J. Donovan, *Conflict and Crisis: The Presidency of Harry S. Truman, 1945–1948* (New York: W. W. Norton, 1977).

30. All these assertions are documented by Israeli scholars Simha Flapan, *The Birth of Israel: Myths and Realities* (New York: Pantheon Books, 1987), pp. 81–118, and Pappe, *The Making of the Arab-Israeli Conflict 1947–1951*), pp. 47–86 (the civil war) and pp. 102–134 (the Israeli-Arab conflict, May through December 1948). Also excellent on the issue of the significant military advantage held by Israel is Stephen Green, *Taking Sides: America's Secret Relations with a Militant Israel* (New York: William Morrow, 1984). See also the comprehensive work by Israeli scholar Benny Morris, *Righteous Victims: A History of the Zionist-Arab Conflict, 1881–1999* (New York: Alfred A. Knopf, 1999), pp. 189–258.

31. Avi Shlaim, *The Iron Wall: Israel and the Arab World* (New York: W. W. Norton, 2000), pp. 35–36.

32. Pappe, *The Making of the Arab-Israeli Conflict*, p. 96. He provides extensive documentation to support this claim.

33. See the detailed study based on recently declassified official government documents by the renowned Israeli scholar Avi Shlaim, *Collusion Across the Jordan: King Abdullah, the Zionist Movement, and the Partition of Palestine* (Oxford: Clarendon Press, 1988).

34. For one important analysis of the transformation of Palestine into Israel, see Nathan Krystall, "The De-Arabization of West Jerusalem, 1947–1950," *Journal of Palestine Studies* 27, no. 2 (winter 1998): 5–22.

35. Pappe, *The Making of the Arab-Israeli Conflict,* pp. 47–101. Other Israeli scholars have contributed to this understanding of events. See, for example, Flapan, *The Birth of Israel: Myths and Realities,* and Simha Flapan, *Zionism and the Palestinians* (London: Croom Helm, 1979). See also Benny Morris, *The Birth of the Palestinian Refugee Problem, 1947–1949* (Cambridge, UK: Cambridge University Press, 1987); Benny Morris, *1948 and After: Israel and the Palestinians* (Oxford: Oxford University Press, 1990); and Benny Morris, "Operation Dani and the Palestinian Exodus from Lydda and Ramleh in 1948," *Middle East Journal* 40 (winter 1986): 82–109. Unfortunately, even though Palestinians have been writing about their dispossession for at least a half-century, their accounts have been dismissed as false. Some of these include Nafez Nazzal, *The Palestinian Exodus from Galilee in 1948* (Beirut: Institute for Palestine Studies, 1978); Walid Khalidi, ed., *From Haven to Conquest: Readings in Zionism and the Palestine Problem until 1948* (Beirut: Institute for Palestine Studies, 1971); Sami Hadawi, *Bitter Harvest: Palestine 1914–1979* (New York: Caravan Books, 1979); Mohammad Tarbush, *Reflections of a Palestinian* (Washington, DC: American-Arab Affairs Council, 1986); Fawaz Turki, *The Disinherited: Journal of a Palestinian Exile, with an Epilogue, 1974,* 2nd ed. (New York: Monthly Review, 1974); Nur Masalha, *A Land Without a People: Israel, Transfer, and the Palestinians, 1949–1996* (London: Faber and Faber, 1997); Ghada Karmi and Eugene Cotran, eds., *The Palestinian Exodus, 1948–1998* (Reading, UK: Ithaca Press, 1999).

36. Khalidi, *From Haven to Conquest*; see especially the monumental work by Walid Khalidi, ed., *All That Remains: The Palestinian Villages Occupied and Depopulated by Israel in 1948* (Washington, DC: Institute for Palestine Studies, 1992).

37. In addition to sources cited above, see Tom Segev, *1949: The First Israelis* (New York: The Free Press, 1986); Sami Hadawi, *Palestinian Rights and Losses in 1948: A Comprehensive Study* (London: Saqi Books, 1988); Nur Masalha, *Expulsion of the Palestinians: The Concept of Transfer in Zionist Political Thought, 1882–1948* (Washington, DC: Institute for Palestine Studies, 1992); Michael Palumbo, *The Palestinian Catastrophe* (London: Faber and Faber, 1987).

38. See Israel Shahak, "A History of the Concept of 'Transfer' in Zionism," *Journal of Palestine Studies* 18, no. 3 (spring 1989): 22–37, plus the many sources cited previously and below.

39. Nur Masalha, "The Historical Roots of the Palestinian Refugee Question," in Naseer Aruri, ed., *Palestinian Refugees: The Right of Return* (London: Pluto, 2001), p. 43.

40. Morris, *Righteous Victims*, pp. 21–22, quoting Theodor Herzl (edited

by Rafael Patai), *The Complete Diaries of Theodor Herzl,* vol. 1 (New York: Herzl Press and T. Yoseloff, 1960), p. 88 (entry for June 12, 1895).

41. Zeev Sternhell, *The Founding Myths of Israel: Nationalism, Socialism, and the Making of the Jewish State* (Princeton: Princeton University Press, 1998), pp. 43–44.

42. Morris, *Righteous Victims,* p. 168.

43. Sternhell, *The Founding Myths of Israel,* pp. 47–73.

44. Ibid., pp. 3–46 and passim; and Shabtai Teveth, *Ben-Gurion and the Palestinian Arabs: From Peace to War* (New York: Oxford University Press, 1985), pp. vii–x.

45. Masalha, "The Historical Roots of the Palestinian Refugee Question," p. 38 (quoting from a letter from Ben-Gurion to his son); Morris, *Righteous Victims,* p. 253, 169; Masalha, "The Historical Roots of the Palestinian Refugee Question," p. 39.

46. Teveth, *Ben-Gurion and the Palestinian Arabs,* p. 181.

47. For the experience of an "elite" refugee, see Ghada Karmi, "The 1948 Exodus: A Family Story," *Journal of Palestine Studies* 23, no. 2 (winter 1994): 31–40.

48. Shlaim, *The Iron Wall,* p. 31.

49. Segev, *1949: The First Israelis,* p. 28.

50. Pappe, *The Making of the Arab-Israeli Conflict,* p. 98. On Plan D, see also Walid Khalidi, "Plan Dalet: Master Plan for the Conquest of Palestine," *Journal of Palestine Studies* 18, no. 1 (autumn 1998): 3–70, including text of the plan, maps, and other supporting information.

51. Pappe, *The Making of the Arab-Israeli Conflict,* p. 96. Deir Yassin was a peaceful Palestinian village five miles west of Jerusalem in which, on April 9, 1948, Menachem Begin's Irgun massacred 254 people—mostly old men, women, and children—then mutilated, raped, disemboweled, and paraded their corpses through the streets of Jerusalem. Begin bragged about this "triumph" in Menachem Begin, *The Revolt: Story of the Irgun* (London: W. H. Allen; and New York: Henry Schuman, 1951), p. 162, though he expunged it from the revised edition published (New York: Nash Publishing, 1977). A particularly important piece, a firsthand account of the massacre, by a retired Israeli colonel and military historian who was sent by the Haganah to observe the attack on Deir Yassin is Meir Pa'il, "A Jewish Eye-Witness: An Interview with Meir Pa'il," in McGowan and Ellis, *Remembering Deir Yassin: The Future of Israel and Palestine,* pp. 35–46. The eleven additional essays in this volume are also of great historical value; I. F. Stone, "The Other Zionism," in *Underground to Palestine: And Reflections Thirty Years Later* (New York: Pantheon Books, 1978), pp. 258–259. Also see Sabri Jiryis, *The Arabs in Israel* (Beirut: Institute for Palestine Studies, 1969; reissued New York: Monthly Review Press, 1976), p. 91; Flapan, *The Birth of Israel,* pp. 94–96. New evidence has recently come to light of other massacres similar to that at Deir Yassin. See, for example, "The Tantura Massacre, 22–23 May 1948," *Journal of Palestine Studies* 30, no. 3 (spring 2001): 5–18 (this is a collection of testimonies of survivors), and Ilan Pappe, "The Tantura Case in Israel: The Katz Research and Trial," *Journal of Palestine Studies* 30, no. 3 (spring 2001): 19–39.

52. Masalha, "The Historical Roots of the Palestinian Refugee Question," p. 45.

53. Pappe, *The Making of the Arab-Israeli Conflict*, pp. 97–98.

54. Ilan Pappe, "Israeli Perceptions of the Refugee Question," in Aruri, *Palestinian Refugees*, p. 72.

55. Farsoun with Zacharia, *Palestine and the Palestinians*, p. 127. Also see Rosemary Sayigh, *Palestinians: From Peasants to Revolutionaries* (London: Zed Books, 1979), who provides invaluable detailed oral histories from Palestinians who fled to Lebanon and still remain in refugee camps there.

56. *Facts and Figures About Palestinians* (Washington, DC: Center for Policy Analysis on Palestine, 1992), p. 13.

57. BADIL, *Palestinian Refugees in Exile: Country Profiles* (Bethlehem: BADIL Resource Center for Palestinian Residency and Refugee Rights, 2000 (48 pp.), quoting from *UNRWA Registration Statistical Bulletin for the Fourth Quarter, 30 November 1999* (Amman, Jordan: UNRWA-HQ, Department of Relief and Social Services, 1999).

58. Salman Abu-Sitta, *The Palestinian Nakba: The Register of Depopulated Localities in Palestine* (London: The Palestinian Return Center, 1998), puts the total number of refugees (including those registered with UNRWA) at 5,115,095. This figure may be on the high end, but UNRWA's 3.6 million is definitely understated. A figure that may be more accurate—higher than UNRWA's and less than Abu-Sitta's—comes from calculations by Rosemary Sayigh. She determines the number of refugees at 4,750,000. Rosemary Sayigh, "Dis/Solving the 'Refugee Problem,'" *Middle East Report* 28, no. 2 (summer 1998): 19–23.

59. Rosemary Sayigh, *Too Many Enemies: The Palestinian Experience in Lebanon* (London: Zed Books, 1994).

60. Farsoun with Zacharia, *Palestine and the Palestinians*, pp. 123–170, provides an analysis of the differing experiences of Palestinians in the diaspora by class, religion, occupation, and political orientation in differing host countries. For an experience of exile from an upper-class refugee, see Ghada Karmi, "After the Nakba: An Experience of Exile in England," *Journal of Palestine Studies* 28, no. 3 (spring 1999): 52–63. A more searing account may be found in Turki, *The Disinherited: Journal of a Palestinian Exile*. For the situation of Palestinians in Israel, see Elia Zureik, *The Palestinians in Israel: A Study in Internal Colonialism* (London: Routledge and Kegan Paul, 1979). A good overall analysis of the situation of refugee communities in the various Arab countries is Abbas Shiblak, "Residency Status and Civil Rights of Palestinian Refugees in Arab Countries," *Journal of Palestine Studies* 25, no. 3 (spring 1996): 36–45. For the situation of Palestinians in Lebanon, see Cheryl A. Rubenberg, "Palestinians in Lebanon: A Question of Human and Civil Rights," *Arab Studies Quarterly* 6, no. 3 (summer 1984): 194–221; Rosemary Sayigh, *Too Many Enemies*; Rosemary Sayigh, "Palestinians in Lebanon: Harsh Present, Uncertain Future," *Journal of Palestine Studies* 25, no. 1 (autumn 1995): 37–53; and Jaber Suleiman, "The Current Political, Organizational, and Security Situation in the Palestinian Refugee Camps in Lebanon," *Journal of Palestine Studies* 29, no. 1 (autumn 1999): 66–80. A good account of conditions in a West Bank camp is Muna Hamzeh, "Dahaysha Diary: A View from the Camp," *Journal of Palestine Studies* 30, no. 2 (winter 2001): 41–60. On the experience of the Palestinian community in Kuwait, see Ann M. Lesch, "Palestinians in Kuwait," *Journal of Palestine Studies* 20, no. 4 (summer

1991): 42–54; Shafeeq Ghabra, "Palestinians in Kuwait: The Family and the Politics of Survival," *Journal of Palestine Studies* 17, no. 2 (winter 1988): 62–83; and Yann Le Troquer and Rozenn Hommery al-Oudat, "From Kuwait to Jordan: The Palestinians' Third Exodus," *Journal of Palestine Studies* 28, no. 3 (spring 1999): 37–51.

61. The most detailed description and analysis of Arab life under this military regime (very similar in all aspects to what Israel imposed over the West Bank and Gaza after 1967) is Jiryis, *The Arabs in Israel*, pp. 9–75 and passim. Also see As'ad Ghanem, *The Palestinian-Arab Minority in Israel, 1948–2000: A Political Study* (Albany: State University of New York Press, 2001), pp. 11–29 and passim, and Zureik, *The Palestinians in Israel: A Study in Internal Colonialism*.

62. Avishai, *The Tragedy of Zionism*, p. 317 and 313–325.

63. For the specifics of the forced internal migration, see G. Kossaifi, "Demographic Characteristics of the Arab Palestinian People," in Khalil Nakhleh and Elia Zureik, eds., *The Sociology of the Palestinians* (London: Croom Helm; and New York: St. Martin's, 1980), p. 21. The most important study of the situation of the Palestinian-Arab community living in Israel is Zureik, *The Palestinians in Israel: A Study in Internal Colonialism*. Also see Segev, *1949: The First Israelis*, pp. 68–91; he presents a detailed account of the process by which the Israeli government confiscated the homes, shops, machinery, furniture, jewelry, citrus (and other) groves/orchards, banks, bank accounts—literally all property—from the departed refugees and turned it over to new Jewish immigrants to Israel. A more recent article is Phillipa Strum, "Israel's Democratic Dilemma," *Reform Judaism* 14, no. 2 (winter 1985–1986). See also Vered Levy-Barzilai, "Know Thy Neighbor—But Don't Hire Him," *Ha'aretz Magazine*, July 12, 2001. For the period 1948–1966, see Jiryis, *The Arabs in Israel*. Also see Uri Davis, "Israel's Zionist Society: Consequences for Internal Opposition and the Necessity for External Intervention," in EAFORD and AJAZ, *Judaism or Zionism: What Difference for the Middle East?* (London: Zed Books, 1986), pp. 177 and following; Uri Davis, *Israel: An Apartheid State* (London: Zed Books, 1987); and Ian Lustick, *Arabs in the Jewish State: Israel's Control of a National Minority* (Austin: University of Texas Press, 1980).

64. Segev, *1949: The First Israelis*, pp. 68–92.

65. Atif Kubursi, "Valuing Palestinian Losses in Today's Dollars," in Naseer Aruri, ed., *Palestinian Refugees: The Right of Return* (London: Pluto, 2001), pp. 217–218.

66. The law is more complex than the essentials I have stripped it to here. It is also related to the Development Authority (Transfer of Property) Law, to the functions of the Custodian of Abandoned Property, the Jewish National Fund, and the Jewish Agency. For a detailed discussion of these laws and relationships, see Walter Lehn with Uri Davis, *The Jewish National Fund* (London: Kegan Paul International, 1988), pp. 130–38 and passim.

67. Israel seized property and land from some 39,000 Palestinians who escaped expulsion and remained in Israel. It was never returned, and these individuals never received compensation although they are citizens of Israel. See Joseph Schechla, "The Invisible People Come to Light: Israel's 'Internally Displaced' and the 'Unrecognized Villages,'" *Journal of Palestine Studies* 31,

no. 1 (autumn 2001): 22. Also see BADIL, *Palestinian Refugees in Exile*, p. 37, and Jiryis, *The Arabs in Israel*. Also see Masalha, "The Historical Roots of the Palestinian Refugee Question," p. 54, and Jan Abu Shakrah, "Deconstructing the Link: Palestinian Refugees and Jewish Immigrants from Arab Countries," in Aruri, ed., *Palestinian Refugees*, pp. 208–216. *Adalah* News Update, "Government Refuses to Provide Information on Moveable Property of Palestinian Refugees," January 28, 2000, available online at BADIL Resource Center. Kubursi, "Valuing Palestinian Losses in Today's Dollars," pp. 217–251. Sayigh, "Dis/Solving the 'Refugee Problem,'" pp. 18–20, has almost no data on the refugees in Syria. The information here on Palestinians in Syria is taken from BADIL, *Palestinian Refugees in Exile: Country Profiles*, pp. 30–36.

68. Shlaim, *The Iron Wall*, pp. 81–82.

69. Ibid., p. 83.

70. Ibid., p. 84.

71. Ibid., p. 91.

72. Cheryl A. Rubenberg, *Israel and the American National Interest: A Critical Examination* (Urbana: University of Illinois Press, 1986), pp. 52–87.

73. For detailed portraits of these individuals, see John W. Amos II, *Palestine Resistance: Organization of a National Movement* (New York: Pergamon Press, 1980), pp. 43–67. Amos is best on Fateh leaders. For an analysis of Popular Front leaders, see Basil R. al-Kubaisi, *The Arab Nationalist Movement, 1951–1971: From Pressure Group to Socialist Party*, submitted to the faculty of the School of International Service of the American University in partial fulfillment of the requirements for the degree of Doctor of Philosophy in International Studies, February 1972, available from UMI Dissertation Information Service.

74. On Fateh's early objectives, see Helena Cobban, *The Palestine Liberation Organization: People, Power and Politics* (New York: Cambridge University Press, 1984), p. 16; Amos, *Palestine Resistance*, p. 56.

75. For an excellent analysis of inter-Arab politics, see Malcolm Kerr, *The Arab Cold War: Gamal `Abd al-Nasir and His Rivals, 1950–1969*, 3rd ed. (New York: Oxford University Press, 1971).

76. Cheryl A. Rubenberg, *The Palestine Liberation Organization: Its Institutional Infrastructure* (Belmont, MA: Institute of Arab Studies, 1983), p. 6. The political structures of the PLO included the Palestine National Council (PNC) as a parliamentary body with sole legislative authority, and the Central Council, an advisory body to the Executive Committee, which was charged with executing the decisions of the PNC. This basic structure was never changed. The PLO was permitted to have a military wing, but it consisted of three Palestinian contingents under the control of Arab countries, had no independence, and was not involved in guerrilla or other military activities.

77. See Kerr, *The Arab Cold War.*

78. See Farsoun with Zacharia, *Palestine and the Palestinians,* p. 178, for the characterization of the Palestine Nationalist Movement and its comparison with the PLO. The French writer Jean Genet went to the Palestinian fedayeen bases in Jordan in the fall of 1970 and remained there until the end of May 1971, and then intermittently until the end of 1972. He subsequently memorialized what he perceived as their bravery, idealism, flexibility of identity, and heroism in a very moving novel, Jean Genet, *Prisoner of Love* (New York, NY:

Review Books, 2003; originally published in Paris by Editions Gallimard, 1986).

79. These included, in order of strength: Fateh, founded in 1957–1958, ideology—nationalist, leader—Yasser Arafat. Popular Front for the Liberation of Palestine, founded in 1967–1968, ideology—initially pan-Arab, later, Marxist, leader—George Habash. Democratic Front for the Liberation of Palestine, founded in 1969 out of a split with PFLP, ideology—Marxist-Leninist, leader—Nayif Hawatmeh. PFLP–General Command, founded in 1968 out of split with PFLP, ideology—leftist/nationalist, leader—Ahmad Jibril. Saiqa, founded in 1968 by Syria, ideology—Syrian Ba'athist, leader—Mohammed Khalifah. Arab Liberation Front (ALF), founded in 1969 by Iraq, ideology—Iraqi Ba'athist, leader—Abdel Rahim Ahmad. The Palestine Liberation Front (PLF), founded in 1977 out of a split with the PFLP–General Command, ideology—nationalist/pragmatic, leader Abd al-Abbas. The Palestinian Popular Struggle Front (PPSF), founded in 1968, ideology—class struggle, leader—unknown. The leaders of Saiqa and the ALF changed several times according to dominant political trends in each country. The PLF and the PPSF always had extremely small bases of support and were marginal to the politics of the PLO except when Arafat needed allies and these groups were willing to accommodate him.

80. For excellent overall perspectives, see Shlaim, *The Iron Wall*, pp. 218–264, and Baruch Kimmerling, *Zionism and Territory: The Socio-Territorial Dimensions of Zionist Politics* (Berkeley: University of California Press, Institute of International Studies, 1983). See also Donald Neff, *Warriors for Jerusalem: The Six Days that Changed the Middle East* (New York: Linden Press/Simon and Schuster, 1984); Green, *Taking Sides: America's Secret Relations with a Militant Israel*; and Yehoshafat Harkabi, *Israel's Fateful Hour* (New York: Harper and Row, 1986). The best source for Syria during this period is Patrick Seale, *Asad of Syria: The Struggle for the Middle East* (London: I. B. Tauris, 1988), pp. 169–184 and passim. For the Egyptian perspective, see Mahmoud Riad, *The Struggle for Peace in the Middle East* (New York: Quartet Books, 1981). The standard Israeli version is presented by Michael Brecher, *Decisions in Crisis: Israel 1967 and 1973* (Berkeley: University of California Press, 1980), and a plethora of others readily available. On Jordan, see Clinton Baily, *Jordan's Palestinian Challenge, 1948–1983* (Boulder: Westview, 1984), and Madiha Rashid al-Madfai, *Jordan, the United States, and the Middle East Peace Process, 1974–1991* (Cambridge, UK: Cambridge University Press, 1993).

81. Morris, *Righteous Victims*, p. 327.

82. Masalha, "The Historical Roots of the Palestinian Refugee Question," p. 61 and notes.

83. Morris, *Righteous Victims*, p. 328.

84. Joseph Massad, "Return or Permanent Exile?" in Aruri, ed., *Palestinian Refugees*, p. 108.

85. For a text of the resolution, see Moore, *The Arab-Israeli Conflict III*, pp. 1034–1035.

86. On early Israeli policies vis-à-vis Jerusalem, see Martha Wenger, "Jerusalem: A Primer," *Middle East Report* 23, no. 3 (May–June 1993): 9–12. Also see Chapter 5 in this book.

87. Morris, *Righteous Victims*, p. 341.

88. Abba Eban, "The Central Question," *Tikkun: A Bimonthly Jewish Critique of Politics, Culture, and Society* 1, no. 2 (n.d. [ca. 1986]): 21.

89. Meron Benvenisti with Ziad Abu-Zayed and Danny Rubinstein, *The West Bank Handbook: A Political Lexicon* (Jerusalem: The West Bank Data Base Project/Jerusalem Post, 1986, distributed by Westview Press, Boulder, CO), p. 67. Also see Meron Benvenisti, *1986 Report: Demographic, Economic, Legal, Social, and Political Developments in the West Bank* (Jerusalem: West Bank Data Base Project, 1986); David Kahan, *Agriculture and Water Resources in the West Bank and Gaza, 1967–1987* (a project of the West Bank Data Base Project) (Jerusalem: Jerusalem Post, 1987); Fawzi A. Gharaibeh, *The Economies of the West Bank and Gaza Strip* (Boulder: Westview, 1985); Abbas Alnasrawi, "The Economics of the Israeli Occupation of the West Bank, Gaza, and South Lebanon," *Scandinavian Journal of Development Alternatives* 6, no. 1 (March 1987): 20, 24–25; Simcha Bahiri, *Industrialization in the West Bank and Gaza* (a project of the West Bank Data Base Project) (Jerusalem: Jerusalem Post, 1987, distributed by Westview Press, Boulder, CO).

90. Two articles that provide in-depth detail are Cheryl A. Rubenberg, "Palestinian Human Rights Under Israeli Rule," *Church and Society* (a publication of the Presbyterian Church, U.S.A.) (March/April 1987): 9–34, and Cheryl A. Rubenberg, "Twenty Years of Israeli Economic Policies in the West Bank and Gaza: Prologue to the Intifada," *Journal of Arab Affairs* 8, no. 1 (spring 1989): 28–73.

91. On the 1982 war in Lebanon, see Cheryl A. Rubenberg, "The Israeli Invasion of Lebanon: Objectives and Consequences," *Journal of South Asian and Middle Eastern Studies* 8, no. 2 (winter 1984): 3–28; Rubenberg, *Israel and the American National Interest*, pp. 254–328; Ze'ev Schiff and Ehud Ya'ari, *Israel's Lebanon War* (New York: Simon and Schuster, 1984); Noam Chomsky, *Fateful Triangle: The United States, Israel and the Palestinians*, updated ed. (Boston: South End Press, 1999), pp. 1–8 and 181–568; Michael Jansen, *The Battle of Beirut: Why Israel Invaded Lebanon* (London: Zed Books, 1982); George W. Ball, *Error and Betrayal in Lebanon: An Analysis of Israel's Invasion of Lebanon and the Implications for U.S.-Israeli Relations* (Washington, DC: Foundation for Middle East Peace, 1984); and Itamar Rabinovich, *The War for Lebanon, 1970–1983* (Ithaca: Cornell University Press, 1984).

92. These included the airline hijackings, the Munich disaster, and Ma'a lot. Israel's responses to either guerrilla incursions or terrorist attacks were always ten times more destructive of lives and property. See Chomsky, *Fateful Triangle*, pp. 188–196, and David Hirst, *The Gun and the Olive Branch: The Roots of Violence in the Middle East* (London: Futura/Macdonald, 1977), pp. 303–338. For a firsthand account by one of the participants in the airline hijackings (female), see Leila Khaled, *My People Shall Live: The Autobiography of a Revolutionary* (London: Hodder and Stoughton, 1973).

93. On the significance of the 1977 PNC and the clear formulation of the "two-state" solution, see Gresh, *The PLO: The Struggle Within*, pp. 177–210. Several good analyses of European relations with the PLO include David Allan and Alfred Pijpers, eds., *European Foreign Policy Making and the Arab-Israeli Conflict* (The Hague: Martinus Nijhoff, 1984); Harvey Sicherman, "Europe's

Role in the Middle East: Illusions and Realities," *Orbis* 28, no. 4 (winter 1985): 803–828; and Ilan Greilsammer and Joseph Weiler, eds., *Europe and Israel: Troubled Neighbors* (Berlin: de Gruyter, 1988).

94. The most detailed and sophisticated analysis of the transformations in PLO objectives is Alain Gresh, *The PLO: The Struggle Within—Toward an Independent Palestinian State* (London: Zed Books, 1983), p. 14. On the democratic secular state concept, see Cobban, *The Palestine Liberation Organization*, p. 16; Abu Iyad (Salah Khalaf) with Eric Rouleau, *My Home, My Land* (New York: Times Books, 1981), pp. 65 and 139; and Gresh, *The PLO: The Struggle Within,* pp. 9–57, esp. 17–18.

95. In the aftermath of the October 1973 Yom Kippur War, the UN Security Council passed Resolution 338. It grew out of a U.S.-Soviet accord worked out in Moscow and presented to the Security Council. Resolution 338 was simply a call for a cease-fire and a reiteration of Resolution 242 adopted by the council after the June 1967 Six Day War. Both resolutions stipulated that the conflict should be resolved through an international conference, under the auspices of the UN Security Council, with the United States and the Soviet Union acting as cochairs, and with all parties (permanent council members, Arab states, and Israel) participating. Like Resolution 242, Resolution 338 stipulated that resolution of the conflict should be based on land for peace—that is, Israel's withdrawal from the territories it conquered in 1967 in exchange for treaties of peace and normalization of relations. Also like Resolution 242, Resolution 338 referred to the Palestinians merely in terms of the need to "resolve the refugee problem." And for this reason, the PLO initially declined to accept the resolution.

96. For the official translation of the PNC document, see "Palestine National Council, 'Political Communique,' Algiers, 15 November 1988," reprinted in *Journal of Palestine Studies* 18, no. 2 (winter 1989): 216–223. For the declaration of independence, see "'Palestinian Declaration of Independence,' Algiers, 15 November 1988," reprinted in *Journal of Palestine Studies* 18, no. 2 (winter 1989): 213–216.

97. For the joint statement, see *New York Times*, December 8, 1988. See also "Palestinian National Council, 'Political Communique,' Algiers, 15 November 1988." For an excellent analysis of the significance of the nineteenth PNC, see Rashid Khalidi, "The Resolutions of the 19th Palestine National Council," *Journal of Palestine Studies* 19, no. 2 (winter 1990): 29–42.

98. For a text of the address, see "Yasir Arafat, Speech Before the Forty-third Session of the United Nations General Assembly on the Question of Palestine, Geneva, 13 December 1988," reprinted in *Journal of Palestine Studies* 18, no. 3 (spring 1989): 161–171.

99. For the text, see "Yasir Arafat, Text of Press Conference Statement, Geneva, 14 December 1988," reprinted in *Journal of Palestine Studies* 18, no. 3 (spring 1989): 180–181.

100. On the institutions of civil society Palestinians created before the intifada, see Joost Hiltermann, *Behind the Intifada: Labor and Women's Movements in the Occupied Territories* (Princeton: Princeton University Press, 1991).

101. See M. Cherif Bassiouni and Louise Cainkar, *The Palestinian Intifada, December 9, 1987–December 8, 1988: A Record of Israeli Repression*

(Chicago: Data Base Project on Palestinian Human Rights, 1989); Norton Mezvinsky, ed., *Report: Human Rights Violations During the Palestinian Uprising, 1988–1989* (Tel Aviv: Israeli League for Human and Civil Rights [English], 1990); Al-Haq, *Punishing a Nation: Human Rights Violations During the Palestinian Uprising, December 1987–December 1988* (Jerusalem: Al-Haq—Law in the Service of Man [West Bank Affiliate of the International Commission of Jurists], 1988); and Al-Haq, *Protection Denied: Continuing Israeli Human Rights Violations in the Palestinian Occupied Territories, 1990* (Jerusalem: Al-Haq—Law in the Service of Man [West Bank Affiliate of the International Commission of Jurists], 1991). On the intifada in general, see David McDowall, *Palestine and Israel: The Uprising and Beyond* (Berkeley: University of California Press, 1989); Zachary Lockman and Joel Benin, eds., *Intifada: The Palestinian Uprising Against Israeli Occupation* (Boston: South End Press, 1989); Jamal Nassar and Roger Heacock, eds., *Intifada: Palestine at the Crossroads* (New York: Praeger, 1990); and Ze'ev Schiff and Ehud Ya'ari, *Intifada: The Palestinian Uprising—Israel's Third Front* (New York: Simon and Schuster, 1990).

102. For analyses of Arafat and the PLO on Iraq, see George T. Abed, "The Palestinians and the Gulf Crisis," *Journal of Palestine Studies* 20, no. 2 (winter 1991): 29–42; Lamis Andoni, "The PLO at the Crossroads," *Journal of Palestine Studies* 21, no. 1 (autumn 1991): 54–64; Muhammad Hallaj, "Taking Sides: Palestinians and the Gulf Crisis," *Journal of Palestine Studies* 20, no. 3 (spring 1991): 41–47; and Farsoun with Zacharia, *Palestine and the Palestinians*, p. 246.

103. For a detailed analysis, see Cheryl A. Rubenberg, "The Gulf War, the Palestinians, and the New World Order," in Tareq Y. Ismael and Jacqueline S. Ismael, eds., *The Gulf War and the New World Order: International Relations of the Middle East* (Gainesville: University Press of Florida, 1994), pp. 317–346.

104. See Friedemann Buettner and Martin Landgraf, "The European Community's Middle Eastern Policy: The New Order of Europe and the Gulf Crisis," in Ismael and Ismael, *The Gulf War and the New World Order*, pp. 77–115, and John Palmer, "The European Community," *Middle East International* (London), no. 406 (August 16, 1991), pp. 17–18.

105. Lesch, "Palestinians in Kuwait," pp. 42–54; Ghabra, "Palestinians in Kuwait: The Family and the Politics of Survival," pp. 62–83; and Le Troquer and al-Oudat, "From Kuwait to Jordan: The Palestinians' Third Exodus," pp. 37–51.

106. See Richard Falk, "Reflections on the Gulf War Experience: Force and War in the UN System," in Ismael and Ismael, *The Gulf War and the New World Order*, pp. 25–39; Enid Hill, "The New World Order and the Gulf War: Rhetoric, Policy, and Politics in the United States," in Ismael and Ismael, *The Gulf War and the New World Order*, pp. 184–223.

107. Louis J. Cantori, "The Middle East in the New World Order: Political Trends," in Ismael and Ismael, *The Gulf War and the New World Order*, pp. 451–472; Raymond Baker, "Islam, Democracy, and the Arab Future: Contested Islam in the Gulf Crisis," in Ismael and Ismael, *The Gulf War and the New World Order*, pp. 473–501. Also see Cheryl A. Rubenberg, "The Bush Administration and the Palestinians: A Reassessment," in Michael W. Suleiman, ed., *U.S. Policy on Palestine from Wilson to Clinton* (Normal, IL: Association of Arab-American University Graduates, 1995), pp. 195–221.

108. For a text of the final resolutions, see "20th Palestine National Council Meeting, Political Statement, Algiers, 28 September 1991," reprinted in *Journal of Palestine Studies* 21, no. 2 (winter 1992): 151–155.

109. Edward W. Said, *Peace and Its Discontents: Gaza-Jericho, 1993–1995* (New York: Vintage, 1995), p. xxiv.

110. For a series of important documents, see "Special Document," *Journal of Palestine Studies* 21, no. 2 (winter 1992): 117–149.

111. For a detailed examination of the content of each of the ten rounds, see Camille Mansour, "The Palestinian-Israeli Peace Negotiations: An Overview and an Assessment," *Journal of Palestine Studies* 22, no. 3 (spring 1993): 5–31. For analyses of Madrid, see George T. Abed, "The Palestinians in the Peace Process: The Risks and the Opportunities," *Journal of Palestine Studies* 22, no. 1 (autumn 1992): 5–17; Haydar `Abd al-Shafi and Nabil Shaath, "Reflections on the Peace Process," *Journal of Palestine Studies* 22, no. 1 (autumn 1992): 57–77; "Special Document File: The Madrid Peace Conference," *Journal of Palestine Studies* 21, no. 2 (winter 1992): 117–149); Naseer Aruri, *The Obstruction of Peace: The U.S., Israel, and the Palestinians* (Monroe, ME: Common Courage Press, 1995), pp. 111–216.

112. For accounts by three of the participants, see Mahmoud Abbas (Abu Mazen), *Through Secret Channels* (Reading, UK: Garnet, 1995); Yossi Beilin, *Touching Peace: From the Oslo Accord to a Final Agreement* (London: Weidenfeld and Nicolson, 1999); and Uri Savir, *The Process: 1,100 Days That Changed the Middle East* (New York: Vintage Books, 1999).

113. For background, see John King, *Handshake in Washington: The Beginning of Middle East Peace?* (London: Ithaca, 1994), and Bassam Abu-Sharif and Uzi Mahnami, *The Best of Enemies: The Memoirs of Bassam Abu Sharif and Uzi Mahnami* (New York: Little, Brown, 1995).

2

Accords and Agreements: Whither Peace?

The Oslo accords were formulated with convenient ambiguity that, for example, did not expressly forbid the construction of new settlements and left the decision about how much and which territory Israel would "give up" in the hands of Israel. A true depiction of the process would have revealed just how much the [Palestinian Authority] gave up on almost every issue. . . . The negotiating process reflected the nature of relations between Israel and the Palestinians. These are the relations between the ruler and the ruled, those who hold all the keys and those who are begging for just one.

—Amira Hass[1]

The disparity in power is so vast that it makes you cry.

—Edward Said[2]

In this chapter I analyze and contextualize the original Oslo Accords, formalized in the Declaration of Principles on Interim Self-Government (DOP), as well as the major and not-so-major agreements subsequently signed by Israel and the Palestinians between 1993 and 2000 (collectively, these are referred to as the Oslo agreements). I also examine the July 2000 Camp David and the January 2001 Taba negotiations, both of which ended without an agreement. I illuminate the motivations, the intentions, and the expectations of the major parties at Oslo and analyze the outcomes for each party. Finally, I look at the issue of refugees and their right of return to illustrate the fundamental flaws in the Oslo agreements.

As Chapter 1 illustrates, the Palestine Liberation Organization (PLO), though in a vulnerable position, entered the Oslo negotiations believing it had already made every possible concession. The PLO expected the peace process to be about the modalities of implementing an independent Palestinian state in the West Bank and Gaza with East

Jerusalem as its capital. Israel, by contrast, considered its recognition of the PLO to be its fundamental concession. It intended to utilize the process to transform the PLO into a security apparatus that would function as Israel's surrogate in policing the Palestinians and guaranteeing Israeli security. Israel expected the outcome to involve some sort of truncated Palestinian entity—something "less than a state," in Yitzhak Rabin's words—in the West Bank and Gaza that would exercise limited autonomy over most aspects of the Palestinian domestic sphere. Israel did not intend to give up its settlements (with the possible exception of those in Gaza and a few small isolated ones in the West Bank), its control over the borders with Jordan and Egypt, or its sovereignty over East Jerusalem or to permit the refugees to return. It attempted to obfuscate these objectives through the language of constructive ambiguity in the DOP and by dividing the process into two phases—interim status, and final status. Yasser Arafat and the majority of PLO leaders were either unable or unwilling to comprehend that reality.

Throughout this analysis, I will emphasize the enormity of the power disparity between Israel and the Palestinians.[3] For example, Israel's success in pressuring the PLO, in the DOP, to defer discussion of the most important issues (settlements, borders, refugees, and Jerusalem) to final-status negotiations allowed Tel Aviv to create facts on the ground throughout the negotiating process. These included, among other things, confiscation of land, construction of settlements and bypass roads, house demolitions, and deportations. The minutia of details Israel imposed on every agreement, in the wake of grand generalities, cumulatively rendered impossible the emergence of a viable state in the end. In essence, Israel structured the accords to ensure that the Palestinian objective of a sovereign independent state in the Occupied Territories would be subordinated to the Israeli goal of maintaining as much territory and control as possible while pacifying the Palestinians with the symbols of nationalism and statehood.

The announcement of the Oslo Accords, in light of the previous failure to reach agreement on any issue during the two years and ten rounds of talks under the Madrid formula, raises many questions.[4] The most compelling are: How did the Oslo Accords come about? and Did Israel fundamentally alter its position on the Palestine issue? The majority of analysts credit the Labor Party, in particular its leadership—Prime Minister Yitzhak Rabin and Foreign Minister Shimon Peres—with a fundamental break from the past that committed Israel to a just and lasting peace with the Palestinians. For instance, revisionist Israeli historian Avi Shlaim, writing in 2000, termed the Oslo agreements "a major breakthrough in the century-old conflict between Arabs and Jews in Palestine

. . . 'historic' because they reconciled the two principal parties to the Arab-Israeli conflict."[5] The following challenges that interpretation.

Prelude to Oslo

The Structure of Leadership in Israel and the Political Consensus

Investigating the relations between the Labor and Likud Parties together-er with their key leaders provides insight into the consistency and consensus of Israel's policy toward the Palestine issue.[6] The most important aspect of such an inquiry resides in an examination of national unity governments and the revolving door among crucial Israeli leaders. For example, in 1984 Labor and Likud agreed to a national unity formula for governing in which the office of prime minister would rotate every twenty-five months. Thus, from 1984 through 1986, Shimon Peres (Labor) was prime minister with Yitzhak Shamir (Likud) as foreign minister and Yitzhak Rabin (Labor) as defense minister. In the second part of the rotation, from 1986 through 1988 (Shamir was the prime minister, Rabin the defense minister). Likud won elections in 1988, but the national unity arrangement was maintained until March 1990 when Labor withdrew from the coalition. Likud governed alone until 1992. Elections that June brought the Labor Party back with the Rabin-Peres team. Significantly, however, Rabin retained (from the Shamir government) Elyakim Rubinstein (Likud), as head of the Israeli delegation for talks with the Palestinians in the Madrid process. After Rabin's assassination in November 1995, Peres became prime minister with Ehud Barak (Labor) as foreign minister. Yet Barak, a career military officer and former chief of staff of the Israeli Defense Forces (IDF), was on record as believing that "the politicians . . . conceded too much to the PLO [at Oslo I]."[7] He also abstained from the Knesset vote on Oslo II.[8] Likud returned to govern in June 1996 when Benjamin Netanyahu was elected prime minister. He appointed David Levy (Likud) as foreign minister and gave Ariel Sharon (Likud) a special portfolio to enable his participation in the cabinet. In May 1999, Labor ascended once more with the election of Ehud Barak as prime minister. He named David Levy foreign minister while giving Shimon Peres a new portfolio as regional development minister. February 2001 saw a renewed national unity government. Ariel Sharon, who orchestrated the 1982 war in Lebanon (with Barak as deputy commander of the IDF), a war designed to liquidate the PLO as a means of destroying Palestinian nationalism in the Occupied Territories, became prime minister. Shimon Peres, initiator of the Oslo process, became foreign minister and remained so during the first two years of the the Al-Aqsa intifada, which saw every vestige of the Palestinian Authority (PA) destroyed and the Oslo process declared dead.

The foregoing leads to several conclusions: regardless of their differences (some real, some rhetorical, on various domestic and foreign issues), there has been remarkable cooperation between the Labor and Likud Parties. Additionally, there has been a revolving door of leaders from both parties serving in a variety of governmental configurations. Moreover, it should be noted that a country's basic foreign policy and national interest do not shift with each election or new government. The dictum in the United States that foreign policy stops at the water's edge has meant in practice that both Democratic and Republican U.S. governments have pursued the same fundamental interests, even though the means to those ends have differed markedly at times. In Israel, as in the United States, there have been disputes over tactics and rhetorical flourishes, but there has not been deviation from the essential tenets of the state's interests vis-à-vis Palestine. Put simply, Israel will not withdraw from the West Bank; it will not dismantle the major settlement blocs; it will not share sovereignty in Jerusalem; it will not allow the return of the refugees; and it will not countenance the existence of a sovereign state between itself and Jordan. (Some right-wing leaders in Israel consider this stance inadequate and advocate annexing the whole of the Occupied Territories together with expulsion of the Palestinian population.) Israeli analyst Yisrael Harel commented on the similarities of Labor and Likud in the context of the January 2003 elections: "The message, 'to hone the differences between Labor and Likud,' is intellectually tempting. But when you get right down to it there is nothing to hone. . . . In fact, the difference . . . between Labor and Likud lies in no more than temperament and the sense of belonging to a particular camp or social milieu."[9]

The Motivations of Shimon Peres and Yitzhak Rabin

Shimon Peres is given credit for being the architect of Oslo and initiating a regionwide peace process (something for which he shared the Nobel Prize). It is true that Peres had a grand vision for the Middle East in which he conceived of Israel as the linchpin of a new regional order. Peres believed that if the Israeli-Palestinian conflict could be solved, then Jordan would sign a peace treaty with Israel and that Syria—isolated by virtue of the Palestinian and Jordanian accords in addition to the

1979 Egyptian treaty—would more readily agree to a settlement on Israel's terms. The resolution of these issues, Peres reasoned, would in turn allow Israel to expand throughout the Middle East—diplomatically, commercially, and economically. He saw the region as a vast market for Israeli technology, expertise, goods, and services. Additionally, he believed such a new regional order—a Pax Israelia, if you will—would lessen the potential military threats to Israel, allowing it to transfer resources into manufacturing sectors for export without jeopardizing its absolute regional military superiority. Peres also argued that such a situation would contribute to a greater international acceptance of Israel and to its increased integration into European economic and political circles.[10]

Based on this vision as well as his subsequent advocacy of the Oslo process, Peres can be credited with inspiring the attempt to resolve the conflict. But even though a solution to the Israeli-Palestinian conflict was the prerequisite to all other steps, that did not mean Peres considered Palestinian nationalist aspirations for an independent state as the path to that end. Rather, he believed that he could terminate the conflict with the Palestinians without breaching Israel's traditional positions, then use that "peace" to further Israel's regional and international interests.

At the practical level, Israel's participation in the secret Oslo talks with the PLO was initiated by Peres's deputy foreign minister, Yossi Beilin, *without* Peres's knowledge or blessing.[11] Beilin writes that he feared telling Peres—of whose support he was uncertain—because in addition to his own reservations, Peres would have to tell Rabin, who was likely to torpedo the talks. When Peres was told, he "wasn't happy" and when Rabin was made aware, he "was not enthusiastic." Beilin continues: "Our feeling" was that "he [Rabin] was personally unimpressed by what . . . had been achieved so far."[12] The implicit sense conveyed by Beilin, then, is that neither Peres nor Rabin took Oslo very seriously. They were not particularly happy about it, but because they did not give it much weight, they did not scuttle it.

The secret talks in Oslo commenced in January 1993 under the direction of Beilin, who, after revealing their existence to the foreign minister, reported directly to Peres. Rabin was not informed of this back channel until May. The Israeli participants were two academics—Yair Hirschfeld and Ron Pundak (who apprised Beilin). The main PLO participant was an economist—Ahmad Qurai' (Abu Ala), who briefed Mahmud `Abbas (Abu Mazen), one of Arafat's most senior advisers and to whom Abu Mazen reported.[13] Hasan Asfur, a political adviser, and Maher al-Kurd, an economic adviser, accompanied Abu Ala. In May, as the talks began to gel, Peres dispatched two highly skilled legal analysts to join the Oslo group—Uri Savir, the director-general of the foreign ministry, and his legal adviser, Joel Singer. Since the 1970s, Singer had been involved in scrutinizing international agreements to which Israel was a party. His expertise in such matters was of the highest order.[14] The Palestinians had no legal advice until the agreements were a fait accompli. On August 19, the Egyptian lawyer Taher Shash (who had been a participant in the 1978 Camp David summit), read the Declaration of Principles and told Arafat that the legal language was acceptable but that the Oslo agreements were worse than what Anwar Sadat had achieved for the Palestinians at Camp David.[15] Indeed, Arafat was the sole decisionmaker on every issue for the Palestinian side, and he did so, with Abu Mazen, in complete secrecy.

Fifteen sessions were held over an eight-month period. When in August 1993 Singer and Savir were satisfied that the agreement compromised none of Israel's red lines, they presented their work in four documents: the Declaration of Principles; a letter from Chairman Arafat to Prime Minister Rabin; a letter from Arafat to Norwegian foreign minister Johan Joergen Holst; and a letter from Rabin to Arafat.[16]

Rabin meticulously examined every word of each document and concluded, most significantly, that they "do not contradict the Allon Plan" for the West Bank to which he had been committed since 1967.[17] Rabin's devotion to that plan, reiterated repeatedly in public and private pronouncements, was firm and unequivocal. The Allon Plan (named for Israeli labor minister Yigal Allon; see note 18), devised in 1967, calls for Israeli retention of the Jordan Valley, including the Allenby border crossing with Jordan; absorption of the Judean desert region; and creation of a vastly expanded greater Jerusalem that would connect the three areas (see Map 2.1). The plan indicates that a Palestinian autonomous area—whatever its final boundaries—would be an island (or islands) surrounded by Israeli territory, settlements, and military installations.[18]

In addition to the West Bank, however, there was Gaza. Reflecting the frustrations of suppressing the intifada in Gaza, Rabin had on several occasions expressed a desire for the whole of it to fall into the sea. Gaza was so overpopulated, impoverished, economically nonviable, and politically volatile that it was essentially ungovernable. The intifada had erupted in Gaza, and it was the most active area during the uprising. The DOP gave the Palestinians primary responsibility for Gaza, providing for the withdrawal of the Israeli civil-military administration. The IDF would redeploy from the muddy streets and open sewers of the teaming refugee camps to the Jewish settlements and the border areas.

Map 2.1   Allon Plan (1967) for the Ultimate Distribution of West Bank and Gazan Territories Between Israel and the Palestinians

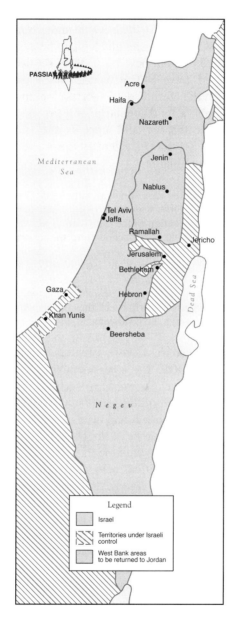

Source: Palestinian Academic Society for the Study of International Affairs (PASSIA), Jerusalem, http://www.passia.org/palestine_facts/MAPS/1967-allon-plan.html. Accessed January 2003. Reprinted with permission of PASSIA.

A further consideration for Rabin was that Hamas and Islamic Jihad, two militant Islamist organizations, were gaining support in the Occupied Territories, especially in Gaza, and the prime minister hoped that Arafat and the nationalist PLO could undermine their influence. But Rabin's hopes were more than ideological: he expected the neutralization to be effected through new PA security services that would not, as Rabin commented, have B'Tselem (the Israeli Information Center for Human Rights in the Occupied Territories) looking over their shoulders.[19] In other words, a fundamental premise of permitting the establishment of the PA was that it would suppress its own people—especially the Islamists, but any future dissident groups as well. Still, Rabin was reluctant. According to Shlaim:

> Rabin's conversion to the idea of a deal with the PLO was clinched by four evaluations. . . . First, was the advice of Itamar Rabinovich, the head of the Israeli delegation to the talks with Syria, that a settlement with Syria was attainable. . . . Second were the reports from various quarters that *the local Palestinian leadership had been finally neutralized*. Third was the assessment of the Israeli Defense Forces' chief of military intelligence that *Arafat's dire situation, and possible imminent collapse, made him the most convenient interlocutor for Israel at that particular juncture*. Fourth were the reports of the impressive progress achieved through the Oslo channel.[20]

The "impressive progress" refers to Palestinian capitulation to Israeli demands in the DOP. The assessment concerning Arafat's "dire situation" was not incorrect. As we have seen, in the aftermath of the Gulf War, the PLO was isolated, emasculated, without financial resources and political support. It had been excluded from participation in any aspect of the Madrid process; the United States had abrogated a low-level, short-lived dialogue with the PLO; and Israel had suppressed the intifada without any political achievements for the Palestinians. Thus, Israel rightly assumed it could extract major concessions from the PLO without having to make compromises of equal magnitude. In fact, Israel's singular substantive adjustment in the DOP was to recognize and negotiate with the PLO—something it had vowed it would never do. But this was not the PLO of the 1970s and 1980s; this was a PLO perilously close to collapsing. Its weakness and pliability were demonstrated during the course of the Oslo talks. Moreover, despite Israeli dogma about the political implication inherent in talking with the PLO, negotiations in reality meant process, not substance.

In the final analysis, Rabin (like Peres) agreed to Oslo because he believed it served Israel's interest of self-preservation as a Jewish and

Zionist state. He had come to reject the idea of annexation because, short of expelling the Palestinian population, its incorporation into Israel would so fundamentally alter the demographic balance of the state that it would cease to be Jewish. He had also come to believe— mainly as a consequence of the intifada—that perpetual military occupation of the West Bank and Gaza was undermining the strategic effectiveness of the IDF for waging war and was having a corrosive effect on domestic society. Additionally, Rabin believed that by making a deal with the PLO and giving it responsibility for security in Gaza, the PLO would rein in Hamas and Islamic Jihad and end their military activities against Israel.[21] The Israeli historian Zeev Sternhell put it succinctly: "If Rabin and Peres agreed to negotiate with the Palestinians . . . [it was] because this solution was the most rational simply from the point of view of Israeli national interest."[22]

The Motivations of Yasser Arafat

Reversing the questions we asked previously: Why did Yasser Arafat agree to participate in the secret negotiations in Oslo? and Why, as the limitations of Israel's position became apparent, did he continue to negotiate? First, it is necessary to reiterate that Arafat alone (with Abu-Mazen and Abu Ala in subsidiary roles) made the decisions to enter the talks and to remain engaged. There was no collective PLO decision-making. The main reason for Arafat's engagement in Oslo was the weakness and isolation of the PLO after the Gulf War. He believed that direct negotiations with Israel, after years of Tel Aviv's refusing to deal with the PLO, was a significant coup. In the words of one of his biographers, "Arafat . . . desperately wanted, perhaps the only thing he wanted [was] the recognition of the PLO as the representative of the Palestinian people. . . . It was the survival of the PLO that had been his principal concern."[23] As well, his own personal survival was of paramount concern. Thus, Oslo presented an opportunity for personal and organizational recognition and political rehabilitation.

Arafat had made repeated instructions to the delegates at Madrid to remain steadfast on traditional PLO positions—Jerusalem, the refugees, water, political prisoners, settlements, self-determination, and Israeli withdrawal from all the territories it occupied in 1967—in accordance with United Nations (UN) resolutions and international law. Yet he made concessions at Oslo on every one of these issues and, moreover, failed to insist on either international laws or UN resolutions as the terms of reference for the DOP. This proved to be an enormous and ultimately fatal error for the Palestinians. Aside from humiliating the

Madrid negotiators, it illustrated the extent to which Arafat surrendered fundamental Palestinian rights and interests merely in exchange for Israeli recognition. It appears, as one Palestinian analyst suggested, that Arafat believed he could gain something from Israel only by conceding in advance most of the Palestinians' history and claims. In the analyst's words, Arafat's position meant:

> We are prepared to live in peace with you, if only you accept the principle of talking to us. As if talking to, and being recognized by, your enemy is your major goal. As if the principle of hard work, determination and committed struggle could be shortcut by throwing all your cards on the table in return for which Israel only conceded something called "limited autonomy" and "limited recognition."[24]

This seems to be an incredibly shortsighted and inept diplomatic negotiating stance for a man who had spent his life leading an organization that purported to represent the interests of all Palestinians. Indeed, whereas Peres and Rabin did not deviate from their principle of Israeli national interests, Arafat appears to have completely lost sight of Palestinian national interests.

Fears about the eclipse of Arafat's own leadership were also major factors leading to his participation. During the intifada, a new indigenous, independent, and unified leadership emerged in the Occupied Territories (though the PLO attempted to hijack it financially and organizationally); it provided structure, organization, and inspiration to the uprising. Arafat perceived these individuals—especially those he was unable to co-opt—as competitors. Moreover, Palestinians from the West Bank and Gaza were participating in the Madrid conference, and they were receiving an enormous amount of positive international attention. Thus, even they were perceived as competitors. So by conducting his own secret talks with the Israelis, Arafat hoped to undermine the prestige and popularity of the Palestinian leaders from within the Occupied Territories.[25]

Arafat did not convene the Palestine National Council (PNC) to ratify the Oslo Accords (undoubtedly, the difficulties he had in winning support for participation in Madrid at the Algiers PNC were on his mind). Nevertheless, circumventing the PNC was a violation of the very basis of the PLO. Instead, Arafat convened the PLO executive committee, although not until September 3 (after Israel and the PLO negotiators had signed off), and there is where he sought ratification of the DOP. However, two of the PLO's most prominent leaders—Mahmoud Darwish and Shafiq al-Hout—resigned, and a significant number abstained. The resolution in favor of the DOP passed the cabinet by only one vote (compare the vote in the Knesset: 61 supported and 50 opposed). Arafat also faced opposition from intellectuals and political leaders in the Occupied Territories as well as organized opposition from Hamas, Islamic Jihad, the leftist Popular Front for the Liberation of Palestine, and the Democratic Front for the Liberation of Palestine. The Palestinian masses also took note of Arafat's failure to even address the issue of political prisoners. At the time of the signing of the DOP, there were some 5,000 political prisoners and administrative detainees languishing in Israeli jails as a consequence of the struggle to end the occupation. In a typical peace settlement, an exchange of prisoners would be the first priority, preceding any further agreements. Yet the prisoner issue was not even raised until the May 1994 Gaza-Jericho agreement (known as Cairo II) and was never fully resolved.[26] None of this, however, distracted Arafat from his enthusiasm over negotiations with Israel and Washington's new embrace.

The Oslo Process Documents

The Declaration of Principles: Oslo I (September 13, 1993)

It is important to examine the DOP in detail because it constitutes the foundation on which succeeding Israeli-Palestinian agreements were based.[27] The DOP was essentially a blueprint for the conduct of future negotiations; it was ambiguous, open to interpretation, and contained no Israeli commitments on Palestinian nationalist aspirations for an independent state. The DOP declared: "The aim of the Israeli-Palestinian negotiations [is] . . . to establish a Palestinian Self-Government Authority . . . for a transitional period not exceeding five years, leading to a permanent settlement based on Security Council Resolutions 242 and 338." The authority would be established in Gaza and Jericho first to be followed later in other unspecified "populated" areas. "Permanent status *negotiations* will commence . . . not later than the beginning of the third year . . . and will cover remaining issues including: Jerusalem, refugees, settlements, security arrangements, borders, relations and cooperation with other neighbors" (emphasis added).[28] Significantly, prior to Oslo and, in particular, at Madrid, the PLO had been steadfast in its opposition to an interim accord unless the principles of a final settlement were agreed in advance. In the DOP, the PLO accepted the

Israeli position of a five-year transition period without a prior agreement about the nature of a permanent settlement.

Importantly, the domain of the Palestinian Authority is functional, not territorial. This means that the PA can exercise authority over the Palestinian people in specified areas, but it has no sovereignty over land, resources, or borders. This constraint is spelled out, for example, in the nature of the PA's jurisdiction. The DOP provided for elections "under agreed supervision and international observation" for a "Council"—the governing authority. The council could legislate matters concerning "education and culture, health, social welfare, direct taxation, and tourism. . . . [and a] Palestinian police force, as agreed upon." Self-government, then, meant administration of people, not control of territory.

Once the council was set up, it would "establish a strong police force, while Israel will continue to carry the responsibility for defending against external threats as well as responsibility for overall security of Israelis for the purpose of safeguarding their internal security and public order." Moreover, "the withdrawal of the military government will not prevent Israel from exercising the powers and responsibilities not transferred to the Council." Herein lies the real function of the PA from Israel's perspective: a "strong police force" whose main purpose would be to guarantee Israel's security; Israel would remain the top cop.

Israel would withdraw from the Gaza Strip and redeploy from the Jericho area. *Redeployment*, however, has a substantially different meaning than *withdrawal*. It implies merely that the IDF will be moved from one area—in this context from the center of major Palestinian cities—and reconstituted in another nearby area—just outside of and around the cities. As Prime Minister Rabin makes clear in his statement (quoted at length below), the IDF would remain in the territories—redeployed from the urban centers to less provocative locations—but at the ready whenever Israel determined there was a need for its intervention.

The DOP also established joint liaison committees for every issue and eventuality. The liaison committees, as well as future negotiations, gave Israel a decisive advantage—indeed, a veto—over the resolution of any question owing to the enormous power disparity between the two sides. The talks in Oslo began in a context of power asymmetries that then became institutionalized in every document signed between Israel and the PLO—beginning with the DOP.

In addition to the foregoing, several other aspects of the agreement require explication: "Permanent peace will be based on [UN] Resolutions 242 and 338." This may appear straightforward, but the resolutions meant very different things to the two parties. In 1988, when the PLO accepted these resolutions as a basis for peacemaking, it did so grounded on the international consensus as to their meaning (i.e., that Israel would withdraw to the June 1967 borders from *all* the West Bank, Gaza, and East Jerusalem). Subsequent PLO diplomacy focused on the establishment of an independent Palestinian state emerging in those areas. However, Israel never accepted this interpretation of the resolutions or the linkage. It contended that the resolutions required Israel to withdraw from only some, but not all, of the territories. And it never acceded to a Palestinian state in the sense of national sovereignty. The DOP does not clarify the two contradictory interpretations of the resolutions, and it does not mention a Palestinian state, self-determination, or Palestinian national rights. These omissions undermined the possibility that Palestinian aspirations would be realized at any future time.

The terms *occupation* or *occupied* also do not appear anywhere in the DOP. In fact, in the documents used at the Madrid conference, Israel (with U.S. backing) had substituted the term *disputed areas* for *Occupied Territories*. As such, the designation was carried over into the DOP. Substantively, this meant that there was no Israeli commitment to end the occupation because there was no "occupation," only "disputed" areas.

As noted, the most serious issues—borders, settlements, security arrangements, refugees, and so on—were deferred for later negotiation (with an implied Israeli veto). The Palestinians had to proceed without any clear idea concerning the character of the future about which they would be negotiating. Additionally, negotiations were to determine the elections for the governing council as well as its structure and responsibilities. Israel would control who would be eligible to vote in the elections, how many seats the council would have, and how it would function, as well as the areas of jurisdiction for which it would be responsible. It is explicit in the DOP that the council would have an extremely limited jurisdiction. Moreover, even the Basic Law (the constitution for the self-governing authority) was to be negotiated between Israel and the Palestinians—Israel would have a veto over the Palestinian constitution-to-be.

Finally, the DOP required that all matters related to economic development must be negotiated or decided in a liaison committee (again, with an implied Israeli veto). These specifically include water resources, electricity, energy, transport, trade, industry, and more. Thus, the DOP constrains the PA from independently pursuing the development of its economy in a manner it deems most efficacious, if Israel does not agree with its plans.[29]

What Was Achieved by the DOP?

What, then, did the parties achieve from signing the DOP? Arafat received Israeli recognition of the PLO, his most cherished goal. In international circles, in particular the United States, Arafat "the terrorist" became Arafat "the statesman." He obtained permission for himself and certain selected others to administer civilian affairs in two areas of Palestine—Gaza and Jericho—and a promise that in the future they could exercise autonomy over additional areas. He also obtained a promise of future negotiations. It should be noted that the DOP salvaged Arafat—politically and financially. Certainly Arafat hoped—even believed—that in the future he could translate the DOP into a situation more in keeping with PLO objectives. But hope and conviction are different than a legal agreement that specifies limitations on the final outcome.[30]

Israel made certain, both implicitly and explicitly, in the articles, annexes, protocols, and other parts of the DOP the bounds beyond which the Palestinians could not go. In a September 21, 1993, speech to the Knesset, Prime Minister Yitzhak Rabin articulated these limits:

> This agreement [i.e., the DOP], which permits the Palestinians to run their affairs, safeguards the following issues for Israel: Unified Jerusalem remains under Israel's rule, and the body that will run the lives of the Palestinians in the territories will have no authority over it. . . . There are no differences of opinion in this House over the eternalness of Jerusalem as Israel's capital. United and unified Jerusalem is not negotiable. . . . The Israeli settlements in Judea, Samaria, and Gaza will remain under Israel's rule without any change whatsoever in their status. . . . The IDF will continue to bear overall responsibility for the security of the Israeli settlements in the territories, the security of every Israeli staying in the territories, and for external security— namely for the defense of the current confrontation lines along the Jordan River and for the Egyptian border. . . . The Israeli government's freedom to determine its positions [on all final status issues is preserved by the DOP] leaving all the options open. . . . The might of the IDF—the best army in the world—is available for our use if, God forbid, we are faced with such a challenge [from the Palestinians]. . . . Above all, I want to tell you that this is a great victory for Zionism.[31]

What did Israel achieve from signing the DOP? Most important, it was credited with making a historic compromise—a genuine commitment to settle, justly and fairly, the 100-year Palestinian-Israeli conflict. This won the Jewish state international accolades, a warmer welcome and greater integration into the European Community, and new acceptance in the Arab world. Indeed, within a few short years, Peres's vision for the Middle East appeared well on the way to becoming reality. In 1994, Jordan concluded a full peace treaty with Israel, and negotiations with Syria, under the auspices of the United States, were in progress. "By 1996 Israel had established diplomatic relations with fifteen Arab states, with Morocco and Tunisia leading the way. In the Persian Gulf region, Oman and Qatar were the first to do business with Israel."[32] Moreover, "the majority of states of the Arab League [had] establish[ed] official and unofficial relations with Israel, brought about the virtual lifting of the Arab boycott and attracted investment from all over the world."[33] The Middle East and North Africa Economic Conference was established as an annual event, with Israel as a full and active participant. "Israel seemed set on a course leading to integration in the politics and economy of the Middle East."[34] Finally, as a consequence of the Oslo process, Israel created an opening that led to full diplomatic relations with India, China, and "like" countries.[35]

Cairo I

In what became a hallmark of all future agreements between the Palestinian Authority and Israel, the second accord was signed five months later than the period stipulated in the DOP. Israel and the Palestinians initialed the first Gaza-Jericho agreement (Cairo I— February 9, 1994).[36] The Israeli negotiating team was composed of top IDF officers, led by Major-General Amnon Lipkin-Shahak, head of military intelligence and the number-two man in the IDF. The Palestinian delegation was led by Nabil Sha'ath, a former businessman and one of Arafat's senior political operatives. Four months of intensive talks resulted in two partial agreements. One involved security and military issues, focusing on the PLO's responsibilities for maintaining order among the Palestinians under its jurisdiction and protecting Israel's security, as well as on modes of control on the Gaza border with Egypt and the Jericho border with Jordan. Israel assumed unilateral jurisdiction over both boundaries. The second agreement was another statement of principles concerning the transfer of authority to the PA. Together, they further refined the limitations on PA governance and delineated the expectations of the PA regarding Israel's security needs.

The DOP had set the terms of reference for future negotiations; the Cairo agreement transformed ambiguity into fixed constraints on Palestinian self-rule. Shlaim, who believes the Oslo Accords were a "historical breakthrough," admits that Cairo I "tilted very heavily toward the Israeli position. The IDF had managed to impose its own conception of the interim period. . . . The outstanding feature of the agreement was thus to allow the IDF to maintain a military presence in and around the areas earmarked for Palestinian self-government."[37] Prime Minister Rabin was more explicit in an address to the Knesset:

> The Palestinians will have a policing authority regarding civilian issues, *subject to several constraints.* . . . [It] allows blanket [IDF] protection of . . . the settlements in the Gaza Strip. . . . [There are] constraints on Palestinian building and other issues. . . . In other areas—such as religion, archaeology, water, electricity, construction and planning, telecommunications, postal services, and population registration affairs—*the transfer of power will be subject to certain constraints in order to secure essential Israeli interests.* . . . [It] stipulates that a liaison committee . . . will be established to . . . decide on the principles concerning the entry of persons who left Judea and Samaria in 1967. Take note we are not talking about refugees from 1948 but about people displaced in 1967. . . . This clause stipulates that all decisions on this issue must be made unanimously by all the members of the [joint liaison] committee. In other words, without Israel's agreement, the committee will not be able to determine how many people will be allowed in and in what stages.[38]

It is remarkable that Arafat would sign away the right of his people who were displaced in 1967 to return to their homes. But it is also evident that even on civilian issues, such as religion and postal services, Arafat agreed to subordinate the self-governing authority to Israel's interests. Clearly, Arafat's personal interest in political resurrection via an agreement with Israel that recognized the PLO and Arafat's leadership, and permitted his return to any part of Palestine, was more important than the content of the agreement and the interests of the Palestinian people.

Israel's persistent emphasis on security is a pronounced feature in every document relating to the peace process. Almost every issue revolves around some aspect of Israel's security needs, and Palestinians are required in virtually every article to guarantee them. Conversely, Palestinian security needs are nowhere addressed. Yet as became evident within days of the signing of Cairo I, Palestinians were vulnerable to Israeli security abuses. On February 25, 1994, Dr. Baruch Goldstein, a U.S.-born physician-settler, armed with a Galil assault rifle, which is standard issue in the IDF, entered Al-Ibrahimi mosque (the mosque of Abraham), containing the Tomb of the Patriarchs in Hebron, walked past the Israeli troops (stationed there to protect worshippers), and shot and killed twenty-nine Muslims at prayer.[39] Goldstein was killed after he was overcome by surviving worshippers; however, settlers from nearby Kiryat Arba constructed an elaborate shrine in his memory to which thousands of settlers made pilgrimage in the ensuing years. It is of significance to note that Hamas (formed in late 1987) did not carry out its first suicide bombing until April 1994, two months after the Al-Ibrahimi massacre.[40]

Hebron, wherein some 450 extremist settlers implanted themselves in 1968 in a fortified enclave in the heart of 160,000 Palestinians, is particularly prone to strife; but the city is also a microcosm of the conflict between settlers and Palestinians in the Occupied Territories (see Chapter 4).[41]

Cairo II

Israel considered the February 9 agreement partial and insufficiently precise in stipulating the autonomy limitations and security responsibilities of the Palestinian Authority. Thus, negotiations continued for another four months until a second Gaza-Jericho agreement was signed (Cairo II—May 4, 1994).[42] Taken together, the myriad agreements that constitute these documents suggest a determined Israeli effort to impose the maximum number of controls on, and obstacles to, the possibility of Palestinians actually succeeding at self-rule.[43] For example, it was agreed in this document that the Israeli occupation laws and military orders, which had controlled every aspect of Palestinians' lives since 1967, were to remain in force unless they were amended by "mutual agreement."[44] It was further agreed that Israel had the right to continue arresting, interrogating, and imprisoning any Palestinian, including those who came from the areas under Palestinian jurisdiction.

Palestinians and Israelis negotiated for eight months in Paris to achieve an economic agreement. The Israel-PLO Protocol on Economic Relations was signed on April 29, 1994. It was incorporated as Annex IV into the Cairo II accord of March 31, 1994, and is generally referred to as the economic protocol or the Paris protocol.[45] The protocol, which runs to the hundreds of pages, covers all economic sectors and activities, including the PA's economic relations with Israel and other countries. By its terms, the Palestinians agreed to a customs union with Israel and to Israel's collection of import, valued-added taxes (VAT), excise, and other taxes. In essence, the agreement preserves the structure of economic domination that Israel established over the West Bank and Gaza beginning in 1967.[46]

Several provisions of the economic protocol illustrate the continuing structural inequalities. Palestinians are prohibited from having their own currency (depriving them of making monetary policy, including determining interest rates and currency value); they cannot set tariffs or VAT (although they are permitted a 2 percent leeway). The PA may collect income taxes.

Trade relations remain bound by Israeli trade policy, and imports and exports are rigidly controlled. For example, the protocol specifies what goods the PA may import (from places other than Israel) and in what quantity. There are also complex restrictions on exports (both to Israel and other countries), and the protocol imposes a de facto customs union with Israel. The customs union essentially aims at keeping the West Bank and Gaza Strip economically integrated with Israel. With regard to labor, the protocol states that "both sides will attempt to maintain the normality of movement of labor between them." However, this clause is modified by the proviso that each side has the right to "determine from time to time the extent and conditions of the labor movement in its area."[47] In practice, this is solely an Israeli prerogative, because it is the Palestinian labor force that is dependent on employment in Israel, not the reverse. Additionally, Israel retains control over electricity, energy, transport, trade, water, and the like. Moreover, as in every accord, there are numerous specific limitations that amount to a Catch-22 for the Palestinians. For example: "Each side . . . will take into consideration the concerns of the other side in its industrial policy."[48] In other words, as they attempt to construct a manufacturing sector, Palestinians must take into consideration the interests of Israeli industrialists whose highly technologized firms compete successfully on the global market.

Israel will collect VAT and customs duties on all goods destined for the West Bank and Gaza as well as continue to collect taxes on the salaries of all Palestinians working in Israel. All these moneys are to be remitted to the PA. However, this seemingly practical clause afforded Israel the opportunity to withhold from the PA, at its discretion, moneys that were due the Palestinians. Thus, for example, from the time the Al-Aqsa intifada erupted in September 2000, Israel seized all taxes that legally should have accrued to the PA—a sum amounting to NIS 1.7 billion (1.7 billion new Israeli shekels). The government then began preparing legislation to allow private Israeli citizens to sue the PA for damages incurred during the course of the uprising with compensation to be paid from the confiscated Palestinian funds.[49] In short, the protocols embodied in Annex IV did not give the PA the necessary means to achieve sustainable economic growth.[50]

Of the four documents concluded up to this time—the DOP

(September 1993), Cairo I (February 1994), and Cairo II and its Annex IV (May 1994), Israeli analyst Meron Benvenisti wrote:

> A perusal of hundreds of the agreements' pages can leave no doubt about who is the winner and loser in this deal. By seeing through all the lofty phraseology, all deliberate disinformation, hundreds of pettifogging sections, sub-sections, appendices and protocols, one can clearly recognize that Israeli victory was absolute and Palestinian defeat abject.[51]

Nevertheless, on July 1, 1994, Yasser Arafat, accompanied by his Tunisian coterie, made a triumphant arrival in Gaza. This became a symbol for the imminent return of all Palestinian refugees, despite the fact that the refugee question had yet to be discussed in negotiations (being deferred in the DOP for final-status talks). Indeed, most Palestinians had no idea of the concessions Arafat had made in exchange for his legal presence in Gaza. The vast majority believed that there was a genuine peace process under way and that within five years (the time frame stipulated in the DOP) they would have an independent state in the West Bank, Gaza, and East Jerusalem. Given such high expectations, when the life situation of ordinary Palestinians began to seriously deteriorate, and when the five-year deadline for a final settlement passed without any political achievements, Palestinian frustration was overwhelming—ultimately spilling over into the Al-Aqsa intifada, the second uprising.

The Agreement on Preparatory Transfer of Powers and Responsibilities

On August 29, 1994, another agreement was signed for the purpose of implementing Israel's actual transfer of authority to the PA for administration of aspects of civilian life in Gaza and Jericho. The accord (Israel and the PLO Agreement on Preparatory Transfer of Powers and Responsibilities) became known as Early Empowerment.[52] It further spelled out the limitations and restrictions, as well as the obligations and responsibilities, incumbent on the PA when it assumed self-government in the areas of education, culture, health, social welfare, tourism, taxation, and policing.[53]

Many of the constraints the accords imposed on the Palestinians were made manifestly clear on October 5 when Prime Minister Rabin announced before the Knesset his detailed plans for a permanent settlement. His definition of *final settlement* differed drastically from that of

Palestinian and other observers (excepting the United States) of the meaning of Oslo. Rabin stated the following:

> The permanent solution lies in the territory of the State of Israel made up of Eretz Yisrael as it was under the British Mandate . . . and alongside it, a Palestinian *entity* that will be the home of the majority of the Palestinian residents of the Gaza Strip and West Bank. We want the entity to be *less than a state*. . . . The borders of the State of Israel . . . will exceed the borders that existed prior to the Six Day War. We will not return to the lines of 4 June 1967. . . . [we will maintain] a united Jerusalem—to *include* also Ma'ale Adumim and Giv'at Ze'ev [West Bank settlements]—as the capital of Israel, under Israeli sovereignty. . . . The *security border* for the defense of the State of Israel will be situated in the *Jordan Rift Valley* [the eastern salient of the West Bank] *along the broadest possible interpretation of that term.* The changes will *include* . . . the Etzion Bloc, Efrat, Betar *and other settlements*. There will be settlement blocs . . . [throughout] Judea and Samaria. . . . I must stress the activity to build security components at the Israeli settlements: fences, by-pass roads, lights, electronic gates. The by-pass roads are aimed at enabling Israelis to move without crossing the Palestinian population areas. . . . [We will maintain] *responsibility for external security* on the *borders with Egypt and Jordan*, in the *airspace over all the territories*, and in *the naval space in the Gaza Strip*.[54]

This caused some (including this author) to wonder whether the Palestinians were listening to the Israeli prime minister. Did they think, somehow, that the "peace of the brave" would transcend political realities? I cannot provide the answer, but (as is discussed immediately below) all of Rabin's positions were incorporated into Oslo II, the Interim Agreement that Israel and the Palestinians signed three weeks later.

Oslo II

On September 28, 1995, in Washington, D.C., the parties signed the next major accord (the Israeli-Palestinian Interim Agreement on the West Bank and the Gaza Strip, or Oslo II).[55] As with other agreements, this ran to hundreds of pages, the interstices of which contained the Rabin limitations plus many others. It reiterated earlier agreements but made additional provisions for elections for the Palestinian Legislative Council to which Israel would transfer authority in the sectors previously specified. It specifically committed Israel to release Palestinian prisoners and detainees in the West Bank and Gaza (though not in East Jerusalem) who had committed offenses prior to September 13, 1993.

Most important, the accord also divided the West Bank into three areas of jurisdiction. Area A would consist of about 3 percent of the West Bank, including the densely populated urban areas of Ramallah, Jenin, Nablus, Qalqilya, Tulkarem, and Bethlehem. Hebron (the largest Palestinian city) was explicitly excluded, its fate being deferred to a later date. Area A would be under the PA's jurisdiction. Area B, which included a network of some 400 Palestinian villages and adjoining rural lands that comprised approximately 27 percent of the West Bank, would be controlled jointly by Israel and the PA. Area C, encompassing 70 percent of the West Bank, included the settlements and their bypass roads, military encampments, Israeli-designated state land, and almost all the agricultural land of the Palestinians. Area C was under exclusive Israeli control.[56] Israel was to redeploy from Area A locations; however, Palestinians could not move from one part of Area A to another without passing through Area B, which meant a series of checkpoints, road-blocks, and the necessary permits to get through. Entrances and exits to Gaza were also under Israeli control.[57] Oslo II thus created a series of isolated Palestinian cantons and completely severed the West Bank from Gaza. Analysts have described it as an "archipelago" or a "slice of swiss cheese" (see Map 2.2).

This situation, combined with a unilateral Israeli prohibition on Palestinians in the West Bank and Gaza from entering Jerusalem, created a schizophrenic condition. For instance, life in downtown Ramallah seemed perfectly normal. The withdrawal of IDF troops gave residents a new sense of freedom, and social life blossomed. Cafés, restaurants, coffee shops, galleries, businesses, research centers, and the like opened and flourished. Yet a Ramallah resident with family in Bethlehem could not visit them (and vice versa) because the road between the two cities passes through Jerusalem. A resident of Ramallah or Bethlehem or from anywhere in the West Bank or Gaza with a serious illness could not obtain medical attention at one of the major Palestinian hospitals in Jerusalem. Ramallah residents who were students or professors at Birzeit University (a few kilometers outside the city but inside Area B) frequently found that they could not reach the university because of an IDF roadblock. A Muslim from anywhere in the Occupied Territories could not pray at Al-Aqsa mosque; a Christian could not worship at the Church of the Holy Sepulcher. A Ramallah Christian could not even attend the Church of the Nativity in Bethlehem. Palestinians from the West Bank could not enter Gaza, and vice versa—on and on across all the Occupied Territories.[58]

Nevertheless, even this limited redeployment generated strong opposition from many sectors in Israel. Benjamin Netanyahu, who

Map 2.2   The Olso II Agreement (1995) Showing Areas A, B, and C

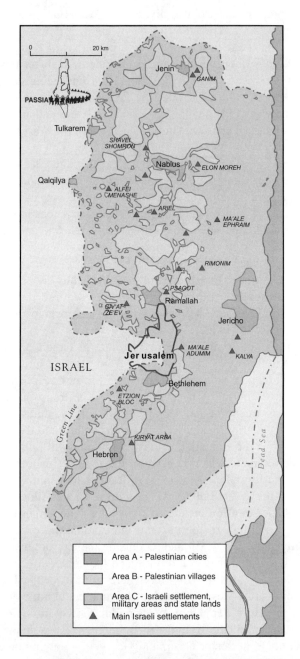

Area A - Palestinian cities
Area B - Palestinian villages
Area C - Israeli settlement, military areas and state lands
▲ Main Israeli settlements

Source: Palestinian Academic Society for the Study of International Affairs (PASSIA), Jerusalem, http://www.passia.org/palestine_facts/MAPS/Oslo-2.html. Accessed January 2003. Reprinted with permission of PASSIA.

became prime minister less than a year later, gave an inflammatory speech in which he declared:

> Today the surrender agreement called Oslo II was placed before the Knesset. . . . The Jewish majority of the State of Israel did not approve this agreement. We shall fight it and we shall bring down the government. . . . Rabin is causing a national humiliation by accepting the dictates of the terrorist Arafat.[59]

Posters and effigies of Rabin dressed in a Nazi uniform appeared throughout the country, and the airwaves were full of invective and incitement. On one radio program, novelist Moshe Shamir declared:

> Yitzhak Rabin is not a Nazi officer as he [is] presented. . . . But Rabin does collaborate with the thousands of Nazi officers whom he brings to the heart of Israel, and he hands it over to them, under the command of their leader, Adolf Arafat, to carry forward the plan of the destruction of the Jewish people.[60]

On November 4, 1995, a West Bank settler, Yigal Amir, a student of fundamentalist rabbis who preached that Rabin had given away the sacred Land of Israel, assassinated the prime minister.[61] The Knesset recommended to the president that he ask Shimon Peres to form a new government. On November 22, Peres became prime minister and Ehud Barak foreign minister.

On January 20, 1996, the Palestinians held elections for the Legislative Council that was seated in Ramallah. Prior to the election, Israel had made the final determination of who was eligible to vote and who was entitled to run for seats in the council. At the same time, Arafat maneuvered among clans, religious groups, and locales to ensure Fateh's dominance in the outcome. Voter turnout was remarkably high—79.7 percent of the 1 million–plus registered voters actually cast ballots. Reflecting the continuing strong support for Arafat and the peace process, Fateh won fifty of the eighty-eight seats, independents took thirty-seven seats, and FIDA (the pro-Oslo party that split from the Democratic Front for the Liberation of Palestine in 1993) claimed one seat.[62] Seven of the independents were Islamists; the remainder were mostly pro-Fateh. Thus, in reality, Fateh controlled seventy-one of the eighty-eight seats. Nevertheless, most observers—international and local—considered it to be a reasonably fair election.

In early January 1996, Peres gave the General Security Services (GSS) permission to assassinate a Hamas leader, Yahya Ayyash, the alleged mastermind behind several earlier suicide attacks. Whether Ayyash engineered these events remains unclear, but it is known that the head of GSS (who most strongly pushed for the assassination) was about to be removed from his post for failing to protect Rabin, and he badly wanted to be remembered for some "success."[63] Ayyash was killed on January 5, 1996, by means of a booby-trapped cellular phone with the assistance of a Palestinian collaborator. Hamas immediately declared Ayyash a martyr and promised revenge. Shortly thereafter, Hamas carried out four suicide bombings that killed approximately sixty Israelis. Five years later, a senior Israeli military commentator, analyzing the folly of Israel's policy of assassination, wrote the following about the Ayyash incident: "In retrospect, it is indisputable that the Ayyash assassination was the fuse which ignited the wave of terror attacks; it occurred at a time of sustained quiet, in a period when the sides were engaged in peace process talks."[64]

In an atmosphere of extreme tension, the United States, at Israel's behest, convened an international conference—thirty-one countries and the PA were in attendance—in Egypt to condemn terrorism. The focus, however, was strictly on Palestinian terrorism. The Ayyash incident was not mentioned, and Arafat came under intense pressure to increase security and prevent terrorist attacks. At the meeting's close on March 13, 1996, all participants pledged (in the Sharm al-Sheikh Declaration) to support "the Middle East peace process . . . to promote security and stability; and to prevent the enemies of peace from achieving their ultimate objective of destroying . . . peace."[65] In May, the PA and Israel concluded an agreement affirming their intention to begin final-status talks.[66] The election one month later of Netanyahu, who had campaigned on an anti-Oslo platform, stalled that process entirely.

The Secret Agreement.   Immediately after the Interim Agreement was signed, a secret, unofficial agreement (the Framework for the Conclusion of a Final Status Agreement Between Israel and the Palestine Liberation Organization) was forged between Mahmoud Abbas (Abu Mazen) and Yossi Beilin. It set forth an outline for final-status negotiations. With Netanyahu's election, the accord was locked away and did not resurface until September 2000, when, in the wake of the collapse of the Camp David summit, *Newsweek* magazine first published the full text.[67] It did not play a role in talks between the two parties, yet it remains of historical significance, and in some quarters during the Al-Aqsa intifada, it was mentioned as a possible final-status proposal.

The Interim Intifada.   Even though the rhetoric of Rabin and Peres was about peace, Netanyahu boldly proclaimed—in word and deed—that the peace process was over. In four months, the new prime minister demolished homes, confiscated land, initiated construction of new settlements, and arrested Palestinians at a frenetic pace. The quality of life for Palestinians declined precipitously, and throughout the West Bank and Gaza tensions escalated—it became a tinderbox. The match came in the middle of the night on September 25, 1996, when Israel blasted open a 2,000-year-old passage, known as the Hasmonean Tunnel, under the Haram al-Sharif. The tunnel, 480 meters long, runs along and under one wall of the Al-Aqsa mosque. One gate emerges at the Wailing Wall directly below the Dome of the Rock, the other at a cistern located below Islamic Waqf property. The government claimed the tunnel was opened to facilitate tourism in the Old City. Palestinians perceived it as an arrogant and provocative statement about Israel's right to all of Jerusalem and as a physical threat to the stability of the holy buildings (the Dome of the Rock and Al-Aqsa mosque) under which the tunnel extended. Shlaim wrote that the tunnel "constituted a symbolic and psychological affront to Palestinians and a blatant Israeli violation of the pledge to resolve the dispute over Jerusalem through negotiations, not via a *fait accompli*."[68]

Palestinian frustration erupted in protests that spread throughout the West Bank and Gaza. In three days, Israeli soldiers killed eighty Palestinian civilian demonstrators and injured some 1,500. Palestinian policemen then turned their guns on the soldiers, killing fifteen and wounding dozens. Israeli-PA security cooperation appeared shattered, and the peace process seemed to be at an end. Continuing tensions brought U.S. diplomatic pressure to bear on both sides to resume negotiations. Three months later, in January 1997, the most controversial agreement between the Palestinians and Israel was signed in Washington; this was the Hebron Protocol.

The Hebron Protocol

Part of Oslo II had involved an Israeli commitment to redeploy from Hebron no later than six months after its signing (i.e., March 28, 1996). Peres, however, suspended the redeployment because of the bombings in the wake of the Ayyash assassination. (He also failed to carry out the prisoner releases.) Netanyahu declared that there would be no redeployment and termed the agreement "canceled." In response to the upsurge in violence and Netanyahu's intransigence, the U.S.-sponsored talks that began in October in Taba, Egypt, aimed at getting the peace process back on track. That meant in practice redirecting attention to the Hebron redeployment. Under an impending crisis with the United States if he

refused to participate in negotiations, Netanyahu made a tactical decision to engage in the process without compromising his principles.
Washington rewarded the prime minister's engagement by fully supporting the Israeli position on Hebron. Nevertheless, negotiations lasted
for three months until the Israel and the Palestine Liberation
Organization Protocol Concerning the Redeployment in Hebron, commonly know as the Hebron Protocol, was signed at Erez Crossing on
January 15, 1997.[69] It was the shortest agreement between the two parties, yet it contained the most explicit loss for Palestinians.[70]

The Hebron Protocol divided the city into two distinct sectors. In
one sector (designated H-2, constituting 20 percent of the city, including its commercial center, the choicest real estate, and Al-Ibrahimi
mosque), Israel would have full control. That is, the 450 Jewish settlers
(representing 0.3 percent of the population) would have complete freedom of action under exclusive IDF protection (see Map 2.3). Moreover,
by expanding and according formal recognition to an exclusive settler
enclave under Israeli control in Hebron, the protocol implicitly sanc-
tioned this and other settlements (heretofore considered illegal)
encroaching on Hebron and other cities (e.g., Joseph's Tomb in Nablus
and Rachel's Tomb in Bethlehem).

Israel would redeploy from the remaining 80 percent of the city (the
H-1 sector), wherein the 160,000 Palestinians were permitted to exercise autonomy and the PA—subject to numerous restrictions and limitations—would be responsible for security. The protocol also required
Israel to make three additional redeployments in other West Bank areas
within eighteen months, conditional on Palestinians meeting their
"security responsibilities"; it was stipulated that "Israel alone will
decide the[ir] timing and scope."[71]

Netanyahu implemented the first redeployment from Hebron—to
the joy of Palestinians living in the H-1 sector. Yet even though his cabinet and the Knesset approved the full Hebron Protocol, Netanyahu subsequently refused to carry out the other two redeployments. Moreover,
the following month, the prime minister took another dramatic and
provocative move with regard to Jerusalem. On February 19, 1997, he
announced a plan for the construction of a new settlement, Har Homa,
on Jabal Abu Ghneim. Located on the southeastern border of Jerusalem
less than 2 kilometers north of Bethlehem in an area of 2 square kilometers, Har Homa will complete the circle of Jewish settlements around
Jerusalem, completely severing contact between Arab East Jerusalem
and the remainder of the West Bank. With his usual rhetorical flourish,
Netanyahu declared, "The battle for Jerusalem has begun. . . . I do not
intend to lose";[72] he also outlined his plan for the construction of 6,500

Map 2.3 The Hebron Protocol, 1997

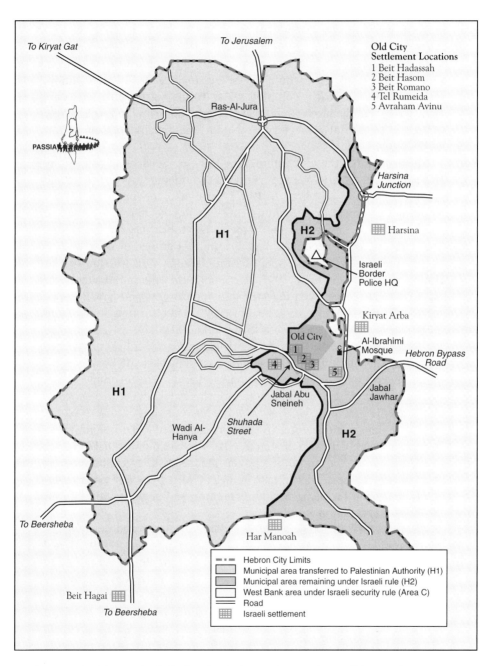

To Kiryat Gat

To Jerusalem

**Old City
Settlement Locations**
1 Beit Hadassah
2 Beit Hasom
3 Beit Romano
4 Tel Rumeida
5 Avraham Avinu

PASSIA

Ras-Al-Jura

Harsina
Junction

H1

H2

Harsina

Israeli
Border
Police HQ

Kiryat Arba

Old City

Al-Ibrahimi
Mosque

Hebron Bypass
Road

H1

Jabal Abu
Sneineh

Jabal
Jawhar

Wadi Al-
Hanya

Shuhada
Street

H2

To Beersheba

Har Manoah

	Hebron City Limits
	Municipal area transferred to Palestinian Authority (H1)
	Municipal area remaining under Israeli rule (H2)
	West Bank area under Israeli security rule (Area C)
	Road
	Israeli settlement

Beit Hagai

To Beersheba

Source: Palestinian Academic Society for the Study of International Affairs (PASSIA), Jerusalem, http://www.passia.org/palestine_facts/MAPS/Hebron-1997.html. Accessed January 2003. Reprinted with permission of PASSIA.

housing units for 30,000 settlers. One Israeli scholar wrote of the decision: "It was a blatant example of the Zionist tactic of creating facts on the ground to preempt negotiations. . . . [It] prejudiced not only the negotiations on the future of Jerusalem but those on a final settlement for the West Bank as a whole."[73] Israeli analyst Daniel Ben Simon, reflecting on the nearly completed Har Homa settlement five years later, wrote that the motivation for its construction was "to break, at any price, the territorial contiguity in which Palestinians are concentrated."[74]

In response to the prime minister's 1997 announcement concerning Har Homa, demonstrations again erupted throughout the West Bank and Gaza. In response, on March 6, 1997, Netanyahu announced that Israel would not carry out the remaining two redeployments to which he had committed Israel in the Hebron Protocol. The following day, the United States vetoed a UN Security Council resolution critical of Israel's decision to build a settlement on Jabal Abu Ghneim. Construction of Har Homa began on March 18, 1997, one month after the initial announcement, and clashes between Palestinian demonstrators and Israeli troops escalated. Between March 6 and March 20, Israeli troops killed eight Palestinians and wounded more than 1,000. On March 21, the United States vetoed a second UN Security Council resolution critical of Israel's settlement policy; that same day, a Hamas suicide bomber blew up a Tel Aviv café, killing three women. The Israeli government then suspended all further negotiations with the Palestinians except those that concerned security.[75]

Netanyahu's settlement activity was not limited to Jerusalem: in the first six months of 1997 (compared to the first six months of 1996), the prime minister used enormous government subsidies to increase by more than 50 percent sales of new homes in West Bank and Gaza settlements.[76] During the same period, economic and social conditions for the Palestinians plummeted.[77]

In this tense atmosphere, an undeclared group carried out two suicide bombings in Jerusalem on July 30 and September 4, 1997. Israel and the United States immediately condemned the PA for its failure to fulfill its security obligations and demanded that it arrest every Islamist in the Occupied Territories. Washington then inserted itself more directly on behalf of Israel's security by introducing the U.S. Central Intelligence Agency (CIA) as coordinator between Israeli and Palestinian security services. It birthed an agreement on December 17, 1997 (the Israel and the Palestinian Authority Memorandum on Security Understanding).[78] The accord was focused exclusively on Israel's security needs, held the PA responsible for all acts of violence, and demanded that the PA utilize all measures against its people to bring about a cessation of violence and guarantee Israel's security.

Reflecting the overwhelming despair and frustration of the Palestinian community at this moment, Edward Said wrote:

> I have not heard one Palestinian applaud or even mildly approve the marketplace bombs last week. They were stupid, criminal acts that have brought disaster on our people. . . . How dare . . . Netanyahu . . . demand that Islamic militants be summarily arrested and Israeli security guaranteed? . . . Israel, in its mania for security, has retained control of every exit and entrance into the territories, and it alone is responsible for West Jerusalem where the attacks took place. . . . [The peace process] has impoverished our people whose per capita income has been slashed by half; we have lost our ability to move around freely, confined to the dreadful little Bantustans . . . obliged to watch more settlements being built and more land taken, more houses destroyed, more people evicted, and . . . collective punishments meted out without proportion or reason.[79]

Ron Pundak, one of the original Israeli negotiators of the DOP, wrote an extensive piece at this juncture, cataloging the long list of Israeli failures to comply with commitments it made in the DOP and in subsequent agreements with the PLO/PA.[80]

To the intense frustration of the Palestinians, Israel continued to hold up implementation of a safe passage between Gaza and the West Bank, construction of the Gaza airport and seaport, the release of political prisoners, plus the construction of an industrial park in Gaza. Dahaniya Airport was finally opened on November 24, 1998, the Qarni Industrial Estate on December 14, 1998, and a safe passage on October 25, 1999; however, Israel closed all three in October 2000. Although construction was initiated on the seaport, Israel imposed continuous impediments to its completion, and it was not finished. The prisoner question was also never adequately resolved. Moreover, though for a time Israel transferred to the PA the taxes it collected from Palestinian laborers in Israel, it later suspended the transfers.

On September 25, 1997, Netanyahu ordered the assassination of another Hamas leader, Khalid Meshal. More than previous assassinations, this one had a variety of unintended consequences. First, it failed when Meshal's bodyguards overcame and captured the Mossad agents involved. Second, was perpetrated in Amman and carried the potential of future Hamas operations outside Israel, whereas heretofore they had been confined to the Occupied Territories and Israel. Third, it revealed Israel's possession of chemical and biological weapons. The assassination attempt involved the injection of a slow-acting agent into

Meshal's ear. So much was at stake that King Hussein of Jordan phoned U.S. President Bill Clinton and demanded that he obtain from Israel the antidote to the poison so that Jordanian doctors could save his life.[81] Meshal survived, but the incident sent shockwaves throughout the territories, compounding tensions and giving rise to unfounded (but nonetheless potent) rumors that Israel was planning to use poison weapons against the population. Yet the critical issue for the Palestinians remained the constantly expanding settlements. Though the Palestinians said so repeatedly, the Israelis seemed unable to come to terms with the fact that they could have land *or* peace but not land *and* peace.

Wye I

Palestinian-Israeli negotiations, suspended in March 1997, remained frozen (except for the CIA-sponsored security talks) for nineteen months. The situation on the ground continued to deteriorate to such an extent that the United States became concerned and persuaded Netanyahu to meet with Arafat in an attempt to break the impasse.[82] President Clinton convened a summit at the Wye Plantation in Maryland, and after difficult negotiations the Wye River Memorandum was signed on October 23, 1998.[83] In it, Israel agreed to redeploy, in three stages, from 13 percent of the West Bank. Each redeployment would be divided into three phases, with the first and the second scheduled and the third unspecified, all conditioned upon the PA's adherence to Israel's security requirements. As with previous agreements, each redeployment was linked to an Israeli evaluation of the PA's performance in fulfilling its security obligations. These entailed a PA commitment to abide by a detailed work plan whereby it promised to cooperate with the CIA and Shin Bet (Israeli intelligence) in tracking down and arresting extremists from Hamas and Islamic Jihad. It included a somewhat nebulous Palestinian commitment to "outlawing and combating terrorist organizations" and "preventing incitement" and a pledge to "systematically and effectively combat" the organizations' infrastructure. This gave the PA sweeping power to detain and arrest anyone for almost anything. The PA was also required to issue a legally binding decree against "all forms of incitement to violence" and to establish mechanisms for acting systematically against all expressions or threats of violence. Arafat further agreed to convene the Palestine National Council to expunge the 1964 Palestinian charter of all clauses that inferred the destruction of Israel.[84] In return for Israel's signature on the agreement, the United States pledged to enhance "Israel's defensive and deterrent capabilities" and upgrade the U.S.-Israeli strategic alliance. Washington also promised to cover the cost of the redeployment, including paying for new bypass roads and infrastructure related to the needs of the settlements.[85] The latter provided perceptible U.S. acceptance of the settlements, in contrast to preceding administrations that had considered them "illegal" and "obstacles to peace." (See Map 2.4.)

Israel fulfilled the first stage of the redeployment but matched it with an equal amount of settlement construction. The PA convened the PNC in Gaza on December 14 and voted to cancel the charter.[86] Despite scrupulous Palestinian adherence to all provisions in the Wye agreement, Israel repudiated it two days later.[87] Netanyahu announced that it was suspending the next two redeployments unless the PA agreed to a set of six additional requirements.[88] Among them, the PA was required to publicly announce that it was "renouncing the intention to declare a state unilaterally"; immediately "take measures against those who violate the anti-incitement order"; immediately jail "at least 22 of the 30 Palestinian wanted fugitives"; "reduc[e] the size of the Palestinian police force to 30,000"; and give an "explicit" public announcement reaffirming Israel's interpretation of the prisoner issue (i.e., "prisoners with blood on their hands will not be released").[89] The PA refused to adhere to the new Israeli demands, and the peace process once again seemed to have reached a dead end.

Palestinians were intensely frustrated at this point not only by the stalled peace process and the worsening economic conditions but also by the failures of their own leadership. The PA had emerged as a corrupt, dictatorial, and repressive regime, which after Wye became even more oppressive (see Chapter 6). The combination of disasters bearing down on Palestinians was explosive.

Wye II

On May 17, 1999, Ehud Barak was elected prime minister. Initially, he sought to put the Palestine question on the back burner and to pursue a treaty with Syria. When Damascus failed to capitulate to Israeli demands regarding a final border, Barak then turned his attention to the Palestinians. Subsequent negotiations centered on reinvigorating the first Wye agreement (Wye I) and resulted in a second Wye agreement (Wye II) on September 4, 1999, signed in the Egyptian city of Sharm al-Sheikh (see Map 2.5).[90] In this memorandum of understanding, Israel agreed to implement, in three stages, the second redeployment specified in the Hebron Protocol. The date and extent of territory of the third redeployment were left unspecified. The agreement also committed the

Map 2.4 The Wye River Memorandum, 1998

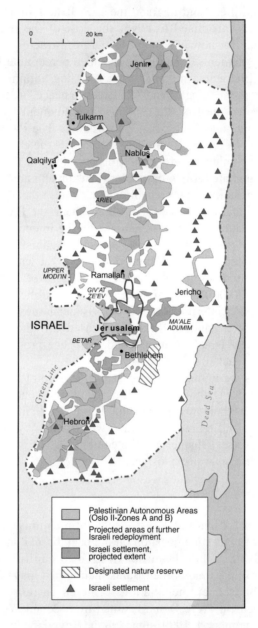

Source: Palestinian Academic Society for the Study of International Affairs (PASSIA), Jerusalem, http://www.passia.org/palestine_facts/MAPS/Wye Memorandum-1998.html. Accessed January 2003. Reprinted with permission of PASSIA.

Map 2.5   The Divisions in the West Bank
Including the Disarticulated
Palestinian Areas and Some
New Israeli Settlements After
Sharm al-Sheikh, 1999

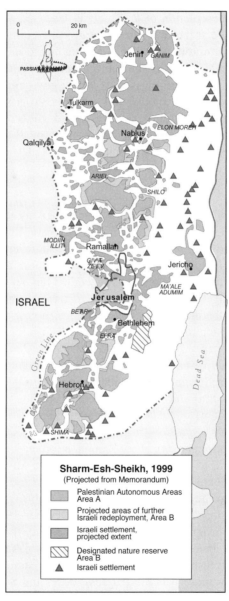

Sharm-Esh-Sheikh, 1999
(Projected from Memorandum)

- Palestinian Autonomous Areas Area A
- Projected areas of further Israeli redeployment, Area B
- Israeli settlement, projected extent
- Designated nature reserve Area B
- ▲ Israeli settlement

Source: Palestinian Academic Society for the Study of International Affairs (PASSIA), Jerusalem, http://www.passia.org/palestine_facts/MAPS/Sharm-Esh-Sheikh-1999.html. Accessed January 2003. Reprinted with permission of PASSIA.

parties to a resumption of final-status negotiations and required Israel to begin the release of Palestinian political prisoners, to facilitate the construction of a safe passage between Gaza and the West Bank, and to permit Palestinian construction of a seaport in Gaza. The PA reagreed to the pledges it made at the first Wye meeting concerning Israel's security. All the Israeli commitments had been negotiated in previous agreements—several as far back as the Cairo agreements of 1994—but had been suspended or canceled by various Israeli governments. In Wye II, as previously, each Israeli pledge was qualified by a series of appendices, modifications, and annexes. Yet Barak, like his predecessor, implemented excessively harsh policies on the ground that further contributed to the misery and impoverishment of the Palestinians.[91]

The Road to Camp David

In the aftermath of Wye II, Barak once again turned his attention to Syria, hoping that with U.S. help he could finalize a treaty; this, however, was an affront to Palestinian sensitivities. Moreover, he reneged on nearly all the commitments he had made in Wye II. The prime minister carried out the first phase of the redeployment as scheduled but delayed implementing the second stage for nearly five months (until March 21, 2000) and never carried out the third stage. Thus, after seven years of negotiations, on the eve of the summit at Camp David, the PA exercised autonomy or self-government over only 18.2 percent of the West Bank. Barak did not release the political prisoners as promised. He refused to honor his promise to transfer to the PA three small villages near Jerusalem (Abu Dis, Al-Eyzaria, and Sawahra) and he approved a rash of house demolitions as well as tenders for new housing in the settlements.[92] He also took no action when settlers began constructing new settlements (euphemistically known as hilltop strongholds). Haim Ramon, a former Labor government minister, characterized Barak in an interview: "Ehud was actually against Oslo, his government abandoned the path for peace."[93]

Barak delayed the commencement of final-status talks by deferring the naming of a lead negotiator until late October 1999. Even then, Israel stalled any progress, and by the end of January the parties were at an impasse.[94] On January 24, 2000, Israel and the PA agreed to begin again with multiple-level (issue-by-issue) final-status negotiations; however, by May there was no progress. After the Syrian track collapsed in March, Barak resumed interest in a settlement with the Palestinians and unilaterally set a deadline of a few months to conclude a final treaty with the PA. President Clinton obliged Barak's interests and convened negotiations between the two sides at Bolling Air Force

Base near Washington, D.C. These talks began on March 21 and ended in deadlock on April 20. Barak pursued another track simultaneously and in secret, in Stockholm, Sweden, that commenced in late April with the redoubtable Abu Ala in charge together with Hassan Asfur and Muhammad Dahlan. On the Israeli side, Internal Security Minister Shlomo Ben Ami and lawyer Gilead Sher presided. Those talks accomplished nothing.

The failure of all these negotiating tracks highlights the fundamental flaws in the Oslo formula; indeed, the impasse stemmed directly from the original DOP and its subsequent incarnations. The Palestinians expected, now that the five-year transition period had passed, that negotiations would be about resolution of the final-status issues based on the assumptions they brought to Oslo at the outset. They wanted an Israeli commitment to withdraw from the Occupied Territories and to dismantle the settlements. They wanted to set final borders for a territorially contiguous and sovereign state in the West Bank, Gaza, and East Jerusalem and to facilitate an acceptable solution to the refugee issue. But Israel's red lines remained as they always had been. From the perspective of the Palestinians, it seemed that seven years of negotiations had been about process rather than substance—which they were. Yet Israel's basic positions had been accommodated in the DOP. If Arafat had hoped that Israel would alter those positions during the interim period, he badly misread Israeli political history. If he genuinely did not comprehend the DOP, that puts him in the company of numerous others, but it excludes him from the group that is considered to include leaders.

President Clinton, at the insistence of Barak, convened a summit at Camp David on July 11, 2000, with the stated aim of resolving all final-status issues and brokering a final peace treaty. Clinton exerted intense pressure on Arafat, who did not want to come (he argued that conditions were not ready for a final agreement—especially because Israel had not yet implemented undertakings agreed to previously).[95] Arafat did, however, elicit a promise from Clinton that if the talks failed the U.S. president would not blame the Palestinians. Clinton, however, did just that in a July 28 appearance on Israeli television.[96] Pundak observes: "The traditional approach of the [U.S.] State Department, which prevailed throughout Barak's tenure, was to adopt the position of the Israeli Prime Minister. . . . The American government seemed sometimes to be working for the Israeli Prime Minister."[97] The summit lasted for two weeks until July 25, when the parties announced that no comprehensive accord could be reached. Much has been made of Barak's generous offers and Arafat's congenital inability to make peace. The following examines what happened at Camp David.

The Camp David Summit

Barak came to Camp David with an ultimatum for Arafat: conclude a final peace treaty on Barak's terms or the alternative "is a situation far grimmer than the status quo."[98] Barak believed that Arafat would have to agree because he (Barak) "could mobilize the world—especially the US—to isolate and weaken the Palestinians if they refused to yield."[99] He demanded that all the interim steps—including the unfulfilled Israeli commitments from Oslo II, Hebron, Wye, and so on—be nullified in lieu of a final settlement with no fallback provisions for further negotiations. On that much all analysts of Camp David agree. Dispute occurs over what Barak offered the Palestinians as a final settlement. There are no official records of Camp David, so much of what appears in the media and elsewhere is speculation—some more informed than others. One commentator, however, was present at the summit—Robert Malley, former special assistant to President Clinton for Arab-Israeli affairs during the Clinton years, accompanied the president to Camp David. Of Israel's allegedly generous offers, Malley has written:

> It is hard to state with confidence how far Barak was actually prepared to go. His strategy was predicated on the belief that Israel ought not to reveal its final positions—not even to the United States—unless and until the endgame was in sight. . . . Strictly speaking, there never was an Israeli offer. . . . The Israelis always stopped one, if not several, steps short of a proposal.[100]

If the United States did not know what Barak was actually offering, neither did the Palestinians. Negotiating in the absence of meticulous proposals and precise maps, and being dependent on ambiguous and shifting positions, would surely be disadvantageous in any situation. The approach provides an interesting contrast to the assiduously detailed documents that accompanied each stage of the interim process. Moreover, in the absence of exactingly enumerated written commitments and maps, anything to which the Palestinians agreed at the summit could have been annulled later by the Israeli government. This, in fact, had been the history of the Oslo agreements. However, it is possible (based primarily on Israeli sources) to reconstruct some of the positions Israel put forward at Camp David. The analysis that follows is based on a compendium of sources; I utilized points only if they were confirmed by two or more sources (see note).[101]

Israel demanded that at least sixty-nine West Bank settlements (Barak was evasive about Gaza) and 85 percent of the settlers would remain, constituting approximately 10 percent of the West Bank. In addition to the settlements, Barak further demanded that certain areas comprising another 10 percent of the territories be under temporary Israeli control for an interim period of not less than twelve years. These included parts of the Jordan Valley and the full border with Jordan, as well as the border with Egypt. In the Jordan Valley (and the surrounding mountain passes), Israel would retain troops, early-warning stations, and military bases. Israel would also retain permanent control of all border crossings (see Maps 2.6 and 2.7).

The Palestinian entity, then, would be bisected by settlement blocs and bypass roads, which would inevitably mean checkpoints, road-blocks, permits, and other troubles. It would consist of four disarticulated cantons on the West Bank: Jericho; a southern canton extending to but not including Abu Dis; a northern area including Nablus, Jenin, and Tulkarm; and a central canton including Ramallah. The Gaza Strip would constitute a fifth canton; it was unclear if Israel would withdraw or if the settlements would remain on the southern coastal region and the northern salient, dividing the strip below Gaza City.

Israel offered no specific proposals on how West Bank water sources would be utilized. Yet the settlement blocs to be annexed to Israel include most of the West Bank water aquifers (one of the main reasons they had been situated there in the first place). The absence of concrete proposals for sharing water, combined with the foregoing, suggests that Israel would continue to control and utilize most West Bank water.

On the question of refugees, Barak would only agree to an unspeci-fied satisfactory solution—not a position Arafat could have presented to his people. The prime minister did make very clear, however, that there could be no right of return. Instead, he spoke about a family reunifica-tion program, to be controlled by Israel, that *might* agree to allow some 10,000 refugees to enter Israel.

On Jerusalem, the prime minister was vague but suggested that Palestinians could have control over Arab neighborhoods in East Jerusalem, although the Jewish and Armenian sectors would remain under Israeli sovereignty. The problems with this proposal, in addition to carving up the Old City, are apparent to anyone who has visited East Jerusalem: there are no more all-Palestinian neighborhoods because since 1967 Israel has implanted, house by house, small Jewish enclaves in every district. Moreover, Israel demanded to retain sovereignty over the Haram al-Sharif, though the Palestinians might be permitted some undefined religious supervision over the holy sites. Most astonishingly with regard to Jerusalem, Barak insisted that Israel would construct a Jewish synagogue on the Harem al-Sharif within the boundaries of the Muslim sacred compound.[102]

Map 2.6   Barak's "Generous Offer" at Camp David (2000) Showing the Division of Palestinian Areas into Cantons Bisected by Settler Bypass Roads

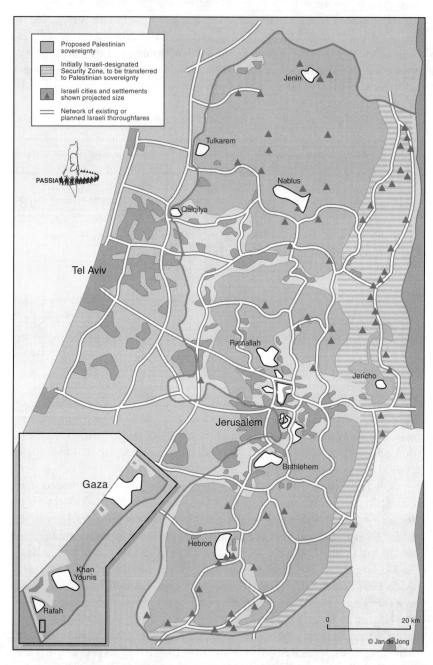

■ Proposed Palestinian sovereignty

▨ Initially Israeli-designated Security Zone, to be transferred to Palestinian sovereignty

▲ Israeli cities and settlements shown projected size

= Network of existing or planned Israeli thoroughfares

PASSIA

Jenin

Tulkarem

Nablus

Qalqilya

Tel Aviv

Ramallah

Jericho

Jerusalem

Bethlehem

Gaza

Hebron

Khan Younis

Rafah

0   20 km

© Jan de Jong

Source: Palestinian Academic Society for the Study of International Affairs (PASSIA), Jerusalem, http://www.passia.org/palestine_facts/MAPS/1wbgs_campdavid.html. Accessed January 2003. Reprinted with permission of PASSIA.

Map 2.7 The Gaza Strip: Jewish Settlements and Major Palestinian Population Centers

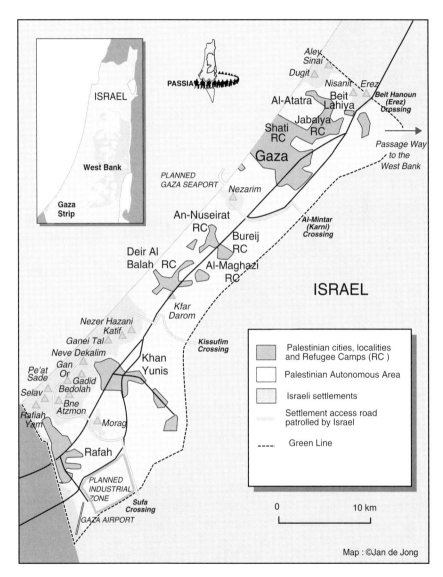

ISRAEL

West Bank

Gaza
Strip

Aley
Sinai
Dugit
Nisanit   Erez
PASSIA
Al-Atatra   Beit   Beit Hanoun
Lahiya   (Erez)
Crossing
Jabalya
Shati   RC
RC
Gaza
PLANNED
GAZA SEAPORT   Nezarim
Passage Way
to the
West Bank

An-Nuseirat
RC
Bureij
RC
Deir Al
Balah RC
Al-Maghazi
RC

Al-Mintar
(Karni)
Crossing

ISRAEL

Kfar
Darom
Nezer Hazani
Katif
Ganei Tal
Neve Dekalim
Pe'at   Gan
Sade   Or
Selav   Gadid
Bedolah
Bne
Atzmon
Rafiah   Morag
Yam
Rafah

Khan
Yunis

Kissufim
Crossing

PLANNED
INDUSTRIAL
ZONE   Sufa
Crossing
GAZA AIRPORT

	Palestinian cities, localities and Refugee Camps (RC)
	Palestinian Autonomous Area
	Israeli settlements
	Settlement access road patrolled by Israel
-----	Green Line

0   10 km

Map : ©Jan de Jong

Source: Palestinian Academic Society for the Study of International Affairs (PASSIA), Jerusalem, http://www.passia.org/palestine_facts/MAPS/gaza-2000.html. Accessed January 2003. Reprinted with permission of PASSIA.

Mainstream analysts of the fiasco that was Camp David—even those who are willing to question the line that Arafat was to blame—place the collapse on issues of process. They conclude that the problems were poor timing, bad chemistry and mistrust, mutual misunderstandings, political missteps, tactical clumsiness, electoral deadlines, miscommunication, insufficient communication, and the like. All of these were present. Yet in the final analysis, Camp David failed not because of procedural mistakes but because Israel remained unwilling, after seven years of interim agreements, to come to terms with the minimal requirements of Palestinian nationalist aspirations.

The Peace Process: Peace or Merely Process?

Analyzing the failure of the Oslo process from the perspective of the Palestinians suggests several conclusions. There are numerous problems in each document concerning every issue. At the most fundamental level, however, each arises from the enormous power imbalance between Israel and the PLO. Power asymmetries were always unequal, but the PLO entered the process at one of the lowest points in its history. Conversely, Israel was at the apex of its political and military achievements, and it enjoyed a full strategic partnership with the United States. Thus, the PLO could not influence even the most basic elements for peace in the DOP framework, and with every new agreement Israel was able to extract additional concessions. Moreover, when Israel failed to implement the agreements to which it did commit itself, the Palestinians were powerless to compel it to do so or to make it pay a price for noncompliance.

The DOP provided the structure for all subsequent agreements, and it essentially grew out of the warm personal relations that developed at Oslo between Abu Ala and Uri Savir. Nevertheless, Savir was a highly skilled lawyer accustomed to dealing with the details of international agreements. Abu Ala was an economist with no legal background. The DOP was ambiguous enough to convince Abu Ala, Abu Mazen, and Arafat that it was the first step, on a direct road, to a sovereign independent Palestinian state in the West Bank, Gaza, and East Jerusalem. Yet thanks to the legal expertise of Savir, it contained all the legal safeguards necessary to protect Israel's interests and prevent such a state from coming into being. The fact that this—warm, trusting personal relations—is a deeply flawed approach to conducting negotiations over the future of ones' people is obvious.

Another aspect of the DOP that hurt the Palestinians was the separation of interim from final status. This put them at an enormous disadvantage: the Palestinians did not actually know what they were negotiating about because Israel was not being clear, at least in a legal sense, concerning what the final status was to be. In the end, the separation permitted Israel to unilaterally determine the nature of the final outcome. Additionally, in practice, separating the two stages allowed Israel to indefinitely prolong even the initiation of final-status talks (contrasted with the five-year interim period stipulated in the DOP) in what some analysts have termed a policy of the permanence of temporary arrangements. It also bought Israel time to construct massive new facts on the ground.

Substantively, the most important defect in the DOP by far is that it is not based on any aspect of international law or UN resolutions relating to the Israeli-Palestinian conflict. There is no mention in the DOP of occupation, self-determination, UN Resolutions 181 and 194, or any other of the relevant UN resolutions—for example, UN Resolutions 2253 (on Jerusalem); 2535B (setting forth the inalienable rights of the Palestinians); 2649 (affirming Palestinian right to self-determination); 2851 (condemning settlements as illegal, etc.); 3236 (reaffirming the Palestinian rights to self-determination, sovereignty, refugees' right of return); and many others.[103] Indeed, by surrendering inclusion of the supporting UN resolutions, the Palestinian positions were immeasurably weakened. There is also a glaring failure in the DOP to mention any of the significant provisions in the body of international law that bear specifically on this conflict (e.g., the 1949 Fourth Geneva Convention, which specifies the status and treatment of persons in occupied territories, the Universal Declaration of Human Rights, and others).[104] Consequently, because the DOP is not based on law, rights, or precedent but on a political agreement between two parties that are *depicted* as symmetrical, the Palestinians had no recourse to the international legal instruments that should have been available to them.

Resolution 181 (the original partition resolution) provided the basis in law for an independent Palestinian state. Resolution 194 stipulated the right of refugees to return or to receive compensation, and its absence permitted the complete exclusion of the refugee problem. The DOP did not clarify its reference to UN Security Council Resolution 242 (stating the inadmissibility of the acquisition of territory by force and calling for Israeli withdrawal from the territories occupied in the 1967 war). However, rather than reflecting the consensual understanding of the international community, it was worded in such a way—constructive ambiguity—that Israel's interpretation prevailed (i.e., Israel was not required to withdraw from *all* the Occupied Territories). This meant that Palestinians were in the position of having to bargain over how much and from which areas Israel would withdraw.

Additionally, Israel's substitution of the term *disputed* for *occupied* in reference to the territories in effect excused it from its obligations under international law as an occupying power. The new phrase rendered irrelevant the major legal instruments noted above to which Palestinians had recourse under conditions of occupation. There is also no mention in the DOP of the Palestinian right to self-determination—a right specifically enshrined in numerous UN resolutions—in addition to the general right of oppressed peoples to self-determination. Again, the PLO forfeited the potential to make use of these international norms and laws in its negotiations with Israel. The failure to ground the DOP in international legal instruments also resulted in the loss of recourse for the Palestinians when Israel violated Palestinian rights subsequent to Oslo (e.g., land confiscation, settlement expansion, house demolitions, ill treatment of prisoners, and collective punishment).[105]

An additional significant failure of the DOP was that no provision was made for an impartial mediator in the event that Israel failed to fulfill its obligations. Thus, the United States, with Israel's blessing, assumed the role of "honest broker" yet unequivocally supported Israel throughout.

Finally, the Oslo process fell victim to the tyranny of security. Israel continuously demanded that the Palestinians *guarantee* Israel's security—a somewhat odd demand considering the vast resources Israel holds to maximize Israeli security and the utter insecurity of Palestinians. Nevertheless, every time one or two individuals from the territories (even from areas under Israeli control) perpetrated an act of violence, Israel used the security requirement to claim that the PA had failed to carry out its obligations under Oslo. Israel then wrapped itself in self-righteousness and proceeded to suspend negotiations, halt redeployments, construct new settlements, impose curfews, delay safe passage, impose closures, and so on.[106] The most important issue that fell victim to the flaws of Oslo is that of the refugees.

The Refugees and the Right of Return

The dispossessed refugees from 1948 are at the heart of the Palestine question (see Chapter 1). The major international legitimation for refugee rights is UN General Assembly Resolution 194 (III) of 1949, which calls for either repatriation of or compensation to the refugees.[107]

The same resolution established the UN Palestine Conciliation Commission, which set guidelines for future negotiations on the refugees as well as for Jerusalem and the boundaries of the Palestinian and Jewish states in Palestine.[108] The UN General Assembly has reaffirmed Resolution 194 regularly during each session, with the exception of 1951. It has also expressed regret over its nonimplementation. (Of note, the United States voted for the resolution annually until 1993—the start of the peace process.) There have been additional UN General Assembly resolutions supporting Palestinian refugee rights, as well as a host of additional rights.[109] For example, in 1996 the UN General Assembly, in Resolution A/RES/51/129, reaffirmed that

> Palestinian Arab refugees are entitled to their property and to the income derived therefrom, in conformity with the principles of justice and equity. [It] requests the secretary-general to take all appropriate steps . . . for the protection of Arab property, assets, and property rights in Israel and to preserve and modernize the existing records.[110]

There are other major legal instruments that support the Palestinians' right of return.[111] These include the 1951 Geneva Convention Relating to the Status of Refugees and its 1967 Refugee Protocol; the 1954 Convention Relating to the Status of Stateless Persons; and the 1961 Convention on the Elimination or Reduction of Statelessness.[112] Additionally, there are specific provisions concerning refugee rights in numerous other international documents that apply to the Palestinians. These include the 1949 Fourth Geneva Convention; the Universal Declaration of Human Rights (article 13.2): "Everyone has the right to leave any country, including his own, and to return to his country"; the Convention on the Elimination of all Forms of Racial Discrimination (article 5[d] [11]): "A state may not deny, on racial or ethnic grounds, the opportunity to return to one's country"; the International Covenant on Civil and Political Rights (article 12.4): "No one shall be arbitrarily deprived of the right to enter his own country"; and the Human Rights Committee, in particular its general comment on article 12 of the International Covenant on Civil and Political Rights (the Human Rights Committee monitors implementation of this covenant).[113] Finally, the two major human rights organizations globally—Amnesty International and Human Rights Watch—support the Palestinian right of return. They explicitly base their positions on the aforementioned international legal instruments. In March 2001, Amnesty International issued a policy statement on the Palestinian refugees' right of return:

With regard to the specific issue of Palestinian exiles, Amnesty International believes. . . . Their right to return has been recognized by the United Nations since UN General Assembly Resolution 194 (III). . . . The right of Palestinians to return continues to be recognized by authoritative bodies within the UN system for the protection of human rights. In March 1998, the Committee on the Elimination of Racial Discrimination . . . was unequivocal about the obligations of Israel in relation to the right of return of the Palestinians. It stated: "The right of many Palestinians to return and possess their homes in Israel is currently denied. The State party should give high priority to remedying this situation. Those who cannot repossess their homes should be entitled to compensation." The UN General Assembly Resolution A/RES/51/129 of December 1996 affirms that "Palestinian Arab refugees are entitled to their property and to the income derived therefrom . . . reaffirms the right of all persons displaced as a result of the June 1967 and subsequent hostilities to return to their homes or former places of residence in the territories occupied by Israel since 1967." . . . Amnesty International calls for Palestinians who fled or were expelled from Israel, the West Bank or Gaza Strip [from 1948 onward], along with those of their descendants . . . to be able to exercise their right of return. . . . Where possible, Palestinians should be able to return to their original home or lands. If this is not possible— because they no longer exist, have been converted to other uses . . . they should be allowed to return to the vicinity of their original home. Palestinians who choose not to exercise their right to return should receive compensation for lost property.[114]

Human Rights Watch likewise issued a declaration in 2001; it states:

Human Rights Watch has long defended the right of refugees and exiles to return to their homes. . . . Human Rights Watch similarly urges that this right be recognized for all displaced people in the Middle East, regardless of religion or nationality. In the case of the peace agreement currently being negotiated [between Israel and the Palestinians], the agreement should recognize this right for Palestinian refugees and exiles from territory located in what is now Israel. . . . This right is held not only by those who fled a territory initially but also by their descendants. . . . The right persists even when sovereignty over the territory is contested or has changed hands. If a former home no longer exists or is occupied by an innocent third party, return should be permitted to the vicinity of the former home. As in the case of all displaced persons, those unable to return to a former home because it is occupied or has been destroyed, or those who have lost property, are entitled to compensation. However compensation is not a substitute for the right of return. . . . Like all rights, the right of return binds governments. No government can violate this right. Only individuals can elect not to exercise it.[115]

It thus seems fair to say that many within the international community support the right of Palestinians to return to their homes or to be compensated for their losses.[116]

The Israeli Position

From the outset, Israel has made its position on the refugees perfectly clear: it bears no responsibility for their fate, it will not permit their return, and it will pay no compensation for confiscated property. Successive prime ministers consistently reiterated this stance, and Barak's proposals at Camp David reflected it as well. From 1949 through the Oslo process, Israel has not deviated from this stance.

The basis of this rejectionism is far more complex than mere political stubbornness. It resides in the concept of a Jewish people. This construct is a Zionist-Israeli legislative and juridical claim that defines Israel not as the state of its citizens but as the state of the Jewish People. Government of Israel "Guidelines" state: "The Jewish people have an eternal, historic right to the Land of Israel, the inalienable inheritance of our forefathers."[117]

The concept is defined to include every Jew anywhere on the globe. It is codified in the Basic Law of Return, which provides that every Jew in the world has an automatic right of return by virtue of being Jewish and upon return is immediately granted Israeli citizenship with full rights under the law. Non-Jews, even those born in the country, are thus excluded from the right of return. Israel's mission, according to the Jewish people, is the in-gathering of world Jewry. Moreover, because it is the state of the Jewish people, Israel argues that allowing Palestinians to return would "endanger the *Jewish* character of the State."[118] This demographic concern goes to the heart of the Israeli stance. Complicating the issue even more is the belief among religious Jews (and some right-wing nonreligious Jews) that the West Bank—Judea and Samaria, as they have renamed it—constitutes the *real* Land of Israel—the Eretz Yisrael of biblical times, the original home of the Jewish people. Returning this land to non-Jews is, for such people, unthinkable.

Thus, for most Israeli Jews, the Palestinians have no right of return. Because Israel is a Jewish state, permitting Palestinians to return would undermine that Jewish exclusivity and character. This position has a further dimension: the issue of transfer, that is, the expulsion from the State of Israel (including the Occupied Territories) of the Palestinians currently residing there.

Some Israeli intellectuals, as well as a larger group of Palestinian intellectuals and nonallied individuals, believe that the most just and equitable solution is for Jews and Arabs—and others—to live together as equal citizens of a genuinely democratic secular state in Palestine/ Israel. It is interesting to observe that the majority of Jews living in the Diaspora today (greater than the number of Jews in Israel), though professing unquestioning loyalty to Israel, have chosen to live in secular democratic states—the United States in particular but also Britain, France, and throughout the Western democracies.

As noted, in the DOP the refugee issue was relegated to final-status talks, and before departing for the 2000 Camp David summit, Prime Minister Barak declared that Israel would not accept the right of return or UN Resolution 194. In a press conference following the failure of the summit, Barak stated that Israel bore no responsibility for the refugee problem because the Arab world had started the 1948 war and had called on the Palestinians to leave the country.[119]

On January 1, 2001, the Knesset enacted legislation on securing the denial of the right of return by a vote of 56-12. The law prohibits any prime minister "from committing to or making an agreement" for the repatriation of Palestinian refugees without first securing approval by at least sixty-one members of the Knesset.[120] A caveat entitles the interior minister, with the consent of the defense minister and the Knesset's Foreign Affairs and Defense Committee, to set guidelines for refugees to enter the country each year based on humanitarian considerations. After the final vote (on the third reading), Yisrael Katz, a member of the Knesset, declared that the law "would ensure that Israel remains a Jewish and democratic state."[121] Clearly, it will ensure the former.

The Palestinian Position

Prior to the outbreak of the 1987 intifada in the Occupied Territories, the focus of the PLO's activities; its social, political, and guerrilla base; and its most devoted constituency had been the refugees in the camps in Jordan, Lebanon, and Syria. Moreover, as a national movement, it represented all the refugee (and nonrefugee) Palestinian constituencies. The intifada, however, shifted the focus of the PLO's attention to the Occupied Territories, and the international diplomacy that followed (i.e., the U.S.-PLO dialogue, the Madrid conference, and the DOP and the subsequent Oslo process) sharpened that focus. As a consequence, the refugee question was sidelined in the heady quest for statehood, and Arafat appeared to forget that he was the representative of *all* Palestinians throughout the diaspora. During the seven years of the Oslo process, the only places the refugee question appeared to have salience were in international forums in Europe and the United States (and, of course, among the refugees themselves).

Traditionally, the PLO has been unwavering in its insistence on the refugees' right of return according to UN Resolution 194. Yet in spite of that resolution and the additional very strong international instruments supporting the Palestinians' right of return, the PA was induced during the Oslo process to adopt a position of so-called pragmatism, or realism. This shift was primarily the result of three factors: the PA's weakness vis-à-vis Israel in the negotiations; the absence of any of the relevant legal referents in the DOP; and intense Israeli and U.S. pressure. Officially, Yasser Arafat continues to maintain that the right of return must be part of any final settlement. Yet he has authorized numerous close advisers to make statements compromising that right, for example, by suggesting that if Israel recognizes the right of return in principle, in practice the refugees can return to the Palestinian state in the West Bank and Gaza.[122] Other officials have suggested that once the Palestinian state comes into being, refugees in the diaspora could be given passports issued by the Palestinian state so that they would be "emigrant communities," residing outside of Palestine.[123] Sari Nusseibeh, whom Arafat appointed as the PA's Jerusalem affairs representative after Faisal Husseini's death, published an article in *Ha'aretz* stating that "it is clear that Israel will not accept the Palestinian demand that four million refugees return to within its borders, after a Palestinian state is established beside it. Therefore we Palestinians must formulate a solution which takes this refusal into account."[124] In October 2002, Nusseibeh and Ami Ayalon (former head of the Israeli intelligence services) toured the United States promoting an agreement they signed in September that renounced the right of return except to a new Palestinian state.[125] Palestinian academic Rashid Khalidi wrote that the issue for Palestinians is

> to determine whether a *symbolic* acceptance that an injustice has been done to the Palestinian people, via acceptance of the right of return in principle, combined with an attempt to right it, via implementation of this right in some specific and clearly defined fashion, will satisfy a sufficient number of Palestinians, while remaining acceptable to a sufficient number of Israelis, to constitute a viable solution to this question.[126]

Khalidi lists a variety of possible solutions to the refugee problem, all of which involve significant compromises to the right of return.

Finally, Mahmoud Abbas (Abu Mazen), architect of the DOP and close adviser to Yasser Arafat, in the October 1995 secret agreement with Beilin, effectively signed away refugee rights. Though the document remained secret and unofficial, it became the model for the set of understandings that constituted the framework for the negotiations at Taba in January 2000.[127] Article 7.1 of the Beilin–Abu Mazen secret agreement states:

> Whereas the Palestinian side considers that the right of the Palestinian Refugees to return to their homes is enshrined in international law and natural justice, it recognizes that the prerequisites of the new era of peace and co-existence, as well as the realities that have been created on the ground since 1948, have rendered the implementation of this right impractical. The Palestinian side thus declares its readiness to accept and implement policies and measures that will ensure, in so far as this is possible, the welfare and well being of these refugees.[128]

Put simply, the PA sacrificed universally acknowledged refugee rights and the most fundamental interest of millions of its people for an illusory Palestinian state. It is one more issue on which the Palestinians have had to compromise—this time to abandon—their objectives.[129]

Yet because of the enormous significance of the refugee question to all sectors of the Palestinian community—those in the Occupied Territories as well as throughout the diaspora—the PA's capitulation on this issue contributed to the disaffection and disillusionment of West Bank and Gaza Strip Palestinians with Arafat and the PA (see Chapter 6). Additionally, Israel's intransigence on the refugee question is perceived among Palestinians as proof that Israel does not want real peace and that its engagement in the Oslo process was a sham from the outset. All of this has added fuel to the uprising.

What Will Be the Fate of the Refugees?

The refugee question will be resolved based on the parameters set by Israel and the United States. *Ha'aretz* revealed exactly what those limitations were. They include the following: Israel will assume no blame or moral responsibility for the refugee situation; at most, it will express regret for the suffering the conflict has caused the Palestinian people. But as Barak stated, "This will not, under any circumstances, be based on an expression of guilt or responsibility." Some of the refugees will be permitted to return to the new Palestinian state should one ever emerge. But Israel will determine the number of those allowed to return—it may even vet each personally—and it will supervise the process of return in a joint committee with the Palestinians. The vast majority of the refugees will be rehabilitated where they now reside. Israeli foreign minister David Levy stated in this regard: "They must be rehabilitated in the places they live in order not to create a situation that could blow up later on."[130]

An international body will be set up to compensate and rehabilitate the refugees. Israel will participate in this organization, but only in a symbolic way. According to Barak, Israel does not have sufficient financial resources to contribute monetarily, so the economic burden of solving the refugee problem will fall largely on the shoulders of the international community. Israel will, however, have a major influential role in the organization in the allocation of funds that it can use as a lever for policy and economic pressure. There will be no personal/individual compensation to the refugees; rather, funds will be used for the collective rehabilitation of the refugees, the dismantling of the camps and the construction of permanent housing, and the development of sources of employment and welfare services. The compensation arrangement will be final; the refugees will be unable to make further claims on Israel. The United Nations Relief and Works Agency for Palestinians will be dismantled.[131]

The Road to the Al-Aqsa Intifada: The Mitchell Commission and the Final Talks at Taba

A month after the collapse of talks at Camp David, Barak provided Ariel Sharon with 1,200 heavily armed riot police and permission to lead a delegation of Likud officials on a tour of the Haram al-Sharif. It was another provocative Israeli declaration of sovereignty over all of Jerusalem, and Palestinians were outraged by it. Young men on the Haram al-Sharif threw stones and sandals at the riot police, who responded with tear gas and rubber bullets. Twenty-four Palestinians were seriously injured. The following day, September 29 (a Friday, the Muslim day of communal prayer), Israel stationed 2,000 IDF sharpshooters and riot police around the Haram. Demonstrations and protests erupted in Jerusalem and spread throughout the West Bank and Gaza. At day's end, six Palestinians were dead and dozens injured. So began the Al-Aqsa intifada that continues to this day.

On October 16–17, President Bill Clinton, in an attempt to quell the violence and restore Israel's security, orchestrated a summit in Sharm al-Sheikh.[132] This meeting produced a truce between the PA and Israel, as well as an agreement to cooperate with a fact-finding committee that came to be known as the Mitchell Commission—under the stewardship of former U.S. Senator George Mitchell. Six days later, however, on October 22, Barak announced that the peace process was suspended. On November 7, Peres and Arafat met, unsuccessfully, to try to implement the Sharm al-Sheikh truce. Both of these efforts failed as a consequence of the basic Israeli approach to the uprising: Israel viewed the Al-Aqsa intifada as a security crisis rather than as a symptom of a political exigency. Instead of recognizing the futility of obstructing the needs and rights of the Palestinian people, Tel Aviv considered only how to employ force to suppress the uprising.[133]

Then, on December 21, 2000, Clinton summoned Israeli and Palestinian leaders to Bolling Air Force Base in preparation for a peace initiative he was about to announce. On December 23, the U.S. president gave both sides his plan for a final-status treaty.[134] On January 21, 2001, in Taba, Egypt, Israel and the PA opened talks based on the Clinton parameters for a final settlement.[135] The positions of the two sides were not formally codified; thus, there have been many interpretations as to exactly what was agreed to (and what was not) at Taba. In February 2002, the European Union (EU) released a document that outlined the positions of each side on permanent-status issues at Taba. The paper has no official status, but according to the European Union, both parties acknowledged that it was a relatively fair representation of their side's proposals.[136] According to the EU document, both sides made concessions they had previously eschewed, but because all this exists in the realm of the theoretical, it is difficult to evaluate the meaning of the positions—none of which, in any case, were radical departures from Camp David. After suspending the negotiations for two days in the midst of the January 21–27 talks because two Israelis were killed, Israel withdrew entirely on January 27. The following day, Barak repudiated all the Israeli proposals made at Taba, terming them "null and void."[137] Once again, Israel and the United States blamed Arafat for the failure despite the fact that he had not rejected the U.S.-Israeli proposals. Israel held elections on February 6, 2001, Barak was defeated, and Ariel Sharon was elected prime minister. No further negotiations were held between Israel and the Palestinians, and the violence escalated.

The Oslo Peace Process: Victim of Power Disparities

The massive power imbalance between Israel and the PLO/PA resulted in agreement after agreement that served Israel's interests and compromised Palestinian objectives. At the same time, disparities allowed Israel to dictate policies and undertake unilateral actions on the ground that violated both the letter and the spirit of the peace accords. Israel imposed closures and curfews; confiscated Palestinian land; restricted Palestinian water usage; constructed new settlements and settler bypass roads; prohibited workers from entering Israel; demolished houses; and in general created a serious deterioration in the living conditions of the Palestinians in the West Bank, Gaza, and East Jerusalem. The PA was powerless to stop any of these actions or even to undertake initiatives of its own to pressure Israel. Moreover, by the end of the seven-year peace process, many Palestinians perceived Arafat and the PA as functioning solely as Israel's policemen—arresting Israel's most-wanted and attempting to ensure Israel's security. In Chapter 3, I investigate Israeli policies in the West Bank, Gaza, and East Jerusalem that created enormous hardships for the Palestinians.

Notes

1. Amira Hass, "Reality as Presented by the Ruled," *Ha'aretz* (Jerusalem, daily, English), August 8, 2001.

2. Edward Said, "Occupation Is the Atrocity," *al-Ahram* (Cairo, weekly, English), August 16–22, 2001.

3. An excellent comparison of the military asymmetries between the PA and Israel in the al-Aqsa intifada is provided by Amira Hass, "Here Is the Real Balance of Power," *Ha'aretz,* August 15, 2001. Also see "Israel Manufactures Chemical and Biological Weapons," *Yediot Ahronot* (Israel, daily, Hebrew), September 14, 1998, translated in *News from Within* (Israel, monthly, English) 14, no. 10 (November 1998): 31.

4. For an analysis of the failure of Madrid, see Naseer Aruri, *The Obstruction of Peace: The U.S., Israel, and the Palestinians* (Monroe, ME: Common Courage Press, 1995), pp. 169–216, and Camille Mansour, "The Palestinian-Israeli Peace Negotiations: An Overview and Assessment," *Journal of Palestine Studies* 22, no. 3 (spring 1993): 5–31.

5. Avi Shlaim, *The Iron Wall: Israel and the Arab World* (New York: W. W. Norton, 2000), pp. 517 and 518.

6. An excellent book that dissects the original myths and shows their continuity over time is Zeev Sternhell, *The Founding Myths of Israel: Nationalism, Socialism, and the Making of the Jewish State* (Princeton: Princeton University Press, 1998).

7. Shlaim, *The Iron Wall*, p. 523.

8. Ran HaCohen, "Mideast War—Really Imminent?" available online at anti-war.com, accessed July 24, 2001.

9. Yisrael Harel, "Its Roots are Not in the Left," *Ha'aretz,* January 23, 2003.

10. See Yossi Beilin, *Touching Peace: From the Oslo Accord to a Final*

Agreement (London: Weidenfeld and Nicolson, 1999), pp. 155–56 and 214, and Avi Shlaim, "Prelude to the Accord: Likud, Labor, and the Palestinians," *Journal of Palestine Studies* 23, no. 2 (winter 1994): 5–19.

11. Beilin, *Touching Peace*, pp. 62–63.

12. Ibid., pp. 68–75.

13. In his book on the Oslo process, Abu Mazen provides literal transcripts of the meetings among Abu Ala and the Israelis. Mahmoud `Abbas (Abu Mazen), *Through Secret Channels* (Reading, UK: Garnet, 1995). Beilin, *Touching Peace*, and Uri Savir, *The Process: 1,100 Days That Changed the Middle East* (New York: Vintage Books, 1999), are crucial for understanding the Israeli side.

14. Avi Shlaim, "The Oslo Accord," *Journal of Palestine Studies* 23, no. 3 (spring 1994): 24–40.

15. Said K. Aburish, *Arafat: From Defender to Dictator* (London: Bloomsbury, 1998), p. 255.

16. For the text of these four documents and supporting materials, see *Journal of Palestine Studies* 23, no. 1 (autumn 1993): 111–124. For an excellent analysis of the four, see Burhan Dajani, "The September 1993 Israeli-PLO Documents: A Textual Analysis," *Journal of Palestine Studies* 23, no. 3 (spring 1994): 5–23. For a PLO defense of the agreement, see Nabil Shaath, "Interview: The Oslo Agreement," *Journal of Palestine Studies* 23, no. 1 (autumn 1993): 5–13. For the Palestinian opposition, see Haydar `Abd al-Shafi (head of the Palestinian delegation to Madrid), "Interview: The Oslo Agreement," *Journal of Palestine Studies* 23, no. 1 (autumn 1993): 14–19.

17. See, for example, Meron Benvenisti, *Intimate Enemies: Jews and Arabs in a Shared Land* (Berkeley: University of California Press, 1995), pp. 171, 173.

18. Israeli labor minister Yigal Allon devised the Allon Plan in the aftermath of the June 1967 Six Day War. It became the unofficial bottom line of the Labor Party (Likud often had more ambitious objectives) regarding the West Bank thereafter. See Benvenisti, *Intimate Enemies*, pp. 61–66, and Shlaim, *The Iron Wall*, pp. 256–258 and 262–264.

19. Rabin is also quoted as saying: "I prefer the Palestinians to cope with the problem of enforcing order in the Gaza [Strip]. The Palestinians will be better at it than we were because they will allow no appeals to the Supreme Court and will prevent the [Israeli] Association for Civil Rights from criticizing the conditions there by denying it access to the area. They will rule there by their own methods, freeing—and this is most important—the Israeli army soldiers from having to do what they will do." *Yediot Ahronot* (Israel, daily, Hebrew), September 7, 1993, translated by Aruri, *The Obstruction of Peace*, p. 210.

20. Avi Shlaim, "The Oslo Accord," *Journal of Palestine Studies* 23, no. 3 (spring 1994): 31–32 (emphasis added).

21. David Makovsky, in *Making Peace with the PLO: The Rabin Government's Road to the Oslo Accord* (Boulder: Westview, 1996), argues that the desire to use the PLO to counter Hamas and Islamic Jihad was the main factor motivating Rabin.

22. Sternhell, *The Founding Myths of Israel*, p. 339.

23. Aburish, *Arafat: From Defender to Dictator*, p. 254. Other biographies of Arafat include Andrew Gowers and Tony Walker, *Behind the Myth: Yasir Arafat and the Palestinian Revolution* (New York: Olive Branch, 1992);

and Alan Hart, *Arafat: Terrorist or Peacemaker?* (London: Sidwick and Jackson, 1984).

24. Edward W. Said, *Peace and Its Discontents: Gaza-Jericho, 1993–1995* (New York: Vintage, 1995), p. 36.

25. See, for example, the analysis by Joseph Massad, "Return or Permanent Exile?" in Naseer Aruri, ed., *Palestinian Refugees: The Right of Return* (London: Pluto, 2001), pp. 106–107.

26. For analyses of the prisoner issue, see Allegra Pacheco, "The Train That Passed Them By: Oslo and the Release of Palestinian Political Prisoners," *Challenge*, no. 47 (January–February, 1998); Yifat Susskind, "Palestinian Political Prisoners," *Middle East Report* (fall 1996); Joel Beinin, "The Oslo Process—Back on Track?" *MERIP Press Information Notes*, PIN 8 (October 7, 1999); Stephen Sosebee, "Tension Builds Over 3,500 Palestinian Prisoners Israel Holds in Defiance of Its Oslo Commitments," *Washington Report on Middle East Affairs* (May/June 1998); and Allegra Pacheco, "The Prison Factory: An Interview with Adv. Allegra Pacheco," *Between the Lines* (Jerusalem, Israeli-Palestinian monthly, English), July 2001.

27. For a legal analysis of the Oslo Accords and their subsequent agreements, see Raja Shehadeh, *From Occupation to Interim Accords: Israel and the Palestinian Territories,* Cimel Book Series, no. 4 (London: Kluwer Law International/Academic Publishers, 1997).

28. "Israeli-PLO Declaration of Principles, Washington, D.C., 13 September 1993," *Journal of Palestine Studies* 23, no. 1 (autumn 1993): 115–121.

29. For an analysis of the DOP, see Laura Drake, "Between the Lines: A Textual Analysis of the Gaza-Jericho Agreement," *Arab Studies Quarterly* 16, no. 4 (fall 1994): 1–36.

30. See Yasser Abed Rabbo (who became minister of culture and information in the PA), "Is Oslo Dead? What Went Wrong?" Direct submission, *Palestine Media Center*, September 22, 2001. He discusses the extremely negative consequences for the Palestinians resulting from their reliance on the trust and goodwill that developed among the negotiators of the DOP in Oslo rather than insisting on exacting clauses, distinct maps, and the like. Savir, in *The Process,* refers repeatedly to the "warm" relations among the negotiators.

31. "Yitzhak Rabin, Statement to Knesset on Israeli-Palestinian Declaration of Principles, Jerusalem, 21 September, 1993," reprinted in *Journal of Palestine Studies* 23, no. 2 (winter 1994): 138–141.

32. Shlaim, *The Iron Wall*, p. 600.

33. Beilin, *Touching Peace*, p. 3.

34. Shlaim, *The Iron Wall*, p. 600.

35. Ze'ev Schiff, "The Mistakes of Oslo," *Ha'aretz*, September 14, 2001.

36. See "Israel-PLO Partial Agreements on Implementation of Declaration of Principles, Cairo, 9 February 1994," in *Journal of Palestine Studies* 23, no. 3 (spring 1994): 147–151.

37. Shlaim, *The Iron Wall*, p. 524.

38. "Yitzhak Rabin, Speech to the Knesset on Gaza-Jericho Agreement, Jerusalem, 11 May 1994 (excerpts)," *Journal of Palestine Studies* 24, no. 1 (autumn 1994): 141–143 (emphasis added).

39. A very good detailed summary of the event is Palestine Human Rights

Information Center, *The Massacre in al-Haram al-Ibrahimi al-Sharif: Context and Aftermath* (Jerusalem: Palestine Human Rights Information Center, 1994).

40. Ministry of Foreign Affairs, *Suicide and Car Bomb Attacks in Israel Since the Declaration of Principles (September 1993)* (Government of Israel, June 2002), and Elizabeth Rubin, "The Most Wanted Palestinian," *New York Times*, June 30, 2002.

41. For good background on Israeli objectives in Hebron, see the Israeli historian Sternhell, *The Founding Myths of Israel*, pp. 318–339.

42. "Israel-PLO Agreement on the Gaza Strip and the Jericho Area, Cairo, 4 May 1994," in *Journal of Palestine Studies* 3, no. 4 (summer 1994): 118–126 (partial). Also see "Special Document: Israel-PLO Protocol on Economic Relations, Paris, 29 April 1994," *Journal of Palestine Studies* 3, no. 4 (summer 1994): 103–118. The full text and annexes of these and all other documents are available online at Israeli Ministry of Foreign Affairs, "The Peace Process: Reference Documents" (hereinafter Israeli Ministry of Foreign Affairs online documents).

43. For a detailed analysis of this accord, see Said, *Peace and Its Discontents*, pp. 67–83.

44. See Raja Shehadeh, "Questions of Jurisdiction: A Legal Analysis of the Gaza-Jericho Agreement," *Journal of Palestine Studies* 23, no. 4 (summer 1994): 18–25.

45. "Israel-PLO Protocol on Economic Relations, Paris, 29 April 1994," *Journal of Palestine Studies* 23, no. 4 (summer 1994): 103–118, and Israeli Ministry of Foreign Affairs online documents.

46. On Israel's economic policies during the occupation, see Meron Benvenisti, *1986 Report Demographic, Economic, Legal, Social, and Political Developments in the West Bank* (Jerusalem: West Bank Data Base Project, 1986); David Kahan, *Agriculture and Water Resources in the West Bank and Gaza, 1967–1987* (a project of the West Bank Data Base Project) (Jerusalem: Jerusalem Post, 1987); Simcha Bahiri, *Industrialization in the West Bank and Gaza* (a project of the West Bank Data Base Project) (Jerusalem: The Jerusalem Post, 1987); Sara Roy, *The Gaza Strip Survey* (Jerusalem: West Bank Data Base Project, 1986).

47. "Israel-PLO Protocol on Economic Relations, Paris, 29 April 1994," *Journal of Palestine Studies* 23, no. 4 (summer 1994): 111–113.

48. Ibid., p. 115.

49. Gideon Alon, "State Plans to Allow Private Damages Suits Against the PA," *Ha'aretz*, March 25, 2002.

50. This data is taken from the excellent overall analysis by Leila Farsakh, "Economic Viability of a Palestinian State in the West Bank and Gaza Strip: Is It Possible Without Territorial Integrity and Sovereignty?" *MIT Electronic Journal of Middle East Studies* 1, no. 5 (May 2001): 43–57. Several good analyses include Emma Murphy, "Stacking the Deck: The Economics of the Israeli-PLO Accords," *Middle East Report* 25, nos. 3 and 4 (May–June/July–August 1995): 35–38; Samir Hleileh (in an interview with Joe Stork), "The Economic Protocols Are the Price We Had to Pay for the Agreement," *Middle East Report* 24, no. 1 (January–February 1994): 7–9; Jennifer Olmsted, "Thwarting Palestinian Development: The Protocol on Economic Relations," *Middle East Report* 26, no. 4 (October–December 1996): 11–13 and 18; and

Sara Roy, "De-Development Revisited: Palestinian Economy and Society Since Oslo," *Journal of Palestine Studies* 28, no. 3 (spring 1999): 64–82.

51. Meron Benvenisti, *Ha'aretz*, May 12, 1994.

52. "Israel and the PLO, Agreement on Preparatory Transfer of Powers and Responsibilities, Erez Checkpoint, Gaza, 29 August 1994," reprinted in *Journal of Palestine Studies* 24, no. 2 (winter 1995): 109–155. See also Israeli Ministry of Foreign Affairs online documents.

53. See Naseer H. Aruri, "Early Empowerment: The Burden, Not the Responsibility," *Journal of Palestine Studies* 24, no. 2 (winter 1995): 33–39.

54. "Prime Minister Yitzhak Rabin, Speech to the Extraordinary Knesset Session on the Interim Agreement (Jerusalem: 5 October 1995, excerpts)," in *Journal of Palestine Studies* 25, no. 2 (winter 1996): 137–139 (emphasis added).

55. "Israeli-Palestinian Interim Agreement on the West Bank and the Gaza Strip, Washington, 28 September 1995," partially reprinted in *Journal of Palestine Studies* 25, no. 2 (winter 1996): 123–140. See also Israeli Ministry of Foreign Affairs online documents.

56. Shlaim, *The Iron Wall*, p. 528, gives different percentages as regards the three jurisdictions.

57. For analyses of the practical implications of this division, see Graham Usher, *Dispatches from Palestine: The Rise and Fall of the Oslo Peace Process* (London: Pluto, 1999), pp. 55–175; Edward Said, *The End of the Peace Process: Oslo and After* (New York: Pantheon, 2000), esp. pp. 74–107; and LAW, *Apartheid, Bantustans, Cantons: The ABCs of the Oslo Accords* (Jerusalem: LAW, the Palestinian Society for the Protection of Human Rights and the Environment, 1998).

58. But a pointed article in *Ha'aretz* demonstrated the "fictional distinction" between Areas A and B when it came to Israeli security concerns. See Baruch Kra, "Background/Fuzzy 'A' and 'B' Definition Costs Lives," *Ha'aretz*, August 31, 2001.

59. Quoted in Shlaim, *The Iron Wall*, p. 551.

60. Quoted in ibid.

61. For a detailed analysis of the ideology, theology, and rabbinical teaching and organization that fomented Yigal Amir (the assassin), see Israel Shahak and Norton Mezvinsky, *Jewish Fundamentalism in Israel* (London: Pluto, 1999), pp. 113–149 and passim.

62. On the Palestinian elections, see Lamis Andoni, "The Palestinian Elections: Moving Toward Democracy or One-Party Rule?" *Journal of Palestine Studies* 25, no. 3 (spring 1996): 5–16; Khalil Shikaki, "The Palestinian Elections: An Assessment," *Journal of Palestine Studies* 25, no. 3 (spring 1996): 17–22; Ahmad S. Khalidi, "The Palestinians' First Excursion into Democracy," *Journal of Palestine Studies* 25, no. 4 (summer 1996): 20–28; 'Ali Jarbawi, "Palestinians at a Crossroads," *Journal of Palestine Studies* 25, no. 4 (summer 1996): 29–39.

63. Shlaim, *The Iron Wall*, p. 556.

64. Uzi Benziman, "Think Again About Assassination Policy," *Ha'aretz*, October 21, 2001.

65. "The Sharm al-Shaykh Declaration, Sharm al-Shaykh, Egypt, 13

March 1996," reprinted in *Journal of Palestine Studies* 25, no. 4 (summer 1996): 137–138.

66. "Israel and the PLO Joint Communique on the Permanent Status Negotiations, Taba, Egypt, 5–6 May 1966," reprinted in *Journal of Palestine Studies* 25, no. 4 (summer 1996): 139–140.

67. For full text of the Beilin–Abu Mazen document, see "Framework for the Conclusion of a Final Status Agreement Between Israel and the Palestine Liberation Organization, 31 October 1995," reprinted in *Ha'aretz*, September 21, 2000.

68. Shlaim, *The Iron Wall*, pp. 576–577.

69. "Israel and the Palestine Liberation Organization Protocol Concerning the Redeployment in Hebron (Agreed Version), Erez Crossing, 15 January 1997," reprinted in *Journal of Palestine Studies* 26, no. 3 (spring 1997): 132–145 (partial). See also Israeli Ministry of Foreign Affairs online documents.

70. For two good analyses of the Hebron Protocol, see Lamis Andoni, "Redefining Oslo: Negotiating the Hebron Protocol," *Journal of Palestine Studies* 26, no. 3 (spring 1997): 17–30; and Edward Said, "The Real Meaning of the Hebron Agreement," *Journal of Palestine Studies* 26, no. 3 (spring 1997): 31–36.

71. "Israel and the Palestine Liberation Organization Protocol Concerning the Redeployment in Hebron (Agreed Version), Erez Crossing, 15 January 1997": 132–145 (partial).

72. Shlaim, *The Iron Wall*, p. 581.

73. Ibid., pp. 581–582.

74. Daniel Ben Simon, "Wall-eyed at Har Homa," *Ha'aretz Week's End*, February 15, 2002.

75. See *Report on Israeli Settlement in the Occupied Territories* (Washington, DC: Foundation for Middle East Peace) 7, no. 3 (May–June 1997); and Applied Research Institute–Jerusalem, *The Har Homa Settlement and the Uprooting of Abu Ghneim Forest* (Jerusalem: Applied Research Institute–Jerusalem, March 18, 1997).

76. Shlaim, *The Iron Wall*, p. 584.

77. *Economic and Social Conditions in the West Bank and Gaza Strip, Quarterly Report, summer 1997* (Gaza: United Nations, Office of the Special Coordinator in the Occupied Territories, October 4, 1997). Also see *Quarterly Report, winter-spring 1997* (Gaza: United Nations Office of the Special Coordinator in the Occupied Territories, April 1, 1997).

78. "Israel and the Palestinian Authority Memorandum on Security Understanding, 17 December 1997," reprinted in *Journal of Palestinian Studies* 27, no. 3 (spring 1998): 147–148.

79. Said, *The End of the Peace Process*, pp. 188–189.

80. Ron Pundak, "From Oslo to Taba: What Went Wrong?" *Survival* 43, no. 3 (autumn 2001): 31–45.

81. See Ciechanover Commission, *Summary of the Report on the Mishal Affair* (Jerusalem: 17 February 1998 [excerpts]), reprinted in *Journal of Palestine Studies* 27, no. 4 (summer 1998): 146–150.

82. See Naseer Aruri, "The Wye Memorandum: Netanyahu's Oslo and Unreciprocal Reciprocity," *Journal of Palestine Studies* 28, no. 2 (winter 1999): 17–28.

83. "The Wye River Memorandum and Related Documents: Special Document File," and "Israel and the PLO, The Wye River Memorandum, Washington, 23 October 1998," reprinted in *Journal of Palestine Studies* 28, no. 2 (winter 1999): 135–139 (partial plus other related documents at pp. 139–146). See also Israeli Ministry of Foreign Affairs online documents.

84. "Israel and the PLO, The Wye River Memorandum, Washington, 23 October 1998," reprinted in *Journal of Palestine Studies* 28, no. 2 (winter 1999): 135–146.

85. "U.S. Secretary of State Madeline K. Albright, Letter of Assurance to Israeli PM Benjamin Netanyahu, Washington, 23 October 1998," reprinted in *Journal of Palestine Studies* 28, no. 2 (winter 1999): 139. See also "U.S. Ambassador to Israel Edward Walker and U.S. Special Envoy Dennis Ross, Four Letters of Clarification to Israel, Tel Aviv and Washington, 29–30 October 1998," reprinted in *Journal of Palestine Studies* 28, no. 2 (winter 1999): 143–145.

86. "Yasir Arafat, Speech at the Palestinian Conference to Affirm Renunciation of the PLO Charter, Gaza, 14 December, 1998 (excerpts)," reprinted in *Journal of Palestine Studies* 28, no. 3 (spring 1999): 146–148.

87. Shlaim, *The Iron Wall*, p. 605.

88. "Prime Minister's Office, List of Palestinian 'Unfulfilled Commitments' Under the Wye River Memorandum (Jerusalem: 15 December 1998," reprinted in *Journal of Palestine Studies* 28, no. 3 (spring 1999): 154.

89. Ibid. See also "Prime Minister Benjamin Netanyahu, Address to the Likud Central Committee, Tel Aviv, 27 December 1998 (excerpts)," reprinted in *Journal of Palestine Studies* 28, no. 3 (spring 1999): 154–156.

90. "Israel and the PLO, Sharm al-Shaykh Memorandum on Implementation of Outstanding Commitments of Agreements Signed and the Resumption of Permanent Status Negotiations, Sharm al-Shaykh, Egypt, 4 September 1999," in *Journal of Palestine Studies* 29, no. 2 (winter 2000): 143–146. See also Israeli Ministry of Foreign Affairs online documents.

91. Ron Pundak, "From Oslo to Taba: What Went Wrong?" pp. 5–6.

92. Robert Malley and Hussein Agha, "Camp David: The Tragedy of Errors," *New York Review of Books*, August 9, 2001, p. 59; and "How Generous Is Generous," in *Crossroads of Conflict: A Special Report* (Washington, DC: Foundation for Middle East Peace, 2000), pp. 2–4.

93. Haim Ramon, "Interview," *Zman Tel Aviv* (Israel, Hebrew), March 2, 2001, translated by Ron Pundak in "From Oslo to Taba: What Went Wrong?" p. 8.

94. Malley and Agha, "Camp David," p. 59.

95. Robert Malley, "Fictions About the Failure at Camp David," *New York Times*, July 8, 2001.

96. For a transcript of the president's remarks, see "President Bill Clinton, Remarks to Israeli Television on the Moving of the US Embassy to Jerusalem and the Camp David Summit, Washington, 28 July 2000 (excerpts)," reprinted in *Journal of Palestine Studies* 30, no. 1 (autumn 2000): 158–161. See also Israeli Ministry of Foreign Affairs online documents.

97. Ron Pundak, "From Oslo to Taba: What Went Wrong?" p. 13.

98. Malley and Agha, "Camp David: The Tragedy of Errors."

99. Malley and Agha, "Camp David," p. 60.

100. Ibid., p. 62.

101. The two most important sources are Ron Pundak (one of the Israeli negotiators of the DOP), "From Oslo to Taba: What Went Wrong?" and Jerome Slater, "Israel, Anti-Semitism and the Palestinian Problem," *Tikkun: A Bimonthly Jewish Critique of Politics, Culture, and Society* (May/June 2001). Also see Gush Shalom, *Shedding Some Light on Barak's "Generous Offers"* (Tel Aviv: Gush Shalom [Israeli Peace Bloc], 2000; Alain Gresh (translated by Wendy Kristianasen), "The Middle East: How the Peace Was Lost," *Le Monde Diplomatique*, September 1, 2001; Abu Mazen (translated by the Middle East Media and Research Institute), "Had Camp David Convened Again, We Would Take the Same Positions," *al-Ayyam* (Ramallah, Palestinian daily, Arabic), July 28, 2001; PA Special Dispatch, Parts 1 and 2, nos. 249 and 250 (August 2, 2001); Aluf Benn, "The Selling of the Summit," *Ha'aretz*, July 27, 2001; Akram Hanieh, "The Camp David Papers: A Special Document File," *al-Ayyam*, in seven installments between July 29 and August 10, 2000, abridged from a translated version with permission of author, reprinted in *Journal of Palestine Studies* 30, no. 2 (winter 2001): 75–97 (Hanieh is editor in chief of *al-Ayyam*, a close adviser to Arafat, and part of the Palestinian team at Camp David). Also helpful: Malley and Agha, "Camp David"; Deborah Sontag, "Quest for Mideast Peace: How and Why It Failed," *New York Times*, July 26, 2001; Abd al Rahreem Malouh (a member of the PLO's executive committee), "Why Did the Palestinians Turn Down Barak's 'Generous Offer'?" *News from Within* 17, no. 5 (July 2001): 16–18. Others: "How Generous Is Generous?" Foundation for Middle East Peace: Special Report (Washington, DC: Foundation for Middle East Peace, winter 2000); Robert Fisk, "Sham Summit Promised Little for the Palestinians," *The Independent* (UK), December 29, 2000; Meron Benvenisti, "Oslo—Without Illusions," *Ha'aretz*, March 8, 2001); Gershon Baskin, *What Went Wrong: Oslo—The PLO, Israel, and Some Additional Facts* (Jerusalem: Israel/Palestine Center for Research and Information, August 2001); Gershon Baskin, *Negotiating the Settlements: The Success of Right-Wing Political Entrapment against Peace* (Jerusalem: Israel/Palestine Center for Research and Information, November 1, 2000).

102. Ron Pundak, "From Oslo to Taba: What Went Wrong?" p. 15.

103. UN General Assembly Resolution 181 (II), November 29, 1947; for text, see "UN General Assembly Resolution 181 (Partition Plan) on the Future Government of Palestine, 29 November 1947," in Mahdi F. Abdul-Hadi, *Documents on Palestine I: From the Pre-Ottoman Period to the Prelude of the Madrid Middle East Conference* (Jerusalem: Palestinian Academic Society for the Study of International Affairs, 1997), pp. 172–183. UN General Assembly Resolution 194 (III), December 11, 1948 (refugees' right of return or compensation), text in "UN General Assembly Resolution 194, 11 December 1948," in Abdul-Hadi, *Documents on Palestine I*, pp. 192–193. All other resolutions are available online at Palestine-UN.org. See "UN General Assembly Resolution 2253 (ES-V), *Measures Taken by Israel to Change the Status of the City of Jerusalem*, 4 July 1967," A/RES/2253 (ES-V) (demands that Israel rescind and desist actions in the city); "UN General Assembly Resolution 2535 B (XXIV), *The Inalienable Rights of the People of Palestine*, 10 December 1969," recalled and referred to in "UN General Assembly Resolution 2672 (XXV), *United Nations Relief and Works Agency for Palestinians in the Near East*, 8 December 1970," A/RES/2672 (XXV)A-D (reaffirms the inalienable rights of

the Palestinian people including right to self-determination and calls on Israel to repatriate the refugees immediately); "UN General Assembly Resolution 2649, *The Importance of the Realization of the Right to Peoples' to Self-determination and the Speedy Granting of Independence to Colonial Countries and Peoples' for the Effective Guarantee and Observance of Human Rights,* 30 November 1970," A/RES/2649; "UN General Assembly Resolution 2851 (XXVI), *Report of the Special Committee to Investigate Israeli Practices Affecting Human Rights of the Population of the Occupied Territories,* 20 December 1971," A/RES 2851 (XXVI) (condemns annexation of territory, settlements, demolition of houses, transfer and expulsion, torture and ill-treatment, collective punishment); "UN General Assembly Resolution 3236 (XXIX), *Question of Palestine,* 22 November 1974," A/RES/3236 (XXIX) (affirms right of self-determination, sovereignty and right of return).

104. For a text of the Fourth Geneva Convention, see U.S. House of Representatives, Committee on Foreign Affairs, "Geneva Convention IV: Protection of Civilians in War," *Human Rights Documents: Compilation of Documents Pertaining to Human Rights* (Washington, DC: U.S. Government Printing Office, 1983), pp. 414–461. The first three Geneva Conventions plus the Hague Conventions of 1899 and 1907 may be found in this source as well. For the conventions relating to refugees and stateless persons, see "Convention Relating to the Status of Refugees, 1951," in Ian Brownlie, ed., *Basic Documents on Human Rights,* 3rd ed. (Oxford: Clarendon, 1992), pp. 64–81; "Convention Relating to the Status of Stateless Persons, 1954," in Brownlie, ed., *Basic Documents on Human Rights,* pp. 82–97; "Convention on the Reduction of Statelessness, 1961," in Brownlie, ed., *Basic Documents on Human Rights,* pp. 98–105; "Protocol Relating to the Status of Refugees, 16 November 1966," in Committee on Foreign Affairs, *Human Rights Documents,* pp. 135–138; "Convention Relating to the Status of Refugees," in Committee on Foreign Affairs, *Human Rights Documents,* pp. 121–134.

105. For an excellent analysis, see W. Thomas Mallison and Sally V. Mallison, *The Palestine Problem in International Law and World Order* (Essex, UK: Longman, 1986).

106. A similar analysis is made in the draft *Peace Without Justice: Abandoning Rights in the Oslo Process* (New York: Center for Economic and Social Rights, April 14, 2000), pp. 18–22.

107. UN General Assembly Resolution 194 (III), December 11, 1948 (refugees' right of return or compensation), in "UN General Assembly Resolution 194, 11 December 1948," in Abdul-Hadi, *Documents on Palestine I,* pp. 192–193.

108. By 1952, the United Nations Palestine Conciliation Commission (UNCCP) had ceased all protection functions toward the refugees and confined its operations to collecting records and documenting refugee properties in Israel—functions that have continued through the present day.

109. All these UN resolutions may be found online at Palestine-UN.org. See "UN General Assembly Resolution 2253 (ES-V), *Measures Taken by Israel to Change the Status of the City of Jerusalem,* 4 July 1967," A/RES/2253 (ES-V) (demands that Israel rescind and desist actions in the city); "UN General Assembly Resolution 2535 B" (XXIV), *The Inalienable Rights of the People of Palestine,* 10 December 1969," recalled and referred to in "UN General

Assembly Resolution 2672 (XXV), *United Nations Relief and Works Agency for Palestinians in the Near East*, 8 December 1970," A/RES/2672 (XXV)A-D (reaffirms the inalienable rights of the Palestinian people, including right to self-determination, and calls on Israel to repatriate the refugees immediately); "UN General Assembly Resolution 2649, *The Importance of the Realization of the Right to Peoples' to Self-determination and the Speedy Granting of Independence to Colonial Countries and Peoples' for the Effective Guarantee and Observance of Human Rights,* 30 November 1970," A/RES/2649; "UN General Assembly Resolution 2851 (XXVI), *Report of the Special Committee to Investigate Israeli Practices Affecting Human Rights of the Population of the Occupied Territories,* 20 December 1971," A/RES 2851 (XXVI) (condemns annexation of territory, settlements, demolition of houses, transfer and expulsion, torture and ill-treatment, collective punishment); "UN General Assembly Resolution 3236 (XXIX), *Question of Palestine,* 22 November 1974," A/RES/3236 (XXIX) (affirms right of self-determination, sovereignty, and right of return).

110. Quoted in Amnesty International, Israel and the Occupied Territories/Palestinian Authority, *The Right to Return: The Case of the Palestinians,* March 30, 2001 (MDE 15/013/2001), p. 4.

111. For a good analysis of the nature, meaning, and utility of each of the documents and the organizations, see Susan M. Akram, "Reinterpreting Palestinian Refugee Rights Under International Law," in Aruri, ed., *Palestinian Refugees,* pp. 165–194. Also see John Quigley, "Displaced Palestinians and the Right of Return," *Harvard International Law Journal* 39, no. 1 (1998): 193–198.

112. "Convention Relating to the Status of Refugees, 1951," in Brownlie, ed., *Basic Documents on Human Rights,* pp. 64–81; "Convention Relating to the Status of Stateless Persons, 1954," in Brownlie, ed., *Basic Documents on Human Rights,* pp. 82–97; "Convention on the Reduction of Statelessness, 1961," in Brownlie, ed., *Basic Documents on Human Rights,* pp. 98–105; "Protocol Relating to the Status of Refugees, 16 November 1966," in Committee on Foreign Affairs, *Human Rights Documents,* pp. 135–138. An important companion to the documentary sources is Amnesty International, *Refugees: Human Rights Have No Borders* (New York: Amnesty International Publications, 1997).

113. "Geneva Convention IV Protection of Civilians in War (1949)," in Committee on Foreign Affairs, *Human Rights Documents,* p. 427; "Universal Declaration of Human Rights (1948)," in Brownlie, ed., *Basic Documents on Human Rights,* pp. 21–27; "Declaration on the Elimination of All Forms of Intolerance and Discrimination Based on Religion and Belief (1981)," in Brownlie, ed., *Basic Documents on Human Rights,* pp. 109–112; "International Covenant on Civil and Political Rights (1966)," in Brownlie, ed., *Basic Documents on Human Rights,* pp. 125–143; "International Convention on the Elimination of All Forms of Racial Discrimination (1966)," in Brownlie, ed., *Basic Documents on Human Rights,* pp. 148–161.

114. Amnesty International, "The Right to Return: The Case of the Palestinians."

115. This is a document in three parts: (1) "Relevant Background," "Human Rights Policy on the Right of Return," *Human Rights Watch World Report 2001: Israel, the Occupied West Bank, Gaza Strip, and Palestinian*

Authority Territories (New York: Human Rights Watch, 2001); (2) "Human Rights Watch Policy on the Right to Return," *Human Rights Watch World Report 2001* (the quote in the text is entirely from this document); (3) "Letter to Israeli Prime Minister Barak," *Human Rights Watch Urges Attention to Future of Palestine Refugees, December 22, 2000.*

116. Two excellent comprehensive documents are LAW, *The Dormant Right: The Continuing Violation of the Right of Return* (Jerusalem: Palestinian Society for the Protection of Human Rights and the Environment [LAW], 2001), and BADIL, *The Right of Return: Campaign for the Defense of Palestinian Refugee Rights*, 2nd ed. (Bethlehem: Resource Center for Palestinian Residency and Refugee Rights [BADIL], 2002). An additional source of interest is Elia Zureik, *Palestinian Refugees and the Peace Process* (Washington, DC: Institute for Palestine Studies, 1996).

117. In Mallison and Mallison, *The Palestine Problem in International Law and World Order,* p. 250. The "Guidelines" were originally a statement of the Likud Party platform; however, in 1977 they were approved by a majority vote of the Knesset, thus representing official Israeli policy.

118. See, for example, the analysis in LAW, *The Dormant Right: The Continuing Violation of the Right of Return*, pp. 2–3.

119. Pappe, "Israeli Perceptions of the Refugee Question," p. 74.

120. Nina Gilbert, "Knesset Makes Palestinian 'Right of Return' Tougher," *Jerusalem Post* (English), January 2, 2001.

121. Ibid.

122. Ziad Abu Zayyad, "The Palestinian Right of Return: A Realistic Approach," *Palestine-Israel Journal of Politics, Economics, and Culture* 1, no. 2 (spring 1994): 77.

123. Jaber Suleiman, "The Palestine Liberation Organization: From Right of Return to Bantustan," in Aruri, ed., *Palestinian Refugees*, pp. 99–100.

124. The original article was published simultaneously in *Ha'aretz* and *al-Quds* (a Palestinian daily) on September 24, 2001. The quotation is taken from an analysis by Danny Rubinstein, "An Exception to the Rule," *Ha'aretz*, November 11, 2001.

125. BADIL, Press Release, "Responses to Nusseibeh-Ayalon Initiative" (Jerusalem: BADIL Resource Center, October 3, 2002); Itim News Service, "Sari Nusseibeh Opens Drive to Waive Right of Return," *Ha'aretz*, October 2, 2002.

126. Rashid Khalidi, "Observations on the Right of Return," *The Palestinian Right of Return* (Cambridge, MA: American Academy of Arts and Sciences, paper no. 6, 1990), p. 5 (emphasis added).

127. Naseer Aruri, "Towards Convening a Congress of Return and Self-Determination," in Aruri, ed., *Palestinian Refugees*, pp. 266–267.

128. For full text of the Beilin–Abu Mazen document, see "Framework for the Conclusion of a Final Status Agreement Between Israel and the Palestine Liberation Organization, 31 October 1995," reprinted in *Ha'aretz*, September 21, 2000. Included with the document are several articles: Akiva Eldar, "Reaching for an Agreement: A Look at the Beilin-Abu-Mazen Agreement)"; Akiva Eldar, "A Gesture to Shimon Peres: In the Furor over the Temple Mount, the Fact that Barak Had Not Budged an Inch Was Missed)"; and Akiva Eldar, "Arafat Welcomed the Beilin-Abu-Mazen Document."

129. For a good overall critique of the PLO on the refugee issue, see

Suleiman, "The Palestine Liberation Organization: From Right of Return to Bantustan," pp. 87–104.

130. Aluf Ben, "Solution to the Refugee Problem," *Ha'aretz*, October 12, 1999, reprinted in "Israel's Scheme to End the Refugee Question," *News from Within* 15, no. 10 (November 1999): 9.

131. Ben, "Solution to the Refugee Problem."

132. "President Bill Clinton, Main Points of Agreement Reached at the Sharm al-Shaykh Summit, Sharm al-Shaykh, Egypt, 17 October 2000," reprinted in *Journal of Palestine Studies* 30, no. 2 (winter 2001): 186 (excerpts).

133. For a good analysis, see Mouin Rabbani, "The Peres-Arafat Agreement: Can It Work?" *MERIP Press Information Notes*, PIN 38 (November 3, 2000).

134. "President Bill Clinton, Proposals for a Final Settlement, Washington DC, 23 December 2000," *Journal of Palestine Studies* 20, no. 3 (spring 2001): 171–175.

135. Much has been made in some sectors about allegedly new Israeli offers to the Palestinians at Taba. Such beliefs were entirely dispelled by military analyst Ze'ev Schiff, "What Was Obtained at Taba Regarding Palestinian Refugees," *Ha'aretz*, September 13, 2001. For the Palestinian view of Clinton's plan, see "PLO Negotiating Team, Reservations Concerning President Bill Clinton's 23 December Proposals for an Israeli-Palestinian Peace Agreement, Ramallah and Gaza, 1 January 2001 (excerpts)," *Journal of Palestine Studies* 20, no. 3 (spring 2001): 155–159.

136. "EU Description of the Outcome of Permanent Status Talks at Taba," *Ha'aretz Weekend Edition*, February 15, 2002. Akiva Eldar wrote several accompanying pieces, including "Dispute over *Ma'aleh Adumim*," "Symbols of Sovereignty," "How Long Is the Western Wall," and "A Negative Balance of Return." The BADIL Resource Center in Bethlehem also produced a comprehensive analysis of the Israeli and Palestinian proposals concerning the refugee question presented at Taba. See BADIL, "Analysis of the Israeli and Palestinian Taba Proposals on Palestinian Refugees with the Full Texts as Annexes, Bethlehem, 13 November 2001 (excerpts)," *Journal of Palestine Studies* 31, no. 2 (winter 2002): 142–159.

137. See the analysis by Uri Avnery in "The Peace Criminal," *Gush Shalom*, July 21, 2001.

3

Life in the
Occupied Territories

The Oslo experiment must be judged, not on the basis of the promises and declarations of its architects, but on the basis of the Israeli policy implemented on the ground.

—Amira Hass[1]

The Oslo Accords failed to produce a permanent status agreement for many reasons, but primarily and most importantly because Israel never committed itself to the one goal that could have made possible such an agreement—a viable, sovereign Palestinian state.

—Henry Siegman[2]

In this chapter, together with Chapters 4–6, I investigate the various areas—collective freedoms, economic well-being, and individual freedoms—in which the Palestinians' quality of life either deteriorated or did not improve following the 1993 Oslo Accords.

The analysis first provides an overview of Israel's practices during the seven-year peace process, with relevant comparisons to Tel Aviv's policies prior to the onset of the Oslo process.[3] For those wishing more information on the pre-Oslo period, the notes provide a host of sources. Palestinians living in Area A (i.e., those areas designated pursuant to Oslo II to be under the control of the Palestinian Authority [PA]) enjoyed a number of specific individual freedoms within the boundaries of PA jurisdiction that heretofore they had not experienced. Yet they, too, were constrained and ultimately suffered as a consequence of Israel's restrictions on collective freedoms and economic development.

Most of the policies discussed here are interrelated as to their consequences for Palestinians. And examining them individually results in some repetition, but this is an appropriate analytical approach.[4] The analysis is organized as follows: (1) collective freedoms (social and economic); (2) collective freedoms (land, settlement, and water); (3) collective freedoms (economic development and well–being); and (4) individual freedoms.

Collective Freedoms:
Social and Economic Dimensions

Types of Closures: General, Partial, Internal, and Total

During the period of the Oslo process, the fate of Palestinian economy and society was more directly and negatively affected by Israel's imposition of closures (as well as the attendant checkpoints, roadblocks, and permits) than by any other policy during this period. In general, *closure* means that Palestinians and Palestinian goods may not enter Israel unless a permit has been previously obtained. Israel determines who, what, and how many of each will be allowed to enter Israel. Prior to 1993, Israel occasionally instituted closures on the Palestinian population, but they tended to be relatively brief and the consequences far less drastic than after 1993. Closures function solely to restrict the movement of Palestinian persons and products: Israeli citizens (including settlers), goods, tourists, and so on freely cross the boundaries. Israel has employed four types of closures since 1993, although they have not always been distinct in practice. Consequently, Palestinians often found themselves in violation of one form of closure when they believed that another was in effect.[5] The four types of closures (general, partial, internal, and total) are outlined below.

General Closure. The West Bank and Gaza have been under a *general closure* since 1993. (It was in effect prior to September 1993, continued thereafter, and was officially declared in October 1994.) General closure has involved the sealing off of the Occupied Territories from Israel; the separation and isolation of Gaza and the West Bank from each other and both from East Jerusalem; and the enforced isolation of the West Bank and Gaza from other countries. Under the policy of general closure, Israel has placed overall restrictions on the movement of labor, goods, and factors of production between the West Bank and Gaza and Israel; prohibited Palestinians in the Occupied Territories from entering Jerusalem; and drastically limited the movement of persons and goods between the West Bank and Gaza. It has involved prolonged delays and extensive searches at checkpoints and border crossings; however, individuals and goods that have valid permits have usually been allowed to move, after lengthy delays at checkpoints, if they pass inspection. But, as B'Tselem notes: "Approvals [permits] were granted sparingly and according to criteria unknown to Palestinians."[6]

Partial Closure. Partial closures include the general closure plus additional restrictions but fall short of total closure. They can apply to goods or persons, to imports, and, more commonly, to exports. They have been most frequently directed at Palestinian laborers in Israel and are typically applied to a specific locale or group of workers rather than the West Bank and Gaza as a whole. Several examples will illustrate the point. In January 1996, all Gazan workers were prohibited from coming to Israel. In February 1996, all West Bank and Gazan workers under age forty-five were prevented from working in Israel. In March 1996, the coastal waters off Gaza were closed to the Palestinian fishing industry.[7]

Internal Closure. Internal closure is a siege imposed on towns, villages, refugee camps, and areas in the West Bank and Gaza Strip that prevents exit and entry. Israel established the policy of *internal closure* in 1996. This involves the restriction of all movement within the West Bank and Gaza—from village to village, from village to city, from refugee camp to town, and so on. Persons are prohibited from moving anywhere for any reason outside their locale. When an internal closure is in effect, Palestinians are imprisoned in their respective communities. It is reinforced by hundreds of new checkpoints and roadblocks manned by the Israeli Defense Forces (IDF). The first internal closure was implemented in March 1996 and lasted for twenty-one days. A second, in September 1996, lasted eighteen days.[8] Subsequently, Israel imposed internal closures for varying periods until the eruption of the Al-Aqsa intifada in September 2000. Thereafter, the West Bank and Gaza were under internal closure (plus general closure) continuously for the entire period of the uprising.[9]

The extent of Palestinian suffering due to closures has been so great that human rights organizations around the globe have forcefully and repeatedly condemned the practice. Here is one of Amnesty International's many statements denouncing the policy:

> Amnesty International called today on the international community to act promptly to end the Israeli policy of closures in the West Bank and Gaza. The confinement of more than 3 million people for 10 months to their own villages or homes by curfews or closures is a totally unacceptable response to the violence of a few. . . . Closures constitute the collective punishment of a whole people. In all cases the closures deny the right to freedom of movement and suffocate economic life. *They are not effective in preventing violent attacks against the Israelis* as the recent suicide bombings have shown.[10]

Total Closure. Through the total closure (also: *blockade* or *siege*), Israel revokes all permits and prohibits all movement of goods and persons from the territories into Israel. Permits are automatically canceled without warning, and there are no exceptions. This condition more than any other harms the labor force, for it results in immediate and indefinite unemployment for every Palestinian who works in Israel. Exports are likewise prohibited, and most imports are disallowed.[11] Israel imposed a total closure on the West Bank and Gaza in September 2000, and it remains in effect as of publication of this book (early 2003).

The United Nations Educational, Scientific, and Cultural Organization has illustrated the magnitude of the effect of total closure by presenting the number of closure days annually in the context of potential workdays. The average annual potential workdays lost (excluding weekends and Jewish and Muslim holidays) for the years 1993–2000 was 278 days.[12] The Palestine Economic Policy Research Institute and independent researcher Liala Farsakh have calculated the cumulative annual losses to the Palestine economy as a consequence of closure days (see Table 3.1).[13]

Roadblocks and Checkpoints

Closures require military forces at roadblocks and checkpoints to interdict individuals, vehicles (including cars, public taxis, buses, trucks, ambulances, etc.), and goods from passing arbitrary (and changing) checkpoints and along major roads. In conjunction with closures, roadblocks and checkpoints have had extremely deleterious social and eco-

Table 3.1 Total Closure Days and Monetary Losses to the Palestinians, 1993–2000

Year	Days of Total Closure	Losses in Millions of U.S. Dollars
1993	26	283.8
1994	89	689.6
1995	112	847.0
1996	121	957.0
1997	79	648.0
1998	26	224.0
1999	16	144.0
2000	75	705.0

Sources: Ishac Diwan and Radwan A. Shaban, eds., *Development Under Adversity: The Palestinian Economy Under Transition* (Summary) (Washington DC: Palestine Economic Policy Research Institute and the World Bank, 1999), p. 6 (years 1993–1996). Leila Farsakh, "Economic Viability of a Palestinian State in the West Bank and the Gaza Strip," *MIT Electronic Journal of the Middle East*, no. 5 (2001): 6 (years 1997–2000), available online at http://web.mit.edu/cis/www/mitejmes/issues/200105/farsakh.htm.

nomic effects. Road barriers are used to prevent people and goods (food, medicine, fuel, etc.) from entering or leaving an area. Road-blocks constitute another measure to impede the freedom of movement of the Palestinian population and often have serious consequences when, for example, sick individuals are prevented from getting to hospitals.[14]

Roadblocks can be permanent or temporary. Within a year of the Oslo agreement, Israel established at least fifty-six permanent military roadblocks along its borders—twenty-nine on the 307-kilometer border between the West Bank and Israel, and twenty-seven on the 51-kilometer border between Gaza and Israel—to enforce the general closure.[15] Temporary roadblocks have been erected primarily under conditions of total or internal closure. At times, there have been as many as 200 temporary roadblocks throughout the West Bank and Gaza. In the more remote West Bank villages, roadblocks have impeded people from obtaining food and fuel—collective suffering that is extensively detailed by B'Tselem, the Israeli human rights organization. B'Tselem has been particularly concerned about the effect of roadblocks on Palestinian access to medical care. It reported that between February 1996 and September 2000 "*at least* 30 Palestinians died after a delay in receiving medical treatment due to restrictions on their freedom of movement."[16] In another study on the medical consequences of road-blocks, B'Tselem condemned Israel's "gross restrictions of the right of Palestinians to proper medical treatment."[17]

A final aspect of roadblocks is harassment by soldiers that needless-ly humiliates people and makes ordinary daily life difficult as a consequence of having to wait in long lines, having their papers checked and rechecked, enduring lengthy searches of their vehicles and persons, and so on.[18] *Ha'aretz,* in one of the many articles it has published discussing harassment at roadblocks, wrote:

> Soldiers held up Palestinians for hours at roadblocks. . . . Palestinians were ordered to stay inside their cars, with the windows rolled up, without air conditioning, during the hottest parts of the day. The car keys were confiscated. . . . The soldiers asked for "passage fees" from the Palestinians wishing to cross . . . [they] suffered beatings . . . sol-diers puncture the tires . . . of vehicles . . . Officers have said that these incidents . . . are the mere "tip of the iceberg." . . . Every hour there are dozens of such roadblocks throughout the territories.[19]

The Permit System

Permits that affect everyday aspects of life in the Occupied Territories, including travel, have been integral to the Israeli occupation policies since 1967. Israel issues permits at its discretion. And prior to the Oslo peace process, Israel issued permits primarily for activities (e.g., building a house, digging a well, planting a crop, or opening a business). However, approximately 90 percent of all applications were denied. If a Palestinian proceeded with a project for which he had not received a permit, he was subject to punishment. This became one of the excuses Israel used for demolishing houses.

After 1993, the permit system was expanded to include persons. Since then, individuals have had to secure permits from Israel to travel beyond the confines of their general locale, thereby restricting personal freedom of movement. The ability to obtain a permit determines whether a Palestinian can commute to work, attend a university, travel to see family, and so on.[20] Israel determines the number of permits granted, as well as the individuals entitled to receive them, and it can revoke them for any reason. In this way, Israel regulates the number, age, and identity of Palestinians working in Israel, the traffic (commercial and private) entering Israel, and so on. Most significant in terms of impeding economic development, permits, together with closures and checkpoints, control the movement of exports and imports as well as the movement between Gaza and the West Bank.[21] Since 1993, Israel's mass revocation of individuals' permits at various times has prevented Palestinians from working in Israel, sent unemployment soaring, and created rising poverty throughout the Occupied Territories. Israel's use of the permit system after 1993—in particular its severe restrictions on the issuance of permits—as well as its revocation en masse, are the primary factors in the stagnation and decline of the Palestinian economy subsequent to the signing of the Oslo Accords.

One example illustrates the effect of the permit system: the ability of Gazan students to obtain university education in the West Bank. Two years after signing the Declaration of Principles (DOP, the primary document under Oslo), Israel, at the beginning of the September 1995 academic year, maintained its refusal (in effect since 1987) to issue student permits. Then, in December, it granted 1,000 permits to Gaza students. Little more than a year later, however, in March 1996, Israel revoked all the permits. The cancellation remained in effect until January 1998.[22]

Curfews

"Curfew," in the words of B'Tselem, "is the most sweeping and extreme restriction on freedom of movement imposed on Palestinians in the

Occupied Territories because it imprisons an entire population within the confines of their homes."[23] Israel also imposes curfews on cities, towns, villages, and refugee camps or parts thereof. During a curfew no one can leave his or her home for any reason. Curfews have lasted for periods of one day to three or more months. Prior to Oslo, curfews were a regular feature of life in the West Bank and Gaza. When curfews are in effect, all residents of affected areas are prohibited from going to work or school, shopping for food, seeking medical help, or conducting any other normal activity. Merchants suffer because they cannot open their shops. Children cannot play outdoors. Students miss school. Mothers cannot shop for food for their families. Life simply comes to a halt while heavily armed soldiers patrol the area and enter and search homes. During curfews of long duration, residents of one part of an area (rotated throughout the area), are given two to four hours every five to eight days, to leave their homes to obtain food and other necessities.

Israel continued to make use of curfews after 1993. One example is telling: In Hebron, in February 1994, Jewish settler Baruch Goldstein murdered twenty-nine Palestinians at prayer in the Ibrahimi mosque; after the incident, the 160,000 Palestinian residents of the city were placed under curfew for thirty days. The 450 Jewish settlers, however, were free to live normally. During the eighteen months following the end of the first curfew, twelve more twenty-four-hour curfews of varying days' length were imposed on the Hebron Palestinians for a total of fifty days. Additionally, there were forty nighttime curfews.[24] During every Jewish holiday, the West Bank and Gaza are placed under curfews so that Israelis may celebrate.

After Oslo II (1995), when the PA assumed control of Area A, Israel could no longer impose curfews on the cities and refugee camps under PA jurisdiction. However, it could, and did, continue to impose curfews in Areas B and C throughout the period of the peace process (although to a lesser extent than prior to 1993). With the outbreak of the Al-Aqsa intifada, Israel once again widely employed curfews, including within Area A. Aggregate data on the number and length of curfews throughout the West Bank and Gaza for the seven years are unavailable, even from B'Tselem.[25]

Safe Passage Between Gaza and the West Bank

Prior to the Oslo Accords, Palestinians moved relatively freely between the West Bank, Gaza, and East Jerusalem. After 1993, Israel severed the West Bank and Gaza from each other with a border checkpoint similar to an international crossing between two hostile nations. Only those very few with VIP status or other special permits could traverse the boundary.

The 1993 Oslo Accords stipulated the immediate creation of a safe passage between the West Bank and Gaza to enable Palestinians to pass through Israeli territory from one area to the other.[26] The DOP (article IV) states that the West Bank and Gaza are a "single territorial unit" whose "integrity will be preserved." Nevertheless, year after year, and despite reiteration in subsequent agreements, Israel refused to allow the opening of such a passage.[27]

On October 25, 1999, after a six-year delay, Israel finally consented to opening the safe passage. It was, however, only the first leg of the passage—the southern route between Gaza and Tarqumiya near Hebron. The northern link was not opened. Moreover, it was under Israeli sovereignty, and Israel retained the right to arrest wanted persons on the safe passage. Israel imposed rigid standards for persons and vehicles desiring to use it. Automobile registrations, driver's licenses, vehicle inspections, truck permits, communal taxis, and bus qualifications were strictly regulated, as were individuals who wished to use the road. Israel routinely turned "back agricultural produce and livestock 'not meeting Israeli health specifications,' delayed transport of West Bank export products destined for the Mediterranean coast," and enforced the stipulation that "persons and vehicles using safe passage under these arrangements [security permits] shall neither break their journey nor depart from the designated routes, and shall complete the passage within the designated time stamped on their safe passage cards and permits."[28]

The safe passage was open for less than one year. Israel closed it on October 8, 2000.

Collective Freedoms: Land, Settlements, and Water

Land Confiscation and the Expansion of Jewish Settlements

Between 1967 and 1987, Israel confiscated more than 52 percent of the West Bank (of which the total area is approximately 2,126 square miles) and 40 percent of the Gaza Strip (approximately 140 total square miles). In addition, there was an accompanying process of Judaization of the territories, reflected in Israel's establishment, by 1987, of 104 settlements with 65,000 Jewish settlers in the West Bank and eighteen settlements with 2,150 settlers in Gaza.[29] Moreover, severe restrictions remained on how the lands remaining in Palestinian hands could be used.[30]

Settlements are typically built on hilltops in the West Bank (Gaza has no hills) and tend to be surrounded by fertile agricultural land. All settlements—which should be understood as modern, developed suburbs with spacious villas, recreational centers, schools, swimming pools, landscaping, even industrial parks—are surrounded by security-related infrastructure: fences, security zones, and military outposts, as well as landfills. The growing needs (for security, bypass roads, and other things) of the settlements have required the confiscation of more and more Palestinian lands. Thus, Palestinian land is seized for new settlements, new housing and amenities in existing settlements, and to expand the security cordon. Israel has also taken extensive amounts of Palestinian land for military bases, nature preserves (off-limits to Palestinians), military training areas, bypass roads, security zones, landfills, and so on.

Aside from the nationalist political implications, the more land that is taken from the Palestinians, the less they have to develop a sustainable agricultural economy, to develop an infrastructure that could support industrial development, and to provide housing, social services, and environmental protection to their society. The Jewish settlements and infrastructures also serve to fragment the West Bank and Gaza into isolated areas. Finally, of course, settlements consume massive amounts of water for residential and commercial use, depriving Palestinians of sufficient water for either personal or agricultural/industrial consumption.[31]

The Oslo period witnessed prodigious growth in settlements, the settler population, and supporting infrastructure. In March 2001, the Israeli organization Peace Now and its partner group, Americans for Peace Now, released data on land and settlements. Their statistics show that in the period between September 1993 (the signing of the Oslo Accords) and January 2000, forty-five new settlements were established (bringing the total number of independent settlement localities to more than 200); there was a 52 percent growth in housing in the settlements and a 72 percent growth in the settler population. All governments—Labor and Likud—participated in this expansion. For example, during the first twenty-one months of the Ehud Barak administration, 2,830 new housing units were constructed—more settlement expansion than took place under the Benjamin Netanyahu government.[32] Additionally, by 2002 military facilities in the West Bank occupied some 106 square kilometers, or 2.1 percent of the total area.[33]

Israeli governments use a variety of mechanisms to encourage Israeli citizens to move to the settlements. Some of these techniques include (1) Israel's de facto annexation of settlements; (2) a sophisticated land-use planning system that invests significant resources to expand and develop settlements; and (3) numerous economic incentives, including low interest rates on home mortgages and extensive financing of local councils, intended to raise the standard of living in the settlements. For example, in 2000, Jewish local councils in the West Bank received government grants that averaged 65 percent more than those received by their counterparts inside Israel. Settlements' regional councils received grants averaging *165 percent* more than their counterparts in Israel.[34]

Also during the period 1993–2000, Israel vastly expanded the settler infrastructure—completing, or initiating, the paving of 186 miles of new bypass roads. With the addition of these 186 miles, the total mileage of settler bypass roads was approximately 363 miles (586 kilometers) by September 2000, occupying 1.5 percent of West Bank land.[35] Palestinians were prohibited from using these roads.

In April 2002, Peace Now issued another report revealing that Ariel Sharon, during his first year as prime minister, had approved the establishment of thirty-five additional settlements. In a public statement, it charged that the government "is systematically violating its obligations to the public" and that the new colonies "are not just 'toeholds,' but constitute new settlements in every way because they have independent infrastructure and impact on new sections of land."[36] In August, the organization discovered an additional eight new colonies.[37] In September, *Ha'aretz* revealed one more new settlement "in the heart of the West Bank" (Rehalim) very near to Nablus.[38] By the continuous confiscation of Palestinian land and construction of Jewish settlements, Israel unmistakably signals its intention not to withdraw from the West Bank and Gaza.

Naomi Chazan, member and deputy speaker of the Knesset, commented on the settlements in 2001:

> Settlements were purposely placed in areas that would separate Palestinian population clusters, denying the possibility of Palestinian territorial integrity not only in the West Bank, but also in the Gaza Strip. This intention was reinforced by the by-pass road plan implemented during the past decade [the period of the Oslo process], which impeded Palestinian mobility and . . . totally truncated the West Bank. Behind these concerted actions lay the notion that the mere existence of strategically located settlements would prevent the creation of a Palestinian State.[39]

In a lengthy piece in *Tikkun*, Israeli scholar Ran HaCohen articulated the deeper impact of the settlements:

> The settlements are not just an appendix to the Israeli occupation, they are the occupation itself. They rob the Palestinians of every vital resource and freedom necessary for their life, both as individuals and as a nation. . . . [Then] there is the political significance. By moving Israeli citizens into the Territories, Israeli governments increase the number of citizens who have a vested interest (real estate, etc.) in keeping, expanding, and strengthening the settlements.[40]

Water

Immediately after the June 1967 war, Israel seized control of all the water sources in the West Bank and Gaza and placed them under the authority of military officials in charge of the occupation. In 1982, control was given to Mekorot, the Israeli national water company. Israel exercises control over Palestinian utilization of West Bank and Gaza water by placing restrictions on the digging of wells, by limiting the depth of wells, and by other means such as differential pricing: Palestinians, compared to Israelis, pay almost four times as much for water.[41]

Israel has experienced serious water shortages as well as increasing salinization of its water supply. Thus, by 1986 approximately one-quarter of the water used by Israel annually inside the Green Line for irrigation and consumption came from the West Bank. Israel also uses Palestinian water to fully hydrate the settlements in the West Bank and Gaza Strip, including their swimming pools, lawns, and gardens. Because Palestinian society has been traditionally based on agriculture, Israel's water restrictions have not only caused a serious deterioration in cultivation; they have had profound implications for all other aspects of Palestinian economic and social life.[42]

The total underground water potential of the West Bank is estimated to be 600 million cubic meters per year. About 125 million cubic meters are situated east of the watershed and are not utilized within Israel proper (though Israeli settlers in the West Bank use them). However, the western water table, with a capacity of 335 million cubic meters per year, and the northeastern water table, with some 140 million cubic meters per year, are fully utilized to hydrate Israel. Indeed, of the joint western and northeastern tables, Israel uses the vast majority of the water, whereas the Palestinian population is permitted only about 20 million cubic meters per year.[43] As reported by Meron Benvenisti: "This main water potential of the West Bank . . . is exploited to its limit, in a

ratio of 4.5 percent to the [Palestinians in the] West Bank and 95.5 percent to Israel."[44] Benvenisti elaborates:

> The total amount of water planned for allocation to the Arab sector
> (agriculture and domestic consumption) at the end of the decade
> [1980s] is 137 million cubic meters per year (for about one million
> people) and for the Jewish population, approximately 100 million
> cubic meters (for about 100,000 people [settlers]).[45]

The water situation in the Gaza Strip is even more severe than in
the West Bank. Consistent overpumping, in conjunction with adverse
ecological conditions, have lowered the volume of the water table and
caused seawater to enter it. The water is becoming increasingly salinat-
ed, and what is used for irrigation (90 percent of the total) is damaging
the quality of Gaza's agriculture, particularly citrus.[46] Israeli policies
have seriously worsened this situation. The water available for consumption is additionally becoming increasingly contaminated because
of the lack of proper sewage systems, as well as seepage from untreated
sewage, pesticides, and fertilizers. Palestinians face a myriad of diseases as a consequence of this situation.

Under the 1993 DOP, the Palestinian Water Authority (PWA) was
supposed to be established, although it was required to function in
cooperation with Mekorot. Together, they were to create the joint Water
Development Program. The DOP, however, did not recognize any
Palestinian water rights (i.e., the right of the PA to assess Palestinian
needs and utilize water resources in the Palestinian territories accordingly). Water, like land, remained under Israeli sovereignty. Thus,
Palestinian access remains dependent on Israeli permission. In the 1994
Gaza-Jericho agreement (Cairo I), the PWA was given jurisdiction over
the Gaza coastal aquifer (though none of the West Bank aquifers). This
right, however, was qualified by the proviso that all Israeli settlements
and military installations in Gaza (and the West Bank) were exempted
from PA/PWA authority. The result was that despite formal PA domin-
ion over the coastal aquifer (as well as required cooperation in its maintenance), Israel enjoyed unrestricted access to its water.

In the 1995 Interim Agreement (Oslo II), Palestinian water rights
were recognized for the first time. Still, Israel acknowledged only the
Palestinians' right to quantities of water (to be negotiated between
Israel and the Palestinians), not the right of Palestinians to sovereignty
over the aquifers. Today, control over water utilization remains in
Israeli hands. Palestinians are left with restricted access to water supplies insufficient to meet their current domestic consumption needs
(much less the needs of a growing population)—vastly inadequate to

the agricultural and industrial needs of an economy urgently in need of economic development.[47]

Israel's restrictions on Palestinian water usage for human consumption and agricultural/industrial development, severe in the mid-1980s, became far more stringent in the ensuing years.[48] In July 2000, B'Tselem reported that "the average Israeli consumes for domestic, urban, and industrial [and agricultural] use approximately 128 cubic meters a year, or 350 liters per person a day—*five times more* than the Palestinian per capita consumption." At *an average of 70 liters per day,* Palestinians thus consume less water than the World Health Organization and the U.S. Agency for International Development recommend as the *essential minimum of 100 liters* per person per day.[49] In the Gaza Strip, the imbalance in water consumption between settlers and residents is even greater than the aggregated figures for all the Occupied Territories. Israeli settlers in Gaza consume 584 liters per person per day; Palestinians consume 83 liters per person per day.[50]

The human implications of the foregoing statistics are far more profound than the numbers themselves reveal. There is a severe water crisis every summer in the Occupied Territories. Thousands of Palestinian homes have access to running water for only a few hours, two or three days a week. Despite the supposedly good intentions and spirit of cooperation at Oslo, nothing was done to ameliorate this situation. Every summer since 1993 has witnessed a more severe water shortage than the previous one. Two 1998 commentaries from *Ha'aretz* reflect the situation in a typical year: "More than half a million Palestinians in the West Bank—about a third of the total population—have been without regular running water for two months."[51] In addition,

> Every summer the same sad story repeats itself: a water shortage. The local wells dug by the Palestinian inhabitants cannot meet their needs, while the amount of water supplied by Israel takes into account neither the growth in the Palestinian population nor the pace of economic development. . . . The strict water rationing . . . is almost reminiscent of a people under siege.[52]

Collective Freedoms:
Economic Development and Well-Being

For the Palestinians who anticipated an independent state at the end of the Oslo process, the most important economic concern was planning for self-sustaining economic development. A state cannot be politically independent if it is fully dependent on or subordinate to a stronger economy. Palestinians hoped that as a result of the peace process they would be able to revive and develop their agricultural sector, develop a more technologically advanced, efficient, and productive industrial sector, and provide employment opportunities for the Palestinian labor force in Palestinian enterprises. Not one of these objectives was realized.

The economic situation in the Occupied Territories after 1993 was shaped by three overarching parameters: the legacy of a quarter century of Israeli policies of structural dependency and de-development, the DOP, and the 1994 Economic Protocol. The legacy of structural dependency and de-development proved impossible to overcome—especially when combined with the closures and the new restrictions specified in the Oslo agreements. More specifically, Palestinian economic development was impeded by the retention of Israeli military law after 1993: Israel's control over key factors of production (e.g., land, water, labor, and capital); Israel's control over external boundaries (effectively regulating Palestinian exports and imports, i.e., trade policy); and the ways in which the area was divided. The latter included the division of the West Bank into Areas A, B, and C; the separation of the West Bank from Gaza; and the prohibition on Palestinians from entering Jerusalem—all contributing to the economics of "enclavization."[53] Other causes of economic stagnation include misappropriation of donor aid, corruption in the PA (including kickbacks from private investors and monopolies over critical materials, e.g., gasoline and cement), wasteful and overly optimistic projects (e.g., the Jericho Oasis Casino and Bethlehem 2000), and mismanagement.[54]

Economic deterioration is measurable in statistics. Between 1994 and 1996, West Bank and Gaza gross national product (GNP) per capita income fell by 18.4 percent. Unemployment rose to 28 percent in 1996. In Gaza, unemployment was as high as 39 percent compared to 24 percent in the West Bank. Gross domestic product (GDP) growth was negative in 1996 and 1997 (at –5.1 percent and -0.7 percent respectively). In dollar terms, real per capita GDP in 1993 was about U.S.$1,600; by 1998 it had fallen to U.S.$1,370. In 1999–2000, there was a positive growth in GDP, but this was mitigated by Israel's policies during the Al-Aqsa intifada, demonstrating the extreme fragility of the Palestinian economy.[55]

Additionally, by 1998 the number of people living in poverty—defined as those with a per capita income of less than U.S.$2 per day—stood at 37.2 percent of the population in Gaza and 15.4 percent in the West Bank, up from a combined West Bank–Gaza Strip rate of 14 percent in 1995. That meant that in 1998 25 percent of households in the

West Bank and Gaza were living at or below the poverty line. At the end of 2000, the combined poverty rate for the West Bank and Gaza was 44 percent.[56] In the first quarter of 2001, 55.7 percent of the West Bank population was living below the poverty line, and 81.4 percent were below that line in Gaza. The combined West Bank–Gaza Strip poverty rate was 64.2 percent.[57] The main cause of poverty in the West Bank and Gaza, according to the World Bank, is "because of low economic development" (see Table 3.2).[58]

Palestinian Agriculture

Since the outset of the occupation, Israel has impeded the productivity and growth of Palestinian agriculture. In addition to water restrictions and land confiscation, Israel prohibited capital investment in physical infrastructure and restricted the development of support systems such as marketing and credit as well as regional support systems. Moreover, Israel specified and rigidly restricted what crops Palestinian farmers could grow, where and how they could be marketed, and so on.[59]

The effects of Israel's agricultural policies are readily measurable: between 1969 and 1985 in the West Bank, the agriculture share of GDP dropped from 36.4 to 30 percent; in the Gaza Strip during the same period, the agricultural percentage of GDP declined from 28.3 to 17.8 percent. At the same time, the agricultural labor force as a percent of total labor dropped from 46 percent to 27 percent in the West Bank, and

Table 3.2   Percentage of Population Living in Poverty[a] and Percentage Unemployed,[b] 1995–2002

	% Population Living in Poverty							
	1995	1996	1997	1998	1999	2000	2001	2002
West Bank	10		11	15				55
Gaza	20		40	37				81
Combined	14	26.9		23.2	21	35	50	64
	% Unemployed							
	1995	1996	1997	1998	1999	2000	2001	2002
West Bank and Gaza	18	21	21	16	12	10 to 28	37	46 to 70

Sources: Data obtained from the World Bank, the IMF, UNSCO, and the PCBS.
Notes: a. Poverty line: U.S.$750 per capita per year.
b. Year 2002 estimate as of June 1, 2002; year 2000 compares first and last quarter.

from 32 percent to 18 percent in Gaza.[60] Between 1993 and 1995, the real value of Palestinian agriculture output declined by 40.12 percent—the worst performance of any economic sector. By 1998, the agricultural share of the West Bank and Gaza Strip workforce had dropped to 13.2 percent.[61] The closure policies, plus Israel's control of land, water, trade, and markets, were the primary causes of this deterioration.

Additional practices that negatively affected West Bank and Gaza agriculture—which increased during each year between 1993 and 2000—include uprooting fruit and olive trees, burning crops, limiting the movement of herds, destroying greenhouses, interfering with fishing, and destroying agricultural land.[62] These were carried out both by the IDF (as collective punishment of a family for a security violation by one of its members), and by settlers (sometimes to enlarge settlements, sometimes merely as vigilantism). For example, in 1998–1999, the army and settlers uprooted 21,705 trees and burned tens of thousands of dunums of agricultural land in the West Bank and Gaza Strip.[63] In the Gaza Strip alone, between September 2000 and July 2001, Israel destroyed 16,000 dunums of agricultural land constituting 9 percent of the arable land. During the same period, it destroyed 175 greenhouses in Gaza.[64] In the West Bank and Gaza Strip combined, between September 29, 2000, and February 28, 2001, Israel uprooted 57,928 olive trees, 49,370 citrus trees, 22,270 stone-fruit trees (e.g., plums), 11,514 date trees, 12,000 banana trees, and 30,282 grapevines.[65] The effect of the foregoing is evidenced in one example: the amount of olives pressed in the West Bank and Gaza fell from 126,147 tons in 2000 to 22,155 tons in 2001—a drop of nearly 80 percent.[66] Aggregate data reveal that between September 28, 2000, and September 28, 2002, in the West Bank and Gaza 667,390 trees were uprooted and 3,669,000 square meters of cultivated agricultural land were destroyed.[67]

In Gaza, agriculture has been traditionally concentrated on the production of citrus almost to the exclusion of all other crops. Beginning in 1977, citrus yields began to decline far below their pre-1977 levels, and they have steadily declined since. The reasons for the contraction include the aforementioned actions combined with Israel's restrictions on Palestinian water use, as well as other policies directed at prohibiting the development of citriculture.[68] For instance, military orders make it illegal to plant new trees or replace old, nonproductive ones and require permits to plant fruit trees on a commercial scale—permits that take five or more years to obtain and are rarely issued. In addition, the tax policies applied to the citrus industry impeded its growth. These included land taxes, income taxes, value-added taxes, and export taxes.[69]

Similar laws affecting all agricultural products have been imposed on West Bank farming as well.[70]

The fishing industry provides an additional example of how Palestinian agriculture has fared in the post-Oslo period. The Paris economic protocol stipulates that Palestinians should be permitted to fish in a twenty-mile area (which is the same as prior to the DOP), although in practice Israel typically limits them to a twelve-mile radius. That was further reduced in early 2000 to six miles, and since September 2000 fishermen are confined to a four-mile or less radius.[71] In 1976–1977, fish production totaled 5,100 tons; in 1989–1990 it totaled 300 tons.[72] Israel's delays in authorizing construction of a port that could have accommodated fishing boats also hurt the industry. Palestinians had to continue launching their boats by tractors, pulling them into the sea from the sandy shores of the Gaza coast without docks to assist them.[73] Additional restrictions on fishing include, in the words of the Palestinian Society for Protection of Human Rights and the Environment (LAW): "Fishermen were subject to a certain timetable and limited fishing hours. They were forced to set sail in primitive fishing boats and were prohibited from buying more sophisticated machinery. These technical difficulties increased fishing costs and risked the lives of the fishermen during bad weather."[74]

In this context, it should be noted that while the PA exercises autonomy over most of Gaza (excluding the seventeen settlements and their security and transport infrastructure), the Oslo agreements give Israel sovereign control of all external borders, including the waters off the Gaza coast. Finally, Israel imposes export restrictions on Gaza fish. Permits for export are extremely rare, and those few that have been issued were rendered useless in the context of closures. Significantly, Israel does not even allow fish to be transported from Gaza to the West Bank.

Palestinian Industry

The following statistics with regard to the West Bank reflect the state of Palestinian industry. In the share of industrial contribution to GDP, the West Bank has evidenced a steady decline: in 1968 it stood at 8.2 percent, in 1975 at 9 percent, and in 1980 at 6.5 percent. In 1985, it rose slightly, to 8.1 percent.[75] The industrial share of West Bank and Gaza GNP rose to 17 percent by 1998, but the figures are misleading because the nature of the industrial sector changed very little. It continues to be composed of very small firms: 92 percent of the total employ less than ten persons—the majority of them employ four or less—and only 3 percent employ more than twenty people. Production remains geared to the most elementary products like textiles and apparel, tobacco products, paper goods, leather products, food and beverages, nonmetallic products, furniture, and so on. Such manufacturers do not contribute to research and development or to the production of more technologically sophisticated products that can fuel economic development.[76] In economic terms, there is no spin-off from the production of primary goods.

Unfortunately, the Oslo period has seen an intensification, rather than the reversal, of this pattern. The essential factors of production that were lacking prior to Oslo were not available after the agreements either. Some of the most basic include a plentiful urban water supply; available regular electricity; solid-waste collection; road networks; telecommunications capabilities; and educational facilities. Additionally, industries require markets and the ability to regulate trade, national control over monetary policies, freedom of movement for goods and persons, credit, access to technology, and much more. All of this has been denied to Palestinians. Closures were also a major obstacle as was the Paris economic protocol with its myriad restrictions.

Another cause of the problems in the Palestinian industrial sector is the investment strategy of external investors and the incentives they received from the PA. One aspect of the economic protocol was the agreement to establish joint Israeli-Palestinian industrial zones in the West Bank and Gaza. The appeals for Palestinians were more job opportunities and decreasing dependence on Israel for employment. For Israeli capitalists, the incentive was the opportunity to move factories to an area where overhead and wages were a fraction of those in Israel—for example, NIS 1,500 per month in Gaza versus NIS 5,000 per month in Israel.[77]

Nevertheless, Israel delayed concluding an agreement for the first zone, the Qarni Industrial Estate in Gaza, until December 14, 1998. That accord was not implemented, and on June 22, 1999, Israel and the PA signed a second agreement to open Qarni. A year later—seven years after the start of the Oslo process—the first industrial project opened at a cost of about U.S.$65 million. Thirty-eight companies were operational, employing some 1,200 Palestinians. Included among the plants were a tire-retreading firm, a bedsheet plant, a light-fixture manufacturing company, textile plants, and a website design company. There were also a number of food-processing and agrobusiness firms. Notably, with few exceptions, these factories were manufacturing the same products, albeit on a larger scale, that have been the traditional mainstay of Palestinian industry. The laborers were working for foreign industrialists (who were not intending to reinvest their profits in the Palestine economy), and though this arrangement provided some employment, it contributed nothing to encourage autonomous economic development. Qarni was closed as a result of the Al-Aqsa intifada.

The PA Ministry of Labor projected that when all the industrial zones in the West Bank and Gaza were complete they would employ about 2,966 people.[78] They were not completed, but even had the zones reached maximum productivity, it would constitute only a tiny percentage of the total labor force. For that reason, many Palestinians in the West Bank and Gaza were skeptical from the outset as to the developmental or even the labor-absorptive utility of the industrial zones. They grew increasingly more critical after the PA created a set of tax laws that made the zones a paradise for foreign investors (e.g., seven- to ten-year tax exemptions) but without commensurate benefits to Palestinians.[79] The new laws were followed by reports of corruption among PA officials who awarded licenses.[80] In short, during the years of the peace process, the West Bank and Gaza did not experience any significant industrial development.

Palestinian Labor

Employment opportunities in the Occupied Territories are far fewer compared to the pool of labor that is available. During the first twenty years of the occupation, Israel absorbed a significant portion of the labor force. For example, in 1984, 50,000 Palestinians from the West Bank, constituting 31.5 percent of the West Bank workforce, were legally employed in Israel. Another 20,000 were working there illegally. Similarly, 40,000 workers from Gaza, constituting 46 percent of the workforce, were legally employed in Israel, with another 12,000 illegal workers, including children between the ages of five and fifteen (altogether about 122,000 workers). Most were in sanitation services, construction, and hotel and other services.[81] During the 1980s, Palestinian wages were substantially lower compared to those of Jewish workers in Israel, but they were significantly higher than rates in the West Bank and Gaza. Moreover, the income earned from working in Israel (as well as abroad) fueled an increase in the standard of living for many in the territories and had a ripple effect throughout the Palestinian economy. The problem inherent in this relationship, however, has been that since 1987 Israel's repeated closures have left either large portions, or all, of these workers unemployed.

Many Palestinian workers were also employed in Saudi Arabia and the Gulf States during the 1970s and 1980s and sent considerable sums of money (remittances) back to the Occupied Territories. However, with the downturn in oil prices in the third quarter of the 1980s, many of these workers were sent home. After the 1991 Gulf War, all were expelled. Thus, the local labor force expanded enormously, but the number of jobs did not; in fact, it began to decline, and unemployment in the Occupied Territories started to climb.

On the eve of the 1993 Oslo Accords, there were approximately 116,000 Palestinians working in Israel. By 1996, that number had dropped to 28,000 and then rose to 48,986 in 1999.[82] As a consequence, unemployment in the West Bank and Gaza rose from approximately 18 percent between 1990 and 1993 to 32.65 percent in 1996. It edged down slightly in the next three years to 30.3 percent in 1997, 25.15 percent in 1998, and 22.05 percent in 1999.[83] Unemployment rates in Gaza have been consistently higher than the national average. For example, in 1996 they were 41.1 percent and in 1997 37.5 percent.[84] The PA absorbed some of these shocks by hyperinflating its bureaucracy, but such employment in the service sector contributes nothing to economic development. Because the industrial sector did not reach a self-sustaining level and the agricultural sector contracted, workers cut off from employment in Israel had no work in the Occupied Territories. Thus, Palestinian unemployment soared and poverty levels escalated.

The Airport and Seaport

To enhance the Palestinian freedom of movement of persons and goods, and to fuel economic development, Israel committed itself in the DOP and again in Oslo II to opening a Palestinian airport and a seaport in Gaza. As with safe passage, however, Israel imposed repeated delays; the airport was not opened until November 1998, and the seaport was never officially opened.

Despite the five-year lapse in its inauguration, Dahaniya Airport was an important symbol to Palestinians. However, it remained under Israeli security control. Israel determined that there could be no nighttime flights. It maintained a separate, strictly Israeli, security facility to check all departing and arriving passengers and cargo after PA officials had processed them. Israel specified which country's planes could and could not use the airport and controlled the airspace and all flight patterns. Furthermore, Israel was solely responsible for the security of Israelis who passed through the air terminal.[85] Israel imposed two temporary closures on the airport before shutting it completely in October 2000—less than two years after flights had commenced. Initially, Arafat was allowed, with Israel's permission, to fly his private plane from

Dahaniya. On January 9, 2002, Israel destroyed the airport with aerial bombardments, tanks, and bulldozers.

Construction of the Gaza port facility was also continually postponed.[86] The port held significant potential for Palestinian economic life. First, its construction would provide immediate work for thousands of Gaza citizens—a matter of great urgency given the extremely high unemployment.[87] Its completion would mean that Palestinians could export agricultural and industrial goods directly from Gaza and the West Bank to other countries. They would no longer have to truck them to Ashdod or Haifa ports or pay Israeli customs, duties, and other taxes. They would also be freed from the permit-induced delays that continuously caused Palestinian produce to decay before it reached a ship. Concern that an increase in Palestinian economic independence would negatively affect their own economy was the main reason Israel opposed the port, although it claimed that the port would facilitate the importation of contraband (e.g., weapons).

In August 1999, Israel finally consented to construction, which was to begin on 1 October; however, it was a much scaled-back facility with a far more limited capacity than had been originally conceived. Moreover, Israel insisted on retaining full security control of the port facilities. Actual construction did not commence until nearly a year later, and then it was limited to several buildings. Once under way, construction proceeded very slowly owing to Israeli-imposed delays on materials. Work on the port itself was not begun.

On September 18, 2001, Israel completely demolished the unfinished port facility using aerial bombardments, tanks, and bulldozers. Among the destroyed structures were the fences surrounding the area, all the finished and unfinished buildings, the offices of Palace Needham (the Dutch-French company contracted by the PA to develop the port), and PA port offices (the Palestinian Port Authority).[88]

Development of the Palestinian Economy Under Oslo

In June 2000, the New York–based Council for Economic and Social Rights wrote: "The Palestinian economy is poorer and more vulnerable today than it was at the start of the peace process, and is further, not closer, to the path of sustainable development."[89] B'Tselem also published a comprehensive critique of the effect of the Oslo process on the Palestinian economy.[90]

Most significant in the foregoing are the Israeli impediments to self-sustaining, autonomous economic development, without which an independent state—had one been in the offing—could not have survived. The economic protocol ensured Israel's continued control of land, water, trade, infrastructure, and the like, but Tel Aviv's closure policies were even more devastating. Israel sought to keep the Occupied Territories dependent on it and to assure that the Palestinian agricultural and industrial sectors did not compete with those of Israel. Trade relations illustrate the continuing problem of dependency: of the total Palestinian exports, 95 percent go to the Israeli market, whereas 80 percent of all imports originate in Israel. Worse, by 2000, the Occupied Territories had a trade deficit of 50 percent of GDP.[91] The insecure political situation throughout the seven years discouraged private investment that rightly feared renewed instability. Indeed, private investment fell from U.S.$1,012.23 million in 1992 to U.S.$255.79 million in 1996.[92] Capital infusions by international donor institutions were invested in specific projects (telecommunications, roads, etc.) that were insufficient to generate self-sustaining growth and raise Palestine out of its less-than–third world status.

In the final analysis, not only did a process of self-sustaining growth not occur; by all economic indicators, the Palestinian economy actually regressed during the post-Oslo years. Moreover, what small advances were made have been destroyed by Israel as a result of the Al-Aqsa intifada.

Individual Freedoms

Although Oslo adversely affected collective freedom, the picture of individual freedom is somewhat less apparent. In certain ways and in some regions, individual freedoms improved. In Area A, for example, the overbearing presence of the IDF was gone, and a variety of new activities from businesses to nightlife blossomed. Town arrest and house arrest were minimal between 1993 and 2000. Restrictions on freedom of speech, peaceful assembly, and the press were rarely enforced (although the PA gradually imposed its own limitations in these areas). Palestinians could display their flag and other nationalist symbols without fear of arrest. In many other respects, however, individual freedoms were equally or more restricted than they had been before Oslo.[93]

Overview and Background

The legal status of Palestinians in the Occupied Territories is imprecise, though in practice in the West Bank and Gaza they are considered "alien residents."[94] In Jerusalem, Palestinians are categorized as "permanent residents," but they are "treated not as an integral part of the city's citizen body, rather like some [temporary] non-Jewish foreigners."[95]

Since 1967, Israel has applied three different sets of laws in the West Bank and Gaza, none giving Palestinians the legal rights enjoyed by Israeli Jews—neither the settlers who live in the occupied areas, nor the residents of Israel proper. The various legal systems Israel has used include (1) military orders (MOs); (2) emergency regulations; and (3) Jordanian, Egyptian, and Ottoman law. MOs are regulations issued on a day-by-day basis by the Israeli military governor of the territories. By 1986, a year before the outbreak of the first intifada, there were almost 1,200 MOs in the West Bank and 900 in Gaza, affecting every aspect of Palestinian life.[96] British Mandatory Defense (Emergency) Regulations are orders that were originally imposed in the aftermath of the 1936–1939 Palestinian uprising but were later used by the mandatory government against Jews. When they were employed to repress Jews, Zionist leaders condemned them as abuses of the "basic principles of law, justice and jurisprudence," arguing that they "rob[bed] every settler of his basic rights."[97] After independence, Israel retained this legislation for use against its Palestinian citizens until 1996 and, in 1967, extended it to the Occupied Territories. Jordanian, Egyptian, and Ottoman legal systems have been invoked when the Israeli authorities have found it expedient to do so. For instance, Israel has used Ottoman land laws to legitimize confiscation of Palestinian land.

Prior to Oslo, Palestinians in the Occupied Territories were (and in Areas B and C continue to be) subjected to two different court systems (Israeli settlers have their own separate courts). Civil courts deal with cases in which the occupation authorities have no stake. Judges in these courts are Israeli-appointed Palestinians. Military courts deal with everything falling under the rubric of security or any matter with which the occupation authorities wish to concern themselves. Judges in the military courts are Israelis and are appointed by the area military commander. No regular system of judicial appeal exists, making it virtually impossible to correct judicial errors or to guarantee proper procedures and standards of evidence.[98]

Palestinians in the West Bank and Gaza have had one avenue of appeal. They have the right to petition the Israeli High Court of Justice to overrule a conviction or a decree issued by the military courts or occupation authorities. Israel has gained considerable public relations advantage from this legal innovation; however, several considerations must be noted. The areas of judicial review are few and extremely narrow. The High Court has sustained the supremacy of MOs as the dominant law in the territories. It ruled that the Fourth Geneva Convention is not binding in the Occupied Territories.[99] It confirmed the principle that the military governor is the sole and unchecked legislator for the area, whose orders are beyond the scrutiny of the High Court. In 2002, the court upheld the right of the IDF to destroy the homes of suspected militants and to deport their relatives.[100] Petitions to the court may be made only through Israeli lawyers—Palestinian lawyers may not appear before the court. The losing party in an appeal must pay both the court costs and the lawyers' fees of the winning party. The evidence used to uphold convictions of Palestinians is almost always withheld from their defense attorneys (allegedly for reasons of national security). Finally, only in extremely rare and highly technical cases has the High Court overturned a decision by a military court.[101]

After the Oslo Accords, Palestinians under the jurisdiction of the PA (i.e., those residing in Area A) came under the administration of the PA. Since 1994, the PA has had its own courts for offenses committed in Area A, and the PA is responsible for arresting and incarcerating persons from those places. However, Israel retains the right to arrest an individual from Area A if it considers him/her responsible for a security offense and the PA fails to imprison the person. In Area C (about 70 percent of the Occupied Territories), Israel is solely responsible for security affairs, including the arrests, detentions, and/or charges and convictions in this domain, and the entire Israeli legal apparatus remains in force. In Area B (about 26 percent of the West Bank), both Israel and the PA have security responsibilities, and either one may arrest, detain, and charge persons therein. Thus, whether an individual is arrested by the Israeli or the Palestinian security services determines which laws and court system are applied to the case. The following discussion focuses on Israeli practices (see Chapter 6 for a discussion of PA policies).[102]

Several Israeli legal practices have had deleterious consequences for Palestinians; these include administrative detention, arbitrary arrest and forced confession, torture, house demolitions, the failure of the Israeli government to apply the rule of law in cases of settler violence, political assassinations, and expulsion and deportation. Several of these are discussed below.

Administrative Detention

Administrative detention is the arbitrary imprisonment of an individual for up to six months without charge or trial. After six months, Israel can extend a person's administrative detention for a second six-month period, and so on indefinitely, at the whim of the occupation authorities. Under this policy, many Palestinians have been incarcerated from two to six years.[103] Detained persons may be denied access to a lawyer during the entire detention period. Legislation governing administrative detention was originally introduced in the British Defense (Emergency) Regulations. In 1982, Israel temporarily discontinued administrative detention, although the legislation remained on the books. In July 1985, Israel revived the practice.[104] B'Tselem has the most comprehensive data on numbers of detainees, although it does not always provide the aggregate information sought.

In July 1999, B'Tselem wrote that between the signing of the Oslo Accords in 1993 and May 1999 "Israel has administratively detained some one thousand Palestinians for periods ranging from two months to five and a half years."[105] Furthermore, "Forty percent have been detained for over one year. . . . At least eleven . . . have spent over three consecutive years in administrative detention."[106] In a May 1999 report, B'Tselem documents that in 1997 Israel issued 354 administrative detention orders; in 1998 it issued eighty-two and in the first three months of 1999 it issued seventy-five.[107] B'Tselem concludes:

> The data shows that . . . since the signing of the Declaration of Principles, Israel's policy toward the human rights of the Palestinians in the Occupied Territories has not changed . . . Even though fewer persons suffer from these violations . . . prolonged administrative detention still occurs.[108]

As of January 30, 2003, 1,007 individuals were being held under administrative detention.[109]

Arbitrary Arrest and Forced Confession

Since 1967, every Israeli soldier has had the right to detain any Palestinian person if the soldier has grounds for suspicion that the detainee may have committed a security offense. Persons may be detained for eighteen days without charge and without access to a lawyer, during which time he or she can be subjected to constant interrogation and a punitive and humiliating regime that, according to B'Tselem, usually involves torture.[110] Confessions obtained under such circumstances (written in Hebrew) may be used to convict the individual making the confession; they may also be used as the sole or principal piece of evidence against anyone named by the detainee. Convictions cannot be appealed.[111] Under the Oslo Accords, Israel retained the right to arrest, interrogate, and imprison any Palestinian, including those who came from Area A.[112]

Security Offenses

Israel has used security concerns to justify most measures it has desired to undertake.[113] Moreover, it has refused to define *security* or explain which criteria fulfill Israeli security requirements in any given case. One of the most widely employed infractions involves membership in a terrorist organization. In the early 1970s, Israel declared the PLO a terrorist organization whose sole aim was the destruction of Israel. It further maintained that all Palestinians who were members of the PLO were committed to the destruction of Israel and, therefore, that Israel was morally and legally justified in any action against them on the basis of self-defense and national security. The PLO did not issue membership cards or have any formal criteria of membership, but any Palestinian could be accused of being a member. Thousands of Palestinians were imprisoned on this basis, almost always without being formally charged, much less convicted. Although not challenging Israel's definition of *membership* in the PLO, Amnesty International repeatedly condemned Israel's system as arbitrary, arguing that membership, by itself, did not constitute a punishable offense.[114] After the Oslo Accords, Israel ceased using alleged membership in the PLO as a pretext for arresting individuals. It was replaced, however, by alleged membership in Hamas.

Security offenses do, of course, include the commission of violent crimes. When Israel has evidence that an individual has carried out a violent offense, that person is charged, tried in a military court, and sentenced to a fixed prison term.[115] Meron Benvenisti undertook a systematic analysis of Palestinians imprisoned between 1967 and 1987 and concluded that the maximum possible number of incarcerations for genuine security violations—gunfire, throwing grenades or Molotov cocktails, setting explosive devices, and laying mines—was 21,742. Conversely, detentions for nonviolent political activities (labeled as security offenses) were 578,000.[116] Between 1988 and 1993, some 112,000 individuals were detained without charge for varying lengths of time.[117] B'Tselem provides annual data as a basis for comparison.[118]

After the signing of the DOP, the absolute numbers of individuals arrested and charged declined. In 1994, Israel arrested and charged 6,500 persons with security offenses. In 1995 it charged 1,600 persons and in 1996 1,200. Arrests for security offenses rose sharply in the next three years: in 1997 Israel arrested 13,000 persons, in 1998 11,500, and in 1999, 10,965.[119] As of July 2000, Israel held 1,550 individuals in custody for security offenses, most in prisons inside the Green Line.[120] These are significant numbers in the context of a peace process; notably, all occurred before the eruption of the Al-Aqsa intifada. Moreover, simultaneously, the PA was arresting hundreds of Palestinians.[121] In September 2002, *Ha'aretz* reported that Israel had arrested more than 30,000 individuals during the two years of the uprising and that at the time it was holding some 8,000–10,000 prisoners.[122]

Torture

Israel's use of torture has been widespread from the outset of the occupation to the present.[123] Many organizations have documented and condemned this Israeli practice including B'Tselem, Amnesty International, Human Rights Watch, LAW, and others.[124] B'Tselem notes that Israel is the only Western democracy to have legalized torture; reports that torture in Israel is unexceptional, authorized, and institutionalized; and alleges that Israel uses torture routinely, having tortured thousands of Palestinians.[125] According to B'Tselem researcher Na'ama Carmi, in the post-Oslo period Israel has continued to employ torture during interrogation against 85 percent of all administrative detainees and security prisoners.[126]

Demolition

The demolition of residential housing has been used since the beginning of the occupation, although the reasons for this practice have changed over time. Initially, demolition was employed primarily as collective punishment of families of individuals arrested and charged with a security offense. A related practice, known as "sealing," in which windows are blocked with cement and cinder blocks and doors are hermetically sealed in order to deny persons access to all or part of their homes, is also used.[127] Between 1987 and 1993, 1,383 Palestinian homes were demolished and 296 were sealed.[128] In June 2001, Jeff Halper, an Israeli professor and coordinator of the Israeli Committee Against House Demolitions, noted that Israel had demolished at least 7,000 Palestinian homes since 1967, with more than 500 more demolished during the first ten months of the Al-Aqsa intifada.[129]

After the 1993 Oslo Accords, Israeli policy on house demolitions changed from collective punishment to something else, becoming part of Tel Aviv's overall effort to encourage the emigration of Palestinians—especially from East Jerusalem—and to extend the landmass that

Israel would control in any final settlement with Palestinians.[130] In the words of Amnesty International: "The demolition of Palestinian homes is inextricably linked with Israeli policy to control and colonize . . . the West Bank."[131]

Israel's official reason for bulldozing houses during the Oslo period has been that the houses were constructed without permits. Throughout the occupation, however, Israel rejected nearly every application for such a permit. Yet as families grew larger, expanding a house was a necessity, and building a new house was the dream of every Palestinian family. Meron Benvenisti, writing in *Ha'aretz* in 2002, made the following assessment of house demolitions:

> The destruction of a home is a barbaric act, and taking such a course of action, no matter what the excuse, is an act of terror that comes under the category of a war crime. . . . It would be hard to overstate the symbolic value of a house to an individual for whom the culture of wandering and of becoming rooted to the land is so deeply ingrained in tradition, for an individual whose national mythos is based on the tragedy of being uprooted from a stolen homeland. The arrival of a firstborn son and the building of a home are the central events in such an individual's life because they symbolize continuity in time and physical space. And with the demolition of the individual's home comes the destruction of his world.[132]

Between 1993 and 1999, Israel demolished 962 houses.[133] From September 2000 (the beginning of the second uprising) through July 2002, Israel demolished 632 houses and sealed 414 houses (see Table 3.3).[134]

Settler Violence

The issue of settler violence is examined extensively in Chapter 4 on Hebron. In summary, Jewish settlers in the Occupied Territories have used various forms of violence against Palestinians since 1967.[135] Settlers are heavily armed and are backed by the Israeli military, judicial, and governmental systems, which support them in many ways.[136]

Political Assassination and Unjustified Shooting

Assassination has long been an Israeli practice, as has shooting into crowds of unarmed demonstrators. B'Tselem terms the latter "unjustified shooting," and this policy has caused many Palestinian fatalities.[137] It will be examined in detail in Chapter 8. Data on targeted assassina-

Table 3.3   House Demolitions in the West Bank and East Jerusalem as
Collective Punishment and for Lack of Permits

Year	West Bank	East Jerusalem
2002 (to 3/1/02)	6	4
2001	119	35
2000	12	9
1999	36	23
1998	150	30
1997	239	16
1996	151	17
1995	43	25
1994	121	29
1993	66	48
1992	158	12
1991	327[a]	
1990	220[a]	
1989	509[a]	
1988	299	30

Sources: B'Tselem, *Demolition of Houses Built Without Permits, 1987–2002* (Jerusalem: B'Tselem—the Israeli Information Center for Human Rights in the Occupied Territories, 2002) and B'Tselem, *House Demolition—Statistics* (Jerusalem: B'Tselem—the Israeli Information Center for Human Rights in the Occupied Territories, 2002).

Note: a. West Bank figures include East Jerusalem for years 1989, 1990, 1991.

tions are somewhat more difficult to obtain. Israel first began implementing its policy of political assassination against Palestinians in the 1970s and continued the practice through the 1990s. Palestinian officials were assassinated in Beirut, Stockholm, Nicosia, Limassol, Rome, Paris, Lillehammer (Norway), Tunis, Amman, and elsewhere.[138]

B'Tselem states:

> Israel is the only democratic country that regards such measures as a legitimate course of action. This policy is patently illegal . . . a policy whose implementation involves a high risk of hurting bystanders and from which there is no turning back. . . . Israel must cease assassinating Palestinians immediately.[139]

Indeed, human rights organizations unequivocally condemn the policy of political assassination.[140] In another report, B'Tselem strongly denounces the practice, noting: "Israel did not devise the assassination policy in the wake of the current intifada. . . . It has employed this policy in the Occupied Territories and abroad for over 30 years. . . . There can be no justification of Israel's assassination policy."[141]

Between the signing of the DOP and 2000, there were two documented assassination episodes: the January 1996 assassination of Yahya Ayyash, and the failed September 1997 attempt on Khalid Meshal (in Amman). However, in the period between September 1993 and April 2000, Israel killed 347 Palestinians in the Occupied Territories (compared to 1,124 between December 1987 and September 1993).[142]

During the Al-Aqsa intifada, Israel intensified the policy of assassination, making it quasi-official under the rubric of liquidation. Between September 2000 and September 2002, Israel assassinated 104 Palestinians, additionally killing forty-six civilian bystanders.[143] A July 2002 liquidation was more controversial than most. Israel killed Hamas leader Salah Shehadeh, while he was asleep with his family, with a one-ton bomb dropped by an F-16 fighter jet on a crowded residential neighborhood in Gaza City. Besides Shehadeh, the bombing caused the death of sixteen civilians including eleven children, the wounding of some 140 civilians, and the destruction of an entire neighborhood. B'Tselem called it a "war crime."[144] For more detailed information on Palestinian deaths, see Table 3.4.

One assassination that has particularly negative consequences for Israel occurred on August 27, 2001, when Israel liquidated the head of the Popular Front for the Liberation of Palestine, Abu Ali Mustafa, with IDF rockets fired into his Ramallah office. Mustafa was a puzzling target because no one, including Israel, had ever alleged that he was associated with any violent activities; moreover, the Popular Front's support in the Occupied Territories was no more than 3–4 percent. Its ideology—Marxist, secular, and pan-Arab—appealed to only a handful of individuals, mostly intellectuals.[145] This assassination, however, triggered a chain reaction of violence and counterviolence. Palestinians retaliated for Mustafa's killing with an assassination of their own: on October 17, PFLP operatives gunned down Israeli Tourism Minister Rehavam Ze'evi in a Jerusalem hotel while another faction carried out a suicide bombing in Israel. Tel Aviv responded with massive violence against the Palestinian population throughout the West Bank and Gaza. Indeed, as with every other Israeli assassination, this one too served only to escalate the conflict.

Expulsion and Deportation

Expulsion has been an aspect of Zionist-Israeli thought and practice from the outset of the movement (see Chapter 1). It is important to revisit this issue because of the growing public sentiment among some Israelis in the context of the Al-Aqsa intifada to expel all Palestinians.[146] In a December 2001 poll conducted by the Israeli daily *Ma'ariv*,

Table 3.4   Israeli and Palestinian Deaths Before and After Oslo

Category	Before Oslo: Dec. 9, 1987–Sept. 14, 1993		After Oslo: Sept. 13, 1993–Aug. 31, 2001	
	Occupied Territories	Israel	Occupied Territories	Israel
Palestinian civilians by Israeli security forces	1,070	17	687	19
Palestinian civilians by Israeli civilians	54	21	70	6
Palestinian security forces by Israeli security forces	—	—	102	—
Israeli civilians by Palestinians	47	53	107	176
Israeli security forces by Palestinian civilians	43	17	56	53
Israeli security forces by Palestinian security forces	—	—	24	—
Total Palestinians killed	1,162		884	
Total Israelis killed	160		416	

Sources: B'Tselem, *Persons Killed Before and After Signing of the Declaration of Principles, 13 September 1993* (Jerusalem: Israeli Information Center for Human Rights in the Occupied Territories, 2001), available online at www.btselem.org/Files/site/english/data/ Fatalities_Since_Oslo.asp.

"50 percent of Israelis now favor 'transferring' the Arabs of the West Bank and the Gaza Strip to Arab countries."[147] Pressure for expelling Palestinians continued to grow as the Al-Aqsa intifada became increasingly protracted; the *Christian Science Monitor* wrote about the issue in February 2002:

> Israeli advocates of a mass expulsion of Palestinians are gaining strength and legitimacy. . . . Tourism Minister Benny Elon . . . this week launched a campaign advocating "transfer," a euphemism for expulsion. . . . Prime Minister Ariel Sharon has not repudiated the idea of a mass expulsion. Sharon, says his spokesman, would like to expel the Palestinians, but does not believe this can be carried out under the present conditions. . . . Right-wing rabbis, allied to the settler movement have also issued a series of writings advocating expulsions.[148]

Chapter 9 discusses this issue in more detail, and it is a matter that demands to be taken seriously.

Conclusion

This discussion illustrates that the Oslo process brought the Palestinians no closer to their objective of a viable independent state in the West Bank and Gaza. Collective social, economic, and political punishments destroyed their hopes for economic development and severely restricted their personal freedom of movement. Some of these policies were newly implemented in the aftermath of the Oslo agreements; other policies and practices were simply carried over from the pre-Oslo era as if nothing had changed.

In the seven years between the signing of the DOP and the eruption of the Al-Aqsa intifada in September 2000, Palestinian human rights were not on the agenda of any player in the Oslo process—Israel, the United States, or the PA. Moreover, the letter of the peace process was violated on all issues: the deadline for the end of the five-year transition period came and went without even the opening of final-status talks. Implementation of the West Bank–Gaza safe passage for persons and goods was delayed for six years, only partially completed, subject to stringent Israeli restrictions, and closed a year later. The commitment to permit external access for Palestinians through an airport and seaport was not fulfilled. The three-stage redeployment/withdrawal from all of the West Bank and Gaza except for final-status areas was not carried out. The redeployments that did occur were always less than the agreements stipulated and in every case involved lengthy delays. Releases of political prisoners were delayed or did not occur at all.

Spiraling degeneration in economic circumstances, increasing restrictions on freedom of movement, societal disintegration, and thwarted hopes for the future transformed what had been massive popular support for the peace process into gradual opposition to it, to Israel as a peace partner, and eventually to the PA itself. Indeed, as Chapter 6 demonstrates, Palestinians came to distrust, and finally to disapprove of, the PA both because of its own repressive practices, corruption, and nepotism and because they perceived it as an agent of Israel's objectives in the Occupied Territories. Together, all these disappointments, humiliations, and deprivations resulted in mass rage and despair that finally erupted in the Al-Aqsa intifada.

Chapter 4 examines Hebron—both the city and district—as a microcosm of the problems discussed here. It also introduces an additional element that plagues all West Bank Palestinians and Gazans: settler violence and the Israeli government's collusion in it. Hebron, as I will demonstrate, is both typical and unique. Chapter 5 analyzes Israel's policies in East Jerusalem, and will also expand on issues raised in this section (e.g., house demolitions) and will introduce other issues that, like settler violence, are common throughout all areas of the West Bank and Gaza (e.g., family reunification). It will also introduce issues that are specific to Palestinian Jerusalemites. It further focuses on Jerusalem as a fulcrum for Israel's settlement and bypass road system, where the holy city is the point at which settlement blocs as far flung as the Etzion Bloc in the south, Ma'ale Adumim in the East, and Modi'in Illit and Giv'at Ze'ev in the north (with connections to Ariel and Beit El) will form a contiguous settlement ring across the West Bank, dissecting the Palestinian areas into at least three distinct, isolated cantons.

Notes

1. Amira Hass, "The Revolt of the Guinea-Pigs," *Ha'aretz* (Jerusalem, daily, English), February 21, 2001.

2. Henry Siegman, "Middle East Conflict: Seek Palestinian Confidence in What?" *International Herald Tribune*, July 17, 2001.

3. See, for example, Na'ama Carmi et al., *Oslo, Before and After: The Status of Human Rights in the Occupied Territories* (Jerusalem: B'Tselem—the Israeli Information Center for Human Rights in the Occupied Territories, May 1999).

4. See, for example, LAW, *Israeli Violations of Palestinian Economic Rights* (Jerusalem: Palestinian Society for the Protection of Human Rights and the Environment—LAW, May 2000).

5. See Mervat Rishmawi and Rhys Johnson, *Right to Work: Economic Rights Under Military Occupation* (a report by the Economic, Social, and Cultural Rights Initiative) (Jerusalem: Palestinian Society for the Protection of Human Rights and the Environment—LAW, 1999), pp. 53–67; and Roger Normand and Lucy Mair, *Under Siege: Israeli Human Rights Violations in Palestine* (presented to the 25th session of the United Nations Committee on Economic, Social, and Cultural Rights) (New York: Center for Economic and Social Rights, 2000), pp. 6–8 and passim.

6. B'Tselem, *Policy of Closure* (Jerusalem: Israeli Information Center for Human Rights in the Occupied Territories, n/d). Also see Yehezkel Lein, *Civilians Under Siege: Restrictions on Freedom of Movement as Collective Punishment* (Jerusalem: B'Tselem—the Israeli Information Center for Human Rights in the Occupied Territories, 2001), pp. 2–5 and ff.

7. Rishmawi and Johnson, *Right to Work*, pp. 51–52.

8. Ibid., p. 52.

9. Lein, *Civilians Under Siege,* pp. 6–10 and ff.

10. News release by the International Secretariat of Amnesty International, *Israel and the Occupied Territories: International Community Should ACT Promptly to End Israeli Policy of Closures in the West Bank and Gaza* (London: Amnesty International, July 18, 2001) (MDE 15/066/2001 124/01; emphasis added).

11. Normand and Mair, *Under Siege*, p. 8. Also see Center for Economic

and Social Rights, *Enforcing the International Covenant on Economic, Social, and Cultural Rights: Reports on Israeli Violations* (Palestine Project Series 2) (New York: Center for Economic and Social Rights, January 2000), p. 15.

12. UNESCO, *Report on the Palestine Economy (with Special Report on Palestinian Merchandise Trade* (Gaza City: Office of the United Nations Special Co-ordinator, spring 2000), p. 18.

13. Ishac Diwan and Radwan A. Shaban, eds., *Development Under Adversity: The Palestinian Economy Under Transition* (Executive Summary), (Washington, DC: Joint Report: Palestine Economic Policy Research Institute and the World Bank, 1999), p. 6 (for the years 1993–1996). Leila Farsakh, "Economic Viability of a Palestinian State in the West Bank and the Gaza Strip," *MIT Electronic Journal of the Middle East*, no. 5 (2001): 6 (for the years 1997–2000).

14. See Amos Harel, "IDF Concerned About Soldiers' Abuse of Palestinian Civilians at Roadblocks," *Ha'aretz*, July 23, 2001.

15. Center for Economic and Social Rights, *Progress, Stagnation, or Regression? The Palestinian Economy Under the Oslo Accords* (New York: Center for Economic and Social Rights, June 2000), p. 7.

16. B'Tselem, *Death Following Restrictions on Movement* (Jerusalem: Israeli Information Center for Human Rights in the Occupied Territories, October 2000). Also see Yehezkel Lein, *No Way Out: Medical Implications of Israel's Siege Policy* (Jerusalem: B'Tselem—the Israeli Information Center for Human Rights in the Occupied Territories, 2001), and Leah Uberseder et al., "Report on the Siege," *News from Within* (Jerusalem, monthly, English) 17, no. 5 (July 2001): 3–9.

17. Yehezkel Lien, *Civilians Under Siege,* p. 27; and Lein, *No Way Out.*

18. Yael Stein, *Illusions of Restraint: Human Rights Violations During the Events in the Occupied Territories 29 September–2 December 2000* (Jerusalem: B'Tselem—the Israeli Information Center for Human Rights in the Occupied Territories, December 2000), pp. 26–27.

19. Harel, "IDF Concerned About Soldiers' Abuse of Palestinian Civilians at Roadblocks."

20. Suzanne Goldenberg, "Israel Bars Palestinian Psychiatrist," *The Guardian* (London), June 20, 2001.

21. See Lein, *Civilians Under Siege*; Normand and Mair, *Under Siege*, pp. 6–8 and passim; and Diwan and Shaban, eds., *Development Under Adversity*, pp. 4–5.

22. Birzeit University, *Understanding the Issue: A Background Guide to the Issues Confronting Gaza Students* (three parts) (Birzeit, West Bank: Birzeit University, 1998).

23. Lein, *Civilians Under Siege,* pp. 10–12 and ff.

24. See Shmuel David, *Impossible Coexistence: Human Rights in Hebron Since the Massacre at the Cave of the Patriarchs* (Jerusalem: B'Tselem—the Israeli Information Center for Human Rights in the Occupied Territories, September 1995): 6–7; and LAW, *Hebron Under Siege* (Jerusalem: Palestinian Society for the Protection of Human Rights and the Environment—LAW, n.d. [ca. 1995]).

25. Private correspondence with Nimrod Amzalak, director of Data

Coordination and Fieldwork, B'Tselem—the Israeli Information Center for Human Rights in the Occupied Territories, March 26, 2002.

26. The construction of a safe passage was mandated in the 1993 DOP, "Israel-PLO Declaration of Principles, Washington, DC, 13 September 1993," reprinted in *Journal of Palestine Studies* 23, no. 1 (autumn 1993): Article 17, annex II, p. 119.

27. The 1995 Interim Agreement stipulated that the West Bank and the Gaza Strip were "a single territorial unit, the integrity and status of which will be preserved." "Israeli-Palestinian Interim Agreement on the West Bank and the Gaza Strip, Washington, DC, 28 September 1995," *Journal of Palestine Studies* 25, no. 2 (winter 1996): Article XI.1, p. 127. See also B'Tselem, *Divide and Rule: Prohibition on Passage Between the Gaza Strip and the West Bank* (Jerusalem: B'Tselem—the Israeli Information Center for Human Rights in the Occupied Territories, June 1998).

28. Israeli analyst Aharon Klieman, "Safe Passage: The Rocky Road to a Middle East Peace," *World Affairs* (winter 1998). Also see B'Tselem, *Divide and Rule,* and B'Tselem, *Safe Passage Statistics* (Freedom of Movement File) (Jerusalem: B'Tselem—the Israeli Information Center for Human Rights in the Occupied Territories, October 2000). For analysis, see Graham Usher, "Neither Safe Nor Free," *News from Within* 15, no. 10 (November 1999): 6–8.

29. Figures from John P. Tarpey, "The Economics of Israeli Occupation," *Christian Science Monitor,* May 4, 1988; Meron Benvenisti, *1986 Report Demographic, Economic, Legal, Social, and Political Developments in the West Bank* (Jerusalem: West Bank Data Base Project, 1986), pp. 25–26, 47–51; and Sara Roy, *The Gaza Strip Survey* (Jerusalem: West Bank Data Base Project, 1986), pp. 134–139. For analyses, see Peter Demant, "Israeli Settlement Policy Today," *MERIP Middle East Report,* no. 116 (July–August 1983): 3–13; Mona Rishmawi, *Planning in Whose Interest? Land Use Planning as a Strategy for Judaization,* Occasional Paper no. 4 (Ramallah, West Bank: AI-Haq/Law in the Service of Man—the West Bank Affiliate of the International Commission of Jurists, December 1986); and Raja Shehadeh, *The Law of the Land: Settlements and Land Issues Under Israeli Military Occupation* (Jerusalem: Palestinian Academic Society for the Study of International Affairs, 1993).

30. Benvenisti, *1986 Report*, pp. 25–26, 47–51. Also see Roy, *The Gaza Strip Survey*, pp. 134–139; Tarpey, "The Economics of Israeli Occupation"; Demant, "Israeli Settlement Policy Today," pp. 3–13; Rishmawi, *Planning in Whose Interest?*; and Shehadeh, *The Law of the Land.*

31. Rishmawi and Johnson, *Right to Work*, pp. 16–38.

32. *Ha'aretz*, February 27, 2001, cited in Jerome Slater, "Israel, Anti-Semitism and the Palestinian Problem," *Tikkun: A Bimonthly Jewish Critique of Politics, Culture and Society* 16, no. 3 (May–June 2001): 20.

33. Palestine Monitor, "Israeli Settlements on Occupied Palestinian Territories," *Fact Sheet* (Jerusalem: Palestine Monitor, the Voice of Civil Society published by the Palestinian NGO Network, n.d. [ca. January 2001]). An excellent in-depth study is Applied Research Institute–Jerusalem, *Monitoring Israeli Colonization Activities in the West Bank and Gaza, February 2000–February 2002* (Jerusalem: Applied Research Institute–Jerusalem, 2002).

34. For a detailed analysis of Israeli government efforts to control the

West Bank through land confiscation and settlement construction, see Yehezkel Lein, *Land Grab: Israel's Settlement Policy in the West Bank* (Jerusalem: B'Tselem—the Israeli Information Center for Human Rights in the Occupied Territories, May 2002. It is the most comprehensive work available on this subject.

35. Nasser Qadus, *Development Issues: Conditions and Current Usage of Land in Palestine* (Ramallah: Ma'an Development Center, 2000), p. 1. Also see Applied Research Institute–Jerusalem, *By-Pass Roads—The Israeli Approach Towards a New Apartheid over Palestinians?* (Jerusalem: Applied Research Institute–Jerusalem, May 2001). There is a slight discrepancy between these two sources. I have made the best judgment I can.

36. Dan Izenberg, "Peace Now Blasts New Settlement Points," *Jerusalem Post* (English), March 19, 2002. *Ha'aretz* strongly condemned the new settlements; see "Editorial," *Ha'aretz*, April 26, 2002.

37. Nadav Shragai, "Peace Now: Eight Outposts Set Up in West Bank Last Month," *Ha'aretz*, September 1, 2002.

38. Yair Sheleh, "Settlers: New Settlement Has Been Formed in Heart of West Bank," *Ha'aretz*, September 26, 2002.

39. Naomi Chazan, "Towards a Settlement Without Settlements," *Palestine-Israel Journal of Politics, Economics, and Culture* 7, nos. 3, 4 (Jerusalem, Israeli/Palestinian quarterly, English) (2000): 46–51.

40. Ran HaCohen, "Building Settlements, Killing Peace: Cease-Fire as Spin," *Tikkun: A Jewish Critique of Politics, Culture, and Society*, June 7, 2001. HaCohen is a literary critic for the Israeli daily *Yedioth Ahronoth*; he teaches at Tel Aviv University and is widely published in Hebrew. (Posted in English on Media Monitors Network, May 25, 2001.)

41. Meron Benvenisti and Shlomo Khayat, *The West Bank and Gaza Atlas* (Jerusalem: West Bank Data Base Project, 1988), p. 20.

42. See the analyses by Uri Davis, Antonia E.L. Maks, and John Richardson, "Israel's Water Policies," *Journal of Palestine Studies* 9, no. 2 (winter 1980): 3–31; Research Material, "Israel and the Resources of the West Bank," *Journal of Palestine Studies* 8, no. 4 (summer 1979): 94–104; David Kahan, *Agriculture and Water Resources in the West Bank and Gaza (1967–1981)* (Jerusalem: West Bank Data Base Project, 1987); and Joe Stork, "Water and Israel's Occupation Strategy," *MERIP: Middle East Report,* no. 116 (July–August 1983): 19–24. For a more recent analysis, see Jad Isaac, "The Essentials of Sustainable Water Resource Management in Israel and Palestine," in Janice Terry, ed., *Water Usage in the Middle East* (Special Issue: *Arab Studies Quarterly* 22, no. 2 [spring 2000]): 13–32.

43. Benvenisti, 1986 *Report*, p. 20.

44. Ibid., p. 21.

45. Ibid., pp. 20–22.

46. Roy, *The Gaza Strip Survey*, p. 50.

47. Rishmawi and Johnson, *Right to Work*, pp. 39–46, and Yehezkel Lein, *Disputed Waters: Israel's Responsibility for the Water Shortage in the Occupied Territories* (Jerusalem: B'Tselem—the Israeli Information Center for Human Rights in the Occupied Territories, September 1998), p. 10; "Editorial," *Ha'aretz*, August 20, 1998. Also useful is Hillel I. Shuval, "A Proposal for an Equitable Resolution to the Conflicts Between the Israelis and the Palestinians

over the Shared Water Resources of the Mountain Aquifer," in Terry, *Water Usage in the Middle East,* pp. 33–62.

48. See Yehezkel Lein, *Not Even a Drop: The Water Crisis in Palestinian Villages Without a Water Network* (Jerusalem: B'Tselem—the Israeli Information Center for Human Rights in the Occupied Territories, 2001); Lein, *Disputed Waters*; Jad Isaac, *Core Issues of the Palestinian-Israeli Water Dispute* (Jerusalem: Applied Research Institute–Jerusalem, 1998); Jad Isaac, *A Sober Approach to the Water Crisis in the Middle East* (Jerusalem: Applied Research Institute–Jerusalem, 1994); Jonathan Kuttab and Jad Ishaq, *Approaches to the Legal Aspects of the Conflict on Water Rights in Palestine/Israel* (Jerusalem: Applied Research Institute–Jerusalem, 1993); Aisling Byrne, *Water: The Red Line* (Jerusalem: Jerusalem Media and Communication Center, 1994).

49. Yehezkel Lein, *Thirsty for a Solution: The Water Crisis in the Occupied Territories and Its Resolution in a Final Status Agreement* (Jerusalem: B'Tselem—the Israeli Information Center for Human Rights in the Occupied Territories, July 2000), pp. 1–2. For a good analysis of water and international law, see Jamal L. El-Hindi, "Compensation as Part of Equitable Utilization in the Israeli-Palestinian Water Conflict," in Terry, *Water Usage in the Middle East*, pp. 113–145 (emphasis added).

50. Lein, *Thirsty for a Solution*, pp. 1–2. Also see Amira Hass, "Separate and Unequal on the West Bank," *New York Times*, September 2, 2001.

51. Amira Hass, "Dire Water Shortage in West Bank," *Ha'aretz*, July 27, 1998.

52. "Editorial," *Ha'aretz*, August 20, 1998. Also see Lein, *Disputed Waters*, p. 25. Also see Lein, *Thirsty for a Solution*; Lein, *Not Even a Drop*.

53. For a good analysis of the meaning of this for Palestinians, see Center for Economic and Social Rights, *Enforcing the International Covenant on Economic, Social, and Cultural Rights*, p. 11.

54. On the casino, see Sara Leibovich-Dar, "All Bets Are Off," *Ha'aretz Magazine,* May 24, 2001; Toufic Haddad, "And the Walls Came Tumbling Down: The Jericho Casino," *News from Within* 15, no. 1 (January 1999): 18–23; Alessandra Antonelli, "The Bets Are on Jericho's Casino," *Palestine Report* (Jerusalem, Palestinian biweekly, English) 5, no. 14 (September 18, 1998); Alesandra Antonelli, "An 'Oasis' in Jericho," *Palestine Report* 5, no. 2, June 26, 1998. On Bethlehem 2000, see Muna Hamzeh-Muhaisen, "Will Bethlehem Be Ready for Christmas?" *Palestine Report* 5, no. 27 (December 18, 1998); Nabeel Kassis, "Bethlehem 2000," *UNDP Focus: Special Issue: Bethlehem 2000* 5, no. 4 (December 1999); Matthew Brubacher, "Bethlehem 2000 Update: New Checkpoint to Choke Palestinians," *Palestine Report* 6, no. 10 (August 25, 1999); Muna Hamzeh-Muhaisen, "The Woes of Bethlehem 2000," *Palestine Report* 4, no. 34 (February 13, 1998); Hadeel Wahdam, "Bethlehem 2000: The Occupation of Rachel's Tomb," *Palestine Report* 6, no. 13 (September 15, 1999). See also Sara Roy, "De-Development Revisited: Palestinian Economy and Society Since Oslo," *Journal of Palestine Studies* 28, no. 3 (spring 1999): 64–82.

55. The statistics come from several sources; see World Bank, *West Bank and Gaza Update: Carrying the World Bank Program into the Next Millennium* (a quarterly publication of the West Bank and Gaza Resident Mission)

(Ramallah, West Bank: The World Bank Group, Third Quarter, 1999), p. 2; Center for Economic and Social Rights, *Progress, Stagnation, or Regression?* pp. 12–13; World Bank, *West Bank and Gaza in Brief* (Washington, DC: The World Bank Group, August 2000), p. 1. See also Diwan and Shaban, *Development Under Adversity*, p. 6. Ishac Diwan and Radwan A. Shaban, eds., *Development Under Adversity: The Palestinian Economy Under Transition* (full report) (Washington, DC: Joint Report, Palestine Economic Policy Research Institute and the World Bank, 1999), pp. 15–18; World Bank, *West Bank and Gaza Data Profile* (New York: The World Bank Group, 2000), p. 1.

56. Report from UNSCO, "The Impact on the Palestinian Economy of Confrontations, Mobility Restrictions and Border Closures, 1 October 2000–31 January 2001" (Geneva: United Nations Special Coordinator for the Occupied Territories, Gaza, February 25, 2001), p. 12.

57. The 2002 statistic is from Save the Children, *The Education of Children at Risk* (New York: Save the Children, January 2002).

58. World Bank, *Poverty in the West Bank and Gaza* (New York: World Bank Team in the Social and Economic Development Group of the Middle East and North Africa Region, January 2001), p. 6.

59. Emile Sahliyeh, "West Bank Industrial and Agricultural Development: The Basic Problems," *Journal of Palestine Studies* 11, no. 2 (winter 1982): 58, 55–69; Tarpey, "The Economics of Israeli Occupation"; Kahan, *Agriculture and Water Resources*, p. 14; Benvenisti, *1986 Report*, p. 10; Simha Bahiri, *Industrialization in the West Bank and Gaza* (Jerusalem: West Bank Data Base Project and the Jerusalem Post, 1987, distributed by Westview Press, Boulder, CO), pp. 33–38; and Meron Benvenisti with Ziad Abu-Zayed and Danny Rubinstein, *The West Bank Handbook: A Political Lexicon* Jerusalem, (Jerusalem: West Bank Data Base Project and the Jerusalem Post, 1986, reissued by Westview Press, Boulder, CO, 1986), p. 112. Also see Sara Roy, "The Gaza Strip: A Case of Economic De-Development," *Journal of Palestine Studies* 17, no. 1 (autumn 1987): 56–83.

60. Kahan, *Agriculture and Water Resources*, p. 14. See text and related note for slightly different figures.

61. Center for Economic and Social Rights, *Progress, Stagnation, or Regression?* pp. 21 and 16.

62. Applied Research Institute–Jerusalem, *They Cut Trees, Don't They? An Assessment of the Israeli Practices on the Palestinian Agricultural Sector* (Jerusalem: Applied Research Institute–Jerusalem, March 2001).

63. Applied Research Institute–Jerusalem, *Israeli Unilateral Actions Since the Signing of the Wye River Agreement* (Jerusalem: Applied Research Institute–Jerusalem, 1999).

64. B'Tselem, *Israel's Policy of House Demolitions and Destruction of Agricultural Land in the Gaza Strip*, Information Sheet (Jerusalem: B'Tselem—the Israeli Information Center for Human Rights in the Occupied Territories, February 2002), puts the number of destroyed dunums at 13,500. The figure of 16,000 comes from Fact Sheet, *Crimes Against Housing and Agriculture* (Gaza City: Palestinian Center for Human Rights, June 2002).

65. Applied Research Institute–Jerusalem, *They Cut Trees, Don't They?*, p. 3.

66. "Palestinian Olive Crop Hit by Unrest," *BBC News*, October 11, 2002.

67. MIFTAH, *A Humanitarian Disaster in the Occupied Territories:*

MIFTA Reports (Jerusalem: Palestinian Initiative for the Promotion of Democracy, August 10, 2002).

68. Roy, *The Gaza Strip Survey*, pp. 44–45.

69. On the disadvantageous terms of trade, see ibid., pp. 44–50.

70. On Israel's marketing restrictions, see Kahan, *Agriculture and Water Resources*, p. 88.

71. Gideon Levy, "Closing the Sea," *Ha'aretz Friday Magazine*, February 15, 2002.

72. Ziad Abu Nada and Ayman Jadallah, "Dividing the Mediterranean: Fishing Restrictions in Gaza," *Palestine Report* 5, no. 31 (January 29, 1999).

73. LAW, "Israeli Fishing Restrictions in the Gaza Strip," in *Israeli Violations of Palestinian Economic Rights,* pp. 14–15.

74. "Israeli Fishing Restrictions in the Gaza Strip," p. 14.

75. Kahan, *Agriculture and Water Resources*, p. 14. Also see Sahliyeh, "West Bank Industrial and Agricultural Development," pp. 58 and 55–56; Benvenisti, *1986 Report*, p. 10; Benvenisti with Abu-Zayed and Rubinstein, *The West Bank Handbook*, p. 112; Bahiri, *Industrialization in the West Bank and Gaza*, pp. 33–38; Roy, *The Gaza Strip Survey*, pp. 54–55 and 56–83; Roy, "The Gaza Strip: A Case of Economic De-Development," p. 58.

76. An interesting piece is Ephraim Kleiman, "Israeli-Palestinian Economic Relations: Past Experience and Future Prospects," *TIGER* (Tiger Working Paper Series no. 8) (Warsaw: Transformation, Integration, and Globalization, June 2001).

77. On the industrial zones in general, see Center for Economic and Social Rights, *Progress, Stagnation, or Regression?* pp. 39–43; George Kurzom, "Frontier Industrial Zones," *Prospects for a Self-Sustainable Palestinian Economic Alternative* (Ramallah: Ma'an Development Center, 1999), p. 1.

78. "Building Palestine," *Palestine Report,* June 25, 1999. Also see Deborah Sontag, "Thaw Bolsters Mid-East Hopes," *The Age*, October 9, 1998, and Patricia Golan, "Marketing a Hard Sell Called Gaza Industrial Estate," *Jerusalem Post*, March 29, 1999.

79. A full discussion of the PA's tax breaks for investors is available in "The PA's Tax Paradise for Investors," *Economic News* (Palnet Online, citing *Ha'aretz*, January 13, 2000).

80. Gwen Ackerman, "The Financial Frontier: High Hopes at Qarni." *Jerusalem Post*, July 6, 2000. Also see Applied Research Institute–Jerusalem, *An Assessment of the Israeli Practice on the Palestinian Agricultural Sector, 1–18 October 2000* (Jerusalem: Applied Research Institute–Jerusalem, November 2000), p. 1.

81. Benvenisti, *1986 Report,* p. 11. Also see Thomas L. Friedman, "Israel's Arab Army of Migrant Workers," *New York Times,* December 6, 1987 (Business Section), pp. 1 and 16. Benvenisti with Abu-Zayed and Rubinstein, *The West Bank Handbook*, pp. 78–82.

82. Center for Economic and Social Rights, *Progress, Stagnation, or Regression?* p. 14.

83. Ibid., p. 15.

84. UNESCO, *Report on Economic and Social Conditions in the West Bank and Gaza Strip* (Gaza City: Office of the Special Coordinator in the Occupied Territories, United Nations, spring 1998), p. 17.

85. Quote and statistics from Saud Abu Ramadan, "Gaza Six Years After Oslo," *Palestine Report* 6, no. 13 (September 15, 1999): 3–5.

86. Saud Abu Ramadan, "Fishing for a Gaza Port," *Palestine Report* 6, no. 10 (August 25, 1999): 7–8.

87. Ze'ev Schiff, "The Meeting with Arafat," *Ha'aretz*, July 9, 1999.

88. PMC, "Israeli Occupation Forces Destroy Gaza Port," *Palestine Media Center* (Gaza: Palestinian National Authority, September 18, 2001), and Amira Hass, "IDF Destroys PA, European Offices at Site of Gaza Port," *Ha'aretz*, September 23, 2001.

89. Center for Economic and Social Rights, *Progress, Stagnation, or Regression?* p. 24. Also see George Kurzom, "Introduction," in *Prospects for a Self-Sustainable Palestinian Economic Alternative* (Ramallah: Ma'an Development Center, 1999), p. 1.

90. B'Tselem, *The Palestinian Economy Since the Oslo Accords* (Jerusalem: B'Tselem—the Israeli Information Center for Human Rights in the Occupied Territories, n.d. [ca. 2000]).

91. World Bank, *West Bank and Gaza in Brief* (Washington, DC: The World Bank Group, August 2000), p. 1.

92. Center for Economic and Social Rights, *Progress, Stagnation or Regression?* p. 22. Also see LAW, *Israeli Violations of Palestinian Economic Rights,* pp. 14–23.

93. For several good general analyses, see Center for Economic and Social Rights, *Human Rights Violations Under Oslo: Overview of CESR's Palestine Project* (Palestine Project Series 1) (New York: Center for Economic and Social Rights, January 2000). Diwan and Shaban, *Development Under Adversity*; Center for Economic and Social Rights, *Applying Economic and Social Rights in Palestine* (Palestine Project Series 3) (New York: Center for Economic and Social Rights, January, 2000).

94. Raja Shehadeh, *Occupier's Law: Israel and the West Bank* (prepared for Law in the Service of Man, the West Bank affiliate of the International Commission of Jurists) (Washington, DC: Institute for Palestine Studies, 1985), pp. 61–101. Also see Raja Shehadeh and Jonathan Kattub, *The West Bank and the Rule of Law* (Geneva: International Commission of Jurists, 1980), and Al-Haq, *A Nation Under Siege, Annual Report on Human Rights Violations in the Occupied Territories, 1989* (Ramallah: West Bank affiliate of the International Commission of Jurists, 1990).

95. Jerusalem Unit, *Human Rights Violations in Arab Jerusalem: An Overview of Abuse* (Jerusalem: Palestinian Society for the Protection of Human Rights and the Environment—LAW, March 1999), p. 8; Lea Tsemel, "Personal Status and Rights," in Naseer Aruri, ed., *Occupation: Israel over Palestine* (Belmont, MA: Association of Arab-American University Graduates, 1983). For an excellent analysis of Israel's violations of international law, see Thomas W. Mallison and Sally V. Mallison, *The Palestine Problem in International Law and World Order* (Essex, UK: Longman, 1986), pp. 174–206 and passim.

96. For an analysis of the military orders, see Al-Haq, *Briefing Papers on Twenty Years of Israeli Occupation of the West Bank and Gaza* (Ramallah, West Bank: Al-Haq/Law in the Service of Man, the West Bank affiliate of the International Commission of Jurists, June 1987), pp. 2–3.

97. Statement by Bernard Joseph, later Dov Joseph, of the Jewish

Agency, addressing the Lawyer's Association in Tel Aviv in 1946, quoted in Sabri Jiryis, *The Arabs in Israel* (Beirut: Institute for Palestine Studies, 1969, reissued by Monthly Review Press, New York, 1976), pp. 11–12.

98. Thus, for example, "confessions"—typically extracted under torture—from individuals detained by the military may not be appealed; neither may objections be raised during the period while a confession is being obtained. See the analysis in American Friends Service Committee, *A Compassionate Peace: A Future for the Middle East* (report prepared for the American Friends Service Committee) (New York: Hill and Wang, 1982), pp. 28. Also see Amnesty International, *Report and Recommendations of an Amnesty International Mission to the Government of the State of Israel, 3–7 June 1979* (London: Amnesty International Publications, 1980) (AI Index MDE/15/02/80); Tsemel, "Personal Status and Rights," pp. 58–61; Shehadeh, *Occupier's Law,* pp. 76–101; and Paul Hunt, *Justice? The Military Court System in the Israeli Occupied Territories* (a report jointly prepared by Al-Haq/ Law in the Service of Man and the Gaza Center for Rights and Law, the Gaza Strip Affiliate of the International Commission of Jurists (Ramallah, West Bank: Al-Haq/Law in the Service of Man, 1987).

99. Except for Israel, nearly every other country in the world considers, according to international law, the territories to be "occupied" and therefore subject to the Fourth Geneva Convention. See, for example, Amnesty International, *Amnesty International Calls on High Contracting Parties to Take Measures to Ensure Israel's Respect for the Fourth Geneva Convention, Public Statement* (London: Amnesty International, May 11, 1999) (MDE 15/037/1999), and Amnesty International, *Israel: Fourth Geneva Convention Meeting: An Abdication of Responsibility* (London: Amnesty International, July 15, 1999) (MDE 15/047/1999).

100. On the court's decision on house demolitions, see Moshe Reinfeld, "Court: IDF Does Not Have to Give Demolition Warning," *Ha'aretz*, August 7, 2002; Moshe Reinfeld, "Court Okays Demolition of Bombers' Abu Dis Homes," *Ha'aretz*, September 18, 2002; Moshe Reinfeld, "High Court Okays Demolition of Gaza House," *Ha'aretz*, August 20, 2002; Jeff Halper, "Fortress Israel: The Message of the Bulldozer," *Counterpunch*, August 13–19, 2002. On the court's decision regarding expulsion, see B'Tselem, *Summary of the Judgment of the Supreme Court Regarding Assigned Residence* (HCJ 7015/02; 7019/02) (Jerusalem: B'Tselem—the Israeli Information Center for Human Rights in the Occupied Territories, September 3, 2002).

101. See, for example, the analysis by Shehadeh, *Occupier's Law*, pp. 95–100.

102. Carmi et al., *Oslo: Before and After.*

103. For several good case studies, see Tom Segev, "Waiting for Gillon," *Ha'aretz Week's End,* July 20, 2001. Also see *Israel: Case ISR 180701—Six Months of Administrative Detention for Mr. Abed Rahman al-Ahmar* (International Secretariat of the Organisation Mondial Contre la Torture [the World Organization Against Torture], Geneva, Switzerland, July 18, 2001).

104. Amnesty International, *Amnesty International's Concerns on Administrative Detentions in Israel and the Occupied Territories* (London: Amnesty International, April 25, 1986), reprinted in *Journal of Palestine*

Studies 16, no. 1 (autumn 1986): 199–201. Also see Amnesty International, *Israel/Occupied Territories,* annual.

105. Carmi, *Oslo Before and After*, p. 12. B'Tselem, *Administrative Detention: Statistics* (Jerusalem: B'Tselem—the Israeli Information Center for Human Rights in the Occupied Territories, September 2000). Addameer Prisoners' Support Association, *Administrative Detention* (Jerusalem: Addameer Prisoners' Support Association, 1999), p. 2. Jessica Montelle, *Prisoners of Peace: Administrative Detention During the Oslo Process* (Jerusalem: B'Tselem—the Israeli Information Center for Human Rights in the Occupied Territories, July 1997), p. 3.

106. Montelle, *Prisoners of Peace*, p. 3.

107. Carmi, *Oslo: Before and After*, p. 13.

108. Ibid., pp. 25–26.

109. B'Tselem, *Administrative Detention Statistics* (Jerusalem: B'Tselem—the Israeli Information Center for Human Rights in the Occupied Territories, February 2003).

110. Yuval Ginbar, *Routine Torture: Interrogation Methods of the General Security Service* (Jerusalem: B'Tselem—the Israeli Information Center for Human Rights in the Occupied Territories, February 1998. Also see Amnesty International, *Torture in the Eighties* (London: Amnesty International Publications, 1984) (AI Index ACT 04/01/84), pp. 233–234.

111. Tsemel, "Personal Status and Rights," pp. 58–61; Amnesty International, *Allegations of Ill-treatment and Torture: The Case of Adnan Mansour Ghanem*. Also Shehadeh, *Occupier's Law*, pp. 147.

112. Allegra Pacheco, "The Prison Factory: An Interview with Advocate Allegra Pacheco," *Between the Lines*, July 2001 (available online, accessed February 23, 2003).

113. *Koteret Rashit* (Hebrew), February 25, 1987, translated and printed in *Israel Press Brief* (International Center for Peace in the Middle East) no. 52 (March/April 1987): 10.

114. Amnesty International, *Amnesty International Report 1986* (London: Amnesty International Publications, 1986) (AI Index: POL 01/03/86), pp. 334–338.

115. Lea Tsemel, "The Political Prisoners," in Erik Fosse, Ebba Wergeland, and Ibrahim Abu-Lughod, eds., *Israel and the Question of Palestine,* special double issue, *Arab Studies Quarterly* 7, nos. 2 and 3 (spring/summer 1985): 126.

116. Benvenisti with Abu-Zayed and Rubinstein, *The West Bank Handbook*, pp. 221–222.

117. Carmi, *Oslo: Before and After*, p.11.

118. Ibid.

119. Ibid.

120. PLO, *Prisoners: Interim Issues* (PLO, Negotiations Affairs Department, July 2000), p. 1.

121. Ayman Jadallah and Ziad Abu Nada, "Israel and the Prisoners," *Palestine Report* 5, no. 42 (April 23, 1999): 4–6. Also see Muna Hamzeh-Muhaisen, "The Quagmire of Palestinian Political Prisoners," *Palestine Report* 5, no. 34 (February 19, 1999): 2–4; and Charmaine Seitz, "Palestinian Prisoners in a Slow Boil," *Palestine Report* 5, no. 25 (1998). For analysis, see

Hanthala Palestine, "Prisoners and International Law" (Hanthala Palestine is a Palestinian organization that supports prisoners, n.d.) (available online); PLO, *Prisoners;* "Administrative Detention," report of the Addameer Prisoners' Support Association, 1999 (available online); Stephen Sosebee, "Tension Builds over 3,500 Palestinian Prisoners Israel Holds in Defiance of Oslo Commitments," *Washington Report on Middle East Affairs* (May–June, 1998): 32–34; *Al-Haq Calls on the International Community to Intervene Immediately to Gain the Release of All Palestinian Prisoners Held in Israeli Prisons* (Ramallah, Palestine: Al-Haq: Law in the Service of Man, the West Bank Affiliate of the International Jurists Association, Geneva), July 30, 1998.

122. Danny Rubinstein, "The Intifada Is Becoming More Popular," *Ha'aretz*, October 14, 2002.

123. Amnesty International, *Report 1986*, p. 337. Amnesty International, *Torture in the Eighties* (London: Amnesty International Publications, 1984) (AI Index ACT 04/01/84), pp. 233–34. Amnesty International, *The Case of Adnan Mansour Ghanem;* Thomas Friedman, "Court Finds Israel Framed a Moslem," *New York Times*, May 26, 1987; and Juan Tamayo, "Israeli Court Blasts Security Agents: Jurists Overturn Officer's Conviction After Torture Alleged," *Miami Herald*, May 25, 1987. For more recent information, see Menachem Shalev, "Shin Bet Lied for 16 Years," *Jerusalem Post*, November 1, 1987 (most of the findings of the Landau Commission are reprinted here). Also see "The Landau Commission," *News from Within*, November 15, 1987. For analyses in the U.S. press, see Thomas Friedman, "Israelis Seem Ambivalent on Violence in Domestic War," *New York Times*, November 8, 1987; Juan Tamayo, "Torture Scandal Rocks Israel's Secret Service," *Miami Herald*, December 6, 1987; Jonathan Broder, "Brutal Image of Israeli Security Branch Services Investigation," *Chicago Tribune*, December 7, 1987; Allegra Pacheco, "The Israeli High Court of Justice Decision Regarding Violent Interrogation Methods: A Critique," *News from Within* 15, no. 9 (October 1999): 1–5; Leah Tsemel, "The Supreme Court: Torture Outlaw," *News from Within* 15, no. 9 (October 1999): 6–9; and Ginbar, *Routine Torture: Interrogation Methods of the General Security Service*, pp. 7–8.

124. For one good analysis of Israel's policy of systematically beating Palestinians, see Palestine Human Rights Campaign, "Physicians for Human Rights Press Conference, February 11, 1988" (Jerusalem and Chicago: Palestine Human Rights Campaign, Database Center, February 17, 1988). A group of physicians from the United States toured the West Bank and Gaza and strongly condemned what they witnessed. Also see Anthony Lewis, "Toward the Extreme," *New York Times*, April 24, 1988. See, for example, Yuval Ginbar, *Sheer Brutality: The Beatings Continue: Beatings and Maltreatment of Palestinians by Border Police and Police Officers During May–August, 1997* (Jerusalem: B'Tselem—the Israeli Information Center for Human Rights in the Occupied Territories, August 1997), and B'Tselem, *Beatings, Maltreatment, and Degradation of Palestinians by Israeli Authorities During June–July 1996* (Jerusalem: B'Tselem—the Israeli Information Center for Human Rights in the Occupied Territories, August 1996). An interesting analysis of torture is Neve Gordon, "Torture Is Not to Make People Talk, but to Make Them Remain Silent," *Media Monitors Network* (May 23, 2001) (available online; accessed February 23, 2003); Aryeh Dayan, "The Slide Down the Slippery Slope,"

Ha'aretz, January 18, 2000, and Michael L. Gross, "Just and Unjust Warfare," *Tikkun: A Jewish Critique of Politics, Culture, and Society* 16, no. 5 (September–October, 2001): 45. B'Tselem, *Legislation Allowing the Use of Physical Force and Mental Coercion in Interrogations by the General Security Service* (Jerusalem: B'Tselem—the Israeli Information Center for Human Rights in the Occupied Territories, January 2000), pp. 5–6 and 56–67.

125. Carmi, *Oslo: Before and After,* p. 13. Also see B'Tselem, *Legislation Allowing the Use of Physical Force and Mental Coercion,* pp. 2–3. Also see B'Tselem, *Torture During Interrogations: Testimony of Palestinian Detainees, Testimony of the Interrogators* (Jerusalem: B'Tselem—the Israeli Information Center for Human Rights in the Occupied Territories, November 1994); B'Tselem, *Legitimizing Torture: The Israeli High Court of Justice Rulings in the Bilbeisi, Hamdan, and Mubarak Cases* (Jerusalem: B'Tselem—the Israeli Information Center for Human Rights in the Occupied Territories, January 1997); Ginbar, *Sheer Brutality;* Ginbar, *Routine Torture*; Yael Stein, *Standard Routine: Beatings and Abuse of Palestinians by Israeli Security Forces During the al-Aqsa Intifada* (Jerusalem: B'Tselem—the Israeli Information Center for Human Rights in the Occupied Territories, May 2001); and B'Tselem, *The Killing of Palestinian Children and the Open Fire Regulations* (Jerusalem: B'Tselem—the Israeli Information Center for Human Rights in the Occupied Territories, June 1993.

126. Carmi, *Oslo: Before and After*, p. 12.

127. Palestine Human Rights Campaign, *House Demolitions and Sealings as Practiced Against the Palestinians Living Under Military Occupation* (Jerusalem and Chicago: Palestine Human Rights Campaign, DataBase Center, 1986). Also see Emma Playfair, *Demolition and Sealing of Houses as a Punitive Measure in the Israeli Occupied West Bank* (a report prepared by Al-Haq/Law in the Service of Man) (Ramallah, West Bank: Al-Haq, 1987).

128. B'Tselem, *Planning and Building Statistics* (Jerusalem: B'Tselem—the Israeli Information Center for Human Rights in the Occupied Territories, 2000); also see "Home Demolition," *The Electric Intifada* (a Resource for Countering Myth, Distortion, and Spin from the Israeli Media War Machine), July 22, 2001.

129. Jeff Halper, "The Israeli Army's Campaign of Revenge and Ethnic Cleansing," *The Electronic Intifada,* July 6, 2001.

130. Yuval Ginbar, *Demolishing Peace: Israel's Policy of Mass Demolition of Palestinian Houses in the West Bank* (Jerusalem: B'Tselem—the Israeli Information Center for Human Rights in the Occupied Territories, 1997); Amnesty International, *Israel and the Occupied Territories: Demolition and Dispossession: The Destruction of Palestinian Homes* (New York: Amnesty International, December 1999) MDE 15/59/99); Amnesty International, *Israel: House Demolitions—Palestinians Given 15 Minutes to Leave* (London: Amnesty International, December 1999) (MDE 15/078/1999); Parastou Hassouri, *Bulldozed into Cantons: Israel's House Demolition Policy in the West Bank Since the Signing of the Oslo Agreements, September 1993–March 1998* (Jerusalem: Palestinian Society for the Protection of Human Rights and the Environment—LAW, 1998); Applied Research Institute–Jerusalem, *Behind the Policy of House Demolition: Why Here and Now?* (Jerusalem: Institute of Applied Research—Jerusalem, 1997); Christian

Peacemaker Teams, "Campaign for Secure Dwellings" (Jerusalem: Christian Peacemaker Teams, the Israeli Committee Against House Demolitions, Land Defense General Committee–Palestine, and the Palestinian Society for the Protection of Human Rights and the Environment, 1998); B'Tselem, *House Demolition Statistics* (B'Tselem—the Israeli Information Center for Human Rights in the Occupied Territories, 1998).

131. Amnesty International, *Israel and the Occupied Territories: Demolition and Dispossession: The Destruction of Palestinian Homes* (London: Amnesty International, August 12, 1999 (MDE 15/059/1999), p. 8.

132. Meron Benvenisti, "Systematically Burying Ourselves," *Ha'aretz*, January 18, 2002.

133. B'Tselem, *Planning and Building Statistics* (Jerusalem: B'Tselem—the Israeli Information Center for Human Rights in the Occupied Territories, 2000); also see "Home Demolition," *The Electric Intifada;* and Amnesty International, *Israel and the Occupied Territories*, p. 42.

134. B'Tselem, *Demolition of Houses Built Without Permits, 1987–2002, Statistics* (Jerusalem: B'Tselem—the Israeli Information Center for Human Rights in the Occupied Territories, July 2002); and B'Tselem, *House Demolitions, Statistics* (Jerusalem: B'Tselem—the Israeli Information Center for Human Rights in the Occupied Territories, July 2002).

135. Data on settler violence in the pre-Oslo period may be found in J. Abu Shakrah et al., *Israeli Settler Violence in the Occupied Territories, 1980–1984* (Chicago: Palestine Human Rights Campaign, 1985), pp. 16–26 (see entire work for an excellent analysis of settler violence). Also see Robert I. Friedman, "Terror on Sacred Ground," *Mother Jones* (August/September 1987): 37–43; Daoud Kuttab, "Old City Violence," *Middle East International* (London, bimonthly) (December 5, 1986), pp. 14–15; Yorem Yarkoni, "In Hebrew It's Called a Pogrom," *Kol Ha'ir* (Hebrew) (November 28, 1986); Said al Ghazali and Kate Rouhana, "Anti-Arab Furor," *Al-Fajr* (Jerusalem, Palestinian weekly, English) (November 28, 1986); "Jerusalem Pogrom," *News from Within* 2, no. 40 (December 12, 1986). For the report of the official Israeli government inquiry into settler violence, see *The Karp Report: An Israeli Government Inquiry into Settler Violence Against Palestinians in the West Bank* (released February 7, 1984, Jerusalem), published in English by the Institute for Palestine Studies (Washington, DC: Institute for Palestine Studies, 1984).

136. Ron Dudai, *Tacit Consent: Israeli Policy on Law Enforcement Toward Settlers in the Occupied Territories* (Jerusalem: B'Tselem—the Israeli Information Center for Human Rights in the Occupied Territories, March 2001), p. 1. Also see Amira Hass, "Protected by the 'System,'" *Ha'aretz,* July 24, 2001.

137. Ron Dudai, *Trigger Happy: Unjustified Shooting and Violations of the Open-Fire Regulations During the al-Aqsa Intifada* (Jerusalem: B'Tselem—the Israeli Information Center for Human Rights in the Occupied Territories, March 2002).

138. A detailed account is provided by Ian Black and Benny Morris, *Israel's Secret Wars: A History of Israel's Intelligence Services* (New York: Grove Weidenfeld, 1991), pp. 272–277, 453–455, 466–472, and passim. See also "Assassinations in the '70s," *Between the Lines* 1, no. 9 (August 2001): 9, translated from Moshe Zonder, "Shooting Without Crying Anymore," *Yediot*

Ahronot Weekend Supplement (Jerusalem, Israeli weekly, Hebrew), July 27, 2001. A former Israeli intelligence officer has written two books that provide considerable insight into how that country's secret services operate around the world. See Victor Ostrovsky, *The Other Side of Deception: A Rogue Agent Exposes the Mossad's Secret Agenda* (New York: Harper Collins, 1994), and Victor Ostrovsky with Claire Hoy, *By Way of Deception: The Making and Unmaking of a Mossad Officer* (New York: St. Martin's Press, 1990). Also see Tarik Kafala, "Israel's Assassination Policy," *BBC News* (online), July 24, 2001; Amnesty International, "Israel/Occupied Territories: State Assassination Policy Must Stop," *Amnesty International*, July 4, 2001 (AI Index MDE 15/063/2001—News Service Nr. 114). Also see "Israel/Occupied Territories: Amnesty International Condemns State Assassinations," *Amnesty International*, July 7, 2001 (AI Index MDE 15/007/2001—News Service Nr. 30). Yael Stein, *Israel's Assassination Policy: Extra-judicial* Executions (Jerusalem: B'Tselem—the Israeli Information Center for Human Rights in the Occupied Territories, n.d. [ca. April 2001]).

139. Stein, *Israel's Assassination Policy*, p. 15.

140. Amnesty International, "Israel/Occupied Territories: State Assassination Policy Must Stop"; and Amnesty International, "Israel/Occupied Territories: Amnesty International Condemns State Assassinations."

141. Stein, *Israel's Assassination Policy*, p. 15.

142. Carmi, *Oslo: Before and After*, p. 6.

143. Renata Capella and Michael Sfard, *The Assassination Policy of the State of Israel: November 2000–January 2002* (Jerusalem: Public Committee against Torture in Israel and the Palestinian Society for the Protection of Human Rights and the Environment, October 2002); Gideon Levy, "Time to Stop the Liquidations," *Ha'aretz*, July 28, 2002; Moshe Reinfeld, "Report: 46 Innocent Bystanders Killed in IDF Assassinations," *Ha'aretz*, October 14, 2002.

144. B'Tselem, Press Release, "Israel Adopts the Tactics of Terrorists" (Jerusalem: B'Tselem—the Israeli Information Center for Human Rights in the Occupied Territories, July 23, 2002). For analysis of Israel's policy, see Amos Harel and Aluf Benn, "Kitchen Cabinet Okays Expansion of Liquidation List," *Ha'aretz*, July 4, 2001, who write: "The IDF will from now on be given broader license to liquidate Palestinian terrorists. . . . The new guidelines allow it [IDF] to act against known terrorists even if they are not on the verge of committing a major attack." Also see Tarik Kafala, "Israel's Assassination Policy," *BBC News* (online), July 24, 2001, and Saleh Abdel Jawad, "The Israeli Assassination Policy," *Between the Lines* 1, no. 9 (August 2001): 2–8.

145. For superficial background on Abu Ali Mustafa, see Tamar Shiloh, "Abu Ali Mustafa: 'Right to Struggle,'" London, *BBC News* (online), August 27, 2001; Lawrence Joffe, "Abu Ali Mustafa: Palestinian Leader Who Rejected Peace Accords," *The Guardian* (London), August 28, 2001. See also "Analysis: Death of a Moderate Voice" (editorial) *Ha'aretz*, November 5, 2001. Mustafa was the leader of the PFLP; thus the PFLP retaliated by assassinating Ze'evi, and Israel then retaliated against the whole Palestinian community. A good analysis comes from Amos Harel and Baruch Kra, "Ze'evi Critically Wounded in Jerusalem Assassination Bid," *Ha'aretz*, October 17, 2001. To understand something about Ze'evi and his racist policies, see Ehud Sprinzak, *The*

Ascendance of Israel's Radical Right (New York: Oxford University Press, 1991), pp. 171–175 and passim; and Nur Masalha, *Imperial Israel and the Palestinians: The Politics of Expansion* (London: Pluto, 2000), pp. 176–185 and passim. Robert I. Friedman, "A Report from Israel and Palestine," *The Nation* 273, no. 21 (December 24, 2001): 13–20. Several excellent sources for Israel's destructive policies during the post-Ze'evi assassination period include Al-Haq, *Israeli Forces Place Sieges and Curfews over Every Palestinian City: Twenty-six Palestinians Killed in Four Days* (Jerusalem: Al-Haq, Law in the Service of Man, October 23, 2001); Palestine Media Center, *Israeli Army Slaughters Nine in Village near Ramallah: Massacre in Beit Reema* (Jerusalem: Palestine Media Center, October 24, 2001); Gideon Levy, "Even the Birds Have Gone," *Ha'aretz*, October 26, 2001 (this is a long and very moving human interest story). Also see Amos Harel, "The Futility of the Operation," *Ha'aretz*, October 26, 2001. Amnesty International, *Amnesty International Urges Israel to Stop Attacks on Palestinian Areas* (London: News Release by the International Secretariat of Amnesty International, 23 October 2001) (MDE 15/097/2001 187/01). Aluf Benn, "Israel Rejects U.S. Call for 'Immediate' Withdrawal from Area A," *Ha'aretz*, October 23, 2001.

146. *Financial Times* (London), December 4, 1979; Louise Cainkar and Jan Abu-Shakrah, "9 Palestinians Served Expulsion Orders by Israeli Authorities," DataBase Center on Palestinian Human Rights, Chicago and Jerusalem, DataBase Project on Palestinian Human Rights, January 5, 1988; Louise Cainkar and Jan Abu-Shakrah, "Human Rights Violations Under Israeli Rule: September Report," Chicago and Jerusalem, DataBase Project on Palestinian Human Rights, September 1987; and Benvenisti with Abu-Zayed and Rubinstein, *The West Bank Handbook*, p. 87, and Joost R. Hiltermann, *Israel's Deportation Policy in the Occupied West Bank and Gaza* (a report prepared by Al-Haq/Law in the Service of Man (Ramallah, West Bank: Al-Haq, 1986). For a discussion of this action and its consequences, see `Ali Jarbawi and Roger Heacock, "The Deportations and the Palestinian-Israeli Peace Negotiations," *Journal of Palestine Studies* 22, no. 3 (spring 1993): 32–47. Jarbawi and Heacock are political science professors at Birzeit University. Carmi, *Oslo: Before and After*, p. 16.

147. Robert I. Friedman, "And Darkness Covered the Land," *The Nation* 273, no. 21 (December 24, 2001): 13–20, 13; Danny Rabinowitz, "Talk of Expulsion More Ominous Than Ever," *Ha'aretz*, May 29, 2001. Also see the commentary by Amira Hass, "Keeping a Lid on the Transfer Genie," *Ha'aretz*, September 10, 2001; Uri Avnery, "A Second Nakbah?" report for *Media Monitors Network,* May 19, 2001 (available online); Yael Stein, *Expulsion of Palestinian Residents from the South Mt. Hebron Area, October–November 1999* (Jerusalem: B'Tselem—the Israeli Information Center for Human Rights in the Occupied Territories, February 2000).

148. Ben Lynfield, "Israeli Expulsion Idea Gains Steam," *Christian Science Monitor*, February 6, 2002.

4

Hebron: Caldron of Hate

If you want to know what callousness is, if you want to know what racism is, if you want to know what evil is, if you want to know what injustice is, and if you want to know what malice looks like, Hebron . . . is the best place on earth to find out.

—Gideon Levy[1]

It was a mistake from the start to plant this cancerous growth in the heart of a densely populated Arab town. . . . The second fateful mistake was when they did not uproot the growth after the massacre at the Cave of the Patriarchs.

—Yossi Sarid[2]

Among the various West Bank cities as well as Gaza City, I have chosen to focus on Hebron as a microcosm of the issues discussed in Chapter 3. Because it is a montage of the problems facing Palestinians under occupation, Hebron permits an integrated summation of the complex effects of Israeli policies in one city.

Hebron, however, is unique in that there are five settlements in the heart of the Old City in addition to its being surrounded by settlements, as are other Palestinian cities (see Map 4.1; also see Map 2.3). Moreover, Jewish settlers in the Hebron District are the most ideologically extreme in the Occupied Territories and the most violent; yet they have consistently enjoyed the protection of the Israeli government and judicial system. Thus, examining Hebron affords insight into the issue of settler violence and Israeli government collaboration. This phenomenon is an indirect aspect of Israel's efforts to force Palestinians out of the West Bank. The role of the Israeli authorities in condoning the organized settler violence against Palestinians additionally raises questions about Israel's commitment to the peace process. Although Israel has not

Map 4.1 Hebron District in Detail

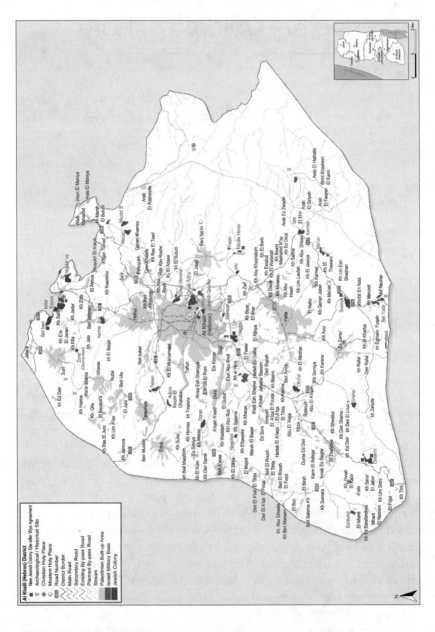

Source: Jad Isaac et al., "Al Khalil (Hebron District)," in Applied Research Institute, *An Atlas of Palestine (The West Bank and Gaza)* (Jerusalem: Applied Research Institute—ARIJ, January 2000), p. 124; and http://www.arij.org/paleye/thahriya/fig4.gif.

officially so proclaimed, many analysts believe that Israel, in any peace settlement, intends to retain Hebron as well as the southern area of Mount Hebron. Israel's direct efforts to expel Palestinian residents from this southern region are an additional focus of the chapter.

Settler Violence

Since the beginning of the occupation in 1967, Jewish settlers in the Occupied Territories have used a variety of forms of violence against Palestinians.[3] Settlers are heavily armed, protected by the Israeli Defense Forces (IDF), and backed by the Israeli governmental system.[4] In the context of the Oslo Accords and the settlers' fear that they might have to relinquish some of the West Bank and Gaza to the Palestinians, settler violence escalated significantly. This increased dramatically during the seven years between 1993 and 2000, and the growing concern in some quarters about government collusion in the violence led the B'Tselem human rights group to publish several major studies on the issue. In one, the organization concludes:

> The administration of most of the law enforcement system in Israel gives expression only to the cheapness of Palestinian life. The treatment of all arms of the law-enforcement system—army, police, State Attorney's Office, and judiciary—of violent offenses against Palestinians is characterized by contempt toward Palestinian complaints and leniency toward the offenders. Whereas a Palestinian who kills an Israeli is punished to the full extent of the law, and sometimes his family as well, it is extremely likely that an Israeli who kills a Palestinian will not be punished at all or will receive only a light sentence.[5]

B'Tselem further argues that the failure to punish settler-vigilantes results from the disinclination of law enforcement to investigate and arrest Jewish offenders; the complacence of the judicial system in inadequately prosecuting those who are arrested; and the automatic grants of pardon and early release from prison given to the few who are convicted.[6] Supporting B'Tselem's findings, in September 2001 *Ha'aretz* reported:

> In the last three years the Judea and Samaria [West Bank] police district has closed 75 percent of the investigative files it opened against Jewish settlers. . . . The most common reasons given for closing files were lack of evidence and *lack of public interest.* . . . In the years 1995–2000, dozens of files were opened. . . . 90 percent [were] closed before October 2000.[7]

In July 2001, *Ha'aretz* provided an insightful analysis of the phenomenon of settler violence in the larger context of Israeli occupation and Palestinian resistance. The analysis was made in conjunction with a report on one particular settler attack on Palestinians, yet it raises important questions about broader issues of occupation and peace.

> There is an endless torrent of such incidents—some more severe than this one, some less—which are taking place throughout the West Bank and which are not being documented. In fact, there was also an endless torrent of such incidents that occurred in various parts of the West Bank even before the outbreak of the present intifada. All these incidents involve a daily diet of harassment, threats and malicious intentions directed against the Palestinians. These incidents took place and are continuing to take place without any connection to the murder of Jews or to shots being fired at them. It is not powerlessness on the part of the Israeli authorities or any decision on their part to look the other way that is protecting Israeli citizens who are attacking Palestinians and which is hiding events from the eyes of the Israeli public. These Israeli citizens [i.e., settlers] who are doing the attacking are being protected by the "system."[8]

In addition, during the occupation, Palestinians in Hebron have been victims of prolonged curfews, closures, and blockades; extreme water shortages; extensive land confiscation; large numbers of house demolitions; and daily insults and humiliations as well as relentless settler vigilantism and "excessive IDF force."[9] Thus, the 1994 massacre by Baruch Goldstein of Palestinians at worship in the Al-Ibrahimi mosque was not an isolated incident. Rather it was one marker on a continuum that began with the first settlers in Hebron in 1968 and which continues through this time.

This chapter focuses on the settlers in and around Hebron and their radical ideology, although other settler groups throughout the West Bank and Gaza are committed to similar ideological viewpoints. As all the major human rights organizations allege, settler violence is one of the most problematic and abusive aspects of the occupation. Moreover, the explicit attempts to expel the Palestinian population from the southern area of the Hebron District are not unique.

Another issue that makes Hebron special is the presence of two international observer groups in the city: the Temporary International Presence in Hebron (TIPH), and the Christian Peacemaker Team (CPT). The experiences of the TIPH and CPT highlight the problems in the oft-repeated call by the Palestinians, especially in the context of the Al-Aqsa intifada, for an international peacekeeping force to protect Palestinians.

Settling Hebron City and Hebron District

The first Jewish settlement in Hebron, Avraham Avinu, was established in 1968 in the middle of a Palestinian neighborhood near the Al-Ibrahimi mosque. The mosque, dating from the ninth century, had been the center of Islamic life in Hebron for centuries. After the Six Day War, the Israeli government imposed the right of worship for Jews in Al-Ibrahimi, which the Israelis call the Ma'arat HaMachpela (the Cave of Machpela). Jews and Muslims revere the site as the burial place of the patriarchs Abraham, Isaac, Jacob, and their wives.[10] Worshipping at the site, however, was not enough for the Gush Emunim (Bloc of Faithful)—a messianic movement led by Rabbi Moshe Levinger, who is committed to the settlement of all of Eretz Israel.[11]

He and his supporters wanted the site to be exclusively Jewish and sought to gain control through a number of means.[12] The first step was the establishment of a permanent Jewish settlement alongside the mosque. To this end, they seized an Arab house, and the Levinger family moved in. At the same time, they began provocations in the mosque. For example, they refused to leave the mosque on Fridays (the Muslim day of communal worship) so that Muslim prayers could not be held. They held Kiddush (the rite of taking wine on the eve of the Sabbath and other occasions) in the mosque—an act that was profoundly insulting to Muslims, who are prohibited from drinking alcohol and who perceived the ingesting of wine in the mosque as an utter desecration. The settlers also hoisted an Israeli flag and in general harassed local Palestinians. These actions created conflict with the Palestinians, and by the end of 1968 Israel permanently stationed IDF troops at the mosque to protect the settlers (who, as noted, are themselves armed by the government).[13] Thus, not only was there a Jewish settlement in the heart of Hebron; there was an Israeli military installation to guard it.

Clearly, the government had a choice about how to deal with the settlers' actions in the late 1960s. The Labor government chose to protect them and to disregard the interests and rights of the Palestinians. In the ensuing years, with new settler expansion and aggression, the government always had choices about how to respond. Initially the Gush was a fringe minority in terms of Israeli society and had little support among the public at large. (More recently, its size and support have grown significantly.) Yet regardless of how egregious the actions, no government has taken the measures required to impose on them the rule of law.

The members of Gush Emunim believe that all of Hebron is Jewish land by divine right. They believe that the city was King David's first capital; thus, it is their duty to resettle the land with Jews and reestablish the city as a Jewish metropolis. By 1976, the settlers had taken over numerous Palestinian-owned buildings and houses in the neighborhood around the mosque, established a *yeshiva* (religious school) called Beit Hadassah, and established dominance over the area. This happened with the support of the government, which, in addition to dispatching IDF troops to protect the settlers, trucked in water, supplied electricity generators, expropriated vast tracts of state land on which settlements could be constructed near Avraham Avinu, and confiscated (under the rubric of security) Arab-owned land for use by settlers.[14] The Israeli government gave Avraham Avinu official recognition in 1979. Today, there are five settlements within Palestinian Hebron.[15]

As the settlers implanted themselves alongside the Al-Ibrahimi mosque, they also began construction on the settlement of Kiryat Arba on confiscated Palestinian agricultural land adjacent to Avraham Avinu.[16] Today Kiryat Arba has a population of some 6,500 and is a stronghold of Gush Emunim. Spree killer Baruch Goldstein, considered a holy saint and martyr by Jewish fundamentalists, is buried there. His grave is a pilgrimage site attended annually by thousands from all over Israel, other settlements, the United States, France, and elsewhere.[17] The government ordered the dismantlement of the shrine, but the faithful continue to come. As of 1998, there were twenty-one settlements surrounding Hebron in what is known as the Hebron District or Mount Hebron.[18]

Settler Violence and Government Collusion

The Gush Emunim is driven by messianism, literalism (especially with regard to Jewish chosenness and the belief in the territoriality of God's covenant), and by their sense of purpose—to redeem Eretz Israel and restore it to its rightful owners. Indeed, redemption and restoration are the leitmotifs of this movement to which all energies are directed. Wrapped in a sense of chosenness and exclusivity, settlers believe that God gave them the land for their exclusive use. The Hebron settlers actually developed a "philosophy" of vigilantism to buttress their practices[19] and have used it to justify their acts of harassment, humiliation, and intimidation against Palestinian residents of the area. In a practical sense, the Hebron settlers' ideology implies that they have the right to engage in any tactics to achieve their objectives—the ultimate one being the expulsion of the Palestinian population. Additionally, they claim that expulsion is a just retribution for a 1929 attack carried out by some Palestinians against Jewish residents of Hebron. Sixty-six Jews were killed, although hundreds of Jews were reportedly saved by Arab neighbors (reports put the number of Jews hidden and saved by their Palestinian neighbors at more than 400).[20] The majority of families who had relatives killed in 1929 have repudiated the Gush Emunim and disavowed any claims on behalf of their loved ones.

Notable is the fact that the Israeli government has seldom punished the settlers. On the rare occasions when an individual has been tried and convicted of an offense—usually murder—he has been given a sentence of only a few years imprisonment, if that, and has invariably been pardoned and released long before completing the term. Israeli analyst Efrat Halper makes the point clearly: "Settler violence, therefore, is not merely sporadic acts of violent individuals or mobs, but a carefully calculated strategy that serves the interest of all the Israeli parties involved."[21]

Rabbi Levinger, the spiritual as well as political and tactical leader of the Gush Emunim, is one of the most violent individuals in this group; yet only once has he been convicted of a crime. In 1990, he served ten weeks in prison for killing an unarmed merchant and was hailed by his followers as a hero when he was released.[22] Though he accepted a plea bargain at trial, he declared in court: "I did not kill an Arab, but I wish I did."[23] In another incident, Levinger shot and killed a Palestinian toddler—for which he was given a few months of community service. Rabbi Levinger has often called on his followers to commit mass suicide if the government moves to evacuate the territories.[24]

In 1972, a U.S.-born fundamentalist rabbi, Meir Kahane, arrived in Hebron and leafleted the city, summoning the mayor, Muhammad Ali Ja'abari, to a public show-trial for his alleged part in the 1929 massacre. He even stormed the mayor's office, demanding his appearance at the trial. The public accounting never took place, but as Ehud Sprinzak writes of Kahane: "His message was always the same. 'The Arabs do not belong here; they must leave.' In this spirit, Kahane initiated an organized operation to encourage the Arabs to emigrate."[25] A partial list of other incidents in Hebron during the 1970s is culled from three Israeli newspapers:

> In 1976 . . . "Tens of [Arab] youths and students from Hebron" were held prisoner in Kiryat Arba, set upon by dogs so that several required hospitalization; [there was] the 1976 expulsion of a judge of a Muslim religious court by the Kiryat Arba settlers after they publicly humiliated him; [throughout 1976–1977 there were] killings, destruction of

vineyards, looting and destruction of property . . . throwing of grenades at Arab houses, destruction of houses. . . .[26]

No one was ever charged for any of these offenses.

By 1980, a group with its origins in Kiryat Arba, known as the Jewish underground, had made several attempts to blow up the Haram al-Sharif (and had formulated more sophisticated plans for a future attack). They had also carried out assassination plots (car bombings) against five democratically elected West Bank mayors. One, Bassam Shak'a of Nablus, lost both legs, suffered severe internal injuries, and was permanently confined to a wheelchair. Nevertheless, no sooner was he released from his lengthy hospital stay than Israel put him under perpetual house arrest, refused to grant him a permit to travel, and stationed IDF guards around his home to screen his visitors. A second mayor, Karim Khalaf of El Bireh–Ramallah, was permanently crippled, although the remaining three escaped without harm. Those charged for the assassination attempts were released after serving two years of a ten-year sentence. Shortly thereafter, Gush settlers exploded a fragmentation grenade in the Hebron market that severely injured eleven children. In March 1982:

> A soldier reported that thirty 12–13 year-old [Palestinian] children were lined up facing a wall with their hands up for five hours in Hebron one very cold night, kicked if they moved. . . . Afterwards the children were taken to prison at an army camp [where their parents were denied the right to see them or to bring them coats].[27]

In October 1982, settlers planted a time bomb in the stands of Hebron's Hussein School soccer field. The explosion occurred minutes before the game was to begin and seriously injured several spectators.[28] Another time a bomb was discovered in the middle of the field. In 1983, three settlers entered the Muslim College of Hebron, threw grenades, and opened fire on students, killing three and seriously wounding thirty-three more. The perpetrators were initially sentenced to life in prison; subsequently, their sentences were reduced to fifteen years, and they were released after serving seven years. In 1984, settlers from Kiryat Arba wired explosives to the fuel tanks of five Palestinian buses expected to be full of travelers. The operation was foiled just before the buses set off.[29] After discussing several of the above actions, Jewish American academic Ian Lustick wrote of Gush Emunim:

> But these were only the most spectacular events in a wave of less serious vigilantism. . . . During that period [1980–1984], the Israeli press reported more than 380 attacks against individuals, in which 23 were

killed, 191 injured, and 38 abducted. Hundreds more attacks were directed at property—automobiles, homes, and shops. Forty-one attacks on Muslim . . . religious institutions were counted.[30]

Hebron in the Context of the Oslo Agreements

The Declaration of Principles (DOP) was signed in September 1993, and Baruch Goldstein carried out his massacre in February 1994.[31] This might have been an opportune time to remove the extremists from Hebron or to restrict their activities. Instead, Prime Minister Yitzhak Rabin chose to punish the Palestinians through curfews, closures, road-blocks, and so on (detailed in previous chapters).[32] He did, however, permit the temporary stationing of international observers in the city. Yet whereas the Palestinians were locked in their homes, settlers freely went about their activities, including celebrating in the streets the "heroic" act and "martyrdom" of Goldstein.

In the 1995 Interim Agreement (Oslo II), which carved up the West Bank and Gaza into Areas A, B, and C, Hebron was given a special status to accommodate settlers' interests. Whereas Israel agreed to the IDF redeployment from the populous urban areas of other West Bank cities, Hebron was divided into two sectors: H-1 and H-2. The Israeli sector, H-2, encompasses 32 percent of the city, which includes 40,000 Palestinians, the 400 settlers in the Jewish quarter, the main (Palestinian) commercial district of the city, Kiryat Arba, and the "surrounding areas deemed necessary for movement of the settlers and the army."[33] The IDF would maintain full control of H-2. In H-1, the remaining 68 percent of the city, the Palestinian Authority (PA) would have restricted autonomy. In contrast to other parts of the West Bank defined as Area A, the PA in H-1 was subject to rigorous limitations—for example, it could have only a maximum of 100 rifles. The status of Al-Ibrahimi mosque was not addressed in the 1995 Interim Agreement; thus, the de facto situation of the post-1994 arrangements would remain in effect. Implementation of the agreement was slated for March 26, 1996, indicating that Hebron would be the last of the West Bank cities from which the IDF would redeploy.

When the scheduled date arrived, Prime Minister Shimon Peres chose to suspend the redeployment. Subsequently Benjamin Netanyahu was elected prime minister, and he had no interest in altering the status quo. Nevertheless, under intense U.S. pressure, Netanyahu signed the January 15, 1997, Hebron Protocol. This was not a new agreement; rather, it merely set out the necessary steps for partial implementation of the Hebron aspect of the 1995 Interim Agreement.[34] The only major

change involved the de jure division of Al-Ibrahimi mosque, which
gave the settlers 70 percent for a synagogue and limited Muslim worship to 30 percent of the site. Additionally, four roads were allocated to
connect Jewish worshipers with the synagogue; one passage was available to Muslims wishing to pray there. Moreover, to protect the settlers,
400 heavily armed Israeli guards, together with three highly sophisticated security systems, were permanently stationed at the site.[35] (Subsequently, the number of soldiers was increased to several thousand
with the support of tanks and artillery.) The division of the city was
implemented shortly thereafter (see Map 2.3).[36] On the morning after
signing the Hebron Protocol, Prime Minister Netanyahu stated:

> We are not leaving Hebron, we are redeploying in a part of Hebron.
> We are staying in all the city's locations where a Jewish settlement
> existed, exists and will continue to exist. The IDF . . . and only they
> will retain control and responsibility and continue to operate without
> any limitations. . . . We don't see you [the settlers living inside the city
> and in Kiryat Arba] as an extraneous appendage, we see you as dear
> brothers. We worry about each and every one of you. You are our rep-
> resentatives in the city of the Patriarchs.[37]

In practical terms, this meant that Israel has absolute control over
H-2 while the PA exercises limited control over H-1. Due to the joint
nature of Area B, Israel (with the PA as a junior partner) has control
over most of the remaining towns and villages of Hebron District. Area
C gives Israel absolute jurisdiction over the remainder of Mount
Hebron, including all settlements as well as Palestinian rural areas (see
Map 4.1). One Israeli analyst described the situation on the ground after
the implementation of the Hebron Protocol:

> The heart of Hebron, including the Old City, remains entirely under
> Israeli control. The market is extremely tense with the presence of set-
> tlers and army trucks; gates and barbed wire block off the central road
> to *Tel Rumeida*. Flanked by Israeli guard towers, *Shuhada* Street
> remains dead silent. There are now twice as many checkpoints as
> before. . . . Traveling within the city proper, one encounters a new
> zone every few hundred meters. At almost every corner stands a
> checkpoint . . . within two weeks after the agreement, the Israeli
> authorities issued five demolition orders for Palestinian homes. . . .
> The claim was that they were obstructing the way for a new by-pass
> road. . . . The Israeli government can legally expel from their homes
> Palestinian residents . . . paving the way for the sort of "ethnic cleans-
> ing" which is already taking place in Hebron's Old City and various
> parts of Jerusalem. . . . Renovations [of homes] are forbidden to
> Palestinians. In downtown Hebron, they may not build anything high-
> er than two stories.[38]

International Observers in Hebron

Two different groups of international observers are stationed in Hebron to protect the Palestinian population. One is the Temporary International Presence in Hebron. In March 1994, owing to the demands of the PA in the aftermath of the Goldstein massacre, Israel agreed to an international presence in the city. In May, a small group of unarmed Norwegian, Danish, and Italian observers began work in Hebron. Four months later, however, in August 1994, Israel demanded that the mission be disbanded. In the 1995 Interim Agreement, a clause was included reestablishing TIPH for deployment during the IDF's redeployment from the city. This time, TIPH had only Norwegian members, its mandate renewable on a monthly basis. However, because Israel chose not to fulfill its agreement to redeploy from Hebron, the mission was not activated. Finally, as part of the 1997 Hebron Protocol, Israel and the PA agreed, in a January 21, 1998, memorandum, to the reconstitution of TIPH, comprising 180 members from six countries: Norway, Italy, Denmark, Sweden, Switzerland, and Turkey. Its mandate was to be renewed every three months with consent of both the PA and Israel. TIPH members met monthly with Israeli and PA security personnel in a Joint Hebron Committee, where they made reports concerning their observations.[39]

TIPH's primary function, in its own words, is

> to create a feeling of security among the Palestinian population of Hebron and contribute in restoring normal life. TIPH pursues this goal by maintaining a constant presence in the streets of Hebron, and by monitoring and reporting developments.[40]

TIPH members had no military or police functions; they could not carry arms (even for self-protection); they could not intervene in conflicts—in fact, they were required to stand aside if they observed a violent incident between Israelis and Palestinians. They were prohibited from interfering with Israeli security, military, or police personnel; and they could not conduct investigations of incidents they observed. TIPH members were also prohibited from talking to the media. In short, TIPH's sole function was to observe the activities of the settlers, soldiers, and Palestinians and report them in a monthly trilateral meeting. Israel set the parameters as well as the limitations on TIPH's mandate. The PA wanted the international force to have a far broader charge, so as to be able to actually protect Palestinians. Israel argued that anything more than observation status would violate its sovereignty. The inequities of the power disparities are obvious.

The second international force in Hebron is the Christian Peacemaker Team. The CPT grew out of a commitment by members of the Mennonite, Anabaptist, Quaker, and Church of the Brethren denominations to utilize their commitment to pacifism, nonviolent intervention, direct action, and justice to attempt to make a difference in real world conflicts. They have teams in Afghanistan, Colombia, Haiti, Mexico, Puerto Rico, and elsewhere. They began their work in Hebron in 1995 after an initial delegation visited the city and met with Palestinian mayor Mustapha Natshe. A formal letter of invitation from the mayor provided the only authorization for their work. The CTP had a twelve-member full-time team, with significant reservists who served as backup when a regular member became ill or was injured. Additionally, the core CTP team oversaw the development of ten projects with their own full-time staffs. One of the most important of these was the Campaign for Secure Dwellings, which linked families in the United States with families in the Hebron District whose houses or land were confiscated or demolished or were under threat of either.

The most significant work the CPT did (and continued to do through the intifada) was nonviolent intervention. CPTers put themselves physically between soldiers with live ammunition and tanks and unarmed Palestinian demonstrators. They put themselves between bulldozers and orchards and homes about to be destroyed. They put themselves between settlers who were harassing, humiliating, or harming Palestinians. They lived with locals, walked the streets, and provided emotional and spiritual sustenance to the Palestinian people of Hebron.[41] Two examples of CPT activities demonstrate the nature of their work:

> All throughout the week [February 1998], CPTers continued to help a Palestinian family build a bathroom and kitchen. The family has lived without these facilities since 1992, because they feared building them would draw the Israeli military's attention to the house . . . [and it would be demolished].[42]
>
> CPTers Pierre Shantz, 24, and Sara Reschly, 26, were arrested today by Israeli police after "getting in the way" of soldiers about to shoot at a Palestinian nonviolent demonstration in Hebron. . . . [They] jumped in front of the soldiers and their guns. They cried: "This is a nonviolent demonstration. They are not throwing rocks." The soldiers, not knowing how to respond, tried to push the CPTers away. They lowered their M-16's, but soldiers threw sound grenades, which sent the crowd scurrying. The demonstration leadership quickly calmed the Palestinians.[43]

How successful were these international peacekeeping groups? One can easily imagine from its mandate that the TIPH was essentially impotent because its observers were unable even to interact with the population. Indeed, as the section below will demonstrate, settler and soldier violence against the Palestinians escalated significantly after the establishment of TIPH in 1997. Palestinian analyst Adam Hanieh summarized: "The Temporary International Presence in Hebron has completely failed to prevent attacks on Palestinians by the Israeli military and settlers before and during the current uprising."[44]

Yet the settlers were hostile to TIPH; they abused them verbally, attacked them physically, and destroyed their property—all under the gaze of the IDF, which did not intervene. Because TIPH members were prohibited from talking with the media, individuals from the CPT often reported their stories. One CPT newsletter stated:

> In the last two weeks, members of the Temporary International Presence in Hebron have suffered both from physical attacks by settlers in Hebron and from a deliberate misinformation campaign waged against them by senior army officials and the Hebron settlers. . . . TIPH members have not been able to go out on patrol, because they only have two cars that the settlers have not damaged, and they are saving those two for emergencies. . . . The Israeli authorities are evidently condoning these acts of hostility against TIPH.[45]

The attitudes of some settlers toward TIPH are expressed here in excerpts from an open letter written by settlers to the TIPH.

> You bear a large share of the blame for the situation, due to your one-sided, knee-jerk support of the Arab terrorist aggressor. Through this behavior you are encouraging the aggressor and sending him a message that he will enjoy international support if he attacks the Jews, using every means against them, however abominable. . . . Unfortunately, the reality is that TIPH has become an anti-Jewish organization that is ready to support every unjust and abominable act on condition that it is perpetrated against Jews. . . . Unfortunately, your organization is part of an international anti-Semitic condition that has been operating against the Jewish People for many generations, a condition . . . which found its worst expression in the terrible Holocaust.[46]

The situation for TIPH became so difficult that in late August 2001 the mission decided it could no longer patrol in the Israeli H-2 sector. In the only interview he ever gave, TIPH Commander Karl-Henry Sjursen told *Ha'aretz:* "Almost everyday Jewish settlers attack our patrols and the Israeli army just watches. So I had to order the withdrawal of our mission from patrolling the Jewish quarter."[47] Sjursen showed the reporter a collection of stones (some quite heavy) that settlers had thrown at TIPH members.

The experience of the CPT has been little better. Its mission is quite different than that of TIPH; it is a very small community motivated only by personal faith and a willingness to die in the cause of justice. Members work primarily by direct intervention to protect Palestinians. The CPT newsletters provide evidence that they have been able to prevent soldiers from opening fire on demonstrators, stopped settler attacks on individuals, impeded—at least temporarily—the destructive work of bulldozers, and other similar activities. But the scope of their operation is so small that they cannot be said to have been effective in protecting the Palestinians of Hebron. Also, given the nature of CPT's modus operandi, it is unlikely to attract a body of persons sufficient in size to afford that protection. Unlike TIPH, the CPT is admired and respected by the Palestinians of Hebron, but the limitations of what it can do are also understood.

The settlers view the CPT with intense hostility and have subjected individuals in the mission to verbal abuse, physical assaults, and death threats. A letter from settlers in 1998 reflects their basic attitude:

> It has been learned that three of your members help and assist Arab terrorists in smuggling explosives used in recent bombings of the Hebron Jewish Community in Israel. For their safety, the above-mentioned [CPT] terrorists are advised to depart from the Land of Israel to their own communities in the next 96 hours.[48]

Most important is the fact that neither the Israeli government, the IDF, nor any other official institution ever defended the the CPT or the TIPH from attacks by settlers. The TIPH was there by virtue of an express Israeli legal agreement and as such was *entitled* to protection. Although CPT does not have the same international legal status, it might be expected that Israel would ensure the safety of a small group of U.S. pacifists residing in an area under its control.

The Meaning of the Peace
Process to Hebron's Palestinians

House Demolitions

Hebron has experienced large-scale house demolitions for reasons of collective punishment as well as settler expansion. Immediately after the 1967 occupation, there was a spate of such demolitions, then they tapered off. During the first intifada, the demolition of Palestinian homes escalated. However, between 1989 and 1993, they once again declined. Subsequent to the beginning of the peace process, house demolitions again rapidly increased.[49] During the Rabin-Peres government, ninety-three homes were demolished; however, the policy was suspended after the clashes that resulted from the September 1996 opening of the Hasmonaen Tunnel under the Haram al-Sharif in Jerusalem. But in January 1997, in the aftermath of the Hebron Protocol redeployment, the policy was reinstituted.[50] In one month following the redeployment, eighteen homes were demolished and "hundreds more [were] slated for demolition."[51] According to the Applied Research Institute, besides demolishing Palestinian houses, Israel, between the signing of the DOP and 1998, confiscated 21,652 dunums (216 hectares) of land in the Hebron District and uprooted 12,950 trees.[52] Six existing settlements were expanded, and in 1999 a completely new settlement was constructed. Conversely, between 1993 and 1998, Israel granted only three permits for residents of Hebron to build houses.[53]

Settler Violence

Eighteen months after the Goldstein massacre, B'Tselem undertook a detailed investigation to ascertain the situation of Palestinians living in Hebron and found that Palestinians were extensively victimized by IDF security forces as well as ongoing settler vigilantism. I will present only a sampling of B'Tselem's findings.

- "In the wake of the [Goldstein] massacre and subsequent Palestinian demonstrations, security forces were present in massive numbers in Palestinian population centers. . . . The security forces used live ammunition excessively [against the demonstrators] . . . [and they] further restricted the Palestinians' freedom of movement, resulting in substantial harm to the routine of daily life in the city."[54]
- "Security forces gunfire killed 27 Palestinians. . . . The number of persons killed in Hebron was appreciably higher than in other West Bank cities."[55]
- "Seven mosques were closed for a fixed period [three to six months]."[56]
- "A total of 50 days of [24-hour] curfew were imposed, 29 [consecutively] immediately followed the massacre [plus] 40 night curfews."[57]
- "Hebron is the only WB city containing checkpoints within the

city. . . . Only Palestinians are checked at checkpoints; the settlers are allowed to pass through freely."[58]

- "Numerous roads were closed to Palestinian traffic. . . . Under army orders, Hebron's main roads were blocked with concrete blocks, cement barrels, concrete fences, and other means. All streets branching off from the road leading from the 'glass Junction' to Kiryat Arba were closed, and the [Palestinian] residents in nearby neighborhoods were forced to travel long distances along alternative routes to reach their homes. The road linking Beit Hadassah to Avraham Avinu was closed to all Palestinian cars, resulting in serious financial loss to numerous businesses in the area; the large vegetable market in the city center . . . was also closed."[59]

- "In several testimonies given to B'Tselem, Hebron's Palestinian residents indicate that security forces personnel beat them severely."[60]

- "Soldiers and police officers handling of cases where settlers injure Palestinians is characterized largely by acquiescence, compromise, and mitigation. . . . Where soldiers have intervened in such incidents, they often injured Palestinians or their property."[61]

One particularly telling incident of settler violence and Israeli government collusion at the highest levels occurred in 1996 when a settler fatally pistol-whipped an eleven-year-old child named Hilmi Shusha. The settler was arrested, but at trial the Israeli judge acquitted him, stating that the "child died on his own as a result of emotional pressure." After numerous appeals by the child's family and their Israeli lawyer, the High Court termed the act a "light killing" and called for a new trial. At the second trial, the settler was sentenced to six months of community service and a fine of a few thousand dollars.[62]

Children: The Settlers' Future

Settler children play a remarkably active role in perpetrating violence against Palestinians. One reason for this is the fact that the authorities are prohibited from arresting children ten years of age or younger regardless of what they do.[63] Kathleen Kern, who spent five years with CPT in Hebron, reported the following in *Tikkun*:

Hebron settler boys between the ages of 5 and 10 wandered the streets in packs, stoning passersby, their homes, and their shops while soldiers looked on. A group of these boys assaulted Sister Ann Montgomery (age 74). When soldiers called us over to a checkpoint and asked to see our passports, the soldiers stood there as the group of about 10 boys proceeded to stone us, hit us with sticks, and throw water at us from the soldiers' water bottles. Despite our requests that the soldiers call the police, they just stood there, sometimes smiling at the boys' behavior. . . . [Eventually the police came] and the little boys, shouting Nazim, Nazim, knew that they could push around police officers with complete impunity.[64]

Another former female CPTer reported a similar story involving children.

As we approached the market, we saw a group of young settler girls trying to enter. . . . One of the girls threw a huge stone at a 75 year-old man, which hit him on the back of the head, causing profuse bleeding. . . . I then noticed an armed man in a white shirt with a black beard and glasses . . . and asked him to try and stop the kids throwing rocks because people were hurt, and tried to explain I had just witnessed an old man being badly hurt. He started screaming at me: "fascist whore," "f———ing Nazi," "Go home," "The Christians massacred the Jews." . . . One of his hands was clenched on his gun. . . . He suddenly came at me "to teach me" and hit me on the right hand side of my head.[65]

In 1994, Micha X. Peled, an Israeli journalist, lived with the settlers in Hebron for three months from which he wrote, directed, and produced a documentary film entitled *Inside God's Bunker*. The documentary is a graphic depiction of settler activities, ideology, and daily life from the perspective of the settlers. It illustrates all the provocations and violence discussed above and additionally focuses on the children of the settlers who range in age from toddlers to teenagers. Children are encouraged by their parents and teachers to be active against Palestinians. Perhaps most striking in the film is the children's uninhibited racism expressed in songs, game-playing, and casual conversation. The lyrics from one of their favorite songs, sung repeatedly, illustrates the point: "The world hates Arabs. The important thing is to kill them one by one. I trod with my feet on my enemy. I bit his skin with my teeth. I sucked his blood with my lips. I still feel I have not done justice to my revenge."[66] Human Rights Watch reported that during a Purim celebration in Hebron on March 11, 2001, "among the crowd were children dressed up as Dr. Baruch Goldstein."[67] Children, of course, were not the only celebrants at the aforementioned Purim festival. *Ha'aretz* notes that on Purim, as on all Jewish holidays, Palestinians are put under total curfew throughout the Occupied Territories so as not to disturb Israeli festivities. But in Hebron the festivities take place under the eyes of the locked-up inhabitants.

> Israelis frolic freely in the streets . . . wildly celebrating their holiday. Is there any other place on earth where the members of one group celebrates the imprisonment of the members of another, where the aggressive dance of the members of the powerful group becomes a commemoration of the imprisonment of an entire city? . . . The day on which this minority celebrates its Purim holiday is also the memorial day of the massacre of 34 innocent [Palestinian] victims, a massacre that happened here only seven years ago.[68]

Land Confiscation, Water Restrictions, and Environmental Pollution

The environment of the Hebron District has also been detrimentally affected by the settlers. The district comprises 105,000 hectares (1,050 square kilometers/405 square miles), of which nearly 25 percent has been expropriated for exclusive Jewish use. The twenty-seven settlements make up a little less than 1 percent. (All Palestinian built-up areas—cities, towns, villages, refugee camps—together constitute only 3.6 percent of the total.) The largest share of confiscated land, some 19.3 percent, is composed of areas that Israel has designated as closed military zones. No Palestinian may live, work, graze animals, or even pass through these areas. There are also four military bases that make up slightly less than 1 percent of the area. Israel has established complete control over 1,200 dunums of forested areas (also closed to Palestinians), making up about 1.5 percent of the area. Furthermore, it has designated 700 dunums as an Israeli nature reserve on about 0.7 percent of the area. Israel owns four of the six quarries in Hebron District (confiscated from Palestinian owners). It has established two exclusive industrial zones—the first on 35,500 dunums (35 square kilometers) southwest of Hebron and Al-Baqa'a, the second on 1,200 dunums south of Hebron known as Meitarim that opened in October 2001.[69] *Ha'aretz* reported that the new zone includes, among other things, a cosmetics company that produces products for the European market, a plant that makes synthetic fuel from sewage, and a dairy plant that produces cheese from goats and sheep grown organically in the region. More plants are expected to open in the near future.[70] Israel also controls a lattice of bypass roads (all of which have buffers of 50–100 meters on either side), with Road 60 constituting a major settler thoroughfare (see Figure 4.1).

The Palestinian economy in the district is based primarily on agri-

Figure 4.1   Effects of Israeli Occupation on the Palestinian Environment

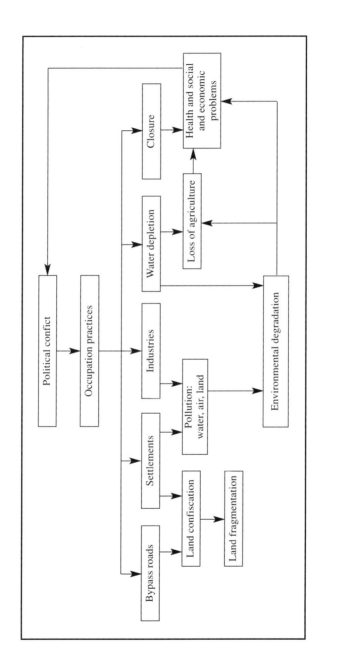

culture and livestock production. In 1967, Israel closed to Palestinian use 85 percent of the available grazing land in the district. Left with only 15 percent, Palestinian shepherds have overgrazed the available land to such an extent that there has been severe degradation of the range plants. In turn, the production of goats and sheep, mainstays of the Palestinian economy and diet, has dropped dramatically.[71] Fifteen percent of the land that Israel has confiscated since 1967 is agricultural. Of the remaining 85 percent, 4,121 hectares are not under cultivation because of insufficient water due to Israeli restrictions on groundwater usage.[72] A frequent type of settler harassment is destruction of agriculture—uprooting olive and fruit trees, wrecking greenhouses, burning crops, polluting or otherwise damaging wells, destroying vineyards, and destroying produce in the markets.[73]

The settlements and military encampments have also seriously contributed to polluting the environment of the Hebron District, especially contaminating the water supply from untreated surface wastewater. As a result, there has been damage to crops and illnesses among the population. Settlers dump domestic solid waste in Yatta and Al-Jalajil, polluting East Hebron and the surrounding area. They also dump solid waste in Ishkloot, affecting the surrounding area. The areas most severely affected by settlement mismanagement of domestic wastewater are Dura and Beit Ummar. The industrial activities of the settlements also cause pollution. For example, wastewater from the wine factory in Kiryat Arba flows to Al-Mazari land, which is on the way from Hebron to Bani Na'im, and affects Um al-Jalajil and Wadi al-Fawwar. Pollution from Kiryat Arba and Kharseena negatively affect the land, crops, and people of Al-Baka'a, Al-Fahs, Um al-Jalajil, and Wadi Jabir. Pollution from the settlements of Ma'on, Carmel, and Otni'el harm the villages of Al-Thahriji, as-Samou'a, and Yatta. Pollution from the settlements of Adora and Telem is harmful to Dura and Tarqumia. The military bases of Har Manooh and Hajay pollute Qalqees, south of Hebron, and the military camp of Kafarooth contaminates Shilta, Dair Qadees, and Shibteen.[74]

Hebron's Water Crisis

One of the major negative environmental effects settlers have on the Hebron District relates to water shortages. In Chapter 3, Israeli water policies (restrictions and limitations vis-à-vis the Palestinians) were examined in detail. The Hebron District, due to topography and low rainfall levels, has always been among the most severely affected areas as a consequence of these water policies. In the post-Oslo period, suffering has become even more pronounced and is due to Israel's failure to fulfill commitments made in formal agreements with the PA as well as discriminatory policies. Summers are particularly difficult for the Palestinian residents of the region. There is insufficient water for human consumption, and the agricultural sector is deprived. In 1998, the water crisis reached extreme proportions.

> Hebron has been the district hit hardest by the shortage, caused largely by the failure of the Israeli water corporation, Mekorot, to supply water per the amounts agreed to in the Water Annex of the Oslo Accords. According to PWA officials, Israel is pumping to the Hebron district only half the negotiated 17,000 cubic meters (CM) of water per day. . . . A black market in water has developed out of the current shortage, whereby water is stolen from aquifers or trucks and sold to needy families at the exorbitant price of 25 NIS [U.S.$6.25] per CM. Palestinian families in Hebron, some of whom now only receive water in trucks once every ten days, are forced out of desperation to pay such prices. The Alia hospital in Hebron has had to turn to black market water, and is currently threatened with closure because of the cost and irregular supply of water. In stark contrast, Israeli colonies in Hebron . . . are supplied with water continuously . . . annual per capita water consumption for colonists is between 650 and 1,714 CM as opposed to 107 to 156 CM in Palestinian areas.[75]

Expulsion of Palestinians from the Southern Area of Hebron District

Israel has undertaken a systematic policy of expelling the Palestinians from the Al-Mufqara region (Yatta region) of the southeastern portion of the Hebron District. An Israeli support group, Ta'ayush, a coalition of organizations from Israel's peace camp who work in partnership with several Palestinian groups in an attempt to halt the expulsions, summarized the issue:

> The Israeli government, military, civil administration, and Jewish settlers have been carrying out a premeditated and coordinated plan to make the South Hebron area "Arab Free." This plan includes repeated expulsions of local residents from their land, destruction of houses, tents, and caves, sealing water wells, uprooting orchards, and preventing the residents from farming their land and tending their livestock. The government pursues this plan while expropriating Palestinian land and issuing injunctions that compromise the residents' right to remain in the region. These actions are carried out in order to exhaust the local Palestinian population and to run them off their land. In the last few months, the rate of evictions has increased and the attempt to ethnically cleanse the whole area is underway.[76]

The Al-Mufqara region of south Hebron is rural and hilly. Most of the land is rocky and difficult to cultivate; therefore, agriculture is limited to small and isolated plots, which are usually located in ravines, where some soil accumulates. The major population center is the town of Yatta, and there are several large villages and a collection of small localized communities of five to six families each scattered throughout the area, with a total population of a few thousand Palestinians. This population largely migrated from the surrounding villages and began to settle in the area in the 1830s, where they lived in natural caves and tents. Originally, these caves were used for temporary shelter; however, according to *Life in the South Hebron Caves,* a book published by the Israeli Defense Ministry, over the years these caves gradually became a permanent living space. The book also discloses that for generations these local farmers (who also raise sheep and goats) have preserved a unique way of life that is inextricably tied to cave-dwelling.[77]

Up until 1947, these farmers cultivated swaths of land that extended all the way to Arad. Following the 1948 war, they became Jordanian residents and were denied access to their land on the Israeli side of the border. In the aftermath of the 1967 war, Israel occupied this region as well as the rest of the West Bank. No sooner did the people return to their land than the occupation authority began to expropriate the Palestinian farmers' land for military bases, drilling zones, nature reserves, and forests. From the early 1980s on, the Israeli government has continually confiscated more land as it began building settlements in the area—Carmel, Ma'on, Sussia, Mezadot-Yhuda (Beit Yatir), Otni'el, and Shim'a. Many of these settlements were constructed in an attempt to create territorial contiguity between border towns inside Israel and the area north of the Green Line. As settlements were erected on expropriated Palestinian land, the government declared the area "state property" (see Map 4.2).[78]

The Beginning of Massive Evictions

The first attempt to carry out a massive expulsion took place in November 1999 when the IDF forcibly removed 750 Palestinians residing in twelve locales.[79] This action was related to demands by settlers from Ma'on that had established the Ma'on farm (a shepherd's ranch) in the region and exerted pressure on the government to evict the Palestinians from nearby areas.[80] In some cases, the soldiers came with eviction orders, and in others they did not display any orders. The

Map 4.2   Southern Hebron District in Detail: Area of Evictions

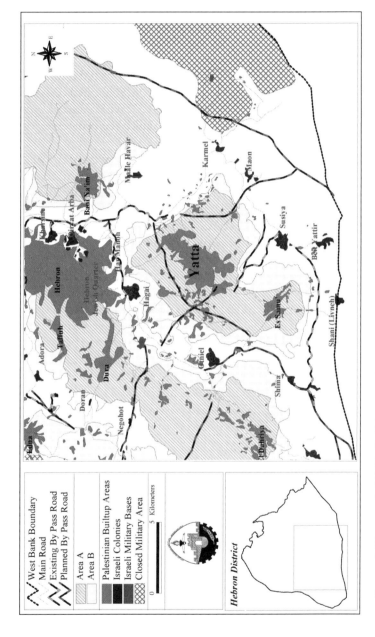

Source: Jad Isaac et al., "Al Khalil (Hebron District)," in Applied Research Institute, *An Atlas of Palestine (The West Bank and Gaza)* (Jerusalem: Applied Research Institute—ARIJ, January 2000), p. 124; and http://www.arij.org/paleye/thahriya/fig4.gif. Reprinted with permission of ARIJ.

expulsions were carried out by a large number of security forces, accompanied by bulldozers that destroyed tents and huts and sealed off the openings of the caves, which were used by the Palestinians as their homes. Hundreds of people, among them many children and infants, were forced to pass the winter without shelter. During spring 2000, after a public struggle in which various political organizations, writers, and public figures participated, the High Court decided that the status quo— as it had been before the evictions—was to be reinstated and that the residents were to be allowed to return to their cave dwellings. Accordingly, the families returned to their land under the protection of this court decision.[81]

Nonetheless, beginning July 3, 2001, another expulsion occurred. For three days, the IDF and the civil administration sowed destruction and carried out mass evictions. This time, the actions were far wider in scope than ever and affected communities throughout the region between Yatta and the Green Line east of the Yatta—as-Samou'a road. These expulsions were carried out without prior warning and involved a large military and civil administration presence. The destruction was systematic in comparison to previous occurrences. Caves that had been sealed in the past were now completely destroyed by bulldozers, which also blocked most of the water wells in the area, ruined crops and property, and killed livestock. Hundreds of people were kicked off their land. Among the people expelled were those who the High Court—in the spring of 2000—had explicitly stated were not to be evicted. During this expulsion campaign, the military even prevented the Red Cross from providing the Palestinians basic humanitarian assistance such as food, blankets, and tents.[82]

Settler Activities: 1999–2000

While these events were occurring in the southern district of Hebron, the situation in Hebron City and the surrounding areas deteriorated as well. Settler violence became more widespread and vicious with the collusion of the authorities, and the IDF itself became more directly involved in the repression of Palestinians. International concern also became more pronounced. In 2001, Human Rights Watch published a report documenting the various abuses, and B'Tselem produced two major studies on the collaboration of the government with vigilante settlers.[83] The following constitutes a representative sample from the Human Rights Watch report detailing the violence. These vignettes demonstrate that little has changed from the 1970s and 1980s, illustrating instead that the peace process has made the settlers more determined and aggressive and the Palestinians more vulnerable.

- August, 2000: "In August, prior to the outbreak of hostilities, settlers from Tel Rumeida destroyed some 350 grapevines belonging to Zakariya al-Bakri."[84]
- October 6, 2000: "Settlers from Tel Rumeida approached the home of the Abu 'Aisha. . . . Young men, aged about 18, [they] proceeded to rip the protective mesh covering the aeration holes of the basement water storage tanks, and dumped an unknown white substance into the water. Chemical analysis later determined . . . [that] the pollution had made the water undrinkable."[85]
- November 1, 2000: "Settlers from Ma'on settlement near Yatta set fire to the grain store of Khalid-al-Umur, burning 150 tons of hay and 30 tons of seed, and causing the death of 7 goats."[86]
- November 2, 2000: [The curfew was lifted for a few hours.] "When the market re-opened, a group of 20 women settlers arrived and began disrupting the market. . . . [They] ripped down all the clothes [displayed] outside and stepped on them, they took some clothes with them. . . . We closed our shops to protect our goods."[87]
- December 8, 2000: "Vandals destroyed more than one thousand phone connections in a switchbox located across the street from the Avraham Avinu settlement, cutting the phone lines of most of the Palestinian population [40,000] inside the Israeli controlled H-2 area."[88]
- February 2001: "The olive grove is the main source of income for the [Munasra] family, bringing in about 18,000 NIS (U.S.$4,500) in a normal year. The entire crop was lost because of the settler attacks. In addition, . . . the settlers poisoned a water cistern on the land."[89]
- April 2001: "It is clear that the majority of physical attacks are initiated by Israeli settlers, and that the IDF has consistently failed in its obligations to protect Palestinians from attacks by Israeli settlers. In effect, settlers are using the protection provided by the IDF to attack Palestinian civilians."[90]
- April 1, 2001: "Settlers burned at least five Palestinian shops and also torched the offices of the Waqf Islamic authority. . . . [They] exploded a gas canister inside a Palestinian store, destroying three Palestinian stores."[91]

Hebron During the Al-Aqsa Intifada

The situation in Hebron only worsened during the second intifada. The individual incidents are too extensive to recount; however, several bear mention. In early July 2001, Israel established a new settlement near Kiryat Arba, and a few days later a Palestinian gunman shot and killed a man at its entrance. *Ha'aretz* reported that

> Immediately, Kiryat Arab's vigilante armies swung into action. Thirsting for revenge, they grabbed hold of Palestinian lands. . . . They burned fields, ignited houses, uprooted trees, and vandalized anything in their path. Cloaked by the twilight dusk, the settlers pressed ahead on their trail of destruction, heading for Palestinian residences in Hebron. They smashed windshields, shattered windows of homes. After rubbing out drawings of the Al-Aqsa mosque, they stamped the Star of David on Palestinian doors. . . . No settler had been impeded; none was arrested. Soldiers stood by. . . . [Subsequently,] the Palestinian residents of Hebron were put under curfew.[92]

A second involves what Colonel (Res.) Moshe Givati, adviser to Security Minister Uzi Landau, termed a "pogrom" at the end of July 2002. Givati, who was in Hebron during the incident, stated that it was "a pogrom against the Arabs of Hebron, with *no provocation on the Palestinian side.*"[93] The spark was the killing of four settlers in a roadside ambush. Shortly after the shooting, and for three days thereafter (during which Palestinians were confined to their homes under a curfew), settlers attacked Palestinian residents of Hebron, broke into homes, destroyed windows and doors, and burned and vandalized everything inside (in some homes they remained and declared their intention to stay permanently). A fourteen-year-old girl was shot dead; a nine-year-old boy was stabbed and critically wounded; and at least fifteen others were seriously injured from beatings. "The security forces stood aside, watched the settlers, and chose to do nothing."[94]

Hebron was the only Palestinian city not under curfew at the end of the summer of 2002 (Israel's reoccupation of the West Bank). However, as in other years, the city was placed under complete curfew during the Jewish High Holy Days. One Israeli journalist wrote:

> The IDF imposed curfew on Hebron's casbah yesterday and opened it to Israeli visitors. The thousands of Israelis strolling Hebron's alleys felt at home. They walked at leisure . . . and had their photographs taken near the closed houses of Palestinians. . . . Israelis were permitted to roam around the casbah. With soldiers protecting them from all

sides, the visitors felt so safe they allowed themselves to explore the dark alleys. Others marched, heads held high, demonstrating their presence. . . . Eliezer Afarsemon [a Hebron settler], in a seemingly euphoric mood, joined the tour. "It's all ours," he explained, pointing at the shut houses. . . . "Would you have believed we'd be here? Walk around like this inside the casbah? We, in Hebron, feel we've won. All of Hebron is now in our control."[95]

Israeli analyst Meron Benvenisti characterized the above:

The celebrations in the shadow of the curfew are an expression of racist, ruthless chauvinism. . . . Much has been said about the brutality, the indifference, and the racist vanity of the decision to put an entire city under curfew to allow a group of extremists to celebrate their mastery over the land and to disseminate messages of hatred and expulsion. But maybe not enough emphasis has been put on the curfew as a form of psychological repression, nothing more than the desire to hide from the consciousness (and perhaps the conscience) the fact of the existence of an entire people, and the hope that the "transfer by the hour will turn into comprehensive transfer."[96]

On October 14, 2002, *Ha'aretz* wrote:

Tensions are running even higher than usual in Hebron this week . . . settlers are forcibly preventing the *muezzin* at the Tomb of the Patriarchs from calling the faithful to prayer. . . . Settlers invaded the Waqf offices, vandalizing the equipment and making a bonfire out of the documents they found in the office, including deeds to all the Waqf property in the city. . . . Settlers broke into a local school, spray-painting the walls with "Death to the Arabs" slogans and painting the walls with stars of David. . . . The incursion into the Waqf offices took place when settlers broke through a wall in a property they had already captured from its Arab inhabitants.[97]

Shortly thereafter, Hebron exploded in violent conflict (see Chapter 9).

The situation of the Palestinians in Hebron is clear. It is not powerlessness on the part of the Israeli government, or even just the decisions of the government to look the other way that protects Israeli citizens who are attacking Palestinians. The government or the "system" is protecting the Israeli citizens who are doing the attacking. As *Ha'aretz* put it:

It was this same system that more than three decades ago, relying on Israel's military force, sent the Jewish citizens of this state to become settlers beyond Israel's recognized borders (irrespective of the fact that some of these settlers thought that they were fulfilling a divine promise), to live on the cultivated and uncultivated lands of the local

Palestinian populace, and to use that populace's springs and wells. The goal of this settlement project [in Hebron] was that, at some future time, the homes of these settlers would ensure the expansion of the area over which Israel enjoys sovereignty. The struggle over the expansion of this area of sovereign control is now [July 2001] in high gear, and it is this struggle that is protecting the attackers, who are loyal soldiers of the "system."[98]

B'Tselem adds: "Israeli leniency extends to all aspects of an incident: from the lack of intervention of soldiers and police present when attacks take place, through superficial and incomplete investigations, to light sentences and pardons of the few settlers convicted of assaulting Palestinians."[99]

Conclusion

The focus in this section has been on Hebron and on the settler movement Gush Emunim. Gush Emunim, however, is active throughout the West Bank and Gaza; moreover, it has given rise to numerous other radical settler organizations, movements, cells, and the like that are also active throughout the Occupied Territories. (Most of these groups are backed by political parties with Knesset representation.) Settler violence has been a significant and continuous problem for Palestinians in the West Bank and Gaza wherever settlers have implanted themselves. The twin objectives of settler violence are conquering land and resources and forcing Palestinians from the West Bank and Gaza.

Yet even more significant is Israeli government acquiescence, compliance, and facilitation of any activities that the settlers undertake. Whether Labor or Likud, the government has collaborated with the settlers at every level of the system. Comprehending this collaboration provides important insight into Israel's intentions with regard to the Hebron District as well as the remainder of the West Bank and Gaza Strip. Indeed, the escalation of settler violence, combined with government collusion, throughout the seven years of the peace process suggests, at the very least, that Israel would like to see the Occupied Territories as *"Arabenrein"* or "Arab-free" as possible.

This chapter additionally suggests that the issue of peacekeepers is far more complex than might be imagined. The PA has demanded on numerous occasions, both before and during the Al-Aqsa intifada, that an international presence to protect Palestinians come to the Occupied Territories. Yet the experience of TIPH strongly suggests that without a broad unrestricted mandate and an autonomous independent armed force, no international peacekeeping mission can succeed in protecting the civilian population. And it is just as clear that Israel will not agree to such a body. Its refusal even to consider international observers in the context of the intifada is telling in this regard, as is Israel's prohibition on the United Nations fact-finding mission that was mandated to look into the situation in Jenin refugee camp in April 2002. Yet in the absence of an international force of any type, it is also apparent that Israel will continue to act with impunity in all matters that are of interest to it.

Settler violence is only one of many governmental tactics to encourage Palestinians to leave the Occupied Territories. In Hebron, we have also seen both direct and indirect efforts to expel Palestinians. It is the same throughout the territories. In Chapter 5, I examine government practices in Jerusalem. Although they are complex and multifaceted, it is clear they have one objective: encouraging the departure of Palestinians.

If the Israeli government is officially evasive about its long-term intentions with regard to Hebron, it has been perfectly clear and unequivocal concerning its objectives toward Jerusalem. Since 1967, Israel has continuously proclaimed that East and West Jerusalem are a single undivided city—Israel's eternal capital—and that Tel Aviv is not open to negotiations concerning any aspect of its status. Thus, in Chapter 5, I investigate the myriad means by which Israel has sought to transform—to Judaize, Israelize, and depopulate of Palestinians—the eastern (i.e., Arab) sector of the city to ensure the permanence of Israeli sovereignty. Examining Israeli policies and practices in East Jerusalem opens a whole spectrum of tactics used to foster the exodus of Palestinians, many of which are applied throughout the West Bank as well.

Notes

1. Gideon Levy, "A Purim Visit to Hebron," *Ha'aretz,* March 17, 2001.
2. Yossi Sarid, "Greater Sodom and Its Daughters," *Ha'aretz* October 9, 2002.
3. Data on settler violence in the pre-Oslo period may be found in J. Abu Shakrah et al., *Israeli Settler Violence in the Occupied Territories: 1980–1984* (Chicago: Palestine Human Rights Campaign, 1985), pp. 16–26 (see entire work for an excellent analysis of settler violence). Also see Robert I. Friedman, "Terror on Sacred Ground," *Mother Jones* (August/September 1987): 37–43; Daoud Kuttab, "Old City Violence," *Middle East International* (London, bimonthly) (December 5, 1986): 14–15; Yorem Yarkoni, "In Hebrew It's Called a Pogrom," *Kol Ha'ir* (Hebrew), November 28, 1986. For the report of the official Israeli government inquiry into settler violence, see *The Karp Report: An*

Israeli Government Inquiry into Settler Violence Against Palestinians in the West Bank (released February 7, 1984, Jerusalem), published in English by the Institute for Palestine Studies (Washington, DC: Institute for Palestine Studies, 1984).

4. Ron Dudai, *Tacit Consent: Israeli Policy on Law Enforcement Toward Settlers in the Occupied Territories* (Jerusalem: B'Tselem—the Israeli Information Center for Human Rights in the Occupied Territories, March 2001), p. 1. Also see Amira Hass, "Protected by the 'System,'" *Ha'aretz*, July 24, 2001.

5. Dudai, *Tacit Consent*, p. 43.

6. Ibid., p. 1.

7. Nadav Shragai, "Police Files Against Settlers Closed—For Lack of Evidence or Interest," *Ha'aretz*, September 24, 2001 (emphasis added); Ron Dudai, *Free Rein: Vigilante Settlers and Israel's Non-Enforcement of the Law* (Jerusalem: B'Tselem—the Israeli Information Center for Human Rights in the Occupied Territories, October 2001); Efrat Halper, "Settler Violence: A Report," *News from Within* 16, no. 9 (December 2000): 19–22. Equally useful is LAW, *Settlers Attack and Harass Palestinians* (Jerusalem: Palestinian Society for the Protection of Human Rights and the Environment—LAW, February 7, 2001). For extensive documentation and lengthy testimonies of Palestinian victims of settler violence, see Dudai, *Tacit Consent*. Two news articles that well illustrate what the settlers do are Amos Harel and Nadav Shragai, "Rioting Settlers Rampage in Arab Villages," *Ha'aretz*, June 7, 2001, and Nadav Shragai, "Vengeance Is Ours, Sayeth the Settlers," *Ha'aretz*, June 20, 2001.

8. Amira Hass, "Protected by the 'System,'" *Ha'aretz*, July 24, 2001.

9. Human Rights Watch, *Center of the Storm: A Case Study of Human Rights Abuses in Hebron District* (New York: Human Rights Watch, 2001), and Shmuel David, *Impossible Coexistence: Human Rights in Hebron Since the Massacre at the Cave of the Patriarchs* (Jerusalem: B'Tselem—the Israeli Information Center for Human Rights in the Occupied Territories, 1995). Also see LAW, *Hebron Under Siege: Accounts* (Jerusalem: Palestinian Society for the Protection of Human Rights and the Environment—LAW, 1999); and Jennifer Laurin, Nizar Qattoush, and Wafa' Safar, *Infringements in Hebron District* (Jerusalem: Applied Research Institute of Jerusalem, n.d. [ca. 2000]).

10. Zeev Sternhell, *The Founding Myths of Israel: Nationalism, Socialism, and the Making of the Jewish State* (Princeton: Princeton University Press, 1998), pp. 318, 332–336; Benny Morris, *Righteous Victims: A History of the Zionist-Arab Conflict, 1881–1999* (New York: Alfred A. Knopf, 1999), pp. 332–336; Ehud Sprinzak, *The Ascendance of Israel's Radical Right* (New York: Oxford University Press, 1991), pp. 88–93 and passim; David K. Shipler, *Arab and Jew: Wounded Spirits in a Promised Land* (New York: Times Books, 1986), p. 103; Noam Chomsky, *Fateful Triangle: The United States, Israel, and the Palestinians*, updated ed. (Cambridge, MA: South End Press, 1999), pp. 123–126, 128–129, and 131; Human Rights Watch, *Center of the Storm*, pp. 11–12.

11. The best source on the ideology of Gush Emunim and the fundamentalists is Israel Shahak and Norton Mezvinsky, *Jewish Fundamentalism in Israel* (London: Pluto, 1999). Also useful for both ideology and practice is Sprinzak, *The Ascendance of Israel's Radical Right*, and Ian Lustick, *For the*

Land and the Lord: Jewish Fundamentalism in Israel (New York: Council on Foreign Relations, 1988).

12. The success of Jewish settlers in taking over Abraham's Tomb (the Tomb of the Patriarchs) in Hebron led, in subsequent years, to a settler takeover of Joseph's Tomb in Nablus and Rachel's Tomb on the Bethlehem border.

13. Sprinzak, *The Ascendance of Israel's Radical Right*, pp. 89–90.

14. Morris, *Righteous Victims*, p. 335.

15. See Map 2.3. Data from "Sites in Hebron," *Hebron: Past, Present, and Forever* (website of the Hebron settlers) (n.d. [ca. 2000]). Also see *Hebron Under Siege: Accounts* (Jerusalem: Palestinian Society for the Protection of Human Rights and the Environment—LAW, n.d. [ca. 1999]).

16. "Sites in Hebron," *Hebron: Past, Present, and Forever*.

17. Shahak and Mezvinsky, *Jewish Fundamentalism in Israel*, pp. 96–112, esp. 111–112.

18. Data on Hebron District from *Settlement Database* (Washington, DC: Foundation for Middle East Peace, 1999), citing *Peace Now* as source for all statistics; and Jennifer Laurin, Nizar Qattoush, and Wafa' Safar, *Infringements in Hebron District* (Jerusalem: Applied Research Institute of Jerusalem, n.d. [ca. 2000]). Some basic information on Hebron District: It is 36 kilometers south of Jerusalem and comprises 105,000 hectares. Total population of the district based on 1997 census data is 389,014, with 119,230 people, or 31 percent of the population, residing in Hebron City. Of the remainder of the district: 35 percent of the population lives in other municipalities (towns); 31 percent in rural villages; and 3 percent in refugee camps.

19. Sprinzak, *The Ascendance of Israel's Radical Right*, pp. 92–93.

20. Ibid., pp. 89–90; and Morris, *Righteous Victims*, pp. 114–115 and 111–120 for context. The quote is from Morris. For the number 400, see Jane Adas, "The Grotesque Situation in Hebron: Where Israeli Soldiers and Settlers Compete to Harass the Inhabitants," *Washington Report on Middle East Affairs* (October/November 1997): 7–8.

21. Efrat Halper, "Settler Violence: A Report," *News from Within* 16, no. 9 (December 2000): 19. B'Tselem has repeatedly documented and condemned the leniency of the government toward the settlers, although to no avail. See, for example, Dudai, *Tacit Consent,* and Ron Dudai, *Free Rein: Vigilante Settlers and Israel's Non-Enforcement of the Law* (Jerusalem: B'Tselem—the Israeli Information Center for Human Rights in the Occupied Territories, October 2001).

22. *Israeli Settler Ideology Dooms Coexistence*, abridged from *Breaking the Siege*, newsletter of the US Middle East Justice Network. Posted on the Green Left Weekly Home Page, no. 138, April 13, 1994, p. 9. Also see Robert I. Friedman, *Zealots for Zion: Inside Israel's West Bank Settler Movement* (New Brunswick, NJ: Rutgers University Press, 1992), pp. 37–39; and Eitan Felner and Roly Rozen, *Law Enforcement on Israeli Civilians in the Occupied Territories* (Jerusalem: B'Tselem—the Israeli Information Center for Human Rights in the Occupied Territories, March 1994), 109 pages, see esp. pp. 68–73. For additional background on Levinger, see Shahak and Mezvinsky, *Jewish Fundamentalism in Israel,* pp. 99–100, 138.

23. Ehud Sprinzak, *The Ascendance of Israel's Radical Right* (New York: Oxford University Press, 1991), p. 165.

24. Theo Haddad, "Current Events: Hebron, Hebron, Hebron," *Trincoll*

Journal, November 14, 1996; and Ian Black and Benny Morris, *Israel's Secret Wars: A History of Israel's Intelligence Services* (New York: Grove Weidenfeld, 1991), p. 350.

25. Sprinzak, *The Ascendance of Israel's Radical Right*, p. 56. Also see Yair Kotler, *Heil Kahane* (New York: Adama Books, 1986), pp. 83–92 and passim.

26. Chomsky, *Fateful Triangle*, p. 270, citing Uri Avneri, *Ha'olam Haze* (Israeli, Hebrew), December 22, 1982; Rafik Halabi, *Koteret Rashit* (Israeli, Hebrew), March 16, 1983; and Chaim Bermant, *Jerusalem Post*, March 22, 1983. For an extensive discussion of settler violence and the leniency of the judicial system including the enumeration of dozens of incidents, see Felner and Rozen, *Law Enforcement on Israeli Civilians in the Occupied Territories*.

27. Chomsky, *Fateful Triangle*, p. 125, citing Michal Meron, *Yediot Ahronot*, March 29, 1992, and Amnon Kapeliouk, *Al Hamishmar*, March 26, 1982.

28. Chomsky, *Fateful Triangle*, p. 126, citing Zvi Barel, *Ha'aretz*, October 31, 1982.

29. Sprinzak, *The Ascendance of Israel's Radical Right*, pp. 97–99.

30. Lustick, *For the Land and the Lord*, p. 66.

31. See Palestine Human Rights Information Center, *The Massacre in al-Haram al-Ibrahimi al-Sharif: Context and Aftermath* (Jerusalem: Palestine Human Rights Information Center, 1994).

32. B'Tselem, *Lethal Gunfire and Collective Punishment in the Wake of the Massacre at the Tomb of the Patriarchs* (Jerusalem: B'Tselem—the Israeli Information Center for Human Rights in the Occupied Territories, March 1994); demonstrates at length the multiple punishments imposed on the Palestinians in the aftermath of an Israeli's massacre of Palestinians, whereas Israeli settlers went completely free.

33. "Israeli-Palestinian Interim Agreement on the West Bank and the Gaza Strip, Washington, 28 September, 1995," partially reprinted in *Journal of Palestine Studies* 25, no. 2 (winter 1996): 123–140. For entire document, see Israeli Ministry of Foreign Affairs online documents. Also see the analysis by Lamis Andoni, "Redefining Oslo: Negotiating the Hebron Protocol," *Journal of Palestine Studies* 26, no. 3 (spring 1997): 17–30. The 40,000 figure comes from B'Tselem, *Lift the Prolonged Curfew on Hebron and Hawara* (Jerusalem: B'Tselem—the Israeli Information Center for Human Rights in the Occupied Territories, September 26, 2000); Human Rights Watch, *Center of the Storm*, p. 7, puts the figure at 30,000.

34. "Israel and the Palestine Liberation Organization, Protocol Concerning the Redeployment in Hebron (Agreed Version), Erez Crossing, 15 January 1997," reprinted in *Journal of Palestine Studies* 26, no. 3 (spring 1997): 132–145, including agreement (partial) plus letters, memoranda of understanding, maps, etc., that accompanied the agreement. Israeli Ministry of Foreign Affairs online documents.

35. Information concerning the mosque comes from LAW, *Hebron Under Siege: Accounts* (Jerusalem: Palestinian Society for the Protection of Human Rights and the Environment—LAW, n.d. [ca. 1999]).

36. For other information in this paragraph, see the analysis by Alain

Gresh (English; translated by Wendy Kristianasen), "Hebron: A City Divided," *Le Monde Diplomatique* (Paris, French), February 6, 1997.

37. Quotation in Gresh, "Hebron: A City Divided."

38. Jessi Roemer, "Israeli Re-Deployment from Hebron: The Mirage of Self-Rule," *Challenge* (Tel Aviv, Israeli, monthly, English), no. 42 (1997).

39. Unless otherwise noted, all information about TIPH is from the TIPH website.

40. Ibid.

41. Unless otherwise indicated, all information about the Christian Peacemaker Teams in Hebron (as well as its broader mission) comes from the CPT website.

42. "Hebron Update: January 5–January 14, 1998," Nigel Perry Diary (online), January 15, 1998.

43. Mark Frey, "Hebron: CPTers Arrested for 'Getting in the Way' at a Nonviolent Palestinian Demonstration," *Christian Peacemaker Teams Network*, January 10, 1998.

44. Adam Hanieh, "On Hold: International Protection for the Palestinians," *MERIP Press Information Notes*, PIN 40 (November 28, 2000).

45. Christian Peacemaker Team, *Hebron: CPT Calls for an End to Verbal and Physical Attacks on TIPH*, August 31, 2001, CPT website.

46. David Wilder, "An Open Letter to TIPH," *YeshaNews*, August 1, 2001 (Yesha is the settlers' organization in the West Bank; this is their newsletter).

47. Lorenzo Cremonesi, "Stoned Out of Town: The TIPH Commander Explains Why He Stopped Patrols in Jewish Hebron," *Ha'aretz*, August 26, 2001.

48. "CPT: Dealing with Threats on Your Life," *Hebron Diary*, January 23, 1998 (reprinted in Nigel Perry Diary online).

49. David et al., *Impossible Coexistence*.

50. "Background on House Demolitions," *CPT in Hebron*, February 27, 1997.

51. Ibid. Some estimates are more conservative than CPT's. For example, Laurin, Qattoush, and Safar, *Infringements in Hebron District*, p. 6, write that in the six-month period between July 30, 1997, and December 25, 1997, Israel demolished three houses in Hebron. Amnesty International, *Israel and the Occupied Territories: Demolition and Dispossession: The Destruction of Palestinian Homes* (New York: Amnesty International, 1999) (MDE 15/59/99), p. 21, writes that "on August 19, 1998, Israel demolished eight Palestinian houses."

52. Laurin, Qattoush, and Safar, *Infringements in Hebron District*, p. 6.

53. Amnesty International, *The Destruction of Palestinian Homes*, p. 21.

54. David et al., *Impossible Coexistence*, p. 8.

55. Ibid., p. 8.

56. Ibid.

57. Ibid., p. 9.

58. Ibid., p. 10.

59. Ibid.

60. Ibid., p. 14.

61. Ibid., pp. 19–20.

62. Omar Barghouti, "Palestine's Tell-Tale Heart," in Roane Carey, ed.,

The New Intifada: Resisting Israel's Apartheid (London: Verso, 2001), p. 167.

63. Kathleen Kern, "Settler Violence and September 11: A Report from the Mean Streets of Hebron," *Tikkun: A Jewish Critique of Politics, Culture, and Society* (November/December 2001).

64. Kern, "Settler Violence and September 11: A Report from the Mean Streets of Hebron."

65. Bonnie Gehweiler, "Settler Assaults Guest of Hebron Peacemaker Team," *Washington Report on Middle East Affairs* (February 5, 2001).

66. The words here are found in LAW, *Hebron Under Siege: Accounts*, p. 3. The film was shown on a few PBS stations in the United States in February 1995 but was rejected by most as "too controversial."

67. Human Rights Watch, *Center of the Storm*, p. 52.

68. Gideon Levy, "A Purim Visit to Hebron," *Ha'aretz*, March 17, 2001.

69. LAW, *Israeli Violations of Palestinian Economic Rights* (Jerusalem: Palestinian Society for the Protection of Human Rights and the Environment—LAW, May 2000), chap. 3, tab. 3.

70. Nadav Shragai, "New Settlements in Jordan Valley, Industrial Zone in Hebron," *Ha'aretz,* November 16, 2001.

71. Jad Isaac et al., *Environmental Profile for the West Bank, Volume 3: Hebron District* (Jerusalem: Applied Research Institute–Jerusalem, 1995), chap. 6.

72. Ibid., chaps. 5 and 6.

73. Gideon Levy, "Bitter Harvest," *Ha'aretz Friday Magazine*, October 19, 2001.

74. LAW, *An Overview of the Consequences of Israeli Occupation on the Environment in the West Bank and Gaza Strip* (Jerusalem: Palestinian Society for the Protection of Human Rights and the Environment—LAW, January 2000); and Isaac et al., *Environmental Profile for the West Bank: Hebron District.*

75. Laurin, Qattoush, and Safar, *Infringements in Hebron District*, pp. 6–7.

76. Ta'ayush: Arab Jewish Partnership, *Solidarity Actions with the Inhabitants of South Hebron Area* (January 2002) (posted on *Ta'ayush* website); *Background: The Expulsion of the Palestinian Population of South Hebron* (South Hebron website, which was constructed by Yesh Gvul). Some of the groups participating in the coalition include Bat Shalom/Coalition of Women for Peace; Du Siach; Gush Shalom; Rabbis for Human Rights; HaCampus Lo Shotek, Tel Aviv University; Israeli Committee Against House Demolitions; Kol Aher BaGalil; Left Forum, Haifa University; Machsom Watch; Meretz Youth; Monitoring Committee of the Arab Population in Israel; New Profile; Noga; TANDI; Women and Mothers for Peace (formerly Four Mothers); Women in Black; and Yesh Gvul. The quote used here is from a Yesh Gvul publication, *Background: The Expulsion of the Palestinian Population of South Hebron*. The information in the remaining paragraphs of this section comes from Ta'ayush's website (unless otherwise indicated) and will simply be cited with reference to Ta'ayush.

77. Ta'ayush, *Solidarity Actions with the Inhabitants of South Hebron Area.*

78. Ibid.

79. An especially good analysis of this expulsion and its aftermath is Gideon Levy, "Out in the Cold: Hundreds of Bedouin and Palestinian Farmers Have Lost Their Homes to a Cruel Deal Between the Jewish Settlers and the Authorities," *Ha'aretz Weeks End*, January 28, 2000. Also see Oren Yiftachel and Neve Gordon, "The Lurking Shadow of Expulsion," May 16, 2002, posted online by al-Awda; and Sergio Yahni, "The Struggle Against Ethnic Cleansing in South Hebron Region," *News from Within* 18, no. 2 (February 2002): 24–28.

80. See Yael Stein et al., *Expulsion of Palestinian Residents from the South Mt. Hebron Area, October–November 1999*, Case Report (Jerusalem: B'Tselem—the Israeli Information Center for Human Rights in the Occupied Territories, February 2000). Also see "Mofaz Attends Hard-Line Settlers Event: New Settlement in Hebron," *Middle East Peace Report* 3, no. 7 (Washington, DC: Americans for Peace Now, August 27, 2001).

81. Ta'ayush, *Solidarity Actions with the Inhabitants of South Hebron Area*.

82. Ibid.

83. Dudai, *Tacit Consent*, and Dudai, *Free Rein*.

84. Human Rights Watch, *Center of the Storm*, p. 54.

85. Ibid., p. 55.

86. Ibid., p. 62.

87. Ibid., p. 51.

88. Ibid., p. 55.

89. Ibid., p. 62.

90. Ibid., p. 50.

91. Ibid., p. 53.

92. Daniel Ben Simon, "Primal Passions," *Ha'aretz Friday Magazine*, July 20, 2001.

93. Amos Harel and Jonathan Lis, "Minister's Aide Calls Hebron Riots a 'Pogrom,'" *Ha'aretz*, July 30, 2002 (emphasis added). Also see Editorial, "Fear and Violence in Hebron," *Ha'aretz*, July 30, 2002, and Editorial, "The Rulers of Hebron," *Ha'aretz*, August 13, 2002.

94. Yael Stein, *Standing Idly By: Non-Enforcement of the Law on Settlers, Hebron 26–28 July, 2002* (Jerusalem: B'Tselem—the Israeli Information Center for Human Rights in the Occupied Territories, August 2002); the quotation is from "Conclusions" and all other material in the paragraph from the body of the report.

95. Daniel Ben Simon, "A Leisurely Stroll Through Locked-Down Hebron," *Ha'aretz*, September 24, 2002. Also see Yair Sheleg, "Thousands Flock to Hebron One Day After the Attack," *Ha'aretz*, September 26, 2002; Sarid, "Greater Sodom and Its Daughters"; Yossi Verter, "Official Report Exposed by Sarid Slams Hebron Settlers for 'Thuggery,'" *Ha'aretz*, September 26, 2002.

96. Meron Benvenisti, "The Homeland Purified of Arabs," *Ha'aretz*, September 26, 2002.

97. Arnon Regular and Baruch Kra, "Hebron Settlers Attack Police, Bar *Muezzins* from Tomb," *Ha'aretz*, October 14, 2002.

98. Amira Hass, "Protected by the System."

99. Dudai, *Free Rein*, p. 1, and Stein, *Standing Idly By*.

5

Jerusalem: City of Light, City of Darkness

> We must convert Jerusalem into the central focus of the entire Jewish people. Jerusalem [under the Partition Plan] has not been designated as the capital of the Jewish State. But Jerusalem ever was and must continue to remain the heart of the Jewish nation. It must be, not only a great and expanding center of Jewish settlement, but also the center of all Jewish national and international institutions, the center of the Zionist movement, the center of Knesset Israel, which will embrace every Jew in the land of Israel, as well as those residing outside the Jewish State; the center of world Jewry, a center of learning, culture, the Jewish spirit, of Jewish art, a place of remembrance for all that is connected with the Jewish People generally and with vital sections thereof, whether of the living or the dead. All these must find their focus in Jerusalem. . . . And finally, we know there are no final settlements in history, there are no eternal boundaries and there are no final political claims and undoubtedly many changes and revisions will yet occur in the world.
>
> —David Ben-Gurion[1]

In Chapter 4, I examined the extent of government acquiescence in settler violence in Hebron in both the pre- and post-Oslo periods and documented Israel's efforts to expel Palestinians from the southern district of Mount Hebron. We saw little evidence of an Israeli commitment to withdraw from Hebron in the context of a final peace agreement, illuminating one reason why Palestinians throughout the West Bank and Gaza Strip lost faith in the peace process. For the Palestinians of the Hebron District, Oslo did not improve their lives; it made matters worse, and they in particular became increasingly frustrated with the hardships of daily life.

However, Hebron was officially included in the 1995 Interim Agreement (Oslo II) as one of the cities from which Israel would redeploy and allow Palestinians limited autonomy. By contrast, Jerusalem was not on any agenda of the interim phase of the peace process. Negotiations about its future were deferred in the Declaration of Principles (DOP) to final-status talks. Moreover, although Israel has not explicitly stated that it intends to incorporate Hebron, it has been clear, consistent, and unequivocal from the outset of Oslo that a united Jerusalem will remain Israel's eternal capital and that East Jerusalem will not come under Palestinian control. Israel's agreement to include Jerusalem in the cluster of final-status issues (as with the question over refugees' right of return) did not mean that it was prepared to compromise the status of the city. Rather, it was viewed from Tel Aviv as a carrot to induce Palestinians to participate in the Oslo process.

For Palestinians, Jerusalem is of paramount historical, political, social, and religious significance. It was part of the Palestinian territories that Israel conquered in 1967 and was implicit in UN Resolution 242's injunction concerning the "inadmissibility of the acquisition of territory by force." Thus, Palestinians expected the Oslo process to lead to the eastern, Arab sector of the city becoming the capital of their independent state.

Yet since 1967, Israel, to facilitate its objective of permanent, unified, sovereign control of the city, has pursued a program of de-Arabization in Jerusalem, including policies aimed at reducing the size of the Palestinian population. Simultaneously, it has employed processes of Judaization and Israelization so as to transform Jerusalem into an overwhelmingly Jewish metropolis—demographically, culturally, socially, and politically. With the initiation of the Oslo process in 1993, Israel intensified these policies more thoroughly and systematically. For example, during the 1993–2000 period, several fundamentalist Jewish groups, with government backing, made a concerted effort to seize Palestinian homes in the Muslim and Christian quarters of the Old City and to take over Palestinian neighborhoods bordering on the Old City.[2] The period covering the Oslo process also saw the creation of new settlements, the expansion of existing ones, and the construction of new bypass roads to link settlements in East Jerusalem with settlements throughout the West Bank. Additionally, Israel developed a series of plans that situated Jerusalem as the fulcrum for integrating settlement blocs in the far reaches of the West Bank with a newly expanded metropolitan Jerusalem and, in turn, with Israel proper.

There are two main topics in this chapter: (1) Israel's systematic discrimination against the Palestinian people in municipal East Jerusalem to encourage them to leave the city, including efforts to expel them; and (2) the extension of the city's boundaries to an expanded metropolitan Jerusalem in an effort to further Israeli control in each of the West Bank's three major regions.

The story of Jerusalem begins in 1948 with Israeli actions in the western sector. It is a chronicle of conquest and refugees. In Chapter 1, I discussed the fact that under United Nations (UN) General Assembly Resolution 181 (the partition resolution), Jerusalem was to have a special status as a *corpus separatum* under permanent UN trusteeship. However, as a consequence of the 1948 war and Israeli-Jordanian agreement, Israel occupied and annexed the western sector, which included nine Arab villages and urban quarters.[3] Jordan annexed the eastern sector. The Palestinian residents of the Israeli-appropriated western area had been specific targets of Plan Dalet (detailed in Chapter 1), resulting in the creation of some 60,000 refugees from that area alone who left behind considerable amounts of property, including 10,000 homes.[4] By March 1949, Israel had established most of its government agencies in the city, and by 1951 all but two ministries were located in West Jerusalem. Under the 1950 Absentee Property Law, Palestinian property automatically became property of the State of Israel, which in turn transferred it to Jewish immigrants. By 1951, West Jerusalem was almost fully settled by Jewish families.[5]

The story of East Jerusalem beginning in 1967 is also one of conquest and systematic Judaization and de-Arabization. Israel's policies vis-à-vis East Jerusalem and its Palestinian population since 1967 have been diverse yet focused. Cumulatively, the policies have had a devastating effect on Jerusalem's Palestinians. The two overriding tactics Israel has used have been to sponsor the settlement of as many Jews as possible in the city, and to encourage the departure of Palestinians.[6] Three Israelis who were key urban planners for the development of Jerusalem for nearly three decades, Amir S. Cheshin, Bill Hutman, and Avi Melamed, describe Israel's objectives with regard to East Jerusalem:

> The first was rapidly to increase the Jewish population in East Jerusalem. The second was to hinder growth of the Arab population and to force Arab residents to make their homes elsewhere. [These principles] have translated into a miserable life for the majority of East Jerusalem Arabs, many of whom have chosen to leave the city, as Israel hoped they would. At the same time, Jews have moved into East Jerusalem by the thousands. . . . In the Arab sector . . . not one new Arab neighborhood had been built, and many of the old Arab neighborhoods remain without sewage and paved roads, not to mention sidewalks and streetlights.[7]

Elsewhere, they wrote:

> If Israeli leaders had their way, most of the Arab population of East
> Jerusalem would have left the city long ago. . . . Policy decision after
> policy decision on East Jerusalem showed that Israel was doing
> everything possible to encourage, and at times force, East Jerusalem
> Arabs from the city. . . . In the first years after the 1967 war, Israeli
> leaders seriously considered ways of literally transferring Arabs out
> of Jerusalem.[8]

Discrimination Against the
Palestinians of East Jerusalem

To facilitate the departure of Palestinians, Israel has employed a variety
of policies, including stripping Palestinians of residency rights, making
it virtually impossible for them to secure housing or commercial permits, and demolishing houses, among others. Additionally, Israel has
allocated so few municipal or government resources to the Palestinian
sector that many residents lack basic amenities such as sewage, piped
water, and electricity. Restrictive funding has also negatively affected
the quality of education, health care, and social services available to
Palestinians.[9]

Moreover, each policy contains within it layers of additional discrimination and hardship for Palestinians. For example, confiscation of
Palestinian land for settlement construction has not alleviated the housing shortage for Palestinians because all the new settlements are designated for Jews only. The permit system that prevents Palestinians from
building houses extends to commercial enterprises. Both are typically
refused, the latter contributing to the unemployment problem. Revocation of residency rights exacerbates denial of family reunification and
so on.[10] Israeli professor Jeff Halper described it thus: "Ethnic cleansing
by bureaucratic strangulation? Yes, it definitely is. It is very bureaucratic and very Kafkaesque."[11]

Israel's Objectives:
Land and People in the Immediate Post-1967 Period

Less than a week after the June 1967 war, Israel demolished 135
Palestinian homes and evicted 650 Palestinians from the Mughrabi
Quarter of the Old City to provide space for Jewish worshipers in front
of the Western Wall. Between June 10 and 11, 1967, Israel eradicated
the Sharaf neighborhood in the Old City as well. It demolished 700
buildings (including 1,840 apartments that housed approximately 6,000

Palestinians, and 437 shops that supported 700 workers). Within months, Israel constructed a collection of houses and businesses on the razed area and renamed it the Jewish Quarter based on the historic Jewish presence in the district.[12] In July 1967, Israel declared the reunification of Jerusalem, effecting its de facto annexation. On July 30, 1980, Israel announced that Jerusalem is its "eternal, undivided capital," thereby formally annexing the city.

When Israel proclaimed the reunification of Jerusalem in 1967, it offered the residents of the city citizenship. However, the proposal was predicated on three requirements. Palestinians had to swear allegiance to the State of Israel, demonstrate proficiency in Hebrew, and relinquish citizenship of any other country. (Palestinians held Jordanian citizenship, which they feared giving up—especially in the uncertain aftermath of the war. Notably, Israeli Jews may hold dual citizenship with any country, without conditions.)[13] Thus, the overwhelming majority declined, and Israel assigned Palestinian Jerusalemites the status of permanent residents.

Additionally, in the immediate aftermath of the June 1967 war, Israel redefined the borders of East Jerusalem. Under Jordanian rule, the city had covered 6.5 square kilometers; Israel expanded it to 64 square kilometers (some 70,000 dunums).[14] The newly designated area of East Jerusalem contained twenty-eight Palestinian villages together with their grazing and farming lands. Nevertheless, "Israel had purposely" drawn the new city borders "to include the maximum territory possible, with the minimum possible Palestinian population."[15] Cheshin, Hutman, and Melamed described it thus:

> The government simply issued orders to expropriate [land that was owned by Arabs] . . . taking advantage of a legal system in Israel that gives [Arab] owners little recourse against the authorities taking away private property. . . . In January 1968, Israel carried out its first major expropriation. . . . Some 3,345 dunums were taken from . . . Arab landowners to build the Jewish [settlement] of *Ramot Eshkol*; 486 dunums were expropriated for [a second settlement]. Four months later another 900 dunums. . . . But Israel's land grab in 1968 was nothing compared with the one that occurred at the end of August 1970, when eight separate expropriation orders were carried out, covering 10,000 dunums of land.[16]

By 1970, after three years of occupation, Israel had expropriated more than 16,000 dunums of Palestinian land to construct East Jerusalem.[17] "The idea was to expropriate as much undeveloped land as possible . . . to prevent Palestinians from building."[18]

Following the land confiscations, between 1967 and 1970 there was a ten-year hiatus until 1980, when Israel seized 4,400 dunums from Palestinian landholders. The next appropriation was in April 1991, with the seizure of 1,850 dunums of Jabal Abu Ghanem. (The 1996 initiation of construction of the settlement Har Homa on Jabal Abu Ghanem in the context of the peace process triggered the mass demonstrations and protests discussed in Chapter 2.) When it is completed, the Har Homa settlement will provide housing for 20,000 and will finalize the ring of Jewish settlements around East Jerusalem, accomplishing the Israeli objective of completely isolating East Jerusalem from the West Bank. It will thus have created sufficient facts on the ground that any redivision of the city in the interests of an independent Palestinian state with East Jerusalem as its capital will be physically impossible (see Map 5.1).

According to an Israeli census taken shortly after the June 1967 war, the Palestinian population of the newly delineated East Jerusalem was 66,000, of which 44,000 resided within the boundaries of what had been Jordanian East Jerusalem, with another 22,000 in the surrounding villages annexed to the city.[19] In 1967, there were almost no Jews in East Jerusalem (with the exception of the Mount Scopus area, which was an Israeli-dominated enclave in the Jordanian-controlled West Bank). The small number of Jews, both in the Old City and in the newly expanded territorial boundaries of the city, owed to the fact that both East Jerusalem and the West Bank had been under Jordanian control for twenty years. From this situation came the policy of filling the city with Jewish residents so as to create an overwhelming Jewish majority. All Israeli policies in Jerusalem must be understood in the context of this "demographic imperative."[20]

In a 1972 census, after six years of Israeli settlement in East Jerusalem, Israel declared that the ratio was 73.5 percent Jews to 26.5 percent Palestinians.[21] This success led Israel to define its demographic objective for the city as sustaining the Jewish-to-Palestinian population ratio at 3:1 (i.e., 75 percent to 25 percent).

Encouraging the Palestinian
Population to Leave East Jerusalem, 1967–2000

To maintain this desired demographic ratio, in addition to settling Jews in East Jerusalem, Israel also had to limit Palestinian population growth in the city and encourage Palestinian emigration. Tel Aviv employed many methods to achieve this objective. One policy involved the decision to allocate the barest minimum of funds for infrastructure, education, and services with the expectation that as their quality of life deteriorated, Palestinians would leave.

Map 5.1   Projected Growth of Arab and Israeli Neighborhoods in East Jerusalem

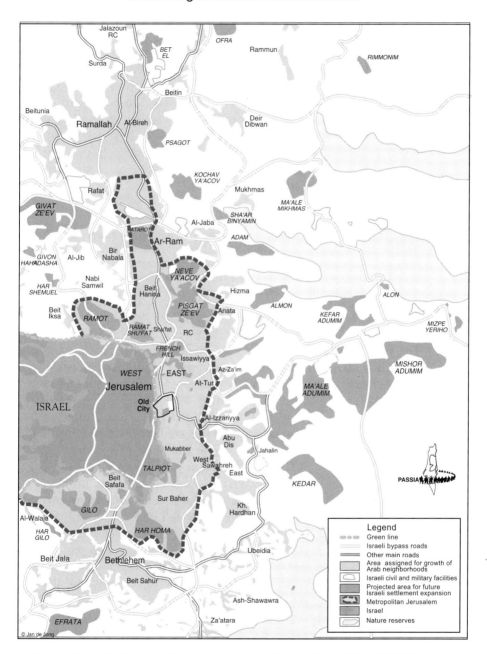

Legend
- Green line
- Israeli bypass roads
- Other main roads
- Area assigned for growth of Arab neighborhoods
- Israeli civil and military facilities
- Projected area for future Israeli settlement expansion
- Metropolitan Jerusalem
- Israel
- Nature reserves

Source: Palestinian Academic Society for the Study of International Affairs (PASSIA), Jerusalem, http://www.passia.org/palestine_facts/MAPS/images/jer_maps/Settlements.pdf. Accessed January 2003. Produced by Jan de Jong. Reprinted with permission of PASSIA.

Palestinian residents of Jerusalem pay the same amount of taxes—in some cases they pay more—as do Jewish residents. The weighty *arnona* (occupancy) tax is especially burdensome, but it is paid into the National Insurance Institute (NII) and is intended to provide benefits and services. Yet Palestinians receive a very small proportion of services relative to the taxes they pay.[22] For instance, there has been virtually no municipal or government funding allocated to Palestinian neighborhoods. After thirty years of occupation, most Palestinian neighborhoods are not hooked up to sewage systems, do not have paved roads or sidewalks, and do not have regular electricity (indeed, lengthy blackouts are typical). Phone service is sporadic. Houses are grossly overcrowded and substandard. The poverty rate is high (an estimated 45–60 percent of the population).[23] Cheshin, Hutman, and Melamed write:

> There are Arab neighborhoods where human waste literally pours out into the streets. Some Arab neighborhoods do not have trash pick-up, and debris piles up in abandoned lots. The streets in many Arab neighborhoods have not even been given names by the local authorities [making mail delivery, among other things, impossible]. . . . Those that have been named still do not have signs. . . . Some East Jerusalem neighborhoods still do not have proper water lines.[24]

The following set of comparisons demonstrates that Jerusalem is not a "united" city. In fact, Jerusalem is a distinctly separated city—divided between a modernized Jewish sector and a backward Palestinian sector.[25] In 1998, according to the Israeli *Jerusalem Statistical Yearbook,* there were 433,600 Jews (68.4 percent) in all of Jerusalem (East and West) and 200,100 Palestinians (31.6 percent).[26] Israel does not disaggregate East from West because it considers the city unified. This ratio of Jews to Palestinians is not quite the desired ideal, but it is close. There are virtually no Palestinians in West Jerusalem, although there are some 170,000 Israeli settlers in East Jerusalem whose indentification and services fall under Jerusalem for purposes of the following chart. Put differently, services for Jerusalem Jews include Jews in both the eastern settlements and western sectors. Palestinians pay 31 percent of the taxes but receive only 2–12 percent of the services of the municipal budget. On a per capita basis, the city spends six times more on each Jewish resident than it does on each Palestinian resident (see Table 5.1).[27]

These comparisons provide clear testimony to the discrimination experienced by Palestinians in Jerusalem. The paucity of services, benefits, and basic municipal obligations illustrates one aspect of Israel's efforts to induce Palestinians to leave the city.

Table 5.1 Comparisons of Municipal Services Between Jewish Jerusalem and Palestinian East Jerusalem

Services	Jewish Jerusalem West and East	Palestinian Sector of East Jerusalem
Population	433,600 (68.4%)	200,100 (31.6%)
Total developmental budget (1999)	383 million NIS	40 million NIS
Transportation budget (1999)	200.5 million NIS	12 million NIS
Town beautification	18 million NIS	2 million NIS
Neighborhood renewal (1999)	6 million NIS	0
Paved roads	There are some 680 kilometers of paved roads, about one kilometer for every 710 Jewish residents.	There are some 87 kilometers of paved roads, about one kilometer for every 2,448 Palestinian residents.
Paved sidewalks	There are about 700 kilometers of paved sidewalks, about one kilometer for every 690 Jewish residents.	There are 73 kilometers of paved sidewalks, about one kilometer for every 2,917 Palestinian residents.
Sewage system	The sewage system is 650 kilometers long—one kilometer for every 743 Jewish residents.	The sewage pipe system is 76 kilometers long—one kilometer for every 2,809 Palestinian residents.
Housing density	The average Jewish dwelling has 3.29 persons with 1.1 persons per room.	The average Palestinian dwelling has 7.4 persons with 2.2 persons per room.
Welfare offices	20	3
Municipal welfare cases	25,691 in 1996	1, 174 in 1996, amounting to approximately 4% of all cases in that year.
Libraries	26	2
Parks	There are 1,079 parks—one for every 447 Jewish residents.	There are 30 parks—one for every 7,362 Palestinian residents.
Neighborhood centers for elderly	115	7
Sports facilities	There are more than 531 sports facilities and 77 more are in the planning and/or construction phase.	There are 33 sports facilities.
Education (1998)	Schools: 414 (public) Classes: 4,498 Pupils/Class: 24 Classrooms constructed, 1988–1999: 1,129	Schools: 35 (public) Classes: 900 Pupils/Class: 30.9 Classrooms constructed, 1988–1999: 286
Garbage collection per neighborhood	100% of neighborhoods have regular collection	40% of neighborhoods have regular collection. Another 40% have "occasional" collection.
Swimming pools	36	None

Sources: Nadav Shragai, "The Sewer Flows in the East, the Money Flows in the West," *Ha'aretz* (Jerusalem, Israeli daily, English), June 7, 2000, special online edition available at www.2.haaretz.co.il/special/mount-e/a/286198.asp. B'Tselem, *Services and Infrastructure* (Jerusalem: Israeli Information Center for Human Rights in the Occupied Territories, 2000), available online at www.btselem.org/Files/site/e....publi....Text/Injustice_in_the_Holy_City/30934.asp; Vitullo, "Israel's Social Policy in Arab Jerusalem," p. 16; *Wi'am* (Cordial Relationships), *Jerusalem* (Bethlehem: Palestinian Conflict Resolution Center 2000), p. 9, available online at www.planet.edu/~alaslah/us/writings/jerusalem.htm.

Education

In keeping with its de-Arabization policy in the city, Israel has invested almost no resources—financial or other—in the educational system of Palestinian East Jerusalem. Public schools are massively overcrowded, and education is substandard.[28] East Jerusalem Palestinian schools are the only ones in Israel to operate on double shifts. Cheshin, Hutman, and Melamed write that Israel considered education

> a tool it could use to try to influence Arab children in East Jerusalem to be supportive of the . . . Jewish State. . . . But no comprehensive plan for expanding the Arab public school system was ever developed. . . . [Moreover, when in 1992] Israel saw the weakening financial situation of the private school system in East Jerusalem [it was perceived] as a great opportunity to extend its influence and control. Israel was prepared to offer the private schools . . . financial assistance, on the condition that Israel be given at least partial control over any school it supported.[29]

The latter involved the censoring of textbooks; the training of teachers by the Israeli education ministry; requiring Hebrew for all students; forbidding any anti-Israeli activity; and allowing government and municipal officials to visit the schools whenever they desired. None of the demands were well received by Palestinian educators, who declined the financial assistance.

As of 1999, Israel's neglect of East Jerusalem schools meant that 30 percent of upper elementary school pupils in East Jerusalem were illiterate. The dropout rate from secondary schools was 40 percent. Some 15,000 young people who were at the age where school attendance was required (i.e., under sixteen) did not go to school. More than half of the 770 classrooms in the public sector are rented and do not meet the standards set by the Israeli education ministry. There are no after-school enrichment programs, no traffic safety courses, no sports or other recreational programs.[30]

Health

Palestinians in East Jerusalem with valid residency identification (ID) cards have health insurance through the Israel National Insurance Institute. Benefits include medical care, income maintenance, wage substitution, child allowances, and rehabilitation.[31] Unlike their Jewish counterparts, however, Palestinian residents are required to prove their residency in Jerusalem to be able to obtain benefits from the NII. This means, in essence, that every time a Palestinian resident of Jerusalem approaches the NII for, say, emergency care, maternity benefits, child allowances, and so on, the NII sends investigators to validate that the person seeking services actually lives in Jerusalem. These residency checks can last up to one year (during which time benefits are not paid). It can also mean that individuals needing hospitalization or emergency care may be turned away because of questions over their residency status.[32] Physicians for Human Rights estimated in 2000 that there were some 10,000 children residing in Jerusalem who were not covered by medical insurance.[33] Of these investigations by the NII, B'Tselem states:

> In implementing this policy, the NII assists Israel in attaining its goal of reducing the number of Palestinians living in Jerusalem. Thus, the NII, instead of promoting a social policy and providing health insurance, has become a tool to advance illegitimate political objectives.[34]

Palestinian health care throughout the Occupied Territories has suffered enormously as a consequence of the closure that has been in place since 1993 and the fact that the five major hospitals serving Palestinians, particularly in terms of specialized care unavailable elsewhere, have been off-limits to West Bank and Gaza Strip residents. Prior to the closure, Palestinians from all over the West Bank and Gaza came to several hospitals (Augusta Victoria, Al-Maqassad, St. John's, St. Joseph's, and the Palestine Red Crescent) for a variety of treatments, including kidney dialysis, cardiovascular, cardiac, and orthopedic surgery and treatment, specialized ophthalmic treatment and surgery, neurosurgery, neonatal care, and others. Patients now have to secure permits from the Israeli government to come to these hospitals, permits that are almost as routinely denied as are those for home construction. Medical personnel as well must secure permits to work at one of the hospitals if they live outside the city. In 1997, the hospitals, collectively, were running a U.S.$12 million deficit and had only a 64 percent occupancy rate.[35]

Policies That Encourage the Departure of Palestinians

Family reunification. Family reunification is an issue that has adversely affected Palestinians throughout the Occupied Territories, but it has been particularly harsh on Palestinian Jerusalemites. When Israel conducted the 1967 census, 66,000 Palestinians resided within the newly defined boundaries of East Jerusalem, but only Palestinians physically present at the time of the census were given permanent residency status.

No one who was out of the city, even if he/she had lived there all his/her life, was accorded this status. Thus, a wife who was visiting her family in Nablus, a child who was studying in the United States, a husband who was working in the Persian Gulf, elderly parents who had fled to Amman during the fighting, and on and on, lost the right to reside in Jerusalem.

To return to Jerusalem, such individuals have had to make formal applications to the Israeli interior ministry under the policy of family reunification. One analyst wrote of the procedure at the interior ministry:

> For the procedures, applicants must present a series of documents such as ID cards, birth certificates, passports, and marriage contracts. Sometimes residents are not in possession of all these documents, often due to inherent problems of living under occupation, so they must acquire them, which is costly [and time consuming]. Furthermore, every application costs what is a prohibitive sum to most families. A family reunification application costs almost 100 dollars, non-refundable if the application is refused. Often, people apply several times for family reunification, and are denied each time. Applicants must wait months, sometimes years, for official responses. Sometimes, no official response is ever received.[36]

Israel's policy on family reunification has altered somewhat over time. Between 1967 and 1973, under intense pressure from the International Red Cross and other international bodies, it permitted a limited number of individuals to return as war refugees. The vast majority of them, however, were residents of the West Bank; only a very few were allowed to return to Jerusalem. Between 1973 and 1993, Israel approved almost no requests for family reunification—and none in Jerusalem. Until 1994, Israel refused to process requests for family reunification submitted by female Jerusalem residents.[37]

From August 1993 through November 1995, in the spirit of Oslo, Israel allowed 2,000 spouses annually to reunite with their families. Again, the vast majority of these were in the West Bank and Gaza; the number in Jerusalem was minuscule. As Yael Stein states, "In general, requests for family reunification by residents of East Jerusalem are not even processed."[38] Moreover, in Jerusalem since December 1995, Israel has refused to register any child born to parents if only one of them (even if the father) is a Jerusalem resident. This is to limit the rate of natural growth. Between November 1995 and the end of 1997, Israel froze the family reunification program altogether. At the end of 1997, the interior ministry had a backlog of 7,470 requests. From January

1998 until September 2000, the program was resumed on the basis of 2,000 spouses per year but again with Jerusalem virtually excluded. Since September 2000, there have been no family reunifications whatsoever.[39]

Israel's policy change in 1995—suspending family reunification altogether—was all the more significant in that the 1995 Interim Agreement (Oslo II) commits Israel "to promote and upgrade family reunification." Moreover, the issue of family reunification has been negatively affected by Israel's closures. For example, after the imposition of the general closure in 1993, Israel established the Procedure for Divided Families, according to which the spouses of Jerusalem residents who lived in the Occupied Territories would be granted periodic permits to stay in Jerusalem after submission of a request for family reunification. The permits were to be issued for three months and would include a permit for the spouse to stay overnight in Jerusalem. Implementation of this policy, however, was problematic. Persons entitled to permits did not always receive them. Most permits did not include permission for overnight stays. Individuals typically had to wait months for a request to be processed. Moreover, each time Israel imposed a total closure, all permits were automatically and immediately revoked. When the closure was lifted, persons had to begin the application process all over again.[40]

Whereas in customary international law the right of persons to marry and live with their families is undisputed, Israel has not recognized the right for Palestinian residents in the West Bank, Gaza, and Jerusalem.[41] According to Kadman:

> Israel's policy has compelled tens of thousands of Palestinians to live apart from their spouses, leaving children separated for prolonged periods from one of their parents. . . . Israel's policy . . . is based on political considerations. . . . The policy's underlying objective is to alter the demography of the Occupied Territories.[42]

Revocation of Residency Rights: The Quiet Deportation

Immediately after its 1967 occupation, Israel dissolved Arab Jerusalem's city council, dismissed and later exiled mayor Ruhi al-Khatib, and issued ID cards to Palestinian residents. As permanent residents, Palestinians travel on temporary *laissez-passers* (travel permits). Until 1995, East Jerusalem Palestinians with valid residency ID cards could leave the city and even live elsewhere, provided they returned to Jerusalem annually to renew their exit permits and ID cards. Only a continuous stay outside the country for seven years, without any intervening re-registration, was cause for the revocation of the status of permanent resident.

Moreover, East Jerusalem residents who moved elsewhere in the Occupied Territories (which Israel consistently encouraged them to do) were not required to have permits to exit and enter Jerusalem; and some, although not many, continued to receive benefits from the NII.[43] These primarily involved the child allotment benefit; however, the benefit applied only to children born to a family before they moved to the Occupied Territories, not to children born afterward. Thus, if a young Jerusalemite couple had one child but the unemployed father found work in Ramallah and they moved there—thereafter having four more children—only the first child received benefits. The most serious restriction prior to 1995 involved the regulation that an East Jerusalem woman who married a man without Jerusalem residency automatically lost her residency right and social benefits, compelling the wife to leave the city and live in her husband's locale. The husband was prohibited from moving to East Jerusalem to live with his wife.

"Center of Life" Policy: A New Restraint

In December 1995, Israel radically altered its policy on the issue of Palestinian residency rights in Jerusalem. The new policy is known as the center of life residency requirement. Palestinians were not informed of the policy change; they learned of it during individual visits to the interior ministry. They also learned of it through a new attitude expressed by the NII. Rather than receiving automatic hospitalization when they were ill, or a child allotment when they gave birth, Palestinians found themselves turned away by hospitals and other service facilities; they were the subject of arbitrary investigations before they received benefits to which they were entitled.[44] Israel also increasingly refused to register newborns of parents who had legal residency status.[45] Between 1995 and 1999, more than 3,000 Jerusalemite Palestinians lost their right to reside in the city. Two Israeli human rights organizations (B'Tselem and HaMoked) illustrate the magnitude and arbitrariness of this policy change for Palestinians from East Jerusalem:[46]

> Palestinians who now go to the Interior Ministry's office in East Jerusalem for whatever purpose are liable to receive notification that their permanent residency permit has expired. They must then return their identity card and leave Israel within fifteen days. Other family members (children and spouses) whose residency rights depend on the

person are also expelled. The ministry applies this policy to every person who had lived or is currently living outside of Jerusalem. . . . As far as residency is concerned, the authorities consider the West Bank to be "outside of Israel," and the same is true as regards those who live in a Jerusalem suburb, a distance of a few kilometers from the city's borders. There are also instances where even Palestinians who have lived their entire lives in Jerusalem have been required to prove that their "center of life" is in Jerusalem. . . . The burden of proof that the individual's "center of life" is in Jerusalem is placed on the Palestinian.[47]

The government's demand that East Jerusalem Palestinians must prove that Jerusalem is their center of life is difficult (if not impossible), complicated, and ultimately decided by a bureaucrat at the interior ministry. Indeed, if proving one's residency was arduous prior to 1995, the new policy has made it more difficult. There are no legal or other appeals available. Among the requirements for proving one's center of life:

1. The individual must present confirmation of place of employment, which must be within the boundaries of Jerusalem.
2. The individual must have copies of all bills for at least the preceding seven years for taxes (e.g., *arnona*), electricity, water, and telephone. Sometimes officials demand to see such bills for the period of an individual's residency in the city. (Considering the number of Palestinian East Jerusalemites who have not had regular water, electricity, or phone service, the demand, by itself, guarantees that many Palestinians will be unable to prove their continuous residency.)
3. The individual must also present confirmation from the NII that he receives annual allotments from the institute.
4. The individual must provide his/her parents' place of residence and demonstrate conclusively whether he/she does or does not live with them. If not, he/she must present a rental contract and there must be evidence of consistent payment. The ministry requires a legal affidavit from an approved attorney indicating that the individual does live in the city.
5. He must have confirmation that all his children have been enrolled in Jerusalem schools since the age of six.[48]

This new policy is particularly grave in light of the difficulties of life in the city—the absence of services, housing, employment, and so on. Palestinians have often been compelled to move elsewhere in the Occupied Territories simply to find employment or a suitable house (Table 5.2).

Table 5.2   Revocation of Residency Rights of East Jerusalem Palestinians,
             1987–1999

Year	No. of Palestinians Whose Residency Was Revoked
1987	23
1988	2
1989	32
1990	36
1991	20
1992	41
1993	32
1994	45
1995	91
1996	739
1997	1,067
1998	788
1999	411

Sources: B'Tselem, *Revocation of Residency in East Jerusalem* (Jerusalem: The Israeli Information Center for Human Rights in the Occupied Territories, 2000), available online at www.btselem.org/Files/site/english/data/The_Quiet_Deportation.asp.

Zoning Laws and Housing Restrictions

Zoning laws.   Zoning laws have primarily applied to areas in East Jerusalem outside the Old City. Although Israel has expanded the Jewish Quarter in the Old City at the expense of the Muslim Quarter, there is no overall zoning plan. Palestinians wishing to build a house, enlarge an existing one, or open a shop in the Old City must obtain a permit from the municipal authority on an individual basis. These requests have been typically denied.

Zoning applies to the other areas of East Jerusalem, outside the old walled enclave. A regional planning board was established to review and evaluate all development projects. According to Cheshin, Hutman, and Melamed, "The board was the guardian of the limitation system . . . [and] was famous for blocking development projects in Palestinian communities in East Jerusalem."[49] For example, Israeli planners zoned vast tracts as green areas that are off-limits to development. Ostensibly, these areas were intended to protect the environment and enhance the beauty of the city by preserving open views of the landscape. In reality, however, green areas have served as a means of containment and demarcation as well as land reserves for future Jewish settlement. For example, Jabal Abu Ghanem was originally zoned green to prevent the neighboring Palestinian villages of Sur Baher and Um Tuba from expanding. Later it was rezoned for construction of the Har Homa settlement.[50] Other areas were left unzoned, but here, too, Palestinian housing and development were prohibited.[51]

Housing restrictions. Housing restrictions and other zoning restrictions were also placed on Palestinians (but not on Israelis). These include the following: Building—residential or commercial—is permitted only in areas that are already built up; it is prohibited in vacant or open spaces. Buildings may be no more than two stories tall. There is a strict limitation on the number of dwellings that can be built in any given area, as well as on the height and size. Thus, for example, whereas a Jewish Jerusalemite owing a plot of 50 square meters can build an eight-story building of 200 square meters, a Palestinian Jerusalemite owning the same size plot can build only a two-story building of 50 square meters.[52] Additionally, as B'Tselem documented, "The Israeli authorities prepared town plans which, instead of developing Palestinian neighborhoods, prevent such development. Over a third of East Jerusalem lacks town-planning schemes, making construction impossible. . . . In fact, Palestinian building is allowed in only 7 % of East Jerusalem."[53] Most building permits are rejected either because of zoning plans or because the land is claimed by Israel as absentee property. Moreover, projects that are submitted to the relevant authorities for approval experience inordinate delays—often as long as ten years—before receiving an answer.[54]

Permits. Permits are an important means by which Israel limits the development of Palestinian neighborhoods and prevents the construction of homes. Between 1967 and 1999, only 12 percent of all new housing units in Jerusalem was built for Palestinians in East Jerusalem (i.e., 21,490 housing units for Palestinians as compared to 122,376 housing units for Jews).[55] As a consequence, considering the Palestinian growth rate since 1967, there is an acute housing shortage and extreme residential overcrowding among East Jerusalem Palestinians.[56] In East Jerusalem as a whole, there are 43,000 homes in Jewish neighborhoods (all built on expropriated Palestinian land), compared to 28,000 homes in Palestinian neighborhoods.[57] The population density of the Palestinian community in East Jerusalem is 2.2 persons per room, twice as high as that for Jewish residents of the city. Some 40 percent of the houses are severely substandard, and about half of all residents rent their homes.[58] (The population density in the Muslim Quarter of the Old City is 487 persons per hectare as compared to the Jewish quarter, where it is 183 persons per hectare.)[59]

House demolitions. Israeli zoning and housing restrictions and the resultant housing shortages have led many Palestinian families to build additions to already existing houses and to build new houses even when denied permits. Israel considers all such construction illegal and eligible for demolition. The demolition rate has been higher in East Jerusalem than anywhere else in the Occupied Territories. For example, between 1993 and 1998—the years of the Oslo peace process—Israel demolished 186 houses in East Jerusalem—ninety-five after the 1995 Interim Agreement alone.[60] The following year (1999), under orders from Prime Minister Ehud Barak, seventeen houses were demolished in East Jerusalem.[61] Also, in 1999, 10,000 Palestinian housing units were declared illegal, and 2,000 were placed under demolition orders (see Table 3.2 in Chapter 3).[62] In September 2002, Israel issued demolition orders for one house and "sealing" orders for three houses because members of the families living in them were alleged by the Israeli Defense Forces (IDF) to be engaged in terrorism.[63] It is believed that this was the first time such collective punishment had been used in East Jerusalem.

New housing projects. Israel has sponsored only two Palestinian housing projects during the period of its occupation of East Jerusalem—the El-Mashrua project in Izariyyeh Village and the Nusseiba housing project in Beit Hania village. These, however, were not undertaken to improve the welfare of the Palestinian community. Rather, they represented another tactic to entice Palestinians to move out of the city limits of East Jerusalem. Israel pledged that Palestinian Jerusalemites who moved to these West Bank hamlets would not lose their Jerusalem IDs, residency rights, or associated services, in particular from the NII. Yet once the Palestinians moved into these projects, Israel reversed itself and revoked their residency rights, including health care and social services.[64] Indeed, "when all was said and done, Arab families who had listened to Israel's promises and left Jerusalem came out the losers."[65]

Land expropriations; zoning laws; commissions for "approval" of development plans; building permits; house demolitions; house takeovers—all have had a cumulative effect. By 1999 in East Jerusalem, 86 percent of the city had been effectively removed from Palestinian control due to expropriation and confiscation; 42 percent of land had been used for settlements, 44 percent for green areas, and 13.5 percent for Palestinian development.[66] Cheshin, Hutman, and Melamed, who were involved in developing these methods, write: "Israel turned urban planning into a tool of the government, to be used to help prevent the expansion of the city's non-Jewish population. It was a ruthless policy, if only for the fact that the needs—to say nothing of the rights—of Palestinian residents were ignored"[67]

Increasing the Number of Jewish Residents

Along with the zoning and housing restrictions Israel placed on the Palestinians, the paucity of services it provided, and so on, Tel Aviv also undertook the construction of modern, highly developed settlements with every amenity, which was conceived as the best means for attracting a large number of Jews to the city. "The idea was to move as many Jews as possible into East Jerusalem."[68] To induce Jews to move into new settlements, the government provided low- or no-interest mortgages, provided tax breaks (e.g., five-year exemptions from municipal taxes), and spent millions on marketing campaigns.[69] It is also notable that Israel pursued a de facto policy of Jews only in its East Jerusalem zoning plans: all the new settlements (which were constructed on land confiscated from Palestinians) are exclusively for Jews. The Israeli High Court upheld this policy based on "the historic reality of homogenous neighborhoods" in the city. Yet when Jews bought or simply took over Arab homes in the Muslim Quarter, "the Israeli courts looked the other way."[70]

More contentious is the settler activity within the Muslim and Christian Quarters of the Old City and in Palestinian neighborhoods along the Old City's walls (e.g., in Silwan, Sheikh Jarrah, Abu Tur, Musrara, A-Tur, Wadi Joz, and Ras al-Amoud). Here, fundamentalist settlers have been involved in the acquisition, one by one, of Palestinian homes, the eviction of their residents, and their replacement by Jewish families. This activity, begun in the 1980s and continuing to the present day, is carried out by messianic religious Jews with ideological roots in and ties to Gush Emunim. There are two main groups: Ateret Cohanim (The Priestly Crown), which concentrates on the Old City's Muslim Quarter, including the area around Herod's Gate as well as the Mount of Olives; and Elad (an acronym for "To the City of David"), which focuses on Silwan. Other groups include Atara L'Yoshna, Magaleh Orot, Torat Cohanim, and the Homot Shalem association. In addition to attempting to "reclaim" the Old City for Jews, they hope to destroy the Haram al-Sharif and re-create the Jewish Temple (see Map 5.2).[71]

Cheshin, Hutman, and Melamed document that the activity of these groups has had "the strong backing of the government" (Labor as well as Likud) and that "the government funneled funds to the East Jerusalem settlers."[72] Money to support these groups also comes from private sources in the United States and elsewhere, most notably from a

Map 5.2 The Old City of Jerusalem

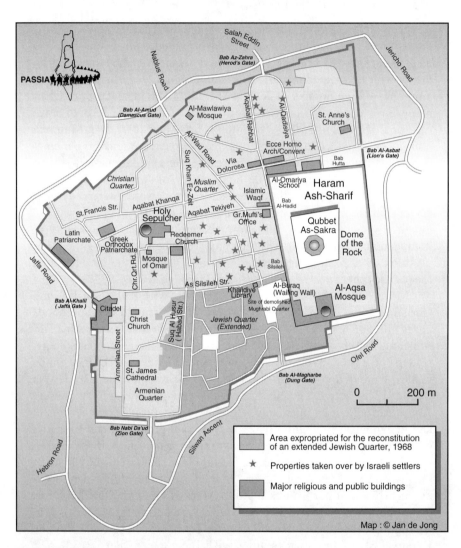

Source: Palestinian Academic Society for the Study of International Affairs (PASSIA), Jerusalem, http://www.passia.org/palestine_facts/MAPS/images/jer_maps/old_city.html. Accessed January 2003. Reprinted with permission of PASSIA.

wealthy Miami businessman, Irving Moscowitz, who alone has funneled tens of millions of dollars to Israeli settler groups to help in the
acquisition of Palestinian homes.[73] The religious zealots were given
inspiration (and, as it was later revealed, money and other assistance)
when, in 1987, the agriculture minister at the time, Ariel Sharon, occupied, with round-the-clock protection from the IDF, a Palestinian home
in the Muslim Quarter. Moreover,

> the government worked behind the scenes to support the settlers in
> east Jerusalem. From Silwan and the Old City to the Mount of Olives
> and Wadi Joz. Millions of dollars of state funds . . . [were] used by the
> settlers to acquire Arab homes. . . . In other cases, the settlement
> activists, with the support of state officials, took advantage of . . . the
> Absentee Property Law . . . to take over Arab homes and evict their
> Arab residents. . . . Without Israeli government support, the acquisi-
> tion of Arab homes in east Jerusalem would have been difficult if not
> impossible. . . . They needed the money and the support of the author-
> ities, and they got both.[74]

Thus, as with the settlers' activity in Hebron, there is not only government acquiescence but also outright support for settler projects in
Jerusalem's Old City and its environs (Map 5.3).

In 1993, Prime Minister Yitzhak Rabin commissioned a committee
to investigate the activities of settlers and their government connections. The findings were released in the Klugman Report, which "clearly showed that the settlers forced Palestinians out of their homes in East
Jerusalem and that many in the Israeli government had supported the
settlers in their efforts. Confronted with this, Israeli leaders on both the
political right and left refused to do anything about it."[75] Indeed, when
in 1998 the Israeli state comptroller, Miriam Ben Porat, notified Prime
Minister Benjamin Netanyahu that an inquiry based on the Klugman
Report would begin within a month unless he ordered otherwise, she
received a directive from the prime minister "to stop the investigation."[76]

On the rare occasions when homes have been purchased legally, the
settlers have been able to offer their owners several million dollars as
an incentive to sell. In the vast majority of cases, however, settlers have
obtained the Palestinian homes either fraudulently or forcefully.[77] The
most common tactic involves government falsification of documents to
classify inhabited Palestinian property as absentee. Once the settlers
obtain the false documents, the Israeli Lands Administration and the
Jewish National Fund allot the fabricated absentee property to the settler groups without offering it up for tender. Moreover, public funds are

Map 5.3   Palestinian Neighborhoods at Risk from Israeli Settlers in East Jerusalem

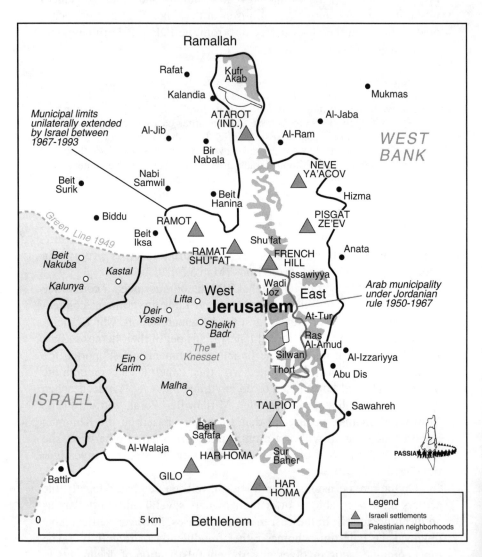

Source: Palestinian Academic Society for the Study of International Affairs (PASSIA), Jerusalem, http://www.passia.org/palestine_facts/MAPS/images/jer_maps/GreaterJerusalem.html. Accessed January 2003. Reprinted with permission of PASSIA.

used to finance all the settlers' expenses—most of which are legal fees, owing to court challenges from Palestinians, and can run into the tens of thousands. A common transaction looks like the following. The settlers provide a counterfeit affidavit to the custodian for absentee property, who in turn declares that the property in question is indeed absentee property. The custodian then transfers the property to the Israeli Development Authority. The Israeli Development Authority transfers the property to Amidar (a government housing company), which, in the final step, rents it to the settler group that produced the altered affidavit in the first place.[78] When financial incentives and fraud have proved insufficient, settlers have resorted to force (with the help of the police and IDF).[79]

During the seven years of the peace process, settler groups have made significant progress: by 2000, they had acquired more than 200 properties in the Old City and nearby neighborhoods through such tactics.[80] Additionally, the Israeli government constructed a Jewish settlement in the heart of Ras al-Amoud (with Moscowitz's financing).[81] The settlement is called Ma'alech Hazaytim and contains 119 apartments, fifty-two of which were occupied by April 2002. In this Palestinian neighborhood of 11,000, the new enclave of "extreme right-wing" settlers will, in the words of *Ha'aretz*, create "Hebron redux."[82]

In April 2002, an article in *Ha'aretz* revealed that the Homot Shalem association, organized by Knesset member Benny Elon (of the National Union Party, which advocates transfer of all Palestinians out of Eretz Israel; Elon was also appointed to Prime Minister Ariel Sharon's cabinet), had secured rights to a Palestinian neighborhood, known as Arab Musrara, alongside the Old City, near Damascus Gate. The group managed to obtain ownership rights to ten compounds and courtyards (about a third of the neighborhood) and has plans to acquire the remainder. Palestinians resided in all the compounds but were slated for eviction so that Jewish families could move in. By September, the group had obtained court orders to evict the Palestinian families and had begun moving in.[83]

Also in April, Elon's group procured a court order to evict several dozen Palestinian families from the Shimon Hatzaddik neighborhood (near the American Colony area) of East Jerusalem and replace them with Jewish families. Twelve Palestinian families were expelled as a result. The Palestinians living in the Shimon district were refugees from 1948 and were housed in the area by the Jordanian authorities after the 1948 war. Elon told *Ha'aretz* that the association's activities there were "just another small step toward returning Zion to Jerusalem"; the goal of the group, he stated, is "to make it impossible to divide the Old City as part of any future diplomatic agreement," and it has the full support of the Israeli government.[84]

In the fall of 2002, the Elad focused its attention on another Palestinian village, Jabal Mukhaber. Despite protests from its Palestinian owner, Elad took over an occupied Palestinian house (the second house acquired by Elad in the village) and announced a plan to build a 600-unit Jewish enclave.[85]

The Expansion of Jerusalem's Boundaries

Settlement of East Jerusalem Before and After Oslo

During the 1990s, in addition to the heightened government-sponsored activity of the settlers in the Old City and its environs and the initiation of construction of Har Homa, Israel engaged in other land confiscations and settlement activities. Israel's objective is to create physical links between existing settlements around Jerusalem, with links extending from Jerusalem to all the major settlements throughout the West Bank, in order to establish an unbroken, physical Jewish presence throughout the area. The concept is based on utilizing Jerusalem as the nucleus from which to connect the Jewish presence in the northern, central, and southern parts of the West Bank.

Israel developed a series of major plans for realizing this end. The first of the three plans was the 1995 Inter-Ministerial Committee Plan approved by Prime Minister Rabin. This was followed by a 1998 scheme known as the Umbrella Municipality Plan. Prime Minister Netanyahu approved it, which incorporated the Inter-Ministerial Committee Plan plus an additional new design (the E1 Plan). In May 1999, within a week after his electoral victory, Prime Minister Barak announced another blueprint for further colonizing the territories, known as the Master Plan.[86]

The Circles of Jerusalem

Municipal Jerusalem. The area Israel defined in 1967 as East Jerusalem (combined with West Jerusalem) is considered *municipal Jerusalem*, or the "first circle." In the eastern part of this sector there are fourteen settlements. Five are quite large, including Gilo, Ramat Allon, East Talpiot, Neve Ya'acov, and Pisgat Ze'ev/Pisgat Omer, with a combined population of 134,900. When Har Homa is completed, it will seal the formal East Jerusalem border. Palestinians remaining in

East Jerusalem will be completely cut off and isolated from their families, friends, and jobs in the West Bank and vise versa (see Map 5.1).

By August 2002, the first phase of construction at Har Homa was nearly complete. The Israeli housing ministry reported that 1,000 homes had been sold and that several hundred people had already moved in. Israel envisions an eventual complex of 6,500 units housing a minimum of 20,000 Israelis, with schools, parks, and shopping malls.[87] The government provides special inducements or subsidies to encourage Israelis to move to Har Homa. Most important are low-interest loans of NIS 100,000 to purchase homes in the settlement (applicable also to Pisgat Ze'ev), with NIS 50,000 rebates if purchased within four months of issue.[88]

Greater Jerusalem.   In 1983, Israel designated an area of the West Bank Greater Jerusalem, or the "second circle" of the city. Greater Jerusalem was to include all the settlements extending to Ramallah in the north, to the Etzion Bloc in the south (including the major settlement of Efrat), to Ma'ale Adumim in the east, and Beit Shemesh in the west. By 1992, 77 percent of the settler population in the West Bank lived in the combined municipal and Greater Jerusalem settlements (see Map 5.4).[89]

There are nine settlements in this second ring, six of which are strategically located and heavily populated. These include Ma'ale Adumim, east of Jerusalem; Givat Ze'ev, north of Jerusalem; Betar Illit, southwest of Jerusalem; Gush Etzion, together with the multiple settlements of the Etzion Bloc, south of Jerusalem and south of Bethlehem; Modi'in Illit, north of Jerusalem and west of Ramallah; and Efrat, southeast of Jerusalem and south of Bethlehem. Their combined populations equal some 85,000 persons. Incorporating these settlements into a redefined concept of Greater Jerusalem expands enormously the territory under sovereign Israeli control, binding large, geopolitically located settlements in the northern, central, and southern West Bank to Israel proper.

Metropolitan Jerusalem.   A "third circle" is entirely post-Oslo. It was initiated in December 1993 when Prime Minister Rabin gave official approval to a plan for municipal continuity between Givat Ze'ev and Ma'ale Adumim through the construction of a series of new roads and tunnels. At the same time, he gave approval for the U.S.$42 million Gilo–Gush Etzion road. In 1995, Rabin again provided endorsement for a new project—the Metropolitan Jerusalem Plan. This large-scale development scheme, which on completion will cover an area of some

Map 5.4   Greater Jerusalem with Emphasis on Depth of Area Controlled by Ma'ale Adumim

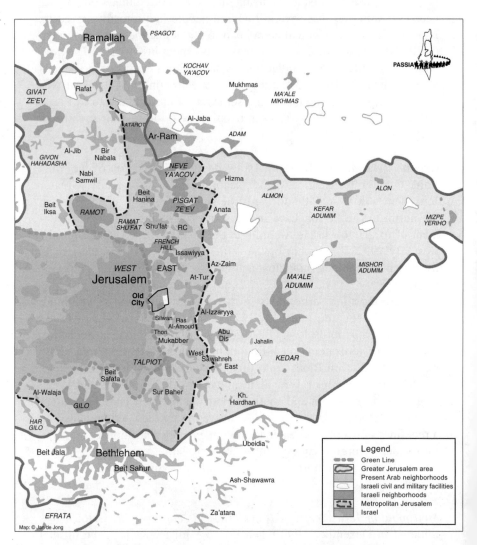

Source: Palestinian Academic Society for the Study of International Affairs (PASSIA), Jerusalem, http://www.passia.org/palestine_facts/MAPS/images/jer_maps/Jlem_camp_david.html. Accessed January 2003. Reprinted with permission of PASSIA.

440 square kilometers and incorporate up to 40 percent of the West Bank, represents a logical extension of the earlier plans, using East Jerusalem as the fulcrum to tie together far-flung settlements, "thicken" existing settlements, and extend Israeli sovereignty over a greater area of the West Bank.[90]

Included in the outer circle of metropolitan Jerusalem is a group of large, widely dispersed, yet shrewdly positioned settlements located across the territory of the West Bank. They include Ariel (northeast of Jerusalem, with a population of 14,440); Beit El (north of Jerusalem on the northern outskirts of Ramallah, with 3,570); Kiryat Arba (southeast of Jerusalem, on the Hebron border, with 6,190); Alfi Menashe (north of Jerusalem, near Qalqilya, with 4,360); and Karmei Shomron (north of Jerusalem, between Qalqilya and Nablus, with 5,370).

Israel's objective in conceiving and implementing this master scheme is the same as for the concept of Greater Jerusalem. First, it is to incorporate as much West Bank territory as possible under Israeli sovereignty; then to connect the settlements in the third circle (metropolitan Jerusalem) with each other through bypass roads and numerous smaller settlements; and finally to join them to the major settlements in the second circle (Greater Jerusalem), thereby linking them to municipal East Jerusalem and Israel proper. The end result will be a situation whereby Israeli citizens populate sovereign Israeli towns throughout the West Bank, all interconnected through infrastructure and military installations, subject only to the authority of the Israeli government. It will fragment Palestinian territory into countless isolated, disarticulated cantons and will remove any question of this being "occupied" territory and the settlement-towns illegal.

As stated earlier in 1998 Israel gave official approval to a new program for annexing territory. Known as the Umbrella Municipality Plan, this scheme calls for the introduction of Israeli civil law (as opposed to military law) in the unincorporated areas of the West Bank, as Israel defines them, around and among the major settlements. (The settlements and settlers are already under Israeli civil law.) Once an area is formally under Israeli civil law, it is automatically part of sovereign Israel. Such legal enactments remove any "occupied," "disputed," or "Palestinian" territory from the agenda for negotiations because the areas would be a priori Israeli.[91]

The E1 Plan was another product of Netanyahu's 1998 grand calculating. It focused on Ma'ale Adumim—in particular on infrastructural, industrial, and public institution development. Moreover, in 1999 the prime minister approved another ambitious plan for connecting the three circles of Jerusalem and incorporating them into Israel. The program calls for the construction of new settlements, the expansion of existing ones, a major increase in the settler population, and an elaborate system of roads, tunnels, other infrastructure, and services to link all the parts into one (see Map 5.5).

Within each of the three circles and among each of the major settlements in each ring are dozens and dozens of smaller colonies—many established after 1995, all connected by special bypass roads, military infrastructure, and so on. Taken together, they provide a gestalt of Israel's future—and of the Palestinians' as well.

Ma'aleh Adumim: A Study of the Most Important Settlement and Its Links

History of Ma'ale Adumim. The original Ma'ale Adumim settlement was established in 1975 on the Jerusalem-Jericho road. The area (some 35,000 dunums) was confiscated from Palestinians who owned the land and had been living on it, and farming or grazing it, for centuries. As is typical, Israel simply declared the area state land and turned it over to settlers. Subsequent confiscations brought the area of the settlement to 43,500 dunums by the early 1990s. The villages that lost the most land in this expropriation were Abu Dis, Al-Izariyyeh, Al-Issawiyyeh, A-Tur, and 'Anata. The agricultural land of the villages and the grazing land of the bedouin that were confiscated extended from the border of Jerusalem on the west to a'Khan al-Ahmad at the approach to the Dead Sea on the east. For the bedouins, as well as for the villagers, loss of their lands meant loss of their agricultural way of life and major transformations in their social life. Today, the area available to the villages together, with a population of approximately 40,000, is some 4,600 dunums. The area of Ma'ale Adumim, with some 26,000 settlers, is 11.5 times greater.[92] (For a view of Ma'ale Adumim and environs, see Map 5.4.)

In contrast to the landless peasants and bedouins, residents of Ma'ale Adumim enjoy a high standard of living, modern infrastructure, green areas, advanced educational and cultural institutions, and numerous other services, benefits, and institutions designed to attract families to the settlement. Residents receive large tax breaks and government-subsidized, highly favorable mortgage terms (as do residents of all settlements). There are hotels and other tourist facilities, and there is an ongoing advertising campaign to attract Christian pilgrims who are coming to Jerusalem and Bethlehem and who seek inexpensive accommodations. Christian American fundamentalists come here by the hundreds. The settlement-town is also well endowed with an industrial park that spreads across 7,500 dunums, in "an area containing unlimited land reserves," and it is

Map 5.5　Detail of E1 Development Plan, 1998

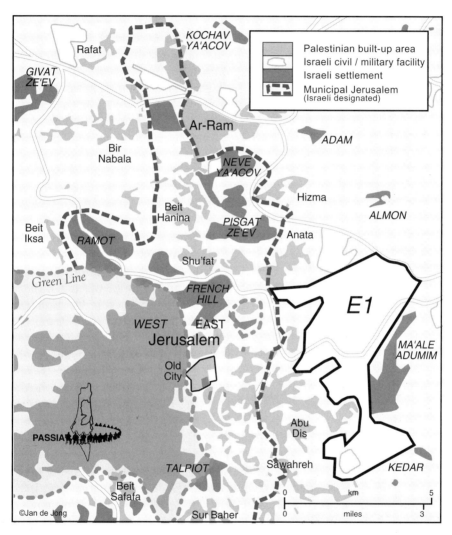

Legend:
- Palestinian built-up area
- Israeli civil / military facility
- Israeli settlement
- Municipal Jerusalem (Israeli designated)

Map labels: KOCHAV YA'ACOV, Rafat, GIVAT ZE'EV, Ar-Ram, ADAM, Bir Nabala, NEVE YA'ACOV, Hizma, ALMON, Beit Hanina, PISGAT ZE'EV, Anata, Beit Iksa, RAMOT, Shu'fat, Green Line, FRENCH HILL, E1, WEST Jerusalem, EAST Jerusalem, Old City, MA'ALE ADUMIM, PASSIA, Abu Dis, TALPIOT, Sawahreh, KEDAR, Beit Safafa, Sur Baher, ©Jan de Jong

0　km　5
0　miles　3

Source: Palestinian Academic Society for the Study of International Affairs (PASSIA), Jerusalem, http://www.passia.org/palestine_facts/MAPS/images/jer_maps/E1developmentplan.pdf. Accessed January 2003. Reprinted with permission of PASSIA.

"among the largest industrial parks in Israel."[93] Because Plan E1 for Ma'ale Adumim specifically mentions its importance as a link with Giv'at Ze'ev in the north and the Etzion Bloc in the south, and because of the strategic and geopolitical importance of each of these settlements independently, the following section briefly examines each.

Giv'at Ze'ev. The Giv'at Ze'ev settlement, like Ma'ale Adumim, lies in the second circle (greater Jerusalem) and is slated to play an important role in the expansion of metropolitan Jerusalem. In 1996, the Israeli government approved a program for the settlement that included 2,650 new housing units plus 20,000 new settlers. The new housing will be constructed on land confiscated from the Palestinian villages of Betunia, Biddo, and Jeib. In March 1997, Israel announced another expansion plan for Giv'at Ze'ev that involves confiscation of an additional 50 acres from Jeib. Then, in March 1997, Israel declared the confiscation of 200 more acres from Betunia and Jeib for the construction of 11,550 additional housing units (see Map 5.6).

The expansion of Giv'at Ze'ev is significant in that when it is completed it will be directly linked with the nearby settlements of Giv'on and Giv'on Hadasha and will lead to the completion of a wall of colonies surrounding the northwestern side of East Jerusalem. Moreover, the master plan envisages Giv'at Ze'ev being connected with Modi'in Illit to the northwest (on the Green Line); Modi'in Illit being directly linked due east to Beit El (just north of Ramallah); and Beit El being connected south to Ma'ale Adumim.[94] This will complete the northern part of the third circle (metropolitan Jerusalem), tying the northern settlements to East Jerusalem through Ma'ale Adumim and through new bypass roads. Some plans on the drawing board hope to see the northern point of this circle at Ariel rather than Beit El. Ariel lies on the road to Nablus, just south of the city, and would obviously significantly expand Israel's reach.

Gush Etzion/Etzion Bloc. A third strategic area for the expansion of Jerusalem is the southward salient that centers on the Etzion Bloc. It comprises some seventeen settlements with a total population of more than 17,000, and is situated south of the Palestinian villages of Bethlehem, Beit Jala, and Beit Sahur. Israel's objective here is also to completely encircle the Palestinian areas from the south, then link the Etzion settlement bloc with southwest Jerusalem on the Green Line and with east-central Jerusalem at Ma'ale Adumim (see Map 5.7).

The importance of the Gush Etzion bloc to Israel's strategy is evidenced in a government-sponsored project to bring English-speakers,

Map 5.6   Detail of Expansion of Giv'at Ze'ev

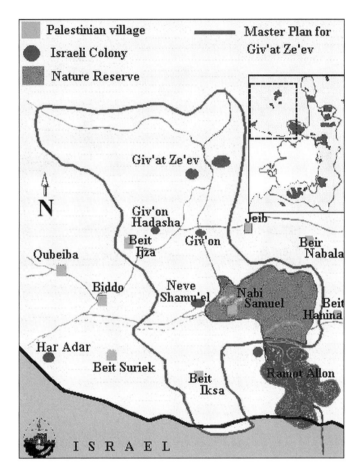

Source: Eye on Palestine, "Giv'at Ze'ev," http://www.arij.org/paleye/
jerusal/fig8.gif. "Monitoring Colonizing Activities in the Palestinian West
Bank and Gaza Strip," Bethlehem, Applied Research Institute—ARIJ.
Accessed September 2002. Reprinted by permission of ARIJ.

Map 5.7 Detail of Etzion Bloc

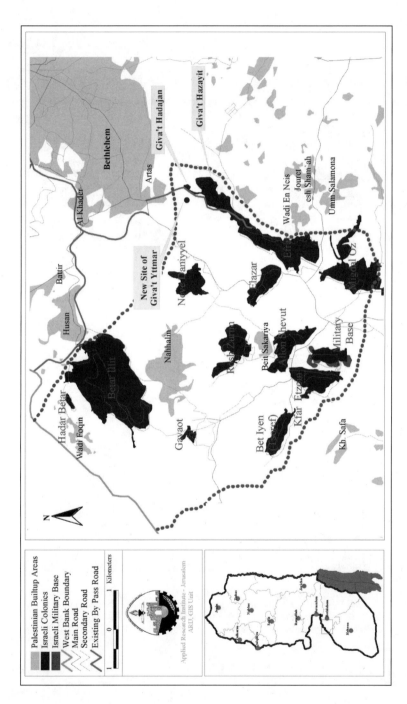

Source: POICA (combined project of the Applied Research Institute—ARIJ, Land Research Center of the Arab Studies Society, and the European Union), Bethlehem, http://www.poica.org/casestudies/etzion-block-expansion/Case Study. Accessed September 2002. Reprinted by permission of ARIJ.

particularly South Africans, to Neve Daniel, a mixed secular/religious settlement in the Etzion Bloc. The World Zionist Organization is working in tandem with the government, to encourage immigrant as well as Israeli families to settle in Neve Daniel. In November 2001, new construction in the settlement was proceeding at a rapid pace. According to *Ha'aretz:* "The village currently has 180 families and totals about 1,000 persons, but . . . these figures could double in the next few years. The initial stage of construction of a planned stretch of 100 housing units has begun on the settlement's western slope." Planners of the project in Neve Daniel see the South African Jewish community as "a logical target group from an ideological point of view."[95] Such planning does not suggest that Israel intends, under any circumstance, to leave the West Bank.

Israel's objective of adding new settlements was further evidenced on March 12, 1997, when the government announced the initiation of construction of Givat Hazayit, a new colony in the Etzion Bloc a few kilometers from Efrat. The settlement is being constructed on 180 hectares with an initial housing projection of 267 units. Givat Hazayit is part of a larger scheme for the Efrat area of the Etzion Bloc that includes two other settlements. One, Givat Yitmar, is being constructed on 23.6 hectares with 397 housing units. The second of the trilogy is Givat HaDajan, being built on 25 hectares with 362 housing units. All three are intended as part of the "thickening" of the Etzion area, squeezing the Palestinians in the region, and finally linking up with East Jerusalem.[96]

On March 24, 2001, Israel announced a master plan for a new town in the Etzion Bloc to be called Giva'ot. It will be located between the settlements of Alon Shuvt and Betar. According to the housing ministry, Giva'ot will have 6,000 housing units and is "intended eventually to be contiguous with . . . Betar, three kilometers away." In the future, it will also be linked with Efrat.[97] Thus, the southern part of the third circle will be complete.

It should be noted that despite the construction of new houses and new settlements, expansion of existing settlements, and the creation of more new roads, there are insufficient numbers of Jews to fill them. Thus, Israel is constantly recruiting Jewish communities (as well as some non-Jewish who are deemed "suitable" for conversion) around the world to immigrate and settle in the Occupied Territories. The efforts with regard to South African Jews were mentioned above. There are also ongoing programs to persuade 200,000 Argentinean Jews to come.[98] In early 2003, the government approved the immigration of 17,000 Falasha Moras (plus 3,000 Falashas) from Ethiopia. These are

black Jews who were forced to convert to Christianity in the nineteenth
century. In 1984, Israel for the first time recognized the Falashas as
Jewish and in 1991 it began airlifts from Addis Ababa that ultimately
totaled 80,000 persons. However, as a community, the Falashas have
fared very poorly in Israel, facing racial discrimination, cultural barriers, high unemployment, and so on. The Falasha Mora were considered
insufficiently Jewish, until Tel Aviv's recent decision to bring them,
since unlike the Falashas, they had continued to identify themselves as
Christians and practiced Christianity.[99] The need for settlers, however,
overcame the question of their Jewishness. The most controversial
group brought to Israel, beginning in 2002, has been a community of
impoverished Peruvian Indians who have no apparent Jewish roots
although they have been willing converts and are enthusiastic settlers.[100] In March 2003, the Jewish Agency announced its readiness for
"quick conversions" for non-Jewish immigrants from Eastern European
countries who are willing to immigrate to Israel and settle in the occupied territories.[101]

Roads: The Glue That Binds the Circles Together

The settler bypass roads that riddle the West Bank play a significant
part in linking together settlements throughout the area and tying them
to Israel. In mid-March 2001, *Ha'aretz* reported that

> The Jerusalem District Planning and Building Committee a few days
> ago approved the plan to build the "eastern ring road" along the capi-
> tal's eastern border. . . . The road will divert [Palestinian] vehicles
> traveling between Bethlehem through Ramallah to a corridor beyond
> Jerusalem's eastern boundary. . . . To pave the 15 kilometer road, 568
> dunums (about 165 Acres) will have to be appropriated from the
> landowners in . . . Arab villages. . . . Work has already begun on one
> of the lateral roads that is to join up with the ring road—the Mount
> Scopus Road. It would connect the Beit Horon-Mishor Adumim route
> in the north to the Beit Sahur-Bethlehem road in the south.[102]

In fact, this road is part of a master road grid that was originally
approved by Prime Minister Netanyahu and ratified by Prime Minister
Barak. It is actually more of a square than a ring with the Old City in
the middle. It includes the completed Road No. 4 in West Jerusalem and
Route 9 in the north. It will have a number of access roads, including
one to Har Homa, the Mount Scopus tunnel road connecting East
Jerusalem with Ma'ale Adumim, the Jerusalem-Jericho bypass, and the
Jerusalem-Ramallah bypass. The road plan includes three tunnels, the

largest of which is 1.8 kilometers in length and will pass under Abu Dis, emerging near Al-Zia'yem. A second tunnel will pass under the Jerusalem airport (Qalandiya) and connect with the Jerusalem-Ramallah bypass to the north and, to the west, with a highway that goes directly to the Mediterranean coastline. This eastern section of this road will slice through the Palestinian neighborhoods of Anata, Issawiyyeh, Hizma, Al-Zia'yem, Asawahra, Al-Tur, Izariyyeh, Abu Dis, Ras al-Amud, and Sur Baher, requiring the confiscation of Palestinian land and demolition of houses; it will also prejudice the political status of final-status negotiations over East Jerusalem. The full road when it is completed is expected to be 45 kilometers in length, requiring the expropriation and destruction of more than 700 hectares of Palestinian agricultural land. Barak authorized the confiscation of 658 dunums to begin work on the eastern ring, and Prime Minister Sharon authorized the confiscation of another 412 dunums. Ten Palestinian homes have already been demolished to make way for the road, and analysts calculate that twenty to thirty more will be destroyed.[103]

Despite what seems like fairly straightforward data with the usual concomitant suffering of the Palestinians at the expense of Israeli expansionism, the real significance of the eastern ring of the Jerusalem road resides in its long-term geopolitical implications. Ultimately, this road, and those that will feed into it from the various outlying settlements—a latticework of settler highways—will give Israel sovereign control over 40 percent of the West Bank and provide it with a physical barrier to reinforce Israeli municipal boundaries in metropolitan Jerusalem.[104] The ring will create a new reality of political separation and territorial discontinuity. Indeed, it is designed not only to connect Israeli settlements but also to prevent territorial contiguity between Palestinian villages.[105] The road system is another means of fragmenting and isolating Palestinian society into disarticulated cantons that preclude the possibility of a viable Palestinian state.

The Geopolitical Significance of Jerusalem

The Jerusalem issue is essential for comprehending the depth and extent of Israel's position relative to fundamental Palestinian objectives in the peace process. I have noted in Chapter 2 that Israel's positions at Camp David were vague, unwritten, and unaccompanied by maps. Still, much is known about Tel Aviv's red lines. Negotiations at the summit were mostly about the percent of territory in the West Bank that Israel would retain under its sovereignty in a final peace agreement. The numbers ranged from 5 percent to 8–9 percent to 10 percent. What is rarely discussed, however, is the meaning behind the numbers. All the settlements together in the West Bank encompass only 8–9 percent of its territory. But these percentages involve a contiguous line of settlement blocs tied together with bypass roads and connected to Jerusalem. Ma'ale Adumim cuts the West Bank in half at its center. When connected to the Etzion bloc and Giv'at Ze'ev, it will mean that a Palestinian state would be broken up, at minimum, into three separate and unconnected cantons (and some analysts suggest that it will be close to sixty-five bantustans). There would be no Palestinian territorial contiguity, and sovereign Israeli towns would surround Palestinians. Israel would have control and sovereignty over the network of West Bank bypass roads. This situation negated the provision in the Declaration of Principles (article IV) that the Palestinian state would have continuity. Map 5.8 illustrates the numerous cantons that would be "Palestine" based on existing settlements and roads.[106]

Concerning the above, Israeli analyst Amira Hass wrote in December 2000:

> How then can anyone assume that a Palestinian could see himself as being independent in his own state, when the simplest of journeys to work or to visit his family would involve daily encounters with foreign soldiers? More than anything, the Al-Aqsa intifada is proving to be an uprising against the settlements and against the Israeli illusion that the Palestinians would accept a reality in which "their independent state" would be sliced through the middle and down its sides by "clusters of settlements."[107]

In January 2003, after two more years of road construction, Hass described the situation:

> Monday marked the official opening of a tunnel that greatly reduces the distance from Ma'aleh Adumim to Jerusalem and from the Jordan Valley to the center of the country. Or, to be more precise, that reduces the distance for Jews traveling . . . Now, Ma'aleh Adumim is almost touching Jerusalem, which embraces Har Homa, which abuts Gilo, and the latter two, thanks to fast roads . . . touch Efrat. . . . A person could travel the length and breadth of the West Bank without ever knowing—not only the names of the villages and cities whose lands were confiscated in order to build the Jewish settlements, but even the fact that they exist. . . . If one looks carefully at the network of roads that have been built and are being built up and down the West Bank and Gaza, for the benefit of the Jews, one might think they had been planned 20 years ago or more to prevent the Palestinians from rising up against the settlements. . . . The people who planned the settlements, large and small, 20 years ago or more also knew that they must

Map 5.8 Settler Bypass Roads Carving Up Palestinian Areas in the West Bank into Isolated Islands

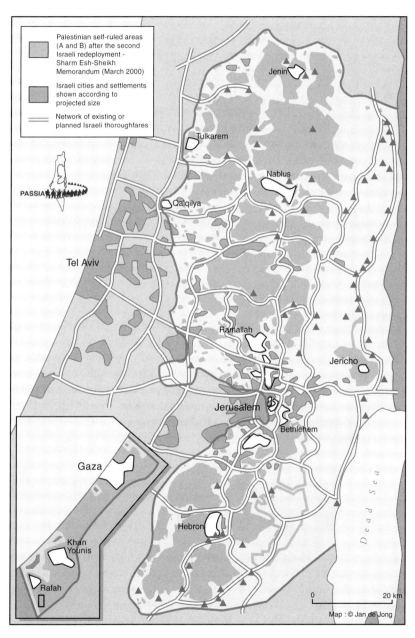

Palestinian self-ruled areas
(A and B) after the second
Israeli redeployment -
Sharm Esh-Sheikh
Memorandum (March 2000)

Israeli cities and settlements
shown according to
projected size

Network of existing or
planned Israeli thoroughfares

PASSIA

Jenin

Tulkarem

Nablus

Qalqilya

Tel Aviv

Ramallah

Jericho

Jerusalem

Bethlehem

Gaza

Dead Sea

Hebron

Khan
Younis

Rafah

0   20 km

Map : © Jan de Jong

Source: Palestinian Academic Society for the Study of International Affairs (PASSIA), Jerusalem, http://www.passia.org/palestine_facts/MAPS/wbgs1.html. Accessed January 2003. Produced by Jan de Jong. Reprinted with permission of PASSIA.

. . . build roads that would isolate every Palestinian city and village, that would divide them from each other and from the main roads, to such an extent that now all it takes is an earthen barrier to block a village's access to the road or to its olive groves, or a city's access to its industrial zone.[108]

Moreover, at the Camp David summit in July 2000, Israel demanded that the Palestinian neighborhoods of Sheikh-Jarrah, Wadi-Jos, Ras al-Amoud, and Silwan remain under Israeli sovereignty, with the Palestinians having some undefined functional autonomy in them. Even the Haram al-Sharif would remain under Israeli sovereignty, though the Palestinians could exercise permanent guardianship—again the meaning was undefined.[109] In short, Jerusalem is to remain an Israeli city, and Palestinian interests have been subsumed in the disparities of power between the two sides. One analyst put it clearly: "The words 'generous offer' say much: they are the words of a conqueror, which the conquered are expected humbly to ratify. They describe a vision of a peace imposed by the strong on the weak."[110]

Conclusion

In this chapter I have demonstrated the hardships and discrimination faced by Palestinian Jerusalemites in the context of Israel's goal of fostering their departure. Many of the policies discussed apply to Palestinian residents of the West Bank and Gaza as well, but nowhere have they been as relentlessly implemented as in East Jerusalem. I also demonstrated the careful Israeli planning that has connected far-flung West Bank settlements through new infrastructure, additional settlements, and expansion of existing ones with Jerusalem and, in turn, with Israel proper. This gives Israel a contiguous, sovereign presence throughout the West Bank and severs Palestinian areas, isolating them into small, disarticulated enclaves incapable of functioning as a viable political or economic entity.

Chapter 6 examines the Palestinian Authority, investigating the corruption, repressive policies, and governing malfeasance that characterized its tenure. The interests of the Palestinian people were poorly served by their leadership on every level. The Palestinian Authority contributed mightily to the worsening life conditions, economic depression, and psychological despair that gripped the people. In some ways, the Al-Aqsa intifada was as much an uprising against the Palestinian Authority as it was against Israel.

Notes

1. David Ben-Gurion, "Speech by David Ben-Gurion at a Meeting of the Executive Committee of the General Federation of Jewish Labor in Palestine, 3 December 1947 (excerpts)," Israeli/Jewish Documents, Mahdi Abdul Hadi, ed., *Documents on Jerusalem* (Jerusalem: Palestinian Academic Society for the Study of International Relations, 1997), p. 77.

2. There are many good accounts of the history of Jerusalem. Perhaps the best is Karen Armstrong, *Jerusalem: One City, Three Faiths* (New York: Ballantine Books, 1996). Also see Henry Cattan, *Jerusalem* (London: al-Saqi, 2000); Gershon Baskin, *Jerusalem of Peace* (Jerusalem: Israel/Palestine Center for Research, 1994); Chaia Beckerman, ed., *Negotiating the Future: Vision and Realpolitik in the Quest for a Jerusalem of Peace* (Jerusalem: Israel/Palestine Center for Research and Information, 1996); and Grace Halsell, *Journey to Jerusalem* (New York: Macmillian, 1987). An excellent documentary source is Palestinian Academic Society for the Study of International Affairs, *Documents on Jerusalem* (Jerusalem: Palestinian Academic Society for the Study of International Affairs, 1996).

3. Avi Shlaim, *Collusion Across the Jordan: King Abdullah, the Zionist Movement, and the Partition of Palestine* (Oxford, UK: Clarendon Press, 1988). The Arab villages annexed to West Jerusalem were Lifta, Deir Yasin, Ein Karem, and al-Maliha. The urban centers annexed to West Jerusalem included al-Qatamon, upper and lower Baqa'a, Mamila, the Abu-Tour-Musara quarter, and Talbiyeh. Together the four villages totaled 28,486 dunums of land (1 dunum equals 1,000 square meters, or roughly one-fourth of an acre), 90 percent of which was owned by Palestinians. For extensive details, see Naseer Aruri, *Whose Jerusalem?* (Boston: Trans-Arab Institute, n.d. [ca. 2000]).

4. LAW, *Human Rights Violations in Arab Jerusalem: An Overview of Abuse* (Jerusalem: Jerusalem Unit of the Palestinian Society for the Protection of Human Rights and the Environment—LAW, 1999), p. 6.

5. Ibid., p. 7. Also see Nathan Krystall, "The De-Arabization of West Jerusalem 1947–1950," *Journal of Palestine Studies* 27, no. 2 (winter 1998): 5–22.

6. For analysis and data, see Kate B. Rouhana, *The Reality of Jerusalem's Palestinians Today* (Jerusalem: Jerusalem Media and Communication Center, 2001), p. 10.

7. Amir S. Cheshin, Bill Hutman, and Avi Melamed, *Separate and Unequal: The Inside Story of Israeli Rule in East Jerusalem* (Cambridge, MA: Harvard University Press, 1999), pp. 10–19. Cheshin was former Jerusalem mayor Teddy Kolleck's adviser on Arab Affairs from 1984 until 1993, then served one year under Kolleck's successor, Ehud Olmert. As Cheshin, Hutman, and Melamed state in the prologue, "The post put him at the center of Israeli policy-making on East Jerusalem during his tenure." Hutman was a senior reporter with the *Jerusalem Post*. From 1992 through 1996, he covered the Jerusalem beat for the newspaper. Melamed served as deputy adviser on Arab affairs from 1991 until 1994 and as adviser from 1994 until 1996. All three are Israeli Jews.

8. Cheshin, Hutman, and Melamed, *Separate and Unequal*, pp. 62–63.

9. For analysis and data, see Rouhana, *The Reality of Jerusalem's Palestinians Today*, p. 10.

10. Yael Stein, *The Quiet Deportation Continues: Revocation of Residency and Denial of Social Rights of East Jerusalem Palestinians* (Jerusalem: B'Tselem—the Israeli Information Center for Human Rights in the Occupied Territories, and HaMoked, Center for the Defense of the Individual, 1998). Yael Stein, *The Quiet Deportation: Revocation of Residency of East Jerusalem Palestinians* (Jerusalem: B'Tselem—the Israeli Information Center for Human Rights in the Occupied Territories, and HaMoked, Center for the Defense of the Individual, 1997). Lea Tsemel and Ingrid Jaradat Gassner, *The Trap Is Closing on Palestinian Jerusalemites: Israel's Demographic Policies in East Jerusalem from the 1967 Annexation to the Eve of the Final Status Negotiations (1996)* (Jerusalem: Alternative Information Center, Memorandum no. 1/96, 1996). Ahmad Rwaidy, *The Israeli Restrictions on Arab Presence and Promotion of Jewish Presence in Jerusalem* (Jerusalem: Jerusalem Center for Women, 1997). Anita Vitullo, "Israel's Social Policy in Arab Jerusalem," *Jerusalem Quarterly File* (Palestinian, English) (Jerusalem: Institute of Jerusalem Studies) (fall 1998): 10–30. Graham Usher, "Returning to the Source: The Politics of Housing in East Jerusalem," *Jerusalem Quarterly File* (winter 1998): 19–22. LAW, Jerusalem Unit, *The Demographic Imperative: Jerusalem 2000* (Occasional Paper Series no. 1) (Jerusalem: Palestinian Society for the Protection of Human Rights and the Environment—LAW, March 2001). LAW, *Human Rights Violations in Arab Jerusalem;* LAW, *The Deportation of Protected Persons* (Jerusalem: Palestinian Society for the Protection of Human Rights and the Environment—LAW, August 1999). Applied Research Institute–Jerusalem, *Expanding Jewish Presence in the Old City of Jerusalem* (Jerusalem: Applied Research Institute–Jerusalem, n.d. [ca. 1998]); Applied Research Institute–Jerusalem, *The Status of Jerusalem Reconstructed: Israel's Unilateral Actions Determine the Future of Jerusalem* (Jerusalem: Applied Research Institute–Jerusalem, n.d. [ca. 1998]); and Foundation for Middle East Peace, *Israel's Uncertain Victory in Jerusalem*, Special Report (Washington, DC: Foundation for Middle East Peace, spring 1999).

11. Jeff Halper, Coordinator of the Israeli Committee Against House Demolitions, in an interview with Kate B. Rouhana, June 22, 1999, quoted in Rouhana, *The Reality of Jerusalem's Palestinians Today*, p. 18.

12. Applied Research Institute–Jerusalem, *Expanding Jewish Presence in the Old City of Jerusalem*, p. 3; American Friends Service Committee, *The Old City of Jerusalem: History in Brief* (Philadelphia: Israel-Palestinian Publishing Program, American Friends Service Committee, n.d.); and LAW, *Land and Settlement Policy in Jerusalem* (Jerusalem: Jerusalem Unit of the Palestinian Society for the Protection of Human Rights and the Environment—LAW, first printed in 1999, reprinted 2000), p. 25.

13. Rouhana, *The Reality of Jerusalem's Palestinians Today*, p. 57.

14. LAW, *Land and Settlement Policy in Jerusalem*, p. 4.

15. Cheshin, Hutman, and Melamed, *Separate and Unequal*, p. 37.

16. Ibid., p. 56.

17. Ibid.

18. Ibid., p. 58.

19. LAW, *Land and Settlement Policy in Jerusalem*, p. 5.

20. Rouhana, *The Reality of Jerusalem's Palestinians Today*, pp. 9–21.

21. LAW, *The Demographic Imperative*, p. 5.

22. The best piece on the multifaceted aspects of taxation and the paucity of services endured by East Jerusalem Palestinians is Vitullo, "Israel's Social Policy in Arab Jerusalem," pp. 10–30.

23. Ibid., p. 14.

24. Cheshin, Hutman and Melamed, *Separate and Unequal*, pp. 124–157.

25. Nadav Shragai, "The Sewer Flows in the East, the Money Flows in the West," *Ha'aretz*, June 7, 2000. B'Tselem, *Services and Infrastructure* (Jerusalem: B'Tselem, the Israeli Information Center for Human Rights in the Occupied Territories, 2000); Vitullo, "Israel's Social Policy in Arab Jerusalem," p. 16.

26. LAW, *The Demographic Imperative*, p. 9, citing *Jerusalem Statistical Yearbook,* 1998.

27. Rouhana, *The Reality of Jerusalem's Palestinians Today*, p. 27.

28. Human Rights Watch, *Second Class: Discrimination Against Palestinian Arab Children in Israel's Schools* (New York: Human Rights Watch, 2001).

29. Cheshin, Hutman, and Melamed, *Separate and Unequal*, pp. 103, 114, 116.

30. *Education* (Jerusalem: Jerusalem Watch, a joint effort between the Palestinian Nongovernmental Organization Network and the Norwegian Association of NGOs for Palestine—Fellesutvalget for Palestina, and hosted by the Palestinian Society for the Protection of Human Rights and the Environment—LAW, March 2000).

31. *Health Services* (Jerusalem: Jerusalem Watch/Palestinian Nongovernmental Organization Network /Fellesutvalget/LAW, March 2000).

32. See, for example, LAW, *The National Insurance Unit and the Violation of the Rights of Pregnant Women and Their Newborn in East Jerusalem* (Jerusalem: Jerusalem Unit of the Palestinian Society for the Protection of Human Rights and the Environment—LAW, 1999), and Hadas Ziv, "Health: A Right, Not a Favor," *Jerusalem Quarterly File*, no. 10 (2000).

33. Quoted in B'Tselem, *Revocation of Social Rights and Health Insurance* (Jerusalem: B'Tselem—the Israeli Information Center for Human Rights in the Occupied Territories, n.d. [ca. 2000]).

34. Ibid.

35. Rouhana, *The Reality of Jerusalem's Palestinians Today*, pp. 39–42.

36. Hanthala, *Residency Rights: Additional Problems* (Jerusalem: Hanthala Palestine, 1999).

37. Noga Kadman, *Families Torn Apart: Separation of Palestinian Families in the Occupied Territories* (Jerusalem: HaMoked, the Center for the Defense of the Individual, and B'Tselem—the Israeli Information Center for Human Rights in the Occupied Territories, 1999).

38. Stein, *The Quiet Deportation Continues*, p. 20.

39. Kadman, *Families Torn Apart*, pp. 11–12.

40. Ibid.; Stein, *The Quiet Deportation.*

41. Kadman et al., *Families Torn Apart.*

42. Ibid., p. 11.

43. Stein, *The Quiet Deportation, pp.* 14–15, and Stein, *The Quiet Deportation Continues*, pp. 7–9. LAW, *ID Confiscation and Removal of Residency Rights* (Jerusalem: Jerusalem Watch/Palestinian Nongovernmental

Organization Network/Fellesutvalget/LAW, March 2000); LAW, *The Deportation of Protected Persons;* Applied Research Institute–Jerusalem, *Palestinian Jerusalemites Are Threatened to Lose Their IDs Under New Israeli Regulations* (Jerusalem: Applied Research Institute–Jerusalem, 1998); Usama Halabi, "Revoking Permanent Residency: A Legal Review of Israeli Policy," *Jerusalem Quarterly File,* no. 9 (2000); Lea Tsemel and Ingrid Jaradat Gassner, *The Trap Is Closing on Palestinian Jerusalemites* (Jerusalem, Israeli Occasional, English) (Memorandum no. 1/96, Alternative Information Center, 1996); Elizabeth Campbell, "Maximum Territory, Minimum Population: The Laboratory for the Policies of Zionist Colonialization," *News from Within* 14, no. 11 (December 1998): 8–13; Manal Jamal and Buthaina Darwish, *Exposed Realities: Palestinian Residency Rights in the "Self Rule Areas" Three Years After Partial Israeli Redeployment* (Bethlehem: BADIL Resource Center for Palestinian Residency and Refugee Rights, and the Alternative Information Center, 1997).

    44. B'Tselem, *Residency and Social Rights* (Jerusalem: B'Tselem—the Israeli Information Center for Human Rights in the Occupied Territories, n.d.).

    45. Hanthala, *Residency Rights: Additional Problems*, pp. 2–3.

    46. B'Tselem, *Revocation of Residency in East Jerusalem* (Jerusalem: B'Tselem—the Israeli Information Center for Human Rights in the Occupied Territories, 2000).

    47. Stein, *The Quiet Deportation*, p. 14.

    48. Stein, *The Quiet Deportation Continues*, p. 15; Rouhana, *The Reality of Jerusalem's Palestinians Today*, p. 61.

    49. Cheshin, Hutman, and Melamed, *Separate and Unequal*, pp. 51–52.

    50. Ibid., p. 37, and LAW, *Land and Settlement Policy in Jerusalem*, p. 14.

    51. Data culled from the following: Cheshin, Hutman, and Melamed, *Separate and Unequal*; LAW, *Land and Settlement Policy in Jerusalem;* Applied Research Institute–Jerusalem, *The Status of Jerusalem Reconstructed: Israel's Unilateral Actions Determine the Future of Jerusalem* (Jerusalem: Applied Research Institute–Jerusalem, n.d. [ca. 1999]); Jerusalem Watch, *Settlements in and Around Jerusalem* (Jerusalem: Applied Research Center–Jerusalem, n.d. [ca. 2000]); Yuval Ginbar, *On the Way to Annexation: Human Rights Violations Resulting from the Establishment and Expansion of Ma'aleh Adumim Settlement* (Jerusalem: B'Tselem—the Israeli Information Center for Human Rights in the Occupied Territories, 1999); Settlement Database, *Settlements in the West Bank* (Washington, DC: Foundation for Middle East Peace, 1999); PASSIA, *1999*, pp. 271–273; Marwan Bazbaz, "Settlement in the West Bank and the Gaza Strip," *Palestine-Israeli Journal of Politics, Economics, and Culture* 4, no. 2 (1999); Matthew Brubacher, "A Reality Check for Jerusalem Settlements: The Case of Gilo," *Jerusalem Quarterly File*, no. 10 (2000).

    52. B'Tselem, *Urban Planning* (Jerusalem: B'Tselem—the Israeli Information Center for Human Rights in the Occupied Territories, n.d.).

    53. B'Tselem, *Urban Planning*.

    54. LAW, *Land and Settlement Policy in Jerusalem*, pp. 8–4; LAW, *The Demographic Imperative;* Applied Research Institute–Jerusalem, *Expanding Jewish Presence in the Old City of Jerusalem;* Applied Research Institute–Jerusalem, *The Status of Jerusalem Reconstructed;* LAW, *Human Rights Violations in Arab Jerusalem*.

55. *House Demolitions* (Jerusalem: Jerusalem Watch/Palestinian Nongovernmental Organization Network/Fellesutvalget/LAW, March 2000).

56. Graham Usher, "Returning to the Source: The Politics of Housing in East Jerusalem," *Jerusalem Quarterly File* 1, no. 1 (1998): 19–22; and B'Tselem, "Discrimination in Planning, Building, and Land Expropriation" (information sheet) (Jerusalem: B'Tselem—the Israeli Information Center for Human Rights in the Occupied Territories, circa 2000).

57. B'Tselem, *Urban Planning*.

58. Vitullo, "Israel's Social Policy in Arab Jerusalem," p. 13.

59. Applied Research Institute–Jerusalem, *Expanding Jewish Presence in the Old City of Jerusalem*, p. 9.

60. LAW, *The Demographic Imperative*, p. 16, and Applied Research Institute–Jerusalem, *Expanding Jewish Presence in the Old City of Jerusalem*, p. 9.

61. LAW, *Settlement Expansion and House Demolition: Jerusalem Under Barak, Part 1* (in three parts) (Jerusalem: Palestinian Society for the Protection of Human Rights and the Environment—LAW, 2001), pp. 6–7. Also see *Jerusalem* (Jerusalem Watch/Palestinian Nongovernmental Organization Network/Fellesutvalget/LAW, March 2000).

62. Jeff Halper, *Jerusalem Facts* (London: Friends of Al-Aqsa, n.d. [ca. 2000]). Also see LAW, *Settlement Expansion and House Demolition: Jerusalem Under Barak, Part 1*), pp. 6–7.

63. Yair Ettinger, "Jerusalem Families Get House Demolition, Sealing Orders," *Ha'aretz*, September 9, 2002.

64. Cheshin, Hutman, and Melamed, *Separate and Unequal*, pp. 150–151.

65. Ibid., p. 150.

66. LAW, *Human Rights Violations in Arab Jerusalem*, p. 12.

67. Cheshin, Hutman, and Melamed, *Separate and Unequal*, pp. 30–32.

68. Ibid., p. 32.

69. See Rouhana, *The Reality of Jerusalem's Palestinians Today*, p. 10.

70. Cheshin, Hutman, and Melamed, *Separate and Unequal*, pp. 60–62.

71. LAW, *Land and Settlement Policy in Jerusalem*, p. 25.

72. Cheshin, Hutman, and Melamed, *Separate and Unequal*, pp. 211–214. The authors discuss at some length the Klugman Report, which was commissioned in 1993 by the Israeli prime minister to investigate the illegal transfers of government funds (via various ministries) to these settlers (pp. 214–215).

73. See, for example, Margot Patterson, "Bingo Tycoon Subsidizes Extremism in Israel," *National Catholic Reporter,* October 18, 2002; Christopher D. Cook, "The Bingo Connection: How an Impoverished Southern California Town Became a Cash Machine for Controversial Jewish Settlements in the Middle East," *Mother Jones,* September/October 2000; Americans for Peace Now, "Controversial Bingo King Bets on ZOA [Zionist Organization of America], Faces California Legislation," *Middle East Peace Report* 3, no. 30 (February 19, 2002); Charlie LeDuff, "California Bingo Hall Plays on World Stage," *New York Times,* November 25, 2002; and Akiva Eldar, "Checkpoints in the Territories and Jerusalem," *Ha'aretz,* February 21, 2002.

74. Cheshin, Hutman, and Melamed, *Separate and Unequal*, pp. 215–216.

75. Ibid., p. 224.

76. Michael Schwartz, "Collusion in Jerusalem: How the Government and

the Settlers Conspire to Take Over Houses and Land," *Challenge*, no. 50 (July–August 1998).

77. Applied Research Institute–Jerusalem, *Initial Construction in the Palestinian Ras El-Amoud Neighborhood* (Jerusalem: Applied Research Institute–Jerusalem, in conjunction with the Land Research Center, 1999); Pope Mussa Bishop, *Jerusalem/al-Quds* (Jerusalem: Coptic Orthodox Church, 1998), available online; Michael Schwartz, "Ras al-Amoud: Noha al-Gul Fighting Alone," *Challenge*, no. 46 (November–December 1997); Applied Research Institute–Jerusalem, *Expanding Jewish Presence in the Old City of Jerusalem* (Jerusalem: Applied Research Institute–Jerusalem, 1997). Also see LAW, *Litigating Silwan: A Case Study of Silwan Village* (Jerusalem: Palestinian Society for the Protection of Human Rights and the Environment— LAW, June 1996). Wadi al-Joz has been as negatively affected as Silwan. See Dalia Habash, "*Wadi al-Joz*: In Focus," *Jerusalem Quarterly File* 1, no. 1 (1998): 43–50.

78. LAW, *Settlement Expansion and House Demolition: Jerusalem Under Barak, Part 2: Settlements and Settlers* (in three parts) (Jerusalem: Palestinian Society for the Protection of Human Rights and the Environment—LAW, 2001), pp. 1–2; Cheshin, Hutman, and Melamed, *Separate and Unequal*, pp. 211–224.

79. Schwartz, "Collusion in Jerusalem: How the Government and the Settlers Conspire to Take Over Houses and Land," p. 4; LAW, *Jerusalem Under Barak, Part 2: Settlements and Settlers*, pp. 2–3.

80. LAW, *Land and Settlement Policy in Jerusalem*, p. 28; Martha Wenger, "Jerusalem Primer," *MERIP Middle East Report*, May–June 1993. Also see Schwartz, "Ras al-Amoud: Noha al-Gul Fighting Alone"; Maureen Meehan, "Eviction of Silwan Family Sets Scene for Accelerated Ethnic Cleansing of Jerusalem," *Washington Report on Middle East Affairs* (January/February 1999): 27, 98; Richard Z. Chesnoff, "Love—and Leave— Thy Neighbor," *Jewish World Review*, July 8, 1998.

81. Patterson, "Bingo Tycoon Subsidizes Extremism in Israel"; Cook, "The Bingo Connection: How an Impoverished Southern California Town Became a Cash Machine for Controversial Jewish Settlements in the Middle East"; and Americans for Peace Now, "Controversial Bingo King Bets on ZOA [Zionist Organization of America], Faces California Legislation."

82. Akiva Eldar, "Checkpoints in the Territories—and Jerusalem," *Ha'aretz Week's End*, February 24, 2002.

83. Nadav Shragai, "More Jews Moving into Arab Musrara," *Ha'aretz*, October 4, 2002.

84. Nadav Shragai, "Jews Buy Up Property in East Jerusalem: Prime Minister Ariel Sharon Encouraged Move into Arab *Musrara* Neighborhood," *Ha'aretz*, April 14, 2002; Nadav Shragai, "Arabs to Be Evicted from Jerusalem Enclave," *Ha'aretz*, April 19, 2002; Nadav Shragai, "Elon Plan Would Encircle Old City with Jewish Outposts," *Ha'aretz*, April 23, 2002.

85. Nadav Shragai, "Jews Move into East Jerusalem House over Protests by Its Arab Owner," *Ha'aretz*, September 4, 2002.

86. Jerusalem Watch, *Metropolitan and Greater Jerusalem* (Jerusalem: Jerusalem Watch/Palestinian Nongovernmental Organization Network/ Fellesutvalget/LAW, March 2000).

87. James Bennet, "Once Disputed Settlement Now Becoming Part of the Israeli Landscape," *New York Times*, August 11, 2002.

88. "Economy Down, but Har Homa Sales Up," *Arutz Sheva Israel National News*, August 2, 2002. Also see Akiva Eldar, "Checkpoints in the Territories—and Jerusalem," *Ha'aretz*, February 21, 2002.

89. Jerusalem Watch, *Metropolitan and Greater Jerusalem*.

90. Ibid.

91. Ibid.

92. Ginbar, *On the Way to Annexation*.

93. Ibid.

94. Applied Research Institute–Jerusalem, *The Status of Jerusalem Reconstructed*, p. 4.

95. Tamar Hausman, "Anglo *Olim* Wooed for New Homes in *Gush Etzion*," *Ha'aretz*, November 16, 2001.

96. Applied Research Institute–Jerusalem, *Givat Hazayit (Um Tale' Hill): A New Israeli Colony in the Southern Vicinity of Bethlehem* (Jerusalem: Applied Research Institute–Jerusalem, 1997).

97. Ziv Maor, "Additional Settlement Planned for Gush Etzion," *Ha'aretz*, March 24, 2001.

98. Joe Eskenazi, "JVS Director Sees Small Signs of Hope During Argentina Visit," *The Jewish News Bulletin of Northern California,* January 3, 2003; Jacob Kovadloff, "Crisis in Argentina," *The American Jewish Committee Publications* (press release), June 23, 2002; Florencia Arbiser, "Americans Seek Solutions for Argentine Community," Jewish Telegraphic Agency, January 22, 2003.

99. Ruth Westheimer and Steven Kaplan, *Surviving Salvation: The Ethiopian Jewish Family in Transition* (New York: New York University Press, 1993); and Tudor Parfitt, ed., *The Beta Israel in Ethiopia and Israel: Studies on Ethiopian Jews* (London: Curzon Press, 1995).

100. Neri Livneh, "Coming Home," *Ha'aretz Weeks End,* July 18, 2002.

101. Amiram Barkat, "Jewish Agency Plans Fast-Track Conversion for Immigrants from CIS [Commonwealth of Independent States]," *Ha'aretz,* March 6, 2003.

102. Nadav Shragai and Baruch Kra, "Committee Approves Jerusalem Ring Road Through West Bank: The Plan Effectively Puts an End to the Possibility That Abu Dis Will Revert to the PA," *Ha'aretz*, March 15, 2001.

103. Applied Research Institute–Jerusalem, *The Circling of East Jerusalem—Roads 45 and 5* (Jerusalem: Applied Research Institute–Jerusalem, 1999). LAW, *A Chronicle of Settlement Activity Since the Wye Plantation Agreement* (Jerusalem: Palestinian Society for the Protection of Human Rights and the Environment—LAW, 1999). Matthew Brubacher, "The Jerusalem Ring Road: The Good, the Bad, and the Explosive," *News from Within* 17, no. 4 (May 2001): 11–13.

104. Brubacher, "The Jerusalem Ring Road," p. 12.

105. Applied Research Institute–Jerusalem, *The Circling of East Jerusalem—Roads 45 and 5*; LAW, *A Chronicle of Settlement Activity Since the Wye Plantation Agreement*; Brubacher, "The Jerusalem Ring Road."

106. Gershon Baskin, "Negotiating the Settlements: The Success of Right-Wing Entrapment Against Peace," November 1, 2000, available online from the

Israel/Palestine Center for Research and Information); Uri Avnery, "The Day Barak's Bubble Burst" (Jerusalem: Gush Shalom, September 15, 2001) (available online); Alain Gresh (translated by Wendy Kristianasen), "The Middle East: How the Peace Was Lost," *Le Monde Diplomatique* (French Daily), September 1, 2001, online English; Stanley Heller, "The Myth of Camp David," *The Struggle* (online); Amira Hass, "The Compromise That Wasn't Found at Camp David," *Ha'aretz*, November 14, 2000.

107. Amira Hass, "Deceptive 'Generosity,'" *Ha'aretz*, December 13, 2000.

108. Amira Hass, "You Can Drive Along and Never See an Arab," *Ha'aretz*, January 22, 2003.

109. Avnery, "The Day Barak's Bubble Burst."

110. Gresh, "The Middle East: How the Peace Was Lost."

6

The Palestinian Authority: Politics, Corruption, and Repression

The leadership of Yasir Arafat *perpetuates* rather than alleviates this horror [i.e., the occupation]: he delivers security to Israel by punishing his own people, lying to them that he is bringing us nearer to self-determination, deceiving them into believing that he acts in their name and interests. With his corruption he has stripped his own people of their resources, squandered their wealth, abused their lives further. What right does he claim to do all this while robbing people, forcing them into monopolies, allowing himself to be accountable to no one as he bribes, bullies, corrupts everyone in his way.

—Edward W. Said[1]

Yasser Arafat and the organizations he has overseen—first the Palestine Liberation Organization and, today, the Palestinian Authority (PLO and PA, respectively)—have been present throughout this analysis although often obscured by the focus on Israel. Chapter 1, however, noted how the PLO, shepherded by Yasser Arafat's skilled leadership, transformed itself from a revolutionary organization dedicated to the liberation of Palestine to a political movement committed to establishing an independent state alongside Israel through the use of diplomacy. Notably, this process occurred during the period of the PLO's greatest strength and international legitimacy. It culminated in the PLO's acceptance of United Nations Resolution 242, the recognition of Israel's right to exist, and an official renunciation of terrorism.

In Chapter 2 I examined Arafat's surrender of Palestinian political and national rights in the context of the PLO's nadir. In the Declaration of Principles (DOP), he conceded that Israel was not required to withdraw from all the territories conquered in 1967 (the West Bank, Gaza, and East Jerusalem), the essence of Resolution 242. Instead, the PLO would negotiate with Israel the areas from which it would withdraw. He agreed to leave to final-status negotiations the most important issues, including the borders, the status of Jerusalem, the fate of the refugees, and the nature of Palestinian sovereignty. The DOP and the subsequent agreements that grew out of it were not a victory for Arafat; rather, they reflected his failure to find a just and equitable solution to his people's problems.

Chapters 3–5 have shown that Israeli policies led to a marked deterioration in the living conditions of the Palestinian people between 1993 and 2000. Building on that analysis, this chapter examines how the Palestinian Authority contributed to the decay of Palestinian society during that same period. At some levels, the roles of Arafat and the PA were determined by Israel's constant demands that they do more to protect Israel's security. Indeed, Israeli-PA security cooperation resulted in gross human rights violations against Palestinians. But there is also clear evidence that Arafat's policies violated human and civil rights.

Indeed, the PA contributed to the suffering of the people it was supposed to represent. Through corruption, economic monopolies, authoritarianism, repression, disdain for democratic processes and judicial fairness, `asha'iriyyah (reviving the *hamayel*, or clan system), nepotism, and other practices, PA policies exacerbated the fragmentation of Palestinian society, increased class and *hamayel* divisions, contributed to the growing economic impoverishment, and were largely responsible for the social disintegration that occurred during this time. In other words, the roles of Yasser Arafat and the PA are central to a comprehensive understanding of the increasing problems and worsening quality of life for Palestinians after September 1993. The frustration and disappointment caused by the PA were part and parcel of the explosive mix that erupted into the Al-Aqsa intifada, the second uprising that began in September 2000. The following examines the PA under three broad categories: *nature of governance; corruption;* and *human rights violations.* These are interconnected.

It is notable, although not mitigating, that the problems with the PA did not occur in a vacuum. The PA was in the Occupied Territories because Israel allowed it to be there, and it functioned within the limits Israel imposed and acted at Israel's behest as a surrogate security force to protect Israeli interests. It was not in Israel's interests that the PA be a democracy. Recall Prime Minister Yitzhak Rabin's comments that Arafat could crack down on political opposition without a supreme court or a B'Tselem breathing down his neck.[2] Moreover, a democracy would have held Arafat accountable for Israel's noncompliance with the principles of the Oslo Accords. Israeli analyst Gershon Baskin writes in this regard: "Israel and the United States are/were afraid of too much Palestinian democracy out of fear that through this democracy anti-peace forces . . . would increase their power. . . . In my view, the absence of democracy is one of the main underlying roots of the Palestinian intifada."[3]

Democracies are messy; people react when their interests are threatened. Citizens are less likely to be taken in by lofty rhetoric when their everyday reality stands in stark contradiction. In dictatorships, only one individual has to be persuaded, and he in turn imposes his decisions on his quiescent people. Thus, Israel and the United States were perfectly contented with Arafat's authoritarian rule—despite the specious demands they made for reform and democracy in the summer of 2002, after Israel's destruction of the PA.

Most of the economic corruption in the PA—in particular the monopolies—involved Israel as well. Israelis were partners with PA officials in the latter's economic aggrandizement. Their activity was quasilegal (sometimes perfectly legal) in Israel and, moreover, benefited the Israeli economy as well as individual entrepreneurs. Where it was questionable, the Israeli authorities tended to overlook irregularities in the interest of peace. But how such arrangements affected the Palestinian people was of no concern to the Israeli government (and neither were the lavish lifestyles and expensive cars and villas of the elites). Indeed, from Israel's perspective, if Arafat's close advisers were materially contented and benefiting from the system, this provided them an incentive to continue playing by Israel's rules of the game. In fact, Israel provided these officials numerous privileges (e.g., VIP passes that allowed them to move freely across the closures, curfews, etc.) so as to sweeten their living situations. None of this, however, justifies or excuses the corruption engaged in by PA officials.

Finally, with regard to the human rights violations, Tel Aviv was indifferent to whatever measures were taken against the Palestinian people as long as Israeli security interests were protected. Israel exerted constant and intense pressure on the PA to arrest more individuals, prohibit incitement, suppress the opposition, and take all possible preventive measures to ensure that no violent incidents would occur. Still, nothing exculpates the PA for its human rights abuses—a great many of which were entirely unrelated to Israel's security needs but rather were perpetrated simply to silence any criticism of Arafat and the PA. It is also true that the personal vested interests PA officials had in the ongoing relationship with Israel outweighed, in all instances, concern for the human rights of the people. In short, PA officials benefited—politically, economically, and socially—from the peace process, which in turn gave them a stake in its perpetuation, despite the fact that it negatively affected the Palestinian people.

Governance

President Arafat

It is important to note at the outset that when Yasser Arafat returned from exile in Tunis to Gaza and Jericho in May and July 1994, he was welcomed with enthusiasm by a majority of Palestinians in the Occupied Territories. Arafat had been not only the leader of the PLO since 1969; more important, he was the personification of Palestinian nationalism, the symbol of Palestinian identity, and the embodiment of Palestinian aspirations. He alone, among the PLO leaders, had enjoyed a special status among Palestinians throughout the diaspora and (though perhaps somewhat less so) in the Occupied Territories, even with the many who supported different political factions. Thus, his return was a momentous occasion and was seen, in the context of the belief held by the majority that the Oslo Accords were the first step on the road to independent statehood, as a success for Arafat as well as for the Palestinian cause.

During the following seven years, however, as a consequence of Arafat's autocratic style, the corruption of those around him, and growing popular awareness of the fatal flaws in the Oslo agreements, his personal popularity fell steadily. In June 1995, one year after Arafat and the PA were seated in Gaza and Jericho, the Jerusalem Media and Communications Center (JMCC) conducted a public opinion poll in the West Bank and Gaza Strip that randomly sampled 1,397 Palestinians.[4] The results were telling. JMCC posed the question: "President Arafat has been considered a symbol of the struggle and aspirations of the Palestinian people and the Palestinian cause. What do you think today?" Only 60.9 percent agreed that "he was and still is a symbol" whereas 22.5 percent believed "he is no longer a symbol for the Palestinian people and cause." The same poll found that only 39.4 percent of West Bank and Gaza Strip individuals supported his leadership. These figures suggest that though a majority of Palestinians still considered Yasser Arafat the symbol of Palestinian nationalism, far fewer trusted his leadership abilities. The data is particularly interesting in that 74.9 percent of the persons polled supported negotiations with Israel for a peaceful settlement.[5] By the time the Al-Aqsa intifada erupted in September 2000, Arafat's standing among his own people was so low—25.7 percent—that if he had attempted to stop the uprising it is probable that he would have been deposed or assassinated. In some quarters, he was even being seen as a collaborator with the Israeli cause. Comprehending this situation is critical to understanding why Arafat did not, as Israel demanded, rein in the elements actively engaged in the uprising, though it is unclear that he would have been successful even had he tried (see Table 6.1).

The Nature of PA Governance

Two broad issues have undergirded the problems of PA governance—in particular with regard to civil institutions and nongovernmental organizations (NGOs), and in respect of the rule of law. The first is the personal style of Yasser Arafat, which in the years prior to Oslo had

Table 6.1   Support for Arafat and Fateh, January 1994–April 2001

Date	Which is the Palestinian personality that you trust most?[a] % Supporting Arafat	Which political party/trend do you trust most?[b] % Supporting Fateh
Jan. 1994		40.4
July 1994		40.9
June 1995	39.4	46.6
Oct. 1995	36.8	41.3
Jan. 1996	41.0	38.9
Feb. 1996	36.3	39.2
Aug. 1996	38.5	34.0
Nov. 1996	44.5	42.0
Dec. 1996	41.2	35.2
Apr. 1997	43.4	38.5
May 1997	39.8	37.9
July 1997	37.6	34.8
Nov. 1997	46.4	40.9
May 1998	38.7	32.9
Aug. 1998	32.6	34.3
Mar. 1999	38.8	37.7
Aug. 1999	28.0	28.0
Sept. 1999	32.0	33.8
June 2000	31.8	34.5
Dec. 2000	25.7	32.1
Apr. 2001	32.3	35.1

Source: This polling data was carried out by the Jerusalem Media and Communication Center—Public Opinion Polls, Jerusalem, Palestine.

Notes: a. Respondents were given a choice of 8–10 local Palestinian leaders and leaders of PLO factions plus "Do not trust anyone," "others," and "no opinion."

b. Choices included Fateh, Hamas, PFLP, Islamic Jihad, NDC, DFFLP, PPP, Fida, "other Islamic parties," "others," "I do not trust anyone," "No opinion."

become increasingly autocratic. Once he returned to Palestine as President Arafat (Al-Ra'ees, or the "Boss"), he became imperious and absolutist, marshaling all power unilaterally in his person. As one analyst wrote concerning Arafat's unprecedented concentration of power:

> He exercises more than sixty functions, which include not only those of a chief executive and chief of state, but also extend to many mundane chores. The fact that those functions include several chairmanships of newly established boards, and no less than twelve new committees of the transitional authority . . . [suggests] that the national project is in trouble.[6]

This observation was made in 1995; the centralization of power in Arafat's hands grew exponentially every year thereafter.

A second underlying issue involves the clash of political cultures between local Palestinians and the PLO cadres—the "returnees" or, somewhat pejoratively, the "Tunisians"—that Arafat brought with him from Tunis to govern. These were mainly men who had left Beirut with Arafat in 1982 and who regrouped in Tunis, running the political affairs of the PLO from there. Their style of governance was centralized, secretive, partisan, elitist, and disdainful of pluralism and democracy.

By contrast, within the Occupied Territories there were many highly educated and experienced individuals in all areas from political leadership to professional expertise. Moreover, the majority of Palestinians in the Occupied Territories had developed a strong commitment to political democracy and civil society.[7] These attitudes grew, to a considerable extent, from their close proximity to Israel. Although these people hated Israel for the occupation, they admired Israel for its democracy compared to the dictatorships in the surrounding Arab countries. This is illustrated in a series of biannual public opinion polls conducted by the Palestinian Center for Policy and Survey Research (CPRS).[8] The following provides one example, but the results were similar each time the question was asked. In December 1996, CPRS asked respondents to rate the "status of democracy and human rights under the PA." Only 8.7 percent evaluated it as "very good" and 34.2 percent as "good." The same question was then posed regarding the United States, Israel, Jordan, and Egypt. On the United States, 44.5 percent rated it "very good" and 24.1 percent rated it "good." On Israel, 53.1 percent rated it "very good" and 25 percent "good." For Jordan, 7.8 percent evaluated democracy and human rights "very good" and 24.6 percent "good." Egypt was rated as 8.4 percent "very good" and 24.4 percent "good."[9] Strikingly, Palestinian respect for the status of human rights and democracy is higher for Israel than for the United States. Yet the significant point is that Arafat and the PA completely ignored the importance of democracy and human rights to the people they were governing and proceeded to rule by fiat.[10]

Additionally, Palestinians in the Occupied Territories had developed a wide variety of institutions of civil society. These began to emerge in the early 1980s as an integral part of the resistance to occupation and gradually developed into a network of professional, efficient organizations. Their origin grew out of the social needs of the Palestinian people—health, legal aid, industry, education, and others. They included the Union of Palestinian Medical Relief Committees, the Palestinian Agricultural Relief Committee, a variety of women's organizations such as the Women's Affairs Center in Gaza, the community "popular committees," the Gaza Community Mental Health Program, and others. Palestinians took pride in these local initiatives nurtured under adversity, and they considered the nascent institutions to be the foundation of their future state.[11]

In the early 1990s, Palestinian civil society underwent a profound transformation, from populist to professional. Voluntary associations with strong links to the community began to give way to professional, salaried NGOs. The new organizations became controversial within Palestinian society—primarily because of the NGOs' dependence on foreign funding and their concomitant need to follow the donors' programs—requirements that were often seriously at odds with the needs of the people.[12] Of concern here, though, is the fact that Arafat was dismissive of the skills, expertise, and dynamism these people could have brought to the PA; moreover, he soon attempted to control and undermine them.

Arafat's first reaction to the NGOs after his arrival in Gaza-Jericho was to ignore them—to treat them and their experience as irrelevant and unworthy of recognition. For a brief period, the new ministries of the PA, the well-known national personalities that returned to lead them, and the general euphoria associated with having a Palestinian government overshadowed the NGOs. Nevertheless, they soon reemerged, energized and potent because of the rapid disenchantment felt by the populace with the PA for its failure to provide services or improve living conditions. Thus, the NGOs continued to meet the basic needs of the populace as they had done prior to the PA's arrival. Moreover, their external financing meant that salaries paid by the NGOs tended to be higher than the average salaries for comparable work in the government sector. For example, a teacher is typically paid between $400 and $600 per month, whereas an average NGO worker earns between $800 and $1,000 per month in the field. Additionally, political opponents of the

PA tended to congregate in the NGOs, and to the extent that criticism of Arafat or the PA was publicly expressed, it most often came from individuals associated with NGOs. All this incurred the wrath of Arafat.

Since their inception, these grassroots groups had been distinguished by their independence, which was a matter of great self-respect to the individuals involved. Yet this very independence was intolerable to Arafat, who was determined not to permit the NGOs to function outside his control. Arafat's attempts to extinguish their autonomy, in turn, made the NGOs detractors of the PA's authoritarian political rule. Soon, the PA was waging a concerted campaign of criticism, harassment, and vilification against the NGOs and their prominent participants. Finally, the atmosphere became so ugly that the Palestinian Legislative Council attempted to pass a law that would regulate relations between the NGOs and the executive.

The Legislative Council drafted a law that was generally acceptable to the NGO community. It defined the relationship between the PA and NGOs; made the NGOs accountable for their practices and finances to both the government and the public (ironic in that no such requirement existed for PA accountability and transparency); and required all NGOs to register with the Ministry of Justice. The bill passed the requisite three readings in the Legislative Council—the final in December 1998—and was forwarded to the executive for Arafat's signature (without which it could not become law). Arafat declined to sign for several months, then returned it to the Legislative Council with an amendment. The NGOs would be required to register not with the Ministry of Justice but with the Ministry of the Interior, placing them directly under the PA's security and intelligence apparatus. Moreover, they would have to obtain a license from Interior, which would be predicated on an investigation and approval by the security services. Initially, the Legislative Council refused to accept the amendment, but several months later it capitulated to Arafat's wishes. The NGOs, however, refused to register under the Ministry of the Interior, and relations between the NGO community and the PA continued to deteriorate thereafter. Loyalty was the preeminent characteristic that Arafat valued in his advisers. Thus, loyalists rather than experts or professionals ran the PA.

The Tunisians and the Security Services

Unlike the Palestinians in the Occupied Territories, the Tunisians had no experience with or concept of democracy, civil society, human rights, press and individual freedom, citizens' rights, and other tenets of democratic rule. They knew only autocracy, paternalism, nepotism, and absolutism, which were the methods by which they exercised control over the Palestinian people.[13] Notably, Arafat's closest advisers and inner circle—the only individuals who had access to him—were all Tunisians.[14] No one locally (from the West Bank, Gaza, or East Jerusalem) was admitted to the inner sanctum.[15] Indeed, the individual who Arafat trusts most and has been his most intimate confidant is not even Palestinian. Muhammad Rashid, an Iraqi, is the only person other than Arafat who has knowledge of the PA's financial accounts.[16] Because of his non-Palestinian origins, Rashid is totally dependent on Arafat—and therefore totally loyal.

It did not take long for the local Palestinians to come to detest the foreigners—for their exclusive proximity to Arafat, for the methods by which they governed, and for their increasingly obvious corruption.[17] Perhaps most galling to the locals were the six separate security services (which eventually became eleven), initially comprising between 35,000 and 40,000 individuals, that Arafat created. In fairness, it must be reiterated that in every Palestinian-Israeli agreement, Israel demanded the creation of a strong Palestinian security force to provide unconditional security for Israel. In the 1995 Interim Agreement (Oslo II), for example, the Palestinians are obliged "to act systematically against all expressions [including verbal] of [Palestinian] violence and terror"; to "arrest and prosecute [Palestinian] individuals suspected of perpetrating acts of violence and terror"; and to "cooperate in the exchange of information as well as coordinate policies and activities" with the Israeli security services.[18]

Arafat, however, took that as license to create multiple security forces, all directly or indirectly under his control. They acted not only to protect Israel, but also interfered in every aspect of Palestinian institutional and individual life. Collectively they were known as the Palestinian Security Services (PSS), and subsumed some eleven different agencies including:

1. The National Security Force (NSF), which coordinated security-related missions and information gathering with Israel's security and intelligence services.

2. The Preventive Security Force (PSF), which was the largest and most powerful of the PA's internal security services. It was involved in preventive actions against Palestinian militants and opposition groups. It was headed by Jibril Rajoub in the West Bank and Muhammad Dahlan in Gaza—two of the most powerful men in the PA.

3. The Presidential Guard (PG) or Force 17 (also called al-Amn al-Ri'asah), which had the specific task of protecting Arafat.

4. Military Intelligence, headed by Musa Arafat, which gathered intelligence on civilian groups and scrutinized the PA's other security services. Like the PSF, it collected information on opposition organizations and individuals, inspected the press, led internal investigations, and so on. It monitored all Palestinians for any expression of opposition to Arafat, and oversaw Palestinian prisoners including interrogations.

5. The Palestinian Police Force (known as the Civil Police or Blue Police), which performed routine policing functions such as traffic control and keeping general order.

6. The General Intelligence Service, which was the official PA intelligence service. It was headed by Amin-al-Hindi and was involved in intelligence gathering inside and outside the territories, counterespionage operations, and developing relations with other foreign intelligence agencies.

7. The Special Security Force (SSF), which operated directly under Arafat. Little is known of its activities.

8. A Civil Defense Force for Emergencies.

9. A Maritime Police or Coast Guard, which guarded Palestinian territorial waters.

10. An Airborne Force or Aerial Police.

11. The County Guard (al-Amn al-Mahafza), which supplied security services to the county governors and their offices. The County Guard summoned people for questioning and resolved local quarrels.[19]

In effect, Arafat created a *mukhabarat* state wherein the intelligence services usurped individual civil liberties and freedom, severely compromised—to the point of rendering impotent—the civilian judiciary, and interfered with the jurisdiction of the Legislative Council, in particular with implementation of the few laws it passed. All of this activity, which directly undermined the rule of law, was undertaken on behalf of the executive, in particular, Arafat's interests.[20]

The Legislative Branch

The Palestinian Legislative Council, first elected in January 1996, was intended to function independently of the executive and to act as a check on its power. Arafat's party, Fateh, controlled seventy-one of the eighty-eight seats, and Abu Ala, Arafat's chief negotiator at Oslo (and on subsequent agreements), was elected speaker. Still, the majority of the council members came from the West Bank and Gaza, and the potential existed for the body to function as envisioned.[21]

The most important initial task facing the Legislative Council was the writing of a constitution for the Palestinian Authority. Yet the constitutional question demonstrates very clearly legislative subservience to executive control. Various nongovernmental groups in Palestinian society consulted over a period of two years about the nature and content of a constitution. They coordinated their discussions with the PLO's National Council Legal Committee and the PA's Ministry of Justice. After two years, they presented the Legislative Council with a draft proposal for the Basic Law for the National Authority in the Transition Period.[22] The Legislative Council debated the proposal, made several minor changes, and in 1997 submitted it to a vote by the council. The Basic Law passed the required three readings (three separate votes), ostensibly making it law. However, as noted, to actually become law it required ratification by President Arafat. He refused to sign it, fearing it would curtail some of his power. He finally signed it in the summer of 2002 when the PA was no longer a functioning entity. One Israeli political analyst adds:

> Israel was also afraid of the Palestinian Legislative Council being able to legislate Palestinian laws that were against Israel's interests or against agreements, thus Israel never challenged Arafat when he declared in private meetings that he could not sign the "Palestinian Basic Law". . . because of Israeli objections.[23]

The PA was left without a constitution and the Palestinian people without the means to ensure democratic processes, to protect citizens' rights, to enforce the rule of law, or to secure constitutional accountability. Additionally, by refusing to sign the Basic Law, Arafat sent the Legislative Council a clear message that he would veto any legislation passed by the council that did not accord with his wishes. As a precedent, this was extremely negative. It rendered the legislative branch impotent from the outset.[24]

The Judicial Branch

The absence of a legal system enshrined in a constitution had a negative impact on the independence, immunity, and integrity of the Palestinian judiciary. Numerous abuses grew out of this situation, some of which are discussed below. However, at a general level the PA executive compromised the judiciary in four main areas. The first involved extreme insecurity for judges. Arafat personally transferred and dismissed judges for no professional reason but because they in some way displeased him or proved insufficiently loyal. At the same time, he appointed judges, who were often unqualified, on the basis of personal and political fidelity or to further his own political support.[25]

The PA primarily relied on clan politics and clan law to rule. For example, to obtain a government job, one has to be from a large clan *(humula)* or belong to Fateh.[26] Handing out carrots—in whatever form—to particular clans to garner support may have served Arafat's personal interests, but it led to serious inter-*hamayel* rivalry and increased the fragmentation in Palestinian society.[27] In the Gaza Strip, in particular, there was a significant increase in interclan violence beginning in 1998, a phenomenon that had remained dormant, at least on a wider community level, for more than two decades. Even more alarming was the increasing reliance on clan or tribal laws—traditional, nonformal mechanisms for settling disputes that are particularly deleterious to women.[28] This reliance on tribal law began to intensify during the first intifada and continued to strengthen thereafter. Thus, although it did not arise specifically under the PA, the PA's practice of undermining the legitimate independent judiciary did nothing to impede people's reliance on this archaic system; indeed, it encouraged it.

A second area of judicial interference involved Arafat's and the PA's failure to execute court decisions. If Arafat did not like a judicial decision, he simply ignored or reversed it. In general, Arafat and the PA treated judicial decisions without seriousness. Arafat often disregarded a law to protect a crony or political ally or, conversely, bypassed the judicial process to punish someone who had criticized him publicly or in some other way offended him.[29]

A third problematic area involved Arafat's establishment, by presidential decree on February 7, 1995, of the State Security Court—a military court—with jurisdiction over security offenses. It began trying individuals so accused in April 1995. The operations of this court were accountable to no one but Arafat. Arrests were arbitrary and trials were held in secret, typically conducted in the middle of the night. Members of the security forces served as judges, and there was no right of appeal. Torture was routine, there were deaths during detention, and death sentences were summary.[30]

Arafat also interfered with the attorney general. The executive appoints the attorney general, who is subject to approval by the Legislative Council, but there are no legal or legislative guarantees preventing the executive from dismissing the attorney general at will. The office is officially part of the executive, but because its mandate is to ensure the rule of law, the attorney general's work actually falls within the responsibility of the judiciary. Between 1995 and 1998, Arafat appointed, then dismissed, two individuals. The first, Khaled al-Kidrah, was dismissed allegedly because of corruption. The second, Fayez Abu Rahmeh, officially resigned but did so, he stated, because "of the difficulties created by pressure and interference from" the executive.[31] Eighteen months passed before, in June 1999, Arafat appointed a successor to Abu Rahmeh, Zuheir Surani. On taking office, Surani's cousin, attorney Raji Surani, warned that his tenure would meet the "same fate as his predecessors, if the executive leadership refuses to come to terms with the supremacy of the law."[32] Surani was no more successful than his predecessors in enforcing the rule of law. There were multiple additional problems with the judiciary that, as will be seen below, were the basis for the extensive human rights violations under the PA.

To summarize the foregoing, the absence of a constitution as a foundation for the rule of law and for the separation of powers resulted in a situation where the executive branch, in particular Arafat, showed flagrant disrespect for the courts and their functionaries. This involved a range of problems, from interference in the judicial process to disregard of court decisions. The compromising of the judiciary, in turn, resulted in increasing reliance on clan or tribal law. The executive obstructed the passage of legislation and refused to sign into law legislation that was passed—most significantly, the constitution (the Basic Law). In short, there was no rule of law in the Palestinian Authority; instead, there was only rule by arbitrary political and security forces (see Table 6.2).

Note that on the three occasions when the question was asked "Do you believe the Palestinian media is free?" only between 20 percent and 27.1 percent believed that it was free. Indeed, the PA's record with the media was an important indicator of the absence of a democratic political culture in Palestine.[33] It is analyzed below.

The System: Neopatrimonialism

In the absence of formal structures of law, constitutionalism, and separate and independent branches of government, in combination with a personalistic, centralizing, and authoritarian leader backed by multiple internal security services, the nature of a political system will be inevitably undemocratic. Rex Brynen, an internationally known Canadian scholar on Palestine, has labeled Palestinian politics "neopatrimonial"—meaning a system that variously combines and overlays the

Table 6.2   Evaluation of Performance of Palestinian Authority Institutional
             Sectors

Date	Very good/ Good[a]	Judicial Authority	Security Forces and Police	Presidential Office	Legislative Council
Sept. 1996	VG	11.1	25.2	29.2	9.6
	G	38.6	37.0	42.8	37.9
Dec. 1996[b]	VG		28.0	39.5	10.6
	G		43.1	35.4	38.3
Apr. 1997	VG	15.2	25.8	33.2	10.7
	G	40.0	50.7	45.4	37.3
June 1997	VG	11.9	21.1	25.6	8.2
	G	39.0	48.0	42.7	37.7
Sept. 1997[c]	VG	12.7	24.2	32.3	9.9
	G	35.9	43.9	41.0	32.5
Dec. 1997	VG	17.3	26.8	34.6	12.8
	G	35.4	45.2	36.6	38.5
Mar. 1998[d]	VG	16.2	31.7	36.6	12.6
	G	37.0	39.6	37.1	36.8
June 1998	VG	17.2	28.5	33.4	12.4
	G	30.7	39.2	37.7	32.3
Oct. 1998	VG	12.6	14.1	17.9	8.5
	G	32.2	36.6	36.7	30.7
Jan. 1999	VG	12.1	14.9	16.2	12.5
	G	35.6	41.3	39.7	36.2
Apr. 1999	VG	8.9	10.3	13.9	9.1
	G	32.7	41.2	39.2	34.3
Oct. 1999	VG	8.8	13.9	14.4	6.1
	G	31.2	38.7	38.6	31.1
Jan. 2000	VG	9.2	15.1	14.2	8.3
	G	32.5	40.4	39.8	33.6

Source: This polling data was carried out by the Center for Palestine Research & Studies-
Survey Research Unit, Ramallah, Palestine.
Notes: a. Respondents were given a choice of very good, good, fair, bad, very bad, no
opinion/do not know.
b. 27.1% believe the Palestinian press is free.
c. 20.0% believe the Palestinian press is free.
d. 24.0% believe the Palestinian press is free.

informal social structures of patrimonialism with the formal and legal
structures of the quasi- or protostate. (Patrimonialism is a political system wherein the power of the ruler is extended through a complex network of functionaries and subordinates. Larger patrimonial networks
are considered an extension of patriarchal mechanisms—or similar to
them in important ways—while also being sustained by patron-client
relationships.) In the Palestinian neopatrimonial system, Brynen argues,
formal lines of responsibility are overwritten by patronage and cliental-
ism; the boundaries of public role and private interest are blurred, with
public office representing an important mechanism for private profit;

and state resources are used to lubricate patron-client networks. At the same time, the state's ability to extract resources (e.g., foreign aid from donor countries or taxes from citizens) and regulate behaviors (e.g., favoritism for loyalists) creates conditions under which the supply of, and access to, scarce goods can be manipulated—which is the fundamental foundation of patronage.[34]

From the outset, the PA engaged in all these corrosive practices. Bribes were required for basic services. Patronage replaced merit. Extortion was the norm in economic transactions. Corruption was present at every level of government. Despite the proliferation of official security services, individuals did not feel secure—indeed, they feared the security services. One consequence was the emergence of armed militias—gangs, in effect. Additionally, due to the repression of any criticism or dissent, political parties other than Fateh became mere shadows of their former selves, and by the end of the seven years of Oslo, even Fateh had fractured into rival groups. There was no political dialogue; indeed, there was hardly any dialogue at all at a society-wide level.[35] In fact, one of the intended results of the PA's rule was to depoliticize and demobilize society—even replacing the ideology of nationalism with a focus on the process of implementing endless interim agreements. This situation had very negative consequences for efforts at mass mobilization during the intifada.

As a result of the new politics, Palestinian society, always fragmented, became far more so. Cleavages among the urban-rural, Muslim-Christian, West Bank–Gaza, *hamayel*, classes, and other lines became more pronounced. Traditionally, individuals' identities and loyalties resided primarily with their *hamula*, although during the 1970s and early 1980s this trend had begun to give way to a relatively more homogeneous society. The first intifada initially built on the growing social integration to build a mass movement that transcended particularistic affiliations, although ultimately it reinforced class and clan identities through divisive political factions. In other words, the party factionalism of the first intifada reproduced to a considerable extent traditional *hamula* ties and loyalties. If any single objective should have topped Arafat's list of priorities, it should have been to unite society on the basis of a common past and the hope for a better, collective future. Strengthening nationalism, not weakening it, should have been paramount. However, Arafat and the PA managed to virtually extinguish Palestinian nationalism rather than reinforce it. These are the essential ingredients of nation-building and state-building, which are the quintessential elements for political and economic development.[36]

Personal and Institutional Corruption

The Surface Manifestations

Corruption undoubtedly exists, to some degree, in most developing and many developed societies. What made it so appalling in the Palestine context was its extent and its manifestly conspicuous public exhibition. Large and lavishly appointed buildings were constructed in the center of Gaza City to house the PA ministries, agencies, and authorities. Also in Gaza, where poverty and squalor are inordinate, Arafat's senior Tunisian cadres built themselves ostentatious villas that stood in stark contrast to the wretched refugee dwellings typically only blocks from the new mansions. The most elaborate and pretentious home was constructed by Abu Mazen, Arafat's link to Abu Ala in the Oslo negotiations and one of his closest advisers. (Moreover, most of the senior officials soon built or bought second lavish villas in Ramallah.) These new ruling elites imported, by the hundreds, young female Filipinos, Sri Lankans, and Indonesians as servants, cooks, and baby-sitters.[37] In Gaza, Palestine's most underdeveloped region and where donkey carts and dirt roads are the norm, the Tunisians drove (or, more accurately, were driven in) Mercedes and other luxury vehicles. Their chauffeurs lounged indolently while they consumed extravagant lunches in an array of exclusive new restaurants—Le Mirage was a favorite, among others. This new elite enjoyed a variety of privileges and rights visibly denied all others. Indeed, PA politics was the politics of exclusion. In this most conservative area of Palestine, Gaza's first and only nightclub was constructed—the Zahra al-Mada'in (Flower of the Cities)—for the entertainment of the Tunisians. Replete with belly dancers, songstresses, and alcohol, including Israel's Maccabee beer, the nightclub appalled Gazans. The once pristine Gaza shoreline became littered with hotels, resorts (one with an Olympic-size pool), and restaurants serving everything from pizza and hamburgers to Chinese, Indian, and Italian cuisine.[38] All this occurred while unemployment in Gaza was approximately 40 percent (and rising rapidly) and more than half of the 1 million Gazans lived in refugee camps. Clearly, the new amenities were not meant to serve Palestinian needs.

Consumer spending was copious and flagrant. New shops carried imported French haute couture that sold faster than the owners could stock it. One example was the wedding of the PA minister of planning, Nabil Sha'ath, shortly after arriving in Gaza. He required multiple sumptuous receptions to celebrate the event. Moreover, the Tunisians were not wealthy before arriving in Gaza (with very few exceptions,

which included both Nabil Sha'ath and Abu Mazen, who were million-
aires in their own right before coming to the Occupied Territories).
Rather, the Tunisians acquired their financial status as a result of the
Oslo process—and not because of any particular service or expertise
they provided. No one is certain exactly where the money for the villas,
cars, and other items came from, but all know it was not from the fruit
of their labor. One observer wrote:

> It is not just Hamas and Islamic Jihad, or bigots in general, who feel
> the shock. Liberals who welcome any challenge to the dour local
> mores feel it too. For almost everyone [in Gaza], the "Tunisians" are
> as alien, as unfit to rule, as those—Turks, British, Egyptians,
> Israelis—who came before them. And because they are actually
> Palestinians, and came as "liberators," the shock is even worse.[39]

The real question, however, is how Arafat amassed the wherewithal to
be able to afford graft on this scale.

The PA's Financial Misdealings

To be clear, Arafat was not just sitting in his office handing out money
in paper bags. In fact, he personally has not been accused of corruption.
Yet Arafat sat at the apex of the pyramid of corruption. Even if he did
not engage in self-aggrandizement, he used, or allowed the use of, the
financial resources intended for the development of Palestine to ensure
the loyalty of his highest officials as well as to guarantee the support of
the masses. The officials had monopolies; the masses had salaries in the
highly inflated bureaucracy. The system of corruption is complex and
involved four interconnected issues that fueled its functioning.

Background and the Hidden Account

The first issue resides in the 1995 Paris Economic Protocol wherein the
Palestinians agreed to a customs union with Israel and to Israel's collection of import taxes, valued-added taxes (VAT), and excise taxes. The
second originates in the relationships that were developed between
Israelis and Palestinians during the process of negotiations beginning
with Oslo and continuing thereafter. The third relates to Arafat's vast
enlargement of the bureaucracy to nearly 100,000 (civilian and securi-
ty/police) that guaranteed him a loyal following because their livelihoods were tied to their fidelity to Arafat. In a situation such as
Palestine, where unemployment was so high and each worker supported

eight to ten people, this was a very significant resource of power. The fourth is a manifestation of the absence of the rule of law and the power and lawlessness of the security services.

As a consequence of the customs and taxation policies specified in the *Paris Economic Protocol,* Israel collected a variety of taxes due the PA, then remitted them to the PA. With regard to import taxes, for example, if televisions were imported into the West Bank via the port in Haifa, the Israeli importer paid an import tax to the Israeli government, which in turn gave it to the PA. Similarly, with VAT taxes garnered on goods purchased from Israel, and excise taxes on fuel, alcohol, tobacco, and the like, the taxes were accumulated by Israel and given to the PA. The income and health taxes Israel extracted from the salaries of Palestinian workers in Israel were likewise turned over to the PA.[40] The Israeli government withheld these taxes in times of conflict with the Palestinians, and there have been allegations, unproved to my knowledge, that even in good times Israel did not always turn over the full amount. During the Al-Aqsa intifada, Tel Aviv withheld all revenue for two years. But that is not the issue here.

Arafat has had and continued to have during the Oslo years numerous secret bank accounts in various cities around the globe. One that he maintained at the Hahashmonaim branch of Bank Leumi in Tel Aviv became public knowledge and caused him considerable embarrassment. In the Occupied Territories, it is known as *al-sondouk al-thani.* The only two people who had access to this account were Arafat and Muhammad Rashid. Between 1994 and January 1997, Israel, at the request of Arafat via an intermediary, transferred NIS 500 million (U.S.$125 million) into this account from the various taxes it collected for the PA.[41] During 1997 alone it is believed that Israel transferred NIS 1.5 billion (U.S.$400 million) into the secret fund in Tel Aviv.[42] This may be contrasted with the NIS 264 million (U.S.$66 million) Israel transferred directly to the PA between 1994 and January 1997.[43]

According to Ronen Bergman and David Ratner, writing for *Ha'aretz,* the money in the secret account was used for three main purposes. First, the foreign donor countries and organizations that made large contributions to the PA, after learning of the corruption, insisted that their moneys be used to initiate self-sustaining economic projects to develop the Palestine economy, not for salaries of PA employees. Arafat then funded his overblown bureaucratic payroll from this account. Second, and also related to Arafat's need to maintain his power base, the secret account was used to pay for a series of activities that ensured mass loyalty to Arafat. Some of these included the martyr allowances to widows and orphans, social services in the Lebanese

refugee camps, and others. The third, and by far the largest share of
the account, was specifically a fallback fund for Arafat and his family
as well as his senior aides, in the event of a coup or some other political misfortune. Given such a cushion, they would be able to safely
leave the country and establish themselves comfortably in exile.[44]
Indeed, in February 2002, *Ha'aretz* reported that "wealthy Palestinians
are in the process of transferring their assets out of the Palestine
Authority."[45]

The taxes that were put into this secret account were intended for
the treasury of the PA to be used for the development of infrastructure
and to fuel economic growth in the West Bank and Gaza. Yet rather than
being used for the benefit of the Palestinian people, this very significant
amount of money shored up Arafat's power base through salaries and
welfare and provided him with security in case of his political demise.
Of course, should Israel choose to, it could deny Arafat access to this
account. Ironically, through this account Israel holds significant power
over Arafat.

Monopolies: Every Minister's Personal Project

Simultaneously with the establishment of the PA, its top officials, with
the blessing of Arafat, assumed control over the essential sectors of the
economy through monopolies that would provide personal wealth.
These officials earned hundreds of thousands of dollars per year from
their monopolies. Moreover, this revenue effectively constituted a transfer of income from poorer economic groups to the new political class,
which used the profits for personal gain or to buy political loyalty.[46]
One Palestinian critic of the monopoly system, Legislative Council
member Hussam Khader, from Nablus, took the risk of speaking publicly:

> They cut up the pie among themselves. The Palestinian leaders
> thought that our economy was some sort of inheritance due them and
> their children. Every honcho got himself a fat slice of the imports into
> the authority. One got the fuel, another got the cigarettes, yet another
> the lottery, and his crony the flour. Gravel is a monopoly belonging
> directly to the security apparatuses, and they earn a fortune from it.
> . . . We are, in fact, talking about a mafia that began to operate in par-
> allel with the conducting of negotiations with Israel. The same men
> who talked politics at Oslo, tried at the same time to forge ties with
> Israeli companies. This mafia now incites against the Palestinian
> Legislative Council. These men will do everything they can to contin-
> ue their activities unsupervised and unmonitored by any other body. A
> weak parliament suits them very well.[47]

Because the Legislative Council was weak and the rule of law non-existent, the development of the Palestinian economy was seriously impeded. For example, there were no laws protecting a company from demands for paybacks, protection, and other forms of extortion. There were no requirements for competition in tenders (bids). There was no organized system for enforcing or collecting debts. There was no law governing mortgages for houses, no way of documenting joint entrepreneurial initiatives, and so on. Thus, legitimate private investors were leery of risking their capital while illegitimate monopolies flourished without any accountability. The absence of financial and other laws explains why private investment, desperately needed for economic development, became so abysmal after initial significant investments.

Several examples will illustrate how the monopolies work. In general, the pattern is as follows: A Palestinian official contracts with an Israeli firm or individual to purchase large quantities of a product at a given price; the official in turn sells the product on the Palestinian market at a greatly inflated price and pockets the profit for his personal benefit. If Palestinian wholesalers had access to an alternate source for the same product at a lower price, the Palestinian security services often attempted to "persuade" the wholesaler to purchase only the product sold by the official monopoly. (This did not occurr with every monopoly, but it was a common enough practice to warrant mention.) At the same time, companies that attempted to sell products in competition with the official monopoly were often subjected to "pressure" from the security services.[48]

There are believed to have been approximately twenty-seven monopolies held by PA officials, including steel, wheat, meat, wood, paint, building materials, feed for sheep and cattle, cement, flour, fuel, gravel, cigarettes, cars, computers, TVs and VCRs, electrical appliances, and others.[49] Several of the top PA officials known to have held one or more monopolies include Muhammad Rashid, senior financial adviser; Mahr al-Kurd, deputy minister of economics and trade; Jibril Rajoub, chief of the PA's preventive security forces in the West Bank; Muhammad Dahlan, chief of Preventive Security Services in Gaza; Abu Ali Shaheen, minister of supply; Nabil Sha'ath, minister of planning; Abu Mazen (Mahmud Abbas), Arafat's chief lieutenant and the number-two man in the PA; Sami Ramlawi, ministry of finance; Hashem Hussein Hashem Abu Nada, economic adviser to Arafat and senior official in the finance ministry; Mou'in Khoury, Arafat's *chef de bureau;* Hikmat Ziad, official on the PA's economics committee; and Maher al-Masri, minister of economy.

In addition, many officials created monopolies for their children, wives, uncles, and aunts.[50] For example, Abu Mazen's son, Yasser Abbas, shared the monopoly on consumer entertainment with Sami Ramlawi. Besides nepotism, there were issues of protection money and bribes. The bribes arose mainly in the context of permits—Palestinians wishing to open a business had to obtain a permit from the PA. The fees for a permit varied from onetime payments to monthly percentages of the business's profits. The fees went to the senior official of whatever agency issued the permit or to the security services. Furthermore, senior security officials and members of the PA frequently demanded from persons already in business regular financial payments for protection. One example is the case of Yusuf al-Baba, a thirty-two-year-old aspiring businessman, who had received a permit from Israel to build a gas station in Nablus. The PA then demanded that he obtain one of its permits. He initially agreed, but when he learned that the permit entailed paying 30 percent of his profits to local Fateh leaders and the PA security forces, he declined. (Because of its strategic importance, gasoline tended to be the commodity most highly subject to fees.) Al-Baba was promptly arrested on January 7, 1997, and his family was unable to learn anything about his whereabouts. Nearly three weeks later, they heard on Israel Radio (Arabic) that he had died in prison. An investigation showed that he had been tortured to death.[51] No one was ever charged or tried in the matter.

Muhammad Rashid held one of the largest monopolies in the territories. His company, the Palestinian Company for Commercial Services (PCCS), had several subsidiaries and controlled a number of markets. One was cement, and all Palestinian contractors were required to buy Nesher brand cement from PCCS. Trucks carrying cement from other manufacturing companies were stopped by the security services and sent home—usually after the drivers were beaten. In 1996, Nesher (an Israeli firm) sold the PA and Rashid more than 1 million tons of cement for which it was paid $50–60 million. Later, it was decreed that Palestinians could purchase cheaper cement from Jordan. Palestinians welcomed the pronouncement, but in practice Israeli officials on the bridge from Jordan subjected the Jordanian trucks to extensive searches, the drivers to humiliating harassments, and so on; as a result, very little Jordanian cement actually arrived in the Occupied Territories. Interestingly, Nesher's CEO, Yitzhak Davidi, told Bergman and Ratner: "We signed our first agreement with the Palestinians even before Arafat arrived in Gaza in 1994. Muhammad Rashid signed on Arafat's behalf." There are no statistics on the amount of profit Rashid has made on this monopoly, but one businessman, Mahmoud al-Fara, revealed his dealings with Rashid. Al-Fara is one of the wealthiest entrepreneurs in the

Gaza Strip. He made his fortune in the United States and was the chief contractor at Dahaniya Airport. Bergman and Ratner report that al-Fara "relates that he feels the heavy hand of the monopolies every day. The Authority's security forces compelled him to buy cement from the Nesher Plant, even though he had reached an agreement with an Egyptian company to import cement at a much lower price."[52]

When a monopoly runs into a problem, Arafat fixes it. For example, the minister who had the monopoly for flour in the West Bank received an "import permit" from a colleague in the ministry of supply and proceeded to import 5,000 tons from Romania via Israel. However, he failed to store the flour properly, and it spoiled. An Israeli associate, contacted through Arafat's office, came to the rescue. He sent a convoy of trucks to the official's Nablus storehouse, loaded the flour, and transported it to Israel, where it was repackaged in fresh sacks so it appeared unspoiled. The PA official then had the spoiled flour returned to the territories and put on the local market. Eventually, when the public discovered that their newly purchased flour was spoiled, the episode became known throughout the Occupied Territories. The Legislative Council convened a committee to investigate; however, the minister of supply, Abu Ali Shaheen, who was determined to protect his turf, ordered his chief of staff not to give the Legislative Council any documents or details related to flour imports. That ended the Legislative Council's investigation. Then Arafat established a ministerial commission of inquiry that, without holding a single meeting, concluded that there had been no improprieties or wrongdoings and that no one should be held accountable. Moreover, a representative of Arafat threatened one member of the Legislative Council, who persisted in raising questions about the affair, that if he did not cease, his parliamentary immunity would be revoked.[53]

Finally, again without exculpating the PA officials, it is important to take note of the wide-ranging Israeli involvement in the monopoly system. Israeli analyst Gershon Baskin commented in March 2001:

> Despite constant warnings by this author and many others of the dangers of direct Israeli involvement in Palestinian corruption, Israeli officials facilitated and encouraged what must be called "the ripping off of the Palestinian people" through shady deals and schemes conducted in broad daylight by tens of former Israeli security officials with agents of the Palestine Authority including Palestinian intelligence officers, policemen, and "advisors" working on behalf of themselves and on behalf of Arafat directly. Many of these deals, if conducted in Israel proper, would have ended with indictments and jail penalties. But in this case they were conducted in "the interest of

peace." This is perhaps one of the most cynical elements of what has emerged over the past eight years. Perhaps even more cynical is that much of that cooperation [continued during the first six months of the Al-Aqsa intifada], and it should not surprise anyone that the first order of Palestinian-Israeli business under Sharon [was] the opening of the Casino in Jericho.[54]

Legislative Council Attempts
to Correct Financial Abuses

Within the PA there is the General Control Office (GCO). In May 1997, it issued a report noting that because of corruption $326 million, rough-ly one-fourth of the PA's budget, had disappeared in 1996. Individuals in the Legislative Council from the Occupied Territories lobbied the council speaker, Abu Ala, to constitute a committee to investigate. He finally agreed but insisted that its mandate be restricted to those areas mentioned in the GCO document. The committee received no coopera-tion from the PA comptroller, any PA ministry, or Arafat. Nevertheless, the committee worked diligently and on July 29, 1997, presented its findings to the council.[55] The council's report on the GCO report went much further than the latter in its investigation of who was responsible for the disappeared money—in fact, its details and names were quite specific, and its revelations provoked a storm of outrage among Pales-tinians. A few of the commission's discoveries illustrate:

- Minister of Health Riad al-Z'anoun approved the purchase from Israel and sale in the Occupied Territories of bad or expired drugs for treating cancer patients; transferred drugs, which were rejected as being of poor quality in the West Bank, to Gaza hos-pitals and clinics; allowed unregistered drugs into the Occupied Territories; and so on. Z'anoun profited personally on all these transactions.
- Minister of Planning Nabil Sha'ath created a scheme whereby he hired individuals at high salaries to work on various PA projects, but by prior agreement the hires agreed to work for less. The dif-ference was pocketed by Sha'ath.
- Minister of Civil Affairs Jamil Tarifi granted, at his discretion, exceptions on import duties, especially on furniture, high-quality electronics, automobiles, and other items. This can involve quite a large loss for the PA because, for example, the import tax on a car is approximately half the price of the car. This scheme worked by having someone from the PA physically present at Israeli ports, instructing the Israelis which goods to exempt.

- On all public works projects, the committee discovered that no tenders (bids) were offered; contractors received permits from specific PA officials to whom, in turn, they gave a kickback.
- Minister of Social Affairs Intisar Wazir (widow of Israeli-assassinated Abu Jihad) was found to have failed to make disbursements to the needy anywhere comparable to the donations and official funds that her office received.

The committee found corruption in eighteen government ministries and recommended criminal charges be brought against three ministers.[56] The investigators also found that there was skimming from foreign donor contributions—in particular when the donor was not strict about accountability and transparency. (After this public scandal, all foreign governments and international organizations demanded reliable accountability as a condition for making a grant; and to the extent possible, they directly funded specific projects rather than permitting funds to pass through the PA.) Finally, the investigation revealed that various PA officials required foreign investors to give them personally a 30 percent share on any investment.

After making its findings public, the Legislative Council voted overwhelmingly in favor of a resolution calling for Arafat to dissolve his cabinet and appoint experts and technocrats rather than political cronies. It also demanded a real separation of powers, with independence for the judiciary and the legislature, as well as a total overhaul of the PA in the interest of greater efficiency. The Legislative Council, as discussed above, had no legal power to enforce the resolution, but many hoped that its stand would generate sufficient public pressure on Arafat that he would make substantive changes.

Arafat, however, treated the charges and demands of the Legislative Council with contempt. One year later, the three criminally accused ministers were still at their posts, corruption continued, and the legislature and the judiciary were no less subject to Arafat's whim than previously. Moreover, instead of streamlining in an effort to increase efficiency, Arafat, when presenting his "new" government, added eight new ministries to the existing twenty-two, with eight additional state ministers without portfolios.[57] According to two analysts, "The only deference Arafat appeared to show to the [Legislative Council's] complaints was to co-opt critical members such as Rafiq Natshe from Hebron and Salah Tamari from Bethlehem—by offering them official positions, appointing Natshe to Labour and creating a ministry to 'combat settlements' for Tamari."[58] Moreover, when some members of the Legislative

Council threatened to reject the new administration, Arafat called special meetings with various council committees and, using his standard carrot-and-stick tactics, pleaded for their support for the sake of national unity, on the one hand, and, on the other, implied threats of force against those who were tempted to hold out. Thus, the Legislative Council approved the new cabinet.

A year later, the continuing chicanery, graft, mismanagement, and general government impotence led twenty prominent Palestinians—including nine members of the Legislative Council—to sign, and publicize, a manifesto entitled "The Homeland Calls Us." Released on November 29, 1999, the document accused Arafat of failing the national cause and of tyranny, corruption, and political deceit. It was unprecedented in its direct attack on Arafat. The president's response was swift and brutal. Eight of the signers were arrested the following day and tortured in prison; a ninth (Bassam Shak'a, who is confined to a wheelchair as a result of a settler terrorist attack) was put under house arrest. The Legislative Council signatories were immune from arrest, so they were targeted with violence: one was shot, one stoned, and others were beaten. The pressure was so intense that four removed their names from the list. The PA also attempted, unsuccessfully, to have its supporters in the Legislative Council revoke the legislative immunity of council members who had signed, and Arafat announced that all the signatories would be tried in the State Security Court for treason (they never were).[59] But the repression had one major intended effect: the original signatories had hoped that their manifesto would catalyze a movement of popular support among the masses, whose sheer numbers would force Arafat to clean up the government. However, in the wake of the repression visited on such prominent individuals, no one else signed the petition (see Tables 6.3 and 6.4).

Human Rights Abuses

The PA's record on human rights was abysmal. Serious violations include arbitrary arrest and detention without charge or trial; extended detention; absence of judicial procedures to protect defendants; widespread use of torture; deaths in custody; death sentences without a fair trial; repression and arbitrary imprisonment of political opposition; restrictions on freedom of assembly; media censorship; harassment of journalists; breaches of universities' academic freedom; banning books; and emergency laws and executive decrees.[60] The reason for the extensive abuses were

Table 6.3   Corruption in the Palestinian Authority: Percentage of
             Respondents Who Said Yes

Date	Do you think there is corruption in PA institutions?[a]	Do you expect corruption to increase in the future?[b]
Sept. 1996	49.3	40.1
Dec. 1996	52.7	34.0
Apr. 1997	57.0	43.6
June 1997	62.9	48.9
Sept. 1997	64.9	38.2
Mar. 1998	60.7	38.5
June 1998	64.5	47.4
Oct. 1998	66.0	56.8
Jan. 1999	67.7	57.2
Apr. 1999	70.6	54.1
June 1999	71.1	55.2
Oct. 1999	63.4	50.6
Dec. 1999	68.2	53.7
Jan. 2000	62.8	53.7
Apr. 2000	70.7	58.5
July 2000	76.1	53.8
July 2001	83.4	49.1

Source: This polling data was carried out by the Center for Palestine Research & Studies—
Survey Research Unit, Ramallah, Palestine.
   Notes: a. Respondents had the choice of answering yes, no, or not sure.
   b. Respondents had the choice of increase, remain as is, decrease, or don't know/no
opinion.

Table 6.4   Corruption in the Palestinian Authority by Institution: Percentage of
             Respondents Who Said Yes Regarding the Following Institutions[a]

Date	Ministries and Government Offices	Security Forces and Police	Presidency Office	Legislative Council
Oct. 1998	78.8	69.7	34.4	46.3
Jan. 1999	76.1	75.0	42.0	49.4
Apr. 1999	75.6	77.3	39.7	49.2
Oct. 1999	80.0	76.5	41.9	51.1
Jan. 2000	83.5	75.7	48.7	58.6

Source: This polling data was carried out by the Center for Palestine Research & Studies—
Survey Research Unit, Ramallah, Palestine.
   Note: a. Respondents were given the choice of yes, no, or not sure.

twofold. The first derived from Arafat's authoritarianism and intolerance
of opposition, buttressed by the lawlessness of the multiple security services in the context of weak and ineffective judicial and legislative
branches. The second related to Israeli-PA security cooperation.

Israel-PA Security Cooperation

Israel and the United States have exerted extraordinary pressure on Arafat and the PA to incarcerate suspected terrorists (who were identified by Israel) and to prevent them from carrying out attacks against Israel. Moreover, Israel demanded that the PA not release suspected people, once arrested, regardless of their actual or potential guilt or innocence. From Israel's perspective, the raison d'être of the PA was to protect Israeli security. Arafat's attempts to satisfy Israeli demands were the major impetus for the mass arrests and detentions of persons allegedly associated with one of the Islamist groups and, later, with the Popular Front for the Liberation of Palestine (PFLP) and the Al-Aqsa Martyr Brigade (a military off-shoot of Fateh). Moreover, Arafat not only bowed to Israeli and U.S. pressure; he also made mass arrests to strengthen his position at the bargaining table (by showing how efficient he was in meeting the security requirements imposed on him). Israel, however, did not consider Arafat's efforts sufficient and continuously demanded that he do more to stop terrorism.

One example of the excesses involved in Israeli-PA security cooperation, and of the PA's violation of individuals' rights in its quest to satisfy Israel, was the Wadi Qelt affair. This involved three Palestinians—Jamal al-Hindi and two cousins, Shaher a-Ra'i and Yusef a-Ra'i—who were wrongly punished for the murder of two Israeli hikers in 1995 in Wadi Qelt (within Area C). Ohad Bachrach and Uri Shaher were shot at close range while bathing in a spring. According to the human rights group B'Tselem, one of the main characteristics of this case was the relentless pressure exerted by Israel and the United States on the PA to find the killers at any cost.[61]

The three accused Palestinians were affiliated with the leftist PFLP, and in the wake of unsubstantiated rumors that the PFLP was responsible for the murders, Israel's General Security Services (GSS) seized al-Hindi in the middle of the night on August 3, 1995. Al-Hindi was held for over six months, including forty-five days during which he was denied access to a lawyer and was subjected to continuous torture. Finally he broke and told his interrogators, "Give me a specific charge, a clear allegation, and I'll admit to it. Just stop the torture." They replied, "There is an allegation. Tell us how you and Yusef and Shaher killed the Jews in Wadi Qelt." Al-Hindi then proceeded to make up stories, none of which correlated with the circumstances of the murder (e.g., how the Israelis were killed, the type of weapon used, etc.). Later al-Hindi told another GSS officer that he knew nothing about the incident—that he had fabricated the stories to stop the torture. About the same time, he remembered that on the day of the crime he had been working in an Israeli settlement where he had to sign in on entry and sign out on leaving. The records at the settlement confirmed that al-Hindi had indeed been on the site the entire day. Still unwilling to release him, the GSS charged him with membership in an illegal organization (the PFLP) and with recruiting others. He was held for three more months while awaiting trial on these charges; however, his attorney arranged a plea bargain whereby he admitted membership in the PFLP and was sentenced to time already served.

On September 3, 1995, one month after Israel incarcerated al-Hindi, the GSS instructed PA intelligence agents to arrest Yusef and Shaher a-Ra'i as accomplices. Security men seized the two Palestinians in the middle of the night. They were held incommunicado for ten days, were not told the reason for their detention, and were not questioned. They did not have access to a lawyer or appear before a judge. On September 13, again in the middle of the night, they were taken to the Muqata'ah, the PA's headquarters in Jericho, where they were brought before the general military prosecutor, Muhammad al-Bishtawi, who informed them: "You killed the two Jews in Wadi Qelt." Shaher replied that it was not true; al-Bishtawi beat him. Shaher and his cousin then asked for extradition to Israel, where they believed they would receive a fair trial because they were innocent. Notably, based on the Cairo agreement, the PA had no jurisdiction to try individuals alleged to have committed crimes in Area C. Nevertheless, al-Bishtawi refused the request for extradition, and that same night Shaher and Yousef were tried and convicted by the PA's State Security Court.

The trial was held in secret with three military judges and fifteen to twenty soldiers present. The judges did not ask the defendants any questions, and no witnesses were heard. A lawyer was appointed for the defendants, but he was a member of the Preventive Security Services. He was not permitted to talk with Shaher and Yousef before the trial, and he was given only two minutes to speak at the trial. According to sources available to B'Tselem, the PA did not want them extradited to Israel, guilty or innocent, because they wanted to demonstrate that they were fulfilling Israel's demands to crack down on terrorists. The cousins were sentenced to twelve years' imprisonment at hard labor. Both continued to maintain their innocence of the murders. Significantly, however, they were not tried and convicted for those crimes but for "damaging Palestinian interests, disturbing the peace, and distributing political pamphlets."[62]

The deleterious effects on the basic rights of Palestinians resulting from Israel's constant demands that the PA stop terrorism is evident in the case discussed above. The situation grew worse annually until 1998 and the signing of the memorandum at Wye River, when it deteriorated even further as a result of direct U.S. involvement. Some of Israel's specific demands on the PA have already been discussed. At Wye they were expanded to include "zero tolerance for violence and terror"; that the PA had to "take all the measures necessary in order to prevent acts of terrorism"; that there must be no "unwarranted releases" of prisoners; and that the PA must fight "the terrorists, the terrorist base, and the environmental conditions leading to support of terror." (The latter condition would be laughable were not the whole situation so serious: the environmental condition leading to terrorism is, of course, the Israeli occupation.) Furthermore, the PA had to "take all necessary security steps to penetrate the terror organizations and act to destroy them from the inside." The Wye River memorandum essentially held the Palestinian civil society hostage to Israel's security whims. It also gave Israel and the PA license to flagrantly violate the human rights of Palestinians.[63] The direct involvement of the Central Intelligence Agency in the field made the United States complicit in human rights violations against the Palestinians.[64] Subsequent to the Wye meeting, Arafat issued a decree aimed at meeting Israeli and U.S. requirements:

> The PA considers all the following forms of action illegal in all areas under Palestinian governance: incitement of racial discrimination, encouraging acts of violence which violate law, insulting religions, using violence or encouraging the use of violence which harms relations with brotherly or friendly countries, encouraging the masses to effect changes by illegal means or encouraging internal disputes.[65]

This decree went far beyond forestalling violence and terrorism. It prohibited a broad range of speech, including incitement to "strife," which is highly ambiguous and was used to preclude criticisms of Arafat, the PA, and the security services and to suppress any discussion of corruption.

One well-known Israeli writer made the following comment with regard to the power dynamics between Israel and the PA, the limits of Oslo, and the need for a repressive regime:

> The Palestinian Authority oppresses its people and intimidates the press. But . . . oppression may be said to be corollary of the Oslo agreement. The logic is simple: The strong side, Israel, took advantage of its strength, cutting a deal that gave the weak side, the PLO, as little as possible. The designers of Oslo set up, in other words, a situation where people, a great many people, were bound to oppose the deal they had gotten. Although [Israel] lacked the foresight to make

real peace, they did foresee the opposition to the nasty, brutish thing that they did make, and they were careful therefore, to provide the new non-state with a huge police force and plenty of rifles. Imprisonment without trial is the norm. Torture is carried out wholesale. Numerous security organizations vie with one another in extortion, and big brother is everywhere. The curbing of the press is merely a part of this general picture. The most alarming aspect in the story has been the speed with which the press agreed to lay down its weapon, the pen.[66]

Human Rights Abuses by the PA

Because most of the human rights issues have been contextualized in relation to Israel's human rights abuses against Palestinians, the following presents an overview of statistics and brief analyses that illuminate human rights violations by the Palestinian Authority. Abuses occurred in a variety of contexts, which are discussed individually below.

Legal Proceedings

Between 1995 and 2000, forty-nine persons were sentenced to death and executed (twenty-three by State Security Courts, eighteen by military courts, four by "special military courts," and four by criminal courts).[67] The State Security Court and military courts deal exclusively with political opponents of the PA.[68] Twenty-seven persons died while in custody, all, it can be assumed, as a result of torture. Forty-two persons were sentenced in military courts (with eighteen executed). Between 1995 and 2000, there were 200 deaths by gunfire unrelated to any police or security function (see Table 6.5).[69]

Political Prisoners

Amnesty International has established the number of political prisoners—nonviolent opponents of the PA—who were arrested and detained without charge for each year plus the number still in custody from the previous year (see Table 6.6). Amnesty International notes that it adopted many of them as prisoners of conscience. Additionally, these individuals are not all alleged affiliates of Hamas or Islamic Jihad. Most are prominent human rights activists, academics, and intellectuals who had displeased President Arafat for one reason or another.[70]

One example (among many too numerous to list) is that of Eyad Sarraj, a psychiatrist and the founder and director of the Gaza

Table 6.5   Persons Detained by the Palestinian Authority Without Charge

Year	No. of Petitions	Orders of Release	Disposition by Security Service
1997	2	2	2 not implemented
1998	5	4	4 not implemented
1999	57	54	37 not implemented[a]
2000	18	18	15 not implemented

Source: All data from PHRMG, *Resources* (Jerusalem: Palestinian Human Rights Monitoring Group, 2001), available online at www.phrmg.org/resources.htm.

Note: a. In 1999, though the Security Services declined to implement the release of 13 additional orders of release, President Arafat, hoping to garner political favor, gave "presidential pardons" to 13 of the 54 individuals receiving judicial orders of release.

Table 6.6   Political Prisoners Held by the Palestinian Authority

Year	No. Arrested	No. Still in Custody from Previous Year(s)
1996	1,200	300
1997	400	115
1998	450	500
1999	350	300
2000	360	600

Sources: AI, Report 1997 (Palestinian Authority: covering the year 1996) (London: Amnesty International, 1997), www.amnesty.org/ailib/aireport/ar97/MDE21.htm; AI, Report 1998 (Palestinian Authority: covering the year 1997) (London: Amnesty International, 1998), www.amnesty.org/ailib/aireport/ar98/mde21.htm; AI, *Report 1999* (Palestinian Authority: covering the year 1998) (London: Amnesty International, 1999), www.amnesty.org/ailib/aireport/ar99/mde21.htm; AI, *Report 2000* (Palestinian Authority: covering the year 1999) (London: Amnesty International, 2000), www.amnesty.org/ailib/aireport/ar2000/mde21.htm; AI, *Report 2001* (Palestinian Authority: covering the year 2000) (London: Amnesty International, 2001), www..wed.amnesty.org/web/ar2001/.nsf....ntries/Palestinian+Authority?OpenDocument.

Community Mental Health Program and former chairman of the Palestinian Commission on Civil Rights. Sarraj, an independent, was openly critical in the Palestinian press of Arafat and the PA and was arrested three times in as many months in 1997. During the first two incarcerations, the PA verbally abused and threatened Sarraj, but the third time he was held for three months and severely tortured. Additionally, in an attempt to discredit him, the PA planted drugs in his office, then charged him with possession of illegal substances. Because of the doctor's international stature, Arafat and the PA were flooded with calls for his release from across the globe. He was released on bail and he continued to be critical of the PA, though not of Arafat personally, but the torture left serious psychological scars. Other Palestinians who do not enjoy the international support of Dr. Sarraj languished in PA prisons indefinitely and endured far longer periods of torture, sometimes resulting in death; often, even their families did not know of their whereabouts.

In September 2000, Amnesty International issued a special report:

> In the past six years, the Palestinian Authority (PA) has detained dozens of persons, including human rights defenders, journalists, religious figures, writers, government officials, trade unionists and academics for exercising their legitimate rights to freedom of expression. Many have been detained after they expressed or reported criticism, verbally or in writing, of the policies of the PA or the conduct of the peace negotiations with Israel. . . . Almost invariably, the PA has held prisoners of conscience without respect for due process. . . . Almost all were never shown an arrest warrant or brought before a court. . . . Members of the various Palestinian Security Forces have physically attacked journalists while they were going about their duties. The PA has closed down newspapers, research centers, news agencies, television and radio stations . . . and stopped the distribution of newspapers and other publications.[71]

Amnesty International noted that the concerns expressed in this document do not apply to "the 600 long-term political prisoners, who may include prisoners of conscience, who have been held without charge or trial by the PA, some since 1994 and 1995."[72]

Censorship and Self-Censorship

There is a quasi-legal basis for censorship in the PA. Although the Basic Law (constitution) guarantees freedom of speech, press, and association, Arafat has refused to sign it, it has not been ratified, and so it cannot serve as a protection. Conversely, one of the first laws adopted by the PA was the Press and Publication Law of 1995. This was, in effect, an edict from Arafat because the Legislative Council had not yet been elected and could not scrutinize it. This law regulates every publication produced or imported into areas under PA jurisdiction and gives the PA broad powers to regulate the media as well as research centers, news agencies, libraries, and other institutions that process and disseminate information. Its article 37, for example, prohibits the publication on a whole range of issues, including any information harmful to religion or morality or that harms national unity or shakes confidence in the national authority. These, of course, are very broad and ambiguous areas;

moreover, all violations of this law are punishable by imprisonment.[73] The edict's contribution to self-censorship has been considerable.

The November 1998 Anti-Incitement Presidential Decree, discussed above as Arafat's compliance with the Wye River Memorandum, has the force of law as a presidential edict. It was not submitted to the Legislative Council. It also served as an extremely effective tool for self-censorship among Palestinians of all persuasions and professions. Significantly, one of the hallmarks of human rights abuses by the PA, including violations of the right to freedom of expression, is that such depredations usually routinely occur outside any legal framework. There does not appear to have been a single case where an individual's arrest and detention were justified on the basis of the Press and Publication Law or the Anti-Incitement Presidential Decree. The various Palestinian security forces simply arrested and detained individuals at will without even reference to the edicts (or other laws).[74]

From the time of its establishment in 1994, the PA has demonstrated a pattern of violations, progressively restricting the right to freedom of expression through a variety of means, including arrest and detention by various security forces. Many detainees were held incommunicado and subjected to torture. Those arrested were rarely shown an arrest warrant or even informed of the reason for the arrest. Nevertheless, the fact that the arrest took place hours or days after they delivered a controversial speech or wrote a critical article, for example, leaves little room for doubt as to the reasons for detention. As a rule, an individual was invited to have coffee with someone in one or another security service, only to be held in detention for days, weeks, or even months. Typically, detainees were subjected to torture. Rarely has the PA brought anyone to court during their detention. In addition to arrests, the PA on occasion subjected individuals to beatings while they were going about their work. One example involves Munir Abu Rizq, at the time chief editor of *al-Haya al-Jadida* (New Life). On attempting to enter police headquarters in Gaza City in August 1998 to cover a session of a special military court that was trying three men for murder (two of whom were subsequently found guilty and executed), Abu Rizq was severely beaten by the police at the entrance to the station and prevented from covering the event.[75]

Newspapers, research centers, news agencies, and TV and radio stations were arbitrarily closed for several days to weeks and even months. The distribution of publications, especially newspapers, was also restricted. Sometimes the security services confiscated an entire edition of a newspaper because some official found an article offensive. The PA also occasionally resorted to the confiscation of books. For example, in December 1996, the GIS confiscated books at the border coming from Jordan. (Ironically, they were books that Israeli officials had allowed through.) The Palestinian Human Rights Monitoring Group, together with the minister of information, wrote to the GIS asking for a clarification of the agency's actions and asking for the books' release to their owner. The GIS did not respond, and the books were not released.[76] In 1996, Arafat banned all books written by the internationally acclaimed Palestinian intellectual Edward Said. Bookstores that had them in stock were ordered to remove them from the shelves, and importation of the offending volumes was prohibited. By 1998–1999, journalists were arrested for writing about demonstrations and strikes. Newspapers were prohibited from printing pictures of burning Israeli and U.S. flags. It was forbidden to print positive articles about any opposition groups, and security issues could not be discussed in any dimension (see Table 6.7).[77]

Self-Censorship

Self-censorship was widespread under the PA, and a surprising number of individuals admit they practiced it. The problem resides in the ambiguity that surrounds what could be considered an offense at a given time or by a given official. Israeli practices in this area were far clearer: everything that a newspaper printed from obituaries to crossword puzzles had to be submitted to the censor. If the censor did not like it, he cut it, but if it did pass, then journalists and newspapers were rarely punished retroactively. Under the PA, by contrast, writers, academics, journalists, and others had to guess what was and was not acceptable, what crossed an arbitrary, murky, and changing line. If they guessed incorrectly, the consequences could be very severe. Thus, erring on the side of caution became a survival mechanism in a situation fraught with uncertainty. Though understandable from the viewpoint of the individual, the cumulative effect of self-censorship was debilitating for society, because no one had an accurate picture of the political, economic, social, and security situations. Rumors became the main source of information.[78] Moreover, in the words of Palestinian journalist Khalid Amayreh:

> Self-censorship is the worst kind of censorship because it thrives on hypocrisy, sycophancy, and mendacity. And a press whose modus operandi is this trio of immoralities will never be able to help create a healthy society. The opposite is true. The real task of any journalist worthy of the name must be the pursuit of truth, and a journalist's responsibility should be first and foremost to his conscience.[79]

Table 6.7   Status of Human Rights and Democracy Under the Palestinian
            Authority

Date	How do you evaluate the status of democracy and human rights under the PA? (% of respondents who replied very good or good; other choices were bad or very bad)		Do you believe people in the WBGS can criticize the PA without fear? (% of respondents who said yes from a yes/no choice)
May 1994[a]	Very good		
	Good		
May 1995	Very good		50.5
	Good		
June 1996[b,c]	Very good		43.9
	Good		
Sept. 1996	Very good	6.5	
	Good	34.9	
Dec. 1996[d]	Very good	8.7	37.4
	Good	34.2	
Apr. 1997[e]	Very good	11.2	
	Good	38.4	
Sept. 1997	Very good	8.6	35.6
	Good	24.9	
Dec. 1997	Very good	10.8	
	Good	30.1	
Mar. 1998[f]	Very good	9.0	37.1
	Good	28.5	
June 1998	Very good	6.0	39.0
	Good	28.6	
Oct. 1998	Very good	5.1	37.3
	Good	21.9	
Jan. 1999	Very good	6.1	41.0
	Good	25.4	
Apr. 1999	Very good	5.3	38.8
	Good	20.6	
June 1999	Very good	4.7	38.6
	Good	22.7	
Oct. 1999	Very good	5.8	38.1
	Good	26.0	
Dec. 1999	Very good	3.5	30.5
	Good	19.8	
Jan. 2000	Very good	6.1	30.3
	Good	24.9	
Apr. 2000	Very good	2.6	28.7
	Good	19.9	
July 2000	Very good	3.5	32.2
	Good	17.1	
July 2001	Very good	3.1	
	Good	17.5	

Source: This polling data was carried out by the Center for Palestine Research & Studies—Survey Research Unit, Ramallah, Palestine.

Notes: a. 54.8% concerned about repression of opposition to PA.

b. 30% of people said freedom of expression was worse after arrival of PA than before (under Israel).

c. 37.7% believe the Palestinian media under PA show failure to uphold freedom of expression and democracy.

d. 35.5% believe country is heading toward democracy.

e. 11.3% thought government was heading toward democracy.

f. 28.4% believe the government is heading toward democracy.

The Assault on Universities and Civil Society

Throughout the occupation, Palestinian universities have fought for independence and autonomy. They were at the forefront in resisting Israel, especially during the first intifada, while developing into fine academic institutions that produced well-trained professionals in virtually every field. Universities are among the most important institutions of civil society, and their lively student electoral politics were a microcosm of Palestinian society. However, within a year of the arrival of the PA, in May 1995, Arafat issued the University Security Administration Presidential Decree. The University Security Administration was placed under the control of Colonel Khalil Arafat, who was given the title of general director and was part of the PSS.

The purpose of the administration was to infiltrate university campuses and to monitor students and professors—what they said inside and outside of class, what organizations and activities they participated in, what they read and wrote, whom they associated with, and so on. Even more ominous, the security apparatus used financial inducements to persuade students to leave their party affiliations and join Fateh. The security people existed on campuses overtly (e.g., as security guards or as members of the University Security Administration who registered to take a degree) and covertly (e.g., students who were paid to work as undercover spies). Whether they were students, University Security Administration officials, or undercover agents, they were required to report daily to their supervisors when someone or something critical of Arafat or the PA was encountered.[80] University officials in Gaza accepted the decree,[81] but in the West Bank, every university refused the establishment of the security service on its campus. West Bank administrators threatened to shut down rather than allow PA security forces on campus.

In response, the University Security Administration made a very public demonstration of its presence in March 1996 at an-Najah University in Nablus, when students were protesting against the arrest of Munther Mushaqi, president of the student council. Some 180 armed men stormed the campus and beat everyone in sight with batons—students as well as professors. They also fired live bullets and tear gas.[82] Long before this event, however, security forces had quietly infiltrated all West Bank campuses and were monitoring professors, classes, students, and activities.

Khalil Arafat issued a series of instructions on the duties and obligations of the administration, violations of which were considered violations of the law. They included such things as "complete coordination and full cooperation should take place between the university guard [the official administration individual on campus] and the student council." Significantly, however, as in other areas under PA control, the department in charge of university security did not have sole jurisdiction. The various other security services had infiltrated the campuses as well and extended their control over what individuals and organizations they could.[83] There were benefits for those who worked for the security services. For example, students who earned low marks in their courses could have a senior security official "talk" with a university professor or even, on occasion, an administrator and request that the grades be changed. This was common practice during the first intifada as well, and most professors strongly resisted entreaties to change grades—especially in West Bank universities. Conversely, students who supported opposition parties or criticized the PA, the peace process, or President Arafat were often arrested and held in detention without charge for periods of several days to weeks and even months.

Professors were not immune from the scrutiny of the security services. Fathi Subub, a professor at Al-Azhar University in Gaza, was arrested, detained, and tortured and lost his job for asking his students in a final exam to write essays on administrative corruption in the PA agencies and administrative corruption at Al-Azhar. Ayyub Othman, professor of English at Al-Azhar, was fired after he publicized incidents of forgery at the university. Ahmed Sa'id Dahlan was denied promotion from assistant to associate professor at Al-Azhar because as head of the teacher union he insisted on a hearing of two professors' cases (one of whom was Ayyub Othman). Abdul Sattar Kassem taught at both an-Najah and Birzeit Universities. After writing an article critical of Arafat, he was shot at the gate to an-Najah. (He survived the assassination attempt and later signed the manifesto "The Homeland Calls Us," for which he was imprisoned.) Professors were also victims of periodic budgetary crises during which the PA claimed not to have the money to pay their salaries. Such crises occurred with astonishing frequency, and some lasted as long as four months.[84]

Conclusion

The Palestinians certainly did not expect, or deserve, to have such leadership. No people deserve such treatment. The governing malfeasance, corruption, and human rights excesses engaged in by Arafat and his coterie of Tunisians led to bitter disappointment and outrage among the Palestinian people. Likewise, Palestinians were highly resentful of the consequences of Israeli-PA security cooperation. It is incontrovertible that the Al-Aqsa intifada was a revolt against Arafat and the PA as much as against Israel and the farce of Oslo. Those who claim that Arafat orchestrated the intifada for political gain after the failure of Camp David are engaging in pure propaganda. By the fall of 2000, Arafat could not have mobilized the mass public on any issue.

In late 1999, several men in Gaza, in different settings and from varying age categories, confided to me that "we were better off under the occupation than under Arafat's rule." These were not cavalier comments but reflected the depth of frustration felt by ordinary people everywhere in the Occupied Territories. Individuals felt immobilized, considering it impossible to struggle on two fronts—against Israel *and* against their own leaders—even more so because as the seven Oslo years moved on it became increasingly difficult for people to distinguish where Israel left off and the PA began. Put simply, the PA's efforts to meet every Israeli requirement made it appear to many Palestinians as surrogates for Israel, or at worst, as collaborators.

The PA—its security apparatuses and its physical institutions—was totally destroyed by Israel in the course of the Al-Aqsa intifada. By the summer of 2002, Arafat was a virtual prisoner in his Ramallah compound, which had been bulldozed except for the sliver of space in which he ate, slept, and conducted business. Ironically, Israel's intense humiliation of Arafat resulted in a short-lived popular resurrection among the masses. At the same time, several of his senior officials were scurrying around attempting to make the reforms demanded by Israel and the United States as a condition for resuming negotiations. The fact that these demands were no more than smoke and mirrors was not lost on the Palestinian people, who wanted real reforms and genuine democracy, not another U.S.-Israeli–imposed regime.

Chapter 7 examines the role of the United States in the peace process. Aside from Israel's rejectionism, U.S. policies are the single most important factor impeding the Palestinians from achieving national and political rights in a viable, independent state alongside Israel. The United States has supported Israel in every position and behavior it has taken vis-à-vis the Palestinians. If one considers the power disparities between Israel and the Palestinians, along with the added weight of Washington's support, the imbalance becomes absurd. Throughout the seven years of Oslo, despite Washington's rhetoric and symbolic flourishes, in reality it acted solely to support Israel. Palestinian rights, interests, and objectives were never part of the U.S. agenda. Understanding the nature and depth of U.S.-Israeli ties will illuminate why the United States has not been an honest broker and never will be. It will also suggest, unfortunately, that unless Israel, by itself, undergoes a radical transformation, Palestinians will not achieve even their minimal objectives.

Notes

1. Edward W. Said, "Are There No Limits to Corruption?" in *The End of the Peace Process: Oslo and After* (New York: Pantheon Books, 2000), p. 180.

2. The quote *"bli bagatz u'bli btzelem"* appears in Gershon Baskin, *What Went Wrong: Oslo—the PLO, Israel, and Some Additional Facts* (Jerusalem: Israel/Palestine Center for Research and Information, n.d. [ca. February/March 2001]).

3. Ibid., p. 2.

4. The Jerusalem Media and Communications Center was founded in 1988 by a group of Palestinian researchers trained in the methods of statistical survey research. Each of their surveys details the methodology and the nature of the sample distribution included in the survey.

5. Jerusalem Media and Communications Center, *Public Opinion Poll No. 7: On Palestinian Attitudes to More than One Year of Autonomy* (Jerusalem: Jerusalem Media and Communications Center, June 1995), pp. 1–7.

6. Naseer Aruri, *The Obstruction of Peace: The U.S., Israel, and the Palestinians* (Monroe, ME: Common Courage Press, 1995), p. 240.

7. On civil society, see Glenn E. Robinson, "The Peace of the Powerful," in Roane Carey, ed., *The New Intifada: Resisting Israel's Apartheid* (London: Verso, 2001), pp. 116–119.

8. The Palestinian Center for Policy and Survey Research is an independent nonprofit Palestinian institution and think tank of policy analysis and academic research founded in 1993. Its director is Khalil Shikaki, who received his doctorate from Columbia University. There are seven other specialist researchers and a highly trained team of 120 field-workers.

9. Center for Policy and Survey Research, *Armed Attacks, PNA Performance, the Palestinian Legislative Council, Corruption* (Ramallah, Palestinian Center for Policy and Survey Research Polls—Survey Research Unit, Poll no. 25, December 1996).

10. See Khalil Shikaki, "The Peace Process, National Reconstruction, and the Transition to Democracy," *Journal of Palestine Studies* 25, no. 2 (winter 1996): 9–11 and passim.

11. "Palestinian Civil Society Under Siege," *On the Record* (newsletter of the Advocacy Project of Grassroots International) 15, no. 2 (June 1, 2001).

12. Several excellent analyses are provided by Grassroots International in addition to "Palestinian Civil Society Under Siege." See "Rising to the Challenge," *On the Record* 15, no. 1 (June 1, 2001); "Betrayed by Oslo," *On the Record* 15, no. 3 (June 6, 2001); "Feeling the Strain: Gaza's Mental Health Crisis," *On the Record* 15, no. 4 (June 12, 2001); "From Small Families to Small Business: Empowering Women," *On the Record* 15, no. 5 (June 21, 2001); "Braking the Cycle of Dependency," *On the Record* 15, no. 6 (June 27, 2001); "The Challenge of Agricultural Development," *On the Record* 15, no. 7 (July 1, 2001); "In Defense of Human Rights," *On the Record* 15, no. 8 (July 9,

2001); and "The Refugee Connection," *On the Record* 15, no. 9 (July 18, 2001). Also excellent on civil society and NGOs is Roni Ben Efrat, "Porcupine Tangos: The Palestinian Authority and the NGOs (Accompanied by the CIA Orchestra)," *Challenge* (Tel Aviv, Israeli, monthly, English), March 14, 2000.

13. See the analysis by Ran HaCohen, "The Palestinian 'State': A Means of Depriving Palestinians Freedom and Equality," *News from Within* (Jerusalem, Israeli, monthly, English) 25, no. 5 (May 1999). Also see Charmaine Seitz, "The Palestinian State—What State Is It In," *Palestine Report* (Jerusalem, Palestinian weekly, English) 6, no. 7 (August 4, 1999).

14. One good analysis is Graham Usher, *Palestine in Crisis: The Struggle for Peace and Political Independence After Oslo* (London: Pluto, 1995), pp. 61–77.

15. Se'eb Erakat, who became his spokesman, was a public exception, but Erakat had no influence on Arafat.

16. Danny Rubinstein, "The Outsider on the Inside," *Ha'aretz* (Jerusalem, Israeli daily, English), January 26, 2001.

17. On the methods by which they governed, see Palestinian Center for Human Rights, *Promoting the Rule of Law and Democracy in Areas Under the Jurisdiction of the Palestinian National Authority: Report 2000* (Gaza Strip: Palestinian Center for Human Rights, 2001), pp. 62–96. Also see Palestinian Human Rights Monitoring Group, *The Palestine Human Rights Monitor: Annual Report 1999* 4, no. 1 (Jerusalem: Palestinian Human Rights Monitoring Group, 2000).

18. "Israeli-Palestinian Interim Agreement on the West Bank and the Gaza Strip," Washington, DC, September 28, 1995, reprinted in *Journal of Palestine Studies* 25, no. 2 (winter 1996); arts. 11, 12, and 14 plus annex 1, pp. 127–130. Also see Israeli Ministry of Foreign Affairs online documents.

19. Gal Luft, "The Palestinian Security Services: Between Police and Army," *Middle East Review of International Affairs* 3, no. 2 (June 1999).

20. One good analysis is Graham Usher, "The Politics of Internal Security: The PA's New Intelligence Services," *Journal of Palestine Studies* 25, no. 2 (winter 1996): 21–34.

21. Abdel Rahman Abu Arafeh et al., *Democratic Formation in Palestine* (Jerusalem: Arab Thought Forum, 1999), pp. 25–38.

22. For background and complete final draft, see Anis al-Qasem, *Draft Basic Law for the National Authority in the Transition Period* (Occasional Document Series no. 5) (Jerusalem: Jerusalem Media and Communication Center, February 1996).

23. Baskin, *What Went Wrong.*

24. For a good analysis of the Legislative Council, see 'Ali Jarbawi et al., *Third Annual Report 1 January 1997 to 31 December 1997* (Jerusalem: Palestinian Independent Commission for Citizens' Rights, 1998), pp. 33–64.

25. LAW, *Executive Interference in the Palestinian Judiciary* (a report by the Independent Judiciary Unit) (Jerusalem: Palestinian Society for the Protection of Human Rights and the Environment—LAW, 1999), pp. 26–35.

26. Iyad Sarraj, "Whispers of the Scared" (translated from the Arabic by Joharah Baker); first appeared in *al-Quds* (Jerusalem, Palestinian daily), October 10, 1998; *Palestine Report*, October 16, 1998, pp. 10–11.

27. A very good analysis of *hamayel* politics is Rita Giacaman, Islah Jad,

and Penny Johnson, "For the Common Good? Gender and Social Citizenship in Palestine," *MERIP Middle East Report* 26, no. 1 (January–March 1996): 11–17. Also good is Hillel Frisch, "Modern Absolutist or Neopatriarchal State Building? Customary Law, Extended Families, and the Palestine Authority," *International Journal of Middle East Studies* 29, no. 3 (August 1997): 341–358.

28. A good analysis of the social disintegration is Sara Roy, "The Crisis Within: The Struggle for Palestinian Society," *Critique: Journal for Critical Studies of the Middle East*, no. 17 (fall 2000): 5–30.

29. LAW, *Executive Interference in the Palestinian Judiciary*, pp. 41–51. Also see LAW, *Reality and Ambitions: Judicial Independence in PA Controlled Areas* (Jerusalem: Palestinian Society for the Protection of Human Rights and the Environment—LAW, 1999).

30. LAW, *Executive Interference in the Palestinian Judiciary*, pp. 52–56. Also see LAW, *Military and State Security Courts in PA-Controlled Areas* (Jerusalem: Palestinian Society for the Protection of Human Rights and the Environment—LAW, 1999). Also see Palestinian Human Rights Monitoring Group, *Death in Custody No Longer Surprising: The Palestine Human Rights Monitor* (Jerusalem, Palestinian occasional, English), a publication of the Palestinian Human Rights Monitoring Group, no. 5 (September–December 1997); and Nina Sovich, "The Death Penalty Under the PA," *News from Within* 15, no. 4 (April 1999). Also for a good analysis of the judiciary, see Jarbawi et al., *Third Annual Report 1 January 1997 to 31 December 1997,* pp. 65–94.

31. LAW, *Executive Interference in the Palestinian Judiciary*, p. 58 (quote) and pp. 57–63 and passim. Also see Abu Arafeh et al., *Democratic Formation in Palestine*, pp. 39–43.

32. Khaled Amayreh, "Palestinian NGOs Under Attack," *al-Ahram Weekly* (Cairo, English), no. 435 (June 24–30, 1999).

33. Amal Jamal, "The Palestinian Media: An Obedient Servant or a Vanguard of Democracy?" *Journal of Palestine Studies* 29, no. 3 (spring 2000): 45–59.

34. Rex Brynen, "The Neopatrimonial Dimension of Palestinian Politics," *Journal of Palestine Studies* 25, no. 1 (autumn 1995): 23–36.

35. Roy, "The Crisis Within: The Struggle for Palestinian Society."

36. Ibid.

37. For extensive details, see Faud Abu Libdeh, Michal Schwartz, and Roni Ben Efrat, "Housemaids in Gaza: The Story of Mela Afandie," *Challenge*, no. 61 (May–June 2000).

38. David Hirst, "Shameless in Gaza," *The Guardian Weekly* (London), April 27, 1997. Donna Abu-Nasr, "Gazans' Bitterness Grows Against Arafat's Elite," *New York Times* (International News), June 10, 1997; Roy, "The Crisis Within: The Struggle for Palestinian Society."

39. David Hirst, "Shameless in Gaza"; and Abu-Nasr, "Gazans' Bitterness Grows Against Arafat's Elite."

40. Ronen Bergman and David Ratner, "The Man Who Swallowed Gaza," *Ha'aretz Weekend Supplement,* April 4, 1997. Also see Michael Schwartz, "A Secret Account in Tel Aviv Funds Arafat's Oppression," *Challenge*, no. 43 (May–June 1997).

41. Bergman and Ratner, "The Man Who Swallowed Gaza."

42. Edward Said, *The End of the Peace Process: Oslo and After* (New York: Pantheon Books, 2000), p. 179.

43. Bergman and Ratner, "The Man Who Swallowed Gaza."

44. Ibid.

45. Amos Harel, "Rich Palestinians Moving Assets Outside PA Areas," *Ha'aretz*, February 24, 2002.

46. Roy, "The Crisis Within: The Struggle for Palestinian Society."

47. The quotation from Hussam Khader is found in Bergman and Ratner, "The Man Who Swallowed Gaza."

48. Amira Hass, *Drinking the Sea at Gaza: Days and Nights in a Land Under Siege* (New York: Metropolitan Books, Henry Holt, 1999), pp. 301–306, 314–315.

49. On PA monopolies, see Michal Schwartz, "The Great Gasoline Scam: Fueling Coexistence," *Challenge*, no. 53 (January–February 1999); Roni Ben Efrat, Assaf Adiv, and Stephen Langfur, "Something's Rotten in the Nonstate of Palestine: Corruption Under Arafat, the Legislators Speak Out," *Challenge*, no. 45 (September–October 1997); Ali Jaradt, "Corruption Is Obstructing the Development of Our Society," *News from Within* 17, no. 3 (April 2001): 21–23; Ilan Halevi, "Self-Government, Democracy, and Mismanagement Under the Palestinian Authority," *Journal of Palestine Studies* 27, no. 3 (spring 1998): 35–48; Murray Kahl, "Corruption Within the Palestinian Authority," report prepared for Congressman Jim Saxton (R–NJ) for use by the U.S. Congress to suspend aid to the PA under the Middle East Peace Facilitation Act, October 30, 1997; and Margaret Warner, "Rating Arafat's Rule," *PBS Online Focus*, May 28, 1997 (transcript).

50. Said, *The End of the Peace Process*, p. 179.

51. Bergman and Ratner, "The Man Who Swallowed Gaza."

52. Ibid. Also see Roy, "The Crisis Within: The Struggle for Palestinian Society," citing the U.S. Department of State (summer 2000), and Tracy Wilkinson and Mary Curtis, "Statehood No Panacea for the Palestinians," *Los Angeles Times*, September 4, 2000.

53. Bergman and Ratner, "The Man Who Swallowed Gaza."

54. Baskin, *What Went Wrong*, p. 2.

55. See Ben Efrat, Adiv, and Langfur, "Something's Rotten in the Nonstate of Palestine."

56. Graham Usher and Tarek Hassan, "More of the Same," *al-Ahram Weekly*, August 13–19, 1998; Abdel-Jawad Saleh, "Something's Missing Here," *al-Ahram Weekly*, September 30–October 6, 1999; and Ben Efrat, Adiv, and Langfur, "Something's Rotten in the Nonstate of Palestine."

57. Usher and Hassan, "More of the Same."

58. Ibid.

59. For the full statement and the list of original signatories, see Palestine Human Rights Monitoring Group, Press Release, "PA Arrested 7 Academics and Politicians Because They Spoke Their Mind" (Jerusalem: Palestine Human Rights Monitoring Group, November 29, 1999); Roni Ben Efrat, "The Manifesto of the Twenty: The Hidden Consensus Finds a Voice," *Challenge*, no. 59 (January–February 2000); Toufic Haddad, "Interview with Abdul Jawad Saleh: 'I Believe This to Be the Beginning of a New Movement for Change,'" *News from Within* 16, no. 1 (January 2000).

60. See Amnesty International, *Five Years After Oslo, Durable Peace*

Must Be Based on Justice (London: Amnesty International, September 1998) (MDE 15/077/1998 09/09/98), and Palestinian Human Rights Monitoring Group, "State of Human Rights in Palestine," *Palestinian Human Rights Monitor*, no. 4 (July–August 1997); Palestinian Human Rights Monitoring Group, *Annual Report 1999: The Palestinian Human Rights Monitor* (Jerusalem: Palestinian Human Rights Monitoring Group, 2000); Amnesty International, *Palestinian Authority: Prolonged Political Detention, Torture, and Unfair Trial* (New York: Amnesty International, December 1996) (MDE 15/68/96 02/12/1996); Palestinian Center for Human Rights, *Annual Report 2000* (Gaza Strip: Palestinian Center for Human Rights, 2001). LAW, *Human Rights in PA-Controlled Areas During 1997* (Jerusalem: Palestinian Society for the Protection of Human Rights and the Environment—LAW, 1998).

61. All of the information on this case study comes from Yehezkel Lein and Renata Capella, *Cooperating Against Justice: Human Rights Violations by Israel and the Palestinian National Authority Following the Murders in Wadi Qelt* (Jerusalem: B'Tselem—the Israeli Information Center for Human Rights in the Occupied Territories, and Palestinian Society for the Protection of Human Rights and the Environment—LAW, 1999).

62. Ibid.

63. For a good analysis, see the Israeli scholar Tanya Reinhart, "The A-Sherif Affair," English version online at http://www.tau.ac.il/~reinhart/political/A-Sharif.html (the article originally appeared in Hebrew in *Yediot Aharonot* [Israeli daily], April 14, 1998; Lein and Capella, *Cooperating Against Justice.*

64. Lein and Capella, *Cooperating Against Justice.*

65. Palestinian Human Rights Monitoring Group, "Political Arrest," *The Palestine Human Rights Monitor* (Jerusalem: Palestinian Human Rights Monitoring Group, March 2000), p. 10. For a good analysis of the human rights abuses growing out of the Wye memorandum including Arafat's presidential decree, see Naseer Aruri, "The Wye Memorandum: Netanyahu's Oslo and Unreciprocal Reciprocity," *Journal of Palestine Studies* 28, no. 2 (winter 1999): 21–22. Human Rights Watch also argued that the security clauses in the Wye memorandum were incompatible with the preservation of human rights in the Occupied Territories; see Human Rights Watch, "An Analysis of the Wye River Memorandum" (New York: Human Rights Watch, November 1998), reprinted in *Journal of Palestine Studies* 28, no. 2 (winter 1999): 162–164.

66. Roni Ben Efrat, "The Telltale Silence of the Post-Oslo Palestinian Press," *Palestinian Diary*, January 28, 2001. Also see Human Rights Watch, *Human Rights Watch Documents Repression and Intimidation by Palestinian Authority in Self-Rule Areas: Criticizes U.S., Israel for Neglect of Human Rights when Demanding Security Crackdown* (New York: Human Rights Watch, October 1997).

67. Palestinian Human Rights Monitoring Group, *Resources* (Jerusalem: Palestinian Human Rights Monitoring Group, 2001).

68. An excellent analysis of the nonfunctioning of these courts is LAW, *Military and State Security Courts in PA-Controlled Territories.*

69. All the statistical information in this section came from Palestinian Human Rights Monitoring Group, *Resources.* For analyses, see Nina Sovich, "The Death Penalty Under the PA," *News from Within* 15, no. 4 (April 1999): 16–18; Palestinian Human Rights Monitoring Group, "Death in Custody No Longer Surprising"; LAW, *Torture and Criminal Liability: The Palestinian*

Security Services (PSS) (Jerusalem: Palestinian Society for the Protection of Human Rights and the Environment—LAW, 2000); Muna Hamzeh-Muhaisen, "Another Execution in Palestine," *Palestine Report* 5, no. 36 (March 5, 1999); LAW, *Military and State Security Courts in PA-Controlled Areas;* LAW, *Capital Punishment in PNA-Controlled Areas* (Jerusalem: Palestinian Society for the Protection of Human Rights and the Environment—LAW, 1999); Palestinian Human Rights Monitoring Group, "The Practice of Torture in the Palestinian Authority," *Palestinian Human Rights Monitor*, no. 3 (May–June 1997); Palestinian Human Rights Monitoring Group, "Preventative Security Services Tortures Innocent Men into Confessing," *Palestinian Human Rights Monitor*, no. 2 (March–April 1997).

70. Amnesty International, *Report 1997* (Palestinian Authority: covering the year 1996) (London: Amnesty International, 1997); Amnesty International, *Report 1998* (Palestinian Authority: covering the year 1997) (London: Amnesty International, 1998); Amnesty International, *Report 1999* (Palestinian Authority: covering the year 1998) (London: Amnesty International, 1999); Amnesty International, *Report 2000* (Palestinian Authority: covering the year 1999) (London: Amnesty International, 2000); Amnesty International, *Report 2001* (Palestinian Authority: covering the year 2000) (London: Amnesty International, 2001).

71. Amnesty International, *Palestinian Authority: Silencing Dissent* (London: Amnesty International, September 2000).

72. One good analysis is Hanthala Palestine, "Prisoners: Palestinians Detained by the Palestinian Authority," Jerusalem, October 1999. Another fair analysis is Kenneth C.W. Leiter, "Life Under the Palestinian Authority," *Middle East Quarterly* (September 1998).

73. Amnesty International, *Palestinian Authority: Silencing Dissent* (London: Amnesty International, September 2000) (MDE 21/016/2000).

74. Ibid.

75. Ibid.

76. Palestinian Human Rights Monitoring Group, "Freedom of the Press, Publications, and Speech in the PA," *Palestine Human Rights Monitor,* no. 3 (May–June 1997).

77. "Internet Against Arafat," *Dagbladet* (Oslo, Norway, translated from the Norwegian), December 28, 1999, online on the *Internews* website.

78. This analysis is well made by Ben Efrat, "The Telltale Silence of the Post-Oslo Palestinian Press." Also see Daoud Kuttab, "Freedom of Expression? Sometimes," *Jerusalem Post,* September 7, 2000, and Daoud Kuttab, "Freedom of Expression Challenges in the Middle East," *CCPJ Reporter* (the Official Newsletter of the Canadian Committee to Protect Journalists), no. 2 (July 1998). Also see Khalid Amayreh, "Self-Censorship—the New Ghoul Haunting Palestinian Journalists," *Palestinian Human Rights Monitor*, no. 1 (January–February 1999); Khalid Amayreh, "The PA Clamps Down (Again) on the Press," *Challenge*, no. 53 (January–February 1999).

79. Amayreh, "Self-Censorship—the New Ghoul Haunting Palestinian Journalists."

80. Palestinian Human Rights Monitoring Group, "Academic Freedom at the Palestinian Universities," *Palestinian Human Rights Monitor* 3, no. 4 (August 1999).

81. In Gaza, the Islamic University feared the repercussions if it refused, and al-Azhar University is a Fatah institution.

82. Palestinian Human Rights Monitoring Group, "Academic Freedom at the Palestinian Universities."

83. Ibid.

84. Bassem Eid, *Academic Freedom at Palestinian Universities* (Jerusalem: Palestinian Human Rights Monitoring Group, August 10, 1999), 20 pages. Also see "Big Brother Enrolls at Palestinian Universities," *News from Within* 15, no. 10 (November 1999).

7

Fateful Triangle: The Palestinians, Israel, and the United States

The cultural identification of the United States with Israel simply by its nature excludes the Palestinians. Palestinians will never be part of the being of the United States and will never be perceived as contributing to U.S. strategy and defense. However perceptions of the Palestinians may change, their viewpoint will never become an integral part of the [national] frame of reference. . . . Like U.S. policymakers for almost a century, [President Bill] Clinton's basic frame of reference was Israel-centered, and despite his superficially friendly ties with Palestinian leaders, he continued until the end of his term to mediate the conflict from a perspective focused primarily on Israel's concerns rather than equally on the concerns of both sides.

— Kathleen Christison[1]

And here we come to the main reason why Israel is able to maintain its occupation for more than a generation despite its manifest illegality and despite efforts to call Israel to account: American administrations and, ultimately, the American Congress.

— Jeff Halper[2]

The U.S. relationship with the Palestinians is inextricably interconnected to the U.S. affiliation with Zionism and Israel. These ties require three levels of analysis. The first involves the perceptions, beliefs, and syllogisms about Israel and the Palestinians that undergird American understanding of and behavior toward the Israeli-Palestinian conflict.[3] The second concerns the institutionalization of one of these beliefs: that which posits Israel as a strategic asset to U.S. national interests. This assumption, predominant after 1967, catapulted the U.S.-Israeli relationship into an all-encompassing strategic partnership, which in turn has prompted Washington to give Israel a free hand in pursuit of its interests vis-à-vis the Palestinians. The third level of analysis includes the diverse collection of pro-Israeli advocacy organizations in the United States and the ways in which they influence the construction and reinforcement of "knowledge" about Israel and the Palestinians, as well as the formulation of official U.S. policy on the conflict. I divide the chapter into two sections: The first is an analysis of the nature of the U.S.-Israeli relationship; the second looks at the specific policies pursued by the Bill Clinton and George W. Bush administrations as they relate to the peace process and the Palestinian-Israeli conflict.

Israel in the United States

Perceptions Toward the Palestinians

U.S. policy toward Palestine and the Palestinians has deep perceptual roots based on a series of beliefs, assumptions, and misconceptions that originated in the nineteenth century and over time have been transformed into "common wisdom," "truth," or "knowledge." Briefly summarized, these postulates included a mythologized Palestine as the land of the bible, the birthplace of Jesus, and, therefore, a Judeo-Christian domain that is an important extension of the West. Its capture by Muslims during the seventh century C.E., and its usurpation and "despoilment" were unfortunate historic wrongs that required correction—considered imminently possible during the nineteenth-century age of progress in the West.[4] In the words of one analyst, "With the onset of missionary involvement in the Levant, the real people of Palestine, their traditions and culture, their towns and villages underwent a 'perceptual depopulation'—a form of ethnic cleansing on the conceptual level."[5] Thus, the Zionist contention that Palestine was "a land without people for a people without land" was readily absorbed into U.S. political culture.[6] If considered at all, Palestinians were dehumanized and regarded as primitive, violent, warlike, and hostile to Christians and Jews.[7]

The belief in a theocratized Palestine that belonged to the West, in turn, assigned an altruistic motive to Western imperialism in the region. Thus, many in the United States considered the British Mandate, and the Zionist project for "redemption" of the Holy Land that it facilitated, as noble and laudable. In particular, many accepted the Zionist proposition that it would bring progress, prosperity, and peace to Palestine. And so when Palestinians rebelled, as they did, for example, in 1936, the U.S. press portrayed them as barbarians prone to fanatical violence and depicted the conflict as either racial (Arab anti-Semitism) or religious (fanatic Muslims killing Jews over a small space at the Western Wall). It was rarely presented as a conflict between two peoples over the same piece of land or as a colonial settler movement that was displacing indigenous peoples.[8]

Over time, Zionists embellished the original missionary-Zionist postulates with new socially constructed assertions. One highly emotive one was the depiction of the genocide of European Jews as a uniquely Jewish phenomenon—the Holocaust—and the manipulation of the guilt and obligation of the West (especially the United States) for not preventing it and for denying immigration rights to Jewish refugees of Nazism.[9] Corollaries to this included the portrayal of Jews as essentialist, eternal victims.[10] Later, Israel was presented as an embattled David against the Arab Goliath. Israeli analyst Jeff Halper writes in regard to these precepts:

> Israel has acted with absolute impunity vis-à-vis international law, and has escaped accountability. It has done so in a number of ways. First it cynically presents itself to the world as a "victim." [Former Premier] Begin was the first to make the Holocaust into a political tool giving moral authority to his policies of aggressive settlement and the invasion of Lebanon, while effectively using Western/Christian guilt to deflect criticism of his policies.[11]

In fact, during the second year of the Al-Aqsa intifada, Israeli leaders began to claim that the Palestinians were an "existential" threat to Israel.[12]

The notion that Israel's security is the driving force in its foreign policy has been so internalized in American culture that the United States has simply overlooked Israel's history of regional aggression. Although it is true that leading up to 1967 Arab leaders frequently made inflammatory and hostile statements regarding Israel (some continue to do so), it is also true that in 1948 Israel, within six months of its founding, defeated the armies of every Arab state in the Middle East, including Palestinian irregulars, and succeeded in a major offensive against Egypt. In 1956, Israel invaded Egypt and in less than ten days occupied the Gaza Strip as well as the Sinai Peninsula down to Sharm al-Sheikh. In six days in 1967, Israel crushed the military forces of Egypt, Syria, and Jordan in a war it initiated, and occupied vast amounts of Arab territory in the aftermath. In 1973, Israel quickly reversed a limited Syrian-Egyptian initiative intended to restore lands that were occupied by Israel in 1967. Not only were the Arab forces defeated; at war's end,

Israel occupied even more Arab territory. In 1978 and again in 1982, Israel invaded Lebanon—the second invasion resulting in an eighteen-year occupation of southern Lebanon.[13] Israel possesses overwhelming conventional military power: it has the fourth strongest military on the globe, and experts acknowledge its capacity to defeat all Arab states combined. It also has a significant (though unofficial) nuclear capability, as well as highly developed chemical and biological weapons. Nevertheless, the construct of an omnipresent Arab threat to Israel's existence and security was objectified in American culture.

Additionally, the ideological truth of Israel as the only democracy in the Middle East—a bastion of Western civilization in a sea of backward dictatorships, Muslim terrorists, and greedy oil sheiks—has had a powerful impact on U.S. perceptions.[14] Indeed, Israel's systematic discrimination against its Arab citizens is rarely an issue for discussion in the United States.[15] Yet as Philippa Strum, former president of the American-Israeli Civil Liberties Coalition, wrote:

> [Palestinian citizens of Israel] . . . are not permitted to serve in the armed forces . . . [which] disqualifies them for such armed service-linked government benefits as government-backed mortgages, government-backed university scholarships, and the regular welfare payments all Israeli families receive per child. The statute covering child payments specifically excludes as recipients families in which a parent has no army service, except Jewish Orthodox families where the father has refused to serve because his religion requires him to serve only God. Thus Arabs who want to serve in the army can neither serve nor receive benefits: Jews who refuse to serve receive benefits. . . . Numerous statistics indicate that Arab municipalities receive far less government funds than do Jewish municipalities for roads, schools, water supply, sewage, etc. Most land in Israel is owned by the Jewish National Fund, which rents it on long-term leases; it will not rent land to Arabs. Much Arab land within Israel proper has been confiscated by the state.[16]

In truth, regardless of the factual circumstances, the beliefs about Israel have continued to resonate with deeply cherished U.S. views of both Jews and Israel: Jews are victims, Israel is a democracy, democracy is good, and Israelis are like us. At best, Arabs and Muslims are the "other." Many levels of American society have contributed to the reinforcement of these precepts, including the mainstream media, commentators and journalists, the intelligentsia, Hollywood, and certain fundamentalist Christian sects.[17] Indeed, the cultural affinity between the two countries became so commingled that the security and survival of Israel became incorporated into the U.S. definition of its own national interest.[18]

Israel as a U.S. Strategic Asset

After the 1967 war (when the United States was mired in the Vietnam War), in which Israel defeated three major Arab states in six days, a new social paradigm or postulate entered American political culture: Israel could serve as a strategic asset, or a surrogate power, to U.S. interests in the Middle East. It could play an important role in undermining Arab nationalism, stemming Soviet encroachment, protecting U.S. oil interests, and shoring up U.S. allies like King Hussein of Jordan, the shah of Iran, and others.[19]

The theory of a U.S.-Israeli special relationship became the cornerstone of U.S. Middle East policy, and as a consequence Washington did not seriously oppose any policy Israel chose to pursue—especially with regard to Palestine and the Palestinians.[20] On some issues, the United States had official policies that were at odds with Israel, but Washington did not use the massive leverage it possessed over Israel (i.e., economic and military aid) to pressure Israel to conform to U.S. positions. It is difficult to comprehend how a state could be considered so weak as to have its existence threatened by its neighbors and at the same time possess the strength to act as a surrogate for the regional interests of the most powerful state in the international system. Yet, such was the mythology surrounding Israel. That the Palestinians were invisible in this paradox is not surprising and Kathleen Christison's observation, that "ultimately . . . Americans had no place in their mind-set for Palestinians and what they had to say about their grievances and aspirations," could not be closer to the truth.[21]

In the 1980s, when some in the United States—although not the government—denounced Israel over the war in Lebanon and its treatment of Palestinians during the first intifada, Israel and its U.S. supporters silenced the critics with a new, pernicious contention equating criticism of Israel with anti-Semitism. Because anti-Semitism was and is a fundamental taboo in U.S. society (as in most civilized societies), the Zionists' ability to parallel the two served as a powerful inducement to self-censorship and silence—especially in the media and among the intelligentsia.[22] In the context of the Al-Aqsa intifada and widespread criticism of Israeli policies, pro-Israel groups resurrected the anti-Semitism slur against individuals and groups that took public positions that were at odds with official Israeli policy.

Shaping Pro-Israel Perceptions

The perception of shared values is at the heart of the U.S.-Israel relationship. It is the substructure that perpetuates all the other assumptions and provides the foundation for the strategic partnership. For example, in a foreign policy speech in November 2001, U.S. Secretary of State Colin Powell stated: "The United States–Israeli Relationship is based on the broadest conception of American national interests, in which our two nations are bound forever together by common democratic values and traditions. This will never change."[23] One only has to consider how anomalous would be "Palestinian" substituted for Israel in the forego- ing, to comprehend the depth of the U.S.-Israel tie and the enormous disadvantage this relationship is to Palestinians in their conflict with Israel. It is for this reason that Israel advocacy groups reinforce the shared values/cultures/democracy postulate as much as they do the strategic asset thesis. The following briefly considers some of the organizations, together with their operating methods, that are involved in this work.

Most of the groups engaged in pro-Israel advocacy are multidimen- sional and immersed in many activities in addition to advocacy. These include charitable work, community social work, education, identity reinforcement, religious enrichment, student integration, and much more. Only about one-third of some fifty or more Jewish American organizations are dedicated solely to work supporting Israel. Many groups are organized nationwide, with branches on college and univer- sity campuses, in every medium-sized town and city, and so on.[24] Only one organization is an official lobby—the American Israel Public Affairs Committee (AIPAC)—and though several other groups engage in lobbying activities vis-à-vis the government, most focus on maintain- ing positive perceptions about Israel within various sectors of society. Of most importance to Israel's interests in terms of influencing policy- making are a group of think tanks that provide the U.S. government with policy papers and senior officials to implement policy.

Media and other watch groups.   Some of the Israel advocacy bodies act as media watchdogs or gatekeepers. Newspaper articles, TV reports, pro- fessors' lectures (on and off campus), student groups, and so on that are critical of Israel are countered with letters to the editor, phone calls, vis- its to editorial and/or administrative offices, demands for equal space, and so forth. Because the watch groups are well organized and their members highly motivated, the targets of their objections may receive hundreds, sometimes thousands, of complaints. One of the most impor- tant groups monitoring media is the Committee for Accuracy in Middle East Reporting in America (CAMERA). Under the category "About CAMERA," the following statement appears on CAMERA's website:

Because public opinion ultimately shapes public policy, distorted news coverage that misleads the public can be detrimental to sound policymaking. . . . Inaccurate and distorted accounts of events in Israel and the Middle East are to be found everywhere from college radio stations to network television, from community newspapers to national magazines, and, of course, on the Internet. In recent years misinformation about the Middle East has also surfaced in fashion magazines, architectural publications, encyclopedias, professional reference works, geography textbooks, travel guides, and even dictionaries. Frequently inaccurate and skewed characterizations of Israel and of events in the Middle East may fuel anti-Israel and anti-Jewish prejudice. CAMERA systematically monitors, documents, reviews and archives . . . these sources, directly contact[s] reporters, editors, producers, and publishers.[25]

Another similar organization is HonestReporting.com. This relatively new online organization "is a fast-action website dedicated to ensuring that Israel receives fair media coverage. We scrutinize the media for anti-Israel bias, and then mobilize subscribers to complain directly to the news agency concerned."[26] All such groups consider the mainstream media to be pro-Palestinian.

Campus Watch is another online group (an off-shoot of the Middle East Forum, founded in the summer of 2002) dedicated to countering pro-Palestinian and anti-Israeli ideas on campuses. It maintains a list of dossiers of professors and institutions and invites students to submit course outlines and report on professors, campus speakers, and events.[27]

Information generators.   Other groups concentrate on producing information to refute alternative claims and explain Israeli positions. The Anti-Defamation League (ADL), originally focused on combating anti-Semitism in the United States, has, since 1967, become the leading organization that generates and disseminates pro-Israel information. For example, it publishes guides for activists that contain "talking points" for "those who want to defend Israel but feel they lack the knowledge or experience to be effective." They include (among others) "How to Advocate to the Media," "How to Advocate on Campus," "How to Advocate to Elected Officials," "Advocating for Israel: An Activists Guide," and "How to Respond to Inaccuracies about Israel." Additionally, the ADL publishes a large number of reports, press releases, crisis updates, backgrounders, archives, and other material on Israel and the U.S.-Israeli relationship.[28] The ADL has also engaged in the compilation and circulation of blacklists of academics and intellectuals (especially those who are Jewish) who support Palestinians.[29]

Other organizations and publications involved in the production of information that advocate for Israel include Information Regarding Israel's Security; *Independent Media Review Analysis; Facts and Logic About the Middle East;* Middle East Media Research Institute; and the Middle East Forum, which publishes the *Middle East Quarterly* and the *Middle East Intelligence Bulletin* plus many others.[30]

When there is a perceived need to bolster Israel's image, as in the summer of 2002 in the wake of Israel's reoccupation of the West Bank, ad hoc groups spring up to manipulate public opinion. At that time, one woman, Jennifer Laszlo Mizrahi, seeded a public relations project with $50,000 of her family's foundation money. With that she raised additional money, then hired a prestigious pro-Israel organization (the Luntz Research Companies) to conduct polls on attitudes toward Israel in various sectors of the U.S. public and to develop a communications strategy to influence public opinion. The Luntz "Communication Manual" was directed at Israeli and U.S. spokespersons and outlined the most effective way to communicate to increase support for Israel. The advice included: "draw direct parallels between Israel and America"; "the language of Israel is the language of America: 'democracy,' 'freedom,' 'security,' and 'peace'"; "explain why a threat to Israel is a threat to America"; "never forget 9/11—it has been forever implanted in the minds and psyches of the American people"; and "the nation that is *perceived* as being most for peace will win this debate" (emphasis added). Subsequently, the airwaves of all major TV stations were blitzed with commercials based on these principles.[31]

Groups that focus on non-Jews. Some organizations sponsor programs in Israel for non-Jewish leaders. The American Jewish Committee (AJC) has been particularly active in this area. Its Project Interchange "is solely dedicated to providing travel seminars in Israel for America's political, civic, ethnic and religious leaders. . . . [It] educates American policy makers and opinion leaders . . . [in] specially-designed seminar programs [that] strengthen relations between the U.S. and Israel, promote mutually beneficial ties between influential Americans and Israelis, and enhance intergroup relations in the United States." The AJC has taken nearly 3,000 leaders on ten-day seminars to Israel through this program, which it fully funds. Participants pay nothing.[32]

Numerous other groups promote U.S. support for Israel through a variety of programs. For example, the American-Israel Cooperative Enterprise functions "to strengthen the U.S.-Israel relationship by emphasizing the fundamentals of the alliance—the values our nations share. . . [by] developing social and educational programs in the U.S. based on innovative, successful Israeli models that address similar domestic problems, and bring novel U.S. programs to Israel. These cooperative activities, which stem from our common values, are called Shared Value Initiatives."[33]

Lobbies. The only officially registered pro-Israel lobby in the United States is the American Israel Public Affairs Committee (AIPAC). It is the most important, though by no means the only, organization active on Capitol Hill. AIPAC and the New York–based Conference of Presidents of Major American Jewish Organizations are the two most influential pro-Israel advocacy groups in the country. While AIPAC focuses on Congress, the Conference of Presidents lobbies the administration.[34]

AIPAC has individuals sitting in every committee and subcommittee in both the House and the Senate to ensure that legislation supportive of Israel's interests is passed. AIPAC's work is buttressed by the financial contributions the Jewish community funnels through pro-Israel political action committees (PACs) that are closely managed by AIPAC itself. For example, in the 1996 election cycle, sixty-one pro-Israel PACs gave a total of $2,738,647 in direct donations. By contrast, six Arab American/Muslim American PACs gave a total of $20,625 in the 1996 cycle.[35] The top eighteen Senate recipients of pro-Israel PAC money were given between $136,320 (Carl Levin, D–Michigan) to $14,000 (Jesse Helms, R–North Carolina). The top twenty House recipients ranged from $30,549 (Jane Harman, D–California) to $10,000 (Elizabeth Furse, D–Oregon). Contributions are carefully targeted to individuals whose committee assignments will involve them in legislation concerning Israel. Some are rewarded for past support of Israel; others, perceived as possible "waverers," are given donations as incentives. Still others, deemed unfriendly, find their opponents' campaign coffers overflowing with Jewish PAC money from around the country.[36] Such was the fate of five-term Georgia Democratic Congresswoman Cynthia McKinney, who was defeated in the August 2002 primaries.[37]

Think tanks. More important than all these organizations combined is a network of think tanks that produces the individuals and the policy planning papers that shape U.S. policy. The two most powerful and influential are the Washington Institute for Near East Policy and the Jewish Institute for National Security Affairs. Others include the Center for Security Policy, the American Enterprise Institute, the Hudson

Institute, the Middle East Forum, and the Jerusalem Center for Public Affairs.[38] The think tanks are discussed below in the analyses of the Clinton and Bush administrations.

The U.S.-Israeli Alliance

The extent of the U.S.-Israeli alliance, or strategic relationship, can be measured in a variety of contexts.[39] One is the dollar amount of economic and military aid the United States provides Israel annually—roughly U.S.$3 billion in direct assistance plus additional generous grants buried in the budgets of various governmental agencies.[40] From 1949 through the end of fiscal year 2000, the total amount of aid to Israel was U.S.$91.8 billion.[41] The measure of Washington's commitment to Israel resides not only in the extraordinary dollar amount; more important, except for one six-month period during Dwight Eisenhower's administration, the aid has not ceased; not even when Tel Aviv has disregarded U.S. requests. Moreover, Washington has never placed conditions on the aid it gives. Even when officials have been less than enthusiastic about Israel's policies, there has not been so much as the threat of withholding aid.[42] Given the amount of money involved, it is clear that if the U.S. government wanted to influence Israel's behavior, it could do so.[43]

To the extent that Americans perceived their affiliation with Israel as intertwined before September 11, 2001, popular and governmental empathy and identification with Israel intensified in the aftermath of the suicide hijackings against U.S. persons and property. Whatever constraints Washington had exercised over Israel's war against the Al-Aqsa intifada vanished overnight, and Tel Aviv was given a green light to do whatever it deemed necessary.[44] Perceptually, all Palestinians became Hamas, and Hamas became the equivalent of Al-Qaida.[45]

Another measure of U.S. support is the protection Washington affords Israel at the United Nations (UN). In the UN Security Council, the United States has worked tirelessly behind the scenes to either prevent resolutions from coming before the council or insisting on language that will spare Israel harsh criticism. It used its veto thirty-four times between September 1972 and December 2002 in support of Israel.[46] For example, during his two terms, the Clinton administration cast three vetoes on behalf of Israel in the Security Council.[47] In the UN General Assembly, where the United States does not have the control it does in the Security Council, U.S. support can be measured in voting patterns. Resolutions supporting Palestinians or rebuking Israel typically result in two votes against (Israel and the United States), with the remainder of the international community in favor. This is illustrated, in

one example, on a November 30, 2000, resolution calling Israel's imposition of "its laws, jurisdiction, and administration on the Holy City of
Jerusalem null and void and with no validity." Only Israel voted against
it. The United States, atypically, abstained.[48]

The alliance is further evident in the extent of intelligence-sharing
between the two countries, the U.S. provision of its most sophisticated
weapons and technology to Israel, and the access and influence that
Israelis and their U.S. supporters have at all levels of government as
well as with the media.[49]

This is not to suggest that Washington and Tel Aviv always see eye
to eye or do not have disputes or disagreements. There have been fric-
tions in this partnership, and typically the media has presented them as
crises. Israel and its U.S. supporters have at times accused the United
States of abandoning Israel, of being traitorous to it, and so on. But
regardless of differences of opinion in a given situation, Washington's
policy toward Israel is characterized by consistency, continuity, and
unremitting support. Conversely, disregard, disinterest, and negation of
fundamental Palestinian national, political, and human rights have distinguished U.S. policy toward Palestine and the Palestinians.[50]

U.S. Policies Toward the Palestinians and Israel

President Clinton and the Peace Process

When Bill Clinton assumed office as president in January 1993, the
Madrid conference, initiated by then–President George H.W. Bush and
then–Secretary of State James Baker in October 1991, was stumbling
toward its tenth fruitless round. Clinton signaled his position on the
Israeli-Palestinian conflict through high-level administrative appoint-
ments. Almost all of them had prior affiliations with the Washington
Institute for Near East Policy, a pro-Israel think tank established in
1985 by two Jewish advocates for Israel: Martin Indyk (director of
research at AIPAC) and Barbi Weinberg (former president of the Jewish
Federation of Los Angeles and an AIPAC vice president). The
Washington Institute for Near East Policy produces a stream of policy
proposals for U.S. Middle East policy.[51] It also plays a major role in
shaping perceptions about Israel in the United States and provides a
training ground for officials who move on to government service.[52]

Every four years the institute convenes the Presidential Study
Group, which produces a blueprint for the next administration's Middle
East policy. In 1992, the institute hosted a special commission on U.S.-

Israeli relations; its final report was entitled *Enduring Partnership*. Eleven of the individuals who participated in this policy-planning study were named to senior positions in the Clinton administration, including Anthony Lake, Madeleine Albright, Stuart Eizenstat, Les Aspin, Dennis Ross, and others.[53] In 1996, the Washington Institute produced a new set of guidelines for U.S. Middle East policy entitled "Building for Security and Peace in the Middle East." Subsequently, the institute boldly declared that this blueprint "played a key role in shaping Middle East policy during the Clinton Administration's second term."[54]

The Jewish Institute for National Security Affairs, another pro-Israel think tank, is, in its own words,

> committed to explaining the need for a prudent national security policy for the United States, addressing the security requirements of both the United States and the State of Israel, and strengthening the strategic cooperation relationship between these two great democracies. . . . [It] communicates with the national security establishment and the general public to explain the role Israel can and does play in bolstering American interests.[55]

It, too, provides policy planning for government implementation and prepares individuals for government service in Middle East posts.[56]

The Individuals That Define and Implement Policy

Clinton's secretary of defense, Les Aspin, and the director of the U.S. Central Intelligence Agency (CIA), James Woolsey, both worked for the Washington Institute for Near East Policy and for the Jewish Institute for National Security Affairs. Sandy Berger was top deputy to the national security adviser. Martin Indyk, former director of the Washington Institute, was positioned as head of the Middle East desk in the National Security Council (later serving as two-term ambassador to Israel and assistant secretary of state for Near East policy). Indyk was an Australian citizen, sworn in as a U.S. citizen in an act of peremptory executive privilege at president-elect Clinton's express wishes.[57] Samuel Lewis, head of the U.S. Peace Council, affiliated with the Washington Institute, and a former ambassador to Israel, was appointed to policy planning at the State Department. Dennis Ross, another former head of the Washington Institute, was appointed to the post of special coordinator for the peace process. Ross was the key U.S. player in the Palestinian-Israeli negotiations during both Clinton terms. He was among the most committed of the pro-Israel advocates in official circles, as well as the most influential. It was his advice that guided all

Washington's policy decisions during Clinton's tenure, and his presence dominated all U.S. talks with the Palestinians and Israelis for eight years.[58]

The perspective of Ross's colleagues at the State Department—Aaron David Miller, Daniel Kurtzer, and Richard Haass, who worked with Ross on the peace process at one time or another during Clinton's eight years—was also Israel-centered, with family and religious ties to Israel. Christison writes that Ross, Miller, and Indyk

> were all personally and emotionally committed to Israel. All had lived in Israel before entering government service; they often vacationed there. Miller and Indyk once told an interviewer that their personal and their professional involvement in the peace process were so intertwined that they could not determine where one left off and the other began.[59]

The aforementioned individuals expressed, at one time or another, their concern for Israel's security as their primary interest. Significantly, there has not been an Arab American in any high government position related to the Middle East. It is unimaginable that Palestinian Americans with expressed sentiments regarding Palestine and the Palestinians comparable to those expressed concerning Israel will ever serve on a U.S. government Middle East policy team.

The Clinton administration came into office with a clear but unspoken directive from the pro-Israel policy strategists: some settlement of the Israeli-Palestinian conflict is desirable. Israel's interests will define the terms (which in any case are incidental) as long as the settlement will serve the purpose of absorbing political shocks in the event of another major crisis in the region (similar to the 1991 Gulf War) that would require U.S. military intervention.[60] Implicit in this position is the assumption that the interests of the United States and Israel are congruent, if not identical.

The approach of the Clinton administration was characterized by its heavy emphasis on the *process* of peacemaking at the expense of *substance*. Ross was committed to the principle—shared by successive Israeli governments—that the United States should not involve itself in substantive issues or put forth ideas of its own. Rather, Ross insisted, the two sides should be allowed to proceed at their own pace, and the United States should adopt a position of strict neutrality. This stance abetted the perception of Washington as an honest broker. Yet given that Israel was the vastly stronger party and in physical control of all the territory under negotiation, and given that the only resource of power available to the Palestinians was verbal argument, this hands-off U.S.

policy strongly favored Israel. It allowed Israel to set the substantive agenda as well as the timetable for talks, to negotiate or not as it saw fit, to create facts on the ground (e.g., land confiscation, settlement expansion), and to renege on commitments it made in the formal agreements (e.g., redeployments) without penalty.[61]

President Clinton consistently presented himself as an honest mediator throughout his tenure—for example, he invited Yasser Arafat to the White House thirteen times, and he gave an empathetic speech toward the Palestinians in Gaza in December 1998. Nevertheless, his first concern was promoting Israel's program and protecting Israel's interests. In reality, Clinton did not function as an honest arbiter and not once spoke positively of a Palestinian state as a possible outcome of the negotiations. If he had, observes William Quandt, "the transition to Israeli acceptance of [that] outcome . . . might have been eased."[62]

When President Clinton left office in January 2001, the Palestinian negotiating team wrote an assessment of his administration's involvement in the peace process. Several of their observations clarify the meaning of the U.S. emphasis on process:

> Under U.S. supervision, the Palestinian-Israeli "peace process" has become a goal in and of itself. A false sense of normalcy has been created because of the on-going process of negotiations. The lack of visible resistance to Israeli occupation from the Palestinian side, except for temporary flare-ups, and Israel's ability to continue negotiations while continuing to build settlements in occupied Palestinian territory has created the false impression that the "process" of achieving peace could substitute for peace itself. Thus, the difficult substantive issues at the core of the conflict . . . have been constantly deflected in order to maintain talks without requiring Israel to face up to its obligations. In fact, the United States' advocacy of "constructive ambiguity" has had disastrous consequences. . . . This lack of implementation [of agreements], combined with the ever-increasing number of Palestinian-Israeli agreements brokered by the United States has caused Palestinians to become increasingly wary of U.S. involvement. . . . The resulting lack of faith in the peace process and the consequent distrust of U.S. promotion of process over substance has made securing a just peace all that more difficult.[63]

Issues During Clinton's First Term

Although Clinton presided over Oslo I (the Declaration of Principles [DOP]), Oslo II, and the Jordanian-Israeli peace treaty, the president remained essentially uninvolved in the day-to-day activities of the peace process during his first term. (It was not until the talks leading to the Hebron Protocol in 1998 that he took an active role.) Secretary of

State Warren Christopher, and even more so Ross, were the hands-on players. Nevertheless, Clinton succeeded in changing the terms of reference for resolving the conflict, primarily with regard to UN Resolution 242 and the status of the settlements. Virtually the entire international community supported Resolution 242—the exchange of land for peace—as the basis for solving the Arab/Palestinian–Israeli conflict. Previously, the United States had demanded of the PLO formal acceptance of Resolution 242 as a precondition to Washington's engaging in talks with it (which the PLO did in 1988). Though the DOP mentions the resolution, it does so in an ambiguous manner. In truth, Israel wanted peace with the Palestinians without relinquishing the land it had conquered in 1967—at least not the majority of it.

As discussed in Chapter 2, the DOP is indistinct about the meaning of Resolution 242, and the accords make no reference to other relevant UN resolutions or international legal referents that supported Palestinian interests. The United States, however, should have been able to take a long-term perspective and understand that a peace not based on equity would not be durable or lasting. Indeed, as Christison notes, the line frequently put forth by the Clinton administration that neither side could expect to attain everything it wanted in negotiations "was clearly addressed to the Palestinians and carried the message that . . . Palestinians must come to the peace process expecting to bargain over the West Bank, Gaza, and East Jerusalem, not to obtain their return."[64]

Clinton and his advisers altered the terms of reference on the issue of settlements, too. Originally, U.S. policy deemed the settlements illegal, which of course they are under international law. However, U.S. presidents had gradually transformed the status of settlements under U.S. policy. President Jimmy Carter was the last to use the term *illegal*. President Ronald Reagan redefined them as "obstacles to peace."[65] For Clinton the settlements were mere "complicating factors."[66] Moreover, with his hands-off policy, Clinton allowed the peace process to stall and afforded Israel the time and space it needed to nearly double the settlements, settler population, and infrastructure in the Occupied Territories.

Congress also enacted legislation against the Palestinians. Shortly after the September 13, 1993, signing of the DOP, it passed a law establishing conditions on U.S. relations with the PLO. This legislation grew out of an earlier congressional law banning all U.S. government dealings with the Palestinian organization. The new law was intended to permit the government to engage in diplomacy with the PLO as well as to provide the Palestinians limited amounts of economic assistance, *conditional* on the PLO's adherence to certain stipulations. The law (the Middle East Peace Facilitation Act of 1994 [Public Law 103-236]) requires the United States to suspend provisions (e.g., diplomatic relations, aid, and other things) with the PLO if the latter fails to carry forth certain requirements (essentially, absolute fidelity to the letter and law of the DOP). The law obliges the U.S. president to submit to Congress every six months written reports of PLO compliance and justification for U.S. aid and engagement. In the event of any individual or group violation of the requirements—primarily acts of violence, although the list was extensive and the requirements broadly framed—the president was constrained in his interaction with the Palestinian group.

Clinton signed the bill.[67] Given that there are no conditions on the aid and support the United States gives to Israel, this law sent a very clear message of how differently the two parties to the peace process would be treated by Washington. Moreover, as time went on, members of Congress attempted to use this law to suspend U.S. assistance to the PA each time there was a violent incident. It became a very large stick that Congress wielded over the Palestinians.

Clinton's Second Term

In Clinton's second term (1997–2001), Madeleine Albright, also previously affiliated with the Washington Institute, replaced Warren Christopher as secretary of state. Sandy Berger became national security adviser, and Dennis Ross continued to play the leading role in shaping U.S. involvement in the peace process. He was supported by Aaron David Miller and Martin Indyk (who later became ambassador to Israel). There were other changes in administration positions, but the continuity of U.S. policy remained unchanged. However, in his second term, President Clinton became more directly and personally active in the peace process.

Clinton's second term coincided with Benjamin Netanyahu's assumption of the prime ministership in Israel. The president spent the better part of his first two years trying to persuade Netanyahu to implement the February 1997 Hebron Protocol, which the prime minister himself had signed and for which the United States richly rewarded him with new commitments and specific advantages. First, Clinton authorized two side documents to the Hebron Protocol, giving Israel considerable leverage in the peace process. Ross's "Note for the Record" and Christopher's "Letter to the Israeli Prime Minister" endorsed Netanyahu's concept of reciprocity (i.e., that Israel would only carry out its commitments to redeploy if there was absolutely no violence on the Palestinian side). Christopher's letter gave U.S. approval to Israel's demand that it alone would decide the extent and location of any further withdrawals without having to negotiate with the Palestinians."[68] Additionally, Clinton's inducements to Netanyahu included early delivery (in January 1998) of the first part of a large shipment of F-15 combat aircraft; a March 7, 1997, veto of a UN Security Council resolution calling on Israel to refrain from East Jerusalem settlement activities; and a March 21, 1997, veto of a Security Council resolution demanding Israel's cessation of construction of the Har Homa settlement on Jabal Abu Ghneim. (This, in fact, was Clinton's third veto for Israel. His first was on a May 17, 1995, resolution condemning Israel's land confiscation in East Jerusalem.)

Still, after a single, limited redeployment, Netanyahu canceled the others. When the prime minister continued to balk, Clinton, at the prompting of Ross, agreed to a new measure to enhance Israel's security. In mid-August 1997, the administration assigned the CIA station chief in Tel Aviv to coordinate efforts between Israel and the Palestinians to prevent terrorism and preempt violence. This was an unprecedented role for the CIA, which Israel rightly perceived as a triumph, whereas the Palestinians saw it as humiliation.[69]

In March 1998, Albright put forward a plan involving concrete steps the Palestinians should take to improve their security performance, as well as a timetable for Israeli redeployment based on the commitments made in the Hebron Protocol. Her efforts bore no fruit, and in October 1998 Clinton summoned Arafat and Netanyahu to the Wye River Plantation for a summit. Clinton's unusual burst of energy in convening Wye was most likely related to his domestic woes (e.g., the Monica Lewinsky scandal and the aftermath of impeachment) and his desire to restore his image as a statesman.[70] The president's participation during the early days of meetings was sporadic, but toward the end he threw himself into a twenty-four-hour negotiating session. The outcome, known as the Wye River Memorandum (see Chapter 2), involved additional Palestinian measures to guarantee Israel's security, the convening of the Palestinian National Council to revoke parts of the 1964 National Covenant (which it had done earlier), and a promise by Israel to implement its prior agreements on redeployments. But because Clinton had previously compensated Israel for its intransigence, the prime minister had little incentive to implement the redeployments. In fact, after a single, limited redeployment, Netanyahu canceled the others.

Ehud Barak's election as prime minister in May 1999 seemed to coincide with a desire by Clinton to remain actively involved in the peace process and preside over its conclusion. The president's historical legacy appeared to be uppermost in his mind at this time, and nowhere could he make as dramatic a contribution as in the Middle East. In line with Barak's priorities, Clinton exercised impressive involvement in attempting to arrange a Syrian-Israeli peace treaty. Following the collapse of the Israeli-Syrian track, the president, pressed by Barak, launched a campaign for a three-way summit on the Israeli-Palestinian issue. Clinton pressured Arafat in early June 2000 and kept it up through July. The Palestinian leader was reluctant, arguing that the time was not right for reaching a full, final agreement. For one thing, there had been no progress in the bilateral final-status talks. In the end, Arafat capitulated, but only after Clinton solemnly promised the Palestinian leader that if the summit failed, he would not hold Arafat responsible.[71]

Given the dead end in each of the three final-status negotiating tracks then in existence (in the Occupied Territories, at Bolling and Andrews Air Force Bases, and in Stockholm), it is difficult to comprehend why Barak and Clinton were so anxious for a major summit. In Clinton's case, it may have been a combination of concern about his legacy and his personal desire to support Barak. Yet he should have had some understanding by this time of the nature of the substantive issues and the extent of the differences between the two sides. Barak clearly had political reasons, as his coalition was collapsing and he needed to rally public opinion with some tangible success. Undoubtedly, he assumed that whatever he offered the Palestinians, they would have no choice but to accept. Additionally, both men were extremely concerned about the possibility that Arafat would unilaterally declare an independent Palestinian state on September 13. In any case, initiating a summit under existing conditions seemed like very poor judgment on Clinton's part.

Nevertheless, Clinton convened the Camp David summit, which occurred during July 11–25, 2000. Although in this venue he attempted to address final-status issues (engaging in substance rather than merely process), Israel set the pace and program of the talks throughout the two weeks. Clinton's role, according to one analyst, was to take, nearly verbatim, Israeli proposals (at times ones that Israeli negotiators had informally discussed with their Palestinian counterparts) and formally present them to the Palestinians as U.S. "bridging proposals."[72]

Out of Camp David came a new myth—the myth of Barak's unprecedented generous offer. The phrase *generous offer* was repeated so many times by so many government officials, media personalities, and policy experts that it soon became the defining fact or truth about Camp David.[73] Supposedly, no further analysis or examination was required. Concomitantly, there was the myth of Arafat's intransigence—

his congenital inability to make peace—and the myth that Arafat planned and orchestrated the Al-Aqsa intifada to extract more concessions from Israel. Israeli analyst Meron Benvenisti comments on the "generous offer" versus "intransigence" constructs:

> A myth in the service of a cause and like all myths, once it has caught on, it becomes more real than reality itself. Israeli society needs the myth, because it is unifying and justifies all actions, clears the conscience, defines the enemy as bloodthirsty and allows society to cope with the tough reality of "no alternative."[74]

Shortly after the close of Camp David on July 25, at Barak's request, Clinton appeared on Israeli television in a strong show of support for the prime minister and the Jewish state. He reiterated U.S. guarantees of increased military aid, an upgrading of the strategic relationship, and his consideration of moving the U.S. embassy to Jerusalem. In early August, the United States and Israel held three days of talks on strengthening their strategic partnership. They worked on a memorandum of understanding that would codify the relationship, reaffirm areas of existing cooperation, and guarantee equipment needs to the Israeli Defense Forces (IDF) for ten years, including aerial refueling capacity and theater missile defense.[75]

Despite the failure of Camp David and the subsequent U.S. actions favoring Israel, Israeli and Palestinian negotiators continued to hold meetings after the outbreak of the Al-Aqsa intifada—through January 2001.[76] It is notable, however, that throughout the period from May 2000 onward, Israel undertook specific preparations for the possibility of an armed conflict if talks broke down completely.[77]

The United States, Israel, the Palestinians, and the Peace Process

As I have argued elsewhere in this book, Israel did not intend to conclude a just and comprehensive peace with the Palestinians. It wanted *peace and land*, not an *exchange of land for peace*. Israel always couched its negotiating positions in terms of its security needs, and the United States is committed, at its deepest cultural, psychological, and political levels, to maximizing Israeli security. The United States supported Israel in every aspect of the process. Both calculated that the weakness of the Palestinians when they entered the Oslo process would guarantee Palestinian compliance. Both were wrong. A century of injustice and almost forty years of occupation had not dulled the Palestinians' pride, identity, and determination to realize their national, political, and human rights. That is why Oslo failed.

Clinton and the Al-Aqsa Intifada

Clinton's comments on Israeli television, and his castigation of the Palestinians as solely responsible for the failure of Camp David, humiliated the Palestinians and created a lasting sense of bitterness. When combined with Ariel Sharon's September 28, 2000, demonstration of Israel's sovereignty over the Haram al-Sharif, the tinderbox built of seven empty years of negotiations and broken commitments was ignited. Israel's reaction to the demonstrations on the day following Sharon's provocation was to dispatch a 2,000-person police and military presence to the Al-Aqsa compound prior to the start of Friday prayers. The presence of the troops on the Haram al-Sharif inflamed the (unarmed) worshipers and led to clashes that resulted in four dead and 220 wounded. Two Palestinians were killed elsewhere in East Jerusalem. The following day, twelve more Palestinians were killed and 500 wounded as demonstrations and clashes spread throughout the Occupied Territories.

The UN Security Council convened on October 3 with some forty-six countries participating to discuss the violence in the Occupied Territories. Washington first attempted to head off the debate. Nevertheless, the council proceeded and by October 5 had a draft resolution. The United States then began lobbying council members to change the language of the resolution, threatening to veto it if it was critical of Israel. Because any resolution was preferable to none, the UN members modified and remodified the language until the United States agreed to abstain rather than use its veto. The October 7 vote on Security Council Resolution 1322 was fourteen in favor, with the U.S. abstention. It condemned the violence in the territories but nowhere mentioned Israel. At the time of the vote, approximately seventy-one Palestinians, fourteen Israeli Arabs, three IDF soldiers, and one Jewish settler had been killed.[78]

In the midst of Israel's military action against the Palestinians, the defense correspondent of *Ha'aretz* reported on October 30 "the largest purchase of military helicopters by the Israeli Air Force in a decade . . . an agreement with the U.S. to provide Israel with 35 Blackhawk military helicopters and spare parts, along with jet fuel, following the purchase, shortly before, of patrol aircraft and Apache attack helicopters." Amnesty International strongly rebuked the arms sale, which contrasted with French and German policies, both of which initiated an undeclared embargo on Israel of defense equipment and materials, at the outset of violence.[79]

On November 14, President Clinton asked Congress to grant extra aid to Israel (U.S.$450 million) in addition to the amount it already receives annually. Out of the new request, the United States would give Israel U.S.$250 million to defray the cost of the Lebanon withdrawal and U.S.$200 million to develop new weapons (e.g., the long-range missile Arrow). The appeal also included a suggestion that Israel's military aid the next year include an extra U.S.$350 million.[80] This petition followed congressional approval on October 28 of the U.S. aid package to Israel for the coming year (U.S.$1.98 billion in military aid and U.S.$800 million in economic assistance).[81]

Clinton's Efforts to Restart Negotiations During the Uprising

On October 16, under the auspices of Egyptian president Hosni Mubarak, Clinton convened a meeting between Arafat and Barak at Sharm al-Sheikh, Egypt. The president encouraged the two parties to declare a cease-fire; pressed the Palestinians to restart the three-way talks among the Israeli and Palestinian security forces and the CIA; and pushed the two sides to compromise on a commission of inquiry into the causes of the violence that would be named by Clinton.[82] CIA Chief George Tenet would oversee a trilateral security arrangement, involving, for the first time, CIA observers in the field in addition to CIA participation in Israeli-Palestinian meetings.[83] One product of this meeting was the so-called Tenet Plan (released on June 13, 2001, by George W. Bush's administration), which addresses the question of how to restore Palestinian contributions to Israeli security.

Issues surrounding the commission of inquiry were particularly sensitive. Arafat had been pleading since the beginning of the uprising for international observers and for an international delegation to investigate the causes of the uprising. Israel had refused both. The U.S. president acceded to Israel's wishes, out of which came the Mitchell Commission (named for George Mitchell; see below). The fruit of this commission (the Mitchell Report, released on May 6, 2001, by the Bush administration) attempts to lay out a political framework for resolving the conflict.[84]

In early November 2000, Israel leaked word that the United States had raised the issue of posting international observers as a buffer in the West Bank and Gaza, and Barak immediately declared that Israel unequivocally rejected the proposal as a reward to Palestinian violence. Clinton, in turn, responded that the United States would not endorse the idea, saying, "Israelis are strongly opposed to it, therefore it can't happen."[85] At the same time, the United States was working hard at the United Nations to prevent the Security Council from passing a resolution that would order UN peacekeeping troops to the region. On December 18, after weeks of high-level pressure, the United States persuaded six other Security Council members to abstain on a pending resolution for 2,000 unarmed UN observers to be deployed in the West Bank and Gaza. This victory prevented the minimum of nine affirmative votes required to pass a resolution while absolving the United States of the need to exercise its veto and risk antagonizing Arab states. Yet simultaneously, the UN human rights commissioner, Mary Robinson, after an extended visit to Israel and the Occupied Territories, accused Israel of using "excessive force" and called for an immediate "international monitoring presence" in the Occupied Territories.[86]

The United States and Israel dismissed Robinson's plea out of hand. Instead of a peacekeeping force, international observers, or an international commission of inquiry, Clinton came up with the Mitchell Commission. On November 26, President Clinton convened the body. The five-member, U.S.-led commission would be chaired by former U.S. senator George Mitchell. Mitchell had been a strong supporter of Israel and a top recipient of pro-Israel PAC money. In addition to Mitchell, the commission was composed of former senator Warren Rodman; former Turkish president Suleiman Demirel, who had presided over the expansion of the Turkish-Israeli strategic alliance in the 1990s; Norwegian foreign minister Thorbojrn Jagland; and European Union representative Javier Solana.

With his delegation constituted, Clinton hastened to assure Israel it would have nothing to worry about. Mitchell and other commission members, on a December visit to the region, reassured Prime Minister Barak that they were there to help, not to pass judgment. They avowed that the commission's purpose was to restore calm and restart negotiations. The Israeli government was not entirely pleased but expressed its gratification that at least the delegates would not be taking a judicial approach and had no intention of serving as a tribunal. Of even greater satisfaction to Israel was Mitchell's decision that the commission would conduct its work entirely from Washington, relying on material submitted to it by Israel and the Palestinian Authority. It would have no local headquarters and carry out no investigations on the ground.[87] Nevertheless, on January 22, 2001, Israel suspended cooperation with the Mitchell Commission, stating that it would renew contacts with the commission "only after high-level talks with the new Bush administration."[88] In contrast, Arafat and the PA were pleased with the inauguration of the Mitchell Commission and closely cooperated with it on all levels despite the fact that it fell far short of the international monitors they had been pleading for.

On May 6, 2001, the Mitchell Commission released its report.[89] George W. Bush was then the sitting president. Stripped to its essentials, the commission demanded that "the PA . . . make a 100 percent effort to prevent terrorist operations and to punish perpetrators . . . [and undertake] immediate steps to apprehend and incarcerate terrorists operating within the PA's jurisdiction." In effect, it held the PA accountable for any act committed by a Palestinian individual or organization, including attacks from within territory formally under Israel's control (i.e., Areas B and C). It stated that Israel "should freeze all settlement activity, including the 'natural growth' of existing settlements" and noted that "the kind of security cooperation desired by [Israel] cannot for long coexist with settlement activity." The report does not specify whether the freeze should be temporary or permanent and whether or not it would include settlements in East Jerusalem and West Bank territory formally annexed by Israel. No reference was made to the illegality of the settlements in international law or of the numerous UN Security Council resolutions characterizing all settlements as illegal.[90]

Some analysts have argued that the Mitchell Report's wording on the settlement issue indicates that the members concluded that Israel's settlement expansion drive was neither a safety valve for Israel's burgeoning population nor a means to provide security for the Israeli heartland. Rather, they contend, the commission came to understand that the importance of the settlements for Israel is as a means of dividing the Palestinian population. In other words, according to this argument, the commission ultimately agreed with Palestinian claims that Israeli settlement policies constitute a purposeful attempt to "segregate the Palestinians in non-contiguous enclaves, surrounded by Israeli military-controlled borders, with settlements and settlement roads violating the territories' integrity."[91] I believe this is, although correct in point of fact, a wishful reading of the report. However, a variety of interpretations can be found in the literature.[92]

With the release of the commission's report, CIA chief George Tenet and William Burns, a new special envoy, were dispatched to the Middle East to attempt to implement a cease-fire based on its recommendations. The PA accepted the plan immediately, whereas Israel (which had access to the report before it was formally published) mounted a campaign against the settlement freeze, which it strongly opposed. In a televised news conference, Prime Minister Sharon stated that Israel would not heed the report's call for a freeze on settlements: "The government regards settlements in all their forms as a vital national enterprise."[93] Yet not wanting to appear the spoiler, Israel seized on the report's demand for a cease-fire and ambiguously accepted Mitchell's plan.[94]

U.S. Policy Under the Bush Administration

President George W. Bush assumed office on January 20, 2001, armed with the latest policy blueprint from the Washington Institute on Near East Policy, entitled *Navigating Through Turbulence: America and the Middle East in a New Century*. The plan suggested that Oslo had run its course and should be replaced. It advised Bush to reserve his intensive involvement (in contrast to Clinton), remain on the sidelines, and let the parties to the conflict decide what they wanted.[95] Bush followed these recommendations to the letter until March 2002, when the Al-Aqsa intifada spiraled out of control and he was forced by his Arab allies to do something (which, as it turned out, was purely cosmetic; see Chapter 8).

The most important organizations, in terms of influence on Bush administration policy formulation, were the Jewish Institute for National Security Affairs (JINSA) and the Center for Security Policy (CSP).[96] In addition, the American Enterprise Institute, the Hudson Institute, the Middle East Forum, and the Washington Institute for Near East Policy all played pivotal roles.[97] Crucial in comprehending the roles of these various institutions is that the same individuals, simultaneously or in succession, served on the boards of directors and in the policy discussion and policy planning groups, as well as in advisory and consulting capacities of each. Richard Perle, chairman of the Defense Policy Board (the Pentagon's advisory board) in the Bush administration, illustrates this cross-institutional fertilization quite well. He is, or has been, a resident fellow at the American Enterprise Institute, a member of the Board of Trustees at the Hudson Institute, a fellow at the Project for the New American Century, and an analyst at the Jerusalem-based (Washington-affiliated) Institute for Advanced Strategic and Political Studies.[98]

The majority of the highest level bureaucrats have either former or existing ties to JINSA, the Washington Institute for Near East Policy, the American Enterprise Institute, the Hudson Institute, and other neoconservative, right-wing, pro-Israel groups. These men, moreover, were not merely pro-Israel, they were strongly pro-Likud and anti-Oslo, and they played a significant role in the warm relationship that developed between Israeli Prime Minister Ariel Sharon and President George Bush and in the administration's alignment with Likud policies. Some of the most influential are Paul Wolfowitz, deputy secretary of defense; Richard Perle; Douglas Feith, undersecretary of defense for policy; and Peter Rodman and Dov Zachkeim, assistant secretaries at the subcabinet rank at Defense; David Wurmser, special assistant to undersecretary for arms control; John Bolton, of the State Department; John Hannah, deputy director of staff, who has a close relationship with Vice President Richard Cheney; and Robert Satloff, national security council adviser. And, with the appointment of Elliott Abrams in December 2002 as the national security adviser for the Middle East, the interests of Israel were well represented throughout the government.[99]

Thus, it does not matter whether a U.S. presidential administration is Democratic or Republican, for the institutions that define policy, as well as the individuals who implement it, are overwhelmingly Israel-centered. The Bush administration was also influenced on Middle East issues by the Christian right, a major bloc in Bush's domestic constituency and which passionately supports Israel.[100]

On June 13, 2001, CIA director Tenet put forward a proposal for a cease-fire between the Palestinians and Israelis (this became known as the Tenet Plan). It called on the PA and Israel to reaffirm their commitment to the security agreements forged at Sharm al-Sheikh (October 2000) and was embedded in the Mitchell Report (April 2001). The Tenet Plan itself focused primarily on a cease-fire, as well as the immediate resumption of security cooperation between the two sides to which senior CIA officials would be a party. Other than the initial reference to the Mitchell Report, it contained no provisions for political negotiations. The Tenet proposals required the PA "to apprehend, question, and incarcerate terrorists . . . [to] stop any Palestinian security officials from inciting, abetting, or conducting attacks against Israeli targets, including settlers . . . move aggressively to prevent individuals and groups from using areas under their . . . control to carry out acts of violence." The plan also called for a 500-meter buffer zone around Palestinian-controlled territory and required the PA to hand over to Israel a list of militants that Tel Aviv claimed were dangerous terrorists.[101]

After six days of intensive negotiations, Israel and the PA reluctantly accepted the Tenet Plan, based, however, on differing interpretations of its meaning. For example, Israel considered the throwing of a stone a breach of the cease-fire and responded with massive firepower. The PA was reluctant, for domestic political considerations, to turn over to

Israel all the wanted men it demanded. A brief period of calm ensued, but the violence soon resumed.[102]

Resolution of the Israeli-Palestinian conflict held little interest for the Bush administration. However, during 2001–2002, Prime Minister Sharon was a frequent White House guest, and he and the administration upgraded U.S.-Israel strategic coordination. Bush accepted Sharon's dictate that there could be no negotiations with the Palestinians until all Palestinian violence ceased. Yasser Arafat was pointedly not invited to Washington. The Bush administration put all the blame for the ongoing violence on the Palestinians while rebuffing all initiatives (European, UN, and others) to send observers to the territories. In early September 2001, the United States sold Israel fifty-two F-16 fighter-bombers in addition to fifty F-16s that it had sold in January 2000.[103] During these months the Al-Aqsa intifada continued, with Israel using a range of tactics, including collective punishments, assassinations, helicopter gunship and F-16 bombardments, reoccupation of Area A, massive house demolitions and crop destruction, and much more. Palestinians retaliated with suicide bombings inside Israel and attacks on soldiers, settlers, and military installations in the Occupied Territories.

In early December, Israel placed Yasser Arafat under house arrest in Ramallah, where he remained thereafter. The United States said nothing until January 24, 2002, when presidential spokesman Ari Fleischer told reporters at an informal briefing:

> The president understands the reason that Israel has taken the action that it takes, and it is up to Chairman Arafat to demonstrate the leadership to combat terrorism. The president continues to believe that it is incumbent on Chairman Arafat to do more, take more steps, and show with action that he is committed to eliminating terrorism and combating it wherever it exists.[104]

No one questioned how Arafat was supposed to exercise leadership and combat terrorism while he was under house arrest.

Some sixteen months into the intifada, *Ha'aretz* published an article that excoriated the United States for its "silence" as Israel prepared for "all-out war" against the Palestinians.

> The Bush Administration has granted Israel its widest military freedom of action since—in an ominous precedent—a Republican Administration turned a blind eye to Ariel Sharon's 1982 invasion of Lebanon. . . . Washington's tacit approval of recent IDF military moves coupled with its continuing pressure on Palestinian leader Yasir Arafat to crack down on militants in his midst, represents a marked

departure from [even] . . . nominal evenhandedness. . . . September 11 has dramatically changed . . . the perception [of Americans]. Israel is seen as the equivalent of New York and the Pentagon. . . . Since Bin Laden is not currently in the headlines, Arafat has been . . . replacing him in the popular view. So Arafat is actually becoming [perceptually] what Sharon wanted him to be, Israel's version of Bin Laden. A decidedly pro-Israel tone among U.S. elected officials has become more evident as November Congressional elections near. In an unprecedented circumstance—and in the face of security threats—there have been no fewer than nine Congressional delegations visiting Israel in the last two weeks. . . . Vowing support for Israel, [they] snubbed Arafat altogether. . . . Former president Bill Clinton embraced Sharon, openly telling his Israeli hosts that the Palestinian leader was to blame for the failure [of the peace process]. . . . At the end of the day, when the fire gets out of control, it may hit American targets here and elsewhere. Then the U.S. will have to do something. But it may be too late.[105]

Indeed, it was too late. In March 2002, with Israeli forces invading Area A throughout the West Bank and Gaza, President Bush made a tepid gesture toward calming the violence by sending Anthony Zinni back to the region to attempt to arrange another cease-fire. On March 25, Zinni presented the "Joint Goals Proposal" to Israel and the PA; it was promoted as a means for immediate implementation of the Tenet Plan. This U.S. plan was, however, even more tilted toward Israeli interests than were Tenet's proposals.[106] Arafat (under house arrest) and the PA (with most of its institutions destroyed) were held responsible for halting the violence, arresting all the militants, confiscating all weapons, destroying weapons factories, preventing suicide bombings, and so on. Again, the focus was simply on a cease-fire and protecting Israeli security. Zinni's plan did not address any of the underlying causes of the intifada or present proposals for a political settlement after the fighting ceased. The fact that the effort failed should surprise no one. Throughout all of Israel's major West Bank invasions and Gaza operations in the spring and early summer of 2002, which culminated in the full reoccupation of the West Bank, a total siege on Arafat's Ramallah compound, and a humanitarian crisis of extraordinary dimensions throughout the West Bank and Gaza Strip, the George W. Bush administration did not pressure Israel to cease and desist. Washington's sole request was that Israel not assassinate Arafat.

Conclusion

The foregoing analysis illustrates the indifference of U.S. policymakers, media, intellectuals, and the mass public toward the Palestinian people.

This disregard is the consequence of several factors, the most important being the extraordinary nature of the U.S.-Israeli relationship. The fate of the Palestinians has been inextricably intertwined with the Zionist project and the State of Israel, and this has put the Palestinians at an enormous disadvantage. Those (whether they be Palestinians or others) who have attempted to explain what the Palestinians have suffered because of Israel have been either discredited or ignored.

So strong is the belief in U.S.-Israeli shared values and Israel's surrogate utility that Washington has been willing to allow Israel to pursue any policy with regard to Palestine and the Palestinians. Moreover, the United States has fully supported—economically, militarily, diplomatically, and in every other way—Israeli policies. This, of course, has been disastrous for the Palestinians. Washington has managed to keep Middle East diplomacy under the sole purview of its domain. Europe, Russia, and the United Nations have all been effectively excluded. Thus, while Israel has the unconditional backing of the United States, the Palestinians are utterly alone. Not only must they confront Israel, which would be difficult enough by itself, but they must face the full diplomatic, political, economic, cultural, and military weight of the United States standing behind Israel. During the two terms of the Clinton administration, Washington promoted itself as an "honest broker" between the two sides when, in fact, there was not any truth to this claim. Thus, the United States is as responsible as Israel for the failure of the peace process and for the eruption of the Al-Aqsa intifada.

One can only assume that if Israel decides to put into practice its much-discussed policy of transfer, the United States will accept that, too (see Chapter 9). It might make a verbal objection, but at the level that matters—economic and military aid—the goods and dollars will continue to flow. None of this can make one optimistic about the future. The only hope resides in average U.S. citizens educating themselves about the conflict and demanding that their government take an active and honest role in bringing about a viable, sovereign Palestinian state in the West Bank, Gaza, and East Jerusalem and a just resolution of the refugee problem.

Chapter 8 illustrates where the foregoing has led. The previous chapters have illuminated the unbalanced and unfavorable (to the Palestinians) agreements of the Oslo process. They have detailed Israel's harsh policies toward the Palestinians living in the Occupied Territories. They examined the failures of the PA—in governance, human rights, corruption, and, perhaps most important, its role in protecting Israel's security (perceived in the minds of many Palestinians as collaboration with Israel and betrayal of its own people). Finally, they revealed the dishonest role of the United States in the peace process— totally supporting Israel on every issue at the expense of the Palestinians. All of these factors combined led to the Al-Aqsa intifada.

Notes

1. Kathleen Christison, *Perceptions of Palestine: Their Influence on U.S. Middle East Policy* (updated ed. with a new afterword) (Berkeley: University of California Press, 1999), pp. 289 and 295–296.

2. Jeff Halper, "Rafah: Holding Israel Accountable," *Independent Palestinian Information Network*, January 14, 2001 (online).

3. The process of transforming perceptions and beliefs into knowledge is called the *social construction of reality*. The best theoretical analysis of this phenomenon is Peter L. Berger and Thomas Luckmann, *The Social Construction of Reality: A Treatise on the Sociology of Knowledge* (New York: Doubleday, 1967).

4. See, for example, Fuad Sha'ban, *Islam and Arabs in Early American Thought: The Roots of Orientalism in America* (Durham, NC: Acorn, 1991).

5. Lawrence Davidson, *America's Palestine: Popular and Official Perceptions from Balfour to Israel Statehood* (Gainesville, University Press of Florida, 2001), p. 9. Also see Bashir Nijim, ed., *American Church Politics and the Middle East* (Belmont, MA: Association of Arab-American University Graduates, 1982), and Dewey Beegle, *Prophecy and Prediction* (Ann Arbor, MI: Prior Pettingill, 1979).

6. The slogan "a land without people for a people without land" was such an integral part of the early Zionist movement that colonized Palestine that its originator is unknown. Countless sources refer to it; here are two recent: Jeff Bander, "The Palestinian Problem: A Historical Review," *The Commentator* (Yeshiva University) 67, no. 8 (February 12, 2003) (online). Bander writes: "Herzl basically ignored the Arab question. . . . The Arabs simply were not there. Thus, 'A land without people, for a people without land,' became the cry of the early Zionists"; Israeli analyst Uri Avneri, in "The Rise of Israel's Right and the Failure of the Peace Movement," *Dialogue Program 2001* (Jerusalem: Palestinian Academic Society for the Study of International Affairs [PASSIA]), May 17, 2001, writes: "For a long time the word 'Palestinian' was taboo because it was an axiom of the Israeli Establishment that there were no Palestinian people, that this was an empty country. The Zionist slogan from the beginning was 'a land without people for a people without land.'"

7. See, for example, Christison, *Perceptions of Palestine,* pp. 3, 8, 9, 19, 24, 37–41, 42–44. See also Davidson, *America's Palestine,* pp. 4–10, 22–26.

8. Davidson, *America's Palestine,* pp. 89–137. Also see Christison, *Perceptions of Palestine*, pp. 16–44. For the classic analysis of Israel as a colonial-settler state, see Maxime Rodinson, *Israel: A Colonial-Settler State?* (New York: Monad, 1973). For a good analysis, see Peter Grose, *Israel in the Mind of America* (New York: Schocken Books, 1984), and Regina Sharif, *Non-Jewish*

Zionism: Its Roots in Western History (London: Zed Books, 1983). Also see Frank E. Manuel, *The Realities of American-Palestine Relations* (Washington, DC: Public Affairs Press, 1949).

9. Two good analyses of how Zionists manipulated the genocide of the Jews of Europe to serve their political ends are Boaz Evron, "The Holocaust: Learning the Wrong Lessons," *Journal of Palestine Studies* 10, no. 3 (spring 1981): 16–26, and Norman G. Finkelstein, *The Holocaust Industry: Reflections on the Exploitation of Jewish Suffering* (London: Verso Books, 2000).

10. See the excellent analysis by the French-Jewish philosopher Maxime Rodinson, *Cult, Ghetto, and State: The Persistence of the Jewish Question* (London: al Saqi Books, 1983), esp. pp. 172–191.

11. Halper, "Rafah: Holding Israel Accountable."

12. Yair Sheleg, "Ya'alon: 'Palestinian Threat Is Cancerous,'" *Ha'aretz* (Jerusalem, Israeli daily, English), August 26, 2002; Nadav Shragai and Gideon Alon, "Settlers Plan PR 'Defeat' of Palestinians; Ya'alon's Remarks Buoy Right, Ire Left," *Ha'aretz*, August 27, 2002; Ari Shavit, "The Enemy Within: The Confrontation with the Palestinians Is an Existential, Cancerous Threat," *Ha'aretz*, August 30, 2002.

13. There are numerous books, many by Israeli scholars, that support this analysis. Some of these include Avi Shlaim, *The Iron Wall: Israel and the Arab World* (New York: W. W. Norton, 2000) (covers the entire history); Ilan Pappe, *The Making of the Arab-Israeli Conflict, 1947–1951* (London: I. B. Tauris, 1994); Patrick Seale, *Asad of Syria: The Struggle for the Middle East* (London: I. B. Tauris, 1988); Tom Segev, *1949: The First Israelis* (New York: The Free Press, 1986), esp. pp. 1–92; Benny Morris, *Righteous Victims: A History of the Zionist-Arab Conflict, 1881–1999* (New York: Alfred A. Knopf, 1999); Ze'ev Schiff and Ehud Ya'ari, *Israel's Lebanon War* (London: George Allen and Unwin, 1984); Boutros Boutros-Ghali, *Egypt's Road to Jerusalem: A Diplomat's Story of the Struggle for Peace in the Middle East* (New York: Random House, 1997); Mohamed Heikal, *The Road to Ramadan* (London: Collins, 1975); David Hirst, *The Gun and the Olive Branch: The Roots of Violence in the Middle East* (London: Faber and Faber, 1977).

14. The classic intellectual study of this phenomenon is Edward Said's *Orientalism* (New York: Random House, 1978). Also see Richard H. Curtiss, *A Changing Image: American Perceptions of the Arab-Israeli Dispute* (Washington, DC: American Educational Trust, 1982); Edmund Ghareeb, ed., *Split Vision: The Portrayal of Arabs in American Media* (Washington, DC: American-Arab Affairs Council, 1983); Jack G. Shaheen, *The T.V. Arab* (Bowling Green, OH: Bowling Green State University, 1985); Michael C. Hudson and Ronald A. Wolfe, eds., *The American Media and the Arabs* (Washington, DC: Center for Contemporary Arab Studies, Georgetown University, 1980).

15. Four excellent examinations of institutionalized Israeli discrimination against its Arab citizens include Sabri Jiryis, *The Arabs in Israel* (Beirut: Institute for Palestine Studies, 1969, reissued by Monthly Review Press, New York, 1976); As'ad Ghanem, *The Palestinian-Arab Minority in Israel, 1948–2000: A Political Study* (Albany: State University of New York Press, 2001); Elia Zureik, *The Palestinians in Israel: A Study in Internal Colonialism* (London: Routledge and Kegan Paul, 1979); Ian Lustick, *Arabs in the Jewish*

State: Israel's Control of a National Minority (Austin: University of Texas Press, 1980). Most analysts consider the situation a form of apartheid.

16. Phillipa Strum, "Israel's Democratic Dilemma," *Reform Judaism* 14, no. 2 (winter 1985–1986): 13.

17. For an excellent analysis of the *New York Times*'s bias toward Israel and the effect of that bias on U.S. foreign policy, see Kathleen Christison, "Just How Much Does the *New York Times* Tilt Towards Israel; and How Much Does It Matter?" *Counterpunch*, August 19, 2002.

18. See, for example, William B. Quandt, *Decade of Decisions: American Policy Toward the Arab-Israeli Conflict* (Berkeley: University of California Press, 1977). For a more critical perspective, see Donald Neff, *Warriors Against Israel: How Israel Won the Battle to Become America's Ally, 1973* (Brattleboro, VT: Amana Books, 1988).

19. See, for example, Stephen Green, *Living by the Sword: America and Israel in the Middle East* (Brattleboro, VT: Amana Books, 1988); Yossi Melman and Dan Raviv, *Friends in Deed: Inside the U.S.-Israeli Alliance* (New York: Hyperion, 1994). The "strategic asset" thesis, i.e., Israel as an asset to American national interests in the Middle East (and elsewhere), has been the dominant perception/assumption/myth since Israel's spectacular victory in the June 1967 war, defeating three major Arab states in six days. For a critique of that assumption, see Cheryl A. Rubenberg, *Israel and the American National Interest: A Critical Examination* (Urbana and Chicago: University of Illinois Press, 1986). For one among hundreds of proponents, see Bernard Reich, *The United States and Israel: Influence in the Special Relationship* (New York: Praeger, 1984).

20. See, for example, Seymour M. Hersh, *The Samson Option: Israel's Nuclear Arsenal and American Foreign Policy* (New York: Random House, 1991).

21. Christison, *Perceptions of Palestine*, pp. 287–288.

22. See, for example, Norman Podhoretz, "J'Accuse," *Commentary*, September 1982, pp. 21–31.

23. Secretary of State Colin Powell, "United States Position on Terrorists and Peace in the Middle East," November 19, 2001, University of Louisville, Kentucky, U.S. Department of State. Also see Farid Jabar, "The Myth of Peace," *News from Within* 18, no. 7 (December 2001): 4–9.

24. See, for example, Edward Tivnan, *The Lobby: Jewish Political Power and American Foreign Policy* (New York: Simon and Schuster, 1987). He presents a very comprehensive analysis of the pro-Israel lobby, its multifaceted tactics, and the various groups that are part of it.

25. Welcome to CAMERA, "CAMERA, The Scope of the Problem, How CAMERA Works," *About CAMERA,* Committee for Accuracy in Middle East Reporting in America (online), accessed February 24, 2003.

26. See Honest Reporting.com—Fighting Media Bias.

27. Will Youmans, "Campus Watch: The Vigilante Thought Police," *CounterPunch*, September 23, 2002. Tamar Lewin, "Web Site Fuels Debate on Campus Anti-Semitism," *New York Times*, September 27, 2002; Marcella Bombardieri, "On Campuses, Critics of Israel Fend Off a Label," *Boston Globe*, September 21, 2002; Editorial, "Academics Blast 'McCarthyite' pro-Israel, U.S. Jewish Web Site," *Ha'aretz*, September 29, 2002.

28. Press Release, "ADL Guide Gives Individuals, Groups Tools for Israel Advocacy," see "Israel," ADL online.

29. ADL, *Pro-Arab Propaganda: Vehicles and Voices* (Washington, DC: Anti-Defamation League, 1983). This booklet contained an enemies list of thirty-one organizations and thirty-four individuals with extensive details on each. The list included some of the most prominent professors in the United States and Israel (e.g., Noam Chomsky, Israel Shahak, Eqbal Ahmad, and others). On November 30, 1984, the Middle East Studies Association (MESA) passed a resolution protesting the "creation, storage, or dissemination of blacklists, enemy lists," etc. Eventually the ADL withdrew this particular publication, but has continued to be active in monitoring individuals and keeping records of their public statements.

30. See, for example, Brian Whitaker, "US Think Tanks Give Lessons in Foreign Policy," *The Guardian* (London), August 19, 2002, and Brian Whitaker, "Selective MEMRI," *The Guardian* (London), August 12, 2002.

31. Matthew E. Berger, "Genesis of a PR Campaign: Using Political Savvy for Mideast Conflict," *Jewish Telegraphic Agency*, August 19, 2002; Joe Berkofsky, "Polls Show Lower Israel Support; As Many in US Blame Both Sides," *Jewish Telegraphic Agency*, August 19, 2002; Nathan Guttman, "Neutrality Isn't Enough for American Jews," *Ha'aretz*, August 18, 2002; Joe Berkofsky, "Jewish Groups Asked to Adopt New Strategy for pro-Israel P.R.," *Jewish Telegraphic Agency*, August 22, 2002; and Luntz Research Companies, *Communicating with America: Key Words, Themes, and Language*, available online at Jewish Internet Association. Nat Ives, "Pro-Israel TV Campaign Draws Fire," *New York Times*, October 1, 2002. Nathan Guttman, "U.S. Jews Open TV Ad Campaign to Burnish Israel's Eroded Image," *Ha'aretz*, October 2, 2002.

32. American Jewish Committee online. Project Interchange online.

33. The American-Israeli Cooperative Enterprise online.

34. An excellent article detailing the ways by which AIPAC and the Presidents' Conference influence the Bush administration's policy on the Israel-Palestine conflict is Michael Massing, "Conservative Jewish Groups Have Clout," *Los Angeles Times*, March 10, 2002.

35. Richard H. Curtiss, "Pro-Israel PAC Donations Soared in Final Months of 1996 Election Cycle," *Washington Report on Middle East Affairs* (April/May 1997): 43–50.

36. In the 1999–2000 election cycle, Jewish PACs contributed a total of $2,044,606. Top Senate receivers included Charles Robb (D–VA), $102,821; Joseph Lieberman (D–CT), $86,000; Gordon Slade (R–WA), $64,250; and Conrad Burns (R–MT), $52,960. The largest recipients in the House included Shelley Berkley (D–NV), $66,951; Sam Gejdenson (D–CT), $29,000; Dennis Hastert (R–IL), $19,500; James Maloney (D–CT), $18,500; and Richard Gephardt (D–MO), $16,500. Washington Report on Middle East Affairs, *Pro-Israel PAC Contributions to 2000 Congressional Candidates, 1999–2000 Cycle* (Washington, DC: Washington Report on Middle East Affairs, 2000).

37. See, for example, Eli Kintish, "Father of Ousted McKinney Spells Defeat 'J-E-W-S,'" *The Forward*, August 23–30, 2002; Sharon Samber, "Congresswoman's Defeat in Primary Seen as Major Victory for Jewish Activists," *Jewish Telegraphic Agency*, August 22, 2002; Editorial, "Mideast Goes to Georgia," *Los Angeles Times*, August 22, 2002; and Matthew Engel,

"Pro-Palestinian Congresswoman Ousted," *The Guardian* (London), August 22, 2002.

38. Two enormously important articles for understanding the role of pro-Israel think tanks are Jason Vest, "The Men from JINSA and CSP," *The Nation*, September 2, 2002, and Whitaker, "US Think Tanks Give Lessons in Foreign Policy."

39. The best recent piece on the nature of the strategic alliance is Stephen Zunes, "Why the US Supports Israel," *Foreign Policy in Focus*, May 2002 online. I highly recommend this article to anyone who wants to understand the strategic-asset thesis. Equally highly recommended is the critique of the strategic-asset thesis by Michael Neumann, "Protect Me from My Friends: Pro-Palestinian Activists and the Palestinians," *Counterpunch*, August 20, 2002.

40. See, for example, Skirl McArthur, "A Conservative Total for U.S. Aid to Israel: $91 Billion and Counting," *Washington Report for Middle East Affairs*, January/February 2001.

41. McArthur, "A Conservative Total for U.S. Aid to Israel: $91 Billion." Also see "Congressional Research Service, Library of Congress, 'Israel: US Foreign Assistance,' Washington, 6 October 1995 (excerpts)," reprinted in *Journal of Palestine Studies* 25, no. 2 (winter 1996): 151–159.

42. One of Israel's more egregious acts was its intentional bombing of a U.S. ship and the killing of U.S. military personnel. Not only was Israel not criticized for this attack; the whole incident was hushed up and removed from the realm of legitimate discourse. See James M. Ennes Jr., *Assault on the Liberty: The True Story of the Israeli Attack on an American Intelligence Ship* (New York: Random House, 1979).

43. Human Rights Watch, *World Report 1995*, "Israeli-Occupied West Bank and Gaza Strip," New York, December 1994, excerpted in *Journal of Palestine Studies* 24, no. 3 (spring 1995): 145–152, 151.

44. See, for example, Camille Mansour, "The Impact of 11 September on the Israeli-Palestinian Conflict," *Journal of Palestine Studies* 31, no. 2 (winter 2002): 5–18.

45. See, for example, Washington Watch, "The Bush Administration's Media Campaign to Pressure Arafat," *Journal of Palestine Studies* 31, no. 3 (spring 2002): 90–98.

46. For an excellent analysis and history of the U.S. vetoes for Israel, including a list of each resolution, its content, and the vote distribution, see Phyllis Bennis, "VETO," *The Link* 36, no. 1 (January–March 2003): 1–13.

47. Solange Habib, Sydney D. Bailey, and Sam Daws, "Table: Subjects of UN Security Council Vetoes," *The Procedure of the UN Security Council*, 3rd ed. (Oxford, UK: Clarendon, 1998); Table of the Veto by Giji Gya and Misaki Watanabe online at Global Policy.

48. Reprinted from *Ha'aretz*, "UN General Assembly Condemns Israel Over Jerusalem," published by the Palestinian Right to Return Coalition, December 1, 2000.

49. An excellent analysis of the U.S.-Israeli intelligence relationship is Ian Black and Benny Morris, *Israel's Secret Wars: A History of Israel's Intelligence Services* (New York: Grove Weidenfeld, 1991). Of more relevance is Andrew Cockburn and Leslie Cockburn, *Dangerous Liaison: The Inside Story of the U.S.-Israeli Covert Relationship* (New York: HarperCollins, 1991).

50. See Cheryl A. Rubenberg, "U.S. Policy Toward the Palestinians: A

Twenty Year Assessment," *Arab Studies Quarterly* 10, no. 1 (winter 1988): 1–43; Cheryl A. Rubenberg, "The U.S.-PLO Dialogue: Continuity or Change in American Foreign Policy," *Arab Studies Quarterly* 11, no. 4 (fall 1989): 1–58; and Cheryl A. Rubenberg, "American Efforts for Peace in the Middle East: 1919–1986," in Roselle Tekiner, Samir Abed-Rabbo, and Norton Mezvinsky, eds., *Anti-Zionism: Analytical Reflections* (a tribute to Rabbi Elmer Berger) (Brattleboro, VT: Amana Books, 1988), pp. 186–256. See, for example, Muhammad K. Shadid, *The United States and the Palestinians* (New York: St. Martin's Press, 1981); Donald Neff, *Fallen Pillars: U.S. Policy Towards Palestine and Israel Since 1945* (Washington, DC: Institute for Palestine Studies, 1995); and Michael W. Suleiman, ed., *U.S. Policy on Palestine from Wilson to Clinton* (Normal, IL: Association of Arab-American University Graduates, 1995).

51. See, for example, Washington Institute's Presidential Study Group, *Building for Peace: An American Strategy for the Middle East* (Washington, DC: Washington Institute for Near East Policy, 1988). This program was the key policy-planning document for the Bush administration.

52. See *What Is the Washington Institute for Near East Policy?* (Washington, DC: Washington Institute for Near East Policy, 2001); and Mark H. Milstein, "Washington Institute for Near East Policy: An AIPAC 'Image Problem,'" *Washington Report on Middle East Affairs*, July 1991.

53. See *What Is the Washington Institute for Near East Policy?*

54. See ibid.

55. Jewish Institute for National Security Affairs, *About JINSA* (Washington, DC: the Jewish Institute for National Security Affairs, 2001), available online.

56. For a complete list of all the Jewish (and pro-Israeli) officials in the Clinton administration, see Avinoam Bar-Yosef, "The Jews Who Run Clinton's Cabinet," *Ma'ariv* (Jerusalem, Israeli daily, Hebrew), translated by Israel Shahak and reprinted in *Journal of Palestine Studies* 24, no. 2 (winter 1995): 148–152.

57. Sheldon L. Richman, "Clinton Hopes Indyk Appointment Will Appease Jewish Leaders," *Washington Report on Middle East Affairs*, March 1993.

58. See, for example, the brief bio that his agent, Harry Walker, uses to promote Ross's speaking engagements. *Ambassador Dennis Ross*, Harry Walker Agency, America's Leading Exclusive Lecture Agency, online.

59. Christison, *Perceptions of Palestine*, p. 304.

60. This analysis is made by Joe Stork, "The Clinton Administration and the Palestine Question," in Michael W. Suleiman, ed., *U.S. Policy on Palestine from Wilson to Clinton* (Normal, IL: Association of Arab-American University Graduates, 1995), p. 255.

61. Christison, *Perceptions of Palestine*, p. 302.

62. William B. Quandt, "Clinton and the Arab-Israeli Conflict: The Limits of Incrementalism," *Journal of Palestine Studies* 30, no. 2 (winter 2001): 26–27.

63. "PLO's Negotiating Team, Assessment of the Clinton Administration's Involvement in the Palestinian-Israeli Peace Process, Ramallah and Gaza, 22 January 2001," *Journal of Palestine Studies* 30, no. 3 (spring 2001): 159.

64. Christison, *Perceptions of Palestine*, p. 297.

65. See Juliana S. Peck, *The Reagan Administration and the Palestinian Question: The First Thousand Days* (Washington, DC: Institute for Palestine Studies, 1984).

66. Christison, *Perceptions of Palestine,* p. 300.

67. For the text of the law, see "Middle East Peace Facilitation Act of 1994: U.S. Congress Conditions on Relations with the PLO (Washington, DC: 30 April 1994," reprinted in *Journal of Palestine Studies* 23, no. 4 (summer 1994): 152–153. The second report was submitted on June 1, 1994. For the text, see "Department of State, Report on PLO Compliance with Declaration of Principles Commitments (Washington, DC: 1 June 1994 (excerpts)," *Journal of Palestine Studies* 24, no. 1 (autumn 1994): 145–149.

68. Quandt, "Clinton and the Arab-Israeli Conflict," p. 27.

69. Ilene R. Prusher, "US Puts CIA on the Case in Mideast," *Christian Science Monitor International*, August 14, 1997; Khader Khader and Musa Qous, "Ross Limits Mission to 'Israel Security,'" *Palestine Report* 3, no. 10 (August 15, 1997); Dean Klovens, "The CIA's Role in the Peace Process," *Middle East Intelligence Bulletin* 3, no. 1 (January 2001).

70. Quandt, "Clinton and the Arab-Israeli Conflict," p. 28, and Christison, *Perceptions of Palestine*, pp. 283–285.

71. Robert Malley and Hussein Agha, "Camp David: The Tragedy of Errors," *New York Review of Books*, August 9, 2001, p. 60.

72. Christison, *Perceptions of Palestine*, p. 302.

73. See, for example, the analysis by Aluf Benn, "The Selling of the Summit: How Ehud Barak Took Advantage of the Isolation and Blackout Imposed by the Americans at Camp David to Win the Israeli-Palestinian Propaganda War," *Ha'aretz*, July 27, 2001.

74. Meron Benvenisti, "Challenging the Myth of Camp David," *Ha'aretz*, August 2, 2001. Additional light is shed on the issue by Gideon Levy, "Just When We Were About to Give Them So Much," *Ha'aretz*, June 17, 2001.

75. "Peace Monitor, 16 May–15 August 2000," *Journal of Palestine Studies* 30, no. 1 (autumn 2000): 132.

76. For a chronicle of these meetings, many of which were bilateral (others included Dennis Ross or CIA representative George Tenet), see "Peace Monitor," *Journal of Palestine Studies* 30, no. 2 (winter 2001): 126–134.

77. See, for example, Ran HaCohen, "The State of the Army, Part 1," May 8, 2000, and "The State of the Army, Part 2: A Cease-fire Which Is Not," June 22, 2000, *Letter from Israel*, direct submission to Internet July 11, 2001, at anti-war.com, and Baruch Kimmerling, "Preparing for the War of His Choosing," *Ha'aretz*, July 12, 2001.

78. For the text of the resolution plus the commentary therein, see "UN Security Council Resolution 1322 on the Violence in Israel and the Occupied Territories (New York: 7 October 2000)," *Journal of Palestine Studies* 30, no. 2 (winter 2001): 157–158.

79. Nicole Krau, "France and Germany Stop Arms Sales to Israel," *Ha'aretz*, December 17, 2000.

80. "Peace Monitor," *Journal of Palestine Studies* 30, no. 2 (winter 2001): 142. See also Nitzan Horowitz, "Clinton Asks Congress for an Extra $450M. for Military Aid to Israel," *Ha'aretz*, November 16, 2000.

81. Nitzan Horowitz, "Congress Set to Okay $2.8 Billion for Israel," *Ha'aretz,* October 28, 2000.

82. "President Bill Clinton, Main Points of Agreement Reached at the Sharm al-Shaykh Summit, Sharm al-Shaykh, Egypt, 17 October 2000," *Journal of Palestine Studies* 30, no. 2 (winter 2001): 186.

83. A superb analysis of all the Sharm al-Sheikh agreements but especially the secret security deals is al-Awda, *Another "Secret Deal,"* International Obervatory for Palestinian Affairs (IOPA), October 19, 2000, online (the analysis was produced by al-Awda—the Palestinian Right to Return Coalition). IOPA is a Geneva-based NGO that "coordinates the work of other NGOs working on issues of the Palestine question. IOPA publishes news and articles about Palestine and circulates information."

84. For an excellent analysis, see Stephen Zunes, "The U.S. Role in the Breakdown of the Israeli-Palestinian Peace Process," *Foreign Policy in Focus: Special Report*, May 2002.

85. "Peace Monitor," *Journal of Palestine Studies* 30, no. 2 (winter 2001): 133.

86. Aluf Benn, "UN Human Rights Chief Calls for International Monitors," *Ha'aretz,* November 18, 2000.

87. Aluf Benn and Amira Hass, "Inquiry Team Will Study Clashes from Washington," *Ha'aretz*, December 11, 2000. Meron Benvenisti, "A Committee of Moral Disgust," *Ha'aretz*, December 14, 2000.

88. Aluf Benn, "Israel Boycotts Mitchell Inquiry," *Ha'aretz*, January 22, 2001.

89. For the complete text of the report, see *Text of the Mitchell Report*, *Ha'aretz*, May 6, 2001.

90. See the analysis by Mouin Rabbani, "The Mitchell Report: Oslo's Last Gasp?" *MERIP Press Information Note*, no. 59 (June 1, 2001).

91. See, for example, the analysis by Mark Perry, "Bush Administration Debates Policy," *Palestine Report*, May 30, 2001.

92. For other good analyses, see Ghassan Khatib, "Why Tenet Will Eventually Fail," *Palestine Report*, June 14, 2001; Daud Abdullah, "The Mitchell Report: Another Fig-Leaf," *Media Monitors Network*, June 2001; Khalid Turaani et al., *Mitchell Report: Framework for Peace?* (Washington, DC: Foundation for Middle East Peace, June 6, 2001).

93. See the analysis by Suzanne Goldenberg, "Sharon Rejects Call for Freeze on Settlements," *The Guardian* (London), May 23, 2001.

94. Amira Hass, "PA Ready for Cease-Fire Based on Mitchell," *Ha'aretz*, May 11, 2001; Amira Hass, "PA Warmly Welcomes Committee Findings," *Ha'aretz,* May 16, 2001; Aluf Benn, "Sharon and Peres Mount Campaign Against Findings of Mitchell Report," *Ha'aretz*, May 10, 2001; Aluf Benn, "Israel Gives OK to Mitchell Report," *Ha'aretz*, May 14, 2001; Aluf Benn, "Israel Opposed to Mitchell Call for Settlement Freeze," *Ha'aretz*, May 16, 2001.

95. See *What Is the Washington Institute for Near East Policy?* More important, for the executive summary of the policy plan, see "Has Oslo Run Its Curse? A Washington Think Tank Offers a Strategy to President-Elect George Bush," *Ha'aretz*, January 17, 2001.

96. See the analysis by Kathleen and Bill Christison, "A Rose by Any Other Name: The Bush Administration's Dual Loyalties," *CounterPunch,* December 13, 2002.

97. Brian Whitaker, "US Think Tanks Give Lessons in Foreign Policy," *The Guardian* (London), August 19, 2002.

98. Irene Gendzier, "Oil, Politics, and the Military in the US 'War on Terrorism,'" *ZNet Mideast Watch,* December 11, 2002, parts 1–3.

99. Kathleen and Bill Christison, "A Rose by Any Other Name"; and Jason Vest, "The Men from JINSA and CSP," *The Nation,* September 2, 2002. The Vest piece is especially useful on the political views and the institutional interconnections of these men.

100. See, for example, Ami Eden, "U.S. Christian Zionists Stage Telethon in Support of 'My People,'" *Ha'aretz,* August 13, 2002; Yigal Schleifer, "Newfound Friends," *Jewish World* (New York), reprinted in *Jerusalem Report,* August 26, 2002; and Yechiel Eckstein, "Christians Aren't the Enemy," *Wall Street Journal,* August 16, 2002.

101. For a text of the Tenet Plan, see *The Tenet Plan: Israeli-Palestinian Cease-fire and Security Plan, Proposed by CIA Director George Tenet, June 13, 2001,* by the Avalon Project at the Yale Law School, available online.

102. See, for example, Amos Harel, Amnon Barzilai, and Daniel Sobelman, "Israel Accepts Tenet Truce, but PA Holds Back," *Ha'aretz,* June 11, 2001; Roger Hardy, "Tenet Plan Open to Interpretation," *BBC News,* June 13, 2001; Derek Brown, "A New and Fragile Ceasefire Takes Shape," *The Guardian* (London), June 13, 2001.

103. Aluf Benn, "Analysis: Best Buddies, up to a Point," *Ha'aretz,* August 26, 2001; Aluf Benn and Natan Guttman, "Bush Puts Blame for Talks Impasse on PA," *Ha'aretz,* August 26, 2001; Nathan Guttman, "Israel, US, Increase Intelligence Links," *Ha'aretz,* September 13, 2001; *Cable News Network,* LP, LLLP, "Israel Buys More F-16s from U.S. Firm," September 7, 2001, CNN online; Bassam Abu-Sharif, "The European Road to Tel Aviv Goes Through Washington," *Media Monitors Network,* September 10, 2001; Nitzan Horowitz and Aluf Benn, "Bush Vows to Pressure PA to End the Violence," *Ha'aretz,* May 4, 2001; Aluf Benn, "U.S. to Honor Nuclear Agreement with Israel," *Ha'aretz,* May 24, 2001; Aluf Benn, "U.S. Strategic Dialogue a Boost for Sharon," *Ha'aretz,* August 23, 2001; Dafna Linzer, "U.S. Backs Israel During UN Meeting on Mideast Conflict," Associated Press, August 20, 2001.

104. Barry Schweid, "White House Backs Arafat Confinement," Associated Press, January 24, 2002.

105. Bradley Burston, "As War Cries Ring Out, U.S. Silence May Signal Rare Free Hand for Israeli Military Moves," *Ha'aretz,* January 24, 2002. In his article, Burston quotes another *Ha'aretz* correspondent, Akiva Eldar, as writing that the September 11 attack on the United States created a new perception wherein "Israel is seen as the equivalent of New York" and "Arafat is actually becoming what Sharon wanted him to be, Israel's version of Bin Laden." Burston does not provide a citation for Eldar's remarks.

106. For a full text of the Zinni proposals, see *Second U.S. "Joint Goals" Proposal, 26 March 2002* (Jerusalem: Jerusalem Media and Communication Center, April 2002).

8

The Al-Aqsa Intifada: Despair Manifest

Since 1967, millions of Palestinians have been under a military occupation, without any civil rights, and most lacking even the most basic human rights. The continuing circumstances of occupation and repression give them, by any measure, the right to resist that occupation with any means at their disposal and to rise up in violence against that occupation. This is a moral right inherent to natural law and international law.

—Baruch Kimmerling[1]

Israel's moves to destroy the Palestinian Authority, thus, cannot be viewed as spontaneous "acts of retaliation." They are part of a calculated plan, long in the making . . . to topple Arafat . . . and end the "historical mistake" [of Oslo].

—Tanya Reinhart[2]

At every stage in the recent troubles, the Israeli forces have been responsible for increasing the level of violence.

—Stanley Heller[3]

Thus far I have argued that the intifada was the inevitable result of four interrelated factors: (1) the deeply flawed nature of the peace accords; (2) Israel's policies on the ground (e.g., closures, curfews, permits, land confiscations, and others) that made Palestinian lives more arduous than they were prior to the signing of the Oslo Declaration of Principles (DOP); (3) the unwavering U.S. support for Israel's policies; and (4) the Palestinian leadership's failure to meet its people's basic needs plus its corruption and repression.

The proximate cause of the uprising—the spark that ignited the flames—was Ariel Sharon's walkabout on the Haram al-Sharif. His presence, together with more than 1,000 troops on the Muslim holy site, sparked strong Palestinian protest. The human rights group B'Tselem conducted an investigation into the sequence of events in the immediate aftermath of Sharon's excursion. It found that the following day (September 29, 2000), a Friday, the Muslim day of communal prayer, Israel arrayed a huge police force around the Haram facing the worshipers when they emerged from the noontime prayer. Many worshipers began throwing stones at the police, who responded with shock grenades and rubber-coated metal bullets. Within minutes the police stormed the Haram, accompanied by massive random firing of weapons. Still firing, the police chased Palestinians who were attempting to exit the Haram. By the afternoon's end, four Palestinians were dead and 200 wounded on and around the holy site. As news of the events spread across the territories, protests erupted throughout the West Bank and Gaza. These demonstrations also were met with lethal fire.[4] In September 2002, the Israeli daily *Ma'ariv* published some startling data concerning Israel's overwhelming use of force: "In the first few days of the intifada, the IDF fired about 700,000 bullets and other projectiles in Judea and Samaria [the West Bank] and about 300,000 in Gaza. All told, about a million bullets and projectiles were used."[5] So began the Al-Aqsa intifada, an uprising that is directly linked to the 1987 intifada.

This chapter is divided into two sections: The first provides a conceptual framework and explores some issues that can help frame an understanding of the evolution of the intifada; the second presents a chronological unfolding of events on the ground.

Conceptual Framework: Analysis and Reflections

Historical Linkages

The Palestinians.   The 1987 intifada was a spontaneous, mass-based, mostly nonviolent movement with a distinct objective: ending the Israeli occupation. Its leadership was composed of local activists representing all the political factions who cooperated in the Unified National Leadership of the Uprising (UNLU). It articulated the goal of the uprising and developed a wide range of tactics that were regularly communicated to the public through leaflets. These included peaceful mass protests, commercial strikes, tax rebellions, burning of identity cards, popular committees to meet the needs of the people, a sustained economic boycott of Israeli products, demonstrations, and limited violence such as stone-throwing and use of homemade incendiaries like Molotov cocktails. The public not only supported the intifada; almost all Palestinians participated in intifada-related activities. For nearly two years, the population was mobilized and engaged despite intense Israeli repression. By the middle of 1990, intifada activity slowed but continued at a low level until the Oslo Accords in 1993.

The uprising persisted mainly because Palestinians believed that their objective—ending the occupation and establishing an independent Palestinian state alongside Israel in the West Bank, Gaza, and East Jerusalem—was attainable.[6] Nevertheless, they paid a high price for this uprising. Israel killed more than 1,240 Palestinians and injured approximately 130,787.[7] Additionally, Israel charged, arrested, and imprisoned between 33,233 and 35,027 individuals.[8]

When the Oslo Accords were signed, the majority of Palestinians saw them as the political result of the intifada. However, as it became apparent to the people that the peace process was not going to achieve this goal and, moreover, that the Palestinian leadership had essentially sold them out, their frustration and rage led to the Al-Aqsa uprising of 2000. Initially that revolt was also a widespread mass movement cutting across all social lines. Yet for a variety of reasons, the second intifada became very different from the first.

Israel. The first intifada also took a considerable toll on Israel. Sixty-four soldiers and 115 civilians were killed.[9] When the uprising began, troops from the Israeli Defense forces (IDF) were stationed in every city, town, village, and refugee camp, essentially functioning as police officers. Israeli soldiers found themselves hunting down stone-throwers in every back alley, dirt street, and side passage—well known to the inhabitants but unfamiliar to the soldiers. Extinguishing this rebellion took more than three years and provoked intense frustration on the part of the IDF. It also diminished the IDF's traditional military preparedness for fighting conventional wars. Israel thus drew the conclusion that something had to be done to alter the situation. Hence, it sought to lessen the IDF's police role and to pacify the Palestinians without fundamentally altering Israeli interests in the territories.

Prime Minister Yitzhak Rabin and others perceived Oslo as a viable solution to this predicament. Palestinians would have responsibility for policing their own people in the most densely inhabited zones, the IDF could redeploy to areas outside the Palestinian towns and cities, Palestinians would have the symbols of a state, and Israel would retain control. The latter would be achieved primarily through the restrictions placed on Palestinian autonomy in the various agreements. Even more advantageous and important, from Israel's perspective, Palestinians would not only be policing Palestinians; the Oslo Accords made them explicitly responsible for guaranteeing Israel's security. One Israeli analyst, Ran HaCohen, observed:

> In some senses, the Oslo "peace process" was a huge success for Israeli colonialism. The "on-going negotiations"—which allow[ed] the Palestinians to choose between either willingly accepting Israel's terms or having them imposed on them unilaterally—enabled Israel to expand settlements on Palestinian lands with virtually no resistance. The Israeli "peace camp" was effectively soothed by false promises of "peace with settlements," American hegemony in the world media silenced any international criticism, and the "process" that was supposed to end Israeli colonialism broke down violently, with about twice as many settlers as seven years earlier.[10]

Accordingly, Israel's solution did not work out as it envisioned. As the peace process progressed, Palestinians' lives deteriorated, and Israel violated both the letter and the spirit of Oslo. For instance, Palestinians became increasingly demoralized and despondent as a consequence of events such as the assassination of Yahya Ayyash, the opening of the archeological tunnel under Al-Aqsa Mosque, the initiation of construction at Har Homa in Jerusalem, continuous confiscation of Palestinian land, and construction of new settlements. Some responded with violence (suicide bombs), but others reacted with peaceful demonstrations. Whatever the form of action, however, Israel retaliated with disproportionate violence, collective punishments of the population, and more provocations. At the same time, it continuously blamed Arafat and the Palestinian Authority (PA) for failing to protect Israel's security and demanded that it take ever more repressive security measures. This coincided with the precipitous decline in the Palestinian economy, increasing unemployment and poverty, and an overall worsening of quality of life. In this environment, the Palestinians resorted to rebellion.

Palestinian Politics and the Nature of the Al-Aqsa Intifada

Paucity of popular participation. Despite its beginning as a popular protest, the Al-Aqsa intifada, unlike the 1987 uprising, was transformed within weeks into an armed conflict involving mainly those Palestinians who had access to weapons. Nevertheless, it consistently had overwhelming popular support, as public opinion polls clearly demonstrate (see Table 8.1).

Table 8.1 illustrates additional significant factors. For one, support

Table 8.1 Public Opinion During the Al-Aqsa Intifada (percentage)

1. Do you support or oppose the continuation of the current Palestinian intifada?

Date	Dec. 2000	April 2001	June 2001	Sept. 2001	Dec. 2001
Support	70.1	80.2	79.0	85.3	80.1
Oppose	17.8	13.3	14.8	12.7	17.1
No opinion	12.1	6.5	6.2	2.0	2.8

2. Do you support the resumption of military operations against Israeli targets as a suitable response within current political conditions?

Date	Dec. 2000	April 2001	June 2001	Sept. 2001	Dec. 2001
Support	72.1	n/a	70.6	84.6	67.5
Oppose	16.8	n/a	14.8	9.9	26.1
No opinion	11.1	n/a	14.6	5.5	6.4

3. Do you see suicide operations as a suitable response within the current political conditions?

Date	Dec. 2000	April 2001	June 2001	Sept. 2001	Dec. 2001
Support	66.2	73.7	68.6	n/a	64.0
Oppose	22.2	15.9	23.1	n/a	26.0
No opinion	11.6	10.4	8.3	n/a	10.0

4. What is your opinion of the Oslo agreement?

Date	Dec. 2000	April 2001	June 2001	Sept. 2001	Dec. 2001
Strongly support	3.2	3.8	4.2	1.6	4.4
Support	35.8	36.6	33.9	28.1	26.6
Oppose	36.0	33.0	34.0	36.4	32.5
Strongly oppose	18.5	19.9	19.9	24.9	29.6
No opinion	6.5	6.7	8.0	9.0	6.9

5. How do you evaluate the performance of the PA?

Date	Dec. 2000	April 2001	June 2001	Sept. 2001	Dec. 2001
Very good	5.2	5.5	6.9	5.7	6.8
Good	50.3	56.3	55.6	56.3	38.1
Bad	23.4	23.9	23.1	25.3	27.0
Very bad	13.9	11.3	11.2	8.3	24.3
No opinion	7.2	3.0	3.2	4.4	3.8

6. The United States acts as sponsor of the peace process and as a mediator in negotiations. How do you characterize its mediation?

Date	Dec. 2000	April 2001	June 2001	Sept. 2001	Dec. 2001
Biased toward Palestinians	1.0	0.4	0.2	n/a	n/a
Neutral	3.1	2.5	1.7	n/a	n/a
Biased toward Israelis	95.1	95.3	96.4	n/a	n/a
No opinion	0.8	1.8	1.7	n/a	n/a

(continues)

Table 8.1   continued

7. Which Palestinian personality do you trust the most?

(Respondents were given a choice of Yasir Arafat; 10 other specific individuals from opposition factions of the leftist and Islamist trends as well as independents; "others"; don't trust anyone; no answer.)[a]

Date	Dec. 2000	April 2001	June 2001	Sept. 2001	Dec. 2001
Yasir Arafat	25.7	32.3	27.8	23.5	24.5
Ahmad Yassin[b]	12.2	8.0	9.8	10.6	12.8
"Don't trust anyone"	31.9	28.3	26.6	26.0	33.1

Source: Polling data was compiled from from five separate, consecutive polls (#'s 39–43) conducted by the Jerusalem Media and Communication Center, Public Opinion Polls, Jerusalem, Palestinian Research Center, available online at www.jmcc.org/publicpoll/results/.
   Notes: a. No one of the other nine individuals received a percentage higher than 4.0 and that varied from poll to poll.
   b. Yassin is the leader of Hamas (the leading Islamist party).
   n/a indicates the question was not asked in that poll.

for the Oslo process had decreased significantly with a maximum of 40 percent of respondents supporting it in any of the five polls. On the issue of trust for Palestinian leaders, Arafat's highest percentage stood at 32.3 percent; his lowest was 23.5 percent. The major opposition leader, Ahmad Yassin, who heads Hamas, received a maximum of 12.8 percent, falling to 8 percent. Conversely, between 26 and 31.9 percent of the people did not trust any leaders in the Palestinian territories. This indicates a high level of alienation among the populace that may partially explain the paucity of popular participation.

There were other reasons why the mass public was not involved despite continuous efforts by nongovernmental organizations to mobilize it. As a result of their professionalization, as well as Arafat's attempts to undermine their legitimacy, they, like the PA, had grown distant from the masses. Another explanation for the lack of popular participation can be found in the overwhelming sense of despair that gripped the Palestinian population. The depth of this despair was such that it tended to immobilize people.

A further reason for the lack of mass participation was that armed groups quickly came to dominate the intifada. Once they emerged as a vanguard, the majority of the population tended to stay away.[11] Popular participation was also deterred by the intensity of Israel's punitive responses, including F-16 air strikes, helicopter gunship missile attacks, blockades, total siege, and so on. Moreover, as a consequence of the division of the territories into Areas A, B, and C, with Israeli forces redeployed outside of the population centers, most of the engagements took place beyond city limits, at Israeli roadblocks and checkpoints. Thus, one had consciously to seek out a confrontation. This was in contrast to the first intifada, during which Israeli troops were stationed on every street corner. The increasingly internally fragmented situation of the West Bank and Gaza—worsened during the intifada by checkpoints and the physical isolation of populated areas through trenches, cement blockades, and so on—made it nearly impossible for people to leave their locales and rendered mass action virtually impossible.

The reduction in popular participation was also due to the deflation of the traditional opposition—the Popular Front, the Democratic Front, and the Palestine People's Party (PPP, formerly Palestine Communist Party [PCP]). During most of the Oslo years, these parties seemed to experience an identity crisis. They did not articulate coherent alternative political platforms or strategies. As a result, their grassroots followings shrank, and they did not regain their pre-Oslo stature. During the Oslo years, the leaders of these groups failed to mobilize the masses around any issue—even social welfare or economic issues. This was due, in considerable measure, to the PA's repression of dissent.

Depolitization was also a consequence of deliberate PA efforts. This resulted, among other things, in a withering of nationalist ideology (i.e., self-determination in an independent state was replaced by focus on a series of interim accords and their implementation or lack thereof). Individuals lost sight of the original objective of their struggle in their preoccupation with the *process* of negotiation that came to overshadow the *substance* (i.e., the goal).[12] Without a clearly defined purpose, individuals are less willing to be politically active. Oslo also brought with it grinding poverty, which had a paralyzing effect on much of the population, which was focused on feeding families. Finally, the lack of mass participation was further related to the PA's security relationship with Israel, which blurred who was the enemy. One analyst expressed this dilemma well:

> The Palestinian political crisis of confidence has more to do with the ambivalence felt by society towards a national authority that has emerged quite authentically from the liberation movement but is organically linked to the State of Israel. Functional cooperation is at its most direct in the domain of security, whether it is to do with joint Israeli-Palestinian patrols in Zone "B" or collaboration between intelligence services at the highest level against the Islamist opposition. . . . Even beyond the formal ties of the autonomy agreements, the real-

ity of the economic dependence of the Palestinian territories on Israel
has fostered networks of interests between the "military-commercial
complex" close to the PA and Israeli officials. . . . In short, the basic
ambiguity of autonomy status condemns the PA to the impossible task
of fighting the national fight while simultaneously collaborating with
the occupier.[13]

Leadership and conflicting objectives. Two other aspects of the Al-
Aqsa intifada were striking: It was essentially leaderless; and it did not
have a clear objective.[14] Arafat was mostly invisible throughout, either
traveling abroad, hunkered down in his Gaza headquarters, or, after
December 2001, under house arrest in Ramallah (where he remained
through February 2003 with a brief reprieve in early summer). Neither
Arafat, nor any other top PA officials, ever stated the objective of the
uprising. In fact, the leadership's goal was simply to restart the negotiating process, curry favor with Washington, garner support from the
international community, and remain in power while not alienating the
Palestinian masses. The public, conversely, would have liked to send
Arafat and his Tunisian coterie packing, and they had no interest in any
objective except ending the occupation. They considered negotiations
an Israeli tactic to create more facts on the ground and deny them their
basic rights.[15] For example, even as early as November 2000, when
Arafat called on all Palestinians to "ensure the intifada [maintains] its
popular character and peaceful course," the militia leaders on the
ground evidenced a divergent perspective. They called for a continuation of the uprising, protests against Arafat's scheduled meeting with
U.S. President Bill Clinton, and "extension of the intifada to include
every street and every Jewish settlement. . . . For those hundreds of
youths who every day take on the might of the Israeli army at checkpoints and settlements across the West Bank and Gaza, in this intifada
'there is no leadership.'"[16]

Not only was the Al-Aqsa intifada essentially leaderless in the
sense of organization, expression of objectives, and tactics; the PA, in
essence, abandoned its own people to the vagaries of Israel's punishing
blows. The PA did not even attempt to function as an agency capable of
offering support to the residents under its jurisdiction. For example,
Palestinian families that tried to ascertain what had happened to a member that Israel had arrested had nowhere to phone and no one to investigate. When the settlers ran rampant in the orchards and fields of
Palestinians in Area A, there was no official agency to turn to for help.
No one from the PA attempted to remove Israeli-installed roadblocks or
to send bulldozers to fill in the trenches that Israel dug around towns.

Writing in *Ha'aretz*, Amira Hass comments: "The PA has been so fragmented that the regime cannot function as a centralized, unified agency.
That fact in itself, incidentally, can serve as proof that the PA's leadership did not plan this uprising."[17] Be that as it may, it was little solace to
the population, which was left to fend for itself in a prolonged wartime
situation. So, too, there was a great deal of bitterness among the people
at Arafat's refusal to activate the 40,000 well-armed Palestinian policemen and send them out to defend the citizenry.[18]

The activists.   Those who were taking part in this intifada generally fell
into one of two broad groupings. The first comprised Arafat and the
senior PA officials, with a smattering of grassroots support. For this
group, the intifada was considered an instrument of diplomatic leverage, in order to prod the international community to pressure Sharon to
return to the negotiations at the point where they had broken off. In fact,
their primary interest appeared to be their own survival.

The second consisted of a loose coalition of some fourteen factions,
running the ideological gamut from Islamic to nationalist. It included
such diverse elements as Islamic Jihad, the Tanzim, the Al-Aqsa
Martyrs' Brigade, Hamas, the Forces of Badr, and others—a majority of
whom were Fatah splinter groups (not, obviously, Hamas or Islamic
Jihad).[19] They emerged mainly because of the competition and factionalism within Fatah. They were not cohesive organizations; and in all
probability, despite their differences with Arafat, if he had demanded a
cease-fire, they would likely have complied. Despite their individual
disorganization, they coalesced under a very broad umbrella calling
itself the National and Islamic Forces (NIF). For the NIF, the intifada
was a means to break out of the Oslo framework and to restore as the
national priority the objective of a genuinely viable and independent
state rather than the "protectorate under Israeli hegemony" that was
Oslo.[20] Tanzim leader Marwan Barghouti put the NIF position clearly:
"'Sharon is Israel's last bullet' before it surrenders to the realization that
it can have either peace and security or occupation and settlement, but
not both."[21] For the NIF and the groups that considered themselves a
part of it, then, the uprising was a war of national liberation in which
the only negotiations to be conducted were those that formalized the
end of the occupation.

During the first intifada, the activists obeyed the orders that were
issued by the UNLU and disseminated through the leaflets. There were
no security organizations, but, as already noted, there was an operational chain of command. In this uprising there were innumerable PA

security organizations, yet they had little contact with the activists and even feared going into the refugee camps where the most radicalized elements were often headquartered.[22] Moreover, the NIF militias did not successfully build a functioning alliance comparable to the UNLU of the first intifada. Their actions were not coordinated either politically or militarily. Their weapons typically included the sniper's bullet, roadside bombs, an occasional mortar round, and a homemade (and highly ineffective) antitank missile. They tended to focus their attacks on settlers, settlements, soldiers, and checkpoints in the Occupied Territories.[23] This was consistent with the political objective of ending the occupation. In addition to the militias, individuals—unaffiliated with any group—carried out military activities. These were mainly the young men who regularly threw stones and Molotov cocktails. The suicide bombers, mostly affiliated with Islamic Jihad or Hamas, primarily targeted civilians inside Israel (discussed below).

The existence of diverse opposition groups with an objective directly counter to Arafat's thoroughly undermines the Israeli claim that Arafat initiated the uprising and was directing all its activities. Indeed, Arafat's position, far from orchestrating the intifada, was actually quite weak. One Israeli analyst wrote: "Arafat, then, appears to have no real strategy for winning the war or for making peace."[24] Another Israeli analyst described Arafat's situation:

> The PA has not turned into a terrorist entity, as recently claimed by many in Israel, including Chief of Staff Shaul Mofaz. It functioned as a weak administration, with limited authority dictated by the agreements with Israel. . . . In recent months, it has become an even weaker and more helpless ruling body, swept along in the wake of the spontaneous outbursts in the Palestinian street. . . . The problem of Yasser Arafat and all the Palestinian leadership is that in order to end the violence . . . they would pay a high price. And the price could be the collapse of their own rule. [If Arafat attempted to disarm the militias] . . . he is likely to pay with his head and the heads of his friends.[25]

In a similar vein, Yezid Sayigh, assistant director for international studies at Cambridge University, wrote in the *Washington Post:*

> Contrary to the Israeli account, [Arafat's] behavior since the start of the intifada has reflected not the existence of a prior strategy based on the use of force, but the absence of any strategy. His political management has been marked by a high degree of improvisation and short-termism, confirming the absence of an original strategy and of a clear purpose, preconceived or otherwise. There has also been minimal Palestinian understanding of how particular modes of political and military behavior might lead to specific end-results.[26]

Yet even after Israel placed Arafat under house arrest in Ramallah, Tel Aviv continued to hold him personally responsible for every violent incident. Moreover, Israel targeted, bombed, and destroyed the facilities of the PA's security services, including its prisons. *Ha'aretz* wrote that "the Israeli attacks on the Palestinian Authority have practically paralyzed the government in the West Bank and Gaza."[27] One wondered, then, how and where Arafat was supposed to deal with the "terrorists." Nevertheless, throughout the intifada, Israel claimed unceasingly that Arafat was in control and he must stop the violence.

Writing some sixteen months after the violence started, analyst Adam Hanieh observed that the most striking result of the conflict "has been the massive erosion of the legitimacy of PA structures."[28] Indeed, particularly in the northern areas of the West Bank (Jenin, Qalqilya, Tulkarm, and Nablus and its environs) and southern Gaza Strip (Rafah and Khan Yunis), the pace and nature of the intifada were not determined by the PA leadership but by street-level activists. In those places, the PA had little, if any, respect. Moreover, in those areas, as elsewhere in the Occupied Territories, the traditionally sharp lines between different political factions had been blurred, and the parties frequently came together to jointly coordinate popular demonstrations, strikes, and military actions in opposition to the PA. Furthermore, "Palestinian criticism of the PA's role has increased alongside the Israeli military escalations. Almost daily demonstrations occur outside the PA headquarters in Ramallah."[29] Hanieh wrote that even the regular Friday marches against the Israeli occupation pointedly stopped outside PA headquarters to demand the release of Palestinian prisoners while critics excoriated the PA's lack of clear direction or strategy:

> The PA's lack of legitimacy in large areas of the West Bank and Gaza Strip shows itself whenever the PA attempts to scale back the intifada to grasp carrots vaguely dangled by the U.S. . . . The PA has forcibly put down large demonstrations each time it has undertaken large arrests of intifada activists to placate the U.S.[30]

Such measures only decreased further the PA's legitimacy among the Palestinian people.

Power and the Definition of Violence

Legitimate and illegitimate use of force.   It is important to emphasize at the outset that the Israeli occupation itself is a form of violence and also that there is a difference between the legitimate and illegitimate use of force. The current state of affairs resulted from a military conquest of the

Occupied Territories and the imposition of an illegitimate military regime over the people through armed force and other forms of repression, and this has controlled every aspect of the lives of the Palestinians. This is not a consensual arrangement between Israelis and Palestinians; it is the commanding domination of one people by another. Moreover, after seven years of the Oslo peace process, all the structures of occupation remained in place. Thus, as Israeli sociologist Baruch Kimmerling points out in the first epigraph at the beginning of this chapter, Palestinians have the "moral right inherent to natural law and international law . . . by any measure . . . and any means at their disposal to rise up in violence against that occupation." Kimmerling further notes that

> the Palestinian right to resist the Occupation is strengthened by the Fourth Geneva Convention's ban on creating irreversible facts on the ground in occupied territories [settlements], and especially the ban on transferring populations [settlers] from the occupying state to the territories it has conquered. . . every violent step taken against the Palestinians—let alone the aggregate of those steps—borders on war crimes.[31]

Israeli historian Ze'ev Sternhell wrote similarly with regard to the second intifada:

> The killing of innocent people [by Israel] is gradually becoming the norm, and that norm is being implemented in the service of a goal that seeks to deprive another people of its freedom and its human rights. . . . This . . . attempt to create symmetry between a just war and a campaign of colonial suppression . . . is a desecration of the memory of those who fell in the 1973 [Yom Kippur War].[32]

Meron Benvenisti broadened the discussion of legitimate and illegitimate uses of force:

> Israelis are demanding for themselves the absolute right to determine when the use of violence is legitimate. Moreover they see themselves as the ones who have a total monopoly over legitimate violence, because violence derives from aggressive enforcement and its justification stems from the absolute imperative of self-defense and from the essential obligation of a ruling authority to maintain law and order and thwart killings and terrorism. All means are valid in trying to destroy any attempts to rebel against the monopoly on legitimate violence. . . . In essence the Israelis are striving to define the violence—theirs' and the Palestinians'—for their own greatest convenience. When it suits them—as in the case of the assassination policy and regulations on opening fire—it is a "war" and when it suits them—such as when soldiers are fired on—it is "attempted murder."[33]

This, of course, is one of the great prerogatives of power. Power names things, and it defines their meaning. Power creates myths. Power writes history from the perspective of those who dominate events. Power seduces the intelligentsia and the media. Finally, the names, definitions, myths, and the like that have been constructed by the powerful to legitimize their dominance are transformed into "truth" and become part of the common stock of knowledge. To speak otherwise—to attempt to speak truth to power—puts one outside the parameters of acceptable discourse and consigns one's words to more power-defined categories ("radical," "anti-Israel," "anti-Semitic," and so on). However, as Benvenisti wrote, "The Palestinians cannot, of course, accept the Israeli definitions of legitimate and illegitimate uses of violence. They cannot agree to describe someone who challenges the occupying regime as a criminal offender."[34] Adding to this perspective, Amira Hass, writing in *Ha'aretz,* stated:

> According to this [Israeli] representation of reality, everything started with the first Palestinian stone, the first Palestinian bullet, and the roadside bomb on the Netzarim-Karni road. There is probably little chance of convincing the Israeli public today that there is a link between that stone, bullet and bomb and the fact that the Oslo years did not offer the Palestinian public a future of independence, nor a hope for social well being. Those who in recent years gladly adopted the victorious, Israeli version of reality . . . cannot be and are not interested in recognising the occupied population's right to rebel. Those who yield to the victim-mindset that is daily fed by Israeli occupation mechanisms; those who count their own dead and wounded while remaining indifferent to the huge number of dead and wounded on the other side, are making no attempt to understand the meaning of the experiment that began in the last decade of the 20th century.[35]

Elsewhere Hass wrote:

> The intifada broke out because the Palestinian public was tired of this situation of occupation that adopts other names, which are user-friendly for 21st century Westerners. But because the Israeli public does not see the occupation, it perceives the uprising as a unilateral and unjustifiable act of aggression, rather than an act of resistance, of a type that has repeatedly taken place throughout human history.[36]

One sector of the Israeli public that clearly sees the occupation for what it is are the more than 500 IDF reservists that have refused to serve in the territories. Their statement, first released on January 25, 2002, says it all:

> We, reserve combat reserve officers and soldiers of the Israeli Defense
> Forces (IDF), who were raised upon the principles of Zionism, sacri-
> fice, and giving to the People of Israel and to the State of Israel. . . .
> We . . . who have served the State of Israel for long weeks every year
> . . . have been on reserve duty all over the Occupied Territories, and
> were issued commands and directives that had nothing to do with the
> security of our country, and that had the sole purpose of perpetuating
> our control over the Palestinian people. We, whose eyes have seen the
> bloody toll this occupation exacts from both sides . . . hereby declare
> that we shall not continue to fight this war of the settlements. [We]
> shall continue serving the IDF in any mission that serves Israel's
> defense. The missions of occupation and oppression do not serve this
> purpose, and we shall take no part in them.[37]

Many of these refusenik soldiers were imprisoned, were fined, and
lost their incomes, causing their families considerable hardship for their
acts of conscience.[38] Yet because they see the truth, they steadfastly
refuse to participate in the repression of the occupation.

Gideon Levy provides one final comment in the discussion of legitimate and illegitimate force:

> Who is a terrorist? Aida Fatahia was walking in the street; Ubei Daraj
> was playing in the yard. She was the mother of three; he was nine
> years old. Both were killed last week by IDF bullets, for no reason.
> Their killing raises once again, in all its horror, the question of
> whether Palestinian violence is the only violence that should be called
> terrorism. Is only car bombing terrorism, while shooting at a woman
> and child is not? Fatahia and Daraj join a long list of men, women,
> and children who were innocent of wrongdoing and killed in the past
> five months by the IDF. In the Israeli debate, their deaths were not the
> result of "terror actions" or "terrorist attacks" and the killers are not
> "terrorists." Those are terms used only for Palestinian violence.[39]

The writer, an Israeli, then asks: Are not massive land expropriations, systematic house destructions, the uprooting of orchards and
groves, cutting off towns and villages from their water source, denying
medical attention to residents, forms of violence? "A pregnant woman
whose baby dies or a patient who died because they couldn't get to the
hospital—something that has become almost routine in the territories—
aren't they victims of terrible violence? What about the behaviour of
soldiers and police at checkpoints, on the roads, everywhere? The
humiliations, the beatings, and the settlers' own violence against
Palestinians—what should that be called?"[40]

The Balance of Force

The existence of the PA and its possession of light weapons allowed
Israel to propagandize this intifada as a war between two equal sides, in

contrast to the 1987 uprising, which could not be seen as other than an oppressed people struggling against a foreign occupier. Israel managed to present its actions in the conflict in the Occupied Territories as a defensive reaction to a well-planned Palestinian scheme for all-out war, despite the fact that in the first three months of the intifada, by the end of December 2000, Israel had killed 359 Palestinians, of whom 243 were civilians; Palestinians had killed forty-two Israelis, of whom seventeen were civilians.[41] At that time, B'Tselem published a forty-eight-page report entitled *Illusions of Restraint* in which it examined events from the outbreak of the intifada until the end of December. It concluded:

> Israel bears primary responsibility for human rights violations in the Occupied Territories. . . . Israel's policy is directed in large part against the civilian population, which is not firing at Israeli civilians or IDF soldiers. . . . Most of those killed or wounded [have been] unarmed. . . . Israel used excessive force in dispersing demonstrations . . . lethal fire in non-life threatening situations is the main cause if deaths of Palestinians. . . . [Israel] did not bother to develop non-lethal methods to disperse demonstrations. . . . As a result . . . [there have been] a large number of casualties among the Palestinians including hundreds of children. IDF shooting also resulted in injuries to people who were not actively involved in the demonstrations, including medical teams and journalists. . . . The numerous restrictions that Israel imposes on freedom of movement of Palestinians in the [Occupied Territories] make the lives of hundreds of thousands of people insufferable, with no justification whatsoever. . . . Curfews imposed on tens of thousands of Palestinian civilians for the convenience of Israeli settlers is flagrant discrimination and preferential treatment of one population over another. Ignoring attacks by Israeli settlers and IDF soldiers' presence at some of the incidents in which the attacks occurred constitute gross breaches of Israel's duty as the occupying power to protect the Palestinian population.[42]

Throughout the uprising, Arafat, who controlled the Palestinian police force, prohibited the 40,000 Palestinian policemen from participating in the fighting against the IDF as an organized force. (A few did participate on an individual basis).[43] This, too, undermines Israel's claim that the PA was waging all-out war. Moreover, *Ha'aretz* (among others) detailed the actual balance of power between the two sides. The following is an abbreviated summation of several articles.

Palestinians deployed the following weapons against Israel: demonstrations at IDF roadblocks and in urban centers, commercial strikes, calls for a boycott of Israeli products, car thefts, and distribution of leaflets; stones—used by the masses, mainly in the first weeks of the hostilities; Molotov cocktails; pistols, rifles, and machine guns; and mortar shells, roadside bombs, explosive devices, and hand grenades; and suicide bombers.

Israel deployed the following against the Palestinians: massive deployments of IDF troops throughout the West Bank and Gaza; F-16 and F-15 fighter-bombers, Apache and Cobra helicopter gunships, and pilotless drones; tanks, armored troop carriers, and armor-plated jeeps; reinforced concrete positions on highways, with observation towers; armored battleships; M16 and Galil assault rifles, heavy machine guns, sniper rifles, bulldozers; bombs, tank and mortar shells, air-to-ground and ground-to-ground missiles; concussion and tear-gas grenades, stun bombs; rubber-coated steel bullets, live bullets, dumdum bullets, artillery shells, nail bombs containing "flechettes" (deadly razor-sharp darts), and booby-trapped bombs; barbed-wire fences, prisons, collaborators; assassination; an official "shoot to kill" policy against demonstrators; armed settlers and settler militias; demolition of homes, PA buildings, civilian institutions; bulldozing of orchards and crops; invasions into Area A; curfews, roadblocks, checkpoints, and a closure on the West Bank and Gaza Strip; limitations on imports of food, medicines, and raw materials; limitations on the marketing of Palestinian agriculture produce; and more.[44]

After these pieces were published, Israel also undertook massive ground force invasions (in addition to prior brief incursions) of Palestinian cities, towns, refugee camps, and villages in Area A; it fully reoccupied the West Bank. The Palestinians constructed a homemade rocket. Of the various Palestinian weapons, the suicide bombings, which are targeted at civilians inside the Green Line, are the most deadly and controversial. Without condoning their use, some effort must be made to understand this phenomenon.

Suicide Bombings

Suicide bombings are undoubtedly the most contentious element of Palestinian resistance. They merit equal condemnation with Israel's killing of civilians; yet it is important to explain why some individuals carry out these acts, as well as why some groups promote their use. The explanation resides neither in the propagandized version of Islam (which says the bombers are brainwashed to believe that if they die martyred they will go to paradise, where some seventy-two virgins await them). Neither is it because they hate Jews and want to kill as many as possible. Fundamentally, the explanation is to be found in despair so overwhelming that these individuals believe they have no future and thus they are willing to sacrifice themselves. In the context of occupation, and Israel's daily assaults on their families and friends, the despair combines with rage and an explosive desire for revenge fuels their actions.[45] Islam (Sunni, at least, which the Palestinians are) absolutely prohibits suicide, and in Arab culture suicide is no more acceptable than in American culture. However, in the struggle agaist occupation many view the suicide bombers as heroes or martyrs. It is, however, strictly a function of the occupation and its repression. Creating despair has been a long-standing Israeli tactic vis-à-vis the Palestinians. As David Ben-Gurion once stated:

> A comprehensive agreement is undoubtedly out of the question now. For only after total despair on the part of the Arabs, despair that will come not only from the failure of the disturbances and the attempt at rebellion, but also as a consequence of our growth in the country, may the Arabs possibly acquiesce to a Jewish Eretz [Greater land of] Israel.[46]

More recently Prime Minister Ariel Sharon stated:

> It won't be possible to reach an agreement with them before Palestinians are hit hard. . . . Only after they are badly beaten so they can get the thought out of their minds that they can impose an agreement on Israel that Israel does not want . . . [will negotiations occur]. . . . They must be beaten: the Palestinian Authority, its forces, and the terrorists. . . . We are at war with a bloodthirsty enemy. . . . [It is] us or them. . . . [They] will have nowhere to go without fear. . . . We have to cause them heavy casualties and then they'll know they can't keep using terror to win political achievements.[47]

Sharon does not use the word "despair" in his comments, but his policy is manifestly intended to break the will of the Palestinian people by force—a program that will assuredly provoke even greater despair. The prime minister had stated on many prior occasions that the most the Palestinians could expect at the end of the conflict was autonomy in 42 percent of the West Bank, a majority of Gaza, and absolutely no presence in Jerusalem.[48]

The response to such despair is not hard to imagine. Given the details of Israel's policies, it seems unnecessary to reiterate why Palestinians would be experiencing profound despair. What makes one individual a suicide bomber and another immobile cannot easily be ascertained. The comments of several writers shed some light:

> All of those enlisted in the army of Palestinian suicide bombers are not obligated to enlist. No one in their society will condemn them as "refuseniks" [Israelis who refuse to serve in the Occupied Territories]

if they limit their activities to demonstrations or even not participate in them. In Israel it is comfortable to believe that they were subjected to "jihad" brainwashing and that it is just a case of pure hatred against Jews for being Jews. But these explanations will not help understand the reality. The answer to what motivates them must be sought elsewhere, just like the answer to the question of why many adults in Palestinian society, who are pained by the phenomena of sanctifying death and the readiness to die, do not dare challenge this.[49]

The analyst proceeds to examine a variety of potentially contributing factors, then concludes:

Potential suicide bombers know that the near future does not promise them a livelihood, decent housing, chances for study and personal development, travel abroad, life in orderly cities, the development of agriculture in their villages or high-tech initiatives. But each of these deficiencies, and all of them together, are not enough to explain the readiness of so many to die at a young age. . . . These deficiencies, of the past and future, build up to internalize a conviction that there is an omnipotent force, a powerful country that since 1967 has dictated and intends to continue dictating the Palestinian society's scope of development and freedom to make decisions. *This is a suffocating, unbearable feeling for the Palestinians, a feeling that the future is not worth living.*[50]

In individuals already consumed by despair, suicide bombings were often triggered by a raging desire for revenge after an Israeli assassination. *Ha'aretz* comments: "The assassinations create an ever-intensifying feeling of rage and hatred. . . . Even official Israeli spokesmen are aware that this method does not prevent terror, and that it actually increases the motivation to use terrorist techniques."[51] A very clear pattern emerged as the intifada continued. Each time there was a period of quiet (on the Palestinian side) or the Palestinians began discussing proposals for peace, Israel carried out an assassination, which in turn provoked a suicide bombing. This then provided Israel with the excuse for massive military retaliation and collective punishment of the entire populace.

This led to a political strategy of retaliation. Given that individuals are willing to become suicide bombers, the question is, Under what circumstances do the political leaders of these individuals decide that a given time is appropriate for such an action?[52]

First, it must be noted that persons without political affiliations or organizational backing carried out some of the suicide bombings. For example, Khalil Abu Ulba, a middle-aged bus driver from Gaza with a wife and eight children, was one out of only 16,000 Palestinians (of a total of more than 3 million) that Israel's intelligence services considered apolitical and reliable enough to retain his permit for working in Israel. On February 14, 2001, he rammed his empty passenger bus into a group of soldiers at a junction south of Tel Aviv, killing eight people. His family and friends confirmed that he was not affiliated with any political movement. But, his wife stated, Abu Ulba had talked about his deep despair over the ongoing siege and economic devastation; of his rage at the intense bombardment and gassing of Khan Yunis that week; and of his anger at the aerial assassination of a Palestinian activist in Jabalya, close to his home, the day before.[53] (It was the tenth Israeli assassination to date.)

In fact, the overwhelming majority of suicide attacks within Israel proper came in retaliation for an Israeli action—an assassination, incursions into Area A, or some other provocation. Typically, Hamas or Islamic Jihad would take credit for the actions; however, as the intifada entered its second year, several dissident Fateh factions claimed responsibility for some of the bombings, as did the PFLP occasionally. A leader in Islamic Jihad told me during an interview: "I hate this violence, I fear for my family. It's not how I want to live. But if we cannot be safe in our cities, they will not be safe in theirs. If they kill our children, we will kill theirs."[54]

One example illustrates: On May 14, 2001, Israeli troops killed five Palestinian policemen manning a PA checkpoint in the West Bank. (Israel claimed it was an error.) In retaliation, a suicide bomber killed five Israelis and wounded forty others at a shopping mall in Netanya. Israel retaliated immediately by bombing the West Bank towns of Nablus and Ramallah with F-16s. This produced two more suicide attacks on May 25—one in Hadera (Israel) and another at a security outpost in Gaza. On June 1, a suicide bomber killed nineteen Israelis at the Dolphinarium disco in Tel Aviv. Arafat condemned the attack and ordered an immediate cease-fire throughout the Occupied Territories. Israel, however, shelled Gaza and killed three women huddled in a tent. That was followed by Israel's assassination by helicopter gunships of three Palestinian activists associated with Hamas. Hamas retaliated with two car bombs in central Israel. Thus, the cycle proceeded. Leaders of the organizations that sponsored suicide bombings argued that they were the only effective weapons Palestinians had against F-16s, tanks, and the arsenal outlined above.[55]

The Al-Aqsa Intifada: Facts on the Ground

Israel's Strategy and Objectives

If, in this conflict, Palestinian objectives wavered between simply returning to the negotiations and fighting until Israel ended the occupation; if its tactics were unorganized and uncoordinated; if its leadership was weak and diverse—the same cannot be said of Israel. After Camp David, Prime Minister Ehud Barak, who was not an enthusiastic supporter of Oslo, was anxious to bring about its termination.[56] His successor, Prime Minister Ariel Sharon, had been an ardent opponent of Oslo from the outset and was dedicated to eradicating Oslo altogether. Ironically, Shimon Peres, an architect of Oslo, was Sharon's foreign minister and presided over its liquidation. As the following illustrates, rather than responding to the Palestinian uprising, Barak, then Sharon and Peres, encouraged it. Sharon, in particular, pursued tactics designed to escalate the intifada with the goals of defeating the Palestinians, eliminating all vestiges of the PA, and dictating the terms of surrender.

Barak: September 2000 to March 2001

When Prime Minister Barak gave Ariel Sharon approval to peregrinate the Haram al-Sharif and to supply him with 1,200 troops for protection, he did so after having had dinner with Yasser Arafat, who warned him that such a provocative action was certain to trigger a mass rebellion. There seems little doubt that Barak understood this even without Arafat's input. Why, then, did he give Sharon the green light? One can hypothesize that Barak, in the frustrating aftermath of the failure at Camp David, welcomed Palestinian demonstrations that he could suppress and thereby remind the Palestinians exactly who was in charge. It may have been that Barak, facing low domestic approval ratings and a faltering governing coalition, believed that allowing Sharon's visit would strengthen his political support and buttress his government.

Supporting the first hypothesis, on October 15, 2000, an operative plan (Field of Thorns) to topple Arafat and the PA was openly discussed by Barak and senior government officials. The plan had been prepared by top officials in the security services during the 1990s and was updated in early 2000. This was two weeks before the first attack by Palestinians on Israeli civilians, which did not occur until November 3. The report stated, among other things, that "Arafat, the person, is a severe threat to the security of the State [of Israel] and the damage that will result from his disappearance is less than the damage caused by his existence."[57]

During the same period, Barak began a propaganda campaign to prepare public opinion for an eventual war. In that effort, his public affairs coordinator, Nahman Shai, released a sixty-page document assembled by one of the prime minister's aides, Danny Yatom, entitled "Palestinian Authority Non-compliance: A Record of Bad Faith and

Misconduct." It was informally referred to as the White Book and put forth such assertions as "Arafat's present crime—'orchestrating the intifada'—is just the latest in a long chain of evidence that Arafat had never deserted the 'option of violence and struggle.'"[58] The publication is composed of lists of crimes supposedly committed by Arafat since the DOP was signed. Yet such assertions fly in the face of the evaluations of Israel's own security services. For example, on April 5, 1998, the head of Shabak (the Israeli Intelligence System or the Israeli Security Services), Ami Ayalon, announced in a government meeting that "Arafat is doing his job—he is fighting terror and puts all his weight against Hamas."[59]

Sharon: March 2001 to October 2002

If Barak prepared the groundwork for all-out war, Sharon would continue it. For Sharon, this conflict was about finishing what he failed to complete in Beirut in 1982: destroying the PLO/PA, defeating Arafat, and extinguishing Palestinian nationalism. One Israeli analyst wrote in *Ha'aretz*:

> Defining the Palestinian national movement and its institutions as a terrorist movement and therefore an illegitimate collective. That's the real meaning of Ariel Sharon's war on "the Oslo disaster"—it's not a war on the articles of the agreements. It is the very recognition of the PLO as the national movement of the Palestinian people that Sharon is still fighting.[60]

Once the Palestinians were broken, Sharon expected to realize the Zionist dream of a Greater Israel from the sea to the River Jordan.[61] He stated that the Palestinians might have a semiautonomous entity on a maximum of 42 percent of the West Bank. That entity, however, would involve some sixty-four disarticulated cantons. Gaza would be similarly fragmented, and Palestinians would be politically excluded from Jerusalem. Another analyst put Sharon's peace plan into clear relief:

> All this is a code for two underlying policies. First breaking the Palestinian resistance once and for all; forcing the Palestinians to accept a mini-state on half the West Bank and Gaza . . . [a state] that will be far from truly sovereign. It will have no territorial contiguity, being squeezed between Israeli settlements, by-pass roads and military checkpoints and facilities. It will have no borders being entirely encircled by Israel, and no control of border crossings. It will be unable to develop a viable economy.[62]

Two factors are of considerable significance in Sharon's ability to prosecute the war by any means and to reject any proposals for resumption of negotiations with the Palestinians. One involves the 2001 inauguration of U.S. president George W. Bush and his administration, which, in contrast to Bill Clinton's administration, held a worldview very similar to the Likud's right wing. The second, and most important, factor was the September 11, 2001, attack on the United States by the Al-Qaida terrorist organization. The latter intensified the Bush-Sharon/U.S.-Israeli relationship in the sense that both were now besieged by the evil of terrorism, which had to be fought at all costs.

Israeli scholar Tanya Reinhart disclosed that the Israeli army had updated its plans for an all-out assault to smash the PA, force out Arafat, and kill or detain its army. The policy (entitled "The Destruction of the Palestinian Authority and the Disarmament of All Armed Forces") was formally presented to the Israeli government on July 8, 2001, by the chief of staff, Shaul Mofaz.[63] If Sharon's intentions were still obscure to some, he made them patently clear on October 17, 2001, when he declared that the Oslo process "is not continuing; there won't be Oslo; Oslo is over."[64] He obviously felt that Israel would not have to pay any price for this policy. For one thing, the semiannual U.S.-Israeli strategic cooperation meetings, which cover all matters of joint concern from military to intelligence, was scheduled to commence on November 15.[65]

The Bush Administration

On November 19, 2001, Secretary of State Colin Powell gave a major foreign policy speech at the University of Louisville in Kentucky entitled "United States Position on Terrorists and Peace in the Middle East."[66] It was a declaration wholly supportive of Israel. Powell's reaffirmation of the U.S. commitment to Israel was also apparent in his declarations repeating the "enduring and ironclad [U.S.] commitment to Israel's security" and affirming that "our two nations are bound forever together by common democratic values and traditions. This will never change." Furthermore, Powell stated that "The Palestinian leadership must make a 100 percent effort to end violence and terrorism. There must be real results, not just words and declarations." And: "the intifada is now mired in the quicksand of self-defeating violence and terror directed against Israel." Powell also instructed the Palestinians that "incitement must stop." No such admonitions were made to Israel.

Powell did not include Sharon's demand for seven days of absolute quiet before any negotiations could proceed; but at the last minute, at Israel's behest, he incorporated the phrase "that without a cease-fire in place, nothing else could progress." An Israeli government source said that the revised formulation "accorded with Israel's stance that it would not negotiate under fire."[67] This prerequisite to negotiations had been a constant Israeli requirement throughout the intifada. Nevertheless, as British correspondent David Hirst wrote in February 2002:

> The last thing Sharon actually wants is that period of calm he claims he does; every time it risks taking hold he has staged one of those "targeted killings" which are bound to provoke a Palestinian response, thereby enabling him, under cover of his "war on terror" to pursue his real, long-term agenda. This pattern has become so obvious that, if anything else, it is now the Israelis who initiate and the Palestinians who retaliate in "self-defense."[68]

In the final analysis, Meron Benvenisti characterized Powell's speech thus: "Powell yielded to Sharon's dictates."[69]

In this environment, an Israeli analyst warned in *Ha'aretz,* "Be prepared, therefore, for the next ploy of an Israeli leader who does not want a peace agreement."[70] Thus, on November 23 Israel assassinated Hamas leader Mahmoud Abu Hanoud (also killing five children on their way to school) at a time when Hamas was upholding a two-month-old agreement with Arafat not to attack targets inside Israel. Gideon Levy wrote in *Ha'aretz:*

> The Abu Hanoud assassination came after the period of relative quiet. . . . [The terror attacks that followed] came after two relatively quiet months in which no mass strikes were perpetrated. The month before was also quiet . . . marred only by one large scale shooting attack . . . and a number of targeted killings of Palestinians.[71]

Alex Fishman, security commentator for the Hebrew daily *Yediot Ahronot,* wrote on November 25:

> We again find ourselves preparing with dread for a new mass terrorist attack inside the Green Line. . . . Whoever gave a green light to this act of liquidation knew full well that he is thereby shattering in one blow the gentlemen's agreement between Hamas and the Palestinian Authority. . . . Whoever decided upon the liquidation of Abu Hanoud knew in advance that that would be the price. The subject was extensively discussed both by Israel's military echelon and its political one, before it was decided to carry out the liquidation. Now the security bodies assume that Hamas will embark on a concerted effort to carry out suicide bombings, and preparations are made accordingly.[72]

Another Israeli analyst noted that

> the majority of serious attacks in recent weeks have not been carried
> out by Hamas cells, but rather Islamic Jihad operatives who refused to
> abide by Arafat's agreements. . . . The assassination of Abu Hanoud
> places the Hamas leadership in a quandary—if they react with a pow-
> erful revenge attack, they will damage Arafat [in his efforts to rebuild
> bridges with Washington]. But if they fail to react, Hamas' prestige
> will be hurt.[73]

There is no question that Sharon knew that killing Abu Hanoud
would result in a severe response, which came in the form of three successive suicide bombings. The first, on November 29, killed three people on an Egged bus near Hadera; credit for these killings was claimed
by Fateh dissidents and Islamic Jihad. Hamas claimed responsibility for
the following two: on December 1, eleven people were killed in two
suicide bombings in the center of Jerusalem, and on December 2, fifteen people were killed in a suicide attack on a bus near Haifa. The
bombings, in turn, afforded Sharon the opportunity to press his case
with the Bush administration that Israel had to use all means to suppress
the intifada. Washington's green light for even more massive Israeli
military action was the one thing that Sharon lacked at this point.[74]

The effects of September 11 were evident when the prime minister
visited the United States on December 3–4, 2001. He was personally
greeted with warmth and received the approval he sought. When Bush
spoke, it was in terms of "we" (the United States and Israel) and of a
common holy war on terror. The president declined to condemn the
Israeli assassinations, the incursions into Palestinian locations in Area
A, or any of Israel's punitive collective punishments against the
Palestinian population. Moreover, he announced the freezing of all
Hamas assets in the United States and declared that Hamas seeks "to
destroy Israel." Bush also issued an ultimatum to Arafat to immediately
dismantle the terrorist organizations, arrest their activists, collect illegal
weapons, and destroy the weapons-manufacturing plants. As well,
Washington continued its steady flow to Israel of the most sophisticated
weapons in the U.S. arsenal.[75] One Israeli analyst commented that "for
a moment there, President George W. Bush sounded like he was out-
flanking Prime Minister Ariel Sharon on the right."[76] Additionally, during Sharon's visit, the U.S. House of Representatives passed (by a
384–11 vote) a resolution "expressing solidarity with Israel in the fight
against terrorism" and demanding a suspension of relations with the
Palestinian Authority if it failed to take any action against terrorism.[77]

Back in Israel, Sharon declared on Israeli television that "Arafat has made his strategic choice: a strategy of terrorism." At the same time Israeli forces launched attacks close to Arafat's home, destroyed his helicopters, and bombed and strafed Rafah and Khan Yunis in the Gaza Strip, destroying hundreds of homes, leveling fields, and uprooting trees. The cycle of Israeli provocation and Palestinian response continued.

Operation Journey of Colors: February 28–March 15, 2002

In February 2002, as Sharon finalized plans for an invasion of the Occupied Territories, he once again traveled to Washington to seek an explicit endorsement of Operation Journey of Colors, a plan to force the Palestinians to accept an unconditional cease-fire. Again, he was not disappointed. U.S. officials repeated in public and private that they understood that Israel had to defend itself by all means. In the words of Mouin Rabbani, the objective behind the plan was "causing the PA to implode as a result of overwhelming military-political pressures [that would leave it] in shambles."[78] Its tactical objective was to totally incapacitate the various militant organizations' ability for sustained action by eliminating their leaderships via assassination.[79] It addition, the strategy was disarming them, destroying their facilities, and arresting their cadres en masse.[80] At the same time, a public opinion poll found that 46 percent of Israel's Jewish citizens favored transferring (i.e., expelling) Palestinians out of the Occupied Territories.[81]

The invasion, which lasted a little more than two weeks, involved Israel's temporary reoccupation of most West Bank and Gaza cities and refugee camps, as well as some towns.[82] All targeted localities were in Area A, the area that the Interim Agreement had designated as being solely under PA control. Israel used massive ground forces in each locale. They were supported by 160–180 tanks and armed personnel carriers that roamed the streets, tearing them apart, crushing cars or any other thing along the streets, and shelling and shooting at schools, stores and shops, hospitals, UN installations, and PA security facilities, as well as any person who appeared.[83] The troops and tanks were accompanied by air cover provided by helicopter gunships and F-16 fighter planes bombing, strafing, and sending missiles for targeted assassinations. Once a locale was taken, the IDF placed the population under curfew, cut electricity, and in many places cut water mains and telephone lines.

The soldiers then demanded that every male between the ages of fourteen and forty-five (in some places it was fifteen to fifty) surrender.

Several thousand men were thus detained at gunpoint, blindfolded, handcuffed, stripped to their underclothing, and made to stand in long lines for hours while soldiers checked the papers of each against a wanted list. Depending on the locale, the men were held from twelve hours to six days. Those held for shorter periods were given no food, water, or medicine and were forbidden from using a toilet. Those held longer were given small portions of bread, water, cucumbers, tomatoes, and yogurt once daily. When they were released, it was always night-time and far from their home locales. In some places, soldiers wrote numbers on the men's arms for purposes of identification. In every holding place, soldiers taunted the men, humiliated them, and some-times kicked or slapped them.[84] By March 12, more than 2,500 men had been arrested. Relatively few, however, were charged (by March 14 the number was approximately 250). Clearly, the wanted men escaped before the IDF arrived.[85]

Once the men in a particular area were shackled and under deten-tion, the IDF conducted house-to-house searches, causing significant damage. Carnage was also caused by aerial bombing of houses, from tank movements and shelling, and shelling from other types of weapons. In the refugee camps of the northern West Bank, damage was especially extensive. In Jenin, Balata, Nur-al-Shams, and Tulkarm, some 1,600 houses were destroyed or seriously damaged.[86] In the camps, as well as other places, hospitals and medical facilities, schools, infrastructure, streets, stores, and colleges and universities sustained severe damage.[87]

In no other area was the ruination of homes as extensive as in the Rafah refugee camp in the Gaza Strip, with a population of 89,000.[88] The demolition of houses had been an ongoing practice in Rafah since the beginning of the intifada; however, as with all other punitive meas-ures, Israel escalated this one as well. By the end of December 2001, fifteen months into the uprising, Israel had completely demolished 368 houses and partially demolished (making them unsuitable for living) 520 houses. This affected some 900 families, or 6,200 persons, who were made refugees for a second time.[89] Shortly before the onset of Journey of Colors, on January 10, 2002, Israeli tanks and bulldozers razed seventy-three additional houses in Rafah, making some 800 per-sons homeless. The inhabitants were given no advance notice of the coming catastrophe and left their homes with nothing except what they were wearing, which in most cases was pajamas because the action was carried out in the middle of the night.[90] Thus, the refugees lost not only their residences but also every possession—furniture, kitchenware, jew-elry, and so on. Gideon Levy wrote in *Ha'aretz:* "The punitive action executed by Israel . . . in particular the mass demolition of homes in Rafah . . . constitutes a war crime. There is no other way to describe the collective punishment of hundreds of innocent civilians who have been left utterly destitute."[91]

Medical facilities and personnel were also direct targets.[92] B'Tselem published a report in March covering the period of February 28 through March 13, 2002, in which it documented the IDF's assault on the medical system.

> IDF gunfire killed five Palestinian medical personnel who were on duty, wounded several members of ambulance medical teams, and damaged ambulances. . . . IDF soldiers have fired at ambulances and prevented medical treatment to the sick and wounded, even leaving some of them in the field, where they bled to death. Also the hospitals have been unable to function because of the damage to the electricity, water, and telephone infrastructure, and the blocking of access to some of them. As a result, the hospitals are unable to receive the wounded and sick, or obtain food and medicines. . . . Red Crescent ambulances that were hit were properly marked and their movement had been coordinated with the Israeli authorities. . . . Since the beginning of the IDF's wide-scale action in the Occupied Territories, there has been a significant increase in human rights violations in the Occupied Territories. *The intentional attacks on medical teams and the prevention of medical teams from treating the sick and wounded have been almost unprecedented. . . . These violations are an integral part of Israeli policies and are accompanied by other grave practices.*[93]

By the end of the second week of Operation Journey of Colors, Israel had killed 170 Palestinians and wounded more than 1,000.[94] *Ha'aretz* published an editorial about the operation:

> The IDF caused deliberate suffering and humiliation to the broader Palestinian population. This cannot be interpreted any other way: the government of Israel, through the IDF, sought to use humiliation as a means of pressure or punishment. There is no other way to understand those photographed scenes of hundreds of people, bound and blindfolded, on their way to interrogation. Chief of Staff Shaul Mofaz was very tardy with his reservations about marking the prisoners with writing on their arms. . . . The idea of humiliation has apparently seeped down to the soldiers from the government.[95]

Despite the wanton death and destruction, Israel did not achieve its main objective (i.e., forcing the PA to accept an unconditional ceasefire or creating its implosion). Tactically, although it discovered some arms caches and a few weapons factories, the militias were not incapacitated, and their will and morale were higher than ever. In the immediate aftermath of the operation, attacks on Israel were stronger and more deadly than prior to it, and the United States, for the first time, expressed some guarded reservations.

President Bush asked Sharon to withdraw from the cities and camps and announced that General Anthony Zinni would return to the area. On March 12, 2002, the United States voted for UN Security Council Resolution 1397, "demand[ing] that both parties halt the violence and cooperate in restarting negotiations." It was, however, a weak resolution and made no critical references to Israeli actions. The United States had successfully watered it down from its original, and far stronger, language.[96]

This sudden U.S. pressure on Sharon occurred in the context of the Bush administration's initial efforts to mobilize an Arab state coalition for a war on Iraq. Vice President Richard Cheney embarked on a charm offensive of Arab capitals just when General Zinni arrived in Israel. Bush, Powell, and other officials had to appear to be doing something to stop the Israeli onslaught so as to persuade Arab leaders to join the new U.S. war effort. Yet when Cheney stopped in Israel, the vice president pointedly snubbed Arafat by declining to meet with him after lengthy consultations with Sharon.[97] Thus, Washington "pressure" could not be interpreted as a change in U.S. policy. It is instructive to note, however, that when Washington did exert pressure, Israel scaled back Operation Journey of Colors accordingly.

Operation Defensive Shield: March 29 to April 28, 2002

The IDF had barely returned to its barracks, with the political leadership expressing its satisfaction at its success in wiping out the terrorist nests, when the Palestinians began to retaliate. Initially, retaliation came in the form of relatively minor attacks on settlers and settlements, but a March 27 Hamas suicide bombing that killed twenty-eight Israelis and injured many more as they were celebrating Passover in Netanya's Park Hotel sparked an Israeli reinvasion of the Occupied Territories. The official goals of this campaign were the destruction of the "Palestinian terrorist infrastructure" and the "isolation" of Yasser Arafat.[98] At the end of the campaign, however, when it was revealed that the IDF had obliterated every institution of civil society, it became clear that the real goal of the campaign was "the destruction of organized Palestinian society."[99] Moreover, while the suicide bombing was cited by Israel as the casus belli for its invasion, a widely reported, detailed plan for the operation had already been completed before the suicide attack occurred.[100]

Thus, Operation Defensive Shield was qualitatively and quantitatively different than anything that had preceded it. Israel reoccupied every major city, refugee camp, and Palestinian locale in the West Bank. The population was placed under a curfew; water, electricity, and phone lines were cut; tanks bulldozed their way through every street and alley, demolishing and vandalizing everything in their path. In some places, swaths of homes were obliterated. In others, soldiers blasted their way from house to house, using Palestinian civilians as "human shields" in a search for militants and expunging or ruining everything in their wake.[101]

In each case the physical damage, as *Ha'aretz* wrote, was "immeasurable in shekels or dollars."[102] It involved virtually total destruction of the external and internal aspects of residences, stores, automobiles, and office buildings. Soldiers smashed, burned, and broke computer terminals; severed cable; removed hard drives; scattered and broke disks, diskettes, printers, and scanners; took away laptops; blasted safes; smashed furniture, TVs, and other household belongings; tore curtains; extracted or vandalized telephone exchanges; burned paper files; broke windows, smashed in doors; filled walls full of holes; wrote obscene graffiti; defecated and urinated on floors and in drawers; destroyed gardens and uprooted trees; and much more.[103] Serge Schmemann, of the *New York Times,* wrote:

> The images are indelible: piles of concrete and twisted metal in the ancient casbah of Nablus, husks of savaged computers littering ministries in Ramallah, rows of storefronts sheared by passing tanks in Tulkaram, broken pipes gushing precious water, flattened cars in fields of shattered glass and garbage, electricity poles snapped like twigs, tilting walls where homes used to stand, gaping holes where rockets pierced office buildings. . . . The infrastructure of life itself . . . has been devastated.[104]

The Systematic Destruction of Institutions and the PA

None of this adequately reflects Israel's methodical decimation of Palestinian civilian institutions—the crux of Operation Defensive Shield. This was accomplished through the systematic seizure of the hard drives from all computers plus the seizure and/or destruction of related files and archives.[105] In other words, it involved the obliteration of all the documentation and records each institution had painstakingly compiled during the seven years of Oslo. The meaning of this is explained by a brief description of some of the affected institutions.[106]

Palestinian Central Bureau of Statistics: The Palestinian Central Bureau of Statistics had spent years collecting and analyzing macro- and microdata on all Palestinian social and economic indices. These included, for the Palestinian population, demographic data; agricultural surveys; animal husbandry; education data; health indices; construction statistics; building licenses; land titles and ownership; housing; trade; taxation; industrial surveys; and much more. This data and survey research represented the necessary foundation for planning for a future state. All was obliterated.

Ministry of Education: This institution held all the lists of current pupils, *tawjihi* (final examination) results going back forty years, lists of teachers, and the entire logistics of the Palestinian school system. These, together with all written documents, books, and printed papers, were destroyed.

Ministry of Health: Here, the ministry's hard drives held all information concerning the state of diseases, medical tests, lists of doctors and nurses, patient medical records, the logistics of the hospitals, and everything pertaining to preventive and curative medicine in Palestine. Nothing remains.

The Ministry of Culture: This ministry building contained extensive collections of Palestinian art and cultural heritage, a department for encouraging children's art, an extensive literature and film collection, and much more. Everything was damaged, and "in every room of the various departments . . . books, disks, pamphlets and documents were piled up and soiled with urine and excrement."[107]

Palestine International Bank: This was considered a pillar of the concept of building a peace process by developing the private sector. The bank was founded in 1997 and served 16,000 clients. The IDF ravaged the bank's computer network. The up-to-date database of accounts, recent transfers, transactions, and checks paid out to and received by customers were all obliterated.

Khalil Sakakini Cultural Center: The IDF destroyed the majority of its archives, documents, and art collection.[108]

Forensics laboratory: This new laboratory in Ramallah was wrecked with demolition charges.

One analyst wrote in *Ha'aretz:* "Gone is the information pertaining to land registration and housing, taxes and government expenditure, car tests and drivers licenses, everything necessary for administering a modern society." Furthermore:

> Years of information built into knowledge, time spent thinking by thousands of people working to build their civil society and their future or trying to build a private sector that would bring a sense of economic stability to their country [were systematically destroyed]. These are the data banks developed in Palestinian Authority institutions . . . and non-governmental organizations and research institutes devoted to developing a modern health system, modern agriculture, environmental protection and water conservation. These are the data banks of human rights organizations, banks and private commercial enterprises, infirmaries, and supermarkets. They were all clearly the targets of destruction in the military operation called Defensive Shield. . . . The IDF translated into the field the instructions inherent in the political echelon's policies: Israel must destroy Palestinian civil institutions, sabotaging for years to come the Palestinian goal for independence, sending all of Palestinian society backward.[109]

All but one of the PA's security installments was demolished, including the police stations and the security organizations headquarters. In Ramallah alone, "80 [percent] of the police infrastructure . . . including the new crime lab and most of the city's jail cells were laid to waste."[110] Files were burned, computers crushed, the information concerning armed underground organizations and all other details pertaining to the [PA] war on terrorism were obliterated. This rendered the PA incapable of any policing or security functions thus making the permanent reoccupation of the territories and the reimposition of the pre-Oslo military administration inevitable.[111]

The human suffering inflicted during this campaign was also extraordinary. The Palestinian Red Crescent reports that 282 Palestinians were killed and 642 were injured.[112] B'Tselem reports that forty-seven Israelis were killed—not including the twenty-eight killed in the March 27 suicide bombing—but does not give statistics on injured.[113] Amnesty International, quoting IDF sources, reported that 4,000 Palestinians were arrested and more than 350 were put under administrative detention.[114] Based on a fact-finding mission Amnesty International carried out in the Occupied Territories, it reported witnessing the intentional targeting and killing of medical personnel and journalists; random firing at houses and people in the streets by the IDF; mass arbitrary arrests carried out in a manner "designed to degrade those detained"; a trail of destruction, including homes, shops, and infrastructure; apartments and homes trashed and looted; cars crushed and lampposts, walls, and storefronts smashed. Amnesty International stated that the IDF had deliberately cut electricity and telephone cables and water pipes, leaving areas without power and water. It further reported witnessing the IDF prohibiting the movement of ambulances, resulting in the needless deaths of injured persons, and firing on medical personnel who attempted to help the wounded. It observed the IDF using Palestinian civilians as human shields.[115]

The IDF policy of using human shields was characterized by *B'Tselem* as "an integral part of the orders they [IDF soldiers] receive" from senior commanding officers. The organization further relates that "the method is the same each time: soldiers pick a civilian at random and force him to protect them by doing dangerous tasks that put his life at risk."[116] For example, soldiers have ordered civilians to

- Enter buildings to check if they are booby-trapped, or to remove the occupants.
- Remove suspicious objects from roads used by the army.
- Stand inside houses where soldiers have set up military positions, so that Palestinians will not fire at the soldiers.
- Walk in front of soldiers to shield them from gunfire, while the soldiers hold a gun behind their backs and sometimes fire over their shoulders.[117]

Defensive Shield put the Palestinian population under a total siege and curfew. People were unable to leave their homes to give birth or bury their dead, much less to obtain food and water. Amnesty International described the situation as a "humanitarian disaster."[118] David Holley, an independent military expert who accompanied Amnesty International's delegation, observed:

> The military operations we have investigated appear to be carried out not for military purposes but instead to harass, humiliate, intimidate, and harm the Palestinian population. Either the Israeli army is extremely undisciplined or it has been ordered to carry out attacks which violate the laws of war.[119]

Human Rights Watch published a forty-page document after an intensive postinvasion investigation in which it stated that "civilians were killed willfully or unlawfully. . . . The IDF used Palestinian civilians as 'human shields' and used indiscriminate and excessive force during the operation. . . . The abuses we documented . . . are extremely serious and in some cases appear to be war crimes."[120]

International outrage at the devastation caused by Operation Defensive Shield (including the military cordon around Arafat's compound in Ramallah, the thirty-nine-day siege of the Church of the Nativity in Bethlehem, and the catastrophic devastation of the Jenin refugee camp) required Washington to undertake some damage control.[121] Thus, the president asked the prime minister to cease and withdraw, and White House Press Secretary Ari Fleischer announced that Secretary of State Powell would go to the region to secure a cease-fire. However, in nearly the same breath, he told reporters that "the president believes that Ariel Sharon is a man of peace."[122] To which Israeli historian Avi Shlaim retorted: "One of the most disturbing aspects of the current crisis is America's complicity in the Israeli onslaught. . . . How many more lives will have to be sacrificed before the Americans understand that General Sharon is part of the problem, not the solution?"[123]

Powell arrived in Jerusalem on April 11, one day after a distinct rebuff of his mission by Sharon, who had launched a new military offensive the previous day.[124] Israeli commentators predicted little hope for Powell's success, and their analyses proved prescient.[125] The secretary left Israel on April 16 with little to show for his efforts; Sharon prosecuted the operation into early May. The dismissiveness displayed toward Powell in Tel Aviv reflected his status back in Washington. The administration's hawks—Vice President Cheney and Secretary of Defense Donald Rumsfeld—persuaded Bush, a pro-Israel president to begin with, that Israel should be supported unconditionally. Moreover, Prime Minister Sharon made a sixth pilgrimage to the White House on June 10 and removed any doubts the president may have been entertaining. Indeed, Bush described Sharon as his teacher and stated in a public forum that the United States was wholly behind Israel. Sharon made full use of the president's carte blanche when he returned home and in mid-June initiated a new military campaign—Operation Determined Path—against the Palestinians.

Operation Determined Path: June 19 to July 3, 2002

Shortly after Operation Defensive Shield was declared a success, with Israeli leaders congratulating themselves on wiping out the terrorist infrastructure, Hamas carried out a major suicide bombing in Tel Aviv on May 7. Once again, the IDF mobilized—this time threatening to invade Gaza. A massive buildup surrounded Gaza almost overnight. It did not, however, develop into a full-scale invasion. Instead, the Israeli government decided not to reoccupy Gaza for the time being but rather to control the Gaza Strip by reconstituting its special operations units in which soldiers disguised as Palestinians carried out undercover operations and launched military incursions when necessary.[126] Instead, the focus would be on the West Bank. Accordingly, the military redeployed and began major operations.

On June 21, Israel's security cabinet approved a plan for an all-out seizure of the West Bank—an invasion already in progress.[127] When it concluded on July 3, Operation Determined Path had resulted in the complete Israeli reoccupation of all the major West Bank cities, refugee camps, and towns. Sharon told his security cabinet that Israel will remain in the Palestinian cities "for a very long time."[128] Senior Israeli officials stated that "not a single word of criticism has been heard from the Americans."[129]

Indeed, rather than criticism, Washington lent its full support to Israel in a very public venue. On June 24, while the reinvasion was in progress, President Bush gave a long-anticipated speech in the Rose Garden outlining "official U.S. policy" on the Israeli-Palestinian conflict that fully reflected all Israel's positions.[130] The president issued a series of commands and conditions to the Palestinians including a "new Palestinian leadership" (i.e., Arafat's ouster) and fundamental reform of the PA as preconditions for Israel's participation in any new peace process. Moreover, the president declared that future talks would lead only to a "provisional" Palestinian state. Unstated by Bush in the speech, but agreed to by the president during the prime minister's visit, was that a noncontiguous Palestinian "state" could occupy no more than 48 percent of the West Bank, with indefinite postponement of a final status agreement.[131] Little was asked of Israel as the president referred to "terrorism" eighteen times; not once did he cite human rights or international law. The speech was, in effect, an abrogation of the Oslo process.

Notably, the president made no reference to the historic March declaration by the Arab League at a Beirut summit to fully normalize relations with Israel in exchange for an end to the occupation (the Saudi Plan).[132] There was also no mention of a regional conference in which all states would participate including a Palestinian state—an idea strongly supported by both the European and Arab states but opposed by Israel. Israeli officials were euphoric on hearing Bush's statement, although Israeli commentators were openly cynical. One wrote: "Bush's statement apparently signals a perpetuation of the armed conflict: it does not signal pauses to ponder possible political solutions."[133] Another penned: "The mouth was that of President Bush, but the hand that wrote the speech was that of Ariel Sharon. Sharon can take credit for the speech: he couldn't dream about a better speech."[134] In contrast, Palestinian outrage was immeasurable.[135]

Reoccupation and Its Meaning for Palestinian Civilians

With the conclusion of Determined Path, the Oslo process had collapsed; the PA, in effect, ceased to function; and Israel was in full occupation of the West Bank.[136] In mid-June, Israel began construction of a wall designed to run the length of the border between Israel and the West Bank and physically separate Israel from the West Bank (see Chapter 9).[137] It divided the West Bank internally into eight distinct and insular geographical entities (Jenin, Nablus, Tulkarem, Ramallah/el-Bireh, Jericho, Bethlehem, and Hebron) with sixty-four subdivisions. All major cities in the West Bank were closed off and isolated by rings of steel fencing. All roads into villages were blocked by dirt barricades or trenches.

The major cities were put under curfews that were enforced with live fire and tear gas. Curfews lasted for varying periods: in Nablus, for example, the population remained under curfew without remission for more than four months.[138] A study by B'Tselem demonstrated that between June 16 and August 15, a period of 1,464 hours, West Bank cities were under curfew for the following number of hours: Jenin, 1,220 hours; Nablus, 1,464; Tulkarm, 1,380; Qalqilya, 825; Ramallah, 1,220; Bethlehem, 1,202; and Hebron, 830.[139] Thus, 2.2 million West Bank Palestinians were imprisoned in their homes during curfew and imprisoned in their area of residence during the few hours that the curfews were lifted.[140]

The Israeli civil administration was reestablished to support the military occupation in controlling the West Bank. This administration supervised and limited Palestinian development through the issuance of permits for every person and every thing.[141] Given these factors, in particular the new permit system in the context of the disarticulation of the territory, it was clear that life for Palestinians in the emerging order would be intolerable.

In late May 2002, the civilian authorities instituted a policy requiring every Palestinian to carry an Israeli-issued permit to move between the eight West Bank regions. The passes, when granted, were issued for one month and allowed for travel between 5 A.M. and 7 P.M. The system gave Israel ultimate power over all aspects of Palestinian lives, including work, education, family visits—anything involving their freedom of movement beyond the geographical confines of their residence.

Initially, few passes were granted, but between May and July the system became institutionalized while the closure of every city, town, and village became more and more hermetic and violent.[142] These were not temporary measures; this was a new and vastly harsher occupation. Of the permit system, Amira Hass of *Ha'aretz* wrote:

> Bureaucratic institutions have a tendency to perpetrate themselves and their methods. . . . People will wait days and weeks for permission to go from one town to the next, and that permission won't be granted—whether because of a lack of manpower, or because of efforts to draft recruits as informants. Every commercial and industrial activity will require the good graces of an Israeli official who will apply his own personal translation to the rules handed down by the Shin Bet and the army, and those rules will change daily.[143]

The psychological implications were also significant.[144] Hass continued:

> The long-term imprisonment in the enclaves is paralyzing the senses, the desire and the ability to initiate, and blocking both individual and collective creativity. But it presumably is pushing more desperate young people to dream about their own destructive reaction to the Israeli policy, no matter how difficult it will be to accomplish.[145]

By the summer of 2002, Palestinians in the Occupied Territories were experiencing an unprecedented humanitarian crisis. Unemployment for the West Bank and Gaza Strip stood at 50 percent, in addition to the 11 percent who had given up hope of ever finding a job.[146] In Gaza, unemployment was nearly 70 percent. Israel had imported some 300,000 foreign workers to fill jobs once held by Palestinians in both Israel and the Occupied Territories, and there was every reason to assume it would continue the practice rather than reemploying Palestinians.[147] Of the Palestinians who were working in September 2002, 59.2 percent earned a salary that left them below the poverty line (defined as NIS 1,624, or U.S.$344, per month for a family of six).[148] Overall, more than 60 percent of Palestinians were existing under the poverty line of less than U.S.$2 per day; in Gaza that number reached 80 percent.[149] The dependency ratio—the number of people dependent on one wage earner—also grew, from 4.8 in 2000 to 7.6 in 2002, a rise of 58.3 percent.[150] By November 2002, annual GNP per capita had fallen to $700 from $2,000 at the start of the intifada.[151]

Some 22 percent of children were suffering moderate, severe, acute, or chronic malnutrition. In Gaza, malnutrition stood at 17.5 percent. One-fifth of all children suffered moderate to severe anemia.[152]

B'Tselem reported that 51 percent of households in the Occupied Territories had reduced the amount of food they consumed while 63 percent reported a deterioration in the quality of food they consumed.[153] The majority of Palestinians survived on the distribution of monetary allocations or foodstuffs by international and religious agencies. Some received money from relatives abroad. The United Nations Relief and Works Agency continued to provide for the refugees, although its budget had been significantly reduced. The Red Cross, UN welfare agencies, and Muslim and Christian charitable organizations helped.[154]

In some instances, Israel prevented humanitarian aid from reaching those in need. The situation deteriorated continually during the fall and at the end of November, the IDF demolished a United Nations World Food Programme warehouse in Gaza. Five hundred thirty-seven tons of food worth $271,000 intended for a monthly distribution to 38,000 destitute Gazans were lost including 413 tons of wheat flour, 107 tons of rice, and 117 tons of vegetable oil.[155]

In addition to the extreme summer water shortage in the Occupied Territories, the government ordered Palestinians to stop all drilling for water in the West Bank and imposed a freeze on the issue of permits for future drillings.[156]

The Palestinian economy was in shambles and unlikely to recover. To cite one example: In the three years before the uprising, Palestinians had invested more than U.S.$5 billion in the tourism sector (hotels, restaurants, a convention center, modern bus stations, shopping malls, a casino in Jericho, and others). These enterprises had either been destroyed by Israel during the intifada or had been bankrupted due to the absence of tourism (or local business) in the context of the violence. After the reoccupation, Israel's policies of curfews, closure, and permits continued to exacerbate this situation, and economists speculated that investors would not recover their capital.[157] Most problematic for economic recovery was Israel's imposition of a back-to-back system on the movement of goods among Palestinian cities. Direct transport of merchandise from town to town was forbidden, forcing trucks to unload once they reached the outer border of a locality and transfer all goods to another truck licensed to operate within that area. The system also made the work of donor countries and institutions complicated, and in late June Israel decreed that goods for donor-funded projects in Gaza would only be allowed entry on a case-by-case basis (which had to be coordinated with Israel in advance).[158]

Gaza was already in severe crisis when the reoccupation of the West Bank was completed. The Gaza Strip was (and had been for many years) completely sealed by an electric fence. There were only three possible entrances and exits, and Israel had absolute control over each one. The welfare of the population in Gaza was completely dependent on the goods that Israel allowed in and kept out. And despite the poverty and unemployment, during April and May Israel had prohibited flour, one of the people's main dietary components, from coming in. It has disallowed (throughout the intifada) cement, iron, and other building materials, thereby preventing construction and exacerbating unemployment. The impact of Israeli control was evident in statistical terms. In April 2000, 3,773 trucks brought goods worth some NIS 97 million into the Gaza Strip from Israel. In April 2002, only 979 trucks were permitted to enter with goods worth NIS 27 million. In April 2000, Gaza exported NIS 28 million in goods; in April 2002, the figure was NIS 424,000.[159]

Of Gaza's three border crossings, Karni was the most important and the most problematic. Goods had to be brought through openings in a high wall that separated the Israeli and Palestinian sides. Gazans were dependent on the procedures in seven sorting cubicles, twenty-three X-ray machines, several pipes sticking out of a concrete wall (used for fluids), and a gigantic parking lot where trucks poured gravel and bags of cement. Every cubicle had two steel doors. When the one facing Israel closed, the other, facing the Palestinian side, opened, and then the goods were unloaded into the cubicle. Two adjacent cubicles were not permitted to operate at the same time, and Israel set the pace at which the X-ray equipment operated. It typically took days, often weeks, and sometimes months for a merchant, contractor, or farmer to get his goods across or bring in materials that were vital to the welfare of the people.[160]

Israel's internal control of the Gaza Strip was no less intense. Gaza was severed into three separate sectors during the intifada, and the Palestinians' ability to move among them was very limited. Palestinians were prohibited from traveling on the main north-south road and had to take a series of backroads and detours to get from one place to another. Half the coastal road was declared off-limits so that the settlers could pass freely. Another checkpoint, known as Abu Houli, was established in April 2002 and separated the southern towns and camps (Rafah and Khan Yunis) from the rest of Gaza. It was not really a checkpoint in the usual meaning because neither cars nor trucks were inspected as they passed through it. Rather, it consisted of a huge gate that was operated by a soldier in a nearby tower. There were no fixed hours for its opening. Cars and trucks began lining up at 5:30 A.M., waiting for the soldier to decide to raise the gate—which he did entirely at his whim as to when and for how long. Huge lines of frustrated travelers were backed up in both directions, yet the gate might be opened for ten minutes or two hours. Never did all those waiting in line pass through at one time.[161] Commerce was negatively affected; students from the south could not get to universities in Gaza City with any regularity; ambulances were not able to get patients to hospitals in a timely manner; and in general the daily existence of every Gazan was further ground down in humiliation and rage. In July, Israel closed the coastline (beach and sea) between Rafah and Dir al-Balah (mid-Gaza).[162]

Conclusion

It is clear from the foregoing that Sharon's intent from the outset was to abrogate the Oslo Accords and reestablish Israeli control over the Occupied Territories. The prime minister methodically gained U.S. support for his objectives through a strategy of gradual escalation combined with a succession of personal visits to Washington. It is incontrovertible that his efforts were abetted by the September 11 tragedy, which led to the deepening of U.S. officialdom's empathy with the "terrorist" threat besieging Israel. Significantly, when Sharon launched the final campaign, Operation Determined Path, the United States did not utter a word of criticism.[163]

The concluding Chapter 9 presents a brief evaluation of the Palestinians' situation more than two years into the Al-Aqsa intifada.

Notes

1. Baruch Kimmerling, "The Right to Resist," *Ha'aretz,* March 27, 2001.

2. Tanya Reinhart, "Evil Unleashed," *Tikkun: A Bimonthly Jewish Critique of Politics, Culture, and Society* 17, no. 2 (March/April 2002): 14–18.

3. Stanley Heller, "Palestinians Are Decidedly of this World," *Commentary and Other Opinion*, May 31, 2001.

4. Yael Stein, *Events on the Temple Mount—29 September 2000* (Jerusalem: B'Tselem—the Israeli Information Center for Human Rights in the Occupied Territories, October 2000). Amnesty International also condemned Israel's excessive use of lethal firepower; see Amnesty International, Press Release, "Israel/Occupied Territories/Lebanon: Amnesty International Calls for UN Investigations," October 9, 2000 (MDE 15/035/2000, News Service Nr. 193).

5. Ben Kaspit, "Jewish New Year 2002—the Second Anniversary of the Intifada," *Ma'ariv* (Jerusalem, Israeli daily, Hebrew), September 6, 2002.

6. Several works on the 1987 intifada include David McDowall, *Palestine and Israel: The Uprising and Beyond* (Berkeley: University of California Press, 1989); Zachary Lockman and Joel Benin, eds., *Intifada: The*

Palestinian Uprising Against Israeli Occupation (Boston: South End Press, 1989); Jamal Nassar and Roger Heacock, eds., *Intifada: Palestine at the Crossroads* (New York: Praeger, 1990); Ze'ev Schiff and Ehud Ya'ari, *Intifada: The Palestinian Uprising—Israel's Third Front* (New York: Simon and Schuster, 1990).

7. The number of deaths comes from Noga Kadman, *1987–1997: A Decade of Human Rights Violations* (Information Sheet) (Jerusalem: B'Tselem—the Israeli Information Center for Human Rights in the Occupied Territories, January 1998), pp. 2–6. The number of injuries comes from Palestine Human Rights Information Center, *Human Rights Update* 2, no. 6 (June 1994): 1, cited in Samih K. Farsoun with Christina E. Zacharia, *Palestine and the Palestinians* (Boulder: Westview, 1997), p. 236. The definition of *injuries* refers to Palestinians who sought medical treatment for injuries resulting from bullet wounds, beatings, and tear gas–related problems.

8. Kadman, *1987–1997: A Decade of Human Rights Violations*, p. 9. And Palestine Human Rights Information Center, *Human Rights Update,* in Farsoun with Zacharia, *Palestine and the Palestinians*, p. 236.

9. Kadman, *1987–1997: A Decade of Human Rights Violations*, pp. 7–8.

10. Ran HaCohen, "The Ideology of Occupation: Israel Tries to Excuse the Inexcusable," *Letters from Israel*, September 4, 2000, at anti-war.com.

11. See the analysis by Ghassan Andoni, "A Comparative Study of Intifada 1987 and Intifada 2000," in Roane Carey, ed., *The New Intifada: Resisting Israel's Apartheid* (London: Verso, 2001), pp. 209–218.

12. See the excellent analysis by Sara Roy, "Palestinian Society and Economy: The Continued Denial of Possibility," *Journal of Palestine Studies* 30, no. 4 (summer 2001): 5–20.

13. Nadine Picadou (translated by Wendy Kristianasen), "Between National Liberation and State-Building: A New Intifada, a New Strategy," *Le Monde Diplomatique*, March 26, 2001.

14. These issues are all well analyzed by Nadine Picadou, ibid.

15. Several good analyses: Mouin Rabbani, "Field of Thorns," *The Nation*, March 12, 2001; Yezid Sayigh, *Arafat and the Anatomy of a Revolt* (Jerusalem: Israel/Palestine Center for Research and Information, August 21, 2001); Joharah Baker, "How to Fight Back," *Palestine Report* (Jerusalem, Palestinian weekly, English), February 13, 2002.

16. See the excellent analysis by Graham Usher, "Whither Yasir Arafat?" OIAP, Geneva, November 12, 2002.

17. Amira Hass, "An Intifada in Search of a Leadership," *Ha'aretz*, December 27, 2000.

18. Bradley Burston, "Background: Sharon Cabinet's War Lobby Revs into High Gear," *Ha'aretz,* March 6, 2002.

19. Gideon Levy, "'If We Get Rid of both Governments, We'll Live in Peace': A Rare Conversation with the Tanzim Fighters," *Ha'aretz Friday Magazine*, March 29, 2001.

20. Rabbani, "Field of Thorns," p. 6.

21. The quotation by Barghouti and the statement following it are from ibid.

22. See the analysis by Akiva Eldar, "Watch Your Back," *Ha'aretz*, March 13, 2002.

23. Rabbani, "Field of Thorns," p. 3.

24. Yossi Alpher, "Sharon's Coercion, Arafat's Fantasies," *Ramallah Online,* December 12, 2001.

25. Danny Rubinstein, "Why Don't They Stop?" *Ha'aretz*, July 2, 2001.

26. Yezid Sayigh, *Washington Post*, August 26, 2001, quoted in Toni Ben Efrat, "The Walls Close In," *Challenge: A Jerusalem Magazine on the Israeli-Palestinian Conflict* (Jerusalem, Israeli, monthly, English), no. 69, September 3, 2001. Also see the much longer piece by Sayigh, *Arafat and the Anatomy of a Revolt.*

27. Danny Rubinstein, "Focus: Israeli Attacks Paralyze PA Government," *Ha'aretz*, March 6, 2002.

28. Adam Hanieh, "Toward Submission or War in Palestine?" *MERIP Press Information Notes,* PIN 82 (January 26, 2002).

29. Ibid.

30. Ibid.

31. Kimmerling, "The Right to Resist."

32. Zeev Sternhell, "Balata Has Fallen," *Ha'aretz*, March 8, 2002.

33. Meron Benvenisti, "The Depth of Animosity," *Ha'aretz*, August 8, 2001. Also see Gideon Levy, "Defining Violence," *Ha'aretz*, March 11, 2001, for a similar analysis.

34. Benvenisti, "The Depth of Animosity."

35. Amira Hass, "The Revolt of the Guinea-Pigs," *Ha'aretz*, February 21, 2001.

36. Amira Hass, "They Don't See Occupation," *Ha'aretz*, August 21, 2001.

37. Quotation in Lev Grinberg, "In Israel, a New-Old Voice of Conscience Awakens," *MERIP Press Information Notes*, PIN 84 (February 22, 2002).

38. Grinberg, "In Israel, a New-Old Voice of Conscience Awakens." Also see Jo Strich, "Israel's Growing Number of War Refuseniks Remain Unbowed," Tel Aviv, Agence France-Presse: News Online, March 21, 2002.

39. Gideon Levy, "Defining Violence," *Ha'aretz*, March 11, 2001.

40. Ibid.

41. B'Tselem, *Fatalities in the al-Aqsa Intifada, Data by Month* (through February 2002) (Jerusalem: B'Tselem—the Israeli Information Center for Human Rights in the Occupied Territories, March 2002).

42. Yael Stein, *Illusions of Restraint: Human Rights Violations During the Events in the Occupied Territories 29 September–2 December 2000* (Jerusalem: B'Tselem—the Israeli Information Center for Human Rights in the Occupied Territories, December 2000), pp. 46–47.

43. Reuven Pedatzur, "Leading Israel to a Needless War," *Ha'aretz,* March 6, 2002.

44. Amira Hass, "Here Is the Real Balance of Power," *Ha'aretz*, August 14, 2001; LAW, *The First Year of the Palestinian Intifada* (Jerusalem: Palestinian Society for the Protection of Human Rights and the Environment—LAW, September 29, 2001); Human Rights Watch, *Israel: Dart Shells Pose Civilian Threat* (New York: Human Rights Watch, June 16, 2001); Sternhell, "Balata Has Fallen"; Sam Kiley, "Shoot-to-Kill Policy Is Exposed in Israel," *Times* (London), December 22, 2002; Stein, *Illusions of Restraint*, pp. 2–9.

45. The most cogent analysis of the motivations of suicide bombers is

Avishai Margalit, "The Suicide Bombers," *New York Review of Books,* January 16, 2003. Also important are Elizabeth Rubin, "The Most Wanted Palestinian," *New York Times,* June 30, 2002, and Amira Hass, "Confessions of a Dangerous Mind," *Ha'aretz,* April 4, 2003.

46. David Ben-Gurion, 1936, quoted in Jeff Halper, "Despair: Israel's Ultimate Weapon," *Information Brief no. 72* (Washington, DC: Center of Policy Analysis on Palestine, March 28, 2001).

47. Prime Minister Ariel Sharon, March 5, 2002; quotations from Sharon's speech to the Knesset reported by Yossi Verter and Gideon Alon, *Ha'aretz,* March 6, 2002.

48. For example, see Sharon's Peace Plan, *MEWNews,* Mideast Web Group 2, no. 1 (January 18, 2001).

49. Amira Hass, "A Future Not Worth Living," *Ha'aretz,* February 20, 2002.

50. Ibid. (emphasis added). Also see Sternhell, "Balata Has Fallen," and Sam Bahour and Michael Dahan, "It's About the Occupation," *Counterpunch,* December 5, 2001. Also see Eyad Sarraj, "Why We Have Become Suicide Bombers," *Mid-East Realities,* Washington, DC, February 2002 (archive 3), online.

51. Baruch Kimmerling, "The Right-Wing Without Its Fig Leaf," *Ha'aretz,* December 3, 2001.

52. The best analysis of the leadership, in particular the Islamic leadership, is Nasra Hassan, "Letter from Gaza: An Arsenal of Believers," *The New Yorker,* November 19, 2002.

53. Rabbani, "Field of Thorns," p. 9.

54. Anonymous, "Informal Interview," author interview, Jerusalem, April 1999.

55. B'Tselem, *Fatalities in the al-Aqsa Intifada, Data by Month* (Jerusalem: B'Tselem—the Israeli Information Center for Human Rights in the Occupied Territories, March 2002).

56. See the analysis by Uri Avnery, "Barak Is Not Rabin," Direct Submission by the International Observatory for Palestinian Affairs (OIPA), Geneva, November 4, 2000.

57. Tanya Reinhart, "Evil Unleashed," *Tikkun: A Bimonthly Jewish Critique of Politics, Culture, and Society* 17, no. 2 (March/April 2002): 14. She notes that details of the document were published in the Hebrew daily *Ma'ariv* on July 6, 2001, and by Amir Oren in *Ha'aretz* on November 23, 2001.

58. Reinhart, "Evil Unleashed," pp. 14–15.

59. Ibid., p. 16, citing *Ha'aretz,* April 6, 1998.

60. Meron Benvenisti, "A Footnote for the Future," *Ha'aretz,* December 13, 2001.

61. See the excellent analysis by Amira Hass, "All the Way from the Sea to the River," *Ha'aretz,* May 30, 2001.

62. Halper, "Despair: Israel's Ultimate Weapon."

63. Reinhart, "Evil Unleashed," p. 16, quoting *Foreign Report* (Jane's Information), July 12, 2001.

64. Ibid., p. 14, quoting *Ha'aretz,* October 18, 2001.

65. Amir Oren, "Semi-Annual US-Israeli Strategic Talks Start Today," *Ha'aretz,* November 15, 2001.

66. For a transcript, see Secretary Colin L. Powell, *United States Position*

on Terrorists in the Middle East, November 19, 2001, Remarks at the McConnell Center for Political Leadership, University of Louisville, Kentucky, U.S. Department of State, online.

67. Aluf Benn and Nathan Guttman, "Powell's Late Revisions Put Spotlight on Cease-fire," *Ha'aretz*, November 22, 2001. Also see Danny Rubinstein, "Powell: End the Intifada—and Occupation," *Ha'aretz*, November 19, 2001.

68. David Hirst, "How Far Will Sharon Go in a War of His Own Choosing?" *Daily Star*, February 20, 2002.

69. Meron Benvenisti, "The Melody of the Imperial Speech," *Ha'aretz*, November 22, 2001.

70. Gideon Samet, "American Betrayal?" *Ha'aretz*, November 16, 2001.

71. Gideon Levy, "It's in Our Hands," *Ha'aretz*, December 15, 2001.

72. Quotation by Fishmen reprinted in Alexander Cockburn, "Sharon or Arafat: Which Is the Sponsor of Terrorism?" *Counterpunch*, December 6, 2001.

73. Danny Rubinstein, "Focus: Murder of a Military Leader Puts Hamas in a Dilemma." *Ha'aretz*, November 24, 2001.

74. Reinhart, "Evil Unleashed," p. 15.

75. See, for example, the analysis by Naseer Aruri, *Dishonest Broker: The U.S. Role in Israel and Palestine* (Cambridge, MA: South End Press, 2003), pp. 201–205.

76. Amos Harel, "Bush-tailed, but Bright-eyed," *Ha'aretz*, December 6, 2001. Also, for Ari Fleisher's press briefing, see Aluf Benn, "PM's Stance Backed by US Ultimatum to PA," *Ha'aretz*, December 3, 2001.

77. Nathan Guttman, "Congress Threatening to Cut Ties with the PA," *Ha'aretz*, December 5, 2001.

78. Mouin Rabbani, "Sharon's Journey of Colors," *MERIP Press Information Notes*, PIN 85 (March 15, 2002).

79. LAW, *Another Extra-Judicial Killing in Ramallah* (Jerusalem: Palestinian Society for the Protection of Human Rights and the Environment— LAW, March 6, 2002); and LAW, *Extra-Judicial Execution in Jenin* (Jerusalem: Palestinian Society for the Protection of Human Rights and the Environment— LAW, March 7, 2002).

80. Rabbani, "Sharon's Journey of Colors."

81. "More Israeli Jews Favor Transfer of Palestinians, Israeli Arabs—Poll Finds," *Ha'aretz*, March 12, 2002, posted online by the *American Committee on Jerusalem*, "Palestine/Israel News," Washington DC, March 12, 2002.

82. The occupied cities included Nablus, Jenin, Qalqiliyh, Tulkarm, Bethlehem, Beit Jala, Ramallah/el-Bireh, and Rafah City in Gaza. The occupied refugee camps included Balata in the Nablus area; Am'ari in the Ramallah area; Dheisheh and A'aydah (Aida) in the Bethlehem area; Far'a and Jenin camp in the Jenin area; Nur al-Shams and Tulkarm camp in the Tulkarm district; and Jabalya, Breij, Khan Yunis, Rafah, and Deir Balah in Gaza.

83. See, for example, BADIL, Press Release, "Israel's War on the Refugee Camps and the Palestinian People" (Bethlehem: BADIL Resource Center, March 7, 2002); Hear Palestine, "Summary of Events," Hear Palestine Press Service, March 7, 2002; Gush Shalom, *Tulkarm Today* (Jerusalem: Gush Shalom, March 9, 2002); Palestine Media Center, *Bloody Friday Forever Engraved in Collective Palestinian Memory* (Ramallah: Palestine Media Center, March 9, 2002); LAW, *Weekly Roundup, 28 February–6 March 2002*

(Jerusalem: Palestinian Society for the Protection of Human Rights and the Environment—LAW, March 7, 2002); LAW, *Weekly Roundup, 7 March–13 March, 2002* (Jerusalem: Palestinian Society for the Protection of Human Rights and the Environment—LAW, March 14, 2002); Palestinian Center for Human Rights, *Weekly Report: On Israeli Human Rights Violations in the Occupied Territories, March 07–13, 2002* (Gaza: Palestinian Center for Human Rights, March 14, 2002).

84. Suzanne Goldenberg, "Mass Arrests Create New Foes for Israel," *The Guardian* (London), March 16, 2002, and Gideon Levy, "In the Name of Us All," *Ha'aretz*, March 17, 2002.

85. Al-Haq, Press Release no. 121, "Al-Haq Calls for an End to Arbitrary Arrest and for Humane Treatment of the Detainees" (Jerusalem: Al-Haq, Law in the Service of Man, March 14, 2002).

86. Amira Hass, "UNRWA: Israeli Raids Have Damaged 1,620 Refugee Homes," *Ha'aretz*, March 11, 2002.

87. See Amnesty International, *Israel and the Occupied Territories: The Heavy Price of Israeli Incursions* (London: Amnesty International, April 12, 2002 (AI Index: MDE 15/042/2002).

88. UNRWA, *Rafah Camp: Camp Profiles* (New York: United Nations Relief and Works Agency for Palestinians, 2002).

89. Applied Research Institute–Jerusalem, *The Refugees of Rafah. . . the Refugee Trip Is Repeated* (Jerusalem: Institute for Applied Research–Jerusalem, January 2002). Also see *The Israeli Aggression Against the Palestinian Civilians and Their Property in Rafah* (Gaza: Almezan Center for Human Rights, September 28 to November 15, 2001).

90. See Yael Stein, *Policy of Destruction: House Demolitions and Destruction of Agricultural Land in the Gaza Strip* (Jerusalem: B'Tselem—the Israeli Information Center for Human Rights in the Occupied Territories, February 2002).

91. Gideon Levy, "Bulldozing Rafah: A Crime Against the Innocent," *Ha'aretz*, January 17, 2002.

92. LAW, *Humanitarian Crisis in the OPTs: Urgent Appeal to the International Community for Intervention* (Jerusalem: Palestinian Society for the Protection of Human Rights and the Environment—LAW, March 13, 2002).

93. B'Tselem, *Impeding Medical Treatment and Firing at Ambulances by IDF Soldiers in the Occupied Territories* (Jerusalem: B'Tselem—the Israeli Information Center for Human Rights in the Occupied Territories, March 2002), pp. 1 and 13 (emphasis added). Also see Mustafa Barghouti, Director, Union of Palestinian Medical Relief Committees (UPMRC), *Joint Appeal, UPMRC and Physicians for Human Rights, Israel*, March 12, 2002.

94. Gideon Levy, "In the Name of Us All."

95. "Editorial," *Ha'aretz*, March 13, 2002.

96. UN Security Council Resolution 1397 (2002), adopted by the Security Council at its 4489th meeting on March 12, 2002.

97. Peter Hirschberg, "Cheney Snubs Arafat, Sharon Humiliates Him," *Ha'aretz*, March 19, 2002.

98. Benziman, "They Let the IDF Win," *Ha'aretz*, April 21, 2002.

99. Uri Avnery, "The Real Aim," *Ma'ariv* (Jerusalem, Israeli daily, Hebrew), April 27, 2002 (translated and posted online by Avnery).

100. Mouin Rabbani, "Bleak Horizons After Operation Defensive Wall," *MERIP Press Information Notes*, PIN 93 (April 30, 2002).

101. See B'Tselem, Press Release, "A Human 'Defensive Shield': IDF Uses Palestinian Civilians as Human Shields" (Jerusalem: B'Tselem—the Israeli Information Center for Human Rights in the Occupied Territories, April 4, 2002). Also see Human Rights Watch, *Israel, the Occupied West Bank and Gaza Strip, and the Palestinian Authorities: In Dark Hour: The Use of Civilians During IDF Arrest Operations* (New York: Human Rights Watch 14, no. 2E, April 2002), and *Ha'aretz* Correspondents, "'Human Shield' Dies as Hamas Man Is Killed by Troops," *Ha'aretz*, August 15, 2002. See Amos Harel, "IDF Admits 'Ugly Vandalism' Against Palestinian Property," *Ha'aretz*, April 30, 2002; Editorial, "Dishonorable Conduct in War," *Ha'aretz*, May 1, 2002.

102. Amira Hass, "Operation Destroy the Data," *Ha'aretz*, April 24, 2002.

103. Ibid.; Amira Hass, "So Much Damage in Just One Hour," *Ha'aretz*, April 23, 2002; Serge Schmemann, "In Israel's Wake, Untold Destruction," *International Herald Tribune*, April 12, 2002; Serge Schmemann, "Attacks Turn Palestinian Dream into Bent Metal and Piles of Dust," *New York Times*, April 11, 2002; John Lancaster, "West Bank's City of Broken Dreams," *Washington Post*, May 7, 2002; Amira Hass, "Someone Even Managed to Defecate into the Photocopier," *Ha'aretz*, April 10, 2002. For extensive detail, see Islah Jad, *Destruction of Palestinian Non-Governmental Organizations in Ramallah* (Ramallah: Palestinian Non-Governmental Organization Network, April 22, 2002). See also Rema Hammami, Sari Hanafi, and Elizabeth Taylor, *Destruction of Palestinian Institutions: A Preliminary Report, 13 April 2002* (Ramallah: Palestinian NGO Emergency Initiative in Jerusalem, April 13, 2002), available online through *The Electric Intifada* website.

104. Schmemann, "In Israel's Wake, Untold Destruction."

105. See Avnery, "The Real Aim," Hass, "Operation Destroy the Data," Hass, "So Much Damage in Just One Hour," and Jad, *Destruction of Palestinian Non-Governmental Organizations*.

106. Information about the damage done to the various institutions taken from Avnery, "The Real Aim," Hass, "Operation Destroy the Data," Hass, "So Much Damage in Just One Hour," Palestine Media Center, *Israeli Occupation Forces Ransack Cultural Center* (Ramallah: Palestine Media Center, April 13, 2002), "Israelis Destroy Offices," *New York Times*, April 16, 2002, Colin Nickerson, "On West Bank, Shattered Cities and Lives," *Boston Globe*, April 14, 2002, Schmemann, "Attacks Turn Palestinian Dream into Bent Metal and Piles of Dust." There were as well numerous examples of less permanently damaged institutions that illustrate simply wanton destruction. At the Medical Relief Committee's Eye Center, every machine was pulled to the floor and smashed. The ophthalmic equipment was likewise demolished. All the eyeglasses were broken and scattered on the floor. The same organization's warehouse for aids for handicapped people was broken into and all prostheses and equipment destroyed. At Max Supermarket (a large modern facility) all the computers were blown up or seized, all of its business records, receipts, and documents gone. Additionally, all private and radio and TV stations, human rights organizations (e.g., Al-Haq, Addameer, MATIN, Mandala Institute, and others), the Ma'an Agricultural Development Center, the Bisan Research Center, and the Health, Development Information, and Policy Institute were

physically defaced and had computers destroyed. Many others were partially ruined.

107. Hass, "Someone Even Managed to Defecate into the Photocopier."

108. For a good analysis of Israel's assault on Palestinian culture during the intifada, see William Dalrymple, "A Culture Under Fire," *The Guardian* (London), October 2, 2002.

109. Hass, "Operation Destroy the Data."

110. Lancaster, "West Bank's City of Broken Dreams."

111. An excellent summation of the consequences of this Israeli operation is Rema Hammami, "Interregnum: Palestine After Operation Defensive Shield," *Middle East Report*, June 26, 2002, reproduced by *Znet: A Community of People Committed to Social Change* (online), June 2002.

112. Palestinian Red Crescent Society, *Deaths and Injuries in the West Bank and Gaza Since March 29, 2002* (al-Bireh: Palestinian Red Crescent Society, April 2002).

113. B'Tselem, *Fatalities in the al-Aqsa Intifada, Data by Month, Statistics* (Jerusalem: B'Tselem—the Israeli Information Center for Human Rights in the Occupied Territories, April 2002). However, in a major position paper, B'Tselem condemned the policy of unrestrained killing. See Ron Dudai, *Trigger Happy: Unjustified Shooting and Violations of the Open-Fire Regulations During the al-Aqsa Intifada* (Jerusalem: B'Tselem—the Israeli Information Center for Human Rights in the Occupied Territories, March 2002).

114. Amnesty International, *Israel and the Occupied Territories: The Heavy Price of Israeli Incursions* (London: Amnesty International, April 2002) (MDE 15/042/2002).

115. An excellent discussion of the human rights violations Israel perpetrated during this operation, including the use of civilians as human shields, is Jessica Montell, "Operation Defensive Shield: The Propaganda War and the Reality," *Tikkun: A Bimonthly Jewish Critique on Politics, Culture, and Society* 14, no. 4 (July/August 2002): 33–41. Also see B'Tselem, *A Human "Defensive Shield": IDF Uses Palestinian Civilians as Human Shields* (Jerusalem: B'Tselem—the Israeli Information Center for Human Rights in the Occupied Territories, 2002).

116. Yael Stein, *Human Shield: Use of Palestinian Civilians as Human Shields in Violation of High Court of Justice Order* (Jerusalem: B'Tselem—the Israeli Information Center for Human Rights in the Occupied Territories, 2002), p. 1.

117. Ibid.

118. Amnesty International, *Israel and the Occupied Territories: The Heavy Price of Israeli Incursions.* Also see Amira Hass, "What Kind of War Is This?" *Ha'aretz*, April 20, 2002, and Amira Hass, "Destruction and Degradation," *Ha'aretz*, May 6, 2002.

119. Amnesty International, *Israel and the Occupied Territories: The Heavy Price of Israeli Incursions.*

120. Human Rights Watch, *Israel, the Occupied West Bank and Gaza Strip, and the Palestinian Authority Territories: Jenin: IDF Military Operations* 14, no. 3 (E) (New York: Human Rights Watch, May 2002).

121. On Jenin, see Brian Whitaker, "UN to Press on with Jenin 'War

Crimes' Report," *The Guardian* (London), May 10, 2002; John Lancaster, "U.N. Envoy Calls Camp 'Horrifying,'" MSNBC News (online), April 18, 2002; David Blair, "Blasted to Rubble by the Israelis," *The Telegraph* (London), April 16, 2002; Justin Huggler, "The Camp That Became a Slaughterhouse," *The Independent* (London), April 14, 2002; Mouin Rabbani, *The Only Truth About Jenin Is the Cover-Up* (Ramallah: Palestinian-American Research Center in Ramallah, April 12, 2002); Rita Giacaman and Penny Johnson, "Who Lives in Jenin Refugee Camp? A Brief Statistical Profile," *Birzeit University*, April 14, 2002; Suzanne Goldenberg, "The Lunar Landscape That Was the Jenin Refugee Camp," *The Guardian* (London), April 16, 2002; Phil Reeves, "Amid the Ruins of Jenin: The Grisly Evidence of a War Crime," *The Independent* (London), April 16, 2002.

122. Fleischer's statement was reported by MSNBC, "United States Calls Sharon 'Man of Peace'" (online), April 11, 2002.

123. Avi Shlaim, "America Must See that Sharon Is the Problem," *The Guardian* (London) (online), April 14, 2002.

124. James Bennet, "In a New Rebuff to US, Sharon Pushes Military Sweep," *New York Times*, April 1, 2002.

125. See, for example, Aluf Benn, "Analysis: Little Hope for Powell's Success," *Ha'aretz,* April 14, 2002.

126. Amos Harel, "Army to Send Covert Unit Back into Gaza," *Ha'aretz*, July 4, 2002. Also see Amos Harel and Daniel Sobelman, "IDF Completes Takeover of Most of Area A: Demolitions in Rafa," *Ha'aretz*, July 3, 2002.

127. John Kifner, "Cabinet in Israel Endorses Seizure of the West Bank," *New York Times*, June 22, 2002, and Aluf Benn, "Analysis: Bringing the Conflict to a Head," *Ha'aretz*, June 23, 2002.

128. Aluf Benn, "Sharon: 'We'll Be in the PA Cities for a Very Long Time,'" *Ha'aretz*, July 4, 2002; Ze'ev Schiff, "The Dangers of a Political Vacuum," *Ha'aretz*, July 4, 2002; Editorial, "Back to Full Occupation," *Ha'aretz*, July 12, 2002.

129. Benn, "Bringing the Conflict to a Head."

130. Transcript of "President Bush Calls for New Palestinian Leadership," the Rose Garden, White House, June 24, 2002.

131. Aluf Benn, "Analysis: Ariel Sharon Agrees to his Own Ideas," *Ha'aretz,* July 5, 2002.

132. The Saudi Plan was introduced on February 17, 2002, by Saudi Crown Prince Abdallah as a comprehensive plan for Middle East peace that included full normalization of relations and peace between Israel and the Arab states in exchange for Israel's withdrawal from the occupied Palestinian territories (West Bank, Gaza, East Jerusalem) and the emergence of an independent Palestinian state plus Israel's withdrawal from Syria's Golan Heights. There was widespread support for the plan throughout the Arab world (as well as in Europe and elsewhere; only Israel and the United States opposed it) and the Saudis hoped to have it formalized at the March 27–28 Arab summit in Beirut. For a variety of reasons the summit did not go as planned with almost half the heads of states absent. Nevertheless, a "final declaration" on a comprehensive peace (reflecting the Saudi proposals) was released. For a text see Arab Heads of State, "Declaration on the Saudi Peace Initiative," March 28, 2002, reprinted in *Journal of Palestine Studies* 31, no. 4 (summer 2002): 182.

133. Uzi Benziman, "Right-Hand Man: The Tail Wagging the Dog," *Ha'aretz,* June 27, 2002.

134. *Yediot Aharonot* (Tel Aviv, Israeli daily, Hebrew), June 25, 2002, translated and reproduced in *World Press,* "International Press Reacts Strongly to Bush's Speech on Middle East," online at worldpress.org, June 28, 2002.

135. BBC, "Palestinian Anger at Bush Speech," London, *BBC News* (online), June 25, 2002, gives a good analysis—if one is needed. For analyses of the President's speech see: Stephen Zunes, "Bush's Speech: a Setback for Peace," *Counterpunch,* June 28/30, 2002; Richard Becker, "Bush's Speech Demands Palestinian Surrender," *International Action Center,* July 2, 2002; Phyllis Bennis, "Bush Mispronounces Middle East Peace," *US Campaign to End the Israeli Occupation,* July 8, 2002; and Ali Abunimah, "Bush's Speech: A Vision of Permanent War," *The Electric Intifada,* June 24, 2002.

136. See, for example, the analysis by Terje Roed-Larsen, "The Death of the Two-State Solution," *al-Hayat* (London, pan-Arab), October 17, 2002.

137. Ilan Pappe, "The Fence at the Heart of Palestine," *al-Ahram* (Cairo, Egyptian weekly, English), July 11–17, 2002, and David Grossman, "Illusions of a Separate Peace," *New York Times* (Opinion), July 12, 2002.

138. Shlomi Swisa, *Lethal Curfew: The Use of Live Ammunition to Enforce Curfew* (Jerusalem: B'Tselem—the Israeli Information Center for Human Rights in the Occupied Territories, October 2002); Sam Bahour, *Perfecting the Violence of Curfew* (Ramallah: al-Awda News, September 3, 2002); Amira Hass, "Curfews Paralyze Six PA Cities," *Ha'aretz,* August 10, 2002; Adam Hanieh, *West Bank Curfews: Politics by Other Means,* MERIP *Press Information Notes,* PIN 100 (July 24, 2002).

139. Swisa, *Lethal Curfew: The Use of Live Ammunition to Enforce Curfew.*

140. Helena Cobban, "Protect Palestinians Now," *Christian Science Monitor,* July 8, 2002.

141. Amira Hass, "The Civil Administration Was Never Disbanded," *Ha'aretz,* July 3, 2002.

142. Ben Lynfield, "Israelis Weigh Responses to Attacks," *Christian Science Monitor,* May 24, 2002; Amira Hass, "Israel Forces Internal Movement Permit on Palestinians," *Ha'aretz,* May 19, 2002; Marwan Bishara, "Israel's Pass Laws Will Wreck Peace Hopes," *International Herald Tribune,* May 22, 2002; Amira Hass, "Indefinite Siege," *Ha'aretz,* June 13, 2002; BBC, "More than 30 International Aid Agencies Condemn Israel," *BBC World Service* (online), July 5, 2002; Amira Hass, "The Real Disaster Is the Checkpoints," *Ha'aretz,* May 21, 2002.

143. Hass, "Indefinite Siege."

144. Particularly good on the long-term psychological consequences of siege, closure, curfew, and the pass system is Amira Hass, "Israel's Closure Policy: An Ineffective Strategy of Containment and Repression," *Journal of Palestine Studies* 31, no. 3 (spring 2002): 5–20.

145. Hass, "Indefinite Siege."

146. Amira Hass, "Palestinian Unemployment Soars to 45 % in Second Quarter," *Ha'aretz,* August 23, 2002, and Amos Harel, "Gilad: Palestinian Society Desperately Poor but Unbroken," *Ha'aretz,* October 14, 2002. For a superb in-depth analysis of the humanitarian situation, see Medécines Sans

Frontières, *Palestinian Chronicles: Trapped by War, July 2002* and *Palestinian Interior: Gaza-Hebron, November 2000–October 2001* (Paris: Medecines Sans Frontieres, July 2002).

147. Danny Rubinstein, "Almost No Sign of Regret," *Ha'aretz*, September 30, 2002.

148. Hass, "Palestinian Unemployment Soars to 45 % in Second Quarter."

149. Harel, "Gilad: Palestinian Society Desperately Poor but Unbroken."

150. Hass, "Palestinian Unemployment Soars to 45 % in Second Quarter."

151. Aron Regular, "Bethlehem Burghers Line Up for Handouts," *Ha'aretz*, December 4, 2002.

152. Catherine Cook, "Palestinian Malnutrition Bodes Ill for the Future," *Ha'aretz*, August 12, 2002; Nathan Guttman and Yair Ettinger, "USAID Reports Hunger Crisis in Territories," *Ha'aretz*, August 6, 2002; Justin Huggler, "One Fifth of Palestinian Children are Chronically Hungry," *The Independent* (London), July 27, 2002.

153. Yehezkel Lein, *Foreseen but Not Prevented: The Performance of Law Enforcement Authorities in Responding to Settler Attacks on Olive Harvesters* (Jerusalem: B'Tselem—the Israeli Information Center for Human Rights in the Occupied Territories, November 2002), p. 5.

154. For an in-depth examination of the economic crisis, see Catherine Bertini, Personal Humanitarian Envoy of the Secretary-General, *Mission Report—11–19, 2002* (New York: United Nations, 2002).

155. Associated Press, "Israel Silent on Food Warehouse Razing," *New York Times*, December 10, 2002; and "UN Agency Calls for Compensation After Israeli Forces Raze Gaza Warehouse," UN News Service, New York, UN News Center, December 2, 2002.

156. Amos Harel and Amiram Cohen, "Eitam Bans Palestinians from Drilling for Water in West Bank," *Ha'aretz*, October 22, 2002.

157. Danny Rubinstein, "Almost No Sign of Regret," *Ha'aretz*, September 30, 2002.

158. Bishara, "Israel's Pass Laws will Wreck Peace Hopes" and Hass, "Indefinite Siege." For a comprehensive analysis of the financial losses to Palestinian businessmen during the intifada, see William Dalrymple, "Profit and Loss," *The Guardian* (London), October 1, 2002.

159. Amira Hass, "No Materials to Build in Gaza," *Ha'aretz*, July 9, 2002.

160. Ibid.

161. Tim Golden, "At Checkpoint in Gaza, Travelers Wait and Wait," *New York Times*, June 12, 2002.

162. Amira Hass, "The IDF Shuts Away the Sea at Rafah," *Ha'aretz*, July 14, 2002. An excellent overview of the human rights situation of Palestinians in the context of the al-Aqsa intifada, with a focus on Gaza and Hebron, was published by Médecins Sans Frontières in October 2001 with an update in July 2002: Médecins Sans Frontières, *Palestinian Interior: Gaza-Hebron November, 2000—October 2001* (Paris: Médecins Sans Frontières, October 2001), and Médecins Sans Frontières, *Palestinian Chronicles: Trapped by War* (Paris: Médecins Sans Frontières, July 2002).

163. Benn, "Bringing the Conflict to a Head."

9

A Future for the Palestinians?

The 4,000 or so residents . . . are essentially trapped. The entrance to
the town is blocked by three haphazard walls of rust-red boulders
courtesy of the Israeli army. Residents periodically open up an alternative, muddy path through nearby olive groves . . . The army routinely detects and closes the paths . . . Locked into their village, the people [were] unable to reach their traditional markets to sell their [olive]
oil . . . no one has money . . . "people are afraid. They don't go out at
night. They're afraid of getting shot. The army comes and breaks into
houses . . . [we] are dying a slow death."
—Deir Istiya village, December 30, 2002[1]

A mobile watchtower, lifted into the air by a crane, surveys Khan
Yunis day and night . . . The wall is a vast, menacing construction
stretching down the coast as far as you can see, separating Khan Yunis
from the Gush Katif settlement . . . soldiers sit poised with machine
guns in the cylindrical bunker at the northern edge of the wall over-
looking the ruins they've made of the Khan Yunis refugee camp . . .
children from the camp play in the shell of a building not far from the
wall . . . A tank then stopped suddenly in the road and . . . started firing everywhere. A helicopter fired a rocket killing 8 more people and
wounding about 100. Later . . . they were shelling the Nasser hospital
. . . The oranges and olives will witness the last of the just-the-people
I met who told me they would never leave.
—Gaza, October 9, 2002[2]

The residents of the camp sat this week and watched mutely as the
iron machines arrived to remove the last remnants of their former
homes and former lives. They sat in circles, each family by itself, on
the earth ramparts around the heavy machines. In the rubble they
occasionally saw a pair of trousers or a doll's head, perhaps a table leg
or a fragment of a painting, a bit of carpet or a crushed pot, but the
machine immediately scooped them up and dumped them with a

crashing noise into trucks that will take them from here to the nearby
landfill, in Wadi Yamoun, leaving behind only clouds of dust.
—Jenin, October 24, 2002[3]

Two years have passed since the beginning of the intifada on
September 28, 2000. Two years that have changed Palestinian lives
completely, two years that have killed so many innocent lives and are
still killing more, and two years that have made people more aware
that unless they have all their rights, they cannot stop the intifada,
even if they want to. They are aware that if they stop, they will loose
more.
—Nablus, September 29, 2002[4]

In the aftermath of Operation Determined Path and the military reoccupation of the West Bank, the future for Palestinians looked bleak. The
the following pages describe the experiences of Palestinian suffering
and provide an overview of the Palestinian situation several months into
the new order. Most striking, perhaps, was that each month following
the reoccupation saw an increase in the number of Palestinians killed,
injured, and arrested, an expansion in home (and commercial) demolitions, and an extension of the military's impunity, as well as the relentless restrictions on freedom of movement (siege, closures, curfews,
etc.). Writing in February 2003, Israeli analyst Gideon Levy commented:

Each passing day in the territories seems to bring with it increasingly
harsh facts that are intended to break the Palestinians . . . Events that
two years ago would have caused an international furor are now part
of the accepted routine . . . The IDF's "permissiveness" is all-perva-
sive in the territories: shooting at stone throwers is now almost taken
for granted.[5]

The essential issue in a final reckoning of the Palestinian quest for a
just peace—the issue that has been at the heart of this book—is power
versus powerlessness. As the chapters thus far have illustrated, the
Palestinians are devoid of power and without allies (including among
the Arab regimes) in their struggle against a powerful state that is fully
supported by the preeminent state in the international system. In considering a Palestinian future, then, I will focus on two general topics: the
punishments, humiliations, and human rights violations Israel visited on
the Palestinians in the aftermath of reoccupation; and (2) the emergence
of a power of a different kind that, I believe, holds hope for the realization of a just and lasting peace for Palestinians.

The Palestinians: A Surfeit of Suffering

Arafat and the Palestinian Authority

With reoccupation, the Palestinian Authority (PA) was dismantled, delegitimized, and discredited. It was powerless to govern its own people or to play any role with external actors. Arafat and the PA attempted to act the parts they once enjoyed, but it was entirely a charade.

On May 2, 2002, Israel allowed Arafat, for the first time in five months, to leave his Ramallah compound. On May 26 he finally signed the Basic Law giving the Palestinians a constitution (it took effect on July 7). On June 6, Israeli tanks destroyed most of the buildings in Arafat's compound, but the president remained somewhat free to move around the West Bank. Israel, however, informed him that if he left the area, he could never return. Subsequently, Arafat promised new presidential elections; sacked half his cabinet to satisfy Israeli and U.S. demands; ordered his people not to attack civilians; agreed to accept the plan proposed by Bill Clinton while he was president; fired Jibril Rajoub (one of his two most senior security chiefs, in charge of the West Bank); and appeared before the Palestinian Legislative Council to condemn every act of terror against civilians. Washington and Tel Aviv, however, continually pronounced Arafat irrelevant; refused to have any contact with him; held him personally responsible for every instance of violence in the territories; and regularly demanded that the Palestinians find a new leader.[6]

Arafat faced his greatest domestic humiliation in June 2002 when members of the Legislative Council voiced such strong aversion to his new government that it was forced to resign to avoid a vote of no-confidence. This opposition reflected the discontent of many members of Fateh—mostly younger and from the West Bank and Gaza (as opposed to returnees)—as well as of the independents, leftists, and Islamists in the council. It was a portent of considerable significance.[7] Moreover, through all of this, Arafat's standing with his own people diminished perceptibly.

On September 19, Israeli troops again attacked Arafat's Ramallah compound, imprisoned him in his office, and demolished and bulldozed every remaining structure. The compound was leveled save for the sliver of office in which Arafat was trapped. He remained besieged until September 30, 2002, when Israel succumbed to the combined pressure of the United States, the United Nations (UN), and European states and allowed him to leave. When he finally emerged, Arafat's personal humiliation and the rubble of his ruined compound seemed like an epitaph for the Palestinian struggle. Israel's siege of Arafat temporarily increased his popularity among the Palestinian masses, who saw the president's personal humiliation as an abasement of the Palestinian nation. It also made them defiant and prepared to carry on the struggle for freedom.[8] Yet his new standing waned almost as quickly as it reappeared.

Arafat failed to read the discontent among his people, or perhaps he simply chose to ignore it, for when he convened the Legislative Council again in late October, he instructed the Fateh leadership to unequivocally order its representatives to vote in favor of the government he presented. Senior PA officials applied all the pressure they could, including physical threats on the lives of parliamentarians if they rebelled against Arafat and voted no-confidence. With the Israeli Defense Forces (IDF) in control of all Palestinian cities and Israel preventing members from Gaza from attending, Arafat swallowed the humiliating situation, apparently more concerned about showing that his regime still existed and that he was still the ruler. Yet while the Legislative Council met and voted to approve Arafat's government, both his regime and his power were a chimera. Thereafter he remained isolated in Ramallah, holed up in what was left of his office, unable to affect Palestinian politics for resistance or peace. All the factions operated independently, neither consulting nor cooperating with the president.[9]

Elections for the Palestinian Legislative Council, demanded by Israel and the United States, were scheduled for January 20, 2003. They were organized by the much-respected president of Birzeit University, Hanna Nasir, but were canceled due to Israel's closures and sieges in the West Bank.[10] During the fall and winter of 2002, acceding to U.S. and Israeli imperatives, a committee established by the PA and headed by cabinet minister Nabil Sha'ath prepared a new draft constitution for a Palestinian state. The 229 articles of the draft were made public in mid-January 2003.[11] In early February 2003, again bowing to U.S. and Israeli pressure, Arafat agreed to appoint a prime minister who would exercise ultimate authority in the PA and accepted the Bush administration's "road-map" as the path to Israeli-Palestinian peace. Abu Mazen (Mahmoud Abbas) received the designation. Still, both Washington and Tel Aviv dismissed these concessions as irrelevant, while Israel looked forward to the impending U.S. war on Iraq as an opportunity to expel Arafat.[12]

An Israeli analyst, Menachem Klein, senior scholar at the Jerusalem Institute for Israeli Studies and professor at Bar Ilan University, provided an insightful analysis of the contradictions in Israel's policy toward Arafat and the PA.

Israel argues that we must have more reforms in the Palestinian administration. . . . [but] reforms cannot be accomplished while Israel's occupation continues. Israel's presence blocks the road to reform. . . . The Israeli authorities have declared repeatedly that Arafat is irrelevant. But they contradict themselves by saying that Arafat is responsible for ordering and coordinating every terrorist attack. . . . Israel will no longer . . . recognize Arafat's authority. . . . But since Arafat has been elected as the Palestinian leader . . . there can be no reform without him. . . . The IDF has reoccupied the Palestinian territories to prevent terror. . . . Yet terrorism continues and Israel continues to demand that Arafat stop it, although Israel has said that Arafat is no longer in charge and that the IDF has taken over responsibility for security. This is illogical. . . . Israel claims that it has reoccupied the Palestinian territories to stop terror, [but] Israel's reoccupation has only increased it by motivating the Palestinians to expel the Israelis. . . . Israel refuses to make any political concessions to Palestinians claiming that this would encourage even greater violence . . . Israel also expands settlements. . . . But expanding settlements encourages terrorism. . . . To end this vicious cycle, Israel must acknowledge that the Palestinians have legitimate claims and make substantial concessions. By refusing to do so, Israel ensures the perpetuation of the conflict. . . . [Israel asserts] that only force will achieve Israel's goals. The authorities claim that this policy has not succeeded because it has not used sufficient force. They also claim that force is defeating the intifada. Neither claim is true. . . . Both Israel and the U.S. . . . [declare that] an Israeli victory over the intifada is the reason why Palestinians themselves are now calling for reform and that the Palestinians are responding to U.S. and Israeli pressure. This is a huge mistake. . . . Palestinians are calling for reforms so that they can have a functioning state, not because they have been forced to do so by Israel and the U.S., but because they are fully convinced that this is good for the Palestinians.[13]

What Do Palestinians Think About Their Future?

The Jerusalem Media and Communication Center released a public opinion poll at the end of September 2002; it indicated that 80 percent of the public supported continuation of the intifada. Some 59.5 percent supported continuation of both popular and military resistance, and 46.1 percent supported military operations inside Israel and the Occupied Territories. Moreover, 64.3 percent supported continuing suicide-bombing operations. On the best means to achieve Palestinian political objectives, 31.9 percent thought that only the intifada could accomplish that goal, and 52 percent believed that a combination of the intifada and negotiations were the best means. Only 3.4 percent strongly supported and 25.1 percent supported the Oslo agreement.[14] The most significant finding was that a large majority of Palestinians desired to persevere with the uprising. Some Palestinians spoke about a new phase in the struggle—one that would be based on nonviolent civil disobedience.[15] The September Jerusalem Media and Communication Center (JMCC) poll did not ask respondents two questions concerning which leaders and factions they trusted, which were typical in previous polls (see Chapter 6). However, in December 2002, the JMCC undertook another comprehensive poll and included these questions. On the issues covered in September, discussed above, there was relatively little change in attitudes. But the response to the "trust" questions was highly significant.

The first question asked: "Which Palestinian leader do you trust the most?" Responses were as follows: Yasser Arafat, 25.5 percent; Ahmed Yasin (head of Hamas), 11.5 percent; eight other prominent individuals received percentages in the range of 1.2 percent (lowest) to 5.2 percent (highest). But 30 percent of respondents said they "don't trust anyone." The second question asked: "Which faction do you trust most?" The responses were thus: Fateh, 28.1 percent; Hamas, 20.1 percent; Islamic Jihad, 5.7 percent; the PFLP, 2.1 percent; with all others receiving lower percentages. However, 31.4 percent of the respondents said they "don't trust any faction."[16] These figures reflect a very high level of alienation among Palestinians.

Given the societal disintegration, the lack of respected leadership, the economic hardships, the military reoccupation, and the total absence of freedom of movement, it was difficult to imagine how the mass public could be mobilized for nonviolent disobedience or any other type of organized action. Yet the fact that the Palestinians would continue to resist, in one form or another, was a given. Too much had been lost to just give up or leave voluntarily.

Reflecting some of the difficulties facing Palestinians, Danny Rubinstein published in *Ha'aretz* a very pessimistic evaluation of the Palestinian situation in late October:

> It is no coincidence that increasingly more civilians—many of them women and children—are victims of recent IDF actions in the West Bank and Gaza. . . . The war now being waged by Israel in the Palestinian territories is no longer against a band of terrorists. . . . [It] has evolved into a war against the entire Palestinian population. The picture now developing in the West Bank does not show 200,000 Israeli settlers besieged in isolated settlements, but rather close to 2 million Palestinians under a protracted siege. Most Arab cities are subjected to . . . curfews that have, to a great extent, paralyzed the economy and the school system. It is no coincidence that the battle over the olive harvest [discussed below] erupted this year. Under IDF patronage, the settlers have become the lords of the extended manor. Dozens of the outposts were built with government and public funds,

and with the encouragement, or acquiescence of, several Israeli governments. These outposts dovetail nicely with the war to extend full Israeli rule over the West Bank. The facts are well known—the number of Palestinian security prisoners grows from one day to the next: it is getting close to the 10,000-prisoner mark.[17]

One commentator suggested in October that "the possibility that the IDF would re-conquer and reoccupy the Gaza Strip . . . has become more concrete of late."[18] There were, indeed, almost daily military operations in Gaza, and between October and December 2002 there were four major assaults involving helicopter gunships, missiles, and tanks that resulted in fifty fatalities.[19]

By January 2003, *Ha'aretz* reported that Gaza had been "indirectly reoccupied" through the establishment of special security zones in the Strip in which

Palestinian movement . . . [was] extremely limited . . . the rules of engagement [were] very permissive . . . all the foliage was uprooted . . . [and which] cover[ed] a large amount of land . . . extend[ing] the entire length of all the lines of contact . . . The second method [was] turning the populated Palestinian areas into disconnected islands . . . by cutting roads and putting forts on main roads.[20]

On January 26, Israel carried out the largest military operation in Gaza since the start of the intifada. The IDF killed thirteen Palestinians and injured forty in Gaza City. It demolished 100 small factories and workshops in which the military alleged that rockets and mortars were being manufactured; destroyed a plant that manufactured trash cans for the municipality, grocery stores, carpentry shops, shops that produced clothing, and other stores. Some 150 families lost their means of support and ten families lost their homes. In addition, the army crumpled roads under tank treads, knocked down telephone and electricity poles, raided dozens of buildings, and demolished two homes. Three buses were destroyed and ten cars flattened.[21]

The impetus for the operation was an IDF allegation concerning weapons production in the factories and workshops. Yet an investigative journalist from *Ha'aretz* visited the swath of destruction the following day and reported that there was no evidence that the factories and workshops were manufacturing weapons.[22]

Human Losses

Deaths and injuries. The Palestinians made no political gains but incurred significant losses during more than two years of the intifada. In addition to the humanitarian crisis, the economic catastrophe, the internal disarticulation of the West Bank and Gaza, the new permit system, the curfews, and so on (see Chapter 8), the human losses require illumination. By the end of December 2002, approximately 1,806 Palestinians had been killed by Israeli soldiers and settlers. Of these, 85 percent were civilians, including 318 between the ages of four months and seventeen years.[23] Moreover, seventy-one Palestinians died after being prevented access to medical care (twenty-one were children, thirteen were newborns). On the other side, 204 members of the Israeli security forces and 444 Israeli civilians (including eighty-three minors) were killed.[24] The number of Palestinian wounded exceeded 21,000.[25] Many of them suffered severe injuries that would leave them physically crippled and economically dependent for the remainder of their lives.[26] (The number of Israelis wounded was approximately 4,000 in the same time period.)[27] In the month of January 2003 alone, Israel killed fifty-two Palestinians.[28]

The status of health care and human well-being. The Israeli chapter of Physicians for Human Rights issued a report in late October on the status of health care in the Occupied Territories. Among other disturbing findings, it stated that during the two years of the intifada the number of stillborn births in the West Bank had increased by 500 percent, and the number of babies born at home had doubled. There were at least thirty-nine cases of births at army roadblocks, 600 cases where the IDF prevented ambulances from moving injured and sick individuals, and about 140 attacks on ambulances and their medical teams. Nearly three-quarters of those who called for an ambulance had to meet it at a military roadblock.[29] Indeed, the infrastructure of the Palestinian health care system was in crisis.

Environmental destruction. In January 2003, the United Nations Environment Programme released a 188-page report documenting the devastation to the Palestinian environment resulting from Israeli practices during the uprising.[30] The study revealed a serious decline in water quality and increasing health problems related to contamination of water supplies, untreated sewage, and solid waste accumulating in population centers. It also illustrated the complex problems resulting from Israel's ever-widening practices of home demolitions and destruction of factories, fields, and trees. Some of the study's conclusions included:[31]

> Depletion of water resources and deterioration of the water supply in the Occupied Palestinian Territories . . . require urgent action . . . The situation is worsened by the discharge of untreated wastewater from

Israeli settlements . . . During the current crisis, the access of municipal maintenance staff to waste water treatment plants has . . . been difficult or impossible as a result of curfews, partial and full closures, and overall worker safety and security considerations. Israeli . . . measures have also raised difficulties in obtaining spare parts and disinfectants such as chlorine. (p. 44)

The ongoing conflict has effectively delayed the approval of many wastewater projects on the ground in Gaza. In addition, since September 2000, municipal personnel encounter severe difficulties in carrying out maintenance tasks due to restrictions on movement and access . . . Palestinian water and wastewater infrastructure has been damaged on several occasions by the Israeli military . . . Palestinians . . . have experienced [difficulties] in obtaining permits or commencing actual construction of plants. (p. 51)

The Jenin municipality, . . . owing to the ongoing conflict . . . [has] been unable to purchase essential spare parts from Israel. A large number of manhole covers [have] been broken and other damages caused to the wastewater system by Israeli tank patrols . . . curfew and closure measures are a severe constraint to the transport of solid waste to locations further away [from population centers]. (pp. 52–53)

The total amount of damage done to the infrastructure of water and wastewater systems in the Occupied Territories by the Israelis during the period September 2000–September 2002 was $1.67 million dollars (p. 56).

Overall problems in solid waste management . . . [1] Disruption of normal solid waste transportation routes due to a number of checkpoints being closed to Palestinian vehicles. [2] Lack of access to normal disposal sites for the same reason. [3] Lack of access to maintenance equipment and spare parts due to delays, transport difficulties caused by roadblocks, curfews and closures, and current import restrictions. [4] Dramatic increase in the waste generated from the destruction of buildings and infrastructure. [5] Introduction of open burning under the current situation. [6] Creation of emergency dumpsites within urban areas, with the associated negative environmental and health impacts. [7] Increase in operational costs, adding to the financial burden of municipalities, whose revenues have fallen sharply. (p. 65)

The UN study also considered the effects of Israeli practices on biodiversity in the Occupied Territories and reached the following conclusions:

Biodiversity is one of the pillars of future sustainable development in the Occupied Palestinian Territories, but it is currently at risk due to: [1] Direct degradation arising from military operations. [2] Increasing

of human population pressure on natural systems from high population growth and the long-lasting refugee crisis. [3] Rapid growth of
Israeli settlements and supporting roads in areas where land is already
scarce. [4] Restrictions on communication, movement and access,
limiting implementation of environmental measures. [5] Construction
of separation fence/wall that effectively blocks movement of terrestri-
al fauna, and cuts the natural ecological corridors. [6] Threats from
solid waste and wastewater pollution. [7] Clearing of land of vegeta-
tion by Israel for security purposes. (p. 95)

Several of the UN report's findings were quite startling. For example, of the 2,180 square kilometers of grazing land in the West Bank and
Gaza, Israel permits the Palestinians use of only 225 square kilometers.[32] Between September 2000 and December 2002, Israel destroyed
14,196 forest trees in the Occupied Territories.[33] And, in the first fifteen
months of the intifada (September 2000–December 2001), Israel demolished 155,343 olive trees, 150,356 citrus trees, 54,223 almond trees,
12,505 date palm trees, 39,227 grape vines, 18,400 banana trees, and
49,851 "other" trees.[34] In February 2002, Gideon Levy reported that
"more than three-quarters of a million trees have been uprooted and
more than 53,000 dunams have been flattened."[35]

In summary, the UN report concludes that depletion of water
resources and deterioration of water quality are the two most serious
problems facing Palestinians in the West Bank and Gaza. Third, in
terms of priority in the West Bank, is land degradation; in Gaza it is
shoreline and marine pollution.[36]

The status of education.   The autumn 2002 school year was a nightmare for Palestinians.[37] The education system—the public system as
well as that run by the United Nations Relief and Works Agency—was
crippled due to curfews and closures. Neither students nor teachers
could reach schools with any regularity, and those who did make it were
traumatized by fear because every journey to a school meant a trip past
tanks, checkpoints, and armed soldiers. Between August 31 (the first
day of the school year) and October 9, West Bank schools were closed
for up to fifteen days. In many locales, the situation was even worse,
and by December 2002 it had deteriorated everywhere in the
West Bank. One man spoke of his frustration, no less felt by every
Palestinian.

> The limitations on our movement in the city are unbearable. This is
> not a normal life . . . An entire neighborhood in the western part of the
> city has been cut off. The residents may not leave on foot or by car.
> They risk their lives to steal into the center [commercial area] of the

city because tanks and personnel carriers are everywhere all the time.
. . . My wife [a teacher] returned soaking wet from the Hawara checkpoint unable to reach her school in the village. Soldiers held her and
her colleagues up in the pouring rain for hours until she gave up and
came home.[38]

Additionally, many schools had been taken over by the IDF for use as
detention centers, and many others had been severely damaged during
the Israeli invasions. One analyst noted, "It is not uncommon for children to be searched and abused by Israeli troops on their way to and
from school or to be subject to tear gas and warning shots near checkpoints."[39] Moreover,

> Exam pass rates in Arabic and math have collapsed, while dropout
> rates are starting to rise for the first time in a decade. . . . Teachers are
> increasingly reporting signs of psychological trauma. . . . It is becom-
> ing ever more apparent that Palestinian children will be paying twice
> over for the crisis in the West Bank and Gaza. Already they have paid
> with the loss of their security, innocence and education. But they will
> also pay with their futures. They will pay with the loss of opportunity,
> development and hope that a sound education brings.[40]

Prisoners. The number of persons imprisoned by Israel during the
intifada was staggering; however, there were no accurate aggregate data
available and equally reliable sources gave different figures even for
monthly records. This was due, in part, to the fact that Palestinians were
held at many different facilities (including prisons administered by the
Israel Prisons Service, the IDF, and the Israel Police Force, as well as at
ad hoc locations that sometimes included settlements). It was also related to Israel's practice of holding individuals incommunicado, without
charge and without access to a lawyer or to their families. Danny
Rubinstein reported in *Ha'aretz* in September 2002 that Israel had
arrested more than 30,000 individuals during the two years of the uprising and that at the time it was holding some 8,000–10,000 prisoners.[41]
B'Tselem does not even attempt to provide aggregate data, but for
September 2002 it reported that there were 4,019 detainees. B'Tselem,
however, does not include prisons run by the Israel Police Force.[42] In
January 2003, B'Tselem reported that 4,815 Palestinians were under
detention—notably more than it counted as imprisoned in September.[43]
Even more striking was the growth in the number of individuals held
under administrative detention. In January 2001, there were sixteen
administrative detainees; in July 2001, there were ten; in January 2002,
thirty-six; in July 2002, 943; in January 2003, 1,007; and by February
2003, there were 1,088.[44]

The conditions under which the Palestinian detainees were held were deplorable although some prisons were worse than others. Everywhere, however, there was severe overcrowding with cramped, unhygienic conditions, poor quality and insufficient food, inadequate access to medical care, and degrading and humiliating treatment often including torture.[45] Amnesty International stated that the manner in which mass detentions were carried out "breached human rights standards."

> They [Israeli security services] treat detained Palestinians in a way apparently designed to humiliate and degrade those arrested. . . . [They] were not brought promptly before a judge, and they were denied access to lawyers and to their families. The Israeli authorities showed an apparent intent to bypass the justice system by increasing the period of incommunicado detention. . . . Most of those still in custody are held without charge or trial. . . . The majority of those detained have been arbitrarily detained, and thousands of Palestinians have been rounded up, humiliated, ill-treated and held in poor conditions as a collective punishment.[46]

Danny Rubinstein again commented in *Ha'aretz* and was less diplomatic than Amnesty International, noting that "every night some 800 prisoners and detainees have to sleep on the floor . . . due to a shortage of beds. . . . Even animals don't live in the conditions given to detainees. . . . The conditions are inhuman and this intolerable situation must not continue."[47] Nevertheless, prison conditions deteriorated even more.[48]

The Olive Harvest

If any single issue illustrated Palestinian powerlessness, it was the autumn 2002 olive harvest. During the intifada, 18,000 olive trees were uprooted, bulldozed, or set ablaze. Land containing olive groves was confiscated, wells were destroyed, and olive fields were declared by the IDF as "closed military zones."[49] By the fall of 2002, manufacturing, tourism, transportation, and construction were in shambles.[50] The olive harvest was expected to account for 10 percent of that year's gross domestic product (GDP).[51]

In the West Bank, where most of the olive groves are located, the olive industry accounts for some 40 percent of agricultural production (excluding livestock) and approximately 70 percent of the production of fruit trees. Some 837,000 dunums—about 45 percent of the arable land—are planted with olive trees in groves that belong to some 70,500 farmers or households.[52] The high level of unemployment—50 percent of the workforce—had resulted in a gradual increase in the number of Palestinians turning to existing sources of income, in particular, during this period, the olive harvest.[53] More than in any previous year, the economic viability of thousands of Palestinian households depended on the ability to complete the cycle of the olive industry: harvesting the olives, extracting the oil, and marketing it.

When the harvest season began, many farmers, due to the reoccupation and its closures, checkpoints, and curfews, were unable to get to their remaining fields. However, those who managed to reach their lands found themselves confronted with violent settlers—a phenomenon that occurs annually. B'Tselem noted that "attacks on olive harvesters by settlers are one aspect of the broader phenomenon of settler violence against Palestinians throughout the year."[54] During the 2002 harvest, however, "the acts of violence against olive harvesters [were] more frequent and intense than in previous seasons."[55]

Jewish settlers throughout the West Bank disrupted the harvest by gathering around harvesters—cursing and insulting them, firing into the air, forcibly preventing them from entering their groves, shooting and throwing stones at workers, and beating them with clubs and rifle butts. In one instance, settlers shot dead a man picking olives on his land in the village of Aqraba, near Nablus, permanently injured the hand of another, and blinded a third in one eye. The settlers also caused deliberate and extensive property damage, including uprooting and burning trees, spilling harvested olives onto the ground, destroying tools used for the harvest, burning cars used to transport the olives, and stealing olives.

The theft of olives was carried out on a systematic scale. In some cases, settlers arrived in Palestinian-owned olive groves, picked the olives, and stole them. In other cases, settlers came to the groves and stole sacks of olives that had already been picked by Palestinians.[56] The theft was justified by settler rabbis—in one instance by a former chief rabbi, Mordechai Eliyahu, who commented in *Ha'aretz:* "Since the land is the inheritance of the People of Israel, planting on this land by gentiles is planting on land that does not belong to them. If someone plants a tree on my land, both the tree and the fruit it yields belong to me."[57]

The villages most subject to settler violence were Aqraba, Yanon, Huwwara, Kufr Dek, Al-Lubban, and Turmus 'Ayya.[58] In Yanon, the violence became so intolerable that the village's residents fled. *Ha'aretz* reported that "the torching of the Yanon village generator and the contamination of the well . . . caused most of the village residents to abandon their homes. The village, which was once home to 150 families, now has less than 10 families living there."[59] In another edition, the Israeli daily wrote: "Every day there are clashes between settlers and Palestinians, often accompanied by gunfire and physical and verbal attacks on Arab farmers."[60] The *Washington Post* reported: "With horses, axes, rifles, stones and fire, Jews . . . [are] cutting and burning trees and beating Palestinian villagers. . . . After driving farmers away, the attackers have stolen ladders and sacks of the crop, and picked the fruit for themselves."[61]

On October 22, the Israeli government announced a ban on all Palestinians from picking olives. The same day, however, it rescinded the ban due to the lack of soldiers to enforce it.[62] (This was also the day the government announced the proscription on Palestinians drilling for water—an order that was not canceled.) At no time during the harvest season did Israel do anything to restrain the settlers or to protect the farmers. As was demonstrated with regard to the situation in Hebron (see Chapter 4), the IDF and security forces colluded with the settlers; in the words of B'Tselem, "they [the IDF] are responsible for the acts of violence that ultimately took place."[63] Another observer noted:

> The attacks on Palestinians . . . have taken place against the backdrop of the Israeli security forces' on-going policy of non-enforcement of the law with regards to violent settlers. This policy is illustrated at all stages of attacks: inadequate preparations for such attacks, even when they are completely predictable; refraining from halting the attacks even when security forces are present at the site, and refusal to thoroughly prosecute the perpetrators.[64]

On October 28, 2002, Prime Minister Ariel Sharon expressed his disapproval of the actions of the settlers. Nevertheless, as B'Tselem noted: "Coming after one month of continuous violence by settlers, and against the background of Israel's long-standing policy of not enforcing the law on violent settlers, these comments can only be interpreted as a cynical attempt to pay lip-service to the principle of law enforcement."[65] Moreover, as a columnist wrote in *Ha'aretz*, the events surrounding the olive harvest were one aspect of Israel's design for "transfer" of the Palestinians.

> Ever since the West Bank was reoccupied and the besieged Arafat no longer has security apparatuses and the Palestinian government has been paralyzed, the Israeli argument about pressure on the population [imposing suffering on the civilians to pressure Arafat to clamp down on terrorists] rings hollow. . . . Curfews, checkpoints, house demolitions, closed factories and ruined farmlands . . . [have] nothing to do with security. The settlers . . . can always claim they shoot at olive

harvesters because the peasants are actually scouts meant to help pre-pare terror attacks—but the clear truth is that it's really a preparation for transfer. There's no other explanation . . . for the sweeping collective punishments in the territories, other than Israeli efforts to make Palestinian life so miserable they'll choose to live elsewhere.[66]

Ze'ev Schiff, one of Israel's most respected military analysts, wrote in the same vein:

> It would be a mistake to regard the settlers' robberies of Palestinian villagers' olive harvests as merely another serious crime. This collective theft signifies a change in the current military conflict between Israel and the Palestinians. . . . For the first time in the current conflict, Israelis are stealing and confiscating Palestinian food. . . . [This] can be seen as laying the groundwork for transfer. . . . Residents have already been forced to leave their homes. . . . With their deeds, the thieves are sending the message that it's not a war on terror in the territories, but a campaign to deepen the poverty and hunger of the Palestinian population. They are burning the olive harvests, damaging the olive trees and preventing the farmers from reaching privately owned groves. This is a classic formula for creating more terrorists.[67]

Indeed, without the ability to control any aspect of their lives, and with oppression omnipresent, Palestinians had few choices. For many, the only choice came down to surviving by emigrating or perishing on their land. In this context, it was no coincidence that the Moledet (Homeland) Party, whose basic platform is transfer, undertook a campaign that included ads in Palestinian newspapers to "offer free help and advice to anyone wanting to emigrate from the West Bank and Gaza."[68]

Hebron Revisited

In November 2002, Hebron again erupted into violence. On November 10, the IDF assassinated Eyad Sawalha, a prominent leader of Islamic Jihad, in Jenin. The organization vowed revenge, which came on November 16 in the form of an ambush by three Jihad men against Israeli military forces in Hebron that killed twelve soldiers and security officers. The attack occurred in an area under sole Israeli control, along the road that links the settlement of Kiryat Arba with Al-Ibrahimi mosque (the Tomb of the Patriarchs). The military was providing security for Jewish worshipers, but no civilians were killed.[69]

After the attack, all Palestinians in Hebron were placed under full curfew; settlers rampaged through the city, destroying cars and property, setting fire to crops and stores, savaging fields and olive groves, and otherwise sewing ruination. The IDF immediately blew up three houses in the vicinity of the attack and six more elsewhere in the city. Under the protection of the IDF, settlers forthwith set up tents and huts at the site of the ambush and announced that that their compound was the base from which would be built a large, new Jewish neighborhood. Prime Minister Sharon called on the army to extract "heavy retaliation."[70]

The settlers rapidly produced a comprehensive plan, accepted by the government, for a tourist promenade (intended for use by Jewish settlers only) in an area 730 meters long and 12 meters wide (about 8.2 dunums), linking Kiryat Arba directly with Al-Ibrahimi. The plan (formalized in an IDF military order) called for the construction of 1,000 housing units along the promenade, necessitating the demolition of 110 Palestinian homes. Moreover, these were not your average homes, for most had been designated as historical sites, having been constructed from the Mamluk period through the Ottoman era.[71] Nevertheless, demolition and construction work began the first week in December. *Ha'aretz* editorialized: "The promenade . . . is another political attempt—more effective than previous ones—to fulfill a long standing plan to create territorial contiguity between Kiryat Arba and Hebron by expropriating [land] in the heart of Hebron."[72]

Meron Benvenisti also commented on the Hebron settler expansion and the government's cooperation:

> For 35 years, Israel has made a supreme effort to take control of the physical space of the West Bank . . . in which the Zionist revolution can be fulfilled. . . . The struggle over physical space is not measured any longer with the establishment of settlements and houses, but through . . . the denial of Palestinian use of the territory in this space—from legal limitations, and through to uprooting crops and preventing olive harvests, prohibitions on vehicular traffic, sieges and closures. . . . The Jewish settlement in Hebron . . . will yet boomerang against its perpetrators.[73]

On January 30, 2003, the IDF commenced what it stated would be at least a month-long campaign in Hebron code-named Hot Winter. Palestinian residents of the city that had been under curfew for two months were informed at the outset of the operation that they would be under continuous curfew for its duration. In the first days of the operation, using tanks and heavy armor, the army bulldozed most of the major streets in the city, carving it into isolated neighborhoods, and imposed military roadblocks, turning it into a dead-end labyrinth. The IDF then bulldozed the entire open-air market in the center of the city, destroying 117 market stalls and leaving as many families without any means of economic support.[74] Subsequent to the demolition of the market, twenty-two additional Palestinian-owned buildings, the majority in the southeastern part of the city, were demolished.[75] One family's situation is illustrative:

> Hebron has never looked as bad as it does now. . . . A deathly silence hangs over the city. It's hard to believe that these houses are bursting with children trapped inside against their will, in terribly crowded conditions. Soldiers and police stand tensely at every corner. . . . All the windows are shuttered, the place almost seems abandoned—just the way the settlers like it. . . . Mohammed Ja'abari, 62, lies on a colorful mattress on the floor. . . . The last time he left the house was in early December when the curfew was temporarily suspended. . . . That was two months ago. . . . He says he felt some heavy pressure in his chest the night before. He woke his sons and begged them to take him to the doctor. But they told him it was impossible . . . they were afraid for his sake and theirs. He has wanted to see a doctor for the last five months, but hasn't been able to. He can't get there on foot and taking a car is completely out of the question. [Israel prohibits Palestinian residents from driving.] Maybe he'll try during the next break in the curfew, which occurs once every four or five days and lasts for an hour and a half. But there is no way to know before hand when the curfew will be lifted. Sometimes they hear the soldiers announcing that the curfew has been reinstated, and only then do they realize that it had been lifted.[76]

A few days later, soldiers

> oversaw the theft of Palestinian lands [by settlers] in south Mt. Hebron . . . preparing the groundwork for transfer. The soldiers acted in direct violation of a court order from December 19, 2002, which ordered the army to allow the Palestinians to plow their fields in the area.[77]

This incident had its origins in late November when Palestinians attempted to till their fields at the start of the plowing season. They were harassed by settlers and prevented by soldiers from entering their land. This situation of daily confrontations continued through the end of January when the Civil Administration gave the Palestinians permission to plow. On February 1, armed with the permits, nine farmers took tractors into their fields and began the tilling ritual. Within hours they were assaulted and beaten by settlers, bound and taken by the IDF to a military encampment, and their tractors were confiscated. The following day settlers took over the Palestinians' fields and, guarded by the IDF, began planting trees. One analyst pointed out that "this incident is part of a systematic campaign to break the ties between Palestinians and their land."[78]

Abusive Treatment of the Palestinians

The headline of an article appearing in *Ha'aretz* provides a good point to start this discussion: "Humiliation Is More Than a Sum of Incidents."[79] Throughout the occupation, Israeli soldiers have mistreated and humiliated Palestinians without sanction or punishment (except in a few egregious cases). These practices did not stop during the seven years of the Oslo peace process, and they escalated during the period of the Al-Aqsa intifada.[80] Some aspects of this phenomenon were noted in previous chapters, and B'Tselem in particular has been exemplary in documenting them. In the aftermath of Israel's reoccupation of the territories, IDF abuse, brutality, and humiliation increased significantly. Such incidents, however, are rarely discussed publicly, because in comparison to gross human rights violations they tend to be considered routine. Yet as much as killings, house demolitions, assassinations, and the like, these daily experiences of humiliation and abuse are deeply imprinted in the Palestinian psyche. As such, some mention must be made of them here.

In general, categories include beatings; harassment, humiliation and excessive delays at checkpoints; the use of Palestinians as human shields; confiscating permits; the so-called lottery (explained below); forcing men en masse, and individually, to strip in front of soldiers; and detaining taxis and their passengers.[81] The following are excerpts from two B'Tselem reports. It is notable that B'Tselem stresses in each of its case studies that what it is presenting "is only the tip of the iceberg in terms of soldiers' current behavior toward Palestinians in the Occupied Territories."[82]

> Twelve Israeli soldiers detained two Palestinian taxis. They dismissed 3 women, a child and an elderly man and proceeded to abuse the nine remaining Palestinians over a period of two hours. . . . The soldiers . . . forcibly removed the driver[s] and [remaining] passengers . . . while yelling and beating them . . . then took the passengers' identity cards. . . . [A] soldier beat Sufia with his helmet and the butt of his gun on the head and left ear. . . . Another soldier arrived and beat him over the head with a metal object. Sufia lost consciousness as a result of the blows. . . . After the nine Palestinians were lined up against the wall, the soldiers began to beat them severely. Among other means, the soldiers struck the men with the butts of their guns and their helmets. Some of the soldiers went to the 2 taxis, broke their windows and slashed the seat covers and tires. The soldiers ordered the Pales-

tinians to beat each other while threatening that if they refused to do so they would be killed. . . . Following two hours of abuse, the soldiers finally let the Palestinians leave. They stoned the victims as they were leaving.[83]

A second account:

> Four soldiers entered a barber shop. . . . For more than an hour they abused five residents of the city. . . . Among other things, the soldiers forcibly cut the hair of two of the men, beat them, and maltreated them and three other Palestinians. The soldiers also used three of the victims as human shields. . . . [As the soldiers approached] Maswadeh [shop owner] and Abu Rumeileh [a barber] closed the barbershop's iron door . . . [the] soldiers started banging on the door. . . . [They] ordered two Palestinian by-standers to call out to the people to open up and threatened to fire into the shop. . . . Maswadeh opened the door. . . . [One] soldier ordered him to sit in one of the barber's chairs and began to cut [his] hair with an electric razor . . . two of the soldiers ordered al-Ajaluni [a customer] to go outside with them, where they beat him. Maswadeh asked the soldier what he was doing, and the soldier slapped him and told him to shut up. . . . The other soldiers ordered a-Rajbi [another customer] to go outside where they searched and beat him. . . . The soldier then ordered Abu Rumeileh to sit in the barber's chair, and proceeded to cut his hair. The electric razor grazed his scalp and when Abu Rumeileh asked him to be gentle, the soldier slapped him. . . . [A] soldier opened a bottle of shampoo and told Abu Rumeileh to open his mouth. When he refused, the soldier . . . tried to force his mouth open. He called the commander to come inside, and hit Abu Rumeileh in the face with a pail. [He] fell to the floor shouting in pain, blood oozing from his nose. The soldier kicked him in the abdomen . . . and threatened to shoot him in the head. . . . The soldiers who had left the barbershop continued to beat the three Palestinians who had been taken outside. A group of Palestinian children began throwing stones at the soldiers. . . . The soldiers took the three Palestinians into the middle of the street, stood them one meter away from each other, rested their weapons on the shoulders of the Palestinians and fired . . . for an extended period of time. . . . [When the soldiers left] they still had the ID cards of the five Palestinians.[84]

In a detailed, five-page story, *Ha'aretz* reported the following:

> The soldiers made Bassam Jarar, a double amputee with kidney disease, and Mohammed Asasa, who is blind in both eyes, get out of the ambulance. Both men had come from dialysis treatment. The soldiers detained them for 10 hours. The IDF spokesman said: "Due to a technical problem, it wasn't possible to check if they were wanted men."[85]

A further practice is known as the lottery:

Israeli Border Police operating in the West Bank . . . have forced
Palestinians they detained to choose whether to have a nose, arm, or
leg broken in a sort of "lottery.". . . Or, they could choose to be shot.
. . . [In other cases] the security forces prepared pieces of paper for
what they called a "lottery" to decide which parts of the Palestinians
bodies would be broken. . . . [In one case] the Border Police . . .
stopped [a Palestinian] while he was traveling in his car and said he
could choose between a broken arm or a broken car. He said he chose
his arm, thinking the [police] would not follow through on the threat.
But the border policeman then broke his arm.[86]

One final example of impunity comes from Khan Yunis, Gaza.

It is still . . . And then . . . a disembodied voice crackles over a loud-
speaker (in Arabic). "COME ON, DOGS. WHERE ARE ALL THE
DOGS OF KHAN YOUNIS? COME. COME. SON OF A BITCH!
SON OF A WHORE! YOUR MOTHER'S CUNT." The boys, no more
than 10 or 11, dart in small packs up the sloping dunes to the electric
fence that separates the camp from the Jewish settlement. They lob
rocks toward two armored jeeps parked at the top of the dune and
mounted with loudspeakers . . . A percussion grenade explodes . . .
bullets from the M–16 rifles tumble end over end and through the
children's slight bodies. . . . Yesterday at this spot the Israelis shot 8
young men . . . this afternoon they kill an 11 year-old . . . and seriously wound four more . . . Children have been shot in other conflicts I
have covered—death squads . . . in El Salvador and Guatemala, mothers and infants lined up and massacred in Algeria, and Serb snipers
put children in their sights . . . in Sarajevo—but I have never before
watched soldiers entice children like mice into a trap and murder them
for sport.[87]

Settlements

Settlements have been at the epicenter of the Palestinians' consuming
rage since the outset of the occupation. In the 1993 Oslo Declaration of
Principles (DOP), Israel pledged not to change the status of the
Occupied Territories pending final negotiations. Yet settlement expansion throughout the peace process was accelerated at a frenetic pace,
continually shrinking and dividing the land that would constitute any
future Palestinian state. Behind the settlement drive during those seven
years lay an elaborate system of government incentives and subsidies
and a powerful network of political support that included both major
parties—Labor and Likud. Perhaps more than any other single issue, it
was the relentless settlement growth, and its concomitant seizures of
Palestinian land, construction of bypass roads, and so on, that led to the
disillusionment and despair of the Palestinians with the peace process

and resulted in the Al-Aqsa intifada. Thus, it is instructive to examine settlement expansion during the period of the uprising.

On March 13, 2002, the Knesset's finance committee approved NIS 135 million for new settlements in the West Bank.[88] In October, *Ha'aretz* revealed that in addition to that money, "billions of shekels slated for the settlements have been concealed in the budgets of the government ministries and offices."[89] It is conservatively estimated that Israel spends more than U.S.$1 billion a year on West Bank and Gaza settlements.[90] One Israeli analyst wrote that "Israel has spent no less than $60 billion on the settlements . . . the equivalent of 20 years American aid."[91] Also in March 2002, Peace Now revealed that Israel, since the election of Ariel Sharon in February 2001, had already established thirty-four new settlements in the West Bank.[92] By December 2002, that number had grown to sixty-six.[93]

B'Tselem published a 100-page document regarding the extent of human rights violations resulting from the establishment of settlements. Among other findings, B'Tselem reported that the settler population in the West Bank at the end of 2001 stood at 380,000, up from 247,000 at the start of the Oslo process. Additionally, it revealed that "while the built-up areas of the settlements constitute only 1.7 % of the land in the West Bank, the municipal boundaries are over three times as large at 6.8 percent. Regional councils constituted an additional 35.1 percent. *Thus, a total of 41.9 % of the area in the West Bank is controlled by the settlements*."[94] Moreover, this 41.9 percent had been de facto annexed to the State of Israel (see Map 9.1). The *New York Times* reported that now "the settlers appear . . . to have the upper hand."[95]

> Settlers continue to build new Jewish homes in the middle of Palestinian Hebron and in the rocky West Bank hills, and to pursue a vision that blends nationalism, messianism and yearning for the good life. . . . The settlers . . . are Israel's "strongest, most successful interest group." . . . Mr. Sharon, an architect for decades of Israel's settlement policy, said this week that evacuation of settlements should not even be discussed. . . . Referring to one of the most isolated and heavily defended settlements, [Sharon stated that] "the fate of Netzarim [in Gaza] is the fate of Tel Aviv." . . . [A settler remarked,] "Catch the land, live on the land, work the land—and no matter how many people are killed, it is yours."[96]

Indeed, so powerful had the settlers become that in the Israeli elections of 2003, they were able to extract a promise from then prime minister Sharon that he would open the Haram al-Sharif to Jewish worship. This in the middle of a ten-day, NIS 2 million campaign, financed by

Map 9.1 Sharon's Proposal for a Final Settlement, 2001

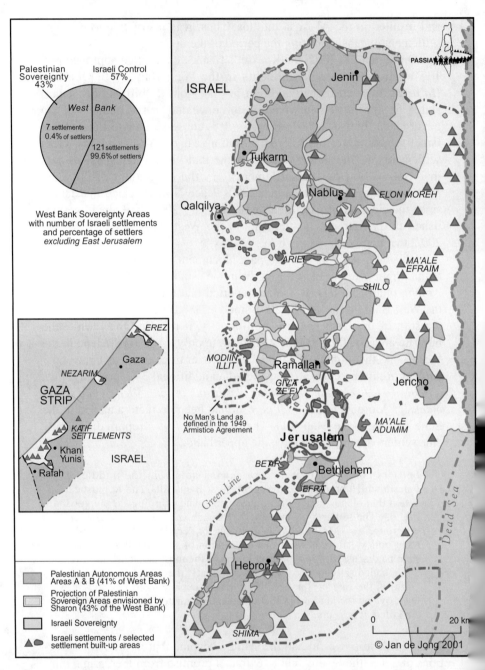

Source: Palestinian Academic Society for the Study of International Affairs (PASSIA), Jerusalem.
http://www.passia.org/palestine_facts/MAPS/sharon-2001.html. Accessed January 2003. Reprinted with permission of PASSIA.

wealthy American Jews, promoting the notion that the "Temple Mount is the heart of the Jewish Nation."[97]

In its concluding remarks on settlements, B'Tselem stated:

> Israel has created in the Occupied Territories a regime of separation based on discrimination, applying two separate systems of law in the same area and basing the rights of individuals on their nationality. This regime is the only one of its kind in the world, and is reminiscent of . . . the Apartheid regime in South Africa. The discrimination against Palestinians is apparent in almost all fields of activity. . . . The settlers, on the contrary, benefit from all the rights available to Israeli citizens living within the Green Line, and in some cases are even granted additional rights. . . . To perpetuate this situation, which is a priori illegal, Israel has continuously breached the rights of the Palestinians.[98]

Notably, the *Washington Post* reported on July 28, 2002, that "the [Bush] administration does not intend to make a significant effort to curb the continued expansion of Israeli settlements in the West Bank."[99] And in early December, the Israeli daily *Ma'ariv* revealed that the housing ministry and the Settlers Council had jointly completed a new plan for increased settlement activity for the subsequent three months that included construction of hundreds of new housing units in fourteen isolated settlements to ensure their permanence.[100]

The Israeli government then announced in late December 2002 that it would construct smart electronic security fences around each West Bank and Gazan settlement. The fences will encompass buffer zones that will extend several hundred meters beyond existing settlement property, meaning the confiscation of more Palestinian lands. This was in keeping with Tel Aviv's intention to limit to 40 percent the amount of territory on the West Bank that would be available for Palestinians. The fences will bring watchtowers, increased military patrols, and, in areas between the fences and the settlements, special rules of engagement (i.e., they will be free-fire zones).[101]

The renowned Jewish philosopher and theologian Marc Ellis lamented this situation in 2002:

> Despite past changes that will continue to occur over the next years, the map of Israel/Palestine will remain essentially as it is today. . . . The control of Israel/Palestine by Israel, its control over the geographic area that stretches from Tel Aviv to the Jordan River, will continue. Israel has not only conquered this area and will control it through direct supervision and surrogates, but the land without significant Palestinian population will be occupied, settled and developed by Israel.[102]

Separation Wall

On June 23, 2002, the Israeli government authorized a plan to construct a security wall running the full length (some 360 kilometers) of the West Bank; it was scheduled to be completed in the summer of 2003.[103] It will have three parts: a northern section, a section encircling Jerusalem, and a southern section. When completed, the reinforced concrete structure will be three times as long and twice as high as the Berlin Wall.[104] The project will involve the expropriation of another 10 percent of Palestinian land.[105]

In addition to the wall itself, on its eastern (Palestinian) side, it will be buttressed by a series of components. The components, which run east to west, will be spread over 30–60 meters, and like the wall itself will all be constructed on confiscated Palestinian land. They include "a trench intended to create an obstacle against tanks, a dirt path that [will] constitute a 'killing zone' onto which access is forbidden, an electric warning fence, a trace path to disclose the footprints of infiltrators, and a two-lane patrol road."[106] There will be heavily fortified watchtowers at regular intervals on the wall, as well as several gates through which Palestinians theoretically can pass to tend their land or return to their village (if, that is, they have secured a valid security permit from the occupation authorities). As with all permits, Palestinian freedom of movement and access will depend on the caprice of the occupiers. When the middle third—the Jerusalem section—of the wall is finished, thirty-five Palestinian families living along the northern edge of Bethlehem will be on the Israeli side of the border because Israel has decided to annex Rachel's Tomb and extend the wall around it.[107]

Work commenced in July 2002 on the northern sector and proceeded rapidly through the fall. By October, construction of the northern segment (110 kilometers) was near completion. As planned, the wall was not built on the Green Line but rather east of it. It swallowed 17,000 dunums of Palestinian agricultural land that had been particularly rich and productive, being cultivated with olive trees, vineyards, seasonal fruit trees, and various kinds of field crops.[108] The wall cuts through other agricultural land, villages, and water resources, including the western aquifer system that provides 51 percent of West Bank water and irrigates the orchards and crops of the northern region.[109] Most deleterious to Palestinian farmers is that the fence cuts through and severs numerous Palestinian properties, creating an impassable wedge between farmers and their lands. A further issue was the fact that villages (seventeen in the northern sector) were situated west of the fence, completely separated from the remainder of the West Bank.[110]

One such negatively affected village was Nazlat 'Isa, located to the north of Tulkarm District, with a population of 2,500 and an area of 622 square meters. On January 7, 2003, the IDF demolished sixty-two shops out of 170 commercial establishments in the village. Subsequently twenty additional businesses were razed. The market was the main source of income for Nazlat 'Isa and, because it is situated near the Green Line, many Israelis traditionally shopped there. Some analysts posited that the destruction was part of Israel's war on the Palestinian economy. This may have been true in part, but the location of the village (along the seam line and between Israel's self-proclaimed military zone beside the wall) suggested that it was slated for bifurcation and destruction to facilitate construction of the wall and its components. However, that its relatively thriving economy was destroyed was certainly one consequence. After the January 7 razing, twenty-eight houses and the remainder of the commercial enterprises were given notifications of intended Israeli demolition.[111]

A second village, East Barta'a, located to the north of Jenin District with a population of 4,000, received military orders in late January 2003 for the demolition of fifty-six commercial shops, twelve private houses, three sewing workshops, and a lamp factory. Like Nazlat 'Isa, East Barta'a is located near the Green Line in the area where the wall and its components are to be built.[112]

The city of Qalqilya was especially negatively affected. It was engulfed on three sides by the wall, depriving its residents of the most minimal freedom of movement. The city forfeited at least 15 percent of its municipal land and more than 50 percent of its agricultural land. It also faced a serious diminution in its water supply because the western aquifer, which lies under it, is now in exclusive Israeli control, and fourteen wells in the city were slated for confiscation.[113] An observer reports what the wall means to the people of Qalqilya:

> Just 2 meters from the wall is a new elementary school. A lookout tower commands the area while children play outside. Random shots ring out whenever a child gets too close to the wall. . . . The map shows how the wall will dissect Qalqilya into a cramped housing area without any room for future expansion, turning it into a refugee camp or an open-air prison. The wall will confiscate 3 of our wells and cisterns and thus deprive our olive trees of the proper irrigation.[114]

In the words of B'Tselem:

> The negative effects of the barrier will not be limited to landowners and residents of enclaves. Places such as *Qalqilya* (38,000 residents)

and *Zita* (2,800 residents), are expected to be closely surrounded by the barrier on three sides. Movement in and out of these locations will be possible from the east only. The repercussions in the case of *Qalqilya* may be particularly severe as the residents of the nearby villages rely on services supplied by the city. The barrier will make access for these residents difficult.[115]

Map 9.2 illustrates the effects of the Israeli fence regime.

One analyst suggested a connection between the wall and transfer: "The wall serves Israel's long-term objective of rendering life for the Palestinians so difficult that they will eventually cross the Jordan River into Jordan and transform the Kingdom into the 'Palestinian State.'"[116]

New Forms of Collective Punishment.

House demolitions. In August 2002, Israel significantly expanded its policy of house demolitions using a new rationale: deterrence. Actually, the policy had been utilized before and during the first intifada but had been dormant for more than a decade. Its renewal was based on an IDF report alleging that Palestinian suicide bombers were in part motivated by the improvement in their family's status because the individual's act was widely viewed as heroic. Thus, the government decided to destroy the homes of anyone who carried out, or allegedly carried out, a suicide attack, participated in any way in its planning, or was involved in other militant activities.[117]

In August, the High Court of Justice gave its approval to the policy (something it had not done in the earlier years of its use) and also accepted the IDF's argument that permitting Palestinians forty-eight hours to appeal demolition orders could endanger the lives of Israeli soldiers. Thus, soldiers could destroy a family home without warning. Of grave concern, too, was the fact that the court's decision left judicial review in the hands of local army commanders. Between August and February 13, 2003, there were 150 demolitions of homes of relatives of alleged militants. That figure compared with sixteen demolitions in the preceding twelve months.[118] By tradition, Palestinians tend to live as extended families in attached compounds so that a single demolition can result in dozens of people suddenly becoming homeless. For instance, in one demolition of a four-story house in Beit Jala, thirty-two innocent civilians including twelve children were rendered bereft of shelter.[119]

Forcible transfer. A second policy implemented by Israel in the summer of 2002 under the rubric of deterrence was the forcible transfer of

Map 9.2   The Separation Wall

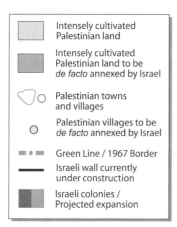

Intensely cultivated Palestinian land

Intensely cultivated Palestinian land to be *de facto* annexed by Israel

Palestinian towns and villages

Palestinian villages to be *de facto* annexed by Israel

Green Line / 1967 Border

Israeli wall currently under construction

Israeli colonies / Projected expansion

The Palestinian city of Qalqilya will be isolated by the wall and illegal Israeli colonies. Approximately 750 acres of Palestinian land will be de facto annexed by Israel.

Map : © Jerusalem Task Force - NAD

Source: Palestine Liberation Organization, Negotiation Affairs Department, Gaza, http://www.nad-plo.org/maps/pre-emp.htm. Accessed February 2003. Produced by the Jerusalem Task Force. Reprinted with permission of the Palestine Liberation Organization Negotiations Affairs Department.

family members of alleged suicide bombers. The cabinet adopted this form of collective punishment in June and selected the first three candidates for deportation in mid-July.[120] Informed in August, they petitioned the High Court of Justice to stop their transfer. On September 3, the High Court approved the forcible expulsion of two of the individuals. The pair, siblings whose brother was assassinated by Israel allegedly for organizing suicide attacks from the West Bank, were summarily dumped on a sandy dune near a Jewish settlement in Gaza. Immediately thereafter, the minister of justice announced that there were other candidates for deportation and that they would be receiving orders soon.[121]

Amnesty International labeled the forcible transfers a "war crime" and wrote "the ruling effectively allows for a grave violation of one of the most basic principles of international human rights law—notably the right of any accused to a fair trial and to challenge any evidence used against them. . . . The unlawful forcible transfer of protected persons constitutes a war crime."[122] B'Tselem's condemnation was equally unequivocal:

> Punishing persons for deeds they did not commit—where the sole reason for the punishment is that they are relatives of individuals suspected of having committed crimes—constitutes collective punishment, which is prohibited by international law. This practice is part of Israel's long-standing policy of inflicting harm on innocent people, in which, for example, Israel has demolished relatives' houses and imposed extensive restrictions on Palestinian movement in the Occupied Territories.[123]

The High Court's involvement in upholding these two IDF policies was not an unusual occurrence. Writing in *Ha'aretz*, Gideon Levy noted that because the court

> validate[d] almost every action of the military in the territories and reject[ed] almost every petition filed by human rights organizations and other groups, the high institution shares in the responsibility for the most serious and cruel actions perpetrated by Israel in the territories. Almost the entire world is talking about war crimes, but [High] Court president . . . and his colleagues give the army's actions the kosher seal, or are silent. When the High Court of Justice rejected petitions on the targeted assassinations carried out by Israel . . . it opened the door to the daily liquidations we are now witnessing.[124]

Between September 2000 and December 2002, the number of targeted assassinations was ninety-seven plus seventy-one bystanders killed during the operations.[125]

Transfer: Mass Expulsion

Throughout the second half of 2002, there was increasingly open discussion in Israel about the option of transfer as a solution to the Palestinian problem.[126] Previously talked about only in private, the issue became part of the open public discourse. A group of former Israeli generals and settlers formed an organization in the summer of 2002 called Gamla. On its website, Gamla published a detailed plan ("The Logistics of Transfer") in which it spelled out all the necessary steps (including an international information campaign) required to expel the Palestinians from the Occupied Territories as well as the Palestinian Israeli citizens of the state.[127] Adding to the climate, Moshe Ya'alon, the new chief of staff, described the Palestinians as "like a cancer."[128] And revisionist historian Benny Morris suggested in an interview that transfer would merely mean finishing what the state's founders began.[129] The High Court's ruling that upheld the IDF policy of expelling relatives of alleged militants was widely viewed as a chilling precedent.[130]

In September 2002, respected U.S. analyst Helena Cobban wrote of the possibility of Israel's using the impending U.S. war on Iraq as a cover.[131] The Jordanian government was "panic-stricken" about the "nightmare" of hundreds of thousands of Palestinians being forced across the border.[132] The Jordanian government asked Tel Aviv for a public declaration that it would not expel the Palestinians during the U.S. assault on Iraq, but Prime Minister Ariel Sharon declined. Tom Segev wrote, "An evil spirit is infiltrating public discourse: the spirit of expulsion."[133] Nearly a year earlier, in a December 2001, a poll conducted by the Israeli daily *Ma'ariv* found that "50 percent of Israelis now favor 'transferring' the Arabs of the West Bank and the Gaza Strip to Arab countries" (see also Chapter 3).[134] Israeli historian Ilan Pappe, who devoted much of his career to researching events in 1948, wrote in October 2002:

> The [Al-Aqsa] uprising . . . has produced in the minds of Israelis—of all walks of life not only within the circles of the right-wing camp—the idea that "we have reached yet another fortuitous juncture in history where revolutionary conditions have developed for solving the Palestinian question once and for all." You can see this new assertion talked about in Israel: the discourse of transfer and expulsion, which had been employed by the extreme right, is now the bon ton of the center. Established academics talk and write about it, politicians in the center preach it, and army officers are only too happy to hint in interviews that indeed should a [U.S.] war against Iraq begin, transfer should be on the agenda.[135]

One article on transfer was written by Amira Hass, who published a lengthy piece in *Znet* magazine (from which the following is excerpted) in February 2003 in the aftermath of the January Israeli elections. She discussed the objectives of several new high government officials regarding transfer, how specific Israeli policies (e.g., closure, settler attacks, denial of movement, etc.) were aimed at making life for Palestinians so desperate that they would "choose" to leave. In addition, there were a number of what she termed "mini-transfers" (Hebron, Yanun, and others). She concluded:

> Until now Israelis and the international community have not shown much interest in the "mini-transfers" and other re-locations within the occupied territories. But opposing such illegal and dangerous prac-tices is extremely necessary, since the threat of mass expulsion is all too real. Recent developments in Israel are disturbing: fundamentalist and apocalyptic beliefs are on the rise, moral considerations have dis-appeared from politics and the IDF has devised new forms of oppres-sion. With international passivity and the absence of Palestinian lead-ers capable of guiding the resistance to the occupation, these are discouraging signs.[136]

The most pointed piece by an Israeli was written for *Ha'aretz* by Shulamit Aloni, who, until the 2003 elections, was a member of the Knesset and a government minister (Meretz Party):

> We do not have gas chambers and crematoria, but there is no one fixed method of genocide. . . . The government of Israel, using the military and its instruments of destruction, is not only spilling blood, but it is also suffocating. What other name can be given to the drop-ping of a one-ton bomb over a dense urban area, when the justifica-tion is that we wanted to murder a dangerous terrorist and his wife? The rest of the citizens, who were killed and injured, among whom are children and women, do not count, of course. How is it possible to explain the expulsion of citizens from their homes at three o'clock in the morning on a rainy night, then depositing bombs in the house, and then departing without warning? When those expelled returned home, the bombs were exploded and a brutal mur-der and destruction of property was thus committed. And what is the justification for what happened in Jenin? . . . . How many does one need to murder and destroy for it to be a crime? – A crime against humanity. . . . Curfew, closure, brutality, murder, destruction of homes of suspects. . . . Curfew and another curfew, arrests and more arrests, destruction of roads, brutality to the residents at road stops. Benny Alon (a minister in the present government), already said "make their lives so bitter that they will transfer themselves willingly."[137]

The fact that Israel has the power to expel the Palestinians is beyond doubt. The fact that there is historical precedent is unquestionable. And that the United States would do little or nothing if Israel undertook such a campaign seemed quite likely.

Israel: In the Aftermath of Reoccupation

How Israelis Envision the Future

Throughout the fall of 2002, the Israeli government repeatedly expressed satisfaction at its military success and vowed not to engage in negotiations with Palestinians until they unilaterally gave up their struggle. Not seeing beyond tomorrow, Sharon and associates seemed to feel that Israel's security and strength were greatly enhanced. Convinced that force was the only thing the Arabs understand and confident in the invincibility of their ability to inflict whatever force was necessary, the Israeli leaders had no concern about the humanitarian, economic, and social crisis in the Occupied Territories.

In despair over his government, Israeli commentator Gideon Levy appealed to his fellow citizens in *Ha'aretz:*

> Is it too much to ask Israelis to take a look, even a glimpse, at what's going on in their backyard? Are we even capable of . . . pay[ing] attention to what is happening in the territories under our occupation? . . . Israel continues to close its eyes, not to see, not to hear and not to know what it is doing to three million people who live less than an hour from our homes. . . . This crass disregard . . . is nothing short of criminal.[138]

Another analyst quoted from a recent book by Daniel Dor:

> "We did not see the millions of Palestinians who were placed under curfew, who were unable to go to work or to school, and who found themselves in the middle of a humanitarian disaster," writes Dor, who assigns the Israeli media a central role in this blindfolding process: "the Israeli press rarely reports what is really happening in the territories."[139]

A third Israeli wrote of the dominant myths that Israeli leaders created for the public, their unquestioned internalization throughout society, and the real intentions of the government:

> The conventional wisdom in Israel is that in 2000, the Palestinians rejected the "generous" Israeli offer for a permanent solution and its

readiness for a Palestinian state, and then the Palestinians initiated the outbreak of the bloody conflict . . . How absurd . . . . During the decade of negotiations, which began in 1991 . . . the Palestinian lands earmarked for that state shrank, and were carved up and divided . . . A bypass road? Land expropriations? Settlement expansion? Uprooted trees? Closure? What's all that compared to talk of Israeli readiness for concessions in some undefined future. Thus the myths became tangible and real—the myth of concessions like the myth of support for a Palestinian state. In January 1991, when Israel began using closures, both to deny freedom of movement for Palestinians into Israel and between the West Bank and Gaza . . . It's convenient to forget that when the closure order was given . . . it wasn't because of mass suicide bombings in Israel. . . . The annexation ambitions were made clear in the interim agreements. First, there was no definition of the areas from which Israel was meant to withdraw . . . signaling that there would be endless foot-dragging at every stage . . . Secondly, the occupied area was divided into three imaginary areas—A, B, and C. In area C, under full Israeli military and civilian control, construction was accelerated on huge by-pass roads and . . . the settlements. On the eve of the second intifada, some 60 % of the West Bank was defined as Area C, meaning off-limits to Palestinian planning and control. When the intifada broke out, the army and settlers worked together to cut off Palestinians from their lands and to tear up what they had planted. Now, the construction of the separation wall involves more land expropriations and destruction of tens of thousands of dunams of farm land, annexing some 30 water wells . . . In crowded Gaza, huge agricultural areas . . . have become fields of death: the settlements, after all, were put in the heart of the agricultural areas. Anyone appearing in any one of these fields is shot, according to the army's rules of engagement. And half of the Gaza coastline . . has been blocked to Palestinians.[140]

The writer then argues that when Israelis do consider the separation wall and the new settlements, they believe that these are "only for security reasons." "It is much more difficult," she writes,

to see the truth—which has perhaps been the [government's] intention since 1994: to use the cover of the myth, the negotiations, and the security talk, to reduce to a minimum, the necessary areas that remain for independent Palestinian development, and with Israeli military force, make the Palestinians accept a "state" that more or less resembles . . . [a] cantons plan.[141]

Israeli historian Zeev Sternhell expressed similar sentiments. Reflecting on the state's history from the time of the Yishuv through the October 1973 Yom Kippur War and its relevance to the current conflict with the Palestinians, he wrote:

> The same conception . . . addiction to force and a destructive culture of government . . . dominates Israeli thinking today . . . even though the Palestinian Authority is in tatters and the majority of Palestinians are begging us to let them go back to being the hewers of wood and drawers of water of the Jews only so they can put food on the table for their children, the Israeli steamroller continues to operate at full-blast, and innocent children, women and men continue to be killed. Those in power are not bothered by the fact that the IDF is recording the blackest page in its history. Indeed, why change a situation that makes it possible to go on ruling the Palestinian territories to the point where a reality without a solution is created?[142]

The myth of Israel's military defeat of the Palestinian terrorist infrastructure was shattered by two major suicide bombings in Tel Aviv on January 5, 2003.[143] There had not been any comparable attacks by Palestinians for months, but in December alone the IDF killed forty-five Palestinians, most of them civilians, and the repression of the reoccupation was felt in every corner of the West Bank. Still, no lessons were learned. Israel retaliated—in a first response—by closing indefinitely Palestinian universities; barring Palestinian officials from attending a long-scheduled conference in London hosted by Prime Minister Tony Blair (which was intended to institutionalize the PA reforms demanded by the United States and Israel); "further restrict[ing] the movement of Palestinians in the territories";[144] firing helicopter gunship missiles at Gaza City; and invading one of the Gaza Strip's refugee camps.[145] Commenting on the suicide bombings and U.S.-European efforts to restart a negotiating process leading to peace between Israel and the Palestinians, *Ha'aretz* editorialized:

> Ariel Sharon and his government have so far rebuffed every political initiative and have used the IDF with destructive brutality that harmed the Palestinian population and often contributed to fanning the flames of hatred and violence. Thus they also share responsibility for the continuing terrible bloodshed.[146]

The U.S.-Israeli Relationship and the Road Map

Despite the death of Oslo, the U.S.-Israeli alliance continued to flourish. In December 2002, George W. Bush's administration, eager to undercut those in the State Department who were promoting negotiations between Israel and the Palestinians, appointed Elliot Abrams as the National Security Council's point man on the Middle East. The selection of Abrams, promoted by the chairman of the Pentagon's Defense Policy Board, Richard Perle, intentionally reinforced those ele-

ments in the U.S. government that believed Washington should back
Sharon unconditionally. Perle had served as an election adviser to
Benjamin Netanyahu between 1996 and 1999, during which he coun-
seled the Israeli to scrap any and all peace attempt, to annex the West
Bank and Gaza, and to foster the immigration of as many Palestinians
as possible.[147] Abrams had consistently opposed the Oslo Accords and,
at the time of his appointment, made clear his opposition to any negotiations between Israel and the Palestinians. One Israeli analyst wrote in
Ha'aretz: "For the Government of Israel, the appointment is a gift from
heaven."[148]

On December 20, the United States vetoed a UN Security Council
resolution that was critical of Israel for a series of attacks on UN workers and facilities in the Occupied Territories. Three UN personnel were
killed and a UN World Food Program warehouse (in Gaza) filled with
foodstuffs was destroyed.[149] The depth of the U.S.-Israeli alliance was
further evident in mid-January 2003 as Washington prepared for war
with Iraq. It sent a high-level liaison team to Tel Aviv "for setting up the
infrastructure for communication and coordination among the IDF, the
Pentagon and American forces in the area during the expected war with
Iraq."[150]

Prime Minister Sharon made a seventh visit to Washington in mid-
October 2002, and Israel requested $12 billion in aid from the United
States in addition to its usual $2.64 billion. President Bush told the
Israelis in December that he supported the new request.[151] The favorable U.S. attitude on increased aid, like the appointment of Abrams, was
considered in Israel (and elsewhere) as demonstrating Washington's
preference for the reelection of Sharon in the January 2003 elections.
One analyst wrote: "The announcement . . . concerning the positive
manner in which the United States views Israel's request for special aid
of $12 billion could not have come at a better time for the Likud."[152]
Ironically, at the same time, and in the context of U.S. war preparations
against Iraq for violating UN resolutions, *Ha'aretz* revealed that "Israel
holds the record for ignoring United Nations Security Council
Resolutions," having violated thirty-two resolutions since 1968.[153] This
did not trouble Washington. But to the prime minister's chagrin,
President Bush handed him a "road map" outlining steps to a
Palestinian state to be in place by the end of 2005.[154]

The essentials of the proposal were hammered out by the Quartet of
the United States, Russia, the European Union, and the United
Nations.[155] It included a three-stage process. During the first stage, the
Palestinians were required to initiate extensive institutional reforms,
including establishment of a prime ministership (i.e., deposing Arafat),

holding elections, and forswearing violent resistance. Nowhere was it spelled out what Palestinians could expect to achieve in return for fulfilling these demands. Israel was requested to halt military activities in civilian areas and freeze settlement construction. The second stage called for a monitoring body composed of members of the Quartet, Palestinian-Israeli negotiations and security cooperation, and restoration of Arab state links to Israel. The third stage called for the establishment of a provisional Palestinian state in the West Bank and Gaza and provided for the possibility of future negotiations about permanent borders that remained undefined. Eventually, there was to be a fourth stage in which an international conference would convene to discuss agreements on Jerusalem, refugees, borders, and settlements—again without any clarity concerning what goals the Palestinians could anticipate achieving.

The road map was even weaker than the DOP.[156] Two prominent U.S. analysts, writing in the *New York Times*, said of the proposal: it "has a little of everything except what is needed most: a detailed blueprint of a comprehensive political settlement and a realistic, internationally monitored way of getting there."[157] Yet despite its overwhelming bias in favor of Israel, Sharon was incensed.[158] *Ha'aretz* reported that "Sharon and his advisors are currently drafting a formulation effectively to torpedo the American plan without making it appear as if that was their intention."[159] One Israeli analyst dismissed the U.S. proposal as "an empty shell . . . that won't be implemented and will join the shelved Clinton, Mitchell, Tenet, and Zinni plans."[160]

In early November 2002, the Labor-Likud unity government of Sharon and Peres collapsed in a dispute over the budget. Sharon appointed Benjamin Netanyahu as foreign minister, called for new elections in late January 2003, and immediately asked Washington for a diplomatic timeout until after the Likud primaries. The Bush administration readily agreed to freeze the road map until after the national elections and the formation of a new Israeli government.[161] In addition, the United States informed Israel that it now considered invalid an agreement that had been worked out in June 2001 by Secretary of State Colin Powell and Shimon Peres (the foreign minister at the time) for a freeze on settlement activity.[162] In a matter of days, Washington negated its own peace proposal—the road map—and gave the green light to Tel Aviv to proceed with settlement construction. Both were additional signals of Washington's preference for Sharon in the coming Israeli elections.

Sharon presented his revisions of the road map in a speech on December 4, 2002, at the Institute of Policy and Strategy's Herzliya conference.[163] He declared that (1) the PA had to comply with demands for security reforms as a precondition to any other step; (2) Israel would not agree to move forward on the road map unless the PA fully met its obligations; and (3) no final status issues would be addressed during the first stage and would be delayed until Israel was ready.[164] One Israeli analyst described the conditions as "something like those the Serbs demanded of the Bosnians."[165] Sharon further indicated that Israel could accept a Palestinian entity on 42 percent of the West Bank (minus Jerusalem) and Gaza.[166] Another Israeli analyst aptly summed up the prime minister's intentions: "its numerous conditions and demands . . . conceal a hidden design—to prolong Israel's occupation and derail the diplomatic process initiated by the U.S."[167] Akiva Eldar wrote:

> Ariel Sharon's principle [is that] the territorial contiguity of the Palestinian state need not be on the ground. It can be over it—on bridges—or under it—in tunnels—in something Sharon refers to as "transportation contiguity." . . . There won't be any elections in the Palestine Authority except for parliament. . . . The Israeli government refuses to allow the European Union, United Nations and Russia to track progress made from one stage of the plan to the next. Israel demands that those three Quartet members adopt the more modest role of helping the United States.[168]

The Palestinians were not happy about the road map either, although for different reasons. Whereas Tel Aviv saw the plan as undermining its fundamental interests in retaining control over the Occupied Territories, the Palestinians saw it as a road*block* to the realization of their legitimate rights. Hanan Ashrawi wrote a somber, incisive critique:

> The "road map" requires a serious Palestinian assessment. . . . From the conceptual, procedural, and substantive point of view . . . the plan still assumes that *gradualism* in the form of a phased approach is [workable] . . . [but] only an *acceleration of the time-frame* would prevent the negative exploitation of the time bought by Israel by deliberate obstructionism. This is especially true of a process that is *"Performance-Based"* instead of relying on clear and objective criteria, requirements and timelines. Combined with *conditionality* . . . the process becomes subject to an endless reservoir of Israeli preconditions that are essentially impossible to fulfill. . . . The *disparity* in conditions and lack of parity in framing the rights and responsibilities of both parties stem from ignoring the *culpability of the occupation*. . . . The unbridled use of force by the Israeli occupation forces . . . has rendered *reciprocity* completely inapplicable and unfair. . . . The glaring lack of *arbitration* and clearly defined mechanisms of *accountability* would render the role of *third parties* largely symbolic, hence

ineffective. . . . The *timing* and the unspecified *mandate* of the "monitoring mechanisms" betray a feeble effort at doing too little too late. . . . The logic of the previous peace process has proved to be a failure, not least in its insistence on *bilateralism* as a means of "conflict resolution.". . . If *multilateralism* is the global mechanism for collective responsibility . . . then the monitoring mechanism of the road map must embody such an approach both in form and substance. . . . The UN must remain the reference. . . . In this way, the micromanagement of and *interference* in Palestinian realities would become legitimate as a form of *positive intervention.* . . . Israel . . . must be held accountable in accordance with the Fourth Geneva Convention and other relevant international charters and agreements. . . . *Selectivity* in citing the Tenet work plan and the Mitchell plan (however inadequate) will also become an encouragement for further Israeli contempt and non-compliance. The most dangerous implications of this approach are in its handling of the Israeli *settlement policy.* . . . Prejudicial and illegal Israeli measures in *Jerusalem* also require firm and immediate intervention pertaining to the siege and isolation, settlement activity, closure of Palestinian institutions, home demolitions, withholding of building permits and ID confiscation. . . . The state with "provisional borders [Israel]," while a unique invention, still offers no promise and no *guarantees* that the interim would not become permanent. . . . Unless the road map clearly spells out the June 4, 1967 borders as being the boundaries of the Palestinian state, the whole exercise runs the risk of generating further conflict and serving Sharon's plans of further land theft and expansion.[169]

The road map, then, did not rectify Oslo's mistakes; rather, it offered the Palestinians even less. Yet the Israeli government deemed it unacceptable. Nevertheless, if the past is prologue, concerning the fate of the road map and the national goals of the Palestinians, it could be assumed that Israel's power compared to Palestinian powerlessness would negate the rights and aspirations of the Palestinians in favor of Tel Aviv's interests, with implicit, if not explicit, support from Washington.

Internal Politics and Elections

On January 28, 2003, Israeli voters went to the polls and gave Ariel Sharon and the Likud Party an overwhelming victory in winning thirty-eight seats in the Knesset to the Labor Party's nineteen. Considering the scandals that plagued Sharon during the campaign, the myriad social problems facing Israel at the time, and the fact that Sharon's Labor Party competitor, Amram Mitzna, pledged to withdraw from most of the Occupied Territories with or without an agreement with the

Palestinians, the outcome suggested that the Israeli public was more comfortable with an elusive "victory" via force over the Palestinians than with a negotiated peace and normalization.[170]

Throughout February 2003, Sharon maneuvered among nine of the twelve other parties (the three Arab parties were, as always, excluded) in the 16th Knesset to form a governing coalition. The coalition was necessary to provide the Likud Party with a parliamentary majority in the Knesset without which it could not govern. Late that month the prime minister announced his government: Likud's thirty-eight seats grew to forty when Yisrael b'Aliya (with two seats) merged with the majority party. Three other parties accepted the prime minister's invitation: Shinui with fifteen seats, the National Religious Party (NRP) with six seats, and the National Union with seven seats. This gave the ruling coalition a total of sixty-eight seats in the 120-member Knesset.

The NRP is officially opposed to a Palestinian state. National Union, which incorporated Moledet and Tkuma, advocates transfer of the Palestinians. Shinui's platform was focused on separating religion from the state and had little to say about the Palestinians. The three right-wing parties not in the government (Shas, United Torah Judaism, and One Nation) held nineteen seats altogether, support transfer (Shas more or less depending on circumstances), and can be counted on to vote with the government on any issue dealing harshly with the Palestinians. The opposition consisted of Labor and Meretz, center-left parties, that together had only twenty-five seats, whereas the three Arab parties (United Arab List, Balad, and Hadash) had only eight seats among them.[171] It was the most right-wing government in Israel's history and boded ill indeed for any just settlement with the Palestinians. On the contrary, it may lead to a catastrophic situation for them.

Israel's power indeed seemed overwhelming in every sphere. It acted with impunity in all matters. Its military, diplomatic, economic, and political strength appeared unchallengeable. Yet appearances do not always provide the full picture. For instance, Israel's economy had been in serious decline. There was a 1 percent negative growth for 2002, unemployment reached 10.4 percent, there was a U.S.$2,400 fall in GDP per capita, a fall in the business sector of 3.1 percent (on top of a 2.4 percent fall in 2001), and a fall in exports (excluding diamonds) of 9.7 percent.[172] In addition, many of Israel's traditional European allies opposed its approach to the Palestinians and took both subtle and strong actions (including economic embargoes and suspension of arms sales) to register their displeasure.[173] More important, however, was the emergence of a different kind of power.

Conclusion: Power of a Different Kind

The hope of a secure and livable world lies with disciplined noncon-
formists who are dedicated to justice, peace and brotherhood.
—Martin Luther King Jr.

Justice is truth in action.

—Benjamin Disraeli

Justice is a certain rectitude of mind whereby a man does what he
ought to do in the circumstances confronting him.
—St. Thomas Aquinas

The foregoing has demonstrated that in terms of conventional power
politics and realpolitik, the Palestinians have little chance of obtaining
even their most minimal objectives and rights. But despite the continued existence of military might, state terrorism, economic weapons, and
all the traditional modalities of power, this is a different era. Globalism
tends to have a bad name, and rightly so when powerful multinationals
exploit and impoverish two-thirds of the globe for the enrichment of a
very few. Yet globalism also involves the globalization of information,
transnational human rights organizations, international solidarity movements, and so on. Although the Palestinians are isolated in the corridors
of traditional power, they are not alone among progressive grassroots
organizations around the globe. Groups that have learned of their plight
and have the capacity to empathize with others are working to inform
and mobilize their fellow citizens to create grassroots movements in
support of the Palestinians. It is my belief that the potential inherent in
such movements can and will have an important impact on global politics, including the question of Palestine, in the coming years.

In these final pages, then, I will consider several grassroots groups,
although there are such a plethora that space does not permit doing justice to each. Primarily, I will look at several Israeli, U.S., and international organizations that I think are most effective. Omission of a particular group does not mean that it is unimportant. Different groups
choose various types of activism and distinct issues on which to focus,
but all, especially taken together, have significance.

The North American office of the International Solidarity
Movement (ISM) originated in the 1960s to support the African
American civil rights movement. Today it trains and deploys individuals from the United States and other countries to carry out nonviolent
direct action as a means to oppose and end Israel's occupation. ISM
sends delegations of activists to work in solidarity with Palestinians,

engaging in such activities as dismantling earthen roadblocks, taking over checkpoints, visiting Palestinians in their homes, providing medical assistance, delivering food and medicine, escorting people who must move despite curfews and closures, rebuilding demolished homes, and many other services. Mustafa Barghouti, a Palestinian physician and head of the Medical Relief Committees, wrote the following about what the work of these people means to Palestinians:

> There is one aspect in which this intifada differs from the first. It has demonstrated the amazing power of people, foreigners, who come here to participate in the Palestinian struggle for justice and independence. Since September 2000, approximately 3,200 people of different nationalities have [come]. . . . Most of these activists arrived here directly from North America, Europe and Scandinavia. . . . The fact that they have come, in such numbers and at their own expense is quite frankly amazing. . . . They also made a tremendous contribution to Palestine and the Palestinian people because of the rest of the world's failure. . . . We have pleaded for international protection. It was not UN troops in smart uniforms who took up positions in our villages and cities, nor was it American soldiers. . . . It was individuals who responded to our calls, and small groups from trade unions and churches, anti-globalization activists, committees from the world social forum, Jewish and Christian groups opposed to the occupation . . . as well as those belonging to Palestinian solidarity groups. These people came, even at the risk of injury, arrest and deportation to stand up to the Israeli occupation, by the Palestinians' side. . . . I think these people are examples of the world's new generation (irrespective of age), and the positive side of globalization. . . . These people have an amazing power. . . . They are the ones that give us confidence that we will be victorious in the struggle for our freedom and independence.[174]

The Christian Peacemaker Teams (see Chapter 4) act very much like the ISM, and they have remained in Hebron during the entire period of the intifada.

Another movement, of a different nature, but also significant, is the divestment campaign. It took its inspiration from the divestment drive initiated by antiapartheid activists who worked to transform South Africa from a race-based state to a secular democracy. The Divest from Israel Campaign was launched in 2001 on major U.S. university campuses, including Harvard, the Massachusetts Institute of Technology (where some 565 signed), Princeton, Tufts, Cornell, and the University of California campuses (where more than 7,000 faculty and students signed), all told some fifty U.S. universities. Petitions, typically initiated by faculty, called for their universities to terminate their investments in Israel. Although no university actually divested from Israel, the debate raged on most campuses and served to inform many who were unaware of the extent of their university's holdings in Israel (e.g., Harvard reportedly has $600 million invested in Israel)[175] or of the situation of the Palestinians under Israeli occupation.

The Boycott Israeli Goods Campaign is an international movement to stop governments from importing products that originate in the Occupied Territories and increasingly from Israel in general. Where governments fail to respond, it works to inform citizens of how to identify the origin of products and encourages them not to purchase. There are also specific campaigns to boycott Starbucks, Caterpillar, Intel, Coca-Cola, and numerous other companies, all of which have strong economic links (and, in the case of Caterpillar, military ties) with Israel. Both the divestment and boycott campaigns have been particularly successful in Europe.

The Cultural Boycott of Israel originated in the United Kingdom but has spread elsewhere, including the United States. It is aimed at denying Israeli academics, artists, musicians, and others the privileged position they enjoy in working and participating in European and North American institutions. It is based on the concept that because Israel is a democracy its citizens are responsible for government actions against the Palestinians. There are various aspects to the general movement, including the Academic Boycott, the Sports Boycott, and others. There is also an international Arms Embargo Campaign. One group that has been particularly active in organizing all the boycotts is Big Campaign (British). A French-based group that has been very active in the many boycotts and has initiated the Call for a Boycott of Israeli Scientific Institutions is Coordination des Scientifiques pour une Paix Juste au Proche-Orient. Global Exchange has for long been active in Palestine and has a current campaign called the Global Campaign to Rebuild Palestinian Homes.

The Palestine Solidarity Campaign is a British-based movement that is activist, informational, lobbyist, and coalition-building. It works on the boycott campaign, on the global campaign to rebuild Palestinian houses demolished by Israel, and the European arms embargo campaign, and it supports the refugees' right of return and highlights human rights abuses.

Several Israeli organizations that work on behalf of peace and justice for the Palestinians are of crucial importance to the grassroots movement for a different kind of power. Gush Shalom is the main Israeli peace bloc. It is politically oriented, progressive, and very activist. It has sister organizations in France, Germany, and elsewhere in Europe. Ta'ayush is an Israeli-Palestinian organization that is progressive and activist. Members of both Gush Shalom and Ta'ayush are constantly present in the Occupied Territories, working in solidarity with Palestinians. Yesh Gvul (There is a Limit) and Ometz Le'sarev (Courage to Refuse) are the main groups that support, advocate, and suffer imprisonment for their refusal to serve in the Occupied Territories. Two similar organizations are New Profile (a feminist group that focuses on antimilitarism in all forms) and Shministim (high school seniors who have declared they will not serve in the territories). All are supported by an international Refuser Solidarity Network. Rabbis for Human Rights is a singular deviation from the perspective of the traditional Orthodox rabbis (the majority of its members are orthodox). It supports peace with the Palestinians in a two-state solution. Women in Black is an activist organization that holds regular vigils to protest Israeli government policies vis-à-vis the Palestinians. It has sister groups in the United States, Canada, throughout Europe, and Australia. Bat Shalom is an organization of Israeli and Palestinian women who work for peace. The Alternative Information Center is a joint Israeli-Palestinian organization that provides information (e.g., the monthly *News from Within*) and continuous activism on behalf of the Palestinians. The Israeli Committee Against House Demolitions fights in court against demolition orders and helps rebuild demolished Palestinian houses. Matzpun petitions and organizes to support the boycotts against Israel.

Some activist Palestinian organizations include the Jerusalem Center for Women, the Palestinian Human Rights Monitoring Group, the Palestinian Center for Human Rights (Gaza), Sabeel (a Christian ecumenical nonviolent group), and the Palestinian Center for Rapprochement Between People (Beit Sahur—nonviolent civil disobedience). Palestinian groups are, of course, severely constrained in their ability to function due to sieges, closures, and curfews.

There are fewer organizations in the United States as compared to Israel that function in solidarity with the Palestinians. That is undoubtedly attributable to the political culture (see Chapter 7). One that has been particularly successful is the Palestine Right to Return Coalition (Al-Awda). It was established in 2000 and has a branch in the United Kingdom. It has mobilized support for the Palestinian refugees' right of return and/or restitution and has disseminated solid information about the Palestinian-Israeli conflict. The Campaign to End the Occupation emerged in late 2002 as a broad-based coalition of progressive groups. It is both informational and activist. A Jewish Voice for Peace is a San Francisco Bay Area–based group that campaigns for an end to U.S. military aid to Israel until the occupation ends, for the refugees' right of return, and for other issues. It is primarily activist. Jews Against the Occupation, a New York group, campaigns for divestment, engages in direct actions (e.g., it disrupted a Jewish National Fund benefit dinner), holds vigils, and organizes protests and demonstrations. It also is primarily activist. Another active U.S. Jewish group is the Not in My Name Coalition. It is based in Chicago and works to delegitimize and end the occupation. Brit Tzedek v'Shalom (Jewish Alliance for Peace), also Chicago-based, is an active group. American Muslims for Jerusalem is very active. The American Friends Service Committee (Quakers) has a strong informational campaign. Two grassroots groups, Sustain the Campaign (working to stopping economic and military aid to Israel) and Stop U.S. Military aid to Israel, are active throughout the United States.

The foregoing is only a sample of the many grassroots groups across the globe that care about the fate of the Palestinians and are working in a variety of ways, transnationally, to bring about a just resolution of this conflict. It is easy to be cynical when surveying the structures and processes of the existing international system. Yet I do not believe that it is utopian to envision an emerging global civil society in which every human life will be considered as precious as every other and with the same inherent dignity and rights.

A positive and just future for the Palestinians is intertwined with a better future for all the globe's citizens. Working in solidarity with the Palestinians also means struggling for a global order in which humane values of peace, justice, economic well-being, and environmental protection will be dominant; and racial, ethnic, religious, and national identities will be secondary to a concern for the welfare of the whole. It also means the delegitimation of militarism—in all its forms.

Notes

1. Tracy Wilkinson, "Palestinian Towns Wobbling on Last Legs," *Los Angeles Times,* December 30, 2002, quoting Saeed Zeidan, a resident of the village. For more on the policy of siege see Yehezkel Lein, *Civilians Under Siege: Restrictions on Freedom of Movement as Collective Punishment* (Jerusalem: B'Tselem—the Israeli Information Center for Human Rights in the Occupied Territories, 2001); B'Tselem, *The Siege* (Jerusalem: Israeli Information Center

for Human Rights in the Occupied Territories, n/d); and B'Tselem, *Policy of Closure* (Jerusalem: Israeli Information Center for Human Rights in the Occupied Territories, n/d).

2. Jennifer Loewenstein, "Khan Yunis: Before the Juggernaut," *Electronic Intifada Diaries,* October 9, 2002. The situation in Khan Yunis continued to deteriorate. In Rafah, also in southern Gaza, conditions were even worse. See, for example, Justin Huggler, "In Rafah, the Children Have Grown So Used to the Sound of Gunfire They Can't Sleep Without It," *The Independent* (UK), December 23, 2002; and Kristen Ess, "Report from Rafah Block 'O'," *Electronic Intifada Diaries,* December 19, 2002. On the issue of "free-fire" see Ron Dudai, *Trigger Happy: Unjustified Gunfire and the IDF's Open-Fire Regulations During the al-Aqsa Intifada* (Jerusalem: B'Tselem— Israeli Information Center for Human Rights in the Occupied Territories, 2002).

3. Gideon Levy, "Scenes from the Rubble," *Ha'aretz*, October 24, 2002. On the devastation of Jenin see Amnesty International, *Israeli Defense Force War Crimes Must Be Investigated/Shielded from Scrutiny: IDF Violations in Jenin and Nablus* (London: Amnesty International, November 2002), MDE 15/143/2002 (77 pages); and Human Rights Watch, *Israel, the Occupied West Bank, and Gaza Strip, and the Palestinian Authority Territories: Jenin: IDF Military Operations*, Vol. 14, no. 3 (E) (New York: Human Rights Watch) May 2002.

4. Amer Abdelhadi, "Nablus: The Intifada, Two Years and Still Going," *Electronic Intifada Diaries,* September 29, 2002.

5. Gideon Levy, "The IDF's 'Permissiveness' in the Territories," *Ha'aretz*, February 9, 2003.

6. An excellent analysis that is highly critical of Israel's policy is Zvi Bar'el, "The Politics of Irrelevance," *Ha'aretz*, January 14, 2003. Also see Yasser Abed Rabbo, "Israel Won't Let Us Reform," *Washington Post*, January 14, 2003. Abed Rabbo is the PA's minister of culture and information and was one of the Palestinians invited to a conference organized by the British government explicitly to deal with PA reform. However, Israel prohibited all the invited Palestinians from attending as part of a sweeping collective punishment for a suicide bombing in Tel Aviv. See Barnaby Mason, "Analysis: London's Palestinian Initiative," *BBC News* (online), January 14, 2003.

7. See the excellent analysis by Palestine Human Rights Center, *Waiting for the Unlikely: PCHR Position Paper on PNA "Reforms"* (Gaza City, Gaza: Palestine Human Rights Center, June 22, 2002).

8. See, for example, the analysis by Graham Usher, "Of Victory and Defeat," *al-Ahram* (Cairo, weekly, English), September 26–October 6, 2002.

9. Danny Rubinstein, "Analysis: The Waning of Yasser Arafat," *Ha'aretz*, October 30, 2002, and Arnon Regular, "PLC Strongly Approves Arafat's New Cabinet," *Ha'aretz*, October 30, 2002.

10. For an excellent analysis of Israel's intentions to prevent elections or any peace effort by the Palestinians, see Danny Rubinstein, "More Punishment," *Ha'aretz*, January 13, 2003, and Danny Rubinstein, "No Nighttime Arrests," *Ha'aretz*, January 27, 2003.

11. Ibid.

12. Aluf Benn, "Background: Enthusiastic IDF Awaits War in Iraq," *Ha'aretz*, February 17, 2003.

13. Menachem Klein, "The Origins of Intifada II and Rescuing Peace for Israelis and Palestinians," *Current Analysis,* Washington, DC, the Foundation for Middle East Peace, October 2, 2002.

14. Jerusalem Media and Communications Center, *Public Opinion Poll # 46: On Palestinian Attitudes Towards the Palestinian Situation and the Second Anniversary of the Intifada, September 21–25, 2002* (Jerusalem: Jerusalem Media and Communication Center, September 2002).

15. Danny Rubinstein, "The Intifada Is Becoming More Popular," *Ha'aretz*, October 14, 2002.

16. Jerusalem Media Communication Center, "On Palestinian Attitudes Towards the Palestinian Situation in General: Opinion Poll # 47," Jerusalem, December 2002.

17. Danny Rubinstein, "A War Against an Entire Population," *Ha'aretz*, October 21, 2002.

18. Gideon Levy, "Beyond the Golden Sands of Gaza," *Ha'aretz*, October 20, 2002.

19. See Amos Harel, "Analysis/Indiscriminate Death from the Air," *Ha'aretz*, December 8, 2002, and Kristen Ess, "Every Day Is a Major Invasion in Gaza," *Electronic Intifada Diaries*, November 18, 2002. For more on the October 8 raid, see Cameron Barr, "Israel Stokes a Cooling Conflict," *Christian Science Monitor*, October 8, 2002; Amos Harel, "Analysis: In Khan Yunis IDF Didn't Internalize What It Is Preaching," *Ha'aretz,* October 9, 2002; and James Bennet, "Sharon Calls Gaza Strike a Success; Says More Will Follow," *New York Times*, October 8, 2002. On December 6, 2002, forty tanks and helicopter gunships invaded Breij refugee camp, leaving ten dead and scores wounded. See Michael Wines, "10 Palestinians Are Killed in Israeli Hunt for a Militant," *New York Times*, December 7, 2002; Chris McGreal, "10 Killed in Raid on Refugee Camp," *The Guardian* (London), December 7, 2002; Justin Huggler, "Israeli Helicopter Attack on Gaza Kills 2 UN Workers," *The Independent*, December 7, 2002; and "Muslim Feast in Gaza Turns to Massacre," *Palestine Chronicle* (Jerusalem), December 7, 2002.

20. Ze'ev Schiff, "Gaza Was Indirectly Reoccupied," *Ha'aretz*, January 22, 2003.

21. Amos Harel and Arnon Regular, "IDF Kills 13 Palestinians in Biggest Operation in Gaza Since Start of Intifada," *Ha'aretz*, January 27, 2003; and Amira Hass, "Weapons of Light Construction," *Ha'aretz*, January 28, 2003. For a lengthy analysis of the incident and its aftermath, see Molly Moore, "Deep in Gaza, a Lopsided Battle," *Washington Post,* February 10, 2003.

22. Hass, "Weapons of Light Construction." This is a long and detailed piece and must be read in full to appreciate the untruth of the IDF allegations and the real reason for the raid—that is, it was carried out on the eve of Israeli elections and Prime Minister Sharon hoped to bolster his, and his party's, showing by a "spectacular" show of force against the Palestinians.

23. B'Tselem, *Statistics: Fatalities in the al-Aqsa Intifada: 29 September 2000–4 January 2003* (Jerusalem: B'Tselem—the Israeli Information Center for Human Rights in the Occupied Territories, January 2003). B'Tselem breaks down the deaths of minors as follows: 58 17-year-olds were killed; 51 aged 16

were killed; 48 aged 15; 41 aged 14; 37 aged 13; 17 aged 12; 11 aged 11; 11 aged 10; 6 aged 9; 10 aged 8; 4 aged 7; 5 aged 6; 3 aged 5; 3 aged 4; 5 aged 3; 4 aged 2; 2 aged 1; 1 6-month-old; 1 4-month-old.

24. B'Tselem, *Statistics: Fatalities in the al-Aqsa Intifada: 29 September 2000–4 January 2003*.

25. Palestine Red Crescent Society, *Total Numbers of Deaths and Injuries—West Bank & Gaza, September 29, 2000–December 31, 2002*, Palestine Red Crescent Society (accessed through B'Tselem website), January 2003.

26. For earlier figures on deaths and injuries plus good analysis, see Danny Rubinstein, "Almost No Sign of Regret," *Ha'aretz*, September 30, 2002; Palestinian Nongovernmental Organization Network, "Two Years of Intifada, Information Brief," *Palestine Monitor* (Ramallah: Palestinian Nongovernmental Organization Network Clearing House, September 28, 2002); MIFTAH, *Special Report: Intifada Update, September 28, 2000–September 6, 2002* (Jerusalem: Palestinian Initiative for the Promotion of Global Dialogue and Democracy, September 15, 2002).

27. Hillel Schenker, "Israel's Dangerous Crossroads," *The Nation*, February 3, 2003.

28. B'Tselem, *Statistics: Fatalities in the al-Aqsa Intifada: Data by Month* (Jerusalem: B'Tselem—the Israeli Information Center for Human Rights in the Occupied Territories, February 2003).

29. Hadas Ziv et al., *A Legacy of Injustice: A Critique of Israeli Approaches to the Right to Health of Palestinians in the Occupied Territories* (Tel Aviv: Physicians for Human Rights—Israel, October 28, 2002). Also see Hadas Ziv et al., *Medicine Under Attack: Critical Damage Inflicted on Medical Services in the Occupied Territories: An Interim Report* (Tel Aviv: Physicians for Human Rights—Israel, April 4, 2002).

30. Pekka Haavisto et al., *Desk Study on the Environment in the Occupied Palestinian Territories*, UNEP/GC, 22/2/add.6 (Geneva: United Nations Environment Programme, January 2003).

31. Ibid.

32. Ibid., pp. 102–103.

33. Ibid., p. 100; and see ARIJ, *Israeli Army Cut 130 Pine Trees and 20 Apple Trees on the Main Road Opposite al-Arrub Camp* (Monitoring Israeli Colonizing Activities in the Palestinian West Bank and Gaza) (Jerusalem: Applied Research Center Jerusalem, January 30, 2003).

34. Haavisto et al., *Desk Study on the Environment*, p. 103.

35. Gideon Levy, "As Ramon Was Launched into Space," *Ha'aretz*, February 19, 2003. In this piece, Levy examines many aspects of the desperate Palestinian situation and contrasts it with the infinitely better situation of Israelis. Also see ARIJ, *An Assessment of the Israeli Practices on the Palestinian Agricultural Sector: September 29, 2000–February 28, 2002* (Monitoring Israeli Colonizing Activities in the Palestinian West Bank and Gaza) (Jerusalem: Applied Research Institute Jerusalem, March 2002).

36. Haavisto et al., *Desk Study on the Environment*, p. 110.

37. For an excellent comprehensive analysis, see Rita Giacaman, Anita Abdullah, Rula Abu Safieh, and Luna Shamieh, *Schooling at Gunpoint: Palestinian Children's Learning Environment in War-Like Conditions*

(Ramallah: Ramallah/Al-Bireh/Beitunia Urban Center, December 2002, reprinted in *Electronic Intifada Diaries* [online], December 6, 2002).

38. Amira Hass, "The Other Nablus I Know" (interviewing H. S., who wished to remain anonymous), *Ha'aretz,* December 24, 2002. See also Ann Gwynne, "Mountain of Fire: Nablus Under Lockdown," *CounterPunch,* January 23, 2003. For more on the issue of freedom of movement see Yehezkel Lein, *Civilians Under Siege: Restrictions on Freedom of Movement as Collective Punishment* (Jerusalem: B'Tselem—the Israeli Information Center for Human Rights in the Occupied Territories, 2001); and B'Tselem, *Freedom of Movement* (Jerusalem: B'Tselem—the Israeli Information Center for Human Rights in the Occupied Territories, n/d).

39. Peter Hansen, "Frightened and Deprived," *International Herald Tribune*, October 9, 2002.

40. Ibid.

41. Rubinstein, "The Intifada Is Becoming More Popular."

42. B'Tselem, *Palestinians Held by Israeli Security Forces During the al-Aqsa Intifada* (Jerusalem: B'Tselem—the Israeli Information Center for Human Rights in the Occupied Territories, February 2003).

43. Ibid.

44. Ibid. See also B'Tselem, "For the First Time Since 1991—Over 1,000 Administrative Detainees" (press release) (Jerusalem: B'Tselem—the Israeli Information Center for Human Rights in the Occupied Territories, January 2003).

45. There are a variety of sources for reports on prison conditions. See Noam Lubell, *The Price of Overcrowding: Findings of a Visit to Kishon Detention Center, June 2002* (Tel Aviv: Physicians for Human Rights—Israel, 2002); Hadas Ziv, *These Worldly Bars: Maltreatment and Neglect at the Israel Prison Services Medical Center* (Tel Aviv: Physicians for Human Rights— Israel, March 2002); and Joseph Algazy, "Fear and Trembling," *Ha'aretz*, January 13, 2003, who examines Israel's policy and practice of torture. See also Defense for Children International/Palestine Section, *Quarterly Child Prisoner Briefing: November 1, 2002–January 31, 2003,* Jerusalem, Defense for Children International/Palestine Section, February 9, 2003; Yasser Akawi, *In Hostile Hands—Palestinian Prisoners at Megiddo* (Tel Aviv: Physicians for Human Rights/Israel, December 2001); LAW, *Hunger Strikes Threatened, Prisoners Tortured, Under-Age Female Prisoners in al-Ramleh* (Jerusalem: Palestinian Society for the Protection of Human Rights and the Environment, October 31, 2002); LAW, *Prisoners Attacked in Ketziot* (Jerusalem: Palestinian Society for the Protection of Human Rights and the Environment, February 4, 2003); LAW, *Lawyers and Prisoners: Poor Conditions in Ofer Detention Center* (Jerusalem: Palestinian Society for the Protection of Human Rights and the Environment, January 14, 2003); LAW, *Palestinian Children in Israeli Jails Face Hardship and Racism* (Jerusalem: Palestinian Society for the Protection of Human Rights and the Environment, January 30, 2003); and Chris McGreal, "Israelis Detain Hundreds Without Trial: Kafkaesque Nightmare Awaits Arrested Palestinians," *The Guardian* (UK), January 24, 2003.

46. Amnesty International, *Israel and the Occupied Territories: Mass Detention in Cruel, Inhuman and Degrading Conditions* (London: Amnesty International, May 2002) (AI Index MDE 15/074/2002), p. 23. Also see Noam

Lubell, *The Price of Overcrowding: Findings of a Visit to Kishon Detention Center, June 2002* (Tel Aviv: Physicians for Human Rights—Israel, 2002); Hadas Ziv, *These Worldly Bars: Maltreatment and Neglect at the Israel Prison Services Medical Center* (Tel Aviv: Physicians for Human Rights—Israel, March 2002); and Joseph Algazy, "Fear and Trembling," *Ha'aretz*, January 13, 2003 (examines Israel's policy and practice of torture).

47. Danny Rubinstein, "One Cause of Palestinian Anger," *Ha'aretz*, January 6, 2002 (discusses the deplorable prisoner situation).

48. Gideon Alon, "800 Prisoners Have No Beds to Sleep On," *Ha'aretz*, October 22, 2002.

49. John Ward Anderson, "Palestinians See New Threat to Livelihoods: Jewish Settlers Accused of Attacking Olive Crop," *Washington Post*, October 23, 2002.

50. For an excellent analysis of the decay of the transportation industry due to Israel's policies, see Atef Saad, "Road Warriors," *Palestine Report*, October 23, 2002. The statistics are staggering: during the two years of the intifada, the transportation industry lost $2 billion and declined to 10 percent of its previous capacity.

51. Jason Keyser, "Olive Harvest a Mideast Conflict," *Washington Post*, October 22, 2002.

52. Yehezkel Lein, *Foreseen but Not Prevented: The Performance of Law Enforcement Authorities in Responding to Settler Attacks on Olive Harvesters* (Jerusalem: B'Tselem—the Israeli Information Center for Human Rights in the Occupied Territories, November 2002), p. 3.

53. Ibid., pp. 3–4.

54. Ibid., p. 6.

55. Ibid., p. 6.

56. Ibid., pp. 6–10, and B'Tselem, Press Release, "Protect the Olive Harvest, Enforce the Law on Violent Settlers" (Jerusalem: B'Tselem—the Israeli Information Center for Human Rights in the Occupied Territories, October 6, 2002). Also see Editorial, "This Year's Palestinian Olive Crop Is Stained by Blood," *Palestine Chronicle* (Jerusalem), October 12, 2002. Gush Shalom, *Harvesting Olives for Peace* (Jerusalem: Gush Shalom, October 17, 2002); Jon Immanuel, "EU's Solana Meets Israeli, Palestinian Officials," *ABC News*, October 6, 2002 (ABCNews, online).

57. *Ha'aretz*, October 25, 2002, quoted in Lein, *Foreseen but Not Prevented*, pp. 8–9. For several other pieces that reflect the settlers' sentiments in their own words, see Orly Halpern, "'Palestinians Don't Exist and Never Will,'" *Ha'aretz* (Anglo File), November 15, 2002; Orly Halpern, "'A Theocracy Would Be Nice,'" *Ha'aretz* (Anglo File), November 15, 2002; and Charlotte Halle, "'Olives Are the Ammunition of the Arabs,'" *Ha'aretz* (Anglo File), November 15, 2002.

58. A good in-depth piece is Amira Hass, "It's the Pits," *Ha'aretz*, October 25, 2002.

59. Editorial, "The Settlers' Persecution," *Ha'aretz*, October 28, 2002. Also see Akiva Eldar, "The Constructive Destruction Option," *Ha'aretz*, October 25, 2002. Also see Uri Avnery, "All Because of One Small Olive," *Counterpunch*, November 5, 2002.

60. Amos Harel and Aron Regular, "Settlers Attack the Olive Pickers,"

Ha'aretz, October 20, 2002, and Anderson, "Palestinians See New Threat to Livelihoods."

61. Keyser, "Olive Harvest a Mideast Conflict." Also see Zvi Bar'el, "A Law unto Themselves," *Ha'aretz*, October 27, 2002, and Mayor Walid Hamad, "Settlers and Trash," *Counterpunch,* November 6, 2002; Justin Huggler, "Settlers Target the Olive Pickers in the Battle for Land," *The Independent*, November 2, 2002; Barbara Demick, "No Olive Branches in the Grove," *Los Angeles Times*, November 7, 2002; and Ian Buruma, "On the West Bank," *New York Review of Books*, December 5, 2002.

62. Palestinian Nongovernmental Organization Network, "Israeli Army Issues Prohibition on Palestinians Harvesting Olives," *Palestine Monitor*, October 22, 2002, and Chris McGreal, "Israeli Retaliation Targets Olive Harvest and Waterholes," *The Guardian* (London), October 23, 2002.

63. Lein, *Foreseen but Not Prevented*, p. 11, 11–19.

64. Ibid., p. 1.

65. Ibid., p. 18.

66. Danny Rubinstein, "The Tangible Fear of Transfer," *Ha'aretz*, October 28, 2002.

67. Ze'ev Schiff, "The Army Must Stop the Olive Thieves," *Ha'aretz*, October 30, 2002. Also see Ze'ev Schiff, "How the Olive Thieves Shamed Israel," *Ha'aretz*, November 11, 2002.

68. James Reynolds, "Israeli Party Helps Palestinians to Emigrate," *BBC News* (online), October 30, 2002.

69. Amos Harel, "At Least 12 Israelis Killed in Hebron Shooting Attack," *Ha'aretz*, November 16, 2002; Amira Hass, "Attack Stuns Arab Residents," *Ha'aretz*, November 17, 2002; Amos Harel and Ido Shai, "Hebron Ambush Scene Dubbed 'Death Alley,'" *Ha'aretz*, November 17, 2002; Adam Keller, "Promenade of Death," *Gush Shalom*, November 18, 2002; BBC, "Sharon 'to Bolster' Hebron Settlers," *BBC News* (online), November 17, 2002; Staff, "IDF Troops Sweep into Hebron," *Ha'aretz*, November 17, 2002; Editorial, "A Catastrophic Response," *Ha'aretz*, November 18, 2002; Aluf Benn and Gideon Alon, "PM Demands 'Quick' Changes in Hebron for Jewish Control," *Ha'aretz*, November 18, 2002.

70. See some of the articles in the preceding footnote. Also see Nadav Shragai, "Background: The Continuity of Hebron's Contiguity," *Ha'aretz*, November 18, 2002; Amira Hass, "Fear and Loathing in Hebron," *Ha'aretz*, November 18, 2002; Alan Philips, "Sharon Supports Settlers' Expansion Move," *The Telegraph* (London), November 19, 2002; Conal Urquhart, "Sharon Threatens to Expand Hebron Enclave," *The Guardian* (London), November 18, 2002; Moshe Gorali, "The Pressure Cooker Explodes in Hebron," *Ha'aretz*, November 20, 2002; James Bennet, "On Hebron Ambush Site, a New Settlement Rises," *New York Times*, November 18, 2002; Amira Hass, "The Shuttered Houses on Holy Days," *Ha'aretz,* November 20, 2002.

71. Esther Zandberg, "Pernicious Promenade," *Ha'aretz*, December 12, 2002; Applied Research Institute–Jerusalem, *A Concrete Arrow in the Heart of Hebron City* (Jerusalem: Applied Research Institute–Jerusalem, November 19, 2002); Amos Harel and Nadav Shragai, "Hebron Settlers Plan to Build 1,000 Units in New Neighborhood," *Ha'aretz*, November 19, 2002; Israeli Committee Against House Demolitions, *A Statement Concerning Israeli*

Military Demolition Order # T/61/02: Hebron Rehabilitation Committee (Jerusalem: Israeli Committee Against House Demolitions, December 8, 2002); Editorial, "A Tourist Promenade in a Battlefield," *Ha'aretz*, December 12, 2002; Arnon Regular, "IDF Starts Work on Hebron Promenade," *Ha'aretz*, December 10, 2002.

72. Editorial, "A Tourist Promenade in a Battlefield."

73. Meron Benvenisti, "The Never-ending Enterprise," *Ha'aretz*, November 22, 2002.

74. Frank Bruni, "Israeli Forces Raid 2 Cities in West Bank," *New York Times*, January 31, 2003; Amos Harel, "IDF Launches Month-Long Operation in Hebron," *Ha'aretz*, January 31, 2003; Gideon Levy, "House Arrest: At 40 Uthman Ibn-Afan Street in Hebron, the Curfew Makes 46 Men, Women and Children Prisoners in Their Own Home," *Ha'aretz Weekly Magazine*, January 31, 2003.

75. Arnon Regular, "Israel Razes 22 Palestinian Structures in Hebron," *Ha'aretz*, February 3, 2003; Justin Huggler, "Israeli Army's 'Hot Winter' Bears Down on Hebron," *The Independent* (UK), February 7, 2003; "Political House Demolitions," *Ha'aretz*, editorial, February 4, 2003.

76. Gideon Levy, "House Arrest," *Ha'aretz*, January 31, 2003.

77. Akiva Eldar, "Yassin's *Hudna*, and the Army's Broken Promises," *Ha'aretz*, February 4, 2003.

78. Ta'ayush, *Another Brutal Attack on Palestinian Farmers* (Jerusalem: Ta'ayush Arab Jewish Partnership, February 1, 2003). Information on this incident is from both Eldar, "Yassin's *Hudna*," and Ta'ayush though there is little difference between them—only that Ta'ayush provides more background.

79. Danny Rubinstein, "Humiliation Is More Than a Sum of Incidents," *Ha'aretz*, January 5, 2003. For a good general piece on humiliation, see "Israeli Soldiers Tell Palestinian Villagers 'We Will Do to You What the Nazis Did to Us,'" *Palestine Chronicle*, January 5, 2003.

80. Two reports that deal with these issues during the peace process are B'Tselem, *Maltreatment and Degradation of Palestinians by Israeli Authorities During June–July 1996* (Information Sheet) (Jerusalem: B'Tselem—the Israeli Information Center for Human Rights in the Occupied Territories, September 1996), and Yuval Ginbar, *Sheer Brutality: The Beatings Continue: Beatings and Maltreatment of Palestinians by Border Police and Police Officers During May–August 1997* (Information Sheet) (Jerusalem: B'Tselem—the Israeli Information Center for Human Rights in the Occupied Territories, August 1997).

81. On the human-shield issue, see Yael Stein, *Human Shield: Use of Palestinian Civilians as Human Shields in Violation of High Court of Justice Order* (Jerusalem: B'Tselem—the Israeli Information Center for Human Rights in the Occupied Territories, November 2002). Also see Chris McGreal, "Israel's Human Shields Draw Fire," *The Guardian* (London), January 2, 2003, and Romal al-Sweiti, "Occupation Soldiers Force Child to Act Like Suicide Bomber for the Camera," *Palestine Chronicle*, January 5, 2003.

82. See, for example, Yael Stein, *Soldiers' Abuse of Palestinians in Hebron, 3 December 2002* (Jerusalem: B'Tselem—the Israeli Information Center for Human Rights in the Occupied Territories, December 2002), p. 12.

83. Yael Stein, *In Broad Daylight: Abuse of Palestinians by IDF Soldiers*

on July 23, 2001 (Jerusalem: B'Tselem—the Israeli Information Center for Human Rights in the Occupied Territories, July 2001). Also see Yael Stein, *Standard Routine: Beatings and Abuse of Palestinians by Israeli Security Forces During the al-Aqsa Intifada* (Jerusalem: B'Tselem—the Israeli Information Center for Human Rights in the Occupied Territories, May 2001).

84. Stein, *Soldiers' Abuse of Palestinians in Hebron, 3 December 2002.*

85. Gideon Levy, "Wanted Men," *Ha'aretz*, November 8, 2002.

86. Nasser Shiyoukhi, "Palestinians Accuse Israeli Security," Associated Press, December 22, 2002. Also see Rubinstein, "Humiliation Is More than a Sum of Incidents," and John Ward Anderson, "Beatings Draw Palestinian Ire: West Bank Residents Allege a Recent Rise in Assaults by Israeli Border Police," *Washington Post* (Foreign Service), January 1, 2003. Anderson chronicles dozens of incidents of abuse and humiliation in addition to the lottery. It's an important piece, especially as it appeared in a U.S. newspaper. Subsequently, the paper editorialized on the subject; see Editorial, "A Brutal Routine," *Washington Post*, January 3, 2003.

87. Christopher Hedges, "Gaza Diary," *al-Awda News*, January 14, 2003. Amira Hass discusses this phenomenon in an article reporting the IDF's destruction of Rafah's two fresh water wells; see Amira Hass, "Danger: Rafah's Fresh Water Wells," *Ha'aretz*, February 5, 2003. On Rafah see Peter Beaumont, "The Lost Children of Rafah," *Dawn* (Pakistan), February 11, 2003; Kristen Ess, "Report from Gaza," *ZNet* (Z Magazine), December 19, 2002; and Kristen Ess, "Rafah: South Gaza Strip," *ZNet* (Z Magazine), January 6, 2003. On the issue of "free-fire" see Dudai, *Trigger Happy: Unjustified Gunfire and the IDF's Open-Fire Regulations During the al-Aqsa Intifada.*

88. Zvi Lavi, "Finance Committee Approves NIS 135m for Settlements," *Ha'aretz*, March 13, 2002.

89. Zvi Zrahiya, "Billions for Settlers 'Hidden' in Ministries' Budgets, MK Says," *Ha'aretz*, October 28, 2002. The ministries hiding money for the settlements included Israel Lands Administration, Transportation, Defense, Industry, Construction and Housing, Agriculture, Religious Affairs, Education and Culture, National Infrastructures, Income Tax, and Local Authorities. The article details the amount of money in each ministry.

90. Molly Moore, "On Remote Hilltops, Israelis Broaden Settlements," *Washington Post*, December 8, 2002.

91. Akiva Eldar, "Guarantees to Perpetuate the Occupation," *Ha'aretz*, January 6, 2003.

92. Peace Now, *34 New Settlement Sites Established Since '01 Elections* (Jerusalem: Peace Now, March 19, 2002; maps available from Dror Etkes).

93. Moore, "On Remote Hilltops, Israelis Broaden Settlements."

94. Yehezkel Lein, *Land Grab: Israel's Settlement Policy in the West Bank* (Jerusalem: B'Tselem—the Israeli Information Center for Human Rights in the Occupied Territories, May 2002) (emphasis added).

95. James Bennet, "Despite Violence, Settlers Survive and Spread," *New York Times*, April 28, 2002.

96. Ibid. Also see the superb piece by Amira Hass, "Five Rules Set by the Kingdom of the Settlements," *Ha'aretz*, January 1, 2003.

97. Nadav Shragai, "PM 'Quietly' Working to Allow Visits by Jews to Temple Mount, *Ha'aretz*, December 26, 2002; and Anat Balint and Nadav

Shragai, "American Magnates Finance New Temple Mount Campaign," *Ha'aretz*, December 31, 2002.

98. Lein, *Land Grab: Israel's Settlement Policy in the West Bank.*

99. Peter Slevin, "Bush Won't Press End to Israeli Settlements: White House Stance Leaves Palestinians Cold," *Washington Post*, July 28, 2002.

100. "Israel Plans Stepped-Up Settlement Activity," Agence France-Presse, December 4, 2002.

101. Amos Harel, "IDF Creating Buffer Zones Around West Bank Settlements," *Ha'aretz*, December 26, 2002, and Nadav Shragai, "All but 10 Settlements Want Electronic Fences: 'Smart' Fences Would Cost NIS 1 Billion," *Ha'aretz*, December 30, 2002.

102. Marc H. Ellis, *Israel and Palestine Out of the Ashes: The Search for Jewish Identity in the Twenty-First Century* (London: Pluto Press, 2002), p. ix.

103. Information on the wall gleaned from the following: Yehezkel Lein, *The Separation Barrier: Position Paper, September 2002* (Jerusalem: B'Tselem—the Israeli Information Center for Human Rights in the Occupied Territories, September 2002); Amira Hass, "The Villagers See the Fence as a Land Grab," *Ha'aretz*, September 30, 2002; Mazal Mualem, "The Security Fence Has Already Netted Some Innocent Victims," *Ha'aretz*, August 19, 2002; LAW, *11,000 Palestinians Between Israel's Apartheid Wall and Green Line* (Jerusalem: Palestinian Society for the Protection of Human Rights and the Environment—LAW, September 25, 2002); LAW, *Israel's Apartheid Wall: We Are Here, They Are There* (Jerusalem: The Palestinian Society for the Protection of Human Rights and the Environment—LAW, 2002); Isabelle Humphries, "Building a Wall, Sealing the Occupation," *MERIP Press Information Note* PIN 107 (September 29, 2002); and Palestinian Environmental NGOs Network, *The Apartheid Wall, Report # 1* (Jerusalem: Palestinian Environmental NGOs Network, November, 2002). A particularly useful piece is Michael Jansen, "A 'Terrible Wall' and What It Entails," *Jordan Times* (Amman, daily, English), November 28, 2002.

104. Humphries, "Building a Wall, Sealing the Occupation." Also see Mustafa Barghouthi, "Construction of Israel's 'Berlin Wall' and the Current Human Rights Situation in the OPT," *Palestine Monitor* (Ramallah), November 18, 2002; Palestinian Environmental NGOs Network, *The Apartheid Wall: Report # 1*. Also see "Beit Amin Fears the Metal Gate as 'Security Wall' Expands," *Palestine Chronicle* (Jerusalem), December 20, 2002.

105. Jansen, "A 'Terrible Wall' and What It Entails."

106. Lein, *The Separation Barrier: Position Paper, September 2002.*

107. On Israel's annexation to Jerusalem of Rachel's Tomb (located in Bethlehem), see Nadav Shragai, "IDF Plan Puts Rachel's Tomb Inside Jerusalem's New Security Borders," *Ha'aretz*, October 29, 2002; Nadav Shragai, "Rachel's Tomb to Be Annexed—De Facto," *Ha'aretz*, September 13, 2002; Editorial, "Grabbing Rachel's Tomb," *Ha'aretz*, September 13, 2002; Gideon Levy, "A Passion for the Grave," *Ha'aretz*, September 15, 2002; and Avirama Golan, "The Politics of Graves," *Ha'aretz*, September 17, 2002. For the relationship between the wall and the tomb, before the fate of the tomb was decided, see Nadav Shragai, "Rachel's Tomb: Beyond or Within," *Ha'aretz*, August 23, 2002.

108. Amnon Barzilai and Jalal Bana, "First Part of Fence Ready Only in

July 2003," *Ha'aretz*, October 23, 2002. See also Chris McGreal, "Tear Gas and Bullets Break Up West Bank Fence Protest," *The Guardian* (London), November 16, 2002.

109. Chris McGreal, "The 1M £-a-Mile Wall That Divides a Town from Its Own Land of Plenty," *The Guardian* (London), November 26, 2001. Also see Dominic Evans, "Britain Criticizes Israel over Settlements, Fence," *Reuters AlertNet* (London) (online), November 5, 2002.

110. Jansen, "A 'Terrible Wall' and What It Entails."

111. *Ha'aretz* staff and agencies, "IDF Razes 62 Shops in Village on Seam Line to Make Way for Fence," *Ha'aretz*, February 7, 2003; B'Tselem, "B'Tselem Calls on Defense Minister: Call Off the Demolition of the Nazlat 'Isa Market" (press release) (Jerusalem: B'Tselem—the Israeli Information Center for Human Rights in the Occupied Territories, January 20, 2003); Mohammed Daraghmeh, "Israeli Forces Demolish Palestinian Shops," *Washington Post,* January 21, 2003; Jonathan Cook, "The Bulldozer's Mandate," *al-Ahram* (Cairo, weekly, English), February 6–12, 2003; ARIJ, *Alarming Demolition Orders in Nazlat 'Isa Village* (Jerusalem: Applied Research Institute Jerusalem, January 21, 2003); LAW, *Weekly Roundup* (Jerusalem: Palestinian Society for the Protection of Human Rights and the Environment, January 16–22, 2003), pp. 3–4.

112. Daniel Ben-Tal, "A Village Divided," *Jerusalem Post* (Jerusalem, daily, English), February 8, 2003; and ARIJ, *Military Orders to Demolish 72 Commercial Shops and Houses in East Barta'a* (Jerusalem: Applied Research Institute Jerusalem, January 21, 2003).

113. Lein, *The Separation Barrier: Position Paper, September 2002;* LAW, *Israel's Apartheid Wall: We Are Here, They Are There;* Jansen, "A 'Terrible Wall' and What It Entails."

114. Susan Brannon, "Qalqilya and the Wall," *Electronic Intifada Diaries,* October 2, 2002. For more information on the wall see Yehezkel Lein, *The Separation Barrier: Position Paper, September 2002* (Jerusalem: B'Tselem—the Israeli Information Center for Human Rights in the Occupied Territories, September 2002); Amira Hass, "The Villagers see the Fence as a Land Grab," *Ha'aretz*, September 30, 2002; LAW, *11,000 Palestinians between Israel's Apartheid Wall and Green Line* (Jerusalem: Palestinian Society for the Protection of Human Rights and the Environment, September 25, 2002); LAW, *Israel's Apartheid Wall: We Are Here, They Are There;* and Michael Jansen, "A 'Terrible Wall' and What It Entails," *Jordan Times* (Amman, daily, English), November 28, 2002.

115. Lein, *The Separation Barrier: Position Paper, September 2002.*

116. Jansen, "A 'Terrible Wall' and What It Entails."

117. A very good exposition of the policy is Ben Lynfield, "Israel Tries to Deter with Demolitions," *Christian Science Monitor*, September 9, 2002.

118. Laura King, "Israel's Demolition Policy Strikes Hard," *Los Angeles Times,* February 13, 2003.

119. King, "Israel's Demolition Policy Strikes Hard." See also "Israeli Army Raids West Bank Camp: US Delivers Rare Rebuke [on house demolitions] to Ally," *Agence France-Presse,* January 4, 2003, for statistics through December. For analysis see Lynfield, "Israel Tries to Deter with Demolitions." See also Arnon Regular and Nathan Guttman, "IDF Razes More Homes

Despite Criticism from State Department," *Ha'aretz,* January 5, 2003. B'Tselem, "Buried Under the Rubble," *B'Tselem Newspaper,* December 19, 2002.

120. Peter Beaumont, "Israel to Deport the Families of Suicide Bombers," *The Guardian* (London), June 24, 2002, and Suzanne Goldenberg, "Israel to Deport Families of Militants," *The Guardian* (London), July 20, 2002.

121. B'Tselem, *Deportation of Family Members to Gaza: Prohibited Collective Punishment* (Jerusalem: B'Tselem—the Israeli Information Center for Human Rights in the Occupied Territories, September 2002). See also B'Tselem, *Summary of the Judgment of the Supreme Court Regarding "Assigned Residence" (HCJ 7015/02); 7019/02* (Jerusalem: B'Tselem—the Israeli Information Center for Human Rights in the Occupied Territories, September 3, 2002).

122. Amnesty International, *Israel/Occupied Territories: Forcible Transfers of Palestinians to Gaza Constitutes a War Crime* (London: Amnesty International, September 3, 2002) (MDE 15/134/2002). Also see Amnesty International, *Israel/Occupied Territories: Forcibly Transferring Relatives of Suspected Palestinian Suicide Bombers Would Violate International Law* (London: Amnesty International, July 19, 2002) (News Service no. 125, MDE 15/120/2002).

123. B'Tselem, *Deportation of Family Members to Gaza: Prohibited Collective Punishment.*

124. Gideon Levy, "The Court's Supreme Test," *Ha'aretz,* January 5, 2003.

125. These figures come from Palestinian Human Rights Center, *Statistics* (Gaza City: Palestinian Human Rights Center, December 2002). B'Tselem provides slightly different figures placing the number of targeted assassinations at "at least 86" with forty bystanders. B'Tselem, *Statistics: Fatalities in the al-Aqsa Intifada: 29 September 2000–4 January 2003* (Jerusalem: B'Tselem—the Israeli Information Center for Human Rights in the Occupied Territories, January 2003).

126. Boaz Fletcher, "Transfer—A Viable Solution," *Arutz Sheva* (Israel, Hebrew), September 5, 2002; Tom Segev, "A Black Flag Hangs over the Idea of Transfer," *Ha'aretz,* May 4, 2002; Editorial, "The Transfer Legacy," *Ha'aretz,* October 8, 2002; Mazal Mualem, "Top Officer Urges Law That Would Permit Expulsions," *Ha'aretz,* August 29, 2002; Nadav Shragai, "Transfer Banner Raised Again," *Ha'aretz,* October 5, 2002; Ali Abunimah, "The Growing Clamor for Ethnic Cleansing," *The Electric Intifada* (online), August 27, 2002; Martin van Creveld, "Sharon's Plan Is to Drive Palestinians Across the Jordan," *News Telegraph* (London), April 28, 2002; Gordon Thomas, "Ariel Sharon's Secret Plan to Remove Palestinians from Israel," *Globe-Intel,* August 20, 2002; Ilan Pappe, "The '48 Nakba and the Zionist Quest for Its Completion," *Between the Lines* (Israel, monthly, English) 2, no. 18 (October 2002); Will Youmans, "Israel May 'Transfer' Palestinians During the War on Iraq," *Counterpunch,* October 9, 2002.

127. Boris Shusteff, *The Logistics of Transfer,* Israel, *Gamla* (online), July 2002.

128. Robert Fisk, "How to Shut Up Your Critics Without a Single Word," *The Independent* (London), October 21, 2002.

129. Benny Morris, "A New Exodus for the Middle East?" *The Guardian* (London), October 3, 2002.

130. Aluf Benn and Amos Harel, "Security Cabinet Approves Plan to Expel Terrorists Kin," *Ha'aretz*, August 1, 2002; Moshe Reinfeld and Gideon Alon, "Court Okays 'Relocating' Two to Gaza," *Ha'aretz*, September 4, 2002; Nathan Guttman and Moshe Reinfeld, "State Department Blasts Decision to Deport Terrorists' Relatives," *Ha'aretz*, September 4, 2002.

131. Helena Cobban, "Stop Ethnic Cleansing in the Middle East Before It Starts," *Christian Science Monitor*, October 10, 2002.

132. See, for example, the analysis by Danny Rubinstein, "In Jordan's Nightmare, the Palestinians Arrive in Waves: Jordanians Are Always Asking American Diplomats About Their Fear That Israel Is Planning a 'Transfer Operation,'" *Ha'aretz*, October 28, 2002.

133. Segev, "A Black Flag Hangs over the Idea of Transfer." Also see Yossi Sarid, "Before Jewish Fascism Takes Over," *Ha'aretz*, October 28, 2002. Another excellent analysis by an Israeli scholar is Ran HaCohen, "Ethnic Cleansing: Past Present, and Future," *Letter from Israel*, Antiwar.com (online), December 30, 2002. Also see Stanley Heller, "Sound the Alarm on Transfer," *The Struggle*, December 23, 2002, online.

134. Danny Rabinowitz, "Talk of Expulsion More Ominous than Ever," *Ha'aretz*, May 29, 2001. Also see the commentary by Amira Hass, "Keeping a Lid on the Transfer Genie," *Ha'aretz,* September 10, 2001; quoted in Robert I. Friedman, "And Darkness Covered the Land," *The Nation* 273, no. 21 (December 24, 2001): 13-20, 13; Uri Avnery, "A Second *Nakbah*?" *Media Monitors Network* (online), May 19, 2001.

135. Ilan Pappe, "The '48 Nakba and the Zionist Quest for Its Completion," *Between the Lines* 2, no. 18 (October 2002).

136. Amira Hass, "Threats of Forced Mass Expulsion," *Znet* (online) (Z Magazine), February 2003. (This is a reprint of an article by the same title from *Le Monde Diplomatique,* February 19, 2003.)

137. Shulamit Aloni, "We Do Not Have Gas Chambers and Crematoria," *Ha'aretz* (translation provided by Zvi Havkin and made available on Gush Shalom's website), March 6, 2003.

138. Gideon Levy, "Eyeless in Israel," *Ha'aretz*, December 15, 2002.

139. Yossi Klein, "Shielded from the Truth," *Ha'aretz,* January 24, 2003, quoting from Daniel Dor, *Me'akhorei Homat Magen* [Behind Defensive Shield] (Babel Publishers and Keshev, the Center for the Protection of Democracy in Israel, 2002) (in Hebrew).

140. Amira Hass, "The Myth of the State and the Reality of the Annexation," *Ha'aretz,* February 12, 2003.

141. Ibid.

142. Zeev Sternhell, "Impasse as the Ideal Solution," *Ha'aretz*, October 11, 2002.

143. See, for example, Chris McGreal, "Bombings Reveal Limits of Israel's Militarism," *The Guardian* (London), January 6, 2003.

144. Aluf Benn, "Analysis: How to Hit Back Without Hurting US," *Ha'aretz*, January 7, 2002. Also Aluf Benn, Amos Harel, and Sharon Sadeh, "Israel, UK Row over Ban on London Conference," *Ha'aretz*, January 7, 2003.

145. See, for example, Jason Keyser, "Israel Closes 3 Palestinian Universities," Associated Press, January 6, 2003.

146. Editorial, "Terror and a Dead End," *Ha'aretz*, January 7, 2003.

147. Roni Ben Efrat, "Sowing the Whirlwind: Israel, America, and the Coming War," *Challenge: A Jerusalem Magazine on the Israeli-Palestinian Conflict* (Jerusalem, Israeli, English), no. 76 (November–December 2002); Kathleen and Bill Christison, "A Rose by Any Other Name: The Bush Administration's Dual Loyalties," *CounterPunch,* December 13, 2002; Ali Abunimah, "Yearning for World War IV: the Israel-Iraq Connection," *The Electronic Intifada,* October 3, 2002; Bill and Kathleen Christison, "Too Many Smoking Guns to Ignore: Israel, American Jews, and the War on Iraq," *Counterpunch,* January 25, 2003.

148. Nathan Guttman, "From Clemency to a Senior Post," *Ha'aretz,* December 16, 2002. Also see Matthew E. Berger, "Abrams Is Point Man on Mideast," *Jewish Telegraphic Agency* (online), December 9, 2002, and Laila al-Marayati, "The Biases of Elliot Abrams," *Counterpunch,* December 16, 2002. Abrams was also infamous for his part in the Iran-contra scandal under President Ronald Reagan. He was convicted for his crimes but pardoned by George Bush Sr. when he was president.

149. Stephen Zunes, "US Declares Open Season on UN Workers," *Foreign Policy in Focus,* January 13, 2003. This constituted the fortieth veto in three decades the United States cast to shield Israel from criticism.

150. Aluf Benn, "Israel, US Kick Off Liaison Operations Ahead of Iraq War," *Ha'aretz,* January 14, 2003.

151. Nathan Guttman and Aluf Benn, "Israel Delivers Special Aid Request to US," *Ha'aretz,* November 27, 2002, and David R. Francis, "Economist Tallies Swelling Cost of Israel to US," *Christian Science Monitor,* December 9, 2002. Aluf Benn, "Bush Favors Special Aid to Israel," *Ha'aretz,* December 15, 2002. The final official request was U.S.$2 billion less than the originally proposed U.S.$14 billion. See Nathan Guttman, "Israel Formally Requests US Aid," *Ha'aretz,* January 7, 2003.

152. Aluf Benn, "A Warm Relationship: Clearly the President Favors the Prime Minister," *Ha'aretz,* January 27, 2003. See also Aluf Benn, "Analysis: Full Back-up from Bush," *Ha'aretz,* December 22, 2002.

153. Shlomo Shamir, "Study: Israel Leads in Ignoring Security Council Resolutions," *Ha'aretz,* October 10, 2002.

154. James Bennet, "US Offers a New Design for Mideast Peace," *New York Times,* October 24, 2002; Aluf Benn, "Burns Arrives to Discuss 'Road Map,'" *Ha'aretz,* October 24, 2002; Aluf Benn, "Sharon Blasts 'Road Map,'" *Ha'aretz,* October 24, 2002; Aluf Benn, "The Road Map: Arafat's Pension, Sharon's Settlements," *Ha'aretz,* October 24, 2002; Ross Dunn, "US Vision for Peace Dismissed by Sharon," *Sydney Morning Herald* (Australia), October 23, 2002.

155. The Quartet consists of the United States, the European Union (EU), the United Nations, and Russia. It came together in Madrid on April 10, 2002, when Secretary of State Colin Powell was en route to Israel and the Occupied Territories. In Madrid, he met with Javier Solana (EU high representative for common foreign and security policy), Josep Pique (Spanish foreign minister; at the time Spain was rotating head of the EU), Igor Ivanov (Russian foreign min-

ister), and Kofi Annan (UN Secretary-General). The four parties hammered out a joint statement on the conflict and agreed to coordinate future efforts for peace. For a (partial) transcript of the statement, see *Communique on the Situation in the Occupied Territories*, Washington, DC, April 10, 2002, reprinted in *Journal of Palestine Studies* 31, no. 4 (summer 2002): 177–178. Also available at U.S. State Department website. On September 17, 2002, the Quartet issued a three-phase plan for an Israeli-Palestinian peace entitled *Statement of the Quartet*, International Information Programs: Middle East/North Africa and Middle East Peace (Washington, DC: U.S. Department of State, September 17, 2002 (available online at usinfo.gov/regional/nea/summit/). Because both Israel and the United States do not wish any other actors to be party to negotiations, on October 15, 2002, the United States reissued the Quartet plan as a U.S. plan entitled *Elements of a Performance-Based Road Map to a Permanent Two-State Solution to the Israeli-Palestinian Conflict* available at Middle East Historical Documents, Mideast Web.org (online), entitled "President Bush's Draft Roadmap to Israel and the Palestinians," Ami Isseroff, ed., and on bitterlemons.org (Palestinian-Israeli Crossfire).

156. See, for example, Charmaine Seitz, "'Roadmap' Poorly Drawn, Say Palestinians and Israelis," *Palestine Report* 9, no. 18, October 23, 2002; Mark Heinrich, "Mideast Peace 'Roadmap' Gets Bumpy Ride," *Reuters*, October 24, 2002; Chris McGreal, "Bush Marks Out Route to Peace in Middle East," *The Guardian* (London), October 18, 2002; Aluf Benn, "Mitchell, Tenet, and the Road Map," *Ha'aretz*, October 31, 2002.

157. Gareth Evans and Robert Malley, "Roadblocks on the Path to Peace," *New York Times*, October 24, 2002.

158. See, for example, Aluf Benn, "Sharon Blasts 'Road Map,'" *Ha'aretz*, October 23, 2002.

159. Uzi Benziman, "Distorting the Map," *Ha'aretz*, October 27, 2002.

160. Benn, "The Road Map: Arafat's Pension, Sharon's Settlements." Also see Meron Benvenisti, "American Goals, Israeli Illusions," *Ha'aretz*, October 24, 2002.

161. Aluf Benn, "No Reply to 'Road Map' Till Likud Vote," *Ha'aretz*, November 8, 2002; Aluf Benn, "Sharon Asked US for a 'Diplomatic Recess' Until After Primaries in Likud," *Ha'aretz*, November 12, 2002; Akiva Eldar, "Sounds of Slumber from Washington," *Ha'aretz*, November 11, 2002; Aluf Benn, "US Agrees to Put 'Road Map' on Hold Until After Elections," *Ha'aretz*, November 13, 2002; Akiva Eldar, "The 'Road Map' Has Been Folded Up," *Ha'aretz*, November 14, 2002.

162. Aluf Benn, "US Backtracks on Peres-Powell Deal over Settlements," *Ha'aretz*, November 27, 2002.

163. For a text of the speech, see *Speech by Prime Minister Ariel Sharon at the Herzliya Conference*, Institute of Policy and Strategy, December 4, 2002 (available online at http://www.herzliyaconference.org).

164. For a preliminary analysis of Sharon's revisions, see Aluf Benn and Gideon Alon, "Sharon Calls for Revisions in 'Road-Map' Principles," *Ha'aretz*, October 29, 2002. For additional analyses after the speech, see Akiva Eldar, "Truth or Consequences," *Ha'aretz*, December 12, 2002; Uzi Benziman, "Sharon's Wink," *Ha'aretz*, December 15, 2002; Chris McGreal, "Sharon's

Deal for Palestine: No Extra Land, No Army, No Arafat," *The Guardian* (London), December 6, 2002.

165. Gideon Samet, "The American Obstacle," *Ha'aretz,* December 18, 2002.

166. Marcia Freedman, "The Sharon Plan Is in Place," *Jewish Week*, December 13, 2002.

167. Benziman, "Sharon's Wink."

168. Akiva Eldar, "People and Politics: War or No War, There's Little Time for US Peace Mover," *Ha'aretz*, January 7, 2003.

169. Hanan Ashrawi, *Road Map* (Jerusalem: Palestinian Initiative for the Promotion of Global Dialogue and Democracy, October 28, 2002) (emphasis in original). Also see Sam Bahour and Michael Dahan, "Roadmap to Nowhere," *Counterpunch*, October 28, 2002, and Editorial, "Quartet's 'Roadmap' Irrelevant to Dramatic Changes on the Ground," *Report* (Foundation for Middle East Peace, Washington, DC) 12, no. 6 (November–December 2002).

170. On the scandal that plagued Sharon, see Jeffrey Steinberg, Anton Chaitkin, and Scott Thompson, "Exposed: Dirty Money Schemes to Steal Election for Sharon," *Executive Intelligence Review,* December 13, 2002, available online; and Hannah Kim, "Follow the Money," *Ha'aretz,* December 20, 2002. *Ha'aretz* had dozens of pieces on this scandal as it was a sensational story in Israel. On Amram Mitzna's platform, see Jason Keyser, "Israel's Labor Party Adopts New Platform with Concessions to Palestinians," *Washington Post,* December 20, 2002. Again, there were dozens of stories in *Ha'aretz*. On Israel's social and economic ills, see Ruth Sinai, "Israel No. 2 in West in Social Inequality," *Ha'aretz,* December 3, 2002.

171. Yossi Verter, "Coalition Hits 68 as National Union Joins," *Ha'aretz,* February 27, 2003.

172. Moti Bassok and Lior Kagan, "1 Percent Negative Growth in 2002 Is Worst in the West," *Ha'aretz,* January 1, 2003.

173. See, for example, Associated Press, "Officials: UK Embargo May Ground Israel's Fleet of Phantom Jets," *Ha'aretz,* January 3, 2003; Peter Finn, "Germany Suspends Arms Sales to Israel," *Washington Post,* April 10, 2002; Jon Henley and Matthew Engel, "French Anger at US Policy on Israel," *The Guardian* (London), February 7, 2002; Amnon Barzilai, "UK Tightening Embargo on Israel," *Ha'aretz*, August 22, 2002; Michael White and Richard Norton-Taylor, "Straw [British Foreign Secretary Jack Straw] Provokes Row over Arms for Israel," *The Guardian* (London), July 9, 2002.

174. Mustafa Barghouti, "Those Who Give Us Hope," *al-Ahram* (Cairo, Weekly, English), 26 September–2 October 2002.

175. David H. Gellis, "Faculty Urge Divestment from Israel," *Palestine Monitor,* May 6, 2002.

Appendix:
Measurement and
Monetary Equivalents

Measurement Equivalents

Unit	Equivalent
1 meter	39.37 inches; 1.0936 yards
1 kilometer	0.62137 mile
1 mile	1.6094 kilometers
1 square meter	1.196 square yards
1 dunum	0.2471 acre; 1,000.0 square meters
1 acre	4.04 dunums; 0.4047 hectare
1 hectare	10.0 dunums; 2.471 acres
1 square kilometer	0.368 square mile
1 square mile	2.59 square kilometers

Source: Kate B. Rouhana, *The Reality of Jerusalem's Palestinians Today* (Jerusalem: Jerusalem Media and Communication Center, 2001), p. 107.

Monetary Equivalents (in 2002)

Shekels (NIS)	Dollars
NIS 1	$0.22
NIS 4.25	$1.00

Bibliography

'Abbas, Mahmoud (Abu Mazen). *Through Secret Channels.* Reading, UK: Garnet Publishing, 1995.

'Abd al-Shafi, Haydar. "Interview: The Oslo Agreement." *Journal of Palestine Studies* 23, no. 1 (autumn 1993): 14–19.

———. "Moving Beyond Oslo." *Journal of Palestine Studies* 25, no. 1 (autumn 1995): 76–85.

Abed, George T. "The Palestinians and the Gulf Crisis." *Journal of Palestine Studies* 20, no. 2 (winter 1991): 29–42.

Abu-Amr, Ziad. *Islamic Fundamentalism in the West Bank and Gaza: Muslim Brotherhood and Islamic Jihad.* Bloomington: Indiana University Press, 1994.

Abu Lughod, Ibrahim, ed. *The Transformation of Palestine: Essays on the Origin and Development of the Arab-Israeli Conflict.* Evanston, IL: Northwestern University Press, 1971.

Aburish, Said K. *Arafat: From Defender to Dictator.* London: Bloomsbury, 1998.

Abu-Sharif, Bassam, and Uzi Mahnami. *The Best of Enemies: The Memoirs of Bassam Abu Sharif and Uzi Mahnami.* New York: Little, Brown, 1995.

Abu-Sitta, Salman. *The Palestinian Nakba: The Register of Depopulated Localities in Palestine.* London: Palestinian Return Center, 1998.

Abu Zayyad, Ziad. "The Palestinian Right of Return: A Realistic Approach." *Palestine-Israel Journal of Politics, Economics, and Culture* 1, no. 2 (spring 1994).

Akram, Susan M. "Reinterpreting Palestinian Refugee Rights Under International Law." In Naseer Aruri, ed., *Palestinian Refugees: The Right of Return.* London: Pluto, 2001, pp. 165–194.

al Asali, Kamil, ed. *Jerusalem in History,* 2nd ed. London: Kegan Paul, 1996.

Amnesty International, Israel/Occupied Territories and the Palestinian Authority. *Five Years After Oslo, Durable Peace Must Be Based on Justice.* New York: Amnesty International, September 1998, MDE 15/77/98.

———. *Five Years After the Oslo Agreement: Human Rights Sacrificed for*

"Security." New York: Amnesty International, September 1998, MDE 02/04/98.

———. *Demolition and Dispossession: The Destruction of Palestinian Homes.* New York: Amnesty International, December 1999, MDE 15/59/99.

———. *The Right to Return: The Case of the Palestinians.* London: Amnesty International, March 30, 2001, MDE 15/013/2001.

———. *Broken Lives—A Year of Intifada.* London: Amnesty International, April 2001, MDE 15/083/2001.

———. *Mass Detention in Cruel, Inhuman, and Degrading Conditions.* New York: Amnesty International, May 2002, MDE 15/074/2002.

———. *Shielded from Scrutiny: IDF Violations in Jenin and Nablus.* London: Amnesty International, October 31, 2002, MDE 15/155/2002.

Amos, John W., II. *Palestine Resistance: Organization of a National Movement.* New York: Pergamon Press, 1980.

Andoni, Lamis. "The PLO at the Crossroads." *Journal of Palestine Studies* 21, no. 1 (autumn 1991): 54–64.

———. "The Palestinian Elections: Moving Toward Democracy or One-Party Rule?" *Journal of Palestine Studies* 25, no. 3 (spring 1996): 5–16.

———. "Re-defining Oslo: Negotiating the Hebron Protocol." *Journal of Palestine Studies* 26, no. 3 (spring 1997): 17–30.

Antonius, George. *The Arab Awakening.* New York: G. P. Putnam and Son, 1946.

Arafeh, Abdel Rahman Abu, et al. *Democratic Formation in Palestine.* Jerusalem: Arab Thought Forum, 1999.

Armstrong, Karen. *Jerusalem: One City, Three Faiths.* New York: Ballantine Books, 1996.

Aruri, Naseer H. "Early Empowerment: The Burden, Not the Responsibility." *Journal of Palestine Studies* 24, no. 2 (winter 1995): 33–39.

———. *The Obstruction of Peace: The U.S., Israel, and the Palestinians.* Monroe, ME: Common Courage Press, 1995.

———. "The Wye Memorandum: Netanyahu's Oslo and Unreciprocal Reciprocity." *Journal of Palestine Studies* 28, no. 2 (winter 1999): 17–28.

Aruri, Naseer, ed. *Occupation: Israel over Palestine.* Belmont, MA: Association of Arab-American University Graduates, 1983.

———. *Palestinian Refugees: The Right of Return.* London: Pluto, 2001.

Avishai, Bernard. *The Tragedy of Zionism: Revolution and Democracy in the Land of Israel.* New York: Farrar Straus Giroux, 1985.

Badeau, John S., et al. *The Genius of Arab Civilization: Source of Renaissance,* 2nd ed. Cambridge, MA: MIT Press, 1983.

Bahiri, Simcha. *Industrialization in the West Bank and Gaza.* Jerusalem: West Bank Data Base Project with the Jerusalem Post, 1987.

Baskin, Gershon. *Jerusalem of Peace.* Jerusalem: Israel/Palestine Center for Research, 1994.

———. *Negotiating the Settlements: The Success of Right-Wing Political Entrapment Against Peace.* Jerusalem: Israel/Palestine Center for Research and Information, November 1, 2000.

———. *What Went Wrong: Oslo—The PLO, Israel, and Some Additional Facts.* Jerusalem: Israel/Palestine Center for Research and Information, August 2001.

Beckerman, Chaia, ed. *Negotiating the Future: Vision and Realpolitik in the Quest for a Jerusalem of Peace*. Jerusalem: Israel/Palestine Center for Research and Information, 1996.

Begin, Menachem. *The Revolt: Story of the Irgun*. London: W. H. Allen; and New York: Henry Schuman, 1951 (rev. ed., New York: Nash Publishing, 1977).

Beilin, Yossi. *Touching Peace: From the Oslo Accord to a Final Agreement*. London: Weidenfeld and Nicolson, 1999.

Benvenisti, Meron. *1986 Report Demographic, Economic, Legal, Social, and Political Developments in the West Bank*. Jerusalem: West Bank Data Base Project, 1986.

———. *1987 Report Demographic, Economic, Legal, Social, and Political Developments in the West Bank*. Jerusalem: West Bank Data Base Project, 1987.

———. *Intimate Enemies: Jews and Arabs in a Shared Land*. Berkeley: University of California Press, 1995.

———. *City of Stones: The Hidden History of Jerusalem*. Berkeley: University of California Press, 1996.

Brown, Nathan J. *Democracy, History, and the Contest over the Palestinian Curriculum*. Washington, DC: Adam Institute, 2001.

Brownlie, Ian Q.C., ed. *Basic Documents on Human Rights*, 3rd ed. Oxford: Clarendon, 1992.

Brynen, Rex. "The Dynamics of Palestinian Elite Formation." *Journal of Palestine Studies* 24, no. 3 (spring 1995): 31–43.

———. "The Neopatrimonial Dimension of Palestinian Politics." *Journal of Palestine Studies* 25, no. 1 (autumn 1995): 23–36.

B'Tselem (Israeli Information Center for Human Rights in the Occupied Territories). *The Killing of Palestinian Children and the Open Fire Regulations*. Jerusalem: Israeli Information Center for Human Rights in the Occupied Territories, June 1993.

———. *Without Limits: Human Rights Violations Under Closure*. Jerusalem: Israeli Information Center for Human Rights in the Occupied Territories, April 1996.

———. *Legitimizing Torture: The Israeli High Court of Justice Rulings in the Bilbeisi, Hamdan, and Mubarak Cases*. Jerusalem: Israeli Information Center for Human Rights in the Occupied Territories, January 1997.

———. *Divide and Rule: Prohibition on Passage Between the Gaza Strip and the West Bank*. Jerusalem: Israeli Information Center for Human Rights in the Occupied Territories, June 1998.

———. *Legislation Allowing the Use of Physical Force and Mental Coercion in Interrogations by the General Security Service*. Jerusalem: Israeli Information Center for Human Rights in the Occupied Territories, January 2000.

———. *Revocation of Residency in East Jerusalem*. Jerusalem: Israeli Information Center for Human Rights in the Occupied Territories, 2000.

———. *Revocation of Social Rights and Health Insurance*. Jerusalem: Israeli Information Center for Human Rights in the Occupied Territories, 2000.

———. *Impeding Medical Treatment and Firing at Ambulances by IDF*

Soldiers in the Occupied Territories. Jerusalem: Israeli Information Center
for Human Rights in the Occupied Territories, March 2002.
———. *A Human "Defensive Shield" : IDF Uses Palestinian Civilians as
Human Shields*. Jerusalem: Israeli Information Center for Human Rights in
the Occupied Territories, 2002.
Carey, Roane, ed. *The New Intifada: Resisting Israel's Apartheid*. London:
Verso, 2001.
Carey, Roane, and Jonathan Shainin, eds. *The Other Israel: Voices of Refusal
and Dissent*. New York: The New Press, 2002.
Carmi, Na'ama, et al. *Oslo, Before and After: The Status of Human Rights in
the Occupied Territories*. Jerusalem: B'Tselem—the Israeli Information
Center for Human Rights in the Occupied Territories, May 1999.
Cattan, Henry. *Jerusalem*. London: Al-Saqi, 2000.
Center for Economic and Social Rights. *Progress, Stagnation, or Regression?
The Palestinian Economy Under the Oslo Accords*. New York: Center for
Economic and Social Rights, June 2000.
Chazan, Naomi. "Towards a Settlement Without Settlements." *Palestine-Israel
Journal of Politics, Economics, and Culture* (Jerusalem, Israeli/
Palestinian quarterly, English), 7, nos. 3, 4 (2000): 46–51.
Cheshin, Amir. *Municipal Policies in Jerusalem: An Account from Within*.
Jerusalem: Palestinian Academic Society for the Study of International
Affairs, 1998.
Cheshin, Amir S., Bill Hutman, and Avi Melamed. *Separate and Unequal: The
Inside Story of Israeli Rule in East Jerusalem*. Cambridge, MA: Harvard
University Press, 1999.
Chomsky, Noam. *The Fateful Triangle: The United States, Israel, and the
Palestinians*, updated ed. Boston, MA: South End, 1999.
Christison, Kathleen. *Perceptions of Palestine: Their Influence on U.S. Middle
East Policy,* updated ed. with a new afterword. Berkeley: University of
California Press, 1999.
Cobban, Helena. *The Palestine Liberation Organization: People, Power, and
Politics*. New York: Cambridge University Press, 1984.
Cohen, Michael J. *Palestine and the Great Powers, 1945–1948*. Princeton, NJ:
Princeton University Press, 1982.
Dajani, Burhan. "The September 1993 Israeli-PLO Documents: A Textual
Analysis." *Journal of Palestine Studies* 23, no. 3 (spring 1994): 5–23.
———. "An Alternative to Oslo? *Journal of Palestine Studies* 25, no. 4 (sum-
mer 1996): 5–19.
David, Shmuel. *Impossible Coexistence: Human Rights in Hebron Since the
Massacre at the Cave of the Patriarchs*. Jerusalem: The Israeli Information
Center for Human Rights in the Occupied Territories, 1995.
Davidson, Lawrence. *America's Palestine: Popular and Official Perceptions
from Balfour to Israel Statehood*. Gainesville: University Press of Florida,
2001.
Diwan, Ishac, and Radwan A. Shaban, eds. *Development Under Adversity: The
Palestinian Economy Under Transition* (Executive Summary).
Washington, DC: Palestine Economic Policy Research Institute and the
World Bank, 1999.
Doumani, Beshara. *Rediscovering Palestine: Merchants and Peasants in Jabal
Nablus, 1700–1900*. Berkeley: University of California Press, 1995.

Drake, Laura. "Between the Lines: A Textual Analysis of the Gaza-Jericho Agreement." *Arab Studies Quarterly* 16, no. 4 (fall 1994): 1–36.

Dudai, Ron. *Free Rein: Vigilante Settlers and Israel's Non-Enforcement of the Law.* Jerusalem: The Israeli Information Center for Human Rights in the Occupied Territories, October 2001.

———. *No Way Out: Medical Implications of Israel's Siege Policy.* Jerusalem: The Israeli Information Center for Human Rights in the Occupied Territories, 2001.

———. *Tacit Consent: Israeli Policy on Law Enforcement Toward Settlers in the Occupied Territories.* Jerusalem: The Israeli Information Center for Human Rights in the Occupied Territories, March 2001.

———. *Trigger Happy: Unjustified Shooting and Violations of the Open-Fire Regulations During the al-Aqsa Intifada.* Jerusalem: The Israeli Information Center for Human Rights in the Occupied Territories, March 2002.

Eban, Abba. "The Central Question." *Tikkun: A Jewish Critique of Politics, Culture, and Society* 1, no. 2 (1986).

Efrat, Roni Ben, Assaf Adiv, and Stephen Langfur. "Something's Rotten in the Nonstate of Palestine: Corruption Under Arafat, the Legislators Speak Out." *Challenge* (Tel Aviv, Israeli, monthly, English), no. 45 (September–October 1997).

Ellis, Marc H. *Toward a Jewish Theology of Liberation: The Uprising and the Future,* 2nd ed. Maryknoll, NY: Orbis Books, 1989.

———. *Beyond Innocence and Redemption: Confronting the Holocaust and Israeli Power: Creating a Moral Future for the Jewish People.* New York: Harper Collins, 1992.

———. "The Future of Israel/Palestine: Embracing the Broken Middle." *Journal of Palestine Studies* 26, no. 3 (spring 1997): 56–66.

———. *Unholy Alliance: Religion and Atrocity in Our Time.* Minneapolis, MN: Fortress Press, 1997.

———. *O, Jerusalem!: The Contested Future of the Jewish Covenant.* Minneapolis, MN: Fortress Press, 1999.

———. *A Year at the Catholic Worker.* Baylor, TX: Baylor University Press, 2000.

———. *Revolutionary Forgiveness: Essays on Judaism, Christianity, and the Future of Religious Life.* Baylor, TX: Baylor University Press, 2000.

———. *Israel and Palestine Out of the Ashes: The Search for Jewish Identity in the Twenty-First Century.* London: Pluto Press, 2002.

Elmusa, Sharif. "The Land-Water Nexus in the Israeli-Palestinian Conflict." *Journal of Palestine Studies* 25, no. 3 (spring 1996): 69–78.

Evron, Boas. "The Holocaust: Learning the Wrong Lessons." *Journal of Palestine Studies* 10, no. 3 (spring 1981): 16–26.

———. *Jewish State or Israeli Nation?* Bloomington: Indiana University Press, 1995.

Farsakh, Leila. "Economic Viability of a Palestinian State in the West Bank and Gaza Strip: Is It Possible Without Territorial Integrity and Sovereignty?" *MIT Electronic Journal of Middle East Studies* 1, no. 5 (May 2001): 43–57.

Farsoun, Samih K., with Christina E. Zacharia. *Palestine and the Palestinians.* Boulder: Westview, 1997.

Felner, Eitan, and Roly Rozen. *Law Enforcement on Israeli Civilians in the*

Occupied Territories. Jerusalem: B'Tselem—the Israeli Information Center for Human Rights in the Occupied Territories, March 1994. 109 pages.

Finkelstein, Norman G. *Image and Reality of the Israel-Palestine Conflict*. London: Verso, 1995.

———. *The Holocaust Industry: Reflections on the Exploitation of Jewish Suffering*. London: Verso, 2000.

Flapan, Simha. *Zionism and the Palestinians*. London: Croom Helm; and New York: Barnes and Noble, 1979.

———. *The Birth of Israel: Myths and Realities*. New York: Pantheon Books, 1987.

Friedman, Robert I. *Zealots for Zion: Inside Israel's West Bank Settler Movement*. New Brunswick, NJ: Rutgers University Press, 1992.

Frisch, Hillel. "Modern Absolutist or Neopatriarchal State Building? Customary Law, Extended Families, and the Palestine Authority." *International Journal of Middle East Studies* 29, no. 3 (August 1997): 341–358.

———. *Countdown to Statehood: Palestinian State Formation in the West Bank and Gaza*. Albany: State University of New York Press, 1998.

Ghanem, As'ad. *The Palestinian Regime: A "Partial Democracy."* Brighton, UK: Sussex Academic Press, 2001.

———. *The Palestinian-Arab Minority in Israel, 1948–2000: A Political Study*. Albany: State University of New York Press, 2001.

Gharaibeh, Fawzi A. *The Economies of the West Bank and Gaza Strip*. Boulder: Westview, 1985.

Ghareeb, Edmund, ed. *Split Vision: The Portrayal of Arabs in American Media*. Washington, DC: American-Arab Affairs Council, 1983.

Giller, Iris. *Death Foretold: Firing of "Rubber" Bullets to Disperse Demonstrations in the Occupied Territories*. Jerusalem: B'Tselem—the Israeli Information Center for Human Rights in the Occupied Territories, 1998.

Ginbar, Yuval. *Israeli Settlement in the Occupied Territories as a Violation of Human Rights: Legal and Conceptual Aspects*. Jerusalem: B'Tselem—the Israeli Information Center for Human Rights in the Occupied Territories, March 1997.

———. *Sheer Brutality: The Beatings Continue: Beatings and Maltreatment of Palestinians by Border Police and Police Officers During May–August, 1997*. Jerusalem: B'Tselem—the Israeli Information Center for Human Rights in the Occupied Territories, August 1997.

———. *On the Way to Annexation: Human Rights Violations Resulting from the Establishment and Expansion of the Ma'aleh Adumim Settlement*. Jerusalem: B'Tselem—the Israeli Information Center for Human Rights in the Occupied Territories, 1998.

———. *Routine Torture: Interrogation Methods of the General Security Service*. Jerusalem: B'Tselem—the Israeli Information Center for Human Rights in the Occupied Territories, February 1998.

Ginbar, Yuval. *Demolishing Peace: Israel's Policy of Mass Demolition of Palestinian Houses in the West Bank*. Jerusalem: B'Tselem—the Israeli Information Center for Human Rights in the Occupied Territories, September 1997.

Golan, Galia. *The Soviet Union and the Palestine Liberation Organization.* New York: Praeger, 1980.

Greilsammer, Ilan, and Joseph Weiler, eds. *Europe and Israel: Troubled Neighbors.* Berlin: de Gruyter Publishing, 1988.

Gresh, Alain. *The PLO: The Struggle Within—Toward an Independent Palestinian State.* London: Zed, 1983.

Grinberg, Lev. "In Israel, a New-Old Voice of Conscience Awakens." *MERIP Press Information Notes*, PIN no. 84, February 22, 2002.

Grose, Peter. *Israel in the Mind of America.* New York: Schocken Books, 1984.

Habash, Dalia. "Wadi al-Joz: In Focus." *Jerusalem Quarterly File* (Jerusalem, Palestinian quarterly, English) 1, no. 1 (1998).

Habib, Solange, Sydney D. Bailey, and Sam Daws. *The Procedure of the UN Security Council,* 3rd ed. Oxford, UK: Clarendon, 1998.

Hadawi, Sami. *Palestinian Rights and Losses in 1948: A Comprehensive Study.* London: Saqi Books, 1988.

Halabi, Usama. "Revoking Permanent Residency: A Legal Review of Israeli Policy." *Jerusalem Quarterly File* (Jerusalem, Palestinian quarterly, English), no. 9 (2000).

Halevi, Ilan. "Self-Government, Democracy, and Mismanagement Under the Palestinian Authority." *Journal of Palestine Studies* 27, no. 3 (spring 1998): 35–48.

Hallaj, Muhammad. "Taking Sides: Palestinians and the Gulf Crisis." *Journal of Palestine Studies* 20, no. 3 (spring 1991): 41–47.

Halper, Jeff. "Despair: Israel's Ultimate Weapon." *Information Brief no. 72.* Washington, DC: Center for Policy Analysis on Palestine, March 28, 2001.

Halpern, Ben. *The Idea of the Jewish State,* 2nd ed. Cambridge, MA: Harvard University Press, 1969.

Hammami, Rema, and Salim Tamari. "The Second Uprising: End or New Beginning?" *Journal of Palestine Studies* 30, no. 2 (winter 2001): 5–25.

Hanieh, Adam. "On Hold: International Protection for the Palestinians." *MERIP Press Information Notes*, PIN no. 40, November 28, 2000.

———. "Toward Submission or War in Palestine?" *MERIP Press Information Notes,* PIN no. 82 (January 26, 2002).

Harkabi, Yehoshafat. *The Fateful Choices Before Israel: Essays on Strategy and Diplomacy.* Claremont, CA: Keck Center for International Strategic Studies, College Press, 1987.

Hass, Amira. *Drinking the Sea at Gaza: Days and Nights in a Land Under Siege.* New York: Metropolitan Books and Henry Holt, 1999.

Hassassian, Manuel. "U.S. National Interests in the Middle East." *Palestine-Israel Journal of Politics, Economics, and Culture* 4, nos. 3 and 4 (1997–1998): 48–54.

Heller, Mark A., and Sari Nusseibeh. *No Trumpets, No Drums: A Two-State Settlement of the Israeli-Palestinian Conflict.* New York: Hill and Wang, 1991.

Hersh, Seymour M. *The Samson Option: Israel, America, and the Bomb.* London: Farber and Farber, 1991.

Hiltermann, Joost. *Behind the Intifada: Labor and Women's Movements in the Occupied Territories.* Princeton, NJ: Princeton University Press, 1991.

Hirst, David. *The Gun and the Olive Branch: The Roots of Violence in the Middle East.* London: Faber and Faber, 1977.

Hudson, Michael C., and Ronald A. Wolfe, eds. *The American Media and the Arabs*, Washington, DC: Center for Contemporary Arab Studies, Georgetown University, 1980.

Human Rights Watch. *Human Rights Watch Documents Repression and Intimidation by Palestinian Authority in Self-Rule Areas: Criticizes U.S., Israel for Neglect of Human Rights when Demanding Security Crackdown.* New York: Human Rights Watch, October 1997.

———. *Center of the Storm: A Case Study of Human Rights Abuses in Hebron District.* New York: Human Rights Watch, 2001.

———. "Human Rights Watch Policy on the Right of Return." *Human Rights Watch World Report 2001: Israel, the Occupied West Bank, Gaza Strip, and Palestinian Authority Territories.* New York: Human Rights Watch, 2001.

———. *Israel, the Occupied West Bank and Gaza Strip, and the Palestinian Authorities: In Dark Hour: The Use of Civilians During IDF Arrest Operations.* New York: Human Rights Watch, 14, no. 2E, April 2002.

———. *Israel, the Occupied West Bank and Gaza Strip, and the Palestinian Authority Territories: Jenin—IDF Military Operations.* New York: Human Rights Watch, 14, no. 3E, May 2002.

Iyad, Abu (Salah Khalaf) with Eric Rouleau. *My Home, My Land.* New York: Times Books, 1981.

Jansen, Michael. *The Battle of Beirut: Why Israel Invaded Lebanon.* London: Zed, 1982.

Jaradt, Ali. "Corruption Is Obstructing the Development of Our Society." *News from Within* (Jerusalem, Israeli, monthly, English) 17, no. 3 (April 2001).

Jarbawi, 'Ali, "Palestinians at a Crossroads." *Journal of Palestine Studies* 25, no. 4 (summer 1996): 29–39.

Jarbawi, 'Ali, and Roger Heacock. "The Deportations and the Palestinian-Israeli Peace Negotiations." *Journal of Palestine Studies* 22, no. 3 (spring 1993): 32–47.

Jarbawi, 'Ali, et al. *Third Annual Report 1 January 1997 to 31 December 1997.* Jerusalem: Palestinian Independent Commission for Citizens' Rights, 1998.

Jiryis, Sabri. *The Arabs in Israel.* Beirut: Institute for Palestine Studies, 1969 (reissued by Monthly Review Press, New York, 1976).

Kadman, Noga. *1987–1997: A Decade of Human Rights Violations.* Jerusalem: B'Tselem—the Israeli Information Center for Human Rights in the Occupied Territories, January 1998.

Kadman, Noga, et al. *Families Torn Apart: Separation of Palestinian Families in the Occupied Territories.* Jerusalem: HaMoked, the (Israeli) Center for the Defense of the Individual, and B'Tselem—the Israeli Information Center for Human Rights in the Occupied Territories, 1999.

Kahan, David. *Agriculture and Water Resources in the West Bank and Gaza (1967–1987).* Jerusalem: West Bank Data Base Project, 1987.

Kahl, Murray. "Corruption Within the Palestinian Authority." Report prepared for Congressman Jim Saxton (R–NJ) for use by the U.S. Congress to suspend aid to the Palestinian Authority under the Middle East Peace Facilitation Act, October 30, 1997.

Kaminker, Sarah. "For Arabs Only: Building Restrictions in East Jerusalem." *Journal of Palestine Studies* 26, no. 4 (summer 1997): 5–16.

Karmi, Ghada, and Eugene Cotran, eds. *The Palestinian Exodus, 1948–1998*. Reading, UK: Ithaca, 1999.

Kern, Kathleen. "Settler Violence and September 11: A Report from the Mean Streets of Hebron." *Tikkun: A Jewish Critique of Politics, Culture, and Society* (November/December 2001).

Kerr, Malcolm. *The Arab Cold War: Gamal 'Abd al-Nasir and His Rivals, 1950–1969*, 3rd ed. New York: Oxford University Press, 1971.

Khalidi, Rashid. "The Resolutions of the 19th Palestine National Council." *Journal of Palestine Studies* 19, no. 2 (winter 1990): 29–42.

———. *Palestinian Identity: The Construction of Modern National Consciousness*. New York: Columbia University Press, 1997.

———. "The Centrality of Jerusalem to an End of Conflict Agreement." *Journal of Palestine Studies* 30, no. 3 (spring 2001): 82–87.

Khalidi, Walid. "Plan Dalet: Master Plan for the Conquest of Palestine." *Journal of Palestine Studies* 18, no. 1 (autumn 1998): 3–70.

———. "The Ownership of the U.S. Embassy Site in Jerusalem." *Journal of Palestine Studies* 29, no. 4 (summer 2000): 80–101.

Khalidi, Walid, ed. *From Haven to Conquest: Readings in Zionism and the Palestine Problem Until 1948*. Beirut: Institute for Palestine Studies, 1971.

———. *All That Remains: The Palestinian Villages Occupied and Depopulated by Israel in 1948*. Washington, DC: Institute for Palestine Studies, 1992.

Kimmerling, Baruch. *Zionism and Territory: The Socio-Territorial Dimensions of Zionist Politics*. Berkeley: University of California Press, Institute of International Studies, 1983.

Kimmerling, Baruch, and Joel S. Migdal. *The Palestinians: The Making of a People*. Cambridge, MA, Harvard University Press, 1994.

Klovens, Dean. "The CIA's Role in the Peace Process." *Middle East Intelligence Bulletin* 3, no. 1 (January 2001).

Kotler, Yair. *Heil Kahane*. New York: Adama Books, 1986.

Krystall, Nathan, "The De-Arabization of West Jerusalem 1947–1950." *Journal of Palestine Studies* 27, no. 2 (winter 1998): 5–22.

LAW (Palestinian Society for the Protection of Human Rights and the Environment). *Human Rights Violations in Arab Jerusalem: An Overview of Abuse*. Jerusalem: Palestinian Society for the Protection of Human Rights and the Environment, 1999.

———. *Israeli Violations of Palestinian Economic Rights*. Jerusalem: Palestinian Society for the Protection of Human Rights and the Environment, May 2000.

———. *Legality and Application: Detentions in PNA-Controlled Areas*. Jerusalem: Palestinian Society for the Protection of Human Rights and the Environment, 2000.

———. *Reality and Ambitions: Judicial Independence in PNA-Controlled Areas*. Jerusalem: Palestinian Society for the Protection of Human Rights and the Environment, 2000.

Lehn, Walter, with Uri Davis. *The Jewish National Fund*. London: Kegan Paul International, 1988.

Lein, Yehezkel. *Captive Corpses (Israel's Refusal to Return Bodies of*

Palestinians Killed in Clashes, or Bombings). Jerusalem: HaMoked, the (Israeli) Center for the Defense of the Individual, and B'Tselem—the Israeli Information Center for Human Rights in the Occupied Territories, 1999.

———. *Human Rights Violations of Palestinians from the Occupied Territories Working in Israel and the Settlements.* Jerusalem: HaMoked, the Israeli Center for the Defense of the Individual, and B'Tselem—the Israeli Information Center for Human Rights in the Occupied Territories, 1999.

———. *Thirsty for a Solution: The Water Crisis in the Occupied Territories and Its Resolution in a Final Status Agreement.* Jerusalem: B'Tselem—the Israeli Information Center for Human Rights in the Occupied Territories, July 2000.

———. *Civilians Under Siege: Restrictions on Freedom of Movement as Collective Punishment.* Jerusalem: B'Tselem—the Israeli Information Center for Human Rights in the Occupied Territories, 2001.

———. *Foreseen but Not Prevented: The Performance of Law Enforcement Authorities in Responding to Settler Attacks on Olive Harvesters.* Jerusalem: B'Tselem—the Israeli Information Center for Human Rights in the Occupied Territories, November 2002.

———. *Land Grab: Israel's Settlement Policy in the West Bank.* Jerusalem: B'Tselem—the Israeli Information Center for Human Rights in the Occupied Territories, May 2002.

———. *The Separation Barrier: Position Paper, September 2002.* Jerusalem: B'Tselem—the Israeli Information Center for Human Rights in the Occupied Territories, September 2002.

Lein, Yehezkel, and Renata Capella. *Cooperating Against Justice: Human Rights Violations by Israel and the Palestinian National Authority Following the Murders in Wadi Qelt.* Jerusalem: HaMoked, the (Israeli) Center for the Defense of the Individual; B'Tselem—the Israeli Information Center for Human Rights in the Occupied Territories; and LAW, the Palestinian Society for the Protection of Human Rights and the Environment, 1999.

Lein, Yehezkel, Yael Stein, and Ron Dudai. *Excessive Force: Human Rights Violations During IDF Actions in Area A: Beit Jala, 6 May 2001; Beit Rima, 24 October 2001; Bethlehem Area, 19–28 October 2001.* Jerusalem: B'Tselem—the Israeli Information Center for Human Rights in the Occupied Territories, 2001.

Lein, Yehezkel. *Disputed Waters: Israel's Responsibility for the Water Shortage in the Occupied Territories.* Jerusalem: B'Tselem—the Israeli Information Center for Human Rights in the Occupied Territories, September 1998.

Lein, Yehezkel. *Not Even a Drop: The Water Crisis in Palestinian Villages Without a Water Network.* Jerusalem: B'Tselem—the Israeli Information Center for Human Rights in the Occupied Territories, 2001.

Leiter, Kenneth C.W. "Life Under the Palestinian Authority." *Middle East Quarterly* (September 1998).

Lesch, Ann Mosely. *Arab Politics in Palestine, 1917–1939: The Frustration of a Nationalist Movement.* Ithaca, NY: Cornell University Press, 1979.

Le Troquer, Yann, and Rozenn Hommery al-Oudat. "From Kuwait to Jordan: The Palestinians' Third Exodus." *Journal of Palestine Studies* 28, no. 3 (spring 1999): 37–51.

Lockman, Zachary, and Joel Benin, eds. *Intifada: The Palestinian Uprising Against Israeli Occupation*. Boston: South End Press, 1989.

Louis, William Roger, and Robert W. Stookey, eds. *The End of the Palestine Mandate*. London: I. B. Tauris, 1986.

Lustick, Ian S. *Arabs in the Jewish State: Israel's Control of a National Minority*. Austin: University of Texas Press, 1980.

———. *For the Land and the Lord: Jewish Fundamentalism in Israel*. New York: Council on Foreign Relations, 1988.

———. "The Oslo Agreement as an Obstacle to Peace." *Journal of Palestine Studies* 27, no. 1 (autumn 1997): 61–66.

———. "*Yerushalayim* and *al-Quds*: Political Catechism and Political Realities." *Journal of Palestine Studies* 30, no. 1 (autumn 2000): 5–21.

Maalouf, Amin. *The Crusades Through Arab Eyes*. New York: Schocken, 1985.

Malley, Robert, and Hussein Agha. "Camp David: The Tragedy of Errors." *New York Review of Books*, August 9, 2001, pp. 59–65.

Mallison W. Thomas, and Sally V. Mallison. *The Palestine Problem in International Law and World Order*. Essex, UK: Longman, 1986.

Mansour, Camille. "The Palestinian-Israeli Peace Negotiations: An Overview and an Assessment." *Journal of Palestine Studies* 22, no. 3 (spring 1993): 5–31.

Manuel, Frank E. *The Realities of American-Palestine Relations*. Washington, DC: Public Affairs, 1949.

Ma'oz, Moshe, ed. *Studies on Palestine During the Ottoman Period*. Jerusalem: Magnes, 1975.

Masalha, Nur. *A Land Without a People: Israel, Transfer, and the Palestinians, 1949–1996*. London: Faber and Faber, 1997.

Massad, Joseph. "Palestinians and Jewish History: Recognition or Submission?" *Journal of Palestine Studies* 30, no. 1 (autumn 2000): 52–67.

McGowan, Daniel, and Marc H. Ellis, eds. *Remembering Deir Yassin: The Future of Israel and Palestine*. New York: Olive Branch, 1998.

Melman, Yossi, and Dan Raviv. *Friends in Deed: Inside the U.S.-Israeli Alliance*. New York: Hyperion, 1994.

Mezvinsky, Norton, ed. *Report: Human Rights Violations During the Palestinian Uprising, 1988–1989* (in English). Tel Aviv: Israeli League for Human and Civil Rights, 1990.

Montelle, Jessica. *Prisoners of Peace: Administrative Detention During the Oslo Process*. Jerusalem: B'Tselem—the Israeli Information Center for Human Rights in the Occupied Territories, July 1997.

Moore, John Norton, ed. *The Arab-Israeli Conflict III: Documents*. Princeton, NJ: Princeton University Press, American Society of International Law, 1974.

Morris, Benny. "The Causes and Character of the Arab Exodus from Palestine: The Israeli Defense Forces Intelligence Branch Analysis of June 1948." *Middle Eastern Studies* (January 1986).

———. "The Harvest of 1948 and the Creation of the Palestine Refugee Problem." *Middle East Journal* 40, no. 4 (autumn 1986): 671–685.

———. "Operation Dani and the Palestinian Exodus from Lydda and Ramleh in 1948." *Middle East Journal* 40 (winter 1986): 82–109.

————. *The Birth of the Palestinian Refugee Problem, 1947–1949.* Cambridge, UK: Cambridge University Press, 1987.

————. *1948 and After: Israel and the Palestinians.* Oxford, UK: Oxford University Press, 1990.

————. "Falsifying the Record: A Fresh Look at Zionist Documentation of 1948." *Journal of Palestine Studies* 24, no. 3 (spring 1995): 44–62.

————. *Righteous Victims: A History of the Zionist-Arab Conflict, 1881–1999.* New York: Alfred A. Knopf, 1999.

Murphy, Emma. "Stacking the Deck: The Economics of the Israeli-PLO Accords." *MERIP Middle East Report* 25, nos. 3 and 4 (May–June/July–August 1995).

Nakhleh, Khalil, and Elia Zureik, eds. *The Sociology of the Palestinians.* London: Croom Helm; and New York: St. Martin's, 1980.

Nassar, Jamal R. *The Palestine Liberation Organization: From Armed Struggle to the Declaration of Independence.* New York: Praeger, 1991.

Nassar, Jamal, and Roger Heacock, eds. *Intifada: Palestine at the Crossroads.* New York: Praeger, 1990.

Nazzal, Nafez. *The Palestinian Exodus from Galilee in 1948.* Beirut: Institute for Palestine Studies, 1978.

Neff, Donald. "Settlements in U.S. Policy." *Journal of Palestine Studies* 23, no. 3 (spring 1994): 53–69.

————. *Fallen Pillars: U.S. Policy Towards Palestine and Israel Since 1945.* Washington, DC: Institute for Palestine Studies, 1995.

Normand, Roger, and Lucy Mair. *Under Siege: Israeli Human Rights Violations in Palestine.* Presented to the 25th session of the United Nations Committee on Economic, Social, and Cultural Rights. New York: Center for Economic and Social Rights, 2000.

Olmsted, Jennifer. "Thwarting Palestinian Development: The Protocol on Economic Relations." *MERIP Middle East Report* 26, no. 4 (October–December 1996).

Owen, Roger, ed. *Studies in the Economic History of Palestine in the Nineteenth and Twentieth Centuries.* Carbondale: Southern Illinois University Press, 1982.

Pacheco, Allegra. "The Train That Passed Them By: Oslo and the Release of Palestinian Political Prisoners." *Challenge* (Tel Aviv, Israeli, monthly, English), no. 47 (January–February 1998).

————. "The Israeli High Court of Justice Decision Regarding Violent Interrogation Methods: A Critique." *News from Within* (Jerusalem, Israeli, monthly, English) 15, no. 9 (October 1999).

Palestinian Center for Human Rights. *Promoting the Rule of Law and Democracy in Areas Under the Jurisdiction of the Palestinian National Authority: Report 2000.* Gaza Strip: Palestinian Center for Human Rights, 2001.

Palumbo, Michael. *The Palestinian Catastrophe.* London: Faber and Faber, 1987.

Pappe, Ilan. *The Making of the Arab-Israeli Conflict, 1947–1951.* London: I. B. Tauris, 1994.

————. "Post-Zionist Critique on Israel and the Palestinians, Part I: The Academic Debate." *Journal of Palestine Studies* 26, no. 2 (winter 1997): 29–41.

———. "Post-Zionist Critique on Israel and the Palestinians, Part II: The Media." *Journal of Palestine Studies* 26, no. 3 (spring 1997): 37–43.

———. "Post-Zionist Critique on Israel and the Palestinians, Part III: Popular Culture." *Journal of Palestine Studies* 26, no. 4 (summer 1997): 60–69.

———. "Israel at a Crossroads Between Civic Democracy and Jewish Zealotocracy." *Journal of Palestine Studies* 29, no. 3 (spring 2000): 33–44.

Peck, Juliana S. *The Reagan Administration and the Palestinian Question: The First Thousand Days.* Washington, DC: Institute for Palestine Studies, 1984.

Podhoretz, Norman, "J'Accuse." *Commentary* (September 1982): 21–31.

Porath, Yehoshua. *The Emergence of the Palestinian Arab National Movement, 1918–1929.* London: Frank Cass, 1974.

———. *The Palestinian Arab National Movement from Riots to Rebellion, 1929–1939.* London: Frank Cass, 1977.

Pundak, Ron. "From Oslo to Taba: What Went Wrong?" *Survival* 43, no. 3 (autumn 2001): 31–45.

Quandt, William B. "Clinton and the Arab-Israeli Conflict: The Limits of Incrementalism." *Journal of Palestine Studies* 30, no. 2 (winter 2001): 26–40.

Quandt, William B., Faud Jabber, and Ann Mosely Lesch. *The Politics of Palestinian Resistance.* Berkeley: University of California Press, 1973.

Quigley, John. "Displaced Palestinians and the Right of Return." *Harvard International Law Journal* 39, no. 1 (1998): 193–198.

Rabbani, Mouin. "The Peres-Arafat Agreement: Can It Work?" *MERIP Press Information Notes*, PIN no. 38 (November 3, 2000).

———. "The Mitchell Report: Oslo's Last Gasp?" *MERIP Press Information Notes,* PIN no. 59 (June 1, 2001).

———. "Sharon's Journey of Colors." *MERIP Press Information Notes*, PIN no. 85 (March 15, 2002).

Reinhart, Tanya. "Evil Unleashed." *Tikkun: A Bimonthly Jewish Critique of Politics, Culture, and Society* 17, no. 2 (March/April 2002): 14–18.

Rempel, Terry. "The Ottawa Process: Workshop on Compensation and Palestinian Refugees." *Journal of Palestine Studies* 29, no. 1 (autumn 1999): 36–49.

Rodinson, Maxime. *Israel: A Colonial-Settler State?* New York: Monad, 1973.

———. *Cult, Ghetto, and State: The Persistence of the Jewish Question.* London: al Saqi Books, 1983.

Roemer, Jessi. "Israeli Re-Deployment from Hebron: The Mirage of Self-Rule." *Challenge* (Tel Aviv, Israeli, monthly, English), no. 42 (March/April 1997).

Rogers, Mary Eliza. *Domestic Life in Palestine.* London: Kegan Paul International, 1862.

Rouhana, Kate B. *The Reality of Jerusalem's Palestinians Today.* Jerusalem: Jerusalem Media and Communication Center, 2001.

Roy, Sara. *The Gaza Strip Survey.* Jerusalem: West Bank Data Base Project, 1986.

———. "The Gaza Strip, A Case of Economic De-Development." *Journal of Palestine Studies* 17, no. 1 (autumn 1987): 56–88.

———. "De-development Revisited: Palestinian Economy and Society Since Oslo." *Journal of Palestine Studies* 28, no. 3 (spring 1999): 64–82.

———. "The Crisis Within: The Struggle for Palestinian Society." *Critique: Journal for Critical Studies of the Middle East*, no. 17 (fall 2000): 5–30.

———. "Palestinian Society and Economy: The Continued Denial of Possibility." *Journal of Palestine Studies* 30, no. 4 (summer 2001): 5–20.

Rubenberg, Cheryl A. "The Israeli Invasion of Lebanon: Objectives and Consequences." *Journal of South Asian and Middle Eastern Studies* 8, no. 2 (winter 1984): 3–28.

———. *Israel and the American National Interest: A Critical Examination.* Urbana and Chicago: University of Illinois Press, 1986.

———. "Twenty Years of Israeli Economic Policies in the West Bank and Gaza: Prologue to the Intifada." *Journal of Arab Affairs* 8, no. 1 (spring 1989): 28–73.

———. "The U.S.-PLO Dialogue: Continuity or Change in American Foreign Policy." *Arab Studies Quarterly* 11, no. 4 (fall 1989): 1–58.

———. "Sovereignty, Inequality, and Conflict: The Conflict over Palestine as a Case Study of the Dysfunctionalism of the Existing International System and the Utility of a World Order Perspective for Comprehending the Conflict." In Michael Dobkowski and Isidor Wallimann, eds., *Research in Inequality and Social Conflict* (vol. 2 of a research annual) (1992): 1–84.

———. "The Gulf War, the Palestinians, and the New World Order." In Tareq Y. Ismael and Jacqueline S. Ismael, eds., *The Gulf War and the New World Order: International Relations of the Middle East.* Gainesville: University Press of Florida, 1994, pp. 317–346.

———. "The Bush Administration and the Palestinians: A Reassessment." In Michael W. Suleiman, ed., *U.S. Policy on Palestine from Wilson to Clinton.* Normal, IL: Association of Arab-American University Graduates, 1995, pp. 195–221.

Ruedy, John, "Dynamics of Land Alienation." In Ibrahim Abu Lughod, ed., *The Transformation of Palestine: Essays on the Origin and Development of the Arab-Israeli Conflict.* Evanston, IL: Northwestern University Press, 1971, pp. 119–138.

Ruether, Rosemary Radford, and Marc H. Ellis, eds. *Beyond Occupation: American Jewish, Christian, and Palestinian Voices for Peace.* Boston: Beacon, 1990.

Rwaidy, Ahmad. *The Israeli Restrictions on Arab Presence and Promotion of Jewish Presence in Jerusalem.* Jerusalem: Jerusalem Center for Women, 1997.

Sabet, Amr G.E. "The Peace Process and the Politics of Conflict Resolution." *Journal of Palestine Studies* 27, no. 4 (summer 1998): 5–19.

Sahliyeh, Emile F. "West Bank Industrial and Agricultural Development: The Basic Problems." *Journal of Palestine Studies* 11, no. 2 (winter 1982): 55–69.

Said, Edward W. *Peace and Its Discontents: Gaza-Jericho, 1993–1995.* New York: Vintage, 1995.

———. "Symbols Versus Substance: A Year After the Declaration of Principles." *Journal of Palestine Studies* 24, no. 2 (winter 1995): 60–72.

———. "The Real Meaning of the Hebron Agreement." *Journal of Palestine Studies* 26, no. 3 (spring 1997): 31–36.

————. *The End of the Peace Process: Oslo and After.* New York: Pantheon, 2000.

Savir, Uri. *The Process: 1,100 Days That Changed the Middle East.* New York: Vintage Books, 1999.

Sayigh, Rosemary. *Palestinians: From Peasants to Revolutionaries.* London: Zed, 1979.

————. *Too Many Enemies: The Palestinian Experience in Lebanon.* London: Zed, 1994.

————. "Dis/Solving the 'Refugee Problem.'" *MERIP Middle East Report* 28, no. 2 (summer 1998): 19–23.

Sayigh, Yezid. "Redefining the Basics: Sovereignty and Security of the Palestinian State." *Journal of Palestine Studies* 24, no. 4 (summer 1995): 5–19.

Sayigh, Yusif A. "The Palestinian Economy Under Occupation: Dependency and Pauperization." *Journal of Palestine Studies* 15, no. 4 (summer 1986): 46–67.

Schiff, Ze'ev, and Ehud Ya'ari. *Intifada: The Palestinian Uprising—Israel's Third Front.* New York: Simon and Schuster, 1990.

Scholch, Alexander. "The Demographic Development of Palestine, 1850–1882." *International Journal of Middle Eastern Studies* 17 (November 1985): 485–505.

Scholch, Alexander, translated by William C. Young and Michael C. Gerrity. *Palestine in Transformation, 1856–1882: Studies in Social, Economic, and Political Development.* Washington, DC: Institute for Palestine Studies, 1993.

Schwartz, Michal. "A Secret Account in Tel Aviv Funds Arafat's Oppression." *Challenge* (Tel Aviv, Israeli, monthly, English), no. 43 (May/June 1997).

————. "Collusion in Jerusalem: How the Government and the Settlers Conspire to Take Over Houses and Land." *Challenge*, no. 50 (July/August 1998).

Segev, Tom. *1949: The First Israelis.* New York: The Free Press, 1986.

————. *One Palestine, Complete: Jews and Arabs Under the British Mandate.* New York: Metropolitan Books and Henry Holt, 1999.

Sellick, Patricia. "The Old City of Hebron: Can It Be Saved?" *Journal of Palestine Studies* 23, no. 4 (summer 1994): 69–82.

Sha'ban, Fuad. *Islam and Arabs in Early American Thought: The Roots of Orientalism in America.* Durham, NC: Acorn, 1991.

Shahak, Israel. "A History of the Concept of 'Transfer' in Zionism." *Journal of Palestine Studies* 18, no. 3 (spring 1989): 22–37.

Shahak, Israel, and Norton Mezvinsky. *Jewish Fundamentalism in Israel.* London: Pluto, 1999.

Sharif, Regina. *Non-Jewish Zionism: Its Roots in Western History.* London: Zed Books, 1983.

Shehadeh, Raja. *The Law of the Land: Settlements and Land Issues Under Israeli Military Occupation.* Jerusalem: Palestinian Academic Society for the Study of International Affairs, 1993.

————. "Questions of Jurisdiction: A Legal Analysis of the Gaza-Jericho Agreement." *Journal of Palestine Studies* 23, no. 4 (summer 1994): 18–25.

————. *From Occupation to Interim Accords: Israel and the Palestinian*

Territories. Cimel Book Series no. 4. London: Kluwer Law International/ Academic Publishers, 1997.

Shiblak, Abbas. "Residency Status and Civil Rights of Palestinian Refugees in Arab Countries." *Journal of Palestine Studies* 25, no. 3 (spring 1996): 36–45.

Shikaki, Khalil. "The Palestinian Elections: An Assessment." *Journal of Palestine Studies* 25, no. 3 (spring 1996): 17–22.

Shlaim, Avi. *Collusion Across the Jordan: King Abdullah, the Zionist Movement, and the Partition of Palestine.* Oxford, UK: Clarendon, 1988.

———. "Prelude to the Accord: Likud, Labor, and the Palestinians." *Journal of Palestine Studies* 23, no. 2 (winter 1994): 5–19.

———. "The Oslo Accord." *Journal of Palestine Studies* 23, no. 3 (spring 1994): 24–40.

———. "Israeli Politics and Middle East Peacemaking." *Journal of Palestine Studies* 24, no. 4 (summer 1995): 20–31.

———. *The Iron Wall: Israel and the Arab World.* New York: W. W. Norton, 2000.

Shu'aybi, Azmi, and Khalil Shikaki. "A Window on the Workings of the PA: An Inside View." *Journal of Palestine Studies* 30, no. 1 (autumn 2000): 88–97.

Snetsinger, John. *Truman, the Jewish Vote, and the Creation of Israel.* Stanford: Hoover Institution Press, 1974.

Sokolow, Nahum. *History of Zionism,* vol. 2. London: Longmans, 1919.

Sprinzak, Ehud. *The Ascendance of Israel's Radical Right.* New York: Oxford University Press, 1991.

Stein, Yael, *The Quiet Deportation Continues: Revocation of Residency and Denial of Social Rights of East Jerusalem Palestinians.* Jerusalem: HaMoked, the (Israeli) Center for the Defense of the Individual, and B'Tselem—the Israeli Information Center for Human Rights in the Occupied Territories, 1999.

———. *Expulsion of Palestinian Residents from the South Mt. Hebron Area, October–November 1999.* Case Report. Jerusalem: B'Tselem—the Israeli Information Center for Human Rights in the Occupied Territories, February 2000.

———. *Events on the Temple Mount—29 September 2000.* Jerusalem: B'Tselem—the Israeli Information Center for Human Rights in the Occupied Territories, October 2000.

———. *Illusions of Restraint: Human Rights Violations During the Events in the Occupied Territories 29 September–2 December 2000.* Jerusalem: The Israeli Information Center for Human Rights in the Occupied Territories, December 2000.

———. *Israel's Assassination Policy: Extra-judicial Executions.* Jerusalem: B'Tselem—the Israeli Information Center for Human Rights in the Occupied Territories, n.d. (ca. April 2001).

———. *Standard Routine: Beatings and Abuse of Palestinians by Israeli Security Forces During the Al-Aqsa Intifada.* Jerusalem: B'Tselem—the Israeli Information Center for Human Rights in the Occupied Territories, May 2001.

———. *Policy of Destruction: House Demolitions and Destruction of*

Agriculture Land in the Gaza Strip. Jerusalem: B'Tselem—the Israeli Information Center for Human Rights in the Occupied Territories, February 2002.

———. *Trigger Happy: Unjustified Shooting and Violations of the Open-Fire Regulations During the Al-Aqsa Intifada.* Jerusalem: The Israeli Information Center for Human Rights in the Occupied Territories, March 2002.

Sternhell, Zeev, *The Founding Myths of Israel: Nationalism, Socialism, and the Making of the Jewish State.* Princeton, NJ: Princeton University Press, 1998.

Stone, I. F. "The Other Zionism." In I. F. Stone, *Underground to Palestine: And Reflections Thirty Years Later.* New York: Pantheon Books, 1978.

Strum, Phillipa. "Israel's Democratic Dilemma." *Reform Judaism* 14, no. 2 (winter 1985–1986).

Suleiman, Michael W., ed. *U.S. Policy on Palestine from Wilson to Clinton.* Normal, IL: Association of Arab-American University Graduates, 1995.

Swisa, Shlomi. *Lethal Curfew: The Use of Live Ammunition to Enforce Curfew.* Jerusalem: B'Tselem—the Israeli Information Center for Human Rights in the Occupied Territories, 2002.

Tamari, Salim. "Palestinian Refugees and the Palestinian-Israeli Negotiations." *Journal of Palestine Studies* 29, no. 1 (autumn 1999): 81–89.

Teveth, Shabtai. *Ben-Gurion and the Palestinian Arabs: From Peace to War.* New York: Oxford University Press, 1985.

Tivnan, Edward. *The Lobby: Jewish Political Power and American Foreign Policy.* New York: Simon and Schuster, 1987.

Trottier, Julie. "Water and the Challenge of Palestinian Institution Building." *Journal of Palestine Studies* 29, no. 2 (winter 2000): 35–50.

Tsemel, Lea. "Personal Status and Rights." In Naseer H. Aruri, ed., *Occupation: Israel over Palestine.* Belmont, MA: Association of Arab-American University Graduates, 1983, pp. 60–67.

———. "The Political Prisoners." In Erik Fosse, Ebba Wergeland, and Ibrahim Abu-Lughod, eds., *Israel and the Question of Palestine,* special double issue of *Arab Studies Quarterly* 7, nos. 2 and 3 (spring/summer 1985).

Tsemel, Lea, and Ingrid Jaradat Gassner. *The Trap Is Closing on Palestinian Jerusalemites: Israel's Demographic Policies in East Jerusalem from the 1967 Annexation to the Eve of the Final Status Negotiations (1996).* Jerusalem: Alternative Information Center, Memorandum no. 1/96 (Jerusalem, Israeli occasional, English), 1996.

Turaani, Khalid, et al. *Mitchell Report: Framework for Peace?* Washington, DC: Foundation for Middle East Peace, June 6, 2001.

United Nations. *The Impact of Closure and Other Mobility Restrictions on Palestinian Productive Activities, 1 January 2002–30 June 2002.* New York: Office of the United Nations Special Co-ordinator with the Government of Norway, 2002.

U.S. House of Representatives, Committee on Foreign Affairs. *Human Rights Documents: Compilation of Documents Pertaining to Human Rights.* Washington, DC: U.S. Government Printing Office, 1983.

Usher, Graham. *Palestine in Crisis: The Struggle for Peace and Political Independence After Oslo.* London: Pluto, 1995.

————. "The Politics of Internal Security: The PA's New Intelligence Services." *Journal of Palestine Studies* 25, no. 2 (winter 1996): 21–34.

————. "Returning to the Source: The Politics of Housing in East Jerusalem." *Jerusalem Quarterly File* (Jerusalem, Palestinian quarterly, English) (winter 1998).

————. *Dispatches from Palestine: The Rise and Fall of the Oslo Peace Process*. London: Pluto, 1999.

Vitullo, Anita. "Israel's Social Policy in Arab Jerusalem." *Jerusalem Quarterly File* (Jerusalem, Palestinian quarterly, English) (fall 1998).

Whitelam, Keith W. *The Invention of Ancient Israel: The Silencing of Palestinian History*. London: Routledge, 1996.

Ziv, Hadas, *A Legacy of Injustice: A Critique of Israeli Approaches to the Right of Health of Palestinians in the Occupied Territories*. Tel Aviv: Physicians for Human Rights–Israel, October 2002.

Zureik, Elia. *Palestinian Refugees and the Peace Process*. Washington, DC: Institute for Palestine Studies, 1996.

Websites for Online Research

Adalah
Palestinian/Arab legal center in Israel
www.adalah.org

Addameer
Prisoners Support Association (Palestinian)
www.addameer.org

The Age
Australian daily newspaper
www.theage.com.au/daily/

Agence France-Presse
News Online
www.afp.com/english/afp/

Al-Ahram Weekly
Leading Egyptian daily newspaper, published in English
www.ahram.org.eg/weekly

Al-Awda
Palestine Right to Return Coalition
http://al-awda.org

Al-Ayyam
Palestinian daily newspaper, Arabic
http://al-ayyam.com

Al-Haq: Law in the Service of Man
Palestinian human rights group
www.alhaq.org/

Al-Hayat al-Jadedah
Palestinian daily newspaper, Arabic
http://www.alhayat-j.com/

Al-Hewar
Forum for intellectuals to exchange views about all Middle East issues
www.alhewar.com

Al-Mezan Center for Human Rights
NGO in Jabalya Refugee Camp, Gaza
www.mezan.org/main.htm

Al-Multaqa Arab Thought Forum
Jerusalem/Palestinian research institute
www.multaqa.org/

Al-Quds
Palestinian daily newspaper, Arabic
http://www.alquds.com

Alternative Information Center
Israel/Palestine—publishes *News from Within*
www.alternativenews.org

American Committee on Jerusalem
Coalition of Arab American organizations; publishes collections of articles
    from various sources
www.acj.org/

American-Israel Public Affairs Committee
AIPAC, pro-Israel lobby
www.aipac.org/

American-Israeli Cooperative Enterprise
Pro-Israel
www.us-israel.org/

American Jewish Committee
Pro-Israel
www.ajc.org

Americans for Middle East Understanding
Published *The Link*
www.ameu.org/

Americans for Peace Now
U.S. support group for Israel's Peace Now
www.peacenow.org/

Amnesty International
www.amnesty.org/

Anti-Defamation League
Pro-Israel
www.adl.org/main_israel.asp

Anti-war
Devoted to the cause of nonintervention especially by the United States; anti-war news, viewpoints, and activities; articles by Ran HaCohen often here
www.antiwar.com/

Apartheid Wall Campaign
Project of the Palestinian Environmental Nongovernmental Organization Network to fight the new separation wall
www.stopthewall.org

Applied Research Institute Jerusalem
Palestinian
www.arij.org

Arab Association for Human Rights
Israeli-Arab site
www.arabhra.org

Arabnet
www.arab.net/

Arab Studies Society
Palestinian
www.orienthouse.org/arabstudies/

Ariga
Israeli News and Analysis
www.ariga.com

Associated Press
http://www.ap.org/

Association for Civil Rights in Israel
www.nif.org/acri/

The Avalon Project at the Yale Law School
www.yale.edu/lawweb/avalon/mideast/mid023.htm

Avnery, Uri
personal website
www.avnery@actcom.co.il

BADIL: Resource Center for Palestinian Residency and Refugee Rights
www.badil.org/

Bat Shalom
Pro-peace Israeli women's group
www.batshalom.org

BBC World Service
www.bbc.co.uk/worldservice

BBC World Service Middle East Page
http://news.bbc.co.uk/hi/english/world/middle_east/default.stm

Bethlehem University, West Bank
http://underattack.bethlehem.edu/

Between the Lines
Bimonthly Israeli/Palestinian journal
www.between-lines.org/

Birzeit University
Research and documentation center
www.birzeit.edu

Bitterlemons.org: Palestinian-Israeli Crossfire
Weekly, run by two prominent intellectuals (Israeli—Yossi Alpher, and
    Palestinian—Ghassan Khatib) to present Israeli and Palestinian view-
    points on prominent issues of concern and controversy, directed toward
    public and policymakers
www.bitterlemons.org/

Boston Globe Online
www.boston.com/globe/

B'Tselem—the Israeli Information Center for Human Rights in the Occupied
    Territories
www.btselem.org

Bustan L'Shalom
Israeli group that promotes land and human rights
www.bustanlshalom.org/

CAMERA
Pro-Israel media watchdog group
http://world.std.com/~camera/

Canadian Committee to Protect Journalists/Canadian Journalists for Free
    Expression
www.cjfe.org

Center for Economic and Social Rights
Independent U.S. foundation
www.cesr.org

Center for Policy Analysis on Palestine (Palestine Center)
Washington, D.C.–based; publishes information briefs, policy briefs, special
    reports, and occasional papers
www.palestinecenter.org/cpap/content.html

Center for Palestine Research and Studies
www.cprs~palestine.org

Center on Housing Rights and Evictions
Palestinian NGO
www.cohre.org

Challenge
Israel monthly journal—progressive
www.hanitzotz.com/challenge/

Chicago Tribune Online
www.chicagotribune.com/

Christian Peacemakers Team, Hebron
http://prairienet.org/cpt/hebron.php

Christian Science Monitor Online
www.csmonitor.com

CNN Online
www.cnn.com

Complete Guide to Palestine's Websites
www.birzeit.edu/links/glance.html

Coptic Orthodox Church, Jerusalem
www.sis.gov.eg/jerusalem/html/quds3.htm

Council for Palestinian Restitution and Reparation
http://rightofreturn.org/

Counterpunch Magazine
www.counterpunch.org/

Dagbladet, Oslo, Norway
www.internews.org/articles/122899_dagbladet/122899_dagbladet.htm

Defense for Children International/Palestine Section
www.dci-pal.org/english/aboutdci.html

Deir Yassin Remembered
www.deiryassin.org/

Deutsch-Israelischer Arbeitskreis fur Frieden im Nahen Osten (German-Israeli
    Work Group on Peace in the Middle East)
www.diak.org

Dheisheh Refugee Camp
Palestinian NGO; focus on human rights
www.dheisheh.acrossborders.org

Electronic Intifada
News and analysis
www.electronicintifada.net/new.html

Eye-on-Palestine
Weekly publication of the Applied Research Institute–Jerusalem, focusing on
    settlement activity
www.arij.org/paleye

Financial Times
London
http://news.ft.com/

Foreign Policy in Focus
www.fpif.org

The Forward
Jewish weekly—pro-Israel
www.forward.com/

Foundation for Middle East Peace
Independent U.S. group that monitors settlements in the Occupied Territories
www.fmep.org

Friends of Al-Aqsa, London
www.aqsa.org.uk/

Gamla
Israeli organization advocating expulsion of Palestinians
http://gamla.org.il/english/

Global-Intel
www.gordonthomas.iel

Global Policy
Site for Security Council resolutions
www.globalpolicy.org/security/membship/veto/vetosubj.htm

Grassroots International
Newsletter and advocacy project for Palestinian civil society
www.grassrootsonline.org/pal_AP.html

Green Left
Australian weekly
www.greenleft.org:au/

The Guardian (London) Online
www.guardian.co.uk

Gush Shalom (Peace Bloc—Israel)
www.gush-shalom.org/

Ha'aretz
The premier Israeli newspaper
www.haaretzdaily.com/

HaMoked Center for Defense of the Individual
Israeli human rights group
www.HaMoked.org.il

Hanthala Palestine
Focuses on international law and human rights
http://hanthala.virtualave.net

Harry Walker Agency
Leading U.S.-based lecture agency
www.harrywalker.com/

Health, Development, Information, and Policy Institute
www.hdip.org

Hear Palestine Press Service
www.hearpalestine/briefing.hearpalestine.org

Hebron Settlers Website
www.hebron.org.il/sites.htm

Honest Reporting.com ("Fighting Media Bias")
Pro-Israel
http://honestreporting.com/

Human Rights Action Project—Birzeit University
www.birzeit.edu/hrap/

Human Rights Watch
http://hrw.org
Devoted to issues of violence in Palestine/Israel
http://www.hrw.org/campaigns/israel/

The Independent
London
http://www.independent.co.uk

Independent Media Center (indymedia)
Network of progressive groups providing information on a range of issues from
    antiglobalization to human rights plus many others
www.indymedia.org.il

Independent Media Review and Analysis
Pro-Israel
www.imra.org.il/

Independent Palestinian Information Network (infopal)
www.infopal.org/palnews

Institute for Palestine Studies
Publishes the *Journal of Palestine Studies*
www.ipsjps.org/

Institute of Jerusalem Studies (Jerusalem)
Palestinian; affiliated with the Institute for Palestine Studies, Washington, D.C.
www.cais.net/ipsjps

International Bank of Reconstruction and Development (World Bank)
www.worldbank.org

International Herald Tribune Online
www.iht.com/

International Observatory for Palestinian Affairs (IOPA)
Geneva-based NGO that collects and puts online articles about the Palestine
    question
www.oiap.org
http://groups.yahoo.com/group/oiap/

International Solidarity Movement
www.freepalestinecampaign.org/

Internetnews
News and articles from Norwegian website Dagbladet, translated into English
www.internews.org/

Islamic Association for Palestine
www.iap.org/ or www.iapinfo@iap.org

Israel National News
www.israelnationalnews.com

Israeli Committee Against House Demolition
http://www.icahd.org/eng/

Israeli Council for Israeli-Palestinian Peace
http://members.tripod.com/~other_Israel

Israeli Defense Force
www.idf.il/English/news/nifg.stm

Israeli Government, Ministry of Foreign Affairs
www.israel.org or www.mfa.gov.il/mfa/go.asp

Israeli-Palestinian Human Rights and Peace Groups
Links to websites
www.ariga.com/humanrights/index.asp

Israel/Palestine Center for Research and Information
www.ipcri.org/

Jerusalem Center for Social and Economic Rights
Palestinian nongovernmental organization
www.jcser.org/main.html

Jerusalem Center for Women
Palestinian NGO that works closely with Israel's Bat Shalom on peace and
    women's issues
www.j-c-w.org/

Jerusalem Forum/Jerusalemites
Amman-based NGO; focuses on education about human dimension of
    Jerusalem
www.jerusalemites.org/

Jerusalem Media and Communications Center
Palestinian—research, publications, and public opinion polling
www.jmcc.org/

Jerusalem Post Online
Israeli daily newspaper, English
http://jpost.com

Jerusalem Quarterly File Online
Palestinian
www.jqf-jerusalem.org

Jerusalem Report
Israeli, English, biweekly
http://www.jrep.com/

Jerusalem Watch Online
Palestinian
www.jerusalemwatch.org/

Jewish Agency for Israel News
http://jafi.org.il/

Jewish Alliance Against the Occupation
www.opentent.org/jews.html

Jewish Chronicle
London
www.jchron.co.uk/

Jewish Institute for National Security Affairs
Pro-Israel
www.jinsa.org/about/about.html

Jewish Internet Association
www.jewishinternetassociation.org/

Jewish Peace Fellowship
www.jewishpeacefellowship.org/

Jewish Telegraphic Agency
Online news service, pro-Israel
www.jta.org/

A Jewish Voice for Peace
www.jewishvoiceforpeace.org

Jewish Voices Against the Occupation
www.jrao.org

Jewish World Online
News, advocacy, pro-Israel
www.jrep.com/Jewishworld/

Jewish World Review Online
Articles and information online, very conservative, pro-Israel
www.jewishworldreview.com/

Jews Against the Occupation
www.angelcities.com/ or www.jewsagainsttheoccupation.org/

Jews for Justice in the Middle East
www.cactus48.com

Jews Not Zionists
www.jewsnotzionists.org/

Jordan Times Online
Amman, Jordanian daily, English
www.jordantimes.com/

Junity (Jewish Unity)
Pro-peace
www.junity.org/

LAW (the Palestinian Society for the Protection of Human Rights and the
    Environment)
www.lawsociety.org

Lawyers Committee for Human Rights
http://lchr.org/

Le Monde Diplomatique Online
French newspaper, English translation; excellent maps of the Middle East
www.en.monde-diplomatique.fr/

Los Angeles Times Online
www.latimes.com/

Ma'an Development Center
Palestinian
www.maan-ctr.org/

Médecins Sans Frontières
www.paris.msf.org/

Media Monitors Network
Posts articles from a variety of sources
http://mediamonitors.net

MERIP Press Information News
www.MERIP.org/pins/pin1.html

MEWNews (Mid East Web Group)
www.mideastweb.org/mewnews/

Miami Herald Online
http://www.miami.com/mld/miamiherald/

Middle East Children's Alliance
Pro-peace
www.mecaforpeace.org/

Middle East Crisis Committee
Pro-peace, publishes *The Struggle*
www.thestruggle.org

Middle East Facts
Pro-Israel
www.mideastfacts.com/

Middle East Forum
Pro-Israel think tank
www.meforum.org/

Middle East Information Center
News and analysis post–September 11
http://middleeastinfo.org/

Middle East Intelligence Bulletin Online
Pro-Israel monthly
www.meib.org/

Middle East International Online (London)
Biweekly independent news on the Middle East
http://meionline.com/

Middle East Media and Research Institute
Pro-Israel
www.memri.org/

Middle East Quarterly Online
Published by the Middle East Forum, pro-Israel
www.meforum.org/meq/

Middle East Report Online
http://www.merip.org/mero.html

Middle East Research and Information Project
Publishes *Middle East Report*, a monthly independent journal on Middle East
   studies
www.merip.org

Middle East Review of International Affairs Online
Online journal providing news, translations from Arabic, and references, pro-
   Israel
www.biu.ac.il/SOC/besa/meria/

Middle Eastern Studies Online
Academic journal; pro-Israel
www.frankcass.com/jnls/mes.htm

Mid-East Realities
News, views, and analysis, monthly magazine
www.middleeast.org/indexnew.shtml

Mideast Watch (ZNET Watch)
www.zmag.org/meastwatch/meastwat.htm

MIFTAH (the Palestinian Initiative for the Promotion of Global Dialogue and
    Democracy)
www.miftah.org

MIT Electronic Journal of Middle East Studies
http://web.mit.edu/cis/www/mitejmes/intro.htm

Mother Jones Online
www.motherjones.com/

MSA News, Scholars Database
Site where prominent intellectuals post articles
http://msanews.mynet.net/~msanews/Scholars/index.html

MUWATIN (the Palestinian Institute for the Study of Democracy)
www.muwatin.org/

The Nation Online
www.thenation.com/

National Catholic Reporter
http://www.natcath.org/

National Public Radio
www.npr.org/

News from Within Online
Monthly publication of the Alternative Information Center
www.alternativenews.org/

New Statesman
London
http://www.newstatesman.com

New York Review of Books
www.nybooks.com/

New York Times International Online
www.newstimes.com

New York Times Online
www.nytimes.com/

NGO Network on the Question of Palestine (UN Department of Political
    Affairs)
www.un.org/Depts/dpa/ngo

Nigel Perry Diary
www.nigelperry.com/diary/

Not in My Name Coalition
Jewish American antioccupation group
www.diak.org/not_in_our_name.htm

The Observer
London
http://observer.co.uk/

On the Record (Grassroots International in Palestine)
www.grassrootsonline.org/pal_AP.html

The Other Israel
Monthly publication of the Israeli Council for Israeli-Palestinian Peace
http://members.tripod.com/~other_Israel/

Palestine Center
News, information, statistics, analysis
www.palestinecenter.org

Palestine Center for Conflict Resolution and Reconciliation
Pacifist NGO in Bethlehem
www.mideastweb.org/ccrr

Palestine Chronicle
http://.palestinechronicle.com/

Palestine Economic Policy Research Institute
www.palecon.org/masdr/main.html

Palestine Independent Media Center (Palestine Indymedia)
http://jerusalem.indymedia.org/

Palestine Information (London)
www.palestine-info.co.uk/mainframe.htm

Palestine-Israel Journal of Politics, Economics, and Culture Online
www.pij.org

Palestine Liberation Organization
www.plo.org

Palestine Media Center
www.palestine-pmc.com/

Palestine Media Watch
www.pmwatch.org/

Palestine Monitor
Website created by Palestine NGO Network as a gateway to civil society
www.palestinemonitor.org/

Palestine National Authority
www.pna.org/

Palestine News Agency—WAFA
Official news agency of the Palestinian Authority
http://www.wafa.pna.net/

The Palestinian NGO Network
A voluntary cluster of Palestinian NGOs that work in a variety of areas
www.pngo.net

Palestine Red Crescent Society
www.palestinercs.org/

Palestine Refugee ResearchNet (McGill University)
www.arts.mcgill.ca/MEPP/PRRN/prfront.html

Palestine Remembered
www.palestineremembered.com

Palestine Report Online
A biweekly journal from the Jerusalem Media and Communication Center; a
    continuation of the print *Palestine Report*
www.jmcc.org/media/reportonline/

Palestine Solidarity Campaign
www.palestinecampaign.org

Palestinian Academic Society for the Study of International Affairs
    (PASSIA)
www.passia.org/

Palestinian Agricultural Relief Committees
www.pal-arc.org/

Palestinian-American Research Center, Ramallah
www.parcenter.org

Palestinian Center for Human Rights
www.pchrgaza.com

Palestinian Center for Peace and Democracy
Canadian NGO in Jerusalem
www.arts.megill.ca/MEPP/ngoproject/pcpd.html

Palestinian Center for Policy and Survey Research
Public opinion polling and other research (affiliated with the Center for
    Palestine Research and Studies)
www.pcpsr.org/

Palestinian Center for Rapprochement
Long history of and commitment to peace
www.rapprochement.org/

Palestinian Central Bureau of Statistics
www.pcbs.org

Palestinian Environmental NGO Network (PENGON)
www.pengon.org/

Palestinian Human Rights Monitor
Bimonthly publication of the Palestinian Human Rights Monitoring Group
www.phrmg.org/monitor.htm

Palestinian Human Rights Monitoring Group
www.lebnet.com/phrmg/

Palestinian Independent Commission for Citizens Rights
Monitors human rights violations by the Palestinian Authority
www.piccr.org/

Palestinian Right to Return Coalition
http://www.al-awda.org/

Palnet
Palestinian news
www.palnet.edu/

PBS Online
www.pbs.org/

Peace Now
Israeli peace group
www.peacenow.org.il/english.asp

Permanent Observer Mission of Palestine to the United Nations
http://palestine-un.org
http://palestine-un.org/peace/frindex.html (includes texts of peace documents
    and treaties relating to Palestine and Israel)
http://palestine-un.org/res/frindex.html (includes texts and information regard-
    ing UN resolutions relating to Palestine)

Physicians for Human Rights
www.phrusa.org/

Physicians for Human Rights—Israel
www.phr.org.il

Project Interchange
U.S. pro-Israel group
www.ajc.org/Israel/ProjectInterchange.asp

Public Committee Against Torture in Israel
www.stoptorture.org.il/

Rabbis for Human Rights (Israel)
www.rhr.israel.net

Ramallah Online
News, media reviews, political analysis
www.ramallahonline.com/

RamallahFlowers
An upgrade of *Ramallah Online*—same content
www.ramallahflowers.com/

Reinhart, Tanya
Personal website
www.tau.ac.il/~reinhart/political/

Search for Justice and Equality
www.searchforjustice.org

September 2000 Clashes Information Center
Online information from Addameer
www.addameer.org/September2000/

South Hebron
Israeli site constructed by Yesh Gvul to provide information about expulsions
     of Palestinians from southern Hebron District
www.southebron.com

Stop US Military Aid to Israel
www.stop-us-military-aid-to-israel.net/5reasons.htm

The Struggle
Publication of Middle East Crisis Committee
www.thestruggle.org/

Sustain Campaign
Works to stop U.S. military and economic aid to Israel
www.sustaincampaign.org

Ta'ayush (Arab-Jewish Partnership)
Israeli peace group
www.taayush.org/

Telegraph Online
News Telegraph–UK
http://www.telegraph.co.uk/

Temporary International Presence in Hebron
www.tiph.org

Tikkun: A Jewish Critique of Politics, Culture, and Society Online
U.S. Jewish magazine, promotes peace and justice
www.tikkun.org

Times (daily); *Sunday Times*
London
http://www.timesonline.co.uk/

Trans-Arab Research Institute
www.tari.org

Trincoll Journal Online
www.trincoll.edu/zines/tj/

Union of Palestinian Medical Relief Committees
www.upmrc.org/

United Nations Development Programme
www.papp.undp.org

United Nations Resolutions on Palestine
www.palestine-un.org

UN Relief and Works Agency
www.un.org/unrwa/

UN Special Coordinator in the Occupied Territories
www.arts.mcgill.ca/mepp/unsco/unfront.html

USAID West Bank and Gaza
www.usaid.gov/wbg/

U.S. Campaign to End the Israeli Occupation
www.endtheoccupation.org

U.S. Department of State
www.state.gov/

Vermonters for a Just Peace in Palestine/Israel
U.S. group from Vermont that supports survival of Palestinian people and an
    end to occupation
www.vtjp.org/

Visions of Peace with Justice in Israel/Palestine
An alliance of Jewish activists working for a just peace
www.vopj.org/

Wall Street Journal Online
http://interactive.wsj.com/

Washington Institute for Near East Policy
Pro-Israel think tank
www.washingtoninstitute.org/

Washington Post Online
www.washingtonpost.com/

Washington Report on Middle East Affairs Online
www.washington-report.org

Wi'am (Palestinian Conflict Resolution Center)
www.planet.edu/~alaslah/

Women's Center for Legal Aid and Counselling
Palestinian NGO
www.wclac.org/

Women in Black
Israeli women's peace group
www.geocities.com/EndTheOccupation/

World Bank Group
www.worldbank.org

Yesh Gvul (Israeli soldiers who refuse to serve in the Occupied Territories)
www.yesh-gvul.org

Yesha Online
Newsletter of the settlers' organization in the West Bank
www.yeshanews.org/

Z Net Magazine Online
www.zmag.org/

Index

471

About the Book

After living for more than three decades under occupation by Israel—and ten years after the Oslo Accords were heralded as the first step toward the resolution of a century of conflict—the Palestinians in the West Bank and Gaza struggle daily with conditions of severe economic, social, and psychological deprivation. What explains the dismal failure of the post-Oslo peace process? What propels the prolonged and devastating upheaval known as the Al-Aqsa intifada? Cheryl Rubenberg's forceful, penetrating critique of the Oslo Accords and their aftermath points to the starkly contrasting objectives of Israel and the Palestinians.

Rubenberg conveys how Israeli policies have eroded Palestinian commitment to a peace process, how U.S. intervention has affected the region, and how pervasive corruption within the Palestinian government has played a role. Her somber conclusion supports the contention that peace in the region, while hoped for by many, depends entirely on unlikely shifts in policy and objectives on all sides. Which leaves the Palestinians further from realizing their aspirations for self-determination than at any time since 1967.

Cheryl A. Rubenberg, an independent analyst and former associate professor of political science at Florida International University, has written on U.S. policy and the Israeli-Palestinian conflict for more than twenty-five years. Her previous publications include *Palestinian Women: Patriarchy and Resistance in the West Bank.*